Europe: A Cultural History

From the beginnings of agricultural society in Africa and the eastern Mediterranean seventeen centuries before Christ up to late twentieth-century mass culture, Rietbergen describes Europe's colourful cultural history in terms of continuity and change as societies developed new ways of surviving, believing, looking at man and the world, and of consuming and communicating. He examines culture through the media of literature, art, science, technology and music.

A major and original contribution to studies of the idea of Europe, this book is distinctive in paying particular attention to the impact of other cultures on Europe and the interaction between Europe and 'other worlds'. Looking beyond ancient and renaissance European cultural history, the author also covers the more recent cultural changes of the last two centuries.

A wide selection of excerpts support and enliven the arguments. From the ancient Babylonian law codes to Pope Urban II's call to crusade in 1095, and from Michelangelo on Italian art in 1538 to the lyrics of Iron Maiden and Sting in the late twentieth century, *Europe: A Cultural History* is a thorough and stimulating overview.

Peter Rietbergen is Professor of Cultural History at the Catholic University of Nijmegen in The Netherlands.

Europe

A Cultural History

Peter Rietbergen

London and New York

First published 1998
by Routledge
11 New Fetter Lane, London EC4P 4EE

Simultaneously published in the USA and Canada
by Routledge
29 West 35th Street, New York, NY 10001

Typeset in Bembo by Keystroke, Jacaranda Lodge, Wolverhampton
Printed and bound in Great Britain by TJ International Ltd,
Padstow, Cornwall

British Library Cataloguing in Publication Data
A catalogue record for this book is available from the British Library

Library of Congress Cataloging-in-Publication Data
Rietbergen, P. J. A. N.
  Europe : a cultural history / Peter Rietbergen.
    p.   cm.
  Includes bibliographical references and index.
  1. Europe—History. 2. Europe—Civilization. I. Title.
  D20.R42   1998
  940—dc21   98-22241
                                                       CIP

ISBN 0–415–17229–2 (hbk)
ISBN 0–415–17230–6 (pbk)

Contents

List of plates   xii
List of maps   xv
Prologue   **xvii**
Europe – a present with a past
Introduction: Europe – a dream? xvii
On the problems of writing a cultural history of Europe xviii
On definitions xx
On the structure and use of this book xxiv
Acknowledgements xxvi

PART I
Continuity and change: new ways of surviving   **1**

1   **Before 'Europe': towards an agricultural and
    sedentary society**   **3**
    Beginnings in Africa and the eastern Mediterranean,
       or the non-European origins of European culture 3
    The advent of agriculture, temple and state 6
    Invasion, conquest and change: the first wave 10
    BABYLON, THE SEVENTEENTH CENTURY BC: THE LAW
       CODE OF HAMMURÁPI 14
    Beginnings in Europe: after the last Ice Age 15
    Invasion, conquest and change: the second wave 19
    A 'marginal' culture? Religion and state formation in
       Israel 20
    A 'marginal' culture? Trade and communication in
       Phoenicia 21
    A 'marginal' culture? Democracy and its limitations in
       Greece 22
    A 'marginal' culture? Tribal society in Celtic Europe 30

The 'birth of Europe' and the Greek 'world-view', or how
to define one's own culture 32
The world of Alexander the Great 34

2   **Rome and its empire: the effects and limits of cultural
    integration**   38
Between the Alps and the Mediterranean, between the
    Etruscan and the Greek worlds: the expansion of the early
    Romans 38
From an informal to a formal empire 42
ROME, THE SECOND CENTURY AD: A LEGAL SYSTEM, A LEGAL
    SOCIETY – THE ROMAN CONTRIBUTION 47
Roman culture 49
The Roman Empire and the worlds beyond 52

3   **An empire lost – an empire won? Christianity and the
    Roman Empire**   58
Developments within the Jewish world: the genesis of
    Christianity 58
From Jews – and Gentiles – to Christians: the role of Jesus
    of Nazareth and his followers 59
Religions in the Roman Empire 61
A sect of 'hopeless outlaws' 62
CARTHAGE, AD 180: ARGUMENTS AGAINST AND FOR THE
    RELIGION OF THE CHRISTIANS 65
Towards an empire Roman as well as Christian 67
Rome and its neighbours in the fourth and fifth centuries AD:
    the division and loss of the political empire – the survival
    of the cultural empire 71
Empire and language 75

PART II
Continuity and change: new forms of belief   79

4   **Towards one religion for all**   81
The Christian world-view: the survival of classical culture
    within the context of Christianity and Europe 81
MOUNT SINAI, AD 547: KOSMAS EXPLAINS THE CHRISTIAN
    COSMOGRAPHY 83
One religion for all: the fusion of Christianity and
    Europe 88

The rise of a new empire: Frankish statecraft and Christian
    arguments 91
Culture and cohesion: the role of ideology and education in
    the shaping of Carolingian Europe, or the 'First
    Renaissance'? 94
The impact of monasteries 98

5   **Three worlds around the Inner Sea: western
    Christendom, eastern Christendom and Islam**   **102**
Confrontation and contact from the sixth century onwards 102
The world of the Prophet: Islam 102
God's kingdom among men: orthodox Christendom 107
A far corner of the earth: Roman, catholic Christendom 110
The Crusades: western Christendom versus Islam and eastern
    Christendom 112
CLERMONT, 26 NOVEMBER 1095: POPE URBAN II CALLS FOR
    A CRUSADE 114

6   **One world, many traditions. Elite culture and
    popular cultures: cosmopolitan norms and regional
    variations**   **119**
Europe's 'feudal' polities 119
The Church and the early states 122
Economic and technological change and the early states 125
Stronger states – stronger rulers? 129
The towns and the early states 131
A Christian world or a world of Christian nations? 136
Elite culture and popular cultures: cosmopolitan norms and
    regional variations 142
LONDON, AD 1378: GEOFFREY CHAUCER DESCRIBES HIS
    WORLD 147
The importance of the universities 151

Interlude: The worlds of Europe, *c.*1400–1800   **159**
A world of villages 160
A world of towns 166
Two worlds? 171

PART III
**Continuity and change: new ways of looking at man
and the world**   **175**

7 **A new society: Europe's changing views of man**   **177**
   The survival of classical culture and the beginnings of
      Humanism 177
   The loss of Byzantium – the gain of Europe: the further
      development of Humanism in Italy 179
   From Humanism to the Renaissance in Italy 184
   ROME, AD 1538: MICHELANGELO TALKS ABOUT ITALIAN ART 187
   Humanism and the Renaissance: Italy and beyond 191

8 **A new society: Europe as a wider world**   **194**
   Economic and technological change and the definitive
      formation of the 'modern' state 194
   From manuscript to typescript 197
   Gunpowder and compass 200
   THE HAGUE, AD 1625: HUGO GROTIUS EXPOUNDS 'THE LAW
      OF NATIONS' 204
   Church and State: the break-up of religious unity 206
   Printing, reading and the schools: education for the masses? 209
   Unity and diversity: printing as a cultural revolution 214
   Europe and its frontiers: nation-feeling and cultural
      self-definition 224

9 **A new society: Europe and the wider world since the
   fifteenth century**   **227**
   The 'old' world and the 'older' world 227
   The 'old' world and the 'new' 233
   The 'Columbian exchange' 236
   EUROPE, THE EARLY SIXTEENTH CENTURY: OPINIONS ON THE
      CONQUEST OF AMERICA AND ITS CONSEQUENCES 242
   Images of America and mirrors of Europe 244
   Further cultural consequences of expansion 251

10 **A new society: migration, travel and the diffusion and
    integration of culture in Europe**   **259**
    Migration, travel and culture 259
    Non-voluntary travel: the cultural significance of migrations 260
    Three types of cultural travel 263

ROME, WINTER 1644–5: JOHN EVELYN VISITS THE ETERNAL
   CITY 275
The practice of travel 277
To travel or not to travel? 280
Travel as an element in growing cosmopolitanism and cultural
   integration 282

**11 A new society: the 'Republic of Letters' as a virtual
   and virtuous world against a divided world**   284
The Republic of Letters: a quest for harmony 284
The Republic of Letters and the ideal of tolerance: theory
   and practice 285
CHATEAU MONTAIGNE, NEAR BORDEAUX, AD 1580: MICHEL DE
   MONTAIGNE ON EUROPE AND 'THE OTHER' 286
The Republic of Letters and its enemies: national cultural
   policies, or the political uses of culture 291
The Republic of Letters, or how to communicate in an
   invisible institution 294
The Republic of Letters and the 'intertraffic of the mind':
   three examples 297

12 A new society: from Humanism to the Enlightenment   301
Humanism and empiricism between 'ratio' and 'revelatio' 301
From scientific empiricism to new visions of man and
   society 304
EUROPE, THE EARLY SEVENTEENTH CENTURY: VIEWS ON THE
   SCIENTIFIC METHOD OF FRANCIS BACON AND RENÉ
   DESCARTES 306
From Humanism to Enlightenment: a long dawn 311
Enlightenment and Romanticism: poles apart? 315

**PART IV
Continuity and change: new forms of consumption
and communication**   321

**13 Europe's revolutions: freedom and consumption
   for all?**   323
Material culture and conspicuous consumption: a process
   of consumer change till the end of the eighteenth century 323
Production and reproduction: a process of economic and
   demographic change till the end of the eighteenth century 327

A process of social and cultural change: the convergence of
elites till the end of the eighteenth century 330

Two 'revolutions': one political, one economic, both
cultural 333

PARIS, 27 AUGUST 1789: THE CULTURAL IMPORTANCE OF THE
'DÉCLARATION DES DROITS DE L'HOMME ET DU CITOYEN' 336

Urban, industrial culture: the regulation and consumption
of time 344

14 **Progress and its discontents: nationalism, economic
growth and the question of cultural certainties** 349

The revolutions and their aftermath 349

Elements of nationalism: the political culture of the
nineteenth century 352

New elites, new mechanisms of cultural diffusion, new
manifestations of culture 355

BASLE, THE MIDDLE OF THE NINETEENTH CENTURY: JACOB
BURCKHARDT (1818–97) CRITICIZES CONTEMPORARY
CULTURE 363

Money and time, goods and leisure: towards a consumer
culture 371

15 **Europe and the other worlds** 374

Europe and its expanding world 374

Europe and Latin America: a severed relationship? 375

The 'old' world and the 'new': North America as a vision
of freedom 377

Capitalism and consumerism: freedom or slavery, progress
or decadence? 380

NEW YORK, 1909: HERBERT CROLY (1869–1930) INTERPRETS
'THE PROMISE OF AMERICAN LIFE' 383

Europe and 'America': a cultural symbiosis or, the growth
of the 'western world' 384

To the 'heart of darkness': Europe and Africa 386

The 'old' world and the 'older' world 390

16 **The 'Decline of the Occident' – the loss of a dream?
From the nineteenth to the twentieth century** 398

The sciences: positivism and increasing relativism 398

BERLIN, 1877: HEINRICH STEPHAN REJOICES IN THE FIRST
GERMAN TELEPHONE SERVICE 399

Europe in hiding, Europe surviving 405
A growing sense of '*fin-de-siècle*' between pessimism and
    optimism 410
A world between wars 415

17 Towards a new Europe?   422

Science, culture and society 422
After the Second World War: deconstruction and
    reconstruction 429
A culture of time versus money 435
From 'familyman' to 'salaryman' – from group identity to
    individual identity? 441
Dimensions of identity – culture as communication: towards
    an 'anonymous mass culture'? 444
EUROPE, SINCE THE 1960s: POPULAR MUSIC – HIGH
    CULTURE? 451

Epilogue
Europe – a present with a future   457

Notes   469
Index   502

List of plates

1 Cave painting at Niaux, France, dated *c*.20,000–10,000 BC   13

2 Engraving showing the pillar with 282 articles of Hammurápi's laws, and the King himself before the sun god, Shamash   13

3 Bronze chariot from a seventh-century BC grave at Strettweg, Styria   18

4 Decoration on a Greek wine-jar, *c*.430/420 BC   27

5 Scene from a funerary monument found at Neumagen, Germany, dated *c*.AD 190   45

6 Mosaic of Empress Theodora, wife of Justinian, dated sixth century, from the church of San Vitale, Ravenna, Italy   45

7 Shrine dedicated to the service of Mithras, located under the Christian church of San Clemente, Rome   63

8 Fresco depicting 'a meal of fraternal love' found in one of the Roman catacombs   63

9 Maps and drawings illustrating the various elements of Kosmas' Christian Cosmology   82

10 Germanic limestone tombstone, eighth century, from Alskog Tjangvide on the island of Gotland, Sweden   82

11 Fifteenth-century fresco cycle in the church at Brancion, France   113

12 Turkish miniature of the archangel Gabriel appearing to Muhammad, from the Topkapi Museum, Istanbul   113

13 Detail from a mid-fifteenth century manuscript on alchemy, in the University Library of Prague   146

14 The teaching of theology at the Sorbonne, from a fifteenth-century French manuscript   146

15 Construction of the Tower of Babel, a miniature in King Wenceslas' Bible *c*.1389–1400   148

16 Water-driven flour-mill on the bank of the River Vltava at Prague, in a colour-wash, pen-drawing by the Dutch artist Roelant Savery, *c*.1610   149

17 A Roman mosaic allegedly depicting Plato's academy, at the National Museum of Naples   186

18 Drawing of a group of bathing soldiers before the Battle of
   Cascina, attributed to Aristotele da Sangallo, 1542   187
19 The scholar-scribe Master Hildebert teaches his pupil Everwin,
   depicted in a handwritten copy of St Augustine's *De Civitate Dei*
   made for Heinrich Zdík, Bishop of Olomouc, *c*.1136–7   203
20 Printer's mark showing a simple printing press, used by Petrus
   Caesar of Ghent, one of the earliest printers, working in the 1470s   203
21 Sixteenth-century engraving showing Francisco Pizarro, the
   Spanish adventurer who conquered the Inca Empire, watching
   the last emperor, Atahualpa, collecting his treasures as a ransom,
   in 1532   241
22 Eighteenth-century engraving showing the observatory for
   astronomical research of the Jesuit mission in Peking   241
23 Sixteenth-century map showing the seven main basilicas in
   Rome   261
24 Jacob Fugger, the Augsburg banker, and his chief accountant,
   Matthäus Schwarz, depicted in the Fugger's headquarters in 1516   265
25 Engraving showing people watching heretics and witches being
   burned in a straw hut, depicted in a text on criminal law and
   procedure, the *Cautio Criminalis* of 1632   286
26 Engraving showing an imaginary conversation, probably on the
   question of Holy Eucharist, between the Pope, a Protestant
   minister and a Jesuit, before Christ, on a French engraving from
   the seventeenth century   287
27 Water-driven organ/automata devised by the learned Jesuit
   Athanasius Kircher (1602–80)   305
28 Eighteenth-century print making fun of science, in a vision of an
   air-borne world   305
29 An engraved broadsheet containing the 1789 'Declaration of the
   Rights of Man and the Citizen' with allegorical illustrations   337
30 The first German railway between Nuremberg and Fürth, in a
   contemporary engraving, 1835   337
31 A view of the Krupp firm's factories at Essen, Germany, in an
   engraving of *c*.1860   347
32 Print by the French artist Gustave Doré, from his *London,
   a Pilgrimage*, 1872, showing the smog- and soot-covered slums   347
33 Lithograph showing the Parisian 'Au Bon Marché', the great
   department store *c*.1870   362
34 German poet J. W. von Goethe contemplating the Roman
   countryside with its ruins of ancient grandeur in a painting by
   Tischbein *c*.1800   363
35 *The Last of England* by Ford Maddox Brown, from the
   mid-1850s   382
36 Engraving showing Livingstone crossing the continent of Africa,
   1853–6   382

37 Engraving showing explorers trying to teach the Bible to
    indigenous rulers such as King Kamrasi of Nyoro, 1863   386
38 Print from *Punch* discussing the question of the veracity of
    Darwin's theories, 1861   387
39 Satirical print of Darwin as and with an ape   387
40 An engraved representation of the Great Exhibition at Vienna
    in 1873, showing the German section of the 'Hall of Machines'   401
41 Engraving showing how machines in the family home could
    free women of heavy household chores   401
42 French artist Raoul Hausmann's 'assemblage' called the
    'Mechanical Head' *c.*1920   425
43 James Watson and Francis Crick, discoverers of the famous
    'double helix' structure of DNA and 1962 Nobel prize winners   425

List of maps

1 Migrations in Western Eurasia, third to first millennium BC   11
2 Extent of Greek influence in the ancient Mediterranean world,
   c.400–300 BC   36
3 Roman Empire in AD 211   46
4 Linguistic boundaries, c.AD 1200 (with eleventh- and
   twelfth-century pilgrimage routes)   145
5 European expansion at the end of the Middle Ages to c.1540   230
6 Agencies and commercial interests of the Fugger trading and
   banking house, c.1500   264
7 Major spheres of European cultural influence, c.1800   392

Prologue

Europe – a present with a past

Es irrt der Mensch, so lang er strebt.
Man shall err as long as he strives.

God, in the 'Prologue' to Goethe's *Faust I*[1]

Introduction: Europe – a dream?

What is Europe? It is, of course, wrong to consider it as a 'natural fact', to call it a continent and to attribute to it the specious security of a distinct geographical entity, as so often happens. If anything, Europe is a political and cultural concept, invented and experienced by an intellectual elite more specifically whenever there was cause to give a more precise definition of what can pragmatically yet simply be described as the western edge of Eurasia, the earth's largest land mass. When was there cause to give such definitions? Often, in a moment or period of crisis, of confrontation. After all, it is only when self-definition is necessary that people become self-reflective, and describe their own identity.

The question why the concept was coined at all leads to another problem, namely, when the concept 'Europe' was first used, and by whom. Of course it is equally important to know what was the content of this concept at different times in history, and for whom and in what way it was a living reality. For the fact that the 'idea of Europe' was often voiced explicitly either as the utopia, or as the propaganda instrument only of an elite, in no way means that it has not become a reality of sorts in the course of time, both for that elite and for far larger groups of people who made and make no claims to that status. As Friedrich Nietzsche wrote: 'Ein Traum, ewig wiederholt [kann] durchaus als Wirklichkeit empfunden und beurteilt werden' ('The continuous repetition of a dream may well turn it into a reality felt and judged').[2]

All these questions and considerations first take us far back into the past before returning to the situation which developed from the nineteenth century onwards and, more specifically, after the Second World War. For it really was only then that politicians, who were mainly economists and lawyers, attempted to bring to fruition what they, interpretively and sometimes manipulatively, presented as the 'idea of Europe', attributing it, in accordance with their idealism, to a long historical tradition.[3] With a view to forever suppressing the chances of Europe once more destroying itself with its own arms, they began to present it as a 'culture' or a 'civilization', as a unity with features distinctly its own. To further the acceptation of what they felt to be a political, military and economic necessity, the 'integration' of Europe, they tried to give it an ideological foundation. As had happened before, 'Europe' once again was held up as an ideal to contemporary society, urging it to realize a dream of cohesion. Yet, in attempting to accelerate the process of unification, these politicians embarked upon a course whose consequences reached much further than in any previous period, pitting an as yet untested belief in the power of a collective, European ideal against the tenacity of older, regional and national allegiances.

Against this background, a historical analysis seems called for of the phenomena that can be considered to have contributed to Europe's cultural cohesion, to its past and present reality.

On the problems of writing a cultural history of Europe

Writing history is a cultural and political, perhaps even a moral dilemma. Indeed, historians of necessity involve their own culture and self in their writing. If they do not create a contemporary picture of the past, few will want to read them. But, if the historian's images are too period-bound, they will quickly fade. My search for Europe is unavoidably a wilful journey along a number of paths, some of which have not yet been taken, while others are obviously well trodden. Whether my stroll leads anywhere is for the reader to decide. It is hoped that this book will provide a time- and place-bound journey through selected fields of Europe's cultural history, guiding readers past various points of recognition and yet stimulating their thought. Regardless of the extent to which one's point of view is determined by the views of earlier travellers, what we see is always new. As a landscape and our perspective of it change during a journey, similarly, when we think about Europe its contours shift and its characteristics rearrange themselves.

Since the seventh century BC, when the term was first used, much has been thought, written and said about Europe, right up to the present day. Europe has been described, respectively, as an Asian princess, a Greek demigoddess, the queen of the world. Europe has been expressed metaphorically in images and words which encode emotions. Europe has also been the result of ways of thinking, of ideologies which actively contributed to the creation of realities. Europe has even become a more or less objective geographical concept. Because of all that, Europe now is a more or less strongly felt bond between those living in it. Europe is situated in that area of tension which links dream to deed, thinking to doing. But it is also a restrictive criterion for those who want to distinguish themselves from an outside world.

What follows does not intend to summarize all this. Nor does it intend to definitely define that which cannot be so defined, namely, what Europe really is, for Europe will continue to change, to be itself in new ways. Europe is a series of world-views, of peoples' perspectives on their reality, sometimes only dreamt or desired, sometimes experienced and realized as well.

This was never more clear to me than when I had finished the first draft of this book. Obviously, a text like the present one is not written or published without being scrutinized by a number of readers, both the critical friends and the professional reviewers, who remain anonymous for the very reason that the publisher asks them to comment on the text in view of its scholarly acceptability and its commercial viability. By and large, their comments have prepared me for the criticism which a book on European culture is bound to receive.

Some critics vehemently accused me of being too irreverent as to the biblical sources of Christian tradition. Others, however, felt that the text should not give such prominence to the influence of Christianity on European culture as it does. They also argued that a cultural history should chastise the Churches for the iniquities perpetrated by them or in their name, showing that Europe's record is far from unblemished.

Some took me to task for not writing about the masses who suffered in the making of Europe, indicating one should expatiate on the human costs of the process, both in Europe and elsewhere. Others, however, asked why in a cultural history there was so much concern for the economic and political background.

Some wondered whether the text did not prove what they always had held, namely that cultural history was nothing but a paean to great men and great ideas. Others noted the dozens of eminent culture makers that I failed to mention, arguing that its art, its literature and its music constitute Europe's most precious heritage and, indeed, its very identity; not surprisingly, perhaps, these past culture makers often proved to be the compatriots of the present reviewers; the latter were not convinced by the argument that an attempt at creating a canon would invite only a host of hostile reactions.[4]

Finally, a few readers were convinced that I was in the pay of the European Union, writing an apologia for the ideologies of its power brokers. Others, however, blamed me for presenting an altogether too bleak view of the reality of the values that are presented as uniquely European, and of the blessings of the unification based upon them.

Indeed, if writing this book has taught me one thing it is the reality of present passions aroused by Europe's past, whether they be religious, moral, nationalist or political in origin. Realizing how genuine these passions are, realizing, also, that Europe continues to change in time, its idea differing from individual to individual, from group to group, I could not but ask myself if I should not give up my project altogether. However, while acknowledging that there may well be some truth in each and all of these critical remarks, considering the pleasure writing this book had given me already I decided

I would rather continue and finish it, trying to present as balanced a view as possible.

On definitions

Writing history means making choices. These choices are made against a background of complex factors, including the problems which writers pose for themselves, their assumptions about the reader's interests and the mass of disorganized details from different and often discordant sources about the past at their disposal. Ultimately, all these factors contribute to the story. But in the last instance, of course, the interpretation given is the result of an effort to ask meaningful, present-minded questions while trying to avoid meaningless, present-minded answers.

Seen against this background, writing a 'cultural history of Europe' is not an easy task. Not only must one determine the chronological scope of such a tale, more importantly one must decide where, both geographically and culturally, Europe begins and ends. This calls for a definition of the two constituent elements of this book: Europe and Culture.

Must everything be described, to the extent that it can be uncovered, which has happened from the North Cape to Gibraltar, from the west coast of Ireland to the Urals – the accepted geographical definition of Europe as a continent? Or should only those developments be emphasized which can help us understand Europe's culture as it is seen today? To avoid a futile attempt at writing an all-inclusive, encyclopedic and, consequently, unreadable book, I have decided to follow the latter approach. However, in doing so choices have been made that limit both the geographical scope of the Europe described in this book and the elements of culture to be discussed therein, knowing that to some readers the restrictions of this text will be somewhat disappointing, not to say painful.

As a result of innumerable geo-economic, geopolitical and cultural-religious developments, some of which can be traced far back into past millennia, while others are of more recent origin, many internal divisions have come into existence creating a multiplicity and diversity of culture in the Europe geographically defined above. Perceptibly the most obvious is the 'dividing line' separating western Europe from what, geographically at least, is called eastern Europe; this 'line', actually a wide transitional zone, sometimes called 'central Europe', stretches from the Baltic to the Balkans and roughly coincides with the present-day states of Poland, the Czech and Slovak Republics and Hungary.

This book mainly, though not exclusively, records events which are observable west of this zone, dwelling somewhat less upon the 'central' European countries and their cultures, and giving little attention to the Balkans and to Russia. Although there are sound scholarly reasons, besides considerations of a politically correct nature, to induce an author to include the cultures of central and eastern Europe in the text, I have chosen not to do so. First of all, I lack the language skills necessary to delve into the relevant literature. More important, however, I believe that this non-inclusion can be defended on the basis of the past itself; with its many 'accidents', it has forged links between a number of regional cultures in western Europe which increasingly have shown a comparable historical development, resulting in a more widely experienced culture that, however diverse in many of its elements, yet has grown towards an overall unity.[5]

One factor determining the relative unity of this area is the way of life and of thinking which was paired with and is still coloured by the development of western Christianity, after the break-up of the Carolingian Empire. However intangible, this development has resulted in a specific cultural sphere. Another, far more important element is the fact that a number of countries in western Europe, while being ruled by 'absolute' monarchs up till the end of the eighteenth century, have yet developed towards consensual and in the end even constitutional government. Over a long period, a tradition of civic societies has evolved, there, characterized by increasing economic and political freedom for the individual and, from the late nineteenth century onwards, also by some sort of collective care for that individual – a mixture of consumerism, liberalism and social democracy. If judged by those criteria, the Europe that now projects itself with such a pretence of historical inevitability is, indeed, only a recent creation;[6] some would even say that this Europe is really a creation of the late nineteenth century.[7]

Due to a number of historical accidents as well as to the absence of certain preconditions, in eastern Europe, such structures and traditions have not developed, or only marginally so. Maybe, in the near future, economic and political developments will result in a growing integration not only of already superficially comparable lifestyles but also of the cultures of western and eastern Europe. In the process, people in the west will be forced to reconsider their notions of what Europe is.

Yet, this cultural-geographical restriction has not solved the problem of choices. Traditionally, histories of Europe begin with an extensive analysis of all that occurred in Egypt, the Near East and Greece from *c*.5000 BC, acting on the assumption that the east coast of the Mediterranean was the 'cradle of European civilization'. As this is indeed where Graeco-Roman culture and Christianity began, to become probably the two most important ideological cornerstones of the concept of 'European' civilization, developments in this region will be described, albeit only sketchily, in Chapters 1, 2 and 3. However, this approach does not do justice to what was occurring at the same time in, for modern concepts, Europe proper and, more specifically, in its western part. Therefore, this aspect is included in the story as well, in Chapters 1 and 2.

Everything, including Europe, exists only by virtue of its contrast or its opposite. Moreover, everyone has an 'unknown side', some characteristics of fears and desires, which define that person. Man, European man as he defines himself, has made and known himself only through a confrontation with the 'other'. Therefore it is crucially important not to forget that from the earliest times onwards but, more visibly and to Europe more profitably, especially between the fifteenth and the twentieth centuries, many influences from outside the area now defined as Europe have played an important, not to say essential role in the shaping of its peoples and their culture. Conversely, Europe has always had a perspective on the world outside Europe as well, the more so as large parts of that world have been dominated by Europe.

Though for the Asian and African parts of the world which came into Europe's orbit that dominance effectively lasted only two centuries, covering the short period of *c*.1750 to *c*.1950, its consequences for the culture of the present world have been enormous. Indeed, if Europe is to be called 'unique', one of the reasons is surely that no other culture has ever influenced the earth as completely, for better or for worse. Also, it is precisely in these two centuries that Europe really came to acquire the characteristics it now prides itself on. It seems to me that in these two centuries the economic importance of Europe's Eurasian, Atlantic and African empires, in its complex interaction with the building of a consumer-oriented, literate, democratic society really constitute the 'miracle of the West'. Consequently, justice must be done to the global aspects of Europe's past, too, if one is to avoid misrepresenting history. Without interpreting the role played in its cultural formation by various non-European worlds and their peoples and cultures, the European world would be incomprehensible.

Many authors whose subject is the 'culture' of Europe only vaguely indicate the actual design and extent of their research. Do they plan to study the 'concept of Europe' only as voiced in ideas which claim for Europe a cultural and spiritual unity, ideas which frequently betray an unspoken yet only barely concealed moral basis and bias? Or is it their aim to study all kinds of 'manifestations of meaning' – for, surely, that is what 'culture' actually is – which in one way or another prove the existence of a real cohesion? If one opts for the latter approach, the central thesis should be that Europe is characterized not only by well-defined concepts of what it is or should be, if such concepts exist at all, but also by behaviour patterns and institutions, by ways of looking at man and society, by the things man makes, all of which collectively may distinguish this area from other parts of the world.

This, then, touches on the much-discussed problem of the difference between on the one hand cultural history conceived as a history of ideas and ideologies, or on the other hand as a far wider ranging history of the great variety of cultural forms, namely the manifestations of man's handling of nature, of himself and of the society he lives in. Both are respectable approaches. As the context in which this book will try to consider what has characterized, and continues to characterize, Europe is so culturally and politically charged, it seems sensible to try to combine both perspectives.

After all, if one would study articulate ideas about Europe without considering them in the context of the time, the circumstances and the social framework they were formulated in, and on the basis of very diverse cultural forms in which they became manifest, there would be a real danger that such ideas would be seen as timeless and universal and that too much value would be attached to them. If the past has anything to teach us, it is that ideas which are proclaimed to have absolute validity are always dangerous.

Looking backwards and forwards, one first has to establish that Europe is made up of a number of traditions that, though each one of them may not be specifically, uniquely 'European', together do constitute a coherent culture, a heritage which is worth exploring from a historical point of view precisely if we want critically to preserve and expand it in order to offer it as a contribution to the welfare of mankind amidst the contributions that have been made and are still being made by other cultures.

Trying to isolate these traditions in their chronological appearance on the European scene, we may first cautiously name the nascent democracy of ancient Greece; we should then go on to the legal structures devised in classical Rome, which protected both life and property, and to the moral values of Christianity that tried to teach that protecting only oneself would not result in a humane society.

Of singular importance is, surely, the tolerance that slowly developed both through interregional and interconfessional contacts within the narrow confines of Europe and through intercultural relations between Europe and the 'other worlds'. The invention of the art of printing was a momentous stimulus not only to the wide distribution of knowledge and to the diffusion of a spirit of criticism and debate, but, perhaps more important, to better education and consequently to more widely spread opportunities for cultural diversity and personal development.

Meanwhile, forms of representative government emerged in intricate inter-action with economic changes that turned Europe from a mainly agrarian society in which, through a complex set of social and legal rules, equality of chances was largely absent, into an industrial society with chances that were, at least in principle, open to everybody. The process that articulated ideas of social equality and social justice eventually resulted in the concept of human rights, a concept not unequivocal but certainly inspiring.

Of course, we should be well aware that as far as the above developments represent ideals, they neither were nor are yet fully realized in practice. On the contrary, Europe has often been untrue to its own heritage. Therefore, without diminishing the great value of that inheritance, it is necessary to evaluate past and present practices precisely to preserve it in as pristine a condition as possible for the future.

This cultural history will try to establish how Europeans, often but certainly not exclusively intellectuals and scholars, shaped their lives, created culture, in increasingly complex manifestations. Many if not all of these manifestations were formed within the fundamental cultural context which Europe acquired from the first century after the birth of Christ. Beginning in this first century AD, a fusion took place between ancient Graeco-Roman traditions and Christianity, in itself originally the product of several Near Eastern, 'Asiatic' religions; it resulted in an often difficult partnership both of resolute rationalism and a religion based on revelation, which introduced elements into the thought of scholarly, religious Europeans that have stimulated a creative tension for two thousand years.

This book also hopes to show how, as a result of this process, many cultural achievements were absorbed as normative values in the self-image of Europe, which was mainly articulated by an intellectual elite. Elites, certainly intellectual elites, form groups whose cohesion is determined by many socio-economic and cultural factors. They share a way of thinking which determines their spoken and – much more powerful – written words, as well as, at least partly, their deeds. In this way they have a strong influence on the cultural expressions of society at large, certainly on those expressions which are encountered on the surface: political and social ideas, the public manifestations of power, customs and manners, and so on.

All this does not mean that the present text deals only with 'elite culture', and omits any reference to 'popular culture'. This is not the place to discuss whether these concepts, also referred to as the 'great' and 'small' traditions, are not too simple and, hence, distorting, to be tenable.[8] Rather, I prefer to stress that precisely the question of what people thought and, more important, how and in which circumstances they acted gives direction to every study of cultural history.

On the structure and use of this book

In view of all these arguments of definition and limitation, any cultural history of Europe is a selection. The result is influenced not only by authors' fields of interest and the scope of their reading, but also by the format of the book to be published, the latter the outcome of a confrontation between a publisher's policy and the presumed audience.

As to the first point, obviously, this book presumes to be a cultural history in the broad sense and therefore has to consider economic, social and political structures and processes as well. Yet as any cultural history is, inevitably, an attempt at a synthesis, trying to recreate and analyse the lifestyle of a number of more or less cohesive groups in a specific region, it cannot give a lengthy, in-depth treatment of these other aspects of the past; readers who want to be thoroughly informed thereof will have to turn either to more specialized works in these fields or to works which pretend to cover European history in all its aspects. Moreover, the nature of a cultural history of Europe which tries to explain present structures and manifestations through an analysis of past developments, almost automatically leads to a selection and discussion of precisely those aspects and episodes which clarify the process of continuity and change that transformed the past into the present.

Writing history, is, therefore, the chronicling of the behaviour and achievements of the 'victors', whether they were individuals or groups, whose actions or concepts contributed to today's cultural fabric. Are the 'losers', those who have been side-tracked by history, not just as important? Can we not learn just as much from the possibilities which once existed but which were never realized, as a result of circumstance – coincidence, the exercise of power, choice? It is an intriguing but unanswerable question. Perhaps we need to establish that, in fact, none of the energy which once existed really has been lost; that all thoughts and trends, even if they have at particular moments been condemned or cast off as too alternative or irrelevant, as heretical even, have only temporarily sunk into oblivion: they may well play a role at any time in the fruitful inter-action between 'past' and 'present' which always creates a 'future'. As William Shakespeare wrote in *The Tempest*: 'Whatever is Past, is Prologue.'

As to the second point, I can be short. A book was envisaged that would be of use to a large audience, implying that, if anything, it should not be so voluminous as to be daunting instead of inviting. I have tried to write such a book.

Besides, I have tried to avoid confining the infinitely complex cultural history of Europe to the straitjacket of an economic or sociological 'grand design' or an all-embracing and explaining theory of culture that I at least have not been able to find.[9] To give some structure to a story that stretches over thousands of years, this book charts Europe's past along the lines of what one may term its four grand phases of continuity and change.

These phases can be summed up in the following catchwords. The effort at survival, characterizing the history of mankind from the beginning, produced a great change in European culture with the transition, from the fifth mil-lennium BC onwards, to an agricultural society, and a rather more secure livelihood. The move towards one, dominant religion in Europe, which really started in the fourth century AD, had enormous consequences for life and thought. With some rhetorical exaggeration, one might say that from the sixteenth century onwards the genesis of a broader view of the world brought European man slowly out of the confines of the village into the orbit of the state, of Europe, and finally even of the other worlds. Last but not least, the development towards mass consumption and communication in the nineteenth and twentieth centuries gave European culture its present characteristics; also, more than anything ever did before, it robbed Europe of many of its traditional cultural forms.

It will be clear that this is not to say that the phases outlined above were peculiar to European history only, for at least the first and second definitely occurred in other regions of our world as well. But it may be maintained that, taken together and seen in their historical interaction, they represent both the result of and a framework for choices that have contributed to Europe's singularity, to its cultural identity as it stands today.

Although it is hoped that the interested lay reader will find this book a stimulating point of entry into European cultural history, it is primarily intended as an introduction for students in their early years of academic study. Some caveats are therefore appropriate.

Cultural histories never follow the strict chronology used by the more traditional political histories. Periodizations like 'the Middle Ages', the 'Early

Modern Period' and 'Contemporary History', long in use, are more or less inadequate, if not actually misleading. The patterns of different areas of culture and, moreover, in different sectors of society, can sometimes remain static for centuries, and sometimes change in quick succession within relatively short periods. Therefore, searching for useful beginnings and endings, for synchronicity, would mean distorting the past only to suit the format of a textbook.

A large number of quotations have been used, hoping that the readers for whom the past is, by definition, a foreign country where people do things differently, will yet feel that they can travel in that country. For the same reason, longer extracts from original sources have been used to provide opportunities for discussion, reflection and further investigation. The annotation of the text is meant to serve both as a bibliography and as an incentive to further reading; therefore, a separate bibliography has not been included.

Acknowledgements

First of all, I would like to thank my colleague, Professor Dr A. Hagen, who, though no historian, through his enthusiasm for the project stands at the beginning of this book.

The way I learnt to experience Europe during my journey has been made decidedly less one-sided by the comments of a number of people who, unlike the anonymous ones referred to above, can and should be mentioned with gratitude. Among them, I would like to give special thanks to my esteemed colleague from Louvain-la-Neuve, Professor Rudolph Reszohaszy, as well as to Professor Paschalis Kitromilides of the University of Athens, Professor Inge Jonsson, of Stockholm University, and Dr Jan van der Harst, University of Groningen. Both they and M. Jacques Walch, former director of IBM Europe, took pains in going through parts of my text, censuring it wherever necessary. The book as it now appears has gained considerably from their often candid criticism, as it did, too, from the observations of those readers who prefer to remain nameless but may yet recognize where their remarks have made a difference.

Yet the book owes equally much to the questions raised by my Nijmegen students, in the lectures and seminars on Mediterranean History, on Intellectual History and on the History of Cultures and Mentalities. With this book I hope to repay a debt of gratitude that every teacher owes to his pupils. The fact that in these programmes Professor Dr J.A.H. Bots and Dr M. Evers for long have been my closest colleagues has added as much to the pleasure of teaching as it does to the necessity to continue asking new questions.

All illustrations have been provided by the Centre for Art Historical Documentation of the Catholic University, at the University of Nijmegen, The Netherlands, which has taken care that all copyrights which were ascertainable have been honoured. Those who think that their right to any of the illustrations has not been honoured, should contact said centre.

Last but not least I want to thank Dr Catherine Brölmann, who put up with this book for a long time and whose meticulous reading saved my text from many inconsistencies. Of course, any defects that remain are solely my own.

Peter Rietbergen
The Dutch Institute, Rome, Italy
The Catholic University, Nijmegen, The Netherlands
July 1994 – November 1997

Part I

Continuity and change

New ways of surviving

1 Before 'Europe'

Towards an agricultural and sedentary society

Beginnings in Africa and the eastern Mediterranean, or the non-European origins of European culture

Already in the seventeenth and eighteenth centuries, some European scholars were searching for the origins of man in a past far remote from and in developments more complex than the simple picture derived by most of their contemporaries from the Christian Bible, which for many Europeans was still the only touchstone of truth, teaching that the earth and man came into existence when God created the universe on the morning of a momentous day in the year 4004 BC.

In 1698, an English medical doctor, Edward Tyson, visited the docks in London, having heard that a chimpanzee was being displayed there. When the animal died, he asked permission to dissect it. He studied all its aspects and functions and compared these with those of humans. Observing many differences, he yet considered the number of similarities to be greater and more significant. His conclusion, published in a book called *Orang-Outang, sive Homo Sylvestris*, 'Orang-Outang, or the Wild Wood Man' (London 1699), was that a fundamental distinction between humans and certain simian types was scientifically untenable.[1] Tyson scrupulously refrained from elaborating on the implications of his observations for the traditional view of man's history as the final, most perfect stage of God's creation. However, these cannot have escaped his more perspicacious readers.

In 1819, a young Dane, Christian Jürgensen Thomsen (1788–1865), was entrusted by the king with the task of beginning the classification of archaeological finds made in Denmark which by royal order were from now on to be sent to Copenhagen. Asking himself how to fulfil his instructions, Thomsen finally decided on a course of action which nowadays would be considered simple logic but was not usual at a time when archaeological objects were mainly judged on their aesthetic merits. He divided his objects according to their material and functional aspects; on the basis of this classification he concluded that the three earliest stages of man's history should be termed the Stone Age, the Bronze Age and the Iron Age, reflecting both growing technological skills and cultural progress. He presented this development as historically significant in itself, thus establishing the study of material culture and of man's past before the invention of writing as an object of scientific study rather than of aesthetics.[2] Some scholars were enthusiastic but the general public could not yet share Thomsen's grand vision of man's past, deeming it too primitive.

In 1847, the Frenchman Jean Boucher de Perthes published a book called *Antiquités celtiques et antediluviennes* (Paris 1847), in which he enumerated the findings of his excavations at Abbeville, on the Somme river. Although some acclaimed him as an important scientist, the majority derided his ideas: how could one possibly accept that there had been any such person as 'antediluvial man'?

Indeed, until well into the nineteenth century such views and their implications were unacceptable, not to say repugnant, to most Europeans, even to the well educated. Civilization, culture, these were the temples and philosophy of the ancient Greeks, the powerful, legal structures of the Romans, the universal norms and values propagated by the Christians. Cave dwellers, whose features were more ape-like than human and who worked with 'primitive' stone tools, simply did not fit into the European self-image. Yet, the progress of archaeological research in the nineteenth and twentieth centuries eventually forced Europe to drastically adjust its self-image, finally even accepting that man had come from Africa, the continent viewed so long as a world of darkness, a world without culture.

In the many millennia between about 1,000,000 and 700,000 years ago, the first hominids left the area in North-East Africa where, even further back in time, they had first lived; while some of them may have moved towards Asia, some migrated in the direction of the Mediterranean, finally settling in present-day Italy and France. We know this only because of the worked stones they left behind: there is not a trace of these people themselves.[3]

Between 700,000 and 400,000 BC, both in Europe and in Africa *homo erectus* probably evolved into *homo heidelbergensis*. As late as *c*.250,000 BC, so-called Neanderthal man entered the scene, named after the region near Düsseldorf, in Germany, where his remains were first found; he actually inhabited the wide region stretching from France and Spain to Uzbekistan, namely from Europe to Central Asia and the Near East. Fossils give us an idea of his appearance: very robust and stocky, on average between 1.55 and 1.65 metres tall, with short legs and a long torso enabling him to cope with the dearth of food resources in winter, when he survived on fat reserves accumulated by gathering in seasons of relative plenty. Neanderthal man's brain volume was, moreover, bigger than that of any other creature. He used these greater cranial capacities to develop a lithic technology, consisting largely of prepared-core flaking, which indicates that he consciously planned his basic survival strategies.[4]

Influenced by the seasons, these earliest inhabitants of Europe travelled around their regions seeking semi-permanent shelter in caves. Gradually, 'conscious' habitation grew, especially with the coming of fire. But these Europeans probably still had no language and therefore lacked the communicative capacity which can, for instance, organize a hunter society.

Meanwhile, a new type of *homo heidelbergensis* had appeared, whom we now call *homo sapiens* but who also is referred to as *Cro Magnon*, named after the French site where he was first discovered; anatomically and behaviourly, he basically resembles modern man. Where and when did he originate? Probably in subtropical and tropical Africa, too, from where he migrated to the Near East, now about 100,000 years ago.

A critical turning point occurred in the years 40,000–35,000 BC. Northern and western Europe as well as the regions around the Alps and the Pyrenees were in the grip of a harsh climate, with glaciers rapidly expanding from the principal mountain ranges. When this 'last' Ice Age had ended, and the world started to get warmer again, the humans gradually spread throughout Europe, via the Mediterranean and the Danube; the widely dispersed Neanderthals, far less capable of surviving, were displaced and finally became extinct.

As proof of the changes that occurred in these millennia, archaeologists have found signs of a far more complex economy, society and culture; hunting was clearly one of the principal strategies for survival, and tools and weaponry became more sophisticated: a more refined technology developed. People looked for dwelling places other than caves; open-air encampments with substantial houses made of wood and bone have been discovered in the plains of Czechoslovakia and southern Russia as well as in France.

Even more fascinating is that people started to create symbolic representations both of themselves and of the world around them.[5] Paintings have been found on the walls of caves, concentrated mainly in southern France and northern Spain. Until 1995, the most revealing were considered those discovered at Lascaux by a group of adventurous boys in the summer of 1940; others are situated in the Pyrenees and at Spanish Altamira. In 1995, a new, and even more spectacular find was made in the Ardèche, where cave paintings depict all kinds of animals hitherto unsuspected in early Europe; they seem to date as far back as 30,000 years. However, the discussion over the interpretation of these artefacts is not yet settled. Was it art for art's sake, or a means to instruct the young men and women of the tribe into the seasonal stages of a hunting economy, with references to the male and female elements in man and society? Then again, the caves may have been used as religious centres, where shamanistic rituals were enacted, and where the paintings reflected trance-like voyages into the world of the animals which were essential to the survival of man.[6] The concentration of cave paintings in what were apparently the most crowded areas of prehistoric Europe may point to the need for ceremonial activities intended to integrate and coordinate the growing population. Besides paintings, representations of humans and animals were made in bone and ivory, splendid examples of which, created *c*.35,000 BC, were found in caves in southern Germany. The many so-called 'Venus' figures are especially fascinating. These female figurines, both stylized and naturalistic, have been found all over central Europe. They may well point to the matrifocal character of these societies.

Did language already exist? The scholarly debate on the origins of language is fraught with vehemently expressed and often contradictory opinions.[7] Theories diverge widely, placing this evolutionary development anywhere between 400,000 and 100,000 BC. As speech preceded writing, there probably will never be any evidence for the exact period of its genesis. Yet the very complexity of the many artefacts or 'art' forms, pointing to a culture which used symbolic representation, intriguingly suggests the possibility of other, perhaps even older, forms of communication.

It is also noteworthy that these cultures, precisely in the articulation of domestic structures and the various 'art' forms, already show their own regional identities, which may have resulted in the formation of separate, self-conscious 'ethnic' groups. For we should not forget that Europe's distinctive physical-geographical features must have favoured the genesis not only of culture in general but also of incipiently diverse cultures: Europe was an incredibly varied landscape in a relatively small corner of the earth, surrounded by seas on three of the four sides, criss-crossed by navigable rivers connecting the inland areas with those seas; it was a region with contrasting but congenial ecologies, with demanding and challenging climates, and with barriers that stimulated development through both seclusion and communication.

The advent of agriculture, temple and state

For hundreds of thousands of years, all humans were hunters and gatherers. So were the inhabitants of North Africa and the Near East until approximately 10,000 BC. In the Sahara, then not a desert but a humid and fertile region, living conditions were favourable and people continued to go on as they always had done, even developing the art of pottery. However, the Near East, the 'land bridge' which allowed African man to move into Europe and Asia, was climatically and geographically somewhat less favoured, as it had been left relatively arid after the last Ice Age. People there had to start collecting wild grasses and to grind them to get some edible seeds – the skeletons of women found there show the spinal distortion this created. When the seeds were sown, first by chance and soon deliberately, agriculture had been 'invented'.[8]

The introduction of a cereal diet from *c.*9000 BC onwards allowed for population growth and, in turn, for the intensification of agriculture. This occurred in the Levantine region (Israel, Palestine, the Lebanon and Syria), in south-eastern Turkey, in southern Russia and in present-day Iraq. From that area, farming spread into Europe, first developing on the coasts of the Black Sea, still then a fresh water lake, as well as into India. Agriculture was soon also taken up in the innumerable small coastal valleys of the eastern Mediterranean and the Aegean islands, where streams, running down from the mountains, deposited their sediment and could be used to irrigate the fields; from there, it spread into parts of Italy, Spain and France.[9]

We have only archaeological evidence on which to base our knowledge of the slow transition to an agrarian economy and society on the European side of Eurasia and of the nature of the lifestyles and the accompanying social and cultural forms which from there spread over large parts of central and south Asia, coastal North Africa and temperate Europe. Still, the process can be reconstructed.

It seems that soon after the introduction of agriculture in the Near East, natural or artificial irrigation as a means to ensure higher yields was developed there, as well as animal husbandry, with the domestication of a limited number of crops and animals,[10] like olive and vine, and woolly sheep. Certain nomadic or semi-nomadic groups now became sedentary, settling more or less permanently in villages, which they often surrounded by earthen or stone walls. Sometimes, these villages were quite large. Thus, for example, the ruins of Çatalhöyük, in Anatolia, give evidence of what almost can be termed a town, built *c.*7000 BC by a people of neolithic cattle breeders; it housed a population of some 10,000 in small dwellings which were entered from the roof. Sculpture and gaily-coloured frescos indicate that these people had thoughts which went far beyond mere physical survival. For reasons as yet unknown, the settlement was deserted some two thousand years later. Another famous example of an early town is the walled city of Jericho, in Palestine, which probably also dates as far back; people continue to live there even now, so it is sometimes referred to as the 'oldest inhabited town in the world'.

This settling process was often accompanied by a transition to institutionalized private ownership. Although it cannot be said that this always led to just and humane structures as we view them, it must be observed that, from a purely economic perspective, this form of production has proven to be the most successful throughout human history: only for his own gain man seems to be driven to produce more and more so that money becomes available for intricate social and cultural structures.

Indeed, where conditions for agriculture were particularly favourable, complex societies and specialized forms of organization developed. The great river valleys led the way: Egypt, where the Nile flooded annually, leaving a narrow strip of fertile mud in the desert from which to reap a rich harvest, and Mesopotamia, the 'Land between the two Rivers', that is, between the Euphrates and the Tigris. The latter not only provided plenty of water for irrigation – artificial irrigation[11] – but, perhaps even more important, allowed for transport between the two emerging food-producing areas of the Near East, northern Syria and the lower reaches of these two rivers. Soon, communities sprang up which based their prosperity both on agriculture and on the manufacture of products not necessary for mere survival, such as tools and weapons made of stone and, later, bronze, or pottery for cooking and to store grain in; they also made added-value products that were ideologically important, to be bought by those who could afford to do so on the basis of their agriculturally produced surplus wealth: things such as costly textiles, artful metalwork and jewellery set with precious stones. Thus, trade networks developed, in which rivers played a significant role, but also overland routes, along which the newly found forms of traction by camel and donkey could be used.

In these as yet mainly agricultural civilizations, which were extremely dependent on water and other natural resources, people were intensely interested in the heavenly bodies, which not only determined night and day but also arranged the seasons and thus were responsible for fertility. These forces could not be interpreted in any scientific way yet, at least not according to science as it is now defined.[12]

In this situation religions had come into existence which worshipped the forces of nature and the heavenly bodies as magical, as divine. It was not long before those who purportedly could make valid pronouncements on their movement or even claimed influence or power over them were especially honoured; dedicating themselves to studying and explaining these things, they became magi, priests, the intermediaries between the divine and the human world. Farmers gladly gave them some of their surplus production in the hope that they would gain the gods' favour.[13] Frequently, a well-defined caste of priests developed, soon basing their power on hereditary claims, administering the religion in which people expressed their relationship to the incomprehensible or ineffable by creating gods. While, first, the gods had been imagined as animals, reflecting the view of the world of a pastoralist-nomadic society, in these urban agricultural communities anthropomorphic images were made as well. These were worshipped in ever more elaborately built cult sites, often centred around mountain-like structures reaching up to the heavens, where they lived, ruling both the skies themselves and all that lived under them. To the temples, the faithful went with their gifts of grain or cattle. From the temples, the priests exercised a growing power over society.

In the most advanced agricultural civilizations the first divisions of time, calendars, were based on a thorough scrutiny of the heavens. In the Nile delta the year was invented, consisting of 365 days which equalled twelve months, each made up of thirty days with leap days to even out the differences. Thousands of years later, the Romans took over this system: in 46 BC, Julius Caesar introduced an improved version of the Egyptian calendar which, with several adjustments, is still used in Europe and the whole of the western world.

As some agricultural societies grew more complex, a more regulated form of administration became necessary, especially when non-working priests started asking farmers for contributions in kind or in money to finance the cost of religious services, and, of course, the clergy themselves.[14] Probably because of the bureaucratic needs arising in these temple societies, the invention of some kind of non-oral communication system to store or transmit information became a necessity. The Inca civilization of Peru developed its system of knotted strings. The Near East developed writing. In the centuries between 3400 and 3200 BC complicated writing systems evolved in Egypt and Mesopotamia, comprised partly of simplified pictures (pictograms), partly of symbols (ideograms), partly of signs for syllables, and partly of one-letter signs. Egyptian 'hieroglyphics' – the Greek for 'holy incisions' – were written on papyrus or incised in stone or clay tablets; this, and Sumerian cuneiform, after the wedge-like signs used in its scripture, became the means of communication in the eastern Mediterranean, a means which was soon adapted to the trade that now developed between the different agricultural civilizations. For it was not only in Mesopotamia that surplus production resulted in all kinds of manufacture and trade. In the entire Near East, rivers, overland routes and the sea, too, brought the various agricultural societies the products that they lacked or desired.

In the narrow but fertile coastal strip of the Levant, cities were inhabited by peoples partly earning their living from agriculture but increasingly turning to trade to attain prosperity. The region became a very important link between the cultures of Egypt, Mesopotamia and of the lands around the Aegean Sea when it transpired that these lacked essential raw materials like copper and tin, for manufacturing bronze weapons and tools, and wood. Thus, cities like Jericho, in the Jordan Valley, as well as Sidon, Byblos and Ugarit, on the coast of present-day Lebanon and Syria, prospered on the basis of trade. In 1975, a team of Italian archaeologists searching the plains of north-western Syria discovered the ruins of the once-great town of Ebla. In it, they found the remains of a huge archive containing tens of thousands of clay tablets covered with cuneiform script.[15] Thanks to these, we now know a lot more about the economic, political and cultural aspects of these early societies: their customs, their rituals, their food, and the way all aspects of life in this region developed through interaction between the four main areas of civilization now existing in the Near East: Asia Minor, or Turkey, northern Syria, Mesopotamia and Egypt. In most of these agriculture-cum-trade societies increasingly complex religious-cultural and sociopolitical structures evolved, based on the possibilities offered by surplus production.

Besides needing temples, which regulated relations between the natural and the supranatural world, these societies usually also had to be defended against internal unrest or external attack. Those who took up these military duties claimed part of the harvest and often appropriated land which farmers then had to work in order to provide them with their living costs and weapons. This is how a second social group came into existence whose members did not work with their hands; they developed into a class of 'nobles', who, frequently in competition with the priests, also began to exercise power over society. Their leaders, whether they turned into absolute monarchs or not, often drew their authority from the interface between religious and military power. Divine powers were sometimes attributed to them, nearly always in connection with the need to comprehend and if possible predict the course of nature, more specifically of the agricultural cycle and the prosperity it brought.

On the fertile borders of the Nile this was the pharaoh, worshipped as 'son of the Sun', who ruled over Upper and Lower Egypt, which had been united in about 3000 BC. The power of these god-kings, who fused religious with military might, was such that the peasantry built the enormous pyramids and temples which were erected in their name.

In Mesopotamia, in the many city-states that divided the fertile lands between the two rivers, initially the priest caste ruled all and everything. It was on their initiative that the gigantic, terraced temple-mountains were built: the traces of these adobe structures still dot the erstwhile rich countryside, now often returned to a desert state. In later centuries the priest-kings had to share or even completely relinquish their power to leaders emerging from the military caste who, however, nearly always induced or forced the priests to divinely legitimize their authority.

On the islands of the Aegean and all around its shores, royal civilizations flourished, too, in the fertile valleys of Mycenae and Tiryns on the Peloponnese as well as on Crete, where, besides agriculture, sea trade became an important source of income.[16] The Cretans also developed their own writing, known as 'linear A', which has not yet been deciphered.

Perhaps one might conclude that the further development of the structure we now know as 'the state' was made possible by two interconnected phenomena occurring within the partly agricultural, partly commercial societies described above: the invention of writing and the development of large-scale trade, together with the introduction of coinage. The former enabled the elaboration of law codes with respect to property and inheritance; the latter made possible the creation of accounting and credit facilities. Together, these formed the basis for a fiscality that could support large armies which, aided by good communication systems and proper logistics, helped the state to acquire power, both internally and externally, and thus, to expand. But these states – whether pharaonic Egypt or the city-states of Mesopotamia and the Aegean – by their growing power and wealth increasingly attracted the unwelcome attention of outsiders, be they driven by hunger or greed.

Invasion, conquest and change: the first wave

Around 5000 BC, the region that is now southern Ukraine and southern Russia, up till the Caspian Sea, was inhabited by a tribal people who, after the burial tumuli they built, are named 'Kurgan' in Russian. They probably spoke a language that is lost now, but which scholars have named proto-Indo-European, for it seems to have been the origin of a number of languages spoken at later times both in Europe and in parts of the Near and Middle East – in present-day Turkey as well as in Iran (formerly Persia) – and in India. In all these languages, linguists have been able to discover striking parallels in the words used for such diverse fields of culture as kinship relations and agricultural practice, for pottery and for numerals. This may indicate that, over a long period of time, the Kurgan people and their language migrated west-, east- and southward.[17] Other scholars claim that people much like them in culture, but perhaps inhabiting a region slightly more to the south, in eastern Turkey, and northern Iraq and Iran, were the ones to start these big migrations and the spread of the languages which resulted in the tongues now spoken in Europe and parts of Asia.[18]

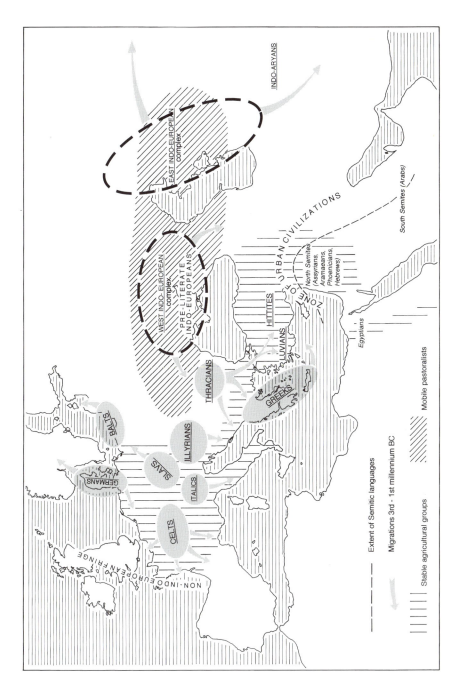

Map 1 Migrations in Western Eurasia, third to first millennium BC

However this may be, it seems certain that these scattered nomadic pastoralist tribes led a frugal life of near-subsistence in the vast tundra or steppe-like plains that stretched from present-day Poland and Hungary through southern Russia to Central Asia and western China. These tribes mostly seem to have been ruled by military elites who maintained their power by using horse-drawn chariots, spears and shields as weapons for swift combat. They worshipped the Sun and the sky gods and, with their horses and wheeled vehicles, were able to travel whenever conditions or their own inclinations drove them to do so. Although their economy included some agriculture and various forms of barter trade, it consisted mainly of cattle grazing. Consequently, a drop in long-term temperature, however minute, greatly affected their economic basis because the amount of pasture available for their herds was reduced. As such climatic changes occurred regularly, they were often forced to leave their homelands and move west, south or east in search of more equable climes.

It was precisely at such times that the wealthy agricultural civilizations around the eastern Mediterranean and in Mesopotamia were viewed eagerly by these belligerent nomads. Nor were they threatened only from the north. Besides the horsemen from the Eurasian plains, the Bedouins from the Syrian and Arabian deserts were equally jealous of their neighbours. Egypt was relatively safe, precisely because the deserts which bordered the Nile were so inhospitable to man. However, not only the 'fertile crescent' – the area of the Euphrates, the Tigris and the coast of the Levant – but also the river valleys of mainland Greece were frequently the target of successful attacks or outright invasions.

Indeed, in the decades after *c.*2200 BC, such tribes from Central Asia settled on the mainland around the Aegean. They spoke an Indo-European language from which Greek later developed. But the invasion by these 'Greeks' was only part of a process that occurred continuously on the Eurasian land mass, resulting in intermittent crises when older societies were uprooted by these invaders. In the two centuries after 2200 BC as well as in the period between *c.*1500 and 1100 BC, nomad leaders gained control not only over the Peloponnese but also over the 'Land between the two Rivers'. Such groups frequently founded new states which, from a cultural perspective, always incorporated a mixture of existing 'native' and new 'foreign' elements. Thus, it was not long before the foreign became native – showing that thinking in such terms can be dangerous.

Hammurápi (1792–1750 BC), the ruler of the city and state of Babylon, in Mesopotamia, was descended from such nomads. He founded a vast empire and became famous as one of the first lawmakers of the western part of the world.[19] A diorite stela more than 2 metres high shows him standing before the sun god Shamash, from whom he accepts the task of writing his 'law code'. In this way he showed that his legal prescriptions conformed to the gods' requirements.

Plate 1 A deer's head in yellow, red, brown and black, from a cave painting at Niaux, France, dated *c.*20,000–10,000 BC. The artist has captured the animal with its head thrown back, its antlers thrust forward, preparing for attack – a scene which must have been part of prehistoric man's daily life
Source: Centre for Art Historical Documentation, Nijmegen, The Netherlands

Plate 2 Engraved diorite stele showing both the 282 articles of Hammurápi's laws, meant to structure a complex society, and the King himself, standing before the sun god, Shamash, receiving the symbols of his power
Source: Musée du Louvre, Paris, France

BABYLON, THE SEVENTEENTH CENTURY BC: THE LAW CODE OF
HAMMURÁPI

The pillar on which Hammurápi's 'law code' is inscribed was discovered by
French archaeologists in Susa, Iran, in 1901–2, and is now in the Louvre
Museum in Paris. Its public function may have been to indicate that 'the law'
could be invoked by anyone who could read or be read to, so that arbitrariness
was to a certain extent abolished.

The text, with its 282 articles, points to a complex, definitely patriarchal
society, characterized by a combination of agriculture and commerce. Intricate
regulations establish the rights and duties of the upper class, the nobility,
towards the state, the temple and the rest of the citizens who were not part of
the nobility, mostly farmers and traders. The prescriptions primarily deal with
land development and use but also address the problems of an already quite
advanced trade system, heavily emphasizing the safeguarding of the rights of
property. In a number of cases the punishment for offences committed by
the nobility against commoners is noticeably less severe than for offences
committed by people against others from their own group: equality before the
law had not been realized, but some forms of public safety had, through the
state's monopoly on public violence.

Many of Hammurápi's laws recur in the oldest laws of the Jews which,
though written much later, especially in the Old Testament books of Exodus
and Deuteronomy, show the influence of Mesopotamia on the societies of the
Mediterranean coast.

1   If a seignior accused another seignior and brought a charge of murder
       against him, but has not proved it, his accuser shall be put to death.
2   If a seignior brought a charge of sorcery against another seignior, but has
       not proved it, the one against whom the charge of sorcery was brought,
       on going to the river [the Euphrates, regarded as god], shall throw himself
       into the river, and if the river has then overpowered him, his accuser shall
       take over his estate; if the river has shown that seignior to be innocent and
       he has accordingly come forth safe, the one who brought the charge of
       sorcery against him shall be put to death, while the one who threw
       himself into the river shall take over the estate of his accuser.
6   If a seignior stole the property of church or state, that seignior shall be put
       to death; also the one who received the stolen goods from his hand shall
       be put to death.
15   If a seignior has helped either a male slave of the state or a female slave of
       the state, or a male slave of a private citizen or a female slave of a private
       citizen to escape through the city-gate, he shall be put to death.
38   In no case may a soldier, a commissary, or a feudatory deed any of his
       field, orchard, or house belonging to his fief to his wife or daughter, and
       in no case may he assign them for an obligation of his.

39 He may deed to his wife or daughter any of the field, orchard, or house which he purchases and accordingly owns, and he may assign them for an obligation of his.

104 If a merchant lent grain, wool, oil, or any goods at all to a trader to retail, the trader shall write down the value and pay (it) back to the merchant, with the trader obtaining a sealed receipt for the money which he pays to the merchant.

106 If a trader borrowed money from a merchant and has then disputed (the fact) with his merchant, that merchant in the presence of god and witnesses shall prove that the trader borrowed the money and the trader shall pay to the merchant threefold the full amount of money that he borrowed.

142 If a woman so hated her husband that she has declared, 'You may not have me,' her record shall be investigated at her city council, and if she was careful and was not at fault, even though her husband has been going out and disparaging her greatly, that woman without incurring any blame at all, may take her dowry and go off to her father's house.

153 If a seignior's wife has brought about the death of her husband because of another man, they shall impale that woman on stakes.

195 If a son has struck his father, they shall cut off his hand.

196 If a seignior has destroyed the eye of a member of the aristocracy, they shall destroy his eye.

198 If he has destroyed the eye of a commoner or broken the bone of a commoner, he shall pay one *mina* of silver.

264 If a shepherd, to whom cattle or sheep were given to pasture, being in receipt of his wages in full, to his satisfaction, has then let the cattle decrease, has let the sheep decrease, thus lessening the birthrate, he shall give increase and profit in accordance with the terms of his contract.

268 If a seignior hired an ox to thresh, twenty *qu* of grain shall be its hire.

269 If he hired an ass to thresh, ten *qu* of grain shall be its hire.

282 If a male slave has said to his master, 'You are not my master', his master shall prove him to be his slave and cut off his ear.[20]

Beginnings in Europe: after the last Ice Age

From about 13,000 BC, the climate in Europe had started to get warmer again, and with the melting of the ice the continent assumed much of the shape it still has. The sea level rose, creating a Baltic Sea considerably larger than the present one, as well as the Zuyderzee – which the Dutch began reclaiming since the early years of our era till they finally converted the last part of it into farmland in the late nineteenth and early twentieth centuries.

With the glaciers receding, north-western Europe also acquired its present contours of high ridges bordering low-lying plains. At the same time, however, the tremendous forces inside the earth continued to work, as they still do, for example in causing northern Scandinavia to rise by a metre per century; many early settlements which, according to archaeological data, were situated on the coast a thousand or more years ago have been unearthed high and dry, inaccessible to any shipping. Meanwhile, western and southern Europe continued to slowly sink, as these regions still do. Over the last millennia, this has caused the disappearance of large coastal plains and the continuous battle of man against water all along these coasts. Sometimes, the process has created huge coastal lakes, like the Marismas in southern Spain, or the Pontine Marshes south of Rome, which became uninhabitable through malaria. Yet again, in other areas the alluvial deposits brought to the sea by Europe's rivers resulted in coastlines prograding steadily: the ancient port of imperial Rome, Ostia, once on the Tyrrhenian Sea, is now situated some 3 kilometres inland.[21] Obviously, these processes, however slow, did deeply affect man's life for all the centuries up till the nineteenth century, when some though certainly not all of them could be halted or even reversed by technological means.

Of more immediate impact to man was the circumstance that with the end of the last Ice Age, the ecology changed, too: the tundra and steppe-like landscape was replaced by dense forests. This process was completed in the whole of Europe by about 10,000 BC. Consequently, the animal population decreased, forcing humans to accommodate their behaviour to a sharply reduced food supply. This seems to have resulted in a different, generally less sophisticated pattern of economic and social organization, evinced by the decreasing production of symbolic forms. Hunting, the exploitation of aquatic resources and the gathering of plant foods, mostly hazelnuts, became the basis of subsistence.[22]

But by the seventh or sixth millennium, a new element slowly began entering this European environment from the Near East, dramatically changing people's lives: now, agriculture and animal husbandry were adopted in Europe, too; staples not native to this region, such as wheat and barley, as well as sheep and goats, were introduced. Farming and cattle-breeding were slowly adopted by the many inhabitants of the great plains characterizing the central-western part of the continent. The process, a slow revolution, beginning in the countries bordering the eastern Mediterranean, first reached Greece and the Balkans, and then spread, by sea, to the islands of the Mediterranean and to Europe's southern shores; by *c.*5000 BC, possibly via the Danube valley which enters deeply into the heartland of Europe, it reached the central regions and began its voyage to the north-west. By this time, both the physical and the cultural landscape of Europe had changed forever.[23]

The limits set on food supply and, consequently, on demographic development, first by a hunter-gatherer and later by a nomadic-pastoralist way of life, were broken. In the agricultural economy that now came to characterize Europe, a new way of life, a new culture evolved, based on the security and prosperity provided by agriculture, in combination with hunting. As in the great river civilizations of the Near East, in Europe, too, agriculture and the surpluses of food and, hence, of wealth that came with it resulted not only in population increase but also in the development of more complex institutions both in the sociopolitical field and in the realm of religion.

Hamlets and villages, mostly palissaded, now covered the temperate woodlands. Houses were built – of stone and clay in the south-east, of timber in central and western Europe. Pottery was introduced, painted in red and white in the Aegean and on the Balkans, decorated in linear patterns in central Europe. People, though still wearing leather clothing and grass capes, began to wear jewellery as well, made not only of shells but also of the very hard to work obsidian.

Extensive burial sites have been discovered, showing graves that were both formal and individual. Shamanistic rituals, including the smoking of narcotic weeds and human sacrifice, characterized religion. Fired clay figurines, mostly female – perhaps referring to woman's prime role in creation and reproduction – have been found in and near many settlements.[24] Culture in Europe, quite possibly a culture which continued to centre around a mother-goddess, became ever more recognizable.[25]

From the fifth millennium BC onwards, various developments slowly altered the area designated as Europe by researchers of prehistoric culture, that is, from Ireland to the Danube and the great rivers of Russia. They can be better charted thanks to the increasing abundance of archaeological findings. This results in an ever more complex picture. Roughly three regions can be distinguished: the north, the middle and the south.

For a very long time, in the cold, relatively unattractive, sparsely populated north the economic, social and political situation did not change much. The agricultural economy remained the principal means of existence; stone remained the primary raw material for tools and weapons and the village remained the main form of settlement. Nevertheless, this culture was able to erect, first, huge wooden temples, like the one discovered in 1997 near Stanton Drew, in south-west England, dating from *c.*3000 BC, and later large stone structures, megalithic monuments, both in the form of circular religious buildings, like the enormous circle at Stonehenge, or the Danish, Dutch and Breton oblong barrow graves. All in all, society here was less affected by the great changes which occurred in the middle and southern regions.

By *c.*5000 BC, agriculture and transport had fully developed in the more temperate parts of Europe, with the introduction of the olive and the grape, as well as of the woolly sheep, and, perhaps a millennium later, of the plough and the wheel. From the south, viticulture eventually reached the frontiers of the temperate zone, in mid-England, the Netherlands, Germany, southern Poland and southern Russia. From a smoking culture, Europe became a drinking culture. Sheep, bred in runs by the women, allowed for the manufacture of textiles; this in its turn revolutionized clothing, which soon became a social sign as well. The wheel and the horse revolutionized both economic and military life: long-distance overland trade and the chariot now became part of European culture.[26] While commerce may have been due to the proximity of these regions to the more complex economic and cultural centres of the

Plate 3 Bronze chariot showing a procession of warriors and other people, some of them leading a (sacrificial?) deer, surrounding a figure (of a mother goddess?) carrying a shallow bowl in which offerings could be placed. From a grave from the seventh century BC found at Strettweg, Styria
Source: Steiermärkisches Landesmuseum, Johanneum, Graz, Austria

eastern Mediterranean, where the kingdoms and cities of the Aegean and the Near East discovered a growing need for the mineral riches of west and central Europe, the chariot may have been brought by the hordes that rode in from the great Eurasian steppe. Not surprisingly, temperate Europe's fertile fields held great attraction for the peoples whom we, retrospectively, call Indo-European, who lived on the plains of central Eurasia. As well as to the Near East and to India, these people turned westward, conquering the older European cultures, changing them, probably, from a more matriarchal to a more patriarchal society, but, of course, being changed by the contact as well.

These chariot-driving peoples brought new techniques. Around *c.*2500 BC, the method of bronze-casting was developed in southern Russia and the northern Near East. This method required enclosed clay-lined furnaces driven by bellows. However, the basic metals of bronze, copper and tin were not widely available in these areas. This must have been one of the prime factors behind the development of long-distance trade within and quickly also outside the Mediterranean. And this trade, in its turn, decisively changed the long-static economies and societies of western and central Europe.[27]

Complex trade routes began to connect the mineral resources of the Carpathians, Austria and southern Germany with the Aegean. The previous existence or the genesis of elites in these regions can now be proven. They 'emerge' from the rich grave-offerings which have been found: chieftains and their families were buried with their horses and bronze chariots, with carefully crafted drinking vessels and beautifully tooled and decorated weapons, all of which indicate prestige but also, of course, surplus wealth. Even in more northern regions, where copper and tin were not available for exchange, skilfully worked bronze was sought; there, amber and fur were used as barter. By 1300–1100 BC, most of south and central Europe were in their 'Bronze Age'.

Invasion, conquest and change: the second wave

The second great wave of invasions in the eastern Mediterranean during the fifteenth and fourteenth century BC, was particularly destructive. While scholarly opinion on this period is characterized by many conflicting interpretations, it seems likely that tribes probably coming from or through the Balkans and Italy penetrated into the eastern part of the Mediterranean where many kingdoms were conquered.[28] Wearing horned helmets and bearing large round shields and spears, these invaders took over power in many places. The Egyptians called them 'sea raiders' because they attacked from the Mediterranean. Indeed, these men conquered the pharaonic kingdom, as is shown by engravings depicting their attacks that cover the walls of the great temple of Medinet Habu, built by Pharaoh Rameses II.

Though many splendid monuments, like the royal palaces of Knossos, on Crete, were lost during these invasions, all sorts of culture, such as language, writing and religion, were retained by the new societies which now came into existence, for the original inhabitants around the Aegean soon mixed with the newcomers.[29]

In consequence of these changes, developments took place all over the eastern Mediterranean; from a modern European point of view, the most interesting ones occurred mainly on the margins of the great civilizations of Egypt and Mesopotamia.

A 'marginal' culture? Religion and state formation in Israel

In about 1000 BC, trading cities – some of them republics, others monarchical city-states – dominated the coastal area occupied by present-day Syria, Lebanon and Israel. Culturally, they fulfilled an ancient and important role as intermediaries between the civilizations of Asia Minor, Mesopotamia and Egypt.[30]

The interior of this region was mainly inhabited by semi-nomadic tribes, some of which had created a monotheistic religion with Yahweh as the only, invisible God. This was an exception in the Near East, where polytheism was the rule and every tribe usually worshipped several gods, represented in human or animal form, although forms of 'henotheism', in which one particular god was seen as the supreme creator, did exist: 'Lord of Heaven and Earth, The Earth did not exist, You have created it', says a text of one of these non-Israelite cultures.

The history of the Israelites, inextricably bound up with their religion, was recorded by a multitude of authors over hundreds of years, till it came to form the *Bible*, from the Greek word for 'Book'. Showing the long, impressive struggle of the Jews to keep their faith with their chosen God, it also shows the slow formation of a Jewish state, out of a tribal community where physical survival was a constant concern, as affirmed by the Bible's manifold food references: God rewarded those who served him well with plenteousness.

In an early period, war erupted between the interior and coastal regions and a number of the Jewish tribes united under kings anointed by priests in Yahweh's name. A new kingdom thus came into being, gaining a governmental, ceremonial and religious centre when King David conquered Jerusalem in about 990 BC. There, Yahweh was worshipped in a splendid temple built by David's son and successor, Solomon.

However, tensions quickly surfaced. On the one hand, the 'modern' kings with their power politics, aided by the cast of priests, strove for centralization and, moreover, sometimes sought support from gods other than the unseen Yahweh. On the other hand, the so-called prophets strove to see the old, holy traditions maintained; acting as self-appointed protectors of the ordinary people, they created their own power base.[31]

When it came to ethics, it was mainly these prophets who pressed the need to live righteously in Yahweh's name. An essential part of this was showing mercy to the less fortunate. The powerful and rich had a duty to protect the poor, since these had virtually no rights to shield them from all sorts of exploitation and oppression. Thus, in the society of ancient Israel, justice was proclaimed to be a religious and moral duty, but certainly not a socially and politically enforceable right.

A 'marginal' culture? Trade and communication in Phoenicia

Since ancient times, trading cities had flourished in Phoenicia, the name given by the Greeks to the fertile but narrow strip between the foothills of the Lebanese and Syrian mountains and the sea. They had originated in places where trade routes from east to west and north to south naturally crossed: here, the Syrian and Palestinian hinterland were connected to the Mediterranean, and Anatolia and present-day Iraq were linked with Egypt. Although the Phoenician region never became politically united, these cities shared similar governmental structures. Moreover, their peoples spoke the same language and often worshipped the same gods.[32]

After the turbulent years between 1500 and 1100 BC, when many great kingdoms in the region were weakened or destroyed by the wave of invasions, these cities took the opportunity to expand, which came when peace returned. They established contacts with the fertile and wealthy valleys around the Aegean but also with Northern Africa, Italy, southern France and eastern Spain. Whenever possible, they even established settlements in these places, to allow part of their own population to emigrate. In this way they introduced many elements from eastern Mediterranean culture into regions which were not as technologically advanced yet.

Somewhere in the middle of the second millennium BC, in the Syrian city of Ugarit the many hundreds of signs used for writing in Mesopotamia had been reduced to some thirty signs. Now, in about 1000 BC, the Phoenicians further developed this system, whereby each sign ('letter') came to stand for only one sound, usually the first sound of the object which the sign had originally been associated with: *alef*, from the first sound for 'cow', became the letter or sound 'a', and so on. This revolutionary discovery can perhaps be explained by the commercial milieu in which it was made. Whereas in the temple-states of Egypt and Mesopotamia reading and writing the complicated sign system was deliberately restricted to a small group of highly educated and hence powerful people, such trading societies as Ugarit and the Phoenician cities needed a simple way of writing that would be easy to learn by a large group who could not afford to spend long years at school.

A 'marginal' culture? Democracy and its limitations in Greece

In the mean time, in Greece the Mycenaean and Cretan civilizations had disappeared. New Judo-European, so-called Dorian, tribes settled there between 1200 and 800 BC. While they took over a number of elements from the previous civilizations, they clung mainly to their own lifestyles.[33] This new society was concentrated around military leaders, local 'rulers' who, however, were more like rustic gentleman farmers than the splendid kings of old who had lived a refined palace culture in large cities. Writing mostly disappeared and bards became the bearers and transmitters of a largely oral tradition, singing the praises of their heroic ancestors in epic poems.

Two collections have survived: the *Iliad*, which tells of the battle between rulers on the Greek mainland and the king of Troy, a city in what is now north-western Turkey, and the *Odyssey*, which describes the fate of one of the heroes of this war, who manages to return home only after a long and difficult journey across the Mediterranean. Both epics were and still are attributed to the poet Homer, who lived *c*.750 BC. While some scholars doubt his authorship altogether, others maintain that even if he was the writer, he certainly was not the only one. While he evidently composed his part of the text by codifying a much older, anonymous, orally transferred tradition, it was added to by later, once more anonymous contributors.

From these poems a 'romantic' or rather chivalrous culture emerges, with valorous men who treated women as the object of desire and war: in the *Iliad*, war breaks out when Helen, a princess, is captured and must be won back – it was a theme that resulted from the Indo-European stock of stories and would become one of the great topics of European literature. It was also an intensely competitive culture, which considered physical prowess to be a sign of power and might. Yet it was a culture which also displayed fascinating elements dating from the period before 1500–1100 BC and the following centuries.

Precisely the oldest elements in these tales have much to teach us about the situation at the end of the previous, second millennium: comparison of Homer's text with the oldest stories from ancient Israel recorded in the first books of the Bible and with the epic poems from Egypt and Mesopotamia shows the fundamental unity shared by the cultures around the eastern Mediterranean, certainly until the invasions of 1500–1100 BC. They shared not only such spectacular stories as the tale of the Flood, which is found in the Noah episode of the Bible's book of Genesis and in the much older Babylonian epic of the hero Gilgamesh – which probably had its historical basis in the huge inundations caused by the breaking of the salt barrier between the Aegean and the great lake that now became the Black Sea, in the fifth millennium BC – but also more profound views on the creation of man and his relations with the divine.

Whereas some scholars think that in Greece this 'oriental' influence had effectively ended with the Dorian invasions, others hold that right down to the eighth century BC the military and economic expansion of the Near Eastern states was such that the eastern Mediterranean remained a cultural continuum – a continuum, however, that during the seventh and sixth centuries was slowly taken over by the Greeks.[34]

However that may be, even as Homer was recording stories from the Greeks' distant and not so distant past, the society which he was part of was already changing. The populations of the Greek communities around the Aegean were growing; this necessitated not only agricultural expansion, but also a turn to trade, to provide an additional means of existence. In the process, the gap between rich and poor seems to have widened. Also, farming villages began to cooperate, creating a new structure called the *polis* – hence 'politics' as the all-inclusive word for socio-administrative, legal and military organization.

In most Greek *poleis*, the tribal monarchy gradually disappeared, to be replaced by government by nobles from the most powerful families who had also, in the past, been military leaders: those who called themselves the community's best men, the *aristoi*. The rivalry between these families frequently led to chaos; sometimes a single person seized power and ruled as a tyrant; at other times efforts to achieve peace resulted in power-sharing between several socio-economic groups.

This is what happened in Athens, during the so-called classical age.[35] When, at the beginning of the fifth century BC, Solon introduced reforms trying to establish the rule of law, faction strife was not eradicated. In the year 508, after nearly one hundred years of war between successive tyrants and aristocratic cliques, Cleisthenes, a nobleman, decided to broaden his power by incorporating the people, the *demos*, in his support base – hence, 'democracy'. Men from the more than one hundred *dèmè*, or neighbourhoods, which comprised Athens were elected by lot to various administrative bodies, the most important of which was the Council of Five Hundred, or *boulè*. However, the People's Council had the last word – each adult male citizen, some 30,000 persons, having the right to vote.

We should be wary of idealizing this situation or comparing it to present-day representative democracy. First of all, attendance at meetings, which took place almost every week, meant the loss of a day's work, especially for those who did not come from the city centre. In practice this probably meant that it was mainly the wealthy citizens who lived in the centre who exercised their democratic rights. Moreover, only the richest citizens could be elected to the most senior positions, since they had the time and education to execute complex administrative tasks, as well as the prestige and financial means to ensure public support for their election. To put an end to the resulting corruption, it was decided that state subsidies would be made available to the poor to enable them to attend the People's Council and various jury courts. This improved the situation yet it still did not prevent the wealthy from frequently winning votes by a show of power, carefully selected charity and sometimes plain bribery, enabling them to attain the offices and positions from which they could continue to exercise the same power. Also, the kind of communication that ensures well-informed decision making among voters was mostly lacking. To start with, most Athenians knew how to read only rudimentarily and hesitantly, if at all.[36] And though people talked about politics a lot, at decisive meetings the political leaders delivering their speeches simply could not be heard by everyone present. Demagogy, or the capacity to somehow influence the *dèmè* and its voters by winning over, first, a small group – e.g. those sitting in the front rows – and through them collect the votes of the larger community, was a widely used means to the ends of various power seekers.

Since equality of property or income was not introduced, the rich could afford to accept the theory and to a certain extent even part of the practice of political democracy. Thus, the poor were given legal equality and they seem to have been free of institutionalized tyranny and exploitation; also, they could at least partly benefit from the practice of consultation and control in the exercise of power. Yet it has to be admitted that two of classical Greece's most influential political thinkers, Plato (428/27–348/47 BC) and Aristotle (384–322 BC), held rather negative views of the democratic system. Plato, in his *Politeia*, sketches democracy as the regiment of unlimited freedom in which all desires exist together. Its obvious anarchy cannot but result in a subsequent phase of tyranny. According to Aristotle, in his *Politika* – part III, 1278–9 – democracy, far from being the *aristè polis*, the 'best form of government for a city-state', is the rule of the poor. Describing the state and its political-constitutional structure, Aristotle presupposed a *polis* of manageable proportions, necessary because in the Greek view democracy was immediate rather than representative. However, he also presupposed a system in which the citizens proper were relatively free from day-to-day toil because immigrant workers, the *metoikoi* – Aristotle himself came from this group – and even outright slaves perform the heavy manual tasks.

Thus, while Greek thinkers have proposed fascinating theories about the various forms of political organization, we should not uncritically proclaim them the progenitors of western, parliamentary democracy.[37] Indeed, both theoretically and practically, their ideas diverged considerably from the ideas and practices that developed in Europe at a far later period. But the discussion their ideas engendered, definitely has been fruitful.

Herodotus (*c.*485–425 BC), a merchant and traveller, who has often been called the 'father of history' because of his *Historiai*, was born in Halikarnassos in Asia Minor but spent most of his life in Athens. In the third book of his 'Histories', he describes a discussion between three men about what is the best, or at least the most preferable, form of government. He attributes the debate to three high-ranking Persians, yet it is clear that he is reproducing a discussion which had been waged among the Greeks for decades and which, in its condemnation of monarchical government, was directed both against the Persians, the Greeks' most dreaded enemies, and against those with monarchic tendencies in Greece itself. Yet, Herodotus' analysis is far from being an ode to democracy; rather, it is an outstanding description of the phases which governments in many Greek *poleis* actually went through; it is a summary of the arguments for and against democracy, oligarchy and monarchy, pointing out, for instance, the ease with which uneducated public opinion can be manipulated, the greed and self-interest of cliques, and the tyranny of a king. These arguments continue to be of vital interest in our own age and, as such, have lost none of their relevance:

> The first speaker was Otanes, and his theme was to recommend the establishment in Persia of democratic government.
>
> 'I think,' he said, 'that the time has passed for any man amongst us to have absolute power. Monarchy is neither pleasant nor good. . . . How can one fit monarchy into any sound system of ethics, when it allows a man to do whatever he likes without any responsibility or control? Even the best of men raised to such a position would be bound to change for the worse – he could not possibly see things as he used to do. The typical vices of a monarch are envy and pride; envy, because it is a natural human weakness, and pride because excessive wealth and power lead to the delusion that he is something more than a man. These two vices are the root cause of all wickedness: both lead to acts of savage and unnatural violence. . . .
>
> A king again, is the most inconsistent of men; show him reasonable respect, and he is angry because you do not abase yourself before his majesty; abase yourself,

and he hates you for being a toady. But the worst of all remains to be said – he breaks up the structure of ancient tradition and law, forces women to serve his pleasure, and puts men to death without trial.

Contrast this with the rule of the people: first, it has the finest of all names to describe it – equality under law; and, secondly, the people in power do none of the things that monarchs do. Under a government of the people, a magistrate is appointed by lot and is held responsible for his conduct in office, and all questions are put up for open debate . . . the state and the people are synonymous terms.'

Megabyzus . . . recommended the principle of oligarchy in the following words: 'In so far as Otanes spoke in favour of abolishing monarchy, I agree with him; but he is wrong in asking us to transfer political power to the people. The masses are a feckless lot – nowhere will you find more ignorance or irresponsibility or violence. It would be an intolerable thing to escape the murderous caprice of a king, only to be caught by the equally wanton brutality of the rabble. A king does at least act consciously and deliberately; but the mob does not. Indeed, how should it, when it has never been taught what is right and proper, and has no knowledge of its own about such things? The masses have not a thought in their head; all they can do is rush blindly into politics like a river in flood . . . let us ourselves choose a certain number of the best men in the country, and give them political power . . . it is only natural to suppose that the best men will produce the best policy.'

Darius was the third to speak.

'I support,' he said, 'all Megabyzus said about the masses but I do not agree with what he said of oligarchy. Take the three forms of government we are considering – democracy, oligarchy, and monarchy – and suppose each of them to be the best of its kind; I maintain the third is greatly preferable to the other two.

One ruler: it is impossible to improve upon that – provided he is the best. His judgement will be in keeping with his character; his control of the people will be beyond reproach; his measures against enemies and traitors will be kept secret more easily than under other forms of government.

In an oligarchy, the fact that a number of men are competing for distinction in the public service cannot but lead to violent personal feuds; each of them wants to get to the top, and to see his own proposals carried; so they quarrel . . . and from that state of affairs the only way out is a return to monarchy – a clear proof that monarchy is best.

Again, in a democracy, malpractices are bound to occur; in this case, however, corrupt dealings in government services lead not to private feuds, but to close personal associations, the men responsible for them putting their heads together and mutually supporting one another. And so it goes on, until somebody or other comes forward as the people's champion and breaks up the cliques which are out for their own interests. This wins him the admiration of the mob, and as a result he soon finds himself entrusted with absolute power, all of which is another proof that the best form of government is monarchy.'[38]

Meanwhile, though a number of Greek cities had opted for a democratic government, one should realize that in Athens, the city we know most about, half of the free-born, adult persons, namely all women, were excluded from politics as, indeed, they were from many other aspects of public life.[39] For legally, too, they were considered unfit to speak or even act for themselves, and had to accept male guardianship all through their life, first of a father or a brother, later of a husband or a son. Their first duty was to bear children, preferably many, as only four in ten would survive infancy. While parents were required to educate their sons in preparation of at least a minimum of participation in the affairs of the city, they kept their daughters in close confinement at home; even there, the females were restricted to the women's quarters. Of formal, literary education for girls, little evidence survives. They took care of the household chores, preparing the meals that, with population growth and the conversion of precious soil from pasture into arable land, came to consist more and more of fish than of meat; incidentally, the women were not supposed to eat with the male members of the family.

Lower-class women may have gone out to work, although in a slave society most menial jobs were taken already; middle- and upper-class girls who had to break their seclusion to go out into the streets never did so unaccompanied; in doing so, they may even have worn a veil. It is also doubtful whether women were allowed to visit the theatre, where the plays were enacted that worded and shaped so much of the views and attitudes of the Athenians. Still, women might participate in the processions honouring some of the gods. In the so-called mystery cults, presided over by priestesses, they even found a domain partly outside immediate male control.

Yet, all in all, Athens and other Greek cities were largely male-dominated societies.[40] Even Greek vase-painting seems to confirm this; whenever women are depicted, both the free-born and the slaves, they are shown serving the men, in the house, in the tavern or in the brothel. Men went out to the gymnasium, participating in the many sports that Greek culture set such store on, precisely because they enhanced the virtues of manly valour. Men went out to the meetings of the fraternities that took care of funerals, allowing for a proper feast on the day of the burial. Men went out to dinner, and drank from the cups adorned with painted scenes representing sexuality in all possible forms, mostly objectifying the female role.

We have to realize that outside marriage free, Athenian women were simply unavailable as sexual partners; slaves or foreign-born prostitutes took that role. We also have to realize that sexuality was not gender-structured, divided into heterosexuality and homosexuality; rather, it was conceived as an act between an active and a passive participant, the active one mostly being male, older and of higher status, as opposed to the passive one, who could be either male or female. From the combination of these factors stemmed a situation wherein it was quite common for men to practise what later has been called homo-sexuality, a word the ancient Greeks themselves did not use. It certainly was not frowned upon or stigmatized if it was lived in an age-structured form, i.e. a form wherein a younger man, eager for education in all fields of life, was sexually subservient to an older one, himself assuming the role of mentor when he too came of age.[41] Some scholars have argued that, at least among the elite, emotional and sexual relationships between adult and slightly younger men prevailed. But while it is true that marriage was more of a social and procreative norm than a sexual and emotive force excluding other attachments, the idea

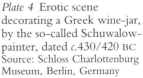

Plate 4 Erotic scene
decorating a Greek wine-jar,
by the so-called Schuwalow-
painter, dated *c.*430/420 BC
Source: Schloss Charlottenburg
Museum, Berlin, Germany

that bisexuality actually was practised widely throughout Greek society may very well be a case of a present situation being given a past legitimation.

Indeed, there is ample material indicating that male–female sexuality was the norm. Even though marriages were always arranged, and the man, marrying around 30, usually was twice as old as the woman, partners often seem to have come to love each other. Yet it is also true that for a man, divorce was very easy indeed, a simple declaration before witnesses being sufficient; women, on the contrary, could separate for only a few very grave causes and had to go through complex legal procedures.

Thus, the position of women in classical Greece much resembled that in traditional Islam. Already the *Iliad* and the *Odyssey* had summarized the female situation: Helen's infidelity created chaos, while Penelope's housebound faithfulness to her husband, presumed dead, restored order. However, the playwright Euripides showed that he realized which problems the prevailing attitudes provoked among the female part of the population when Medea, the heroine of his eponymous tragedy, spoke the words: 'Of all living, thinking beings, we women are the most unlucky.' Nor was the philosopher Plato unaware of the imbalance. He is supposed to have given thanks to nature, first because he was human rather than animal, and second, because he was a man rather than a woman – continuing the enumeration of his good fortunes by adding how lucky he was to be a Greek rather than a foreigner, and lastly, an Athenian citizen living at the same time as Socrates. Though in the later decades of the fifth century BC, ideas about some kind of women's emancipation were voiced, among others by Plato, they were not implemented.

Only in the third and second centuries did women acquire greater freedom, expressed, among other things, in and through education which now became available to elite girls as well as to boys.

However, in dealing with all these questions, we should be aware that the evidence we have is overwhelmingly urban and, indeed, Athenian, as well as upper class. It is hard to judge if the situation was different in other cities and in the countryside. Even the ideas of female beauty may reflect this complex bias: we know that women who could afford to do so, liked to wear a thick layer of white facial make-up which, obviously, indicated that they were not forced to go out working for a living or, worse, had to labour in the fields, as farmers and slaves did. Whether the lips, painted a bright red, and the hair, dyed a golden blond, also indicated a subconscious desire to emphasize a racial difference, is difficult to say.

Political, social and cultural life in the city was mostly concentrated around a holy place, a shrine – generally located on the highest point of the polis, the *akro-polis*, easiest to defend and nearest to heaven – and a meeting place, *agora*, where the adult men from the polis gathered for communal decisions or actions. Young men from the elite were educated not only in reading and writing and in the classical stories about gods and heroes, but also in rhetoric, a way of speaking and thinking which was just the thing for public action and for politics. In these locations, standard Greek language and a specifically Greek cultural pattern developed.

An important aspect of Greek as well as of other Mediterranean cultures was that the gods were represented as humans, admittedly with more power than ordinary mortals but still with the same urges and desires, virtues and vices.[42] This meant that, from the point of view of ethics, the norms which people used to guide themselves in their lives, in society, were determined by social rather than religious or moral considerations. Honour and shame with respect to a person's own group were the dominant values, not guilt and atonement as a result of subjection and surrender to a morally superior or even perfect god. It seems that in the classical era many Athenians spent a considerable amount of their time fighting those whom they thought to have blemished their honour – in court, however, rather than through blood feuds as in the archaic age.[43]

Yet there was little agreement with regard to the foundations of human actions in norms and values. In the fifth century, when the so-called Sophists dominated higher education, they argued that the application of a logical, rational way of thinking which enabled man to discover the rules which seemed to govern the structure of language and nature should also lead him to accept the conclusion that there were no such things as absolute laws, regardless of whether these were handed down by the gods: everything was based on conventions which men had agreed upon among themselves. A thinker like Socrates (469–399 BC) opposed such views, maintaining that laws were solidly anchored in absolute moral norms which existed independent of people, time and place. It is an opposition that still fuels discussions about the validity of values in present-day society.

However, most people did relate their everyday experience to a larger order, as Greek thinking about life and society was embodied in a corpus of myths, in stories about the world of the gods and their relationship to the world of man; actually, myths were collective representations which held man's subconscious visions of the world of landscapes, of nature, but also of family structure and of the community. Thus, myths came to be sources of great authoritative meaning in Greek society, up to the third and second centuries BC.[44]

Related to norm-describing myths, on the interface between the worlds of the gods and of man, was the theatre. Attic drama, in its two forms of tragedy and comedy, developed from the festive celebrations for the fertility god Dionysios. The honour of writing plays for such an event and for the public who attended it led to creative competitiveness between dramatists like Sophocles and Euripides. They and many others produced inspiring texts resulting from this; despite their time-bound context, they often articulate problems which modern Europeans also wrestle with. In tragedy, the relations between man and the gods were a central theme, while comedy developed as a form of political cabaret; both were staged for the edification and enjoyment of the people but also were used for the legitimation of political ideas, for the ideological manipulation of the electorate.[45]

Political, social and cultural structures comparable, in varying degrees, with those in Athens evolved in many Greek *poleis*. Based partly on its sociopolitical constellation, partly on its great wealth, Athens became one of the most powerful city-states in the fifth and fourth centuries BC. But although they repeatedly tried to do so, the Athenian leaders did not succeed in gaining control over the other Greek cities.[46] Nevertheless, the town of Athens became an exemplary centre, attracting talent in diverse fields from all over the Greek world. Relative freedom, an interested public and an economy which had been functioning well for some time led to a vibrant intellectual climate in which many forms of culture developed and were then copied elsewhere in the Greek world.[47] In this way, Athenian Greek culture gained a glory which far exceeded its relative political importance.

Even though the Greek cities had a common identity, not only in their language and in the organization of their polytheistic pantheon but also in the political and philosophical discussions which were central to the cultural life of the elite, they jealously guarded their independence, just like the Phoenician city-states. Partly because policies of aggression and expansion within the Greek world itself frequently succeeded only briefly or failed altogether, most cities had to find other ways of solving the internal problems which occurred, mainly for economic and demographic reasons. Colonization was one such option.

As a result of trade, the Greek and Phoenician cultures had already intersected in the tenth and ninth centuries. Perhaps the Phoenicians, with their expansionist politics in the western part of the Mediterranean, were an example for the Greeks: from the seventh century, many Greek *poleis* began settlements there, at first as trading posts, but quickly as colonies, too. Thus, a variety of cultural elements spread from these Greek cities to southern Italy, southern France and eastern Spain.[48] One element should, of course, be specifically mentioned. In the time of Homer, the Greeks had adopted Phoenician 'alphabetic' writing. Adding to it signs to represent the vowels which the Phoenician system lacked, they greatly facilitated scripture, making it more compact and less equivocal. One of the results of this form of trans-ferring culture was that in southern Italy, dominated as it was by the Greek colonies, first the Etruscans and later the Romans took over the Greek writing system. This is how the 'alpha-bet', this 'Asian' discovery, provided the origins for the system of writing which came to be used first in Europe and then in the whole of the western world.

A 'marginal' culture? Tribal society in Celtic Europe

Meanwhile, in the first millennium BC, life in Europe, beyond the regions the Greeks knew about, had changed again, precisely because, as in the eastern Mediterranean, there too the influences had been felt of new tribes moving south and west from their homelands in Russia and Central Asia. As always, archaeological finds provide evidence of the various developments that ensued.

People continued to live in clans and tribes, dominated by aristocratic families who owed their power to their military leadership and the wealth produced by dependent farmers. Druids and sages, shamanistic medicine men, continued to control the contacts with the other world through magic and various forms of ritual. Lentils were introduced, as well as broadbeans and millet, which now became a staple, being strong and growing quickly. But villages made way for hill forts, large walled-in spaces, probably erected to protect against external attack,[49] and burying the dead in graves was replaced by cremation and the preservation of ashes in funerary urns – hence the name 'Urnfield culture' for this period. This seems to reflect a deeper, spiritual change: rather than stressing the need to preserve the wholeness of the body for the afterlife the corpse was now allowed to decay because it was valueless. In the visual arts, scenes depicted men – warriors – performing heroic deeds: action and glory are the things that remain for posterity, while the soul lives on, borne to another world by birds and boats, symbols which start to occur frequently, also in the boat-shaped stone settings for the buried urns.

This culture and society, which came to dominate a great part of Europe for the next thousand years, has been named Celtic, after the Greek traveller and writer Herodotus, who called the tribes living in these regions *Keltoi*.[50] The Celts or Gauls truly were the builders of a 'Europe before Europe', the carriers of the first civilization which seems to have encompassed the whole continent since *c*.1300–1100 BC, from Brittany to the Balkans and the Baltic.[51] However, it is a civilization which has left only material remains – enormous stone structures, magnificent gold jewellery and many other objects which are evidence of transcontinental trade.

The centres of Celtic culture were, roughly, eastern France, southern Germany and western Czechoslovakia, with a definite core in the Hallstatt region, near the Salzkammergut, and the La Tène-areas near Lake Neuchâtel. There, a number of chiefdoms ruled by military aristocracies controlled rich reserves of copper, silver and tin; they also controlled some of Europe's main waterways – the Seine, Saône and Rhône, the Rhine and the Danube – stretching into the farthest corners of the continent. Their position did not exactly weaken when, once more in the eastern Mediterranean, men took metallurgical techniques one step further, going beyond the making of bronze to the melting of iron. For iron ore was abundantly available in these regions.[52] This resulted in increasingly intricate trade networks, which now also came to include Spain; the great reserves of silver found there allowed the silver coins to be minted which were the motor necessary to the growing economy of the eastern Mediterranean cultures.[53]

Indeed, iron and silver were among the main reasons why, by the ninth century BC, both the Greeks and the Phoenicians decided to settle in the western Mediterranean. The Greeks founded Massalia – Marseilles – which controlled the trade routes to the north, via the Rhône; they also settled in Ampurias, near present-day Barcelona, and traded with the Guadalquivir region, where the so-called 'Tartessos kingdoms' had become wealthy; these were Phoenician foundations, as were the trading posts on Ibiza.

Actually, the whole of Europe now became a series of interlocking systems of trade, connecting Cadiz with the Shetland Islands. We know about this trade from documents like the Massaliote *periplous*, a sixth-century sailor's manual about trade routes from Spain to Ireland. But there also was a trade system linking the Black Sea and the Danube with the shores of the Baltic.

The fact that in these centuries the climate in Europe deteriorated may have had a bearing on these changes as well. Northern Europe became far more humid, and huge tracts of arable land slowly turned into peat bogs in the seventh and sixth centuries BC. People had to find new ways to survive. From the sixth century BC, the Celts, driven by overpopulation in an agricultural society which had reached the limits of its productivity, began to expand to the south and south-east, over the Alps to the rich Italian peninsula and through the Balkans to the world of the Greeks and the empires in Asia Minor.

But if anything, these migratory movements strengthened the already complex trade area; an increase of cultural exchanges became inevitable, as is obvious, for example, from the magnificent *kratèr* found in a chieftain's grave in Vix, France: a bronze drinking vessel, 1.68 metres high, clearly of Near Eastern, Greek-influenced workmanship. It is only one of many finds that tell us that Mediterranean influences slowly began to pervade Celtic culture, just as Celtic motifs turn up in Greek and, later, Roman art.[54]

Regrettably, we know little about the Celts. For although Celtic myths and legends such as the story of King Arthur and the romance of Tristan and Isolde have come down to us, transmitted orally for centuries and written down only at a later stage, there are no sources written by the Celts themselves. Therefore one can only speculate about the precise details of life in this period, which was rediscovered only in the eighteenth century. In the nineteenth century, viewed by a culture which by that time had begun to look for its earliest roots, Celtic civilization was increasingly romanticized as the 'Dawn of Europe'.[55]

The 'birth of Europe' and the Greek 'world-view', or how to define one's own culture

Actually, we have to go back to the early Greeks to see when the name of Europe originated and what those who conceived it meant by it.[56] Europe first and foremost was a geographical term which came into use in classical Greek civilization from the seventh century BC. The Greeks had but a limited idea of the earth's situation: they considered the Mediterranean to be, literally, the midst of all lands; or, as the sixth-century prose writer Hekataios of Miletos told in his 'history', the sea divided the two worlds: Asia, which at first also included North Africa, and Europe.[57] Moreover, they had certain ideas about their own culture which reflected a mental mechanism found all over the world: most cultures define civilization – normality and identity – by describing certain peripheral areas and their inhabitants as not conforming to their own norms, branding them as foreign and even uncivilized; this way of thinking enables people to define what is their 'own' and what is 'another's'.

The ancient Greeks considered that Africa, which was given its independent geographical status several centuries later in the writings of the widely travelled Herodotus, was black and uncivilized, with the exception of Egypt, whence came many of the arts prized by the Greeks.[58] Asia they deemed more civilized but politically and militarily weak. Europe, or rather the Greek sphere of influence – the first mention of Europe, in the seventh century, speaks of 'the Peloponnese, Europe and the islands whose shores are lapped by the sea'[59] – was the most civilized and consequently, it was thought, the strongest region. It was strong because civilization was concentrated in free, independent and – at least according to Greek political and cultural propaganda – democratic city-states which between them maintained a balance of power. These states, sharing the same language, Greek, and the same traditions in the field of religion and other forms of culture, constituted *Hellas*, not a political structure proper but a cultural community, a civilization; it celebrated its cohesion in such manifestations as the games held every fourth year near the great temple of Zeus at Olympia, on the Peloponnese, or in the pilgrimages made to the famous Pythia, the oracle at the sanctuary of Delphi, with its processional way climbing a mountain overlooking the Gulf of Corinth and lined with sumptuous monuments and statues presented by cities and private citizens alike. As a cultural community of independent states, the Greek cities differed greatly – though perhaps not as completely as the Greeks would have it – from the 'other' world, from Asia, where there were large political systems encompassing numerous communities and luxury-indulging despots who ruled these vast territorial unities with brutal force.

And yet, the name 'Europe' was coined in a mythical story about the rape of the maiden Europa, a Phoenician princess, who was abducted by the father of the gods, Zeus, and taken to Crete. Did the Greeks thus recognize and even honour their many cultural debts to the Near East, to Asia? Herodotus did not fail to mention that the alphabet had been a Phoenician invention. And, of course, Plato, who may have travelled south to see the other worlds, wrote admiringly about the religious and philosophical ideas of Egypt.

On a deeper level, the Greeks felt that they could explain how their civilization had been shaped and why it was different. The prime cause was the climate, which was so varied in Europe that four seasons followed each other in one year: the change between cold and warmth ensured that people were flexible and active, both physically and mentally. In Africa and Asia another situation prevailed: there, the temperature was more even, and also warmer, so that body and spirit were less flexible and more sluggish; people in these parts were indolent and inactive, allowing themselves to be led too easily by tyrannical kings and emperors. In short, they were different, foreign, as was expressed in their language, too: they spoke no Greek! They were 'babblers', 'barbarians'. This rather exclusive stance, implying a fairly negative view of most Africans and Asians, nevertheless did not usually lead to discriminatory practices based on race or skin colour.[60]

It will be clear that this geographical and climatological approach and the characteristics attributed to various cultures on the basis of it were only a cover for a fascinating but certainly also biased political and cultural argument, one which not least was intended to support continued Greek independence against the constant threat posed to them by neighbouring countries, especially to the east.[61] It is one of the first examples of the power which a geographical representation, a 'mental' map, can have over man and his ideas.[62] However, despite this intriguing reasoning and also despite the Greeks' conceit, the small city-states in the long run proved not strong enough to effectively resist the expansionist politics of adjoining states.

During the centuries that the Greek *poleis* acquired their character as independent powers, a number of empires came into existence in Asia Minor which threatened that independence. In particular, the empire of the Medes and the Persians, dating back to the sixth century and concentrated in present-day Iran, expanded its power at the expense of the Greek cities that ruled the coast of Asia Minor; its armies even marched to within a short distance of Athens. It is true that Greek coalitions knew how to halt the Persians – in 490 BC at Marathon and in 480/479 at Salamis and Plataiai – but this did not prevent the Persians' pressure being noticeably felt, especially in Greek Anatolia. Precisely in this context, the linguistic distinction between Greek and non-Greek gradually acquired political content, emphasizing the difference between 'Greek freedom' and 'oriental despotism', as is made plain with dramatic power in Aeschylus's famous political play *The Persians*. Thus, the cultural stereotypes developed in the Greek world as a result of the necessity to militarily confront the Persians greatly helped to form a 'national' Greek identity.

Still, in the end even the great alliances between the Greek city-states set up at Athens' initiative were unable to withstand the force of events, the more so because time and time again the *poleis'* mutual jealousy inevitably opened the way for foreign influences.

The world of Alexander the Great

In the fourth century, a young man who became the ruler of Macedonia, a somewhat rustic principality on the northern periphery of the Greek cultural world, finally dealt the death blow to Greek freedom through an extension of Macedonian control over the Greek city-states. Yet at the same time, his actions were instrumental in diffusing Greek culture to an extent until then not realized.

Alexander the Great (356–323 BC) had been raised in the best traditions of 'classical' Athens by his teacher Aristotle. After succeeding to the throne, he followed in his father's expansionist footsteps, conquering not only the whole of 'Greece' proper but also the Greek world of Asia Minor, the trading cities of the Levant, Egypt and large parts of the Persian empire. It is true that his empire did not last – his generals divided the spoils they inherited from him – but in the diverse kingdoms into which the Near East was subsequently split up, an intriguing mixture emerged between many elements from Greek culture and the pre-existing traditions of those regions. This resulted in a civilization which has been called 'Hellenistic'.[63]

From the fourth century BC, urban elites in the world around the eastern Mediterranean often took over the Greek language and literary tradition as well as Greek art; combining these with their own Babylonian, Egyptian, Persian or Syrian heritage they produced a fascinating mosaic; sometimes, the result was a harmonious fusion, at other times one can still see the different parts continuing beside each other in art, religion, literature and the sciences. The world of the polis was past. The time of the cosmo-politan, the citizen of the world, had come. A new culture became visible.[64]

This culture was experienced most strikingly in one of the many cities founded by and named after Alexander. From its birth in 331 BC, Alexandria, in the Nile delta, quickly became an international port, the most prosperous city in the Mediterranean, where the sea routes from east to west and from south to north linked up with the land routes to and through East Africa, the Arabian peninsula and the rich world of further Asia.

Alexandria probably owed much of its cultural standing to its economic function as the gateway through which the Mediterranean, and Europe, could reach the civilizations of Africa and even more of the Orient, of Asia. Transversing Persia, Alexander himself had reached the Indus and thus the confines of the great civilizations of South Asia. When Plutarch, some 500 years later, wrote about Alexander's campaigns, he took care to emphasize that

Alexander had founded many cities there and, indeed, had brought the essence of civilization to these regions, giving them the Greek language and the values cherished by the Greeks, such as the love for one's parents. While thus defining Greece's own culture by juxtaposing it to neighbouring ones, he and other Greek writers could not suppress their admiration for the Zoroastrian culture of Persia, with its vision of the world as a battlefield between good and evil, and man's need to bring justice to all, especially to the poor, and the Hindu culture of India, with its accomplishments not only in the fields of religion, philosophy and cosmology, but also in the applied arts and in technology.

From the third century BC, trade, from the Persian Gulf across the deserts of the Near East, but even more through the Indian Ocean and up the Red Sea, brought the wealth of the Asia to Alexandria: not only diamonds and pearls, pepper and sugar, ebony and sandalwood, ivory and silk, but also cotton and wool. From the Mediterranean world came slaves, and sesame seed, flax and wine, copper, lead and tin.[65] The same trade served as an exchange mechanism for all sorts of ideas perhaps even more than for actual objects, allowing for a diffusion of knowledge and its applications in all fields of culture, in which the question of original invention is hardly ever to be answered, if not actually meaningless.

Such high-tech gadgets as milometers, altimeters, earthquake detectors and armillaries which explained the movements of the planets within our system that could be found in Alexandria were to be found in India and China as well, showing the varied interests, especially, of the maritime and mercantile communities of the Near East and of Asia. In Alexandria, this 'interface' between cultures, in this cosmopolis, where great riches were stored, the phenomena known as libraries and museums first came into existence: cultural institutions the likes of which much later would become focal points of European civilization as well as centres of tradition and renewal. It was precisely the great 'Museion', museum, library and university at the same time, which became a fulcrum of science and learning. This was the milieu where the Homeric tradition was first researched and where Euclid (*c.*300 BC) wrote his textbook on mathematics, the *Elementai*. It was the place where Eratosthenes (280–200 BC), after having put two sticks in the sand and observing the different length of the shadow they cast, decided the earth was not flat, went on to calculate the earth's circumference at 40,000 kilometres – his fault margin later proved to be less than 100 kilometres; it was also the place where, later, Ptolemy (*c.*AD 100–*c.*170) developed the geocentric model of the cosmos as well as naming the continents of the earth and their various parts. It was the town where Archimedes, who hailed from Syracuse, on Greek Sicily, studied applied physics and engineering. It also was the town whose school of medicine was famous all over the Hellenistic world; at an early time, the Greeks, borrowing, perhaps, from Indian insights, had evolved a rational system of diagnosis and treatment, which resulted in such practitioners as Galen, who was a student at Alexandria in the second century AD and the first to describe the circulation of the blood.

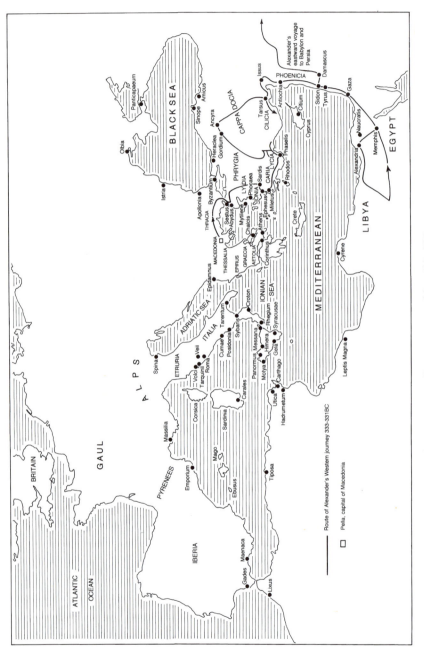

Map 2 Extent of Greek influence in the ancient Mediterranean world, *c.*400–300 BC

ATLANTIC
OCEAN

BRITAIN

GAUL

IBERIA

PYRENEES

Maenaca
Gades
Lixus

Emporium
Ebusus
Mago
Sardinia
Corsica

Tiposa

Massilia

Spina

ETRURIA
ITALIA
ALPS

Veii
Volci
Tarquini
Roma

Carales

Hadrumetum
Utica
Carthago
Motya
Panormus

Cumae
Posidonia
Tarentum
Croton
Sybaris

Messana
Rhegium
Himera
Gela
Syracusae

Leptis Magna

ADRIATIC SEA
IONIAN SEA

Epidamnus

Apollonia

Istria

THRACIA
MACEDONIA
THESSALIA
EPIRUS
AETOLIA
GRAECIA
Corinthus
Athens
Chalcis

Byzantium
Sestus
Abydus
Mytilene
Phocaea
Ephesus
Miletus
Sardis
IONIA
LYDIA
CARIA
LYCIA

Crete

BLACK SEA

Olbia

Panticapaeum

Sinope
Amicus

Heraclea
Gordium
Ancyra

PHRYGIA

CAPPADOCIA

Tarsus
CILICIA

Issus

Antiochia

Phaselis
Rhodos

PHOENICIA

Damascus

Sidon
Tyrus

Citium
Cyprus

Gaza

Alexandria
Naucratis
Memphis

EGYPT

LIBYA

Cyrene

MEDITERRANEAN

Alexander's
eastward voyage
to Babylon and
Persia

—— Route of Alexander's Western journey 333-331BC

☐ Pella, capital of Macedonia

From a political perspective, this 'Hellenistic world' quickly came under pressure from the armies of the nascent Roman Empire which, starting in the second century BC, crossed the borders of the Italian peninsula and within two centuries conquered all lands surrounding the Mediterranean Sea.[66]

Yet despite the decline and fall of the actual political independence of the Greek cities and the rise of hegemonic political structures, the concept of fostering individual spiritual development, of a citizen's (i.e. a free man's) civil rights as opposed to a powerful state, remained in the background. Admittedly, during the following two thousand years of European history most people were not exactly granted much political freedom, at least not until the revolutions of the late eighteenth century AD drastically changed society. However, the core of a theory about the political rights of citizens – whether or not within the context of the immediate but yet limited form of democracy that had been the practice of many Greek cities – was formulated by a number of Greek philosophers; several centuries later this foundation would be given additional strength in the legal systems devised by a number of Roman philosophers and jurists, and embodied in the 'legal state' of Rome. If only for this reason, the role played by Rome in the history of Europe deserves closer attention.

2 Rome and its empire

The effects and limits of cultural integration

Between the Alps and the Mediterranean, between the Etruscan and the Greek worlds: the expansion of the early Romans

In the twenty-second century BC, when the first Greeks settled on the Peloponnese, tribes speaking an Indo-European language and probably coming in from the Near East or Central Asia had entered Italy, settling in the centre of the peninsula. They are now called Latins.

More than a thousand years later there was a new invasion, by a people known as the Etruscans.[1] Their language has been only partly deciphered, with the result that little can be said for certain about their origins. We know them, largely, through the lavish grave goods with which they buried their dead; these are important cultural phenomena, providing an excellent guide to the study of the development of their society; they indicate the lifestyles of the various sociocultural groups as well as the power of the ruling elite. Their societies developed in the fertile region between present-day Florence and Rome; they organized themselves in independent city-states in which a warrior aristocracy formed the elite, ruling over the older, indigenous population. In the eighth and seventh centuries BC, they succeeded in expanding both northwards and southwards. Their power was a result of their wealth, which was based on trade in metalwork and pottery; the quality of their craftsmanship was such that there was a great demand for their products all over the Mediterranean.

The Etruscan elite, eager for the products of the Greek civilization that thrived in the south of Italy, soon adopted alphabetic writing as well; indeed, the oldest known example of Greek writing has been discovered in an Etruscan woman's grave in Osteria dell'Osa. Yet their influence also reached beyond the Alps, penetrating deep into the Celtic world. This was certainly one more of the reasons why, in the sixth and fifth centuries, Celtic tribes, driven by overpopulation and the hope of riches, entered Italy.[2]

One of the cities which the Etruscans had conquered in the seventh century was Rome, a mixed Latin-Samnite community situated in the fertile plain along the banks of the Tiber river, where trade routes linked the sea, and its precious salt, with the interior and the mountains, with their valuable grain and cattle. The legendary 'seven hills' probably served as places where the population of the valley sought protection when it was attacked.

Etruscan kings ruled Rome for more than a century in an often tense partnership with a local aristocracy which was united in an advisory board, the Senate.[3] By the sixth century, the Etrusco-Roman community became fully urban, adopting the characteristics of the south-Italian Greek *poleis*. The aristocrats, known as patricians, based their power on property ownership; as 'patrons' they relied on the backing of their 'clients', a group of dependent farmers. The remaining part of the free citizens, mostly traders and artisans, were known as plebeians.

In about 500 BC – the official date given is the year 509 – the patricians forcibly expelled their Etruscan overlords. Rome became an oligarchic republic, ruled by two magistrates, or consuls, chosen annually from the ranks of the patricians who, assembled in the Senate, now formed the Republic's governing body. Rome was certainly not a democracy of equal citizens. Indeed, the Roman Republic mainly guaranteed the rights – *libertates* – and the property of the aristocracy; their retainers enjoyed only limited rights.[4]

In the following centuries the city of Rome started a struggle for the fertile land in the region. Since the Etruscans had their hands full trying to ward off continued Celtic attacks in the north, Rome was more or less able to do as it pleased, especially to the south.[5] Increasing numbers of Latin cities were forced to recognize Rome's suzerainty, even if they retained their internal self-government when the ruling elites cooperated, that is, if they submitted to Rome's demands. They supplied troops and other aid for the wars which Rome now continued to wage. Besides this, Rome began to establish colonies in strategic positions in conquered areas, partly to relieve the pressure of a growing population in the city itself.

Thus, in the fifth, fourth and third centuries, a process of romanization began, whereby the language and other cultural elements of 'The Town', as it proudly called itself, were imposed on the whole of the region, although, of course, there was also interaction with existing regional cultures; in particular, local deities from subjected cities were incorporated in the Roman pantheon. Contact with, and the gradual subjugation of, Greek colonies in southern Italy had especially far-reaching consequences: many expressions of Greek culture were admired by the Romans and absorbed by the Roman elite.

Meanwhile, in Rome itself political and social contrasts grew with expansion. Not only did wealthy plebeians demand access to power, but also the whole non-governing population insisted on written laws to protect them against magistrates' arbitrariness. The demand for codification was first realized in 451 BC. Moreover, rich patricians and rich plebeians gradually merged into one group of *nobiles*, which in 367 BC led to the requirement that one of the consuls must be a plebeian. In 287 BC, the so-called *concilium plebis*, the gathering of all free male Roman citizens, was given legal status.[6] However, as in Athens, this did not lead to a democracy in the present-day sense. By the second century BC, the body of electors already consisted of approximately

250,000 men and therefore could not possibly assemble. In fact, power lay in the hands of the *de facto* administrators, the nobles, who continued their oligarchic government through their experience in and monopolization of bureaucracy, manipulating the electorate with all available means.

The waging of war became a Roman characteristic in the fourth and third centuries. War was certainly a social 'release'; as so often in history, expansionist politics and the creation of foreign enemies were instruments used to avert internal tensions by giving the population an external challenge. Indeed, many of Rome's wars were not defensive but, under the pretext of preventive action, blatantly aggressive. War was also a way for the Roman elite and sometimes for ordinary men, too, to achieve fame, wealth, status and thus power.

It was almost inevitable that the southward expansion of Rome would result in a conflict with the wealthy and powerful trading city of Carthage, one of the colonies founded by the Phoenicians, or Carthaginians, on the coast of North Africa, which by now controlled parts of southern Italy, Sicily and a large part of the western Mediterranean.[7] When the elder Cato (234–149 BC), one of Rome's most influential statesmen, decided to throw a handful of ripe figs at the feet of his fellow senators, he wanted only to underscore the message he had been proclaiming for some time: 'Carthage must be destroyed', both for its riches as the centre of North African agriculture and for its commercial and political hold over the western sea. From 264 BC already, both cities had been at war; the prize was, indeed, supremacy over the sea, over trade and the wealth which consolidation and further expansion would bring. In 202 BC, a decisive, though by no means the last battle was fought: the Carthaginian general Hannibal was defeated and the road now lay open for Rome's rule over the western Mediterranean.

This only provided a challenge for further expansion. In the period after 197 BC, Roman legions marched against the Celts in the Po valley and even into southern France and Ibero-Celtic Spain. In the same years they marched on Greece, where the city-states were brought into subjection, and on Asia Minor, where the kingdoms of Alexander's successors had to yield to them. The Greek cities retained a measure of internal autonomy, partly as a result of the esteem in which the Roman elite held Greek culture. In the west where, certainly in the transalpine regions, there were no strong state-systems, the fortified cities which formed the centre of Celtic tribal connections were placed under Roman government, often after bloody battles or complete deportation such as happened during Caesar's wars. As in Greece, the local elites were usually allowed to keep their power, on condition that they met Rome's military, fiscal and cultural requirements.

The empire that now began to take shape was partly informal, still based, as it were, on the patron–client relations of early Rome, and partly formal. Its expansion was accompanied by the growing power and wealth of the city which was its centre and its symbol. But the population of Rome was mushrooming at a spectacular rate. On the one hand, this was caused by the increasing number of slaves, the prisoners of war who bred and thus also multiplied slaves.[8] On the other hand, more and more people came to the *Urbs*, 'The Town', in search of fame and fortune, including many impoverished Italian farmers who had lost their property to rich Romans who bought more and more land which they then exploited as large-scale enterprises, often with the help of slaves. Thus, a large section of the city's population was poor, the more so because the Roman economy remained largely artisanal, not branching out into large-scale industries. This led to tensions which became especially manifest in the supply of food.[9]

The proletariat which developed increasingly served as an instrument in the power politics of the rich. Indeed, some have characterized Roman society as a system wherein the wealthy used their money to manipulate and discipline the people's freedom, mostly through the organization of elaborate festivals which were presented as proof that the rulers served the ruled, thus creating symbolic proof of the rulers' right to rule.[10] As it was quite easy to bribe those who, though poor, were free and had the right to vote with promises of 'bread and games', many Roman politicians, who were usually aristocrats, took advantage of this situation. Some were sincere in their use of such 'bought' votes, wanting to bring about political and social change, others only seemed out to increase their own power. In 122 BC, it was decided that the state was to subsidize food supplies for the population and in 58 BC there was even a transition to free distribution of food. All this resulted in an enormous financial burden upon the state, which prompted, as it were, more wars to increase the number of people who could be forced to make financial contributions to the empire, to Rome, to a system which became ever more cruel and exploitative.

However, by now, Roman society itself became dangerously divided.[11] From 91 BC, civil wars raged almost uninterruptedly, coming to an end only with the aristocratic general Gaius Julius Caesar. He had first risen to power by flaunting his class's traditions, courting the common people by going about the streets, giving them magnificent mock battles in the amphitheatre and expending largesse on a grand scale. Charming both men and their wives, acting like a truly populist politician, he strengthened his power base before taking on the governorship of Rome's northernmost province. Operating from there, he regained his wealth and, being both a brilliant albeit ruthless general and a very clever propagandist, acquired his fame as a successful commander in Gaul and Germania. Finally he returned to Rome, not to content himself with another temporal office, to be shared with another ambitious leader, but appointing himself dictator. However, he was murdered in 44 BC by some aristocrats who, as was to be expected, wanted to regain their group's previous position.

Chaos ruled until power was seized by Gaius Octavius, who had the support of the army, which honoured him as Caesar's cousin and adoptive son, and of a sizeable proportion of the old aristocracy, who not only were willing to trade their former independence for law and order but also hoped to continue some of their power under an aristocratic leader.[12] By a deft manipulation of the various power groups in Rome and in the empire, Octavius finally succeeded in rallying the support of the whole realm. Avoiding the trap which so many of his predecessors had fallen into, he liked to uphold the fiction that he ruled as *princeps*, the first of citizens, instead of as the imperial autocrat he obviously was. Yet, in 27 BC, he let himself be 'forced' by the Senate to accept the title of *Augustus*, the Exalted One. His successors are simply known as the Roman emperors.

From an informal to a formal empire

In the first and second centuries AD, the Roman Empire reached its final, enormous extension, spreading its influence over large parts of Europe, the Near East and North Africa, showing its great strengths. Simultaneously, for partly as a result of this expansion, its weaknesses slowly began to appear as well.[13]

Admittedly, in the north-west, England was successfully invaded; the wall built in the border region with present-day Scotland by the Emperor Hadrian came to form a frontier to ward off the 'uncouth' and warring Picts. Prosperous cities with temples and public baths, such as *Verulamium* (York) and *Aquae Sulis* (Bath), arose south of this border. The countryside was covered by army camps and fortified *villae*, manor houses that were also centres of romanized Celtic culture.[14]

However, the wars that were intended to extend the empire eastward to the Elbe were unsuccessful. After many bloody battles with the tribes living in central Europe, Rome finally accepted the Rhine as the *limes*, the frontier of its empire in the north and east. Depending, of course, upon the length of the communication lines with Rome, the areas within its borders underwent intensive romanization, especially in regions around the imperial administrative centres, the cities which sprang up along the line, often around the forts where the Roman legions were garrisoned.[15]

Thus, in Roman Gaul as well as in present-day Belgium and in the Netherlands, a provincial but nonetheless often splendid variety of Rome's culture became manifest, of which the material remains can still be found today, for the outer regions of the empire in everything tried to emulate the glorious centre, Rome. Temples were built where the supranatural was honoured – both the Roman gods and, besides, the older, local ones, romanized but still recognizable to the indigenous people. Aqueducts were constructed, bringing water to the inhabitants, baths were built where they used to relax, amphitheatres were erected where the games were organized, as well as, in the larger centres, theatres where plays were staged. And the people, not only locals but often Roman colonists or retired legionnaires and their offspring, lived there, in dwellings small and great, the more luxurious, many-roomed ones adorned with mosaics and frescos, as in the cities of Italy itself.

To the north-east of the *limes*, the Dacians and Thracians, unruly tribes inhabiting the Balkans up to the Danube, were slowly incorporated into the empire and underwent romanization as well, expressed in, among other things, their language and material culture.

Sending their legions further eastwards, the Romans had also reached the Euphrates and the Tigris; there, however, they were halted by the Parthians, who ruled over an enormous empire in present-day Iraq, but of whom we know relatively little as yet. Though the Emperor Trajan once reached the Persian Gulf, reminiscing about his great predecessor, Alexander, and the eastward journeys he had undertaken, the Parthians did not allow the Romans to use this route to the riches of Asia.

By and large it was Egypt, and more specifically Alexandria, that, via the Arabian peninsula and the Red Sea, still played an important role in the empire's communication with the Orient. The Romans thought a great deal about Asia, writing not only about its geographical but also about its philosophical characteristics and fantasizing about its fabulous wealth. Indeed, so great was the demand for Asian products in the Roman world that according to the writer Pliny the Younger, authorities started to worry about the serious silver drain from the Mediterranean to the world of 'India'.[16] Undoubtedly, the ships that carried gems and gold, silk and spices also carried ideas and beliefs, which then were incorporated in the syncretic religions and philosophies of the Graeco-Roman world of the eastern Mediterranean.

In the south of the empire, on the Mediterranean coast of grain-rich Africa, splendid cities were built, with magnificent colonnaded market squares, temples and amphitheatres. Yet here the deserts and the semi-nomadic Bedouins who lived there created a real boundary beyond which the Romans could not expand: apparently these opponents, knowing the harsh terrain as no others did, were too formidable.[17] Still, this does not mean that the indigenous peoples living here, trading across the sand sea, did not form another interface of culture, by which notions of the world beyond the Sahara crept into the Roman-Mediterranean world as well.

How did this empire hold together? Obviously, an intricate legal-administrative apparatus was needed but, however efficient, by itself it would not have been sufficient to rule effectively such an enormous region. From the point of view of infrastructure, the famous 'Roman roads', with the bridges that allowed them to traverse low-lying valleys or unfordable rivers, were of prime importance, and great energy as well as huge sums were spent on them, so much so that after two thousand years many European roads still follow their course. Constructed by the legions as they advanced further and further from the central milestone that marked the empire's heart in Rome, they allowed the armies to move swiftly from one part of the empire to another, from one camp to another.[18] Both these roads as well as these camps, which often became the nuclei of larger, civilian settlements, provided a network with nodal points that gave cohesion and security; it should be added that they also helped to spread all kind of technical skills and even literacy to the frontier regions of the empire. But for all its military might and efficiency, the empire would not have survived for several centuries if its institutional structure had not been strong.

Beginning with the rule of Augustus, the capstone of the system was the emperor, law-giver, master of life and death.[19] No wonder, then, that his person gradually acquired superhuman traits. And the emperors used this as propaganda to further increase the legitimacy of their power. The tradition of divine rulers, which had already existed for a long time in such kingdoms of the eastern Mediterranean as Egypt and Persia, and which had been adopted by Alexander partly to facilitate his own rule in these regions, was broadened into an 'emperor cult' enforced throughout the empire.[20] The artistic elite at court glorified the emperor with all the means at their disposal, and his images were worshipped in temples. Certainly, in the eyes of the masses the emperor became a sacrosanct figure.

But beside the fact that everyone had to honour and obey the emperor, it was, perhaps, far more important that everyone also had to respect the basic principles of the empire as codified in its legal system. This ensured that all free persons were treated equally by uniform laws, whether they lived in *Londinium* (London) on the Thames, in *Augusta Treverorum* (Trier) on the Rhine, in *Carnuntum*, near Vienna, on the Danube, or in *Doura Europos*, on the Euphrates, in *Hadrumetum* (Hammamet) on the Tunisian coast, or in *Tingis* (present-day Tangier) commanding the Maghrebine coast of the Straits of Gibraltar.

From the first century AD onwards, the empire underwent important changes.[21] Augustus and his successors increasingly controlled the entire system of government. Financially they were able to do so because of the gigantic domains granted to them by the Senate or which they inherited from wealthy citizens who wanted to court their favour; people also were frequently compelled, with varying degrees of force, to bequeath their property to the emperor. Moreover, the emperors gained direct control over a large number of precisely those provinces which were the most prosperous in the empire: Gaul, with its trade, Spain, with its mineral deposits, Syria, where the wealth of Asia was brought to Europe, and grain-rich Egypt. This position enabled them to employ the financial resources of government to consolidate and increase their own power, as well as manipulate the food supply, thus placating the people of Rome. Moreover, the army, certainly in a formal sense, was also under the emperor's control. To win the support of the soldiers, who naturally were an important power factor, the emperors provided them with pensions and promises of farms after they left the army – Spain was romanized not least because of the many veterans who settled there, managing agricultural estates and breeding the horses which the army needed.[22]

As the empire grew, so did its bureaucracy. Many of the new offices were occupied by the emperor's own candidates, who were directly appointed by him. The Senate and the consuls receded more and more into the background. Meanwhile, the legal system, which was principally aimed at guaranteeing the individual's rights, specifically the material ones, was extended. This provided the foundation for a juridical-institutional pyramid with the emperor at its peak: in the administration of justice he was the final court of appeal. Surely, it was this very system, and the rules that it helped uphold, that must be considered one of the central elements in the longevity of the Roman Empire.

Plate 5 A Roman teacher, with the beard of manhood and authority, and his class, reading their parchment scrolls; as schools for the general public were usually crowded, and pupils would use only wax tablets, this probably represents a private class. To embark on a career in an intensely 'legal' society as the Roman Empire, it was necessary to study the three Rs. From a funerary monument found at Neumagen, Germany, dated *c.*AD 190
Source: Landesmuseum, Trier, Germany

Plate 6 The wife of the great Roman 'law-giver', Justinian: Empress Theodora, with her ladies-in-waiting, from the sixth-century mosaics in the church of San Vitale, Ravenna, Italy
Photo: P.J.A.N. Rietbergen

Map 3 Roman Empire in AD 211

SCANDIA

HIBERNIA

BRITANNIA
SUPERIOR

York
BRITANNIA
INFERIOR

GERMANIA
INFERIOR

GALLIA
BELGICA

Trier

GERMANIA
SUPERIOR

GALLIA
LUGDUNENSIS

AQUITANIA

GALLIA
NARBONENSIS

RAETIA

NORICUM Vienna

1
2
3

PANNONIA

DACIA

MOESIA
SUPERIOR

MOESIA INFERIOR

1 ALPES ATRECTIANAE ET POENINAE
2 ALPES COTTIAE
3 ALPES MARITIMAE

LUSITANIA

HISPANIA
BAETICA

HISPANIA
TARRACONENSIS

MAURETANIA
TINGITANA

MAURETANIA
CAESARIENSIS

NUMIDIA

SARDINIA
ET
CORSICA

ITALIA

SICILIA

DALMATIA

MACEDONIA

EPIRUS

ACHAEA

AFRICA

CRETA
ET
CYRENE

THRACIA

BITHYNIA ET PONTUS

GALATIA

ASIA

LYCIA ET
PAMPHYLIA

CYPRUS

CAPPADOCIA

CILICIA

ARMENIA

SYRIA

ARABIA

PARTHIA

AEGYPTUS

--·--·-- Provincial boundaries

ROME, THE SECOND CENTURY AD: A LEGAL SYSTEM, A LEGAL
SOCIETY – THE ROMAN CONTRIBUTION

In the course of several centuries, Roman jurists – legal scholars and lawyers – worked out a system which, as the following extracts clearly show, in many ways still provides the basis of the law in large parts of Europe and, indeed, in consequence of European imperialism from the sixteenth century onwards, in considerable parts of the non-European world. This process began and developed parallel with the expansion of the Roman Empire, when more and more subjected nations and states took over the basic principles of Roman law, which had originally been the law of the city of Rome.

These principles were expounded in the second century AD, in Gaius's *Institutiones*, a basic legal text in which one can recognize such fundamentals as that the spirit of the law prevails over its letter, as well as the increasing emphasis on the claims of equity and the principle of the benefit of the doubt. Gaius's reference to the law of nations, which, according to him, has universal application, is equally important; it includes an acceptance of the human condition in that it presupposes war and the organization of states, as well as the right to property and the necessity of legal commerce. As Roman law was considered to be in conformity with this 'natural' law, it could also claim to be universal, as it were.

> Every people that is governed by statutes and customs observes partly its own peculiar law and partly the common law of all mankind. That law which a people establishes for itself is peculiar to it, and is called civil law [*ius civile*] . . . while the law which natural reason establishes throughout all mankind is followed by all peoples alike and is called the law of nations [*ius gentium*], as being the law observed by all peoples [*gentes*]. Thus the Roman people observes partly its own peculiar law and partly the common law of mankind. . . .
>
> The laws of the Roman people consist of statutes, plebiscites, decrees of the Senate, imperial constitutions, edicts of those possessing the right to issue them, and responses of the learned. . . . An imperial constitution is what the emperor by decree, edict, or letter ordains; it has never been doubted that this has the force of statute, seeing that the emperor himself receives his *imperium* through a statute.
>
> The right of issuing edicts is possessed by the magistrates of the Roman people. . . . The responses of the learned are the decisions and opinions of those who are authorized to lay down the law. If the decisions of all them agree, what they so hold has the force of statute, but if they disagree the judge is at liberty to follow whichever decision he pleases. . . .
>
> The principal distinction in the law of persons is this, that all men are either free or slaves. Next, free men are either freeborn or freedmen. Freeborn are those born free, freedmen those manumitted from lawful slavery.[23]

This last point is explained in more detail in the most famous codification of Roman law, the *Corpus iuris civilis*, which consists of a textbook (Gaius's *Institutiones* mentioned earlier), a series of imperial decrees, the so-called

Codex, and the *Digesta*, a collection of notions mainly about private law. These were all brought together in AD 533, during the reign and on the explicit order of Emperor Justinian. In the *Digests* it is posed that

> Manumissions are also comprised in the law of nations. Manumission is the dismissal from hand, that is, the giving of freedom. For as long as anyone is in a state of slavery, he is subject to hand and control; when manumitted, he is freed from control. This has its origin in the law of nations, seeing that by natural law all were born free and manumission was not known since slavery was unknown; but after slavery made its appearance . . . , the benefaction of manumission followed. . . .
>
> Under this same law of nations, wars were begun, peoples distinguished, kingdoms founded, ownerships marked off, boundary stones placed for fields, buildings erected, commercial relations, sale, hire, and obligations instituted.

Among the general tenets formulated in the *Digests* we read:

> That which is faulty in the beginning cannot become valid with the passage of time.
> . . . No one who has the power to condemn lacks the power to acquit.
> . . . Anything not permitted to the defendant ought not to be allowed to the plaintiff.
> . . . In cases of doubt, the more liberal interpretation should always be preferred.
> . . . In all matters certainly, but especially in the case of law, equity should be given due regard.
> . . . It is right under natural law that no one should increase his wealth through harm or injury to another.
> . . . No one suffers a penalty for what he thinks.
> . . . Every individual is subjected to treatment in accordance with his own action and no one is made the inheritor of the guilt of another.[24]

Being such an intensely legal society, it is perhaps not surprising that in the Roman Empire the position of free women, too, seems to have been rather more closely safeguarded and, from a modern point of view, rather more humane than in Greece. Although Roman society was intensely patriarchical, with the *pater familias* having extensive authority over all members of his household, marriage contracts gave women the right to retain their own property and, indeed, the management of it.[25] They presided over the household, symbolized also in their presence at dinner. Nor was a Roman woman as restricted to her own domain as her Athenian counterpart. Moreover, women were held in far greater public respect than in Greece, occasionally even participating in literary and political life.

Yet there seems to have been a growing aversion to marriage at least in Rome itself, already in the second century BC. As this caused the birthrate to fall, government measures had to be taken – Augustus' rule that a woman was to be free of male guardianship after she had borne three children must be interpreted with this objective in mind as well. One famous censor, Cecilius Metellus, is reported to have delivered a speech in which he said: 'If we could get on without a wife, Romans, we would all avoid the annoyance, but since nature has ordained that we can neither live very comfortably with them nor at all without them, we must take thought for our lasting well-being rather than for the pleasure of the moment.'[26]

Whether he was being ironical or referred to homosexuality as the preferred alternative is doubtful. Yet, as in Greece, and for the same reasons, the practice was widespread and not morally condemned, either. The famous eighteenth-century historian of the Roman Empire, Edward Gibbon, rather scandalized, had to admit that all but one of the first fourteen emperors of Rome were either bisexual or exclusively homosexual.

Despite their greater legal freedom, most females led a restricted existence. Marrying, normally, around the age of 12, Roman girls were first and foremost supposed to bear children and educate them to become proper Roman citizens. Tacitus admonished them to breast-feed their offspring themselves, as the Germanic women did, rather than follow the old custom of employing a wet-nurse. Sex outside the marriage, while considered normal and even status-enhancing for men, was deemed totally unacceptable for women, the more so as their sexuality was seen as insatiable, as noted by the poet Horace in one of his odes; he, of course, was only following Aristotle, who had argued as much in his 'History of Animals'.[27] Reading the many descriptions of women engaging in sexual adventures with as much gusto as men should not blind us to the fact that Roman poets and prose writers really portrayed the lifestyle of only a small elite.

As in Greece, Roman women sought refuge in religion, especially in the many mystery cults that centred round female deities; particularly popular, all over the empire, was the cult of the ancient Egyptian goddess Isis, who was supposed to give women the same power that men had. The poet Juvenal, writing at the beginning of the second century AD, felt forced to comment in some very satirical, even bitter verses upon this phenomenon, a fact which may indicate the still essentially patriarchal character of Roman society.

Roman culture

From the second century BC onwards, the Greek civilization which had become the norm in a large part of the eastern Mediterranean during the later years of Alexander's conquests became embedded in a new world, the expanding Roman Empire. The Mediterranean empire of the Romans spanned three continents, many races and even more religions. It was relatively tolerant. There were hardly any ethnic distinctions within the empire's borders.[28] Status was determined by wealth and the prestige a person acquired by adapting to the culture of the elite via the *paideia*. Indeed, perhaps one of the most important factors contributing to the cohesion of the Roman Empire and its culture was that, regardless of all differences in race, language and religion, the steep way to the top, to a career in the centres of provincial power, or even in the imperial capital, was, in principle, open to all free people living within the *limes*, if they had the ambition to embark on such a road.

The condition, of course, was that one was a Roman citizen. Admittedly, citizenship and the rights that went with it were not given to everybody, but during the first and second centuries, slowly, one town after the other was granted it until, in the second decade of the third century, all free inhabitants of the empire were made citizens – if only to secure their fiscal contribution to the state.

If one were a Roman citizen, one could become a member of the elite, maybe not within one but certainly within two generations, provided one had absorbed the *paideia* ideal which had been the basis of Greek cultural and especially moral-philosophical texts and had been adopted by the Roman elite. It actually meant that one had learned to read, write and especially speak Latin well, within the rhetorical tradition which had developed under Greek influence.[29]

In his *Institutio Oratoria*, 'The Elements of Oratory', the Roman writer Quintilian (*c.*AD 35–96) clearly outlined the elements deemed essential to the education of a proper citizen of the Roman Empire. From a pedagogical perspective, his views are still surprisingly modern.

> Above all, make sure that the infant's nurse speaks correctly. . . . Of course, she should without doubt be chosen on the basis of good moral character, but still make sure that she speaks correctly as well. The child will hear his nurse first, and will learn to speak by imitating her words. And by nature we remember best those things which we learned when our minds were youngest.
>
> [I, 1, 4–5]

> I am not so foolishly unaware of a child's stages of development as to think that young children should be harshly forced to begin with the three R's or should have real work pressed upon them. Above all else we must take care that a child who is not yet old enough to love learning should not come to hate it and dread, even when he is older, an experience which was once bitter. Let his lessons be fun, let him volunteer answers, let him be praised, and let him learn the pleasure of doing well. If, on occasion, he refuses instruction, bring in someone to serve as a rival, someone with whom he can compete; but let him think that he is doing well more often than not. Encourage him with the rewards or prizes in which his age group delights.
>
> [I, 1, 20]

> As soon as a boy has learned to read and write, it is time for him to study with a grammaticus. I won't distinguish between Greek and Latin teachers, although I would prefer that priority be given to a Greek teacher. But both offer the same curriculum. And this curriculum can be divided very briefly into two main subjects: the art of speaking correctly and the interpretation of poetry. However, the curriculum offers much more in the details of the programme than is at first apparent on the surface. For example, the art of speaking and the art of writing are

connected. And flawless reading precedes interpretation. And critical judgement is required in all the cases. . . .

It is not sufficient to have read only poetry. Every kind of writer must be thoroughly investigated, and not simply for his topic or theme, but for his vocabulary, because words often acquire authority according to the writer using them. And your studies with the grammaticus cannot be complete without the study of music because this education should include a discussion of meter and rhythm. You cannot understand the poets if you know nothing about astronomy since the poets so often use the rise and setting of the constellations (to give one example) in indicating time. Nor should this level of education overlook the study of philosophy, not only because many passages in almost every poem require our understanding of an intricate or minute detail of natural science but also because some poets, such as Empedocles among the Greeks, and Varro and Lucretius among the Romans, actually wrote down doctrines of philosophy in verse.

[I, 4, 1–5][30]

All the texts Quintilian referred to were available to those who could afford them; until the first century AD, everything was written on rolls, *volumina*, of papyrus, and then in books, *codices*, consisting of sheets of parchment folded a number of times into pages.

Not surprisingly, to succeed in Rome, a knowledge of Greek itself was to be recommended. In an often extreme philHellenism, the majority of the Roman elite frequently looked up to Greek philosophy, literature and the visual arts. Roman youths from the better families, the future leaders of this upstart empire, completed their education with a tour along the Hellenic cultural centres, and filled their villas and city palaces with Greek, 'classical' art treasures, or copies of them. Those who considered themselves the real heirs to classical Greece, the inhabitants of Athens and of other Greek cities, also in Asia Minor, often looked down on 'barbaric' Rome. 'The Town' itself was deeply offended by this contempt – after all, had not the *Pax Romana* protected Greek civilization against destruction by Asian barbarism?

Despite often slavishly following Greek examples, so much so that, for example, in sculpture Roman copies could hardly be distinguished from Greek originals, the Romans did create a culture of their own. Cicero, the famous orator, spoke and wrote in such a way that he became the norm for Roman rhetoric, for a way of speaking and, thus, thinking that every civilized person was supposed to practise.

In poetry, Horace's lyric odes became classics. Meanwhile, Virgil continued the story of Homer's *Odyssey* with his impressive epic about the tribulations of Aeneas, son of the royal house of Troy who, after his escape from the ruins of his city, was supposed to have fled westward and begot the first Romans: thus, Rome symbolically made itself the heir to the culture of the eastern Mediterranean, but also claimed to have created a new civilization.

Instead of indulging in such mythmaking but propagandistically effective poetry, Tacitus set new standards of prose writing and of a rigorous, 'objective' analysis of history, in his often blood-curdling tales about the vicissitudes of the empire under the rule of the first imperial family.

A certain ease in citing from all these classical, normative texts helped an ambitious man to hold his own amid his rivals and to prove himself as a 'cultured' person. Yet money was certainly a help, if only because it provided ambitious and well-to-do parents from the 'province' who had not been reared in the Roman tradition themselves, with the means to give their children the education and, thus, the opportunities which they themselves had not had.

Thus, the Roman Empire, with its advanced communications network, its *lingua franca* and its relatively open cultural ideal, created an educated elite which, though numerically limited, still may have been the single largest such group in the world before the global changes of the late nineteenth and twentieth centuries. It is doubtful whether, without these foundations, the Europe we know would have come into existence.

The Roman Empire and the worlds beyond

Of central importance for the formation of what we now call European culture was that Rome, which considered itself the cultural heir to Greece but which had, in the mean time, developed its very own characteristics as a result of its expansion, ruled a large part of the area which was already known as Europe. Knowledge about this area steadily increased precisely because of the Romans' expansionist politics.

By the second century AD, the imperial frontier, the *limes*, had reached its furthest extension; yet, even the peoples living beyond it, as, for example, the Germanic tribes, were known to the Romans and influenced by them. Only the north of Scotland, parts of Scandinavia and northern Russia were still uncharted on the Roman maps. The inhabitants of these areas, usually semi-nomads living in tribes, remained unknown. However, they were a constant threat to the empire, which attracted them because of its fabulous wealth. Because they frequently gave in to that lure and tried to cross the empire's borders, with violence if necessary, they were seen as enemies and stigmatized by the Romans as foreign, as a 'babbling', 'barbaric', uncivilized rabble just as the Greeks had described the Romans in earlier times.[31]

Satyrs and titans – these were the terms of abuse, mingled with admiration, used by the Romans to describe the Celts or Gauls when they first came to know them. The Roman writer Ammianus Marcellinus (*c*.AD 330–95) describes their appearance and behaviour as follows: 'Almost all of the Gauls are of tall stature, fair and ruddy, terrible for the fierceness of their eyes, fond of quarrelling and of overbearing insolence'.[32] The geographer Strabo (*c*.64 BC–AD 19) already had told his readers that: 'On whatever pretext you stir them up, you will have them ready to face danger, even if they have nothing on their side but their own strength and courage'. He adds:

> To the frankness and high-spiritedness of their temperament must be added the traits of childish boastfulness and love of decoration. They wear ornaments of gold, torques on their necks and bracelets on their arms and wrists, while people

of high rank wear dyed garments besprinkled with gold. It is this variety which makes them unbearable in victory and so completely downcast in defeat.

Another writer added some information about their customs:

> When several dine together, they sit in a circle; but the mightiest among them, distinguished above the others for skill in war or family connections, or wealth, sits in the middle like a chorus-leader. Beside him is the host and next on either side the others according to their respective ranks. Men-at-arms, carrying oblong shields stand close behind them while their bodyguards, seated in a circle directly opposite, share in the feast like their master.

In short, the Celts were considered irritable, ambitious and belligerent characters, as the Romans had discovered at first hand. The famous *De Bello Gallico*, 'On the Gaulic War', in which the Roman general and later autocrat Gaius Julius Caesar had described his campaigns north of the Alps (58–51 BC), concurs with the handful of earlier and later accounts we have of them.

While Celtic civilization flourished in south and central Europe, partly as a result of the interaction with Rome and the Mediterranean world, society and culture in northern Europe remained largely unchanged for a long time. This area, too, was inhabited by Indo-Germanic peoples who had congregated mainly in Scandinavia, present-day Germany and Poland. In about 90 BC, the Greek writer Poseidonios had called these people the 'Germans', a concept later taken over by the Roman general Caesar. Following Caesar's conquests in present-day France and the various attempts by the first Roman emperors to expand the borders of their empire in the north and east, Roman contact with the 'Germans' steadily grew. In AD 98, the historian Tacitus even devoted a separate study to them, 'On the origins and region of the Germans'.[33]

As the Germans had not yet begun to write their own history, the account by Tacitus is an important supplement to archaeological research. Relying on data procured by Roman officers and other eyewitnesses, he described the peoples who lived beyond the Rhine, the empire's border, but frequently crossed from there into areas occupied by the Romans. On the name 'Germans', Tacitus had ideas of his own. He writes:

> The name Germany . . . is modern and newly introduced, from the fact that the tribes which first crossed the Rhine and drove out the Gauls, and are now called Tungrians, were then called Germans. Thus what was the name of a tribe, and not of a race, gradually prevailed, till all called themselves by this self-invented name of Germans, which the conqueror had first employed to inspire terror.[37]

He continues:

> For my own, I agree with those who think that the tribes of Germany are free from all taint of intermarriages with foreign nations, and that they appear as a distinct, unmixed race, like none but themselves. Hence, too, the same physical peculiarities throughout so vast a population. All have fierce blue eyes, red hair,

huge frames, fit only for a sudden exertion. They are less able to bear laborious work. Heat and thirst they cannot in the least endure; to cold and hunger their climate and their soil inure them.

This verbal portrait is very similar to Ammianus Marcellinus' description of the Celts, indicating that, at least to these Mediterranean observers, all northerners looked very much alike.

In fact the term 'Germans' refers to dozens of tribes which between *c.*800 BC and the beginning of the Christian era occupied the whole region between the Rhine, the Danube and the Weichsel: Burgundians, Franks, Frisians, Goths, Longobards, Saxons, Vandals and so forth.[34] They inhabited that enormous part of Europe which had not fallen into Roman hands, even though some Germanic tribes settled within the empire's borders, especially in present-day Belgium and the Netherlands. We know most about the situation in Scandinavia, northern Germany and the Netherlands; systematic excavations in central and eastern Europe have not yet begun. The Roman writer Pliny the Elder, who died in AD 79 in Pompei, of an attack of asthma shortly after the eruption of Mount Vesuvius, wrote a 'Natural History', which, in fact, was an encyclopedia of all kinds of knowledge, including the data he had collected about the peoples Romans had heard about but did not know much about as yet; he told his readers that the Frisians, in those northern regions, lived on their terps, 'looking like seafaring folk when their lands are inundated, but like shipwrecks when the water recedes.'

Germanic tribes usually consisted of a number of clans, each clan comprising several families who recognized a common, sometimes mythical, ancestor and who lived together in one village – this was not a society which needed cities.[35] Animal husbandry was the dominant economic feature, while barley was the most important staple, used for both food and drink, when made into beer; it was supplemented with various wheats and cultivated vegetables. Culturally, religion was of the greatest importance. The heavens were ruled by fertility goddesses like Freya and Njörd, and war gods like Odin/Wotan and Donar/Thor; priest-kings celebrated sacrifices for them, both in holy groves and in wooden temples.[36]

Political and military power was in the hands of a warrior aristocracy, consisting of families who traced their ancestry back to the gods. For the rest, society was made up of free farmers, who were included in political and military decision-making, and of families whose members were wholly or partly unfree and hence had fewer or no rights. These included, for instance, members of other tribes who had been forced into submission and prisoners of war who had been enslaved.

Many of the Germanic tribes fought fiercely among themselves, driven by a lack of fertile farmland, overpopulation and the hope of the spoils of war. Besides, from the beginning of the first century AD the proximity of the prospering border areas of the Roman Empire provided a constant challenge. These wars were sometimes led by anointed, 'sacred' kings and sometimes by dukes, chosen for the occasion. Thus, in the Cherusci tribe the noble warrior Hermann, or Arminius, was appointed duke to lead his people against the Roman aggressor in AD 9 in the famous and to Rome disastrous battle of the Teutoburger Wald, where three legions are supposed to have been slaughtered.

Besides astonishment at the completely different political and social structure of the Germans, Tacitus' text expresses a certain admiration as well; it almost seems as if he thought these Germans still lived in a happy primitiveness.[38] The observations he made about their way of life point to such fascinating differences as existed then, and still do, between Mediterranean village life and the north European practice of settlement. Tacitus writes:

> They obtain their kings on the basis of birth, their generals on the basis of courage. The authority of their kings is not unlimited or arbitrary. Their generals control them by example rather than command, and by means of the admiration which attends upon energy and a conspicuous place in the front line. . . . The strongest incentive to courage lies in this, that neither chance nor casual grouping makes the squadron or wedge, but family and kinship. . . .
>
> On small matters, the chiefs consult, on larger questions the community, but with this limitation, that even the matters whose decision rests with the people are first handled by the chiefs. They meet . . . on specified days. . . . It is a failing of their freedom that they do not meet at once, when commanded, but waste a second and third day by dilatoriness in assembling. When the throng is pleased to begin, they take their seats carrying arms. Silence is called for by the priests, who thenceforward have power also to coerce. Then kings or chiefs are listened to, in order of age, birth, glory in war, or eloquence, with the prestige that belongs to their counsel rather than with any prescriptive right to command. If the advice tendered is displeasing, they reject it by shouting; if it pleases them, they clash their spears. . . .
>
> Conspicuously high birth or signal services on the part of ancestors confer the rank of chief, even in the case of very young men; they mingle with others of maturer strength and long-tested valour, who are not ashamed to be seen among their retinue. In the retinue itself, degrees are observed, depending upon the judgement of whom they follow. There is great rivalry among the retainers to decide who shall have the first place with his chief, and among the chieftains as to who shall have the largest and most spirited retinue. To be surrounded always by a large band of chosen youths means rank, strength, glory in peace, protection in war. . . .
>
> It is well known that none of the German tribes lives in cities and that they do not even allow houses to touch one another. They live separately and scattered, according as spring, meadow or grove appeals to each man. They lay out their villages not, after our fashion, with buildings contiguous and connected; everyone keeps a clear space round his house.

A 'myth' had been born, for during the next two thousand years this picture, in a way highly flattering to 'the Germans', was influential in shaping the self-image of the inhabitants of the region between the Rhine, the Baltic, the Oder and the Alps, who often have been proud to call themselves the heirs of Tacitus' heroes.

Archaeological research has shown that from *c.*2500 BC onwards, the huge area between the Baltic Sea, the Dnieper River, the Carpathian Mountains and the Oder was inhabited by the so-called proto-Slavic tribes. Their economy and society seem to have centred around agriculture as well as pastoralism. As they left no written records, and did not come within the sphere of influence of the Roman Empire, little is known of them up till the fourth and fifth centuries AD.[39] By then, the combined influence of Rome and of Christianity had created cultural divisions that were a factor in a historical process wherein the inhabitants of the western part of geographical Europe began to consider the continent's Slavic part as being on the margin of the 'civilized' world, or even not belonging to it at all. This image was certainly reinforced by another wave of invasions of warlike tribes from the Eurasian plains, who after conquering these regions mingled with the indigenous population, and then went on to attack the Roman Empire's frontiers.

The work of Ammianus Marcellinus shows how a culture like that of the Romans, based on agriculture, a sedentary population, and a rigid, institutionalized structure regulated by laws, viewed these nomadic pastoralists, who were attracted by the riches of Rome and who, in the course of the fourth century, began to cause the Roman legions more and more trouble:

> The people of the Huns . . . all have compact, strong limbs and thick necks, and are so monstrously ugly and misshapen that one might take them for two-legged beasts. . . . They are so hardy in mode of life that they have no need of fire nor of savoury food, but eat the roots of wild plants and the half-raw flesh of any kind of animal whatever, which they put between their thighs and the backs of their horses and thus warm a little.
>
> They are never protected by any buildings . . . roaming at large amid the mountains and woods, they learn from the cradle to endure cold, hunger and thirst. . . . They are subject to no royal restraint, but they are content with the disorderly government of their important men, and led by them they force their way through every obstacle. . . . They are all without fixed abode, without hearth, or law, or settled mode of life, and they keep roaming from place to place, like fugitives, accompanied by the wagons in which they live.[40]

On the south-eastern frontiers lived

> the Saracens whom we never found desirable either as friends or as enemies [and who], ranging up and down the country . . . laid waste whatever they could find, like rapacious hawks which, whenever they have caught sight of any prey from on high, seize it with swift swoop. . . .
>
> I will now briefly relate a few more particulars about them. Among those tribes whose original abode extends from the Assyrians to the cataracts of the Nile and the frontiers of the Blemmyae [perhaps the Pygmies of Central Africa], all alike are warriors of equal rank, half-nude, clad in dyed cloaks as far as the waist, ranging widely with the help of swift horses and slender camels in times of peace or of disorder. No man ever grasps a plough-handle or cultivates a tree, none seeks a living by tilling the soil, but they continually rove over wide and extensive tracts without a home, without fixed abodes or laws.[41]

Ammianus' descriptions clearly define the elements which he thought were the fundaments of Roman civilization, and which were lacking in the lives of these barbarians. Yet such tribes as the ones he wrote about were not the least important among the factors that, in the end, brought about the collapse of the Roman Empire.

3 An empire lost – an empire won?

Christianity and the Roman Empire

Developments within the Jewish world: the genesis of Christianity

In order to determine the role of Christianity in the Roman Empire it is first necessary to give a general outline of the course of Jewish history preceding the birth of Christ. As a result of internal tension, the temple-state of Israel had early on split into two parts, Israel and Judaea. It lost its independence when both kingdoms collapsed under the expansion of, first, the Late Assyrian Empire (722 BC) and, thereafter, the Babylonians (597 BC). Part of the Jewish population was even carried off into exile to present-day Iraq.

It was precisely in their milieu that cultural traditionalism could flourish, yet now with a new religious element: the oppression of life in exile was seen as Yahweh's punishment for the Jews' deviation from monotheism and the loose lifestyle of many believers. Therefore, the need for repentance and for strict compliance with the religious laws as articulated in the first part of the Old Testament, the so-called 'five books of Moses' or *Pentateuch*, was stressed. However, besides this, the hope grew that a 'Messiah' or 'anointed one' would arise, a king who would renew the bond between the people of Israel and their God and make them mighty once again. The prophets Isaiah, Jeremiah and Ezekiel emphasized the different aspects of this regenerated Judaism.

During this period when they had lost their own sovereignty, many Jews who had not been deported went to more challenging places in the region and thus spread all over the Near East. As they often came to play a leading role in the big trading cities, they were looked at askance by the local populations. The fact of their prosperity and of the obvious difference of their religion sometimes made them easy scapegoats when a community felt the need to exorcize internal tensions, taking them out on 'foreigners'.

Meanwhile, the Persians conquered Babylon and allowed the departed Jews to return to their homeland. The orthodox believers who, having suffered for the good cause during the 'Babylonian Exile', naturally wanted to be the leaders of the kingdom they now restored, soon found they were not the only ones to inhabit it. There were many other groups besides. Some of these were dedicated to the Jewish religion, even though they were not as devoted and strict as the former exiles. Moreover, other religions were now practised in the Jewish state as well. Moreover, in the fourth and third centuries BC the entire Near East increasingly came under the influence of Greek culture.[1] In the course of the second century, the greater part of the Jewish elite was Hellenized. To counter this process, all sorts of orthodox groupings in Jewish society tried to gain greater power: the 'Hassidics', the 'pious ones' and, later, the Pharisees, and especially the zealot sect of the Essenes cherished strongly ritualistic beliefs paired with an intense hatred of foreigners.

External threats in the second and first centuries, first from the Hellenist rulers who picked up the fragments of the imperial dream of Alexander the Great, and later from the Romans, reinforced the need felt by the more faithful Jews for a charismatic leader, a Messiah, who would bring salvation and make Israel independent. In this context all kinds of visions of an approaching 'end of time' and a glorious new beginning were linked to the need to be cleansed of sin. This has become clear from the discovery of the so-called Dead Sea Scrolls, which began in 1947 and continues to the present; it has shown the existence of a group of Jews living at Qumran in the century preceding the birth of Christ who, according to their texts, held a number of these ideas, which later were presented as typically Christian.

From Jews – and Gentiles – to Christians: the role of Jesus of Nazareth and his followers

This was the atmosphere in which Jesus of Nazareth was born, and in which he preached during the first decades of the era that now bears his name in the western world. It was against this background that his disciples interpreted his message: his call for charity, especially towards the poorest, his plea for belief in the one true, invisible God, his warning against the futile attractions of earthly life, and the view he offered of a better world to come. As with so many Jews before them who had gathered around prophets and other leaders, Jesus's followers saw him as a 'Messiah', an 'anointed one', even as the new 'King of the Jews'. They were prepared to die for his – for God's – cause: martyrdom for these Jews was a sign of election, a challenge to the foreign aggressors and a step on the way to realizing Yahweh's kingdom.

Those who grouped themselves around Jesus of Nazareth included not only a small number of faithful disciples, later known as 'apostles', but also an increasing crowd of people from both the Jewish faith and other Near Eastern religions, called heathens, or 'Gentiles' by the Jews. Collectively, they quickly became known as Christians because, in fact, they followed the man who was referred to as 'Chreistos', the Greek word for the Hebrew 'anointed one'.

We only know from the testimonies of his closest followers what it was that attracted people to the new Messiah. In the record of Jesus's teachings written by Matthew, one of his disciples, we read the following:

When he [i.e. Jesus] saw the crowds he went up a mountain. There he sat down, and when his disciples had gathered around him he began to address them. And this is the teaching he gave:

Blessed are the poor in spirit: the kingdom of Heaven is theirs.
Blessed are the sorrowful; they shall find consolation.
Blessed are the gentle; they shall have the earth for their possession.
Blessed are those who hunger and thirst to see right prevail; they shall be
  satisfied.
Blessed are those who show mercy; mercy shall be shown to them.
Blessed are those whose hearts are pure; they shall see God.
Blessed are the peacemakers; they shall be called God's children.
Blessed are those who are persecuted in the cause of right; the kingdom of
  Heaven is theirs.

Another disciple, Luke, gave his own version of what happened on that occasion. He presents Jesus as saying:

to you who are listening I say: love your enemies; do good to those who hate you; bless those who curse you; pray for those who treat you spitefully. If anyone hits you on the cheek, offer the other also; if anyone takes your coat, let him have your shirt as well. Give to everyone who asks you; if anyone takes what is yours, do not demand it back.

Treat others as you would like them to treat you . . . you must love your enemies and do good, and lend without expecting any return; and you will have a rich reward: you will be sons of the Most High, because he himself is kind to the ungrateful and the wicked. Be compassionate as your Father is compassionate.

Do not judge, and you will not be judged; do not condemn, and you will not be condemned; pardon, and you will be pardoned; give, and gifts will be given you.[2]

And yet we know little about Jesus as a historical person;[3] the oldest text accepted as 'gospel' by the Christians, that of Mark, does not even have his birth story.[4] During his lifetime, the Romans conquered most of the Near East and they also held sway over Israel. They saw Jesus as a bothersome rebel, one of the many prophets whose agitation made the Jews such an unruly people. A number of factions among the Jews themselves also viewed Jesus and his disciples as a threat: they felt that they did not need a new king at all, and feared that his actions, enraging the Romans, would only increase Roman pressure on their society. Therefore, the Nazarene was accused of being an enemy of the state. A trial ensued and once he was found guilty it was decided that he should be put to death. According to tradition, this was carried out in AD 33.

Everything else we know about Jesus has largely been derived from the descriptions of his life which were recorded long after his death by his disciples and which, to the followers of Jesus, came to constitute the second, most important part of the Bible; the majority of Jews, of course, who did not acknowledge Jesus as the Messiah, do not accept this 'New Testament'. However, in the gospels, Christ's followers did not want to write a biography according to modern standards but rather to tell stories in which Jesus's message as they interpreted it would be enhanced by the story of his actions. Also, being members of a new faith, their writings were often biased.

Moreover, in the decades and centuries that followed, those writings which provided information and interpretations that, for one reason or another, were displeasing to those of Christ's followers who now were leaders in Christian communities were quickly destroyed. As a result, some of the oldest descriptions, like that of Barnabas, virtually disappeared. What eventually became 'the tradition', the three so-called synoptic gospels of Matthew, Mark and Luke recognized by the Christian Churches, consists of texts which have all been written at least fifty years after the death of Christ. As testimonies to their writers' faith, they are fascinating and to Christians entirely convincing; as historically trustworthy sources on which, moreover, the Christian Churches have long based their claims to power, they are to be read with the greatest caution.

Religions in the Roman Empire

The author Minucius Felix, who lived in the second half of the second century AD, gave a description of how the Roman Empire, which incorporated more and more different cultures because of its expansionist politics, also embraced a multitude of religions. In his dialogue *Octavius* he analysed the way the Romans themselves accepted everything which appeared salutary to them.[5] However, he also criticized a number of what were, according to him, more banal and untrustworthy cults, as for instance, the mystery cult of the Phrygian mother-goddess Cybele and her lover Attis, which had attracted many followers since the third century BC.[6] With the acuity of a twentieth-century religious anthropologist, Minucius Felix particularly targeted the extremely popular Isis cult, which had come to the capital from Egypt:

> Hence it is that . . . we see each people having its own individual rites and worshipping the local Gods – the Eleusinains Ceres, the Phrygians the Great Mother, the Epidaurians Aesculapius, the Chaldaeans Baal, the Syrians Astarte, the Taurians Diana, the Gauls Mercury – the Romans one and all. . . . In captured fortresses, even in the first flush of victory, they reverence the conquered deities. Everywhere they entertain the gods and adopt them as their own; they raise altars even to the unknown deities, and to the spirits of the dead. Thus it is that they adopt the sacred rites of all nations, and withal have earned dominion. . . .
>
> Consider the sacred rites of the mysteries. You find tragic deaths, dooms, funerals, mourning and lamentations of woebegone gods. Isis, with her Dog-head and shaven priests, mourning, bewailing, and searching for her lost son; her miserable votaries beating their breasts and mimicking the sorrows of the unhappy mother. Then, when the stripling is found, Isis rejoices, her priests jump for joy, the Dog-head glories in his discovery. . . . Is it not absurd either to mourn your object of worship, or to worship your object of mourning? Yet these old Egyptian

rites have now found their way to Rome, so that you may play the fool to the swallow and sistrum of Isis, the scattered limbs and the empty tomb of your Serapis and Osiris.[7]

The Roman authorities could accept these cults as long as they had no grave political implications. Thus, the cult of the Indian-Persian god Mithras, whose birth in a cave, last supper before death and ascension into heaven were depicted on the walls of countless underground temples all over the empire, was hugely popular among the soldiers of Rome from the first century AD onwards, and, if only for that reason, even favoured by the emperors themselves. However, sometimes a cult was deemed more threatening, as, for instance, the devotion of the Persian prophet Mani, whose teaching, stressing the battle between good and evil, became very popular in the third century AD. In many of these new religions there was a drift towards monotheism, for like Judaism, which had been gaining influence outside Israel, these cults, too, tended towards the belief in one God. It was this particular tendency which was vigorously opposed, as in Emperor Diocletian's edict of AD 296:

> Excessive idleness . . . sometimes drives people to join with others in devising certain superstitious doctrines of the most worthless and depraved kind. In so doing, they overstep the bounds imposed on humans. . . . Wherefore it is our vigorous determination to punish the stubborn depraved minds of these most worthless people.
>
> We take note that . . . those Manichaeans have set up new and unheard-of sects in opposition to the older creeds, with the intent of driving out to the benefit of their depraved doctrine what was formerly granted to us by divine favour. We have heard that these men have but recently sprung up and advanced, like strange and unexpected portents, from the Persian people, our enemy, to this part of the world, where they are perpetuating many outrages, disturbing the tranquillity of the peoples and also introducing the gravest harm to the communities.
>
> And it is to be feared that . . . they may try, with the accursed customs and perverse laws of the Persians to infect men of a more innocent nature, namely the temperate and tranquil Roman people as well as our entire empire with what one might call their malevolent poisons. . . .
>
> Therefore, we instruct that their followers, and particularly the fanatics, shall suffer a capital penalty, and we ordain that their property be confiscated for our fisc.

A sect of 'hopeless outlaws'

Amidst all these competing sects, the Christians, too, developed into a prominent religious movement all over the Near East, on the Asian periphery of the Roman Empire. Perhaps precisely because they creatively incorporated a great number of characteristics of their competitors, they succeeded in becoming one of the region's major religions within the time span of only one century, between *c.*AD 40 and 140, i.e. 'after Christ's birth', or *Anno Domini* – the Christian way of reckoning time, which, however, was introduced in western Europe only in the eighth century.

Plate 7 A shrine dedicated to the service of Mithras, one of the great competitors of Christ. In the centre is the altar table, showing the winged god riding his bull; around the walls are the seats for the believers who gathered here to share their sacramental meal. The shrine is located under the Christian church of San Clemente, Rome
Photo: Alinari

Plate 8 A fresco depicting a 'meal of fraternal love' or 'Agapè', the cultic meal of the early Christians, found in one of the Roman catacombs
Photo: Marc de Kleine, Nijmegen

Christianity subsequently spread across North Africa and Mediterranean Europe.[8] Of major importance was the preaching of the Apostle Paul who, in the fifth and sixth decades of the first century AD, told his audiences both in Asia Minor and in Rome that Christianity was not reserved to former Jews only but, indeed, was open to every person. He, and a number of his fellow apostles, Jesus's disciples, used the easy communications provided by the empire to travel over vast distances, divulging the word of their teacher and bring his good news to all who wanted to listen. After the fall of Jerusalem, the destruction of the temple and the effective dismantling of the Jewish state by the Romans, in AD 70, Christianity and, for that matter, Judaism were definitely freed of the constraints of ancient Israel.

At first, many viewed Christianity with contempt, as a sect which mainly convinced slaves and women, and was mostly practised underground, an obscure religion to which people surrendered in good or foolish faith. And yet, such was the power of the Christian message that from the second century AD the whole Roman Empire around the Mediterranean gradually began to acquire a Christian character.[9] At least three elements of Christianity were attractive to wide strata of society. Revelation, which could bring even the uneducated to vital truths.[10] Conversion, which gave the Christians the kind of moral excellence formerly attainable only by those who could afford the costly Graeco-Roman education that was supposed to be the model road towards perfection. And lastly, of course, the highly appealing idea of salvation, of a life after death, given to each and every believer, however sinful, because of the redeeming offer made by Christ of his own life, symbolized in the Eucharist – incidentally another food ritual. It gave the Christians a sense of a personal relationship with a personal God, and a perspective from which to judge and, in many cases, endure the vicissitudes of life on earth, so painful to many. No wonder many were attracted by this fundamental vision of man's equality before an impartial God who would justly judge each according to his merits, as well as by the feeling of belonging, the sense of community created by this non-local, indeed 'universal' sect.

The writer Minucius Felix indicates the objections raised against the Christians: their origins in the lowest social strata, their secrecy, their refusal to worship Roman deities and, politically even more unacceptable, the deified emperors, as well as their contempt for this life and their belief in a resurrection of soul and body alike. The propaganda against the Christians was determined, at least in part, by a lack of familiarity with their symbols and rites, which largely had developed underground. However, much of it was the result of pure malice:

> Is it not deplorable that a faction . . . of abandoned, hopeless outlaws makes attacks against the gods? They gather together ignorant persons from the lowest dregs, and credulous women, easily deceived as their sex is, and organize a rabble of unholy conspirators, leagued together in nocturnal associations and by ritual fasts and barbarous foods, not for the purpose of some sacred rite but for the sake of sacrilege – a secret tribe that shuns the light, silent in public but talkative in secret

places. They despise the temples . . . , they spit upon the gods, they ridicule our sacred rites . . . , they pity our priests; half-naked themselves, they despise offices and official robes. What amazing folly! What incredible arrogance! They despise present tortures yet dread uncertain future ones; while they fear to die after death, they have no fear of it in the meantime; deceptive hope soothes away their terror with the solace of a life to come. . . . This plot must be completely rooted out and execrated. They recognize one another by secret signs and tokens; they love one another almost before they are acquainted. Everywhere a kind of religion of lust is also associated with them, and they call themselves promiscuously brothers and sisters, so that ordinary fornication, through the medium of a sacred name, becomes incest. . . .

[They] say that a man put to death for a crime and the lethal wooden cross are objects of their veneration. . . .

What is told of the initiation of neophytes is as detestable as it is notorious. An infant covered with spelt to deceive the unsuspecting is set before the one to be initiated in the rites. The neophyte is induced to strike what seems to be harmless blows on the surface of the spelt, and this infant is killed . . . its blood – oh, shocking – they greedily lap up. . . .

Furthermore, they threaten the whole world and the universe itself and its stars with fire, and work for its destruction . . . ; they say that they are reborn after death from the cinders and ashes.[11]

At first, the Roman authorities were not worried overmuch, regarding the Christians as yet another crazy sect. Soon, however, they were irked by some of the tenets of the Christians' faith, especially its abhorrence of emperor worship, and began to persecute them. Until AD 250, only individual Christians were prosecuted as enemies of the state. Later, their religion as such was made illegal, and bloody, large-scale prosecutions started, which also affected sects like the Manichaeans.

CARTHAGE, AD 180: ARGUMENTS AGAINST AND FOR THE RELIGION OF THE CHRISTIANS

The governor of Roman North Africa, proconsul Vigellius Saturninus, whose seat was in the ancient Phoenician town of Carthage, interrogates six Christians brought before him, three men and three women. The act of interrogation reads as follows:

The proconsul Saturninus said: 'You can secure the indulgence of our lord the emperor if you return to your senses.'

Speratus said: 'We have never done any wrong; we have lent ourselves to no injustice; we have never spoken ill of anyone. . . .'

The proconsul Saturninus said: 'We, also, are religious, and our religion is simple; and we swear by the *genius* of our lord the emperor and pray for his welfare, as you ought to do'. . . .

Speratus said: 'The empire of this world I do not recognize; but rather I serve that God whom no man has seen nor can see with human eyes. I have not committed theft; if I buy anything, I pay the tax'. . . .

The proconsul Saturninus said to the others: 'Cease to be of this persuasion. . . . Do not participate in this madness.'

Cittinus said: 'We have none other to fear except only our Lord God who is in heaven.'

Donata said: 'Honour to Caesar as to Caesar, but fear to God.'

Vestia said: 'I am a Christian.'

Secunda said: 'What I am, that I wish to be.'

The proconsul Saturninus said to Speratus: 'Do you persist in being a Christian?'

Speratus said: 'I am a Christian.' And they all concurred with him.

The proconsul Saturninus said: 'Do you desire some time to reconsider?'

Speratus said: 'In a matter so just, there is no reconsidering.'

The proconsul Saturninus said: 'What are the things in your box?'

Speratus said: 'The Books, and the letters of Paul, a just man.'

The proconsul Saturninus said: 'Take a postponement of thirty days and reconsider.'

Speratus said again: 'I am a Christian.' And they all concurred with him.

The proconsul Saturninus read out the decree from the tablet: ' . . . it is my decision that they be punished with the sword.'

Speratus said: 'We give thanks to God.'

Nartzalus said: 'Today we are martyrs in heaven: thanks be to God.'[12]

In AD 197, the Roman scholar Tertullian wrote his *Apologeticum*, an extensive apologia for the Christians. He analysed their actions, practices and way of life, dismissed all false accusations, and indicated, finally, that the principal objection to them was not their religion but their refusal to recognize the emperor's authority as divine. In passing, he actually reversed the accusation: the Romans themselves feared their rulers more than their gods:

'You do not,' say you, 'worship the gods; you do not offer sacrifice for the emperors'. It follows by parity of reasoning that we do not sacrifice for others because we do not for ourselves: it follows from our not worshipping the gods. So we are accused of sacrilege and treason at once. That is the chief of the case against us, the whole of it, in fact. . . .

So now we have come to the second charge, the charge of treason against a majesty more august. For it is with greater fear and shrewder timidity that you watch Caesar than the Olympian Jove himself. . . . So that in this too you show more fear for the rule of a man. In fact, among you perjury by all the gods together comes quicker than by the *genius* of a simple Caesar. . . . So that is why the Christians are public enemies: because they will not give the emperors vain, false, and rash honours. . . .

We invoke the eternal God, the true God, the living God, for the safety of the emperors. . . . Nothing is more foreign to us than the state. One state we recognize for all: the universe.[13]

Thus, Christianity already defined itself as a universal religion, recognizing no political boundaries: it meant its empire to be of the whole world.

Towards an empire Roman as well as Christian

In the course of the fourth century AD, all official connections between the Roman state and the old religions came to an end. In AD 313, Emperor Constantine (*c*.AD 280–337) and his associate in the eastern part of the empire promulgated what later became known as the 'Decree of Milan'. This was actually a series of orders addressed at the most important civil servants, telling them to put an end to the prosecution of Christians and to give them the same freedom to practise their religion as the worshippers of other religions which flourished in the Roman Empire.

Reading the text of this 'Decree of Milan', the preference for the new religion which most of Constantine's successors would finally give it is noticeable already, despite its attempt to be neutral with regard to all religions:

> When I, Constantine Augustus, as well as I, Licinius Augustus . . . were consider-ing everything that pertained to the public welfare and security, we thought that, among other things which we saw would be for the good of many, those regulations pertaining to the reverence of the Divinity ought certainly to be made first, so that we might grant to the Christians and to all others full authority to observe that religion which each preferred; whence any Divinity whatsoever in the seat of the heavens may be propitious and kindly disposed to us and all who are placed under our rule . . . so that the supreme Deity, to whose worship we freely yield our hearts, may show in all things His usual favour and benevolence.
>
> Therefore, your Worship should know that it has pleased us to remove all conditions whatsoever, which were in the rescripts formerly given to you officially, concerning the Christians, and now any one of these who wishes to observe the Christian religion may do so freely and openly, without any disturbance or molestation. . . . your Worship will know that we have also conceded to other religions the right of open and free observance of their worship for the sake of the peace of our times, that each one may have the free opportunity to worship as he pleases; this regulation is made that we may not seem to detract aught from any dignity or any religion.[14]

As a result of this decree all property which had been confiscated from the Christians was returned to them and the state paid damages to those who had acquired such confiscated property. Not only was the religion of the Christians given equality with other religions, it was also given a decided economic advantage, one which the new Church made use of to extend its power range as an institution. The power of the old religions was gradually eroded and, parallel with this, the flourishing Christian community and its leadership were given the chance to strengthen their own position. On the one hand, measures were taken definitely limiting the appeal of the older religions:

> No person at all, of any class or order whatsoever of men or officials . . . whether he is powerful by the accident of birth or is humble in descent, legal status and fortune, shall sacrifice an innocent victim to senseless statues in any place at all or in any city. He shall not, through more secret wickedness, venerate his household

god with fire, his *genius* with wine, his *Penates* with fragrant essences . . . But if anyone should dare . . . he shall be reported in accordance with the example of a person guilty of high treason.[15]

On the other hand, many privileges were accorded to the new religion. In AD 313, Constantine decreed that:

> Since it appears from many things that the setting at naught of divine worship, through which the highest reverence for the most holy power of heaven is preserved, has brought great dangers to the state, and that the lawful restoration and maintenance of this have bestowed good fortune on the Roman name and extraordinary prosperity on all the affairs of mankind – for it is divine Providence which bestows these blessings – it is our decision that those men who, with due holiness and devotion . . . offer their services in the performance of divine worship, should receive rewards for their labours . . . Wherefore it is my will that those persons in the catholic Church . . . who devote their service to this holy worship – those who are customarily named clerics – shall once and for all be kept completely exempt from all compulsory public services . . . nor be disturbed in any way from devoting themselves completely to serving their own law. For when they render supreme service to the deity, it seems that they confer the greatest possible benefits upon the state.[16]

Eventually – at least, that is how the story goes – Constantine himself became a Christian: on his deathbed, in AD 337, he was baptized.[17] There is no consensus among historians on the question whether this was the result of political opportunism or of religious conviction, although it seems likely that political necessity and a sense of the sociocultural irreversibility of the Christianization process heightened the emperor's own sensibility.[18]

In the process of its rise to pre-eminence, the Christian Church inevitably lost some of its pristine qualities. The idea of *gnosis*, of an inner enlightenment attainable by everyone who strove after it in a life that was, of necessity, torn between matter and spirit, between evil and good, had widely spread in the Near East from the first century onwards and had greatly influenced early Christianity. Stressing individual responsibility, it left little room for a stifling authority structure. As such structures were now developing within the Church, the gnostic ideas were forced into the background. So was, according to many historians, the largely egalitarian relationship between men and women which had characterized the early Church.[19]

Also, Christianity was soon rocked by fierce faction strife. Specifically the doctrines of the divinity of the human Christ and the concept of Holy Trinity, of God the Father, his Son and the Holy Spirit, were hotly debated issues, partly because many could not be convinced by the theological and philosophical basis of these notions. Obviously, either for personal or political reasons, the emperors could and would not tolerate such heated discussions, which led to arguments, fights and even outright schisms. Therefore, they frequently attended the councils during which the Christians tried, usually in vain, to reconcile their differences. They also supported the policies of the Church leaders who persecuted dissenting Christians and tried to root out their ideas. Hence, Constantine himself was present at the Council of Nicea in AD 325. Eusebius, the emperor's contemporary and biographer, describes the drama in his *Vita Constantini*, III, vi–x, *passim*:

> Constantine summoned a general synod, inviting the bishops in all parts with honorary letters to be present . . . at that time there were to be seen congregated in one place persons widely differing from one another not only in spirit but also in physical appearance, and in the regions, places, and provinces from which they came . . . from all the churches which had filled all Europe, Africa and Asia. . . . Present among the body were more than 250 bishops . . . for the council which was to put an end to the controversies.

The Council ended with the promulgation of the famous Nicene Creed, a text which meant to enable the participants to feel reconciled with each other and, thus, to restore unity. The Church, aided by the state, tried to formalize and control public discourse in religious matters, in order to establish an orthodox doctrine. Indeed, Church councils' decisions always were presented as consensual.[20] It all helped to develop a society with an overtly pyramidical, authoritarian pattern of relationships.

However, precisely because the ecclesiastical leadership ruled out any possibility for discussion, the arguments continued unabated. Later, in AD 380 and 381, Emperor Theodosius determined that:

> It is our will that all peoples ruled by our Clemency shall practise that religion which the divine Peter the Apostle transmitted to the Romans; that is, according to the apostolic discipline and the evangelical doctrine, we shall believe in the single deity of the Father, the Son, and the Holy Spirit, under the concept of equal majesty and of the Holy Trinity. We order that those persons who follow this rule shall embrace the name of Catholic Christians. The rest, however, whom we judge demented and insane, shall have the infamy of heretical dogmas, their meeting places shall not receive the name of churches, and they shall be smitten first by divine vengeance and secondly by retribution of our hostility. . . .
>
> The contamination of the Photian pestilence, the poison of the Arian sacrilege, the crime of the Dunomian perfidy, and the sectarian monstrosities . . . shall be abolished even from the hearing of men.[21]

In fact, the result of Constantine's political decisions had been that Christianity became the state religion, so that more and more people felt called on to embrace the new faith. By now, even members of the elite were converting to it, whether out of conviction or from a wish to hold on to their positions. Consequently, Christianity became thoroughly saturated with those elements from the old 'heathen' culture that did not conflict with it, such as classical rhetoric, aspects of philosophy, and many themes and forms from the visual arts. In the end, even the Christian calendar and the veneration of saints and relics showed many aspects of the older, pagan cults.

Thus it was that all around the Mediterranean – including, therefore, a large part of Europe – a situation developed which, on such a large scale, was unique from the perspective of world history, namely, that only one religion governed the society and the culture of a world empire. Moreover, it was not a poly-theistic but a monotheistic religion requiring each person to submit completely to an unseen but yet personal God. Faith, not reason, was its central principle. Anything humanly invented but by the Church leaders considered to be in conflict with professed religion now was condemned as heresy if it could not be fitted into the new theological system, one way or the other.

Indeed, the new religious elite wanted to extirpate completely the power which all sorts of cults and religions, usually older than Christianity, still held over the population. In this, they had the emperors on their side, who increasingly had chosen to attach themselves to Christianity. Indeed, the rulers of the Romans strove for as much unity of thought and action among their subjects as possible and therefore often supported these policies of cultural homogenization. In a decree of AD 357, the Emperor Constantius Augustus told his people:

> No one shall consult a soothsayer or astrologer or diviner. The evil teaching of augurs and practitioners of magic shall become silent. The Chaldeans and magicians and all the rest . . . shall not attempt anything of this sort. The curiosity of all men for divination shall forever cease.[22]

Of course, this certainly did not mean that such practices really disappeared. On the contrary, many Christian priests consciously or unconsciously took over the role of the old magicians and sorcerers, precisely because the population needed a priesthood that could communicate with and if necessary placate the incomprehensible forces of nature.

Everyday life gradually became structured according to the Church's rules. Not only were all sorts of advantages accorded to the new religion and its followers, but also as many elements of the older cultures as possible were adapted to conform to Christian standards in the interest of cultural homogenization. This can be seen from ordinances of 386 and 392:

> On the day of the Sun, which our ancestors rightly called the Lord's Day [Constantine had ordered this in AD 321], the prosecution of all litigation, court business and suits, shall be entirely suspended. No person shall demand the payment of a public or private debt, nor shall there be any cognizance of controversies before arbitrators. . . . Contests in the circuses shall be prohibited on the festal days of the Sun . . . in order that no concourse of people to the spectacles may divert men from the reverend mysteries of the Christian law.[23]

The emperors, most of whom by now had been educated within a Christian culture, were increasingly severe with the remnants of the older cults, often not primarily because they were opposed to them from a religious point of view but because such cults posed a threat to public stability, offering opposition groups an alternative ideology. In AD 395, and again in later years, they ordered that:

> If any images still stand in the temples and shrines, and if they received or do now receive the worship of pagans anywhere, they shall be torn from their foundations. . . . The buildings themselves of the temples which are located in cities or towns or outside the towns shall be confiscated to public use. Altars shall be destroyed in all places.[24]

In AD 425, an imperial edict was promulgated which shows how much had changed in less than a century after Constantine's decision: it was patently obvious that Christianity had become victorious. All ideas which diverged from the governing doctrine were forcefully suppressed. Moreover, the emperor had given the Pope – the bishop of Rome who, as the successor of the Apostle Peter, claimed supremacy in the Church's hierarchy – his unambiguous support as the only spiritual leader of all Christendom:

> We command that the Manichaeans, heretics, schismatics, astrologers, and every sect inimical to the Catholics shall be banished from the very sight of the City of Rome, in order that it may not be contaminated by the contagious presence of the criminals. An admonition, moreover, must be especially issued concerning those persons who by perverse persuasion withdraw from the communion of the venerable Pope, and by whose schism the rest of the common people also are corrupted.[25]

However, this edict also shows that, whatever power the Church had acquired, it still had not managed to force everyone in the Roman Empire into the straitjacket of Christianity.

Rome and its neighbours in the fourth and fifth centuries AD: the division and loss of the political empire – the survival of the cultural empire

Certainly from the first century AD onwards, parallel with its territorial growth the Roman Empire had become increasingly economically dependent on natural resources and manpower which had to be imported from outside its borders. In particular, slaves, who had to keep the system going, could be obtained only by wars of conquest and, when the empire had reached its greatest size, by purchasing them from barbarian middlemen beyond its frontiers. An indication of the 'problem' is that by the end of the first century AD, in Italy alone 2 million of its 6 million inhabitants were slaves; this meant that a fresh supply of 150,000 new slaves was needed annually.

Strangely enough, this resulted in a situation in which the Roman economy became a powerful stimulus to the economies of neighbouring regions. In northern and central Europe, for example, the needs of the enormous Roman army led to increased cattle-rearing among the German tribes beyond the

Rhine, who provided leather for tents, boots, saddles, and other horse gear. Archaeological finds also testify to an increased demand for luxury goods in these areas which provided the empire with raw materials and slaves. Such finds also evidence technological improvements in the various border regions, which were perhaps influenced by increased contacts with the Gallo-Roman world, as shown by the beautiful filigree, gem-encrusted jewellery discovered in a chieftain's grave at Sutton Hoo, in England.

Then, by the second century AD, peoples in northern and central Europe began to move again, partly due to population increases, and partly due to climatic changes and social instability on the eastern periphery of Europe: Poland and western Russia. This led to the Longobards crossing the Danube in the latter part of the century, and the Franks, Frisians and Saxons emerging at the Rhine border, and sometimes crossing it in the first half of the third century. Often, these were war bands of uncertain ethnogenesis, confederated because they were drawn by the weakening of Roman authority in the frontier regions.

Further east, a heterogeneous congeries of Germanic tribes as well as even more loosely organized, roving groups made up of a wide range of ethnic elements, probably originating from the Vistula basin, now entered written history as 'the Goths', the name give them by the terrified people of south-east Europe,[26] who were first confronted with their attacks in the late second and early third centuries.[27] They settled near the Roman border on the Danube and soon even converted to Christianity. There, Bishop Wulfila or Ulfilas (c.AD 310–382/3) decided to give his people the Bible in Gothic. Its earliest known manuscript copy, probably produced in the sixth century, was written in beautiful silver letters on purple vellum; this *Codex Argenteus* is now kept in the University Library at Uppsala. Wulfila had to invent an alphabet to achieve his aim, for his people's civilization was still one without writing.[28] Actually, there never was an original, distinct Goth culture. Yet, during two centuries of raids, invasions, settlements, removals and resettlements, nomadic elements, Germanic influences and the Graeco-Roman culture of the Balkan and the Black Sea coast came to constitute a civilization which was then introduced into western Europe as well.

For when the Huns came from the Eurasian steppe by the end of the fourth century, the Goths penetrated further into the relative safety of the Roman Empire. They eventually conquered the wealthiest regions of its western part. Some of their bands set up a kingdom in northern Italy, based at Ravenna, where the monumental remains of a marvellous mixture of Roman and Germanic cultural elements can still be seen. Others founded a kingdom in southern France, based at Toulouse; they adapted easily to the local Gallo-Roman culture. And in Spain, too, the Roman elements mixed with the German heritage of the Goths, resulting, among other things, in a thriving intellectual life that lasted till the coming of new conquerors in the seventh century.

It produced such great spirits as Isidore, archbishop of Seville (c.560–636), a major scholar in various fields. He wrote a 'History of the Goths' that, significantly, starts with a *Laus Spaniae* (a 'praise of Spain'), indicating the wish of the Goth conquerors to merge with the existing, romanized population; it was a first expression of Spanish 'national' feeling. He also compiled a history of the world, a treatise on astronomy and cosmography, and, most important perhaps, a fascinating work called *Etymologiae*, one of Europe's first encyclopedias and a foundation of philosophy and scholarship for centuries to come.

The coming of the Huns led to the migration of peoples in western Europe, too. One year, at the beginning of the fifth century, the Burgundians crossed the frozen Rhine, settling around Worms, Speyer and Strasbourg. Later, their army was destroyed by the hordes from Asia. This disaster, told and retold countless times in heroic songs by Burgundian bards who embroidered and added to it, finally resulted in the famous *Nibelungenlied*, providing Europe with a fecund legend that was set to music by Richard Wagner in the nineteenth century and, in the twentieth century, filmed in silent but evocative images by the German film-maker Fritz Lang.

Meanwhile, the keepers of the empire, the Christian emperors of the fourth and fifth centuries, clearly understood that not even the new religion could provide the divine protection they had so dearly hoped for. The pressure on the borders from outside increased; now, the tribes and peoples who were driven from central and eastern Europe and Central Asia by the changes that affected their agriculture and cattle-raising became a threat more than ever before.[29] But as the rule of the emperors became weaker, many members of the elites who implemented state power on the regional and local level began to look upon the Church as the one institution that could guarantee the old values, a process that can be witnessed, for example, among the urban elites of Roman Gaul.[30]

Meanwhile, the empire's structural flaws had become glaringly manifest. Its very size was, perhaps, one of the main reasons for its demise; the bureaucracy and economy were unable to adequately mobilize the forces of resistance; communications between the capital and the provinces took too long; on the peripheries there was increasing distrust of the parasitic, wasteful centre, Rome, with its continuous demands for money and goods. As the central power waned, regional differences turned out to be centripetal after all. Now that it was attacked from all sides, it became apparent the empire could no longer be ruled as an economic, military and organizational unity, precisely when it needed this unity most.

Consequently, the main component parts gradually went their own way, disclosing the cultural varieties that had continued to exist underneath the Roman veneer. In the east, Greek had remained the common language, while in the west, Latin had gradually gained the upper hand. Roman unity was indeed lost when central government no longer appeared able to effectively defend the borders. Finally, considerations of a logistic-military nature led to the decision to formally divide the empire in an eastern and a western half, to be ruled in concord by two emperors. In retrospect, this decision inevitably seems foolish. It certainly proved fateful.

From the fourth century onwards, a Greek or Byzantine empire developed in what formerly had been Greece and Asia Minor. This empire considered itself the true heir to ancient Rome, creating a vision of its capital, Byzantium, as the 'new Rome' and renaming it Constantinople in AD 330.[31] The western Roman Empire, the *imperium occidentalis*, the empire of the Occident, became known as the Latin Empire because of the dominant cultural language.

During the last centuries of its existence, the Roman Empire, by now permanently divided, was increasingly forced to adopt a policy of accommodation, with the result that, gradually, not only were foreign peoples allowed in but also they were assimilated with Roman culture. Often, the foreign war bands were positively hailed as the troops which the great senatorial landed families of the empire needed to fulfil the role they increasingly took upon themselves, that of defending and policing the region they dominated, now that imperial authority was weakening. This, of course, contributed to the romanization of the immigrants.

By the late fourth and early fifth centuries, certainly in the northern and western parts of the empire, imperial power was mostly controlled by non-Roman generals and finally passed outright into the hands of newcomers. One such, Theodosius, though a descendant of the Visigoths, a people who only shortly before had been described as a 'barbaric' tribe, yet could become emperor of the west in AD 381. Showing that a loss of memory can be politically expedient, the orator Themistius praised this upstart as the saviour of the old culture, saying:

> The Barbarians have still not defeated the Romans, for after all, form triumphed over formlessness, order over chaos, courage over fear, obedience over disobedience.[32]

But the ideas of this intellectual, who swam with the tide and yet managed to finely articulate the essence of Roman culture in the face of this powerful new leader, were not shared by all 'real' Romans. In AD 399, the somewhat more conservative orator Synesius addressed Emperor Arcadius as follows: 'That these fair-haired people, who arrange their hair in Euboian styles, are our slaves in private but our rulers in public is outrageous, a shocking spectacle'.[33] These words showed an undertone which people in Europe would frequently use when they wanted to brand others, migrants, as a 'danger' to their own position and culture.

Meanwhile, a certain defeatism mastered the empire's inhabitants. The Christian scholar St Jerome (331/47–419/20) wrote:

> I come now to the frail fortunes of human life, and my soul shudders to recount the downfall of our age. For twenty years now and more the blood of Romans has every day been shed between Constantinople and the Julian Alps. Scythia, Thrace, Macedonia, Thessaly, Dardania, Dacia, Epirus, Dalmatia, and all the provinces of Pannonia, have been sacked, pillaged and plundered by Goths and Sarmatians, Quadians and Alans, Huns and Vandals and Marcomanni. How many matrons,

and how many of God's virgins, ladies of gentle birth and high position, have been made the sport of these beasts! Bishops have been taken prisoners, presbyters and other clergymen of different orders murdered. Churches have been overthrown, horses stabled at Christ's altar, the relics of martyrs dug up. . . . The Roman world is failing, and yet we hold our heads erect instead of bowing our necks.[34]

This attitude of proud resignation did not prevent the end of the empire. In August of AD 410, the Goth leader Alaric laid siege to Rome, conquering and sacking it. The one time symbol of the unity and power of the Roman Empire was, for the time being, destroyed. But St Jerome's words indicate the chance of survival which he ascribed to a world no longer Roman but still Christian.

And he was not mistaken. At the end of the fifth entury, some of the war bands who had settled within the empire in the region of the Rhine, Moselle, Somme and Loire were united under one Chlodwig, who shook off the yoke of the romanized rulers of that region and established a kingdom, utilizing the traditional instrument of German politics, the creation of a partly fictive tribal structure with its basis in equally fictive family relationships to create a 'people' now called the Franks.

But as so many Germanic war leaders and their followers had done before him, Chlodwig converted to Christianity; according to tradition, he was baptized in Rheims on Christmas night in AD 497. He may have been persuaded to do so by the assurances of Christian missionaries that such a move would bring him the power and wealth associated with the old empire. Certainly, his descendants used this argument to style themselves the successors of the Roman emperors – and Rheims remained the place where, if possible, the French kings were crowned till the French Revolution, 1500 years later. But whatever Chlodwig's motives, he linked himself and his people with the culture of the Romans, as did a great number of the Germanic tribes who continued to enter the empire that was now definitely lost.

Empire and language

By the fifth century AD, the linguistic map of Europe had become thoroughly complicated. During many centuries of invasions numerous tribes and nations had brought their languages to this part of the world. By and large, most languages originally stemmed from the so-called 'proto-Indo-European', spoken by the semi-nomadic inhabitants of the southern Russian steppes, northern Turkey and Iran somewhere in the millennia between 7000 and 5000 BC.[35] Although this 'original' language does not exist any more and, moreover, its nature and its 'originality' are still hotly debated, efforts at reconstruction have revealed some of its cultural characteristics, which show that the society which used it was a patriarchical one, subsisting both on agriculture and pasturing.

One or more tribes from this linguistic-cultural 'pool' had begun to spread to the Danube area between 5000 and 3500 BC and reached the Adriatic region somewhere before 2000 BC. Meanwhile, they had also moved into Iran and India, where their language developed into the Indo-Iranian tongues, among which are old Persian and Sanskrit, the language of India's oldest and holiest books, the *Vedas* – though it must be said that even now Indians accept the idea that the most venerated elements of their culture came from the outside far less readily than Europeans.[36]

In Europe, the spread and development of the Indo-European languages closely followed the pattern of two millennia of invasions and conquests before the beginning of the Christian era. In Greece, the Greek language has been attested from the fifteenth century BC onwards. In the end, it became the *lingua franca*, the language commonly used in the eastern Mediterranean from the third century BC till the seventh century AD, when it was superseded, there, by Arabic.

The first Indo-European people to spread their language over central and western Europe were the Celts, during the last millennium BC. As the German tribes came in from western Russia, partly by way of Scandinavia, Celtic was largely marginalized; it remained the language of the western periphery of Europe: Ireland, Cornwall and Brittany.

But while the Germanic languages were formed – Gothic, now lost, and the Anglo-Saxon, Scandinavian and German varieties – they also encountered a powerful competitor. Around the Adriatic basin, the Italic languages had evolved, among which Latin soon became the tongue of conquerors. For as the Roman Empire consolidated its hold over ever greater parts of south-west Europe, the spoken or 'vulgar' version of Latin became predominant because it was the language of the political and cultural elite and, soon, also of the new, Christian Church. Indeed, the spreading of the Christian message obviously was favoured greatly by the communication possibilities provided by that highly unified cultural and linguistic structure which was the Roman Empire with its Graeco-Latin civilization, but, in its turn, the spreading of Christianity resulted in the spreading of a Latinized language as well.

Eventually, this complex situation gave birth to the so-called 'Romance' languages, the regional, vernacularized varieties of Latin: Italian, Sardinian, French, Occitan, Spanish, Catalan, Portuguese and, of course, Romanian. These gradually supplanted the languages previously spoken in these regions, whether of yet older Indo-European origin or, as in the case of the only survivor, Basque, even dating back to pre-Indo-European times.

Looking at the map of the Roman Empire in the fourth and fifth centuries AD, one must conclude that the military *limes* had become, to a large extent, a cultural, linguistic frontier, too. South-west of it, the Romance tongues continued to predominate and while in the north-western corner the Germanic languages – English, Frisian, Dutch and German – consolidated themselves, in later centuries there has been considerable interaction with, especially, Latin, and later French. North and east of the frontier, the other Germanic languages flourished largely uninfluenced, though, further east, a last wave of invasions in the sixth and seventh centuries AD brought the Baltic and

Slavonic branch of Indo-European to central Europe and the Balkans; it first branched out into a number of dialects from which, eventually, separate languages stemmed, among them Polish, Czech, Slovak, Serbian, Croat, Bulgarian and, of course, Russian.

Thus, it seems that the secret success of any language is muscle, first, and, perhaps, mission and money second. Greek marched with the armies of Alexander, Latin spread with the legions of the Romans and the missionaries of the Christians and, in later times, Arabic would conquer three continents in the wake of Islamic traders and troops, while, of course, Spanish began its victory in the sixteenth century in the wake of a global conquest both material and spiritual. To a far lesser extent, from the seventeenth century onwards, the Dutch and the French established their language overseas as well. Last, but not least, English first started on its road around the world when the Britons built their empire.

Part II

Continuity and change

New forms of belief

4   Towards one religion for all

The Christian world-view: the survival of classical culture within the context of Christianity and Europe

It is important to note that, within three centuries, a sect, Christianity, originating in a very localized tribal religious tradition, Judaism, had developed into a full-fledged Church, and, moreover, one that encompassed the entire Roman Empire and was by now deemed of such importance that the emperors sought to take it over, showering it with land grants and exempting its priests from public service. Yet this Church, while accepting these privileges, for a long time shied away from the state, maintaining that a true believer could not serve two masters. On the other hand, the Church soon adopted the organizational structure of the empire, with its hierarchy of authorities culminating in the bishops. Moreover, as the structures of the empire grew weaker, the leaders of the Church often felt forced to step in where civic authorities could not cope anymore.

What happened in the mean time to that pseudo-geographical concept, Europe, which was in fact a world-view, a cultural representation of the Graeco-Roman world?[1] For an inhabitant of the Roman Empire like Augustine (AD 354–430), a patrician's son from Thagaste in North Africa who converted to Christianity and later became a saint, the world actually consisted of two parts: an eastern part, which coincided with the continent of Asia, which to him was the Near East, and a western part, which consisted of Europe and Africa, separated but not divided by the Mediterranean:

> The reason why Europe and Africa have been made into two continents lies in this, that all the water from the ocean comes between the two, flowing between their lands and forming the great sea for us.[2]

Thus, Augustine does not attach much meaning to the concept of Europe: even though he knew that another world existed beyond it, what counted for him was the Roman Empire, a unity wrapped around 'our sea'.

As he himself did, too, more and more of that empire's citizens converted to the new religion, which developed in the welter of existing cultures and,

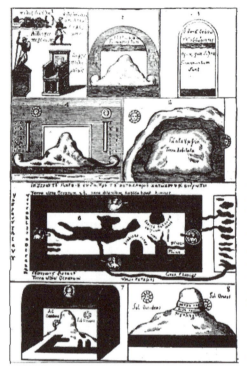

Plate 9 The maps and drawings illustrating the various elements of Kosmas' Christian Cosmology; shown are, among other things, heaven as a dome covering the earth, the pillars that support the firmament, and earth itself, within its surrounding ocean which, again, is encircled by the land inhabited by man before the Flood: the site of paradise
Source: Centre for Art Historical Documentation, Nijmegen, The Netherlands

Plate 10 A Germanic limestone tombstone, eighth century, from Alskog Tjangvide on the island of Gotland, Sweden, showing another cosmology. Its runic inscription dedicates it to the memory of one Jurulv, murdered by relatives. The stone shows the Ship of the Dead below, and in the upper part the deceased's arrival, on Odin's eight-legged horse, at Walhalla, the home of the Gods – a great hall as the ones actually built in Northwestern Europe at that time
Source: Centre for Art Historical Documentation, Nijmegen, The Netherlands

indeed, consciously and unconsciously nourished on many of its elements. Consequently, this new religion soon provided an attractive and, for many, convincing mix of characteristics of other popular religions and systems of thinking. Among these were the teachings connected with the Indian-Persian god Mithras, and also the cult of the Invincible Sun God, who for many years had been the Emperor Constantine's tutelary deity: the rites celebrating the birth of Mithras and the feast of the Sun both helped to shape the Christian feast of 'Christmas', as the birth of the Saviour and the return of Light. Equally influential was the worship of the Egyptian goddess Isis, who, often painted and sculpted as a mother-goddess, with the child Osiris in her lap, clearly became a model for the representation of the Virgin Mary. And, of course, there were the ideas of a number of Greek philosophers including Aristotle and Plato; these were very popular among the Graeco-Roman elites in the years when the Christian Church began to try and influence them. In the cultural synthesis that ensued, the view that people had of the world changed, both in a physical and in a metaphysical sense.

―――――――――

MOUNT SINAI, AD 547: KOSMAS EXPLAINS THE CHRISTIAN COSMOGRAPHY

In about AD 547, the Greek Kosmas, who had become a monk after a life of travelling and trading as far as India, wrote his *Kristianikè Topographia* (Christian Topography). A ninth-century copy of the text can be found in the Vatican Library in Rome, illustrated with the earliest Christian maps.

In this work he tried to reconcile pagan geography and the geographical details known to him with the notions which Christian Holy Scripture seemed to dictate on this subject. Kosmas' view of the world seems to run counter to the global world that had been central to Ptolemaic cosmology. From now on, for more than a thousand years, outside a small part of the scholarly elite most Europeans, including a large part of the Christian priests, would think of the earth as flat, as a vast expanse of land in an even vaster expanse of water, under the vault of heaven. It required particular explanations of the nature of the relations between land and sea, earth and heaven, and the movements of the heavenly bodies.

> We have said that the figure of the earth is lengthwise from east to west and breadthwise from north to south, and that it is divided into two parts: this part which we, the men of the present day, inhabit, and which is all round encircled by the intermedial sea, called the ocean by the Pagans, and that part which encircles the ocean, and has its extremities bound together with those of the heaven, and which men at one time inhabited to eastward, before the flood in the days of Noah occurred, and in which also Paradise is situated. . . .
>
> The northern and western parts of the earth which we inhabit are of very great elevation, while the southern parts are proportionally depressed. For to what extent of its breadth the earth is imperceptibly depressed, it is found to have an

elevation of like area in the northern and western parts, while the ocean beyond is of unusual depth. But in the southern and eastern parts the ocean beyond is not of unusual but of the medium depth. When these facts are considered, one can see why those who sail to the north and west are called lingerers. It is because they are mounting up and in mounting up they sail more slowly, while in returning they descend from high places to low, and thus sail fast, and in a few days bring their voyage to an end . . .

The eastern and southern parts again, as low-lying and over-heated by the sun, are extremely hot, while the northern and western, from their great elevation and distance from the sun, are extremely cold, and in consequence the inhabitants have very pale complexions, and must keep themselves warm against the cold . . .

Since then the heaven and the earth comprise the universe, we assert that the earth has been founded on its own stability by the Creator, according once more to the divine scripture, and that it does not rest on any body. . . .

We therefore first depict along with the earth the heaven, which is vaulted and which has its extremities bound together with the extremities of the earth. To the best of our ability we have endeavoured to delineate it on its western side and its eastern; for these two sides are walls, extending from below to the vaults above. There is also the firmament which, in the middle, is bound together with the first heaven, and which, on its upper side, has the waters according to divine scripture itself . . .

To the extremities on the four sides of the earth the heaven is fastened at its own four extremities, making the figure of a cube, that is to say, a quadrangular figure, while up above it curves round in the form of an oblong vault and becomes as it were a vast canopy. And in the middle the firmament is made fast to it, and thus two places are formed.

From the earth to the firmament is the first place, this world, namely, in which are the angels and men and all the present state of existence. From the firmament again to the vault above is the second place – the Kingdom of Heaven, into which Christ, first of all, entered, after his ascension, having prepared for us a new and living way.

Since the heavenly bodies then, according to divine scripture, are moved in their orbits by invisible powers, and run their course through the north, and pass below the elevated part of the earth, it is possible, with such a configuration, for eclipses of the moon and the sun to be produced. For the angelic powers, by moving the figures on rational principles and in regular order, and with greater speed than lies in us to apprehend, produce these phenomena, plying their labours by night and by day without ever pausing.[3]

Looking at Kosmas' map, the nether world is, by and large, the same as the world of the Christians, Europe and the Holy Land, symbolically centring around Jerusalem and Rome, with Asia and Africa only sketchily represented, not least, obviously, because so little of it was actually known.[4]

In this world, a confrontation between the cosmos as seen through the eyes of the holy book of the Christians and the knowledge and world-view of the

'Ancients', admired by the elite of the Roman Empire and their successors, was inevitable. The resulting tension became structural and, right up to the twentieth century, continued to feed cultural changes in the worlds of those who were raised within Christianity. The genesis and development of ideas in Europe and, inextricably linked with it, of European culture, began to display an alternating rhythm of periods which harked back to classical civilization, and times when more emphasis was placed on an original Christian purity, which gradually became more and more idealized. Always, when the tension became too great, a synthesis which could reconcile both elements was sought. However, a system of ideas which could please and convince everyone was not found.

Three forms of tension, voiced most clearly in the overlapping fields of philosophy, religion and science, seem to have been perennial: between the immortal soul and the mortal body, between good and evil and, intertwined with the first two, between faith, in the unreasoned authority of a higher power, and reason, as the essential capacity of the free-willed human.

One of the central questions repeatedly asked long before the coming of Christianity had been whether everything in the universe, including man, who considers himself a thinking, free agent, actually consists of matter or substance. The Greek philosopher Democritos (*c.*470–360 BC) had already answered this in the affirmative. In his atom theory, he proposed that everything could be traced back to a more or less complex whole of the smallest component parts. The human 'spirit', or soul, is no more than this, disappearing along with the body at death.

Such concepts were unacceptable to Christianity; after all, they were diametrically opposed to the notion of bodily resurrection which was precisely the idea the Church wanted to use to neutralize the second fundamental tension. Christ and his followers had actually fought the presence of misery and injustice on earth, of 'evil', evident to so many, with the promise of a life of eternal goodness and happiness in the hereafter to which both body and soul would be resurrected after death. Although this solution appealed to many, there were those who still asked themselves how a God who was presented as all-good as well as all-powerful and who, moreover, promised man his resurrection had permitted evil to enter the world in the first place.

In the first centuries of the discussions between Christians and other religious-minded intellectuals in the Roman world, all sorts of theories were put forward to solve this dilemma. Some of the most important have collectively become known as *gnosis*, or knowledge. Those who followed this path accepted good and evil, spirit and matter, as essential characteristics of man and, therefore, of God, who had created man. According to them, salvation could be achieved by understanding these characteristics and their consequences. However, this rather personalized way of thinking, popular among a number of Christians ever since, was anathema to the religious authorities; in the early centuries of Christianity all traces of it were gradually eliminated from the accepted tradition.

Within Christianity, the accepted tradition largely followed the ideas formulated by the patrician's son from Thagaste in his major works, the *Confessiones* and the *De Civitate Dei* (On the City of God). Augustine first concluded that man exists because he thinks, considers and doubts. Next, Augustine asked himself how man came into existence and then affirmed that this resulted from the creation by an eternal God who stands outside and above the cosmos and who created space, that is, motion, and time. Augustine's ideas show the influences of the Graeco-Roman culture in which he was raised and in which Christianity had developed as a new system of thought, seeking to synthesize what nowadays many think cannot be synthesized – the unconditional surrender to a revealed God and the physical reality of the world and of man as perceived by man's rational way of thinking. To Augustine, the world, and in it the Church, the only road to salvation, as well as its members, are all imperfect, but yet point to the perfection they will realize when turning to God.

The teaching of Augustine owed quite a lot to the philosophy of Plato (428–348 BC), principally as it had been assimilated and reformulated by Plotinus (*c.*AD 204–70). Indeed, neo-Platonism was perhaps the most important spiritual movement in the later years of the Roman Empire. As a result of studying Plato's philosophy, Christianity constructed itself into a way of thinking and living that could appeal to the cultural elite as well as to the masses. Several of Plato's concepts could indeed be interpreted in such a way that the more intellectual defenders of Christianity could align themselves with these. After all, in his *Symposium* the Athenian philosopher had stipulated that there are two worlds: that of the imperfect body in which people operate with their impressions and senses, and which they can therefore know, and the world of Ideas, the higher principles which, although he is partly unaware of them, exist in every human. In his *Timaios*, Plato had articulated his views on creation: 'Ideas' are the thoughts of the *Nous* (the Intellect or the Divine Soul), in which the *Hen* (the One) has become conscious. These 'Ideas' manifest themselves in the *Psychè* (the Soul) of the world but also in the souls of people, which thus became animate matter.

Inevitably, however, Christian intellectuals also had to come to terms with Aristotle, Plato's most distinguished student. As often happens with students, he had reasoned away from his teacher. Arguing that the Ideas were only 'names', not real things, Aristotle did talk of 'forms', in which undefined matter, substance, was given shape, resulting in physical nature. The 'pure form', which sets everything in motion, is the 'prime mover', pure thought – God, who thinks himself and therefore creates himself. The essence of this Platonic-Aristotelian body of ideas was finally reworked in a Christian sense by theologians like Augustine.

But whereas the founding fathers of Christianity relied heavily on the philosophical speculations of the ancient Greeks, they did not relate at all happily to the latter's physical deductions, the other outcome of their worldview. Indeed, the more analytical natural sciences as developed by the Greeks found little acceptance with the Christian leaders, if only because the preferred course of man was predestined, after all. Man would not reach his destination, the Heavenly City as sketched by St Augustine, by futilely delving into the secrets of microcosm or macrocosm. These were not his to know, nor were they useful to ameliorate a life on earth that, precisely in its suffering, was a preparation for a better life thereafter.

The Christian leaders did encounter difficulties, being opposed by such forceful critics as the scholar Porphyry (AD 234–301/6), Plotinus' student. He denounced the new movement as completely irrational and unphilosophical in his *Contra Christianos*, an attack against which Augustine, for instance, could defend himself only with some difficulty. However, as in purely theological matters, in cosmology and philosophy, too, the Christian emperors soon decided not to tolerate any further discussion of the religion of their choice: the works of men like Porphyry were publicly burnt on Constantine's orders.[5]

Naturally, the ins and outs of these learned discussions eluded the great majority of the new believers. But they were readily convinced by the notion of the existence of Good and Evil, and by the idea that man would escape his own inclination towards Evil and, hence, injustice and misery only by submitting to God, whom one must love as one did one's neighbour; they soon accepted that it was possible to obtain God's mercy and, thus, salvation, only by obeying the teachings and rules of the Church which God's son, Christ, had established on earth. These were the foundations of the views of man and the world held by most 'Europeans' for the following two thousand years.

Meanwhile, in the crisis which ended the political unity of the Roman world in the fourth and fifth centuries, both in the eastern and the western empire intellectuals felt the need to articulate their own identity, to define a common fate; being poets, chroniclers or Church authorities, they were all part of the political elite and wrote their works in the service of state or Church.[6]

In the west, on which the following will mainly concentrate, this common fate gradually became linked to Christianity, now increasingly seen as the one characteristic and indeed redeeming feature of a geographically well-defined world, which by and large coincided with western Europe.

Especially the bishops of Rome, feeling the threat to their power over the Christian world posed by their main competitors, the patriarchs of Constantinople, did their part to form the western half of the empire into an independent religious and cultural region, over which, as by divine right, they also held political dominion. Fundamentally, this claim to supremacy was founded on a passage in the gospel of Matthew – chapter 16, verses 18–19 – wherein the disciple Simon acknowledges Jesus as God's son whereas Jesus tells Simon that as Peter, the Rock, he will be the foundation stone of Christ's Church, with the power to bind and loose in heaven and earth. Hence, a tradition arose in which Peter was proclaimed to have been Christ's first Vicar on Earth and the first bishop of Rome. His grave, reputedly situated in a Roman cemetery several metres below the baroque bronze canopy that now fills the enormous space underneath the cupola of St Peter's in Rome, became a centre of pilgrimage for many believers.

His successors as bishops of Rome – the historical continuity of their line is disputed – mostly came out victorious in the many doctrinal disputes with other Christian groups in the Mediterranean-Christian world of the first four centuries AD. However, though they claimed both temporal and spiritual control over all bishops in the entire Church, effectively, their power, such as it was, was limited to western Europe and all the regions Christianized from there.

With the Greek geographical-climatological notion of Europe being fitted into Christian thought during the early centuries of the Christian era, the conversion of the old elite, schooled in the ideals of *paideia*, ensured that the underlying concepts of man and civilization became part of Christian culture as well. The central text of the Christians, the Bible, and especially the Old Testament, was now interpreted with the Greek geographical names and the concepts implicit therein at the back of the educated readers' minds.

After all, these readers, the faithful, had to explain for themselves why the world as they knew it, the world around 'Our Sea', was so varied, especially in different human species. Also, the political and cultural leaders wanted to show why their civilization was the most important and therefore worth defending.

This resulted in the following construction. Based on a story told in Genesis, the first book of the Old Testament, about Noah, the father of man after the Flood, his three sons were identified with the inhabitants of the three known worlds. Shem became the patriarch of the Semites, the inhabitants of Asia. Ham, who was said to have mocked his father for his drunkenness, and was consequently cursed for it, became the patriarch of the Hamites, the inhabitants of Africa – the story would at a much later date be used by Europeans to argue the inherent cursedness of the Africans. Japheth became the patriarch of the Japhites, the inhabitants of Europe.[7] These descendants of Noah subsequently were to be found in many European texts, like the seventh-century *Historia Brittonum*, in which they populate the three continents. In the encylopedic notes of the contemporary scholar Isidore of Seville, the intellectual light of the Visigoth kingdom of Spain, the origin of Europe's population is attributed to Japheth and his descendants. Not only the Romans but all peoples who had come into contact with the Roman Empire, such as the Franks, were seen as the progeny of one of Japheth's descendants, Alanus.[8] Thus, through Noah, all these 'Europeans' were blessed by God. The very act of that blessing obviously emphasized Europe's special position in the world as the 'Christian world'.[9]

One religion for all: the fusion of Christianity and Europe

In the mean time, many of the 'barbaric' tribes who were invading western Europe absorbed numerous aspects of the conquered region's culture, religious as well as linguistic, adopting Latin or one of its regional variants. The process can best be witnessed in the elites of these peoples, who, even if they did not accept the new religion out of conviction, quickly came to see it as an effective means to retain or increase their power.

Already by AD 403, the Christian intellectual Prudentius had internalized a vision of history in which the Roman Empire had acquired its role as an ideal political and cultural unity precisely to be able, at a later stage, to provide the basis for the spreading of the Christian message which would ultimately save mankind. For him the empire's borders coincided with those of the Christian world: the time had now dawned when belief and reason would merge, a significant pronouncement about the elements which, according to Prudentius, had been introduced by the Christian and Roman cultures, respectively. He observed that, 'Life, but not merit, is given to everyone', since 'an abyss separates the Roman forms of life from the barbaric, just as man is separated from the animals, the mute from those who speak.'[10]

The tribes and peoples from northern and eastern Europe who continued to advance on the prosperous south-west between the fourth and tenth centuries, settling within the Roman-Christian world, were often viewed with disdain by those who had already been romanized for a longer period. One of these tribes were the Longobards, who had conquered northern and central Italy and were felt to threaten the Pope's position. Consequently, in the year 739, Pope Gregory III sought the help of the Frankish leader, Charles Martel, who, formally speaking, was a usurper of the throne formerly held by the Merovingian kings, the descendants of Chlodwig,[11] and therefore needed the Pope's help to legitimize and even sanctify his rule. A papal chronicler wrote:

> The province subject to Roman government was smitten by the wicked Longobards and their King, Liutprand. Coming to Rome, he pitched his tents in the field of Nero, ravaged the Campagna, and forced many Roman nobles to shave and dress in the Lombard fashion. Therefore the man of God [i.e. Pope Gregory III], oppressed with grief on every side, took the holy keys from the grave of the blessed Apostle Peter and sent them by sea to the land Francia, to the most wise Charles [i.e. Charles Martel], who then ruled the Frankish kingdom, by his ambassadors, the most holy Bishop Anastasius and the priest Sergius, to ask the most excellent Charles to free them from this great oppression by the Longobards.[12]

But after one or two generations, the erstwhile inimical newcomers had been assimilated in the Roman-Christian culture as well. The merits and virtues of the civilization which they now made their own are clearly, albeit idealistically described by another chronicler:

> The Longobards . . . have abandoned their barbaric savagery, perhaps because they married natives and begot children who derived something of the mildness and wisdom of the Romans from the blood of their mothers and from the properties of the country and climate. Even now they retain the elegant Latin speech and

polished manners. In the government of their cities and the service of their commonwealth they still copy the skilful methods of the ancient Romans. They are so eager for freedom that they recoil from excess of power and are ruled by the will of consuls rather than of dictators [*imperantes*]. And as it is known that there are three estates among them, consisting of captains, vavasours and people, consuls are chosen, in order that arrogance may be suppressed, not from one estate alone, but from every estate; and lest they be seized with a lust for power, they are changed nearly every year. Hence it happens that almost all the land is divided between the cities . . . and it is almost impossible to find any noble or magnate, even in so wide an area, who does not obey the orders of his city. The cities . . . do not scorn to promote to knighthood and to offices of various ranks young men of inferior condition, and workers engaged in low, even manual trades, whom other peoples thrust out like the plague from the freer and more honourable pursuits. Hence it happens that they far surpass all other cities in the world in wealth and power.[13]

In the mean time, Christianity itself had become at least as expansionist as the Roman Empire had ever been. In about AD 550, St Prosper of Aquitaine argued that:

Christ's mercy was not satisfied only to reach the borders of Rome: it has already brought many peoples who were never compelled by Rome's arms to submit to the lordship of the Church of Christ.[14]

This brings us to a highly important observation. With the demise of the Roman Empire, the Christian Church had become its heir in many respects. It had already taken its bureaucratic structure, which now gave it great strength. Now, it also took on its civilizing role, bringing to a world of 'barbarians', a world of tribal chiefs and their loosely organized kingdoms such important, albeit mundane services as literacy and legislation, which helped create a centralized power, alongside the promise of eternal salvation. Thus, the Roman popes increasingly showed their awareness that they could make use of the fading memory of a once powerful empire to build a new one. In AD 597, Pope Gregory the Great sent the monk Augustine to England; he probably did not do so because he had been struck by the angelic beauty of the blond boys sold in the Roman slave market, but because he remembered that 'Anglia' had once been a thriving part of the Roman Empire, and, relying on the structures, cultural and political, that still remained, might now be induced to submit to the Church's growing dominion.[15] Within less than twenty years, the missionaries sent by the Pope had helped the Anglo-Saxon kings to codify more than ninety laws,[16] not forgetting to ensure the position of the new religion.

Indeed, in the process of Christian expansion that took place between the fourth and tenth centuries and went far beyond the former Roman frontier, a new 'cultural space' came into existence, hesitantly at first but gradually more noticeable. In the eighth century it reached present-day central Germany. This was where the 'wild tribes of Germania' lived, among whom Boniface (*c.*674–754), coming from England, preached and acquired his sainthood. He travelled to Thüringen via 'Bavaria and the border areas of Germania's unknown areas' to convert the heathen tribes there. Later, he was honoured in Rome by the Pope with 'a book in which were written the holy laws of the Church, laid down by the synods of bishops, and an order . . . that he teach the people entrusted to him according to these examples.' As he finished Boniface's biography, the monk Willibald could write about the saint's successes: 'and so it happened that the message of his sermons became known everywhere, to such an extent that his name resounded almost all over Europe'.[17] Christianity and Europe slowly but surely became 'one'.

The rise of a new empire: Frankish statecraft and Christian arguments

The various tribes which had settled in central and western Europe in the last centuries of Roman rule soon developed some sort of state-structure. However, it has to be borne in mind that at least until the twelfth century, power was actually exercised by regional or even local lords and their soldiers, rather than by central authorities, if only because in an illiterate society, to be effective any command had to be given orally, any decison be controlled personally. And illiterate the new post-Roman culture certainly was.

Often, the conquerors or war leaders gave land grants to those of their family or followers who had aided them, creating a lineage-system society; they also confirmed the possessions of those families of the indigenous, older, senatorial aristocracy who had not withstood them, and who enjoyed their income from the farmers not so much by right of their kinship relations with the new ruler, but under an older tributary tradition within the structure of the Roman Empire. Soon, these two systems merged. For even though in these 'proto-states' power relationships were, at the beginning, highly personalized, over the following centuries the situation slowly stabilized. More and more, the new landowners, too, rather than invoking an ever more distant connection with the original conqueror and his successors, ruled their subjects by right of birth, and by right of the functions they had acquired within the state and which often became hereditary. By and large, the farming population of Europe retained its freedom, though, of course, the new rulers eagerly adapted the pre-existing systems of taxation and corvees to their own use.

Sometimes, the new ruling families gradually lost part of their power again to the magnates of their state, precisely because they often needed to buy military support by granting them lands from the princely domain.

Within the sphere of the ancient Roman Empire, however, central rulers always seem to have retained some of their authority, based on the residual notion of a state governed by a lawful sovereign who dispensed justice to the state's subjects.[18] Often, this was enforced by some kind of divine right, invoked through a supposed relationship with ancient heroes, or demi-gods, even though this pagan notion was Christianized as well. Indeed, it was by virtue of this fiction that until the end of the seventeenth century, the English and French kings, after their coronation, laid their healing hands on hundreds or even thousands of people suffering from various illnesses.

Inevitably, princes as well as magnates sought to increase their power by means of dynastic alliances or simple conquest. As indicated above, on the territory of Roman Gaul, the leaders of the tribe of the Franks successfully did so. However, despite the successes of their Merovingian dynasty, the ensuing process of unification by which the remains of the empire of the west largely came to coincide with the world of Roman Christendom always is identified with Charles (*c.*742–814) – whose epithet 'the Great' was added later. He was the energetic and apparently charismatic member of a family who had deposed the Merovingian kings, but, using the tradition of their authority and skilfully manipulating the Frankish nobles, had greatly expanded their royal authority,[19] though, perhaps, even then at the cost of granting them more royal land and even certain sovereign rights.

Yet Charlemagne himself succeeded in gaining control not only of large parts of present-day France, Belgium, Switzerland and the south of the Netherlands already under Frankish power but also of western and central Germany, northern Italy and northern Spain, establishing Christianity among all the tribes which he subdued.

Charlemagne continued an economic policy adopted by his predecessors, realizing that a strong kingdom could exist only on the basis of a strong economy.[20] And a strong economy could not be only an agricultural one, certainly not if it were to produce the surplus and hence the fiscal revenue the Frankish kings needed for their expansionist policy. Trade had to be revived, and, moreover, a common, stable, reliable currency introduced if Charlemagne were to reach his aim. Therefore, he encouraged Frankish trade within the network of important trading towns that connected the northern Netherlands with northern Germany and Scandinavia and, from there, with the further coasts of the Baltic Sea, where trade routes led through Russia, along the Wolga basin, to the Black Sea; thus, Frankish trade reached the markets of the Near East and Central Asia, and, with it, the silver which the Frankish rulers needed to reform the coinage. Of course, Charlemagne also tried to revitalize trade between the Mediterranean coasts of Europe and the trading centres of northern Africa and the Levant. In this, too, he was successful. Both the wealth and the power of the Frankish kingdom grew.

Without anyone realizing what was going on, the Frankish policy was considerably helped by the fact that in the fourth and fifth centuries, another climate change had occurred. Europe now became drier, and water seems to have been in short supply – folklore and legends talk about the problem. But with the seas less stormy, and the Alpine passes open for longer periods during the year, trade could only profit from the new situation.

To further enhance his authority and thus his power, in the year 800, Charlemagne went to Rome, the holy city of Christianity, to be rewarded by the Pope with the imperial crown, thus becoming the first in a long line of 'Holy Roman Emperors'. What happened was later interpreted as follows:

> After handing over the empire to Christ's vicar, Constantine went to Thrace, where Europe ends, and established a city there named after him. That was where the seat of the empire was until the time of Charles, in whose person Pope Adrian transferred the empire from the Greeks to the Germans.[21]

The Roman popes thus were seen to have had the power to give the imperial crown to whomever they wished, in this case transferring the heritage of Rome from the east, from Constantinople, to the west, to Charles's seat at Aachen, where the emperor built a chapel deliberately echoing Roman ecclesiastical architecture.

It seemed as if the glory at least of the western part of the former Roman Empire had been resurrected, as if a true *renovatio imperii* had been realized. The two founts of ideal power, the terrestrial, realized in the 'universal' State, and the celestial, realized in the 'universal' Church, were again in communion. The Church, embodied in the Pope, Christ's Vicar on Earth and established in Rome, and the State, embodied in the emperor who sought his legitimacy at least partly in that state *par excellence*, the Roman Empire, were locked in a holy alliance. Of course, the spiritual support of the Church of Rome and the military power of the empire was of mutual benefit to Pope and emperor – as long as they did not compete for actual supremacy both in religious and secular matters; yet, however profitable it might seem in the short run, the collaboration could not but be problematic in the long run.

Meanwhile, for the intellectuals of Charlemagne's time, mainly writing and philosophizing monks and priests,[22] it was as if God supported this young king from a young people and blessed his victories. Obviously, these victories were a reward for the emperor's piety and his policy of the Christianization of civilization. What could be more meaningful than to define the area over which he claimed dominion as 'Europe' and thus present it once again as a logical, complete unity?[23] Those who articulated imperial propaganda were the men of the Church who now controlled the imperial court – for they were the ruler's trusted collaborators, rather than the regional magnates, who were his competitors. Among others, Charlemagne's principal confidant, Alkuin (*c.*735–804), and the emperor's biographer, Einhard (*c.*770–840) did their best to glorify him as the man who wielded the *regnum Europae*.[24]

Indeed, Charlemagne not only embarked on a policy of Christianization, thus at the same time broadening the power of this court elite, but also attempted to preserve the little that was left in the west of Graeco-Roman civilization and make it fit into the way of life of his court and of the warrior elite of his realm. After all, Charlemagne and his supporters needed an ideology which would give cohesion to the constantly expanding Frankish Empire.

The way in which the Frankish kings placed themselves in the tradition of the ancient Roman emperors and proclaimed themselves the rightful heirs to their empire becomes clear from a letter dating back to 871 which one of Charlemagne's successors, Emperor Louis II, sent to his colleague and 'competitor', the Byzantine *basileus* Basil I. For the Byzantine emperors, trying to uphold the fiction of the one, undivided Roman Empire, were willing to recognize the rulers of the barbarians in the west only when these accepted to be their representatives.

The arguments used by the Franks are mostly derived from the Bible and the merits which the Frankish kings have earned by their own conversion to Christianity and their policies of converting other peoples. However, historical and cultural arguments are also used in another way. The role of the Jews in relation to Christ is interpreted negatively, and the bond between the Franks on the one hand, and Rome and Latin on the other – the city and the language of civilization – are emphasized. Note, too, how the Byzantines' use of Greek and their 'abandonment' of Rome are held against them. In fact, the text presented all the elements which would determine the western European self-image for centuries to come:

> the Frankish race has borne the Lord much very fertile fruit, not only by being quick to believe, but also by converting others to the way of salvation. Hence the Lord rightly warned you: 'The Kingdom of God shall be taken from you and given to a nation which bears him fruit' [Matthew 21.43] God was able, out of stones, to raise up children for Abraham [Matthew 3.9], and so he could also, out of the hardness of the Franks, raise up heirs to the Roman Empire. If we belong to Christ, we are, according to the Apostle, the seed of Abraham [Paul to the Galatians 3.29]; and if we belong to Christ, we can, by his grace, do everything which those who belong to Christ can do. As we, through our faith in Christ, are the seed of Abraham, and as the Jews for their treachery have ceased to be the sons of Abraham, we have received the government of the Roman Empire for our right thinking or orthodoxy. The Greeks for their cacodoxy, that is, wrong thinking, have ceased to be Emperors of the Romans – not only have they deserted the city and capital of the Empire, but they have also abandoned Roman nationality and even the Latin language. They have migrated to another capital city [i.e. Byzantium] and taken up a completely different nationality and language.[25]

Culture and cohesion: the role of ideology and education in the shaping of Carolingian Europe, or the 'First Renaissance'?

The influence of scholars like Alkuin persuaded Charlemagne strongly to advance education everywhere in his empire. Not only were senior clergymen urged to take the lead but also his court nobles, who ruled the various parts of the empire and who were asked to provide their establishments with schools for the children of servants as well as the sons of free men who wanted an education.

The educational ideal was clearly based on a Christian way of life, since a better understanding of Holy Scripture would lead to a morally better and hence more civilized behaviour. Probably in AD 794 or 796, Charlemagne wrote to Abbot Baugulf of Fulda the well-known 'Epistola de litteris colendis' ('Memorandum on the cultivation of learning'), in which he admonished this prelate and all the other ones who were informed in the same way:

> Be it known to You, whose devotion is pleasing to God, that we and our loyal servants have considered it profitable that the bishoprics and monasteries committed by Christ's favour to our guidance should in addition to following the monastic way of life and living together under a holy rule, offer earnest instruction in the study of literature to those who, by the gift of God, are capable of learning, according to the capacity of each of them. Observing a rule imparts order and grace to honourable conduct, and perseverance in teaching and learning does the same for correct speech: so that those who are eager to please God by rightly living may not neglect to please Him by speaking correctly. . . .
>
> For although correct conduct may be better than knowledge, nevertheless knowledge precedes conduct. . . . Because of failure to learn, the uninstructed tongue could only faultily express what devout piety was faithfully dictating to the mind. Hence we began to fear that, there being too little skill in writing, there might also be far too little wisdom in understanding the Holy Scriptures. . . . Therefore we exhort you . . . not to neglect the study of letters. . . . Let men be chosen for this work who have the will and ability to learn and the desire to instruct others. And let this be done with a zeal as great as the earnestness with which we command it. We wish you, as befits soldiers of the Church, to be devout in thought and erudite in speech, chaste in your strict conduct and learned in your eloquence, so that if anyone seeks to see you out of reverence for the Lord or because of your noble and holy life, he may both be edified by your appearance and enlightened by the wisdom he perceives in your reading and singing, and may go home joyfully rendering thanks to Almighty God.[26]

Arguing that this educational policy was only for the benefit of the Church and the clergy, as some critics might be inclined to do, seems misreading the emperor's own political intentions truly to create an educated elite that would contribute both to cultural and religious unity and, hence, to the better governability and well-being of the empire.

The emperor's ideas can be observed from a number of statements. Thus Charlemagne directed the following appeal to a group of theologians:

> Therefore, because we take care constantly to improve the condition of our churches, we have striven with watchful zeal to advance the cause of learning, which has been almost forgotten by our ancestors; and, by our example, also we invite those whom we can to master the study of the liberal arts. Accordingly, God aiding us in all things, we have already corrected carefully all the books of the Old and New Testaments, corrupted by the ignorance of the copyists.

In AD 789 he admonished a number of his senior officials to:

> join and associate to themselves not only children of servile condition, but also sons of free men. And let schools be established in which boys may learn to read.[27]

Reading presupposes texts which can be read. We know that Charlemagne ordered books from all parts of his realm to be collected in the imperial library at Aachen;[28] and as his biographer tells us in the twenty-ninth chapter of the *Vita Karoli*, the emperor ordered the codification of German tribal laws as well as of the German heroic songs, both of which up till then had been transmitted orally.

Through the efforts of Charlemagne – behind whom, of course, we should see his ecclesiastical advisers – the culture of the elite of the Church slowly, and in an adapted form, also became the culture of the secular upper class. In that process the Frankish state, which now included a considerable part of western Europe, gradually acquired a character which was Germanic as well as Christian and, in fact, also Roman, with the remnants of Greek civilization being mainly received through the filter of Rome and through Latin.

The effect of this new culture was that much greater because under Charlemagne a policy of expansion and colonization was initiated which pushed the borders of the Frankish Empire increasingly northwards and eastwards. Even though the Picts and the Frisians, the Goths and the Wends, the Baltics and the Slavs were not subjected, they were still drawn within the cultural influence of the Frankish Empire.

Admittedly, the political unity which a large part of present-day western Europe had formed under Charlemagne was already lost shortly after his death. Yet western Europe's expansionist policies into central Europe, undertaken with the Church's wholehearted cooperation, were pursued by his successors, especially by the rulers of the German states, until, in the fourteenth century, the limit had been reached in the Baltic area, in Poland and in the Balkans. There, they encountered a different form of expansion, that of Greek Christianity and the Byzantine emperors. The elites around Pope and emperor in the west saw Graeco-Byzantine culture as decidedly 'different' and even hostile and threatening, despite its Christian character. Therefore, this region became an uncertain border area, disputed and, consequently, divided culturally, religiously and politically, where people for centuries have been confronted with choices which still tear them apart today.[29]

With the spread of Christianity through missionaries who were supported equally by the popes, the Holy Roman Emperors and the various European princes, the Roman Church took on the organization of religious life in the entire area to the west of the line stretching from the Baltic to the Balkans.[30] A truly transcontinental Church was created and became visible in the persons and the power of bishops and priests, while monasteries and cathedral schools educated new elites, who cherished the same norms and values. As in the south and west, in northern and central Europe, too, the Church and, with it, the cultured elite, now referred to that one and only centre, Rome. These regions, which had never submitted to the Roman Empire, were now fitted into a common, Christian ideology. This ideology was gradually presented more clearly as a universal ideology, as, unquestionably, the very essence of civilization.

To foster this communal ideology, the Church of Rome aimed to give the very diverse peoples and tribes of Europe a common history. In the new history, in which all sorts of legends about people's origins were adjusted or rewritten, the roots of the secular world, the history of power and culture, were sought in the ancient Romans. The Romans, in their turn, were linked by their ancestor, Aeneas, to his forefathers, the Trojans, who were, *en passant*, identified with Greek culture. The roots of the religious world, the history of salvation, naturally went back to the Bible, the Old and the New Testaments. In both spheres it was a history which was presented as having irrevocably reached its completion in Europe, in the west – or, as the historian Otto von Freising (d. 1158) put it:

> As I said earlier, all human powers and possibilities, in this case, wisdom, come from the east, from Babylon, in order to be completed in the west.[31]

In a simple sentence, the specific elements which now were seen as constituting Christian – 'European' – culture were identified: power, to be understood as the result of human knowledge, wisdom, which, in its turn, was to be understood as the product of learning – both, of course, the gift of God. Significantly, for Otto the origin of this wisdom lay in Asia; not, as one might have expected, in the Holy Land, but even further eastward, in Mesopotamia where, it was assumed, God had first created man, had given him the powers of knowledge and had placed him in the garden of Eden.

By now, a definite system of higher education had been worked out, in which the seven *artes liberales* were divided in the *trivium*, namely the triad of grammatica, rhetorica and dialectica, and the *quadrivium*, namely the foursome of arithmetica, geometria, astronomia and musica. The school attached to the imperial palace at Aachen became the prototype for numerous schools founded by the clergy in the following centuries. These establishments now became the real centres of culture in Europe.[32] As a result of these developments, Latin rapidly gained the character of a 'universal' language, facilitating communications between scholars in this growing 'western world' and so contributed in no small degree to the development of certain common forms of civilization in this region.

Still, to term the complex policy sketched above a 'first Renaissance', as has been done, is perhaps misjudging it. It may seem like an attempt at a cultural *renovatio* of the old Roman Empire, but the actual aim was to create the foundations only of a Christian, Frankish Empire; understandably, in view of the fact that this policy was instigated by the Church, there was no trace of an 'objective', independent appreciation of the ancient, pagan culture in its own right.

Roman Christianity did not remain the religion and culture only of an elite. Indeed, it was practised by most people in the western part of Europe, though almost always combined with numerous pre-Christian customs and all sorts of beliefs which the Church termed 'superstition' or even pagan; these included ways of thinking which for one reason or another were anathema to the ecclesiastical authorities, ranging from what was seen as sorcery and witchcraft – though a distinction was made between white and black magic – to sooth-saying and alchemy as well as various forms of astrology and kabala. Still, it is quite clear that well into the seventeenth century, i.e. for more than a thousand years, precisely the clergy continued to act both as official, Church-appointed mediators between man and the divine as well as assuming the roles formerly played by the druids of the Celts or the priests of the German gods, often performing age-old rites which had been condemned by that 'official' Church.

Indeed, as the majority of people in the Carolingian Empire were of Germanic origin, a 'Germanization' of Christianity was inevitable. The Church accepted this situation in a rational as well as emotional and psycho-logical way, Christianizing many cultural phenomena: festivals like the Germanic celebrations of mid-winter and the coming of light were fused with the feast of the nativity of Christ to become an ever more complex Christmas; certain customs as, for instance, the festive annual markets, were linked to the day commemorating the consecration of the local church; and certain people, such as local seers, miracle workers or heroic rulers were, not infrequently, canonized, their cults becoming the feasts of Christian saints.[33] In this way the different regional cultures could be made to merge into the one Christian culture as effectively as possible.[34] Precisely because those cultural elements that most strongly influenced the common people's emotions – though they might be considered pagan and profane by the elite – were now brought within the power of the Church, the diffusion of at least the central ideas of Christianity was much facilitated.

Yet unity was never completely realized. Indeed, deviant ideas, branded as heresies, were constantly formulated, showing that the Church was not able to provide all the answers. Whether because of religious or intellectual scruples, or for economic, political and social reasons, individuals and groups would stand up, and formulate alternative views of man, society and salvation, calling into doubt the certainties, the order and the security provided, at a cost, by the Church. Often, these people would try to reach the masses, using the vernacular instead of Latin, the language of the Church, incomprehensible to most. Thus, criticism, dissent and heterodoxy contributed to the growth of regional cultures, undermining the pretended unity of the Christian world.[35]

The impact of monasteries

The basic institutional structure of the Church as it had developed in the last centuries of the Roman Empire – fundamentally the system of bishoprics and, increasingly, the supremacy of the Roman papacy – continued to exist in most countries of western Europe that developed on territory formerly under Roman rule; it was exported as Christianity itself spread to the north and east through the missionary efforts of its clergy and, often, the zeal of regional magnates and princes. Yet Christianity would not have become a major religious and cultural factor without the contribution of another of the Church's institutions, the monastery.

A monastic tradition – which, of course, is not unique to Christianity but also flourishes in Hinduism and Buddhism – originated in the very regions where Christianity had flowered first, in Palestine, Syria and Egypt. Retreating from the worries of the world into a private sphere of prayer and introspection, men and women went into the desert to live the solitary life of a hermit, or congregating into small communities devoted to pious contemplation. The 'first' Christian monastery proper – with separate establishments for males and females – was founded by St Pachomius in the Nile valley in the fourth century AD. Soon, many communities decided to adopt a common rule, to give cohesion to their congregation.

It was not long before the monastic tradition moved to the north, to the Byzantine Empire – even nowadays, Mount Athos in northern Greece is a veritable cluster of monasteries – and to the west, to northern Africa and to Europe. Mostly, these communities were held in awe by the common people and the rulers alike, even in times of violence and devastation. They were seen as places of God, where men and women communicated with heaven, setting an example to a world that would not or could not live a life of continuous piety.[36]

The mainstream in western monasticism took shape when Benedict of Nursia (*c.*480–543/7) – a Roman of noble ancestry who had entered the Church, and, disappointed with its growing power and wealth, ended up founding a monastery on Monte Cassino – decided to adapt an earlier, anonymous set of guidelines to structure his community. In the following centuries, this rule, later known as the Benedictine Rule, was adopted by hundreds of monasteries all over Europe, finding wide if not exclusive acceptance.

Benedict's ideas resulted in a variety of monastic manifestations. As to the monastery's formal organization, mature men wishing to enter, or boys influenced and inspired by their elders to wish so, usually had to spend some time in the novitiate before being allowed to take the vows of chastity, obedience and poverty and being admitted as monks. The monks as a community elected an abbot, who ruled the monastery as long as he lived, consulting the community when necessary. In female monasteries, the same rules prevailed.

The essence of Benedictine life can be summed up in the two actions of praying and working. Prayer, seven times a day during the span of twenty-four hours, was combined with contemplation, through the study of theology and the reading of devotional literature and, soon, with a life of learning in general. To this end, the monastic *scriptoria*, where monks painstakingly copied the texts that the Church needed, began to manufacture bibles and other texts for daily devotional use.[37] But monasteries also began to collect or transcribe texts of general literary and scientific interest, and to produce original scholarship.

Codifying and commenting on the gospels, the wisdom of the Fathers of the Church and the ideas of all those who somehow had contributed to humanity's welfare, they helped to preserve numerous manuscripts containing the cultural heritage of Antiquity;[38] there even were monks who stressed the need to preserve pre-Christian poetry as important and valuable for Christian culture,[39] although the often explicit sexual contents of, e.g., Roman literature led to the expurgation or even elimination of a good many texts, as of those which too closely scrutinized the secrets of nature, of God's creation. In the twelfth century, the abbey of Cluny in France, one of the grandest and wealthiest in Christendom, owned some 570 volumes of manuscript texts, while the cathedral of Durham, in England, preserved 546, and the cathedral of Bamberg in Germany 365 books.[40]

As centres of learning, with important libraries, many monasteries developed into centres of education as well, producing scholars who, for centuries, have been influential in almost all fields of European culture. Thus, the magnificent monastery of St Gallen, in Switzerland, and later the great abbey of Cluny, to name but two, attracted students from all over Europe, as did the schools attached to the cathedrals, the churches where a bishop resided, seated in his 'cathedra' or bishop's throne.

It was precisely through the monasteries that European women, whose opportunities in secular, male-dominated society were severely restricted, were able to contribute to culture in a major way. The lady Hroswitha, abbess of the monastery of Gandersheim (*c*.930–70) left an important oeuvre of Latin poems on religious themes, an epic devoted to the Emperor Otto I, and a series of plays which make her the first playwright of the post-classical European world.[41] And the lady Hildegard (1098–1179), abbess of the Benedictine monastery of Bingen, gained just fame in a number of fields: as a seer and a visionary, whose literary texts are of great beauty and show her to have been thoroughly conversant with classical literature and philosophy; as an exorcist, who left fascinating texts with medical-magical ideas and conjurations; and also as a musical theorist.[42]

Work in these monasteries was understood as daily, manual labour in the fields, providing sustenance for each monk or nun and, thus, making the monastery as independent as possible of the world and its distracting influences. Consequently, though individual poverty remained the rule, institutional wealth was soon in evidence all over monastic Europe. The majority of monasteries became very rich indeed, both through their own industry and through the often considerable bequests and donations, in money and landed property, from the faithful who wanted the monastics to pray for their souls or to engage the support of these increasingly powerful institutions in all kinds of political manoeuvrings. Monasteries developed into extensive agricultural enterprises that were often worked by numerous tenant farmers who further increased the monastery's wealth with their rents. The more vigorous male monastic orders, choosing to settle in agriculturally unpromising regions, through the reclamation of vast stretches of waste land – as e.g. in parts of

France and England, in the northern Netherlands, and in Pomerania and Silesia – altered the countryside all over Europe.[43] While contributing to the 'Christian aspect' of the landscape, through their cultural influence they altered the European mind as well.

5 Three worlds around the Inner Sea

Western Christendom, eastern Christendom and Islam

Confrontation and contact from the sixth century onwards

With the gradual decline of an empire that had spanned the entire Mediterranean, the 'Inner Sea' became both a bridge and a battleground between the three powers that can be considered the heirs of the Roman Empire's Graeco-Hellenistic and Latin cultures. Between them, they divided this world, both politically and culturally.

In the south-east, the Arabs, driven by the inspiration of Islam, gained mastery over a large part of the sea's Asian and African shores. Islamic civilization, one of the successors to the Roman Empire,[1] was both stimulated by and resulted from opposition to the older Judaeo-Christian tradition and to Greek culture. The power of Islam soon confronted with the Byzantine Empire that had taken shape in the north-east, a state that was also a Church and for a thousand years desperately tried to hold on to the former eastern territories of Rome. And, finally, Islam collided with a Europe narrowly defined, a Europe that, in the north-west, mainly through the drive of the Roman Church, had preserved the culture of ancient Rome to become the civilization of the Frankish world of the Occident. It has been argued that the strength and the longevity of these three empires derived from the vital alliance between state power and monotheistic religion and that, indeed, as long as heresies could somehow be contained, their polit
ical structures could remain intact as well.

The world of the Prophet: Islam

In the sixth century AD, a prophet appeared on the Arabian peninsula who preached a new religion. As with most prophets, for a long time he was not heard by his people. Basically, when Muhammad began his teaching, the culture of the Arabs was the manifestation of a tribal, nomadic economy and society, that interacted fruitfully with a series of prosperous ports, on the perimeter of the largely poor peninsula, which formed a network in which commerce between the coasts of the Mediterranean and the Indian Ocean, and hence East Asia, was conducted via the Red Sea and the Persian Gulf.[2] The

Arabs worshipped many impersonal gods; mainly, these were supranatural forces which materialized in sacred objects, like the famous Black Stone even now revered in Mecca's holy precinct, or *haram*. In Mecca, one of these rich trading towns on the edge of the vast desert, Muhammad was born around 570 of the Christian era, into the Hashemite clan of the wealthy tribe of the Kuraysh.

From AD 610 onwards, Muhammad began receiving messages from Allah, which he soon started to communicate to his relatives. Slowly, his prophecies became more complex. Memorized and transmitted orally by a growing band of disciples, in its entire extent Muhammad's new religion and its precepts was clearly revealed only when, after the Prophet's death in AD 632, his teachings were finally codified in the Koran (the 'Reading'). By then, his followers knew that Allah was the only, invisible and yet omnipotent God, to whom all believers striving after the joys of paradise should profess their faith. In testimony of this, they should lead a life of honesty and piety. They should pray five times a day, they should fast during the month of Ramadan and, if at all possible, at least once in their lives make the pilgrimage (*haj*) to Mecca and Medina, where Muhammad was buried. By then, too, it was clear that Muhammad considered himself the last of a long line of prophets, that ran back to Jesus of Nazareth and to his early Jewish predecessors, to all of whom he obviously owed much. In the second chapter of the Koran, Abraham is mentioned as the father both of the Arabs, via Ishmael, and of the Jews, via Isaac; Abraham is also made the builder of the Ka'ba, the House of Worship at Mecca, where the Black Stone was kept and which now became the central sanctuary of Islam. Indeed, Muhammad acknowledged both the Jewish and the Christian faiths as being parts of a unique triad, the *Ahl al-Kitab* (the 'people of the book'), the three monotheistic religions that had their origin in the Old Testament.

Studying the Koran, as well as the reports about the Prophet's life, one is struck by the similarities both between the teaching and the life of Muhammad as it is now represented, and the tradition that was woven around Jesus; as in Jesus's case, too, all discordant versions of Muhammad's sayings were suppressed and, finally, destroyed after his death to ensure that his successors controlled his tradition as it was embodied in the holy book, the guide *par excellence*. As it reads in the first *sura* or chapter of the Koran, the *Sura al-Fatiha* ('Opening Chapter'), also called the *Umm al-Kitab* ('Mother of the Book'):

In the Name of Allah, the Compassionate, the Merciful

1   Praise be to Allah, the Lord of the Worlds;
2   The Compassionate, the Merciful;
3   Master of the day of Judgement;
4   You alone do we worship, and to You alone we pray for help;
5   Guide us to the straight Way;
6   The Way of those whom You have favoured;
7   Not of those who have incurred your wrath. Nor of those who go astray.[3]

At first, Muhammad's views were not looked upon kindly by the majority of the Meccan people. Hence, in AD 622, the Prophet had to flee, taking refuge in the city of Jathrib, later renamed Madinat al-Nabi (The City of the Prophet) or Medina. This flight, known as the *hegira*, was later taken as the beginning of the Muslim calendar. In Medina, Muhammad's charismatic personality soon made him into a religious as well as a political and military leader. With his followers, who swore to wage a holy war or *jihad* in defence of their new faith and its prophet, he succeeded in capturing Mecca in AD 630. By his death, Islam – the 'abandonment to Allah's will' – had spread over the greater part of Arabia.

As the Prophet had no male children, the position as his successor or *caliph*, both in the religious and in the political leadership, was disputed between on the one hand an elected heir, and, on the other, his son-in-law Ali, the husband of his favourite daughter Fatima.[4] The bloody struggles that ensued shook the community of the believers. Indeed, with the murder of Ali's son Husayn, in AD 680, the *umma* (the Islamic world) finally split into two. The one part, believing in the resurrection of Ali's descendants, formed the Sh'ite community; they live mostly in present-day Iraq. The other, by far the larger group, are known as the Sunnites, those who claim to be the true keepers of the Prophet's tradition. Both groups soon developed doctrinal differences, although they are easily recognizable as stemming from the same root.

Despite and, indeed, sometimes in consequence of the wars of succession, the armies of Islam succeeded in conquering Syria, in AD 639, and Egypt, in AD 642 – the major Near Eastern possessions of the Byzantine Empire. From there, they slowly spread to the west, taking over Byzantine North Africa.[5] In the east, too, Islam was successful. In AD 651, the caliphs even captured faraway Persia. Meanwhile, merchants and traders sailing the Indian Ocean spread Islam to India and to the Far East, as did those who dared follow the desert trail into Central Asia.

Ruling first from Damascus and later from Baghdad, the caliphs had to pacify and unite their vast territories in North Africa and the Near East. On the whole, wherever possible they followed a course of respect for local religion and custom. To ensure their military and political control over their growing realm and its enormous fiscal possibilities, they pursued a policy of colonization, settling persons of unquestionable Islamic rectitude all over their dominions. Yet, in the end, the erstwhile political unity was lost again, precisely because the empire had, after all, grown too big and hence ungovernable.

When, from AD 711 onwards, Islamic forces began to conquer the Iberian peninsula, completing their conquest in AD 718 but for a small pocket of Christian principalities in the unhospitable north-west, the conquerors were not Arabs at all, but Islamicized Berbers from the Maghreb, who soon disclaimed their obedience to the caliph in the east. They set up a number of principalities of their own, of which Cordoba was by far the most powerful. Exploiting the fertile fields of *al-Andalus* (the south), and the rich trade with

North Africa and, from there, with sub-Saharan Africa and the Levant, Islamic Iberia grew wealthy indeed. Soon, the city of Cordoba was a major cultural centre as well, with a huge mosque, founded in AD 786 to rival the main Islamic sanctuaries of Mecca and Jerusalem, and, added to it, an important university and a great library, where students and scholars from all over the Islamic world gathered to study, teach and do research.

Besides Islamic Spain, the Maghreb and Egypt soon claimed independence, too. From the ninth century onwards, the Islamic empire was divided between a number of dynasties and rulers. But still, Islamic culture retained its position, precisely through the strength of its two major unifying factors, the religion as preached by Muhammad and the Arabic language, the language of the holy book.

As the Prophet had declared that he was the last of God's messengers, Islam could not accept a priesthood that would further develop its doctrinal system. Indeed, after many disputes, the Koran itself, as God's revelation of his eternal truths – in the second sura, the *Sura al-Baqara*, it reads: 'This is the Book in which there is no doubt, in it is guidance for those who fear God' – was widely held to be eternal with God and, hence, unchangeable. In consequence, it could not even be translated. This, obviously, was an unworkable situation, for a religion, if it does not live and change, however little, will inevitably disappear. It was not long before a number of learned men claimed the ability to explain all that was unclear in the Koran's 144 suras and in Muhammad's sayings. By the ninth century, the six books of the *Sunna* supplemented the holy book as a source from which rules for Islam could be dictated. Together, the holy book and the tradition of the Prophet now provided the basis for daily life in its religious as well as in all its secular forms, welding together the disparate cultures of the worlds conquered by Islam.

The second factor in this process of unification was the common language, Arabic. It was the language of the holy book, of the first believers and hence the language of the conquerors, of the new elite. Everyone aspiring to a position of influence under the new regime realized not only that conversion to Islam was mandatory but also that Arabic was the language of power. However, to the vast majority of the inhabitants of the Islamic empires, it remained an entirely artificial language. It was memorized – if not always understood, as was the case, too, with Latin in the Christian world – through the recitation of the Koran. But it was not a vehicle for the living cultures. For daily usage these continued to speak their own language; in some regions, though, new languages originated from a mixture of the old, regional tongues and the recently imported one, again comparable to developments in Europe in the wake of the pre-eminence of Latin.

As to Arabic or rather Islamic civilization, it has to be understood that in most of its manifestations it was a splendidly creative continuation of the Graeco-Byzantine culture of the Near East and North Africa, spreading, however, far beyond that world to large parts of Africa and Asia, where it continues to flourish to the present day. Some would even say that the Muslim victory was the final fulfilment of antique civilization, with the God-given power claimed by the early caliphs nothing less than the continuation and perhaps even realization of the political and religious universalism of Constantine, living on in the pan-Islamic tendencies of today.

Yet, in many ways the new Islamic or Islamicized intellectual and artistic elites went far beyond Greek culture. In AD 830, the Caliph al-Ma'mun founded the famous 'House of Wisdom' in Baghdad — a library and an academy for translations as well as for original research. There, such scholars as the Nestorian Christian Husayn ibn-Ishaq, a physician by training, produced translations of the works of Dioscurides, Galen and Hippocrates. This resulted in a medical practice that was greatly superior to the dismal state of health care in the west.

Also in Baghdad, Plato's *Republic* and several of Aristotle's texts were translated, as well as commented upon. For while translating Greek scientific literature, Islamic scholars soon contributed their own ideas to these texts as well. Also, from Greek and Hindu mathematics, they developed the much more sophisticated 'algebra'. Al-Khwarizmi, introducing the Arabic (but actually Indian) numerals — the original nine to which he added the zero — made arithmetic into a simple system, greatly facilitating its use both for scientific and practical purposes, as in education and, of course, commerce.

Based on their empirical observations of heaven and earth, Islamic scholars realized their own discoveries in the fields of technology, producing maps, astronomical charts and nautical instruments. In the decorative arts as well as in architecture, Islamic architects created beauty beyond the examples found in the Hellenistic-Byzantine world, as shown by the great mosques of Djenne and Timbuktu, in sub-Saharan Mali, of Cordoba in Spain, of Cairo in Egypt and of Ispahan in Iran, the palaces of Granada and Delhi, and the calligraphed manuscript Korans found all over the Islamic world.

In literature, too, Islamic writers produced major works. Building on the fecund storytelling tradition of the nomadic past of the Arabs, and adding to it motives and themes from the older folklore of the regions they had conquered, the Egyptian, Greek and Hebrew tales, the great collection of the *Thousand and One Nights* was formed. But long before its final codification in the fourteenth century, numerous stories told by the ill-used Scheherazade — the female teller who, to prevent death for herself and her friends, has to entertain her cruel master with an endless succession of amusing and exciting tales — had found their way to the west in one of the most untraceable but also most persistent ways of cultural transfer, oral communication. Consequently, a considerable part of the stories deemed typically European from times immemorial, and handed down from generation to generation by the storytellers who toured the countryside and the towns in England, France and Germany, first came to Europe from the Islamic world, although their origins often turn out to lay even beyond the Near East, as far as Persia and India. In lyric poetry, too, the Arab world achieved marvellous results that influenced Europe especially via Islamic Spain.

Indeed, it has been said that 'while al-Rashid and al-Ma'mun [two of the early caliphs] were delving into Greek and Persian philosophy, their contemporaries in the West, Charlemagne and his lords, were reportedly dabbling in the art of writing their name'.[6] Exaggerated though this may be, by the eighth and ninth centuries AD, the cultural achievements of the Islamic east far outshone those of the Christian west and continued to do so for several hundred years to come; for a thousand years, the economic and cultural capitals of the world were not London, Paris or even Rome; they were Baghdad, Cordoba and Damascus or, for that matter, Constantinople and, one might add, Hangzhou, Heyan-kyo and Tenochtitlán.

God's kingdom among men: orthodox Christendom

Since the fifth century, the Roman emperors of the east, accepting the impossibility of keeping the entire empire under control, decided to concentrate on their domains of Asia Minor, Syria, Egypt and North Africa, leaving the west, reluctantly, to the Franks, the barbarian usurpers of Italy and Roman Gaul. Byzantium, their capital on the Bosporus, had become Constantinople, a city of great splendour, with magnificent marble palaces sprawling over the hilltops, and crowned by the Hagia Sophia, the Church of Holy Wisdom, with its golden mosaics and enormous cupola a feat not only of architecture and engineering but also of Christian faith.

Indeed, in the Byzantine Empire, Church and State were closely associated, not to say intertwined; they constituted one organic structure, a mimesis, or imitation on earth of the kingdom of heaven. This theocracy was ruled by the *basileus*, the emperor, a semi-sacerdotal figure, God's immediate representative among men.

If anything, Byzantine civilization was the most direct heir of the Graeco-Hellenistic culture that for hundreds of years had dominated the eastern part of the Mediterranean. Yet it was fundamentally influenced by the introduction of Christianity. The Orthodox Church, so called because it claimed to be true to the original Christian faith, became the prime creative element in Byzantine life, shaping both politics and culture. Indeed, political dispute and strife were always connected with if not directly caused by theological issues, if only through the great degree of informed lay participation in Church affairs.

The Byzantine elite, both the patricians of 'The Town' – after all, they thought of Constantinople as the second or rather 'new' Rome – with their huge estates spread all over the empire, and the leading oligarchies of the provincial capitals held to the ideal of the Christianized *paideia*; the higher ideal, however, was union with God through asceticism, which explains the great regard for and even greater power of the many monasteries in the empire.

On the whole, Byzantine society was an educated one. Primary education, widely available, sometimes even at the village level and, what is more, for both sexes – a thing unheard of in the Christian west till some thousand years later – ensured a high level of literacy. Female participation in culture, generally, was extensive, with many aristocratic ladies studying, engaging in research and writing. Scholarship was held in high esteem, fostered both in the great university of Constantinople, founded already in AD 425, and in the important institutions of learning in such major provincial cities as Antioch and, of course, Alexandria.

The empire had its first flowering in the sixth century, especially during the reign of Emperor Justinian, an able administrator who ordered the codification of Roman Law as it then functioned, thus contributing greatly to its survival. The seventh and eighth centuries, however, saw both internal dissension and external assault.

A great conflict broke out when the worship of icons, the images of Christ and the saints, which by many educated believers smacked of idolatry, was forbidden. However, the majority of the population and, even more, the monasteries, the main repositories of the icons and the recipients of the wealth their veneration brought, were furious. Peace was restored only when the images were restored. It gave more power to the monasteries, such as the great complex on Mount Athos, which also became a major factor in economic life, not only in agriculture but also in trade.[7]

Meanwhile, with the advance of Islam in the Near East and North Africa, the empire lost not only a considerable part of its fiscal capacity and hence of its military power – taxes were raised in the remaining parts of the empire, resulting in growing popular unrest – but also the line of defence that shielded its capital. From then on, the empire was set on a course of war against the forces of Islam that it would finally lose with the fall of Constantinople in 1453. There was little consolation in the fact that, in the mean time, its civilization greatly contributed to the formation of Islamic culture.

From the seventh century onwards, cultural contacts with the 'Franks' as the people of the west were often called slowly increased.[8] The great commercial centres of Italy, headed by Venice, which tried to re-establish trade in the Mediterranean after the chaos of the fifth and sixth centuries, were especially influenced by Byzantium. The decoration of the great churches at Ravenna as well as the mosaics and stained glass that still adorn St Mark's basilica evince their Byzantine origins. All over Italy, religious art and, indeed, the liturgy of the Church itself for a long time were influenced by Byzantine examples. And although one may question the claim that western painting originated in the Orthodox east, undisputably religious painting all over the Christian world of Europe was influenced by Byzantine examples, as witnessed by the 'iconic' style of the frescos that decked the walls of the great abbey church at Cluny; also, art production at the court of Charlemagne shows some Byzantine traces.[9]

At least in one field, a really complex and fascinating amalgam seems to have been created. Recent musicological research suggests that what the western Church calls Gregorian chant, the liturgical music of Rome that originated in the fifth century AD, cannot have sounded as we have heard it over the past 150 years. Rather, it must have resembled its actual origins, early Byzantine and perhaps even Jewish music and, moreover, at least in those parts of Roman

Christendom that were influenced by Islam, such as southern Italy and southern Spain, the music that still can be heard in North Africa and the Near East, where the continued orality of transmission has caused traditions to remain much stronger than in Europe.

Yet interaction between 'Rome' and the 'new Rome', the two 'sibling cultures', these two halves of the greater, Christian Europe, was far less intensive than might have been expected,[10] despite the cultural influence of such dynastic ties as the one which in AD 972 brought a Byzantine princess, Theophano, to the west to become the wife of Emperor Otto II.[11] The growing doctrinal differences between the Church of Rome and the Church of Constantinople prevented a more intensive and fruitful exchange.

The Byzantine emperors wanted total control over their Church, both in its institutional and in its theological aspects; effectively, they nominated and deposed the patriarchs who were its nominal leaders. The popes in Rome, on the other hand, claiming supremacy over the entire Christian world, did not accept this situation. A schism was the result, aggravating the already inimical feelings between the two worlds, as both sides did their best to make propagandistic use of the incipient cultural-religious self-consciousness in the west and the east.[12]

With the gradual loss to Islam of its southern territories, from the eighth century onwards Byzantium sought compensation to the north. Its expansion on the Balkans, where the Christian powers from the west were advancing as well, was greatly facilitated by the close links between Church and State. Just as, a century earlier, Charlemagne's conquests in central Germany had profited from Rome's missionary efforts, so the Byzantine rulers extended their power to Bulgaria, Transylvania and Wallachia in the wake of Orthodox missionaries. The fact that, unlike their Roman counterparts, the Greeks did not insist that their language be retained as the language of the holy book, may be the key to the success of their conversion policies among the Slav peoples in the face of Rome's efforts to introduce Latin Christendom in these debated lands. Realizing that the liturgy and the religious texts would be more effectively introduced if translated in the vernacular, such ninth-century missionaries as the brothers Methodius and Cyrillus, unconsciously following the example of Bishop Ulfilas among the Goths, are even said to have devised an alphabet for the till then illiterate Slavs. The so-called Cyrillic writing still retains its use, as, for example, in Russia.[13]

What with their disappointments in the Balkans, and the Byzantine refusal to acknowledge their supremacy, the popes in Rome did everything to incite the Christian princes and powers of the west against their competitors in the east. As economic competition in the Mediterranean grew fiercer as well, concentrating on Byzantium's hold over some of the most profitable trade routes to the Far East, understandably the clash of religious and other interests did nothing to reconcile the two Christian worlds to each other, hindering contact between intellectuals as well – the more so as few western scholars read any Greek.

After another period of decline in the tenth and eleventh centuries, the Byzantine Empire, once more reduced in size – it had lost its Italian possessions, especially Sicily, which had gone first to Islamic conquerors and then to the Norsemen – entered upon a second period of cultural flowering. As far as its influences on the outside world are concerned, one must mention the famous medical School of Salerno that, in a fruitful interaction of Greek-Byzantine, Jewish and Islamic scholars, flourished under the enlightened tutelage of the Norman kings in southern Italy.

To the north-east, the Viking rulers who had established their regime around the two cities of Novgorod and Kiev in the ninth and tenth centuries engaged in diplomatic relations with their Byzantine neighbours.[14] Slowly, Orthodox Christianity was introduced among the 'Russians', showing its cultural creativity in the monasteries with their rich music and their churches painted with icon-like frescos, culminating in the works of the great Andrej Rublev (*c.*1360 to *c.*1430), who decorated the cathedral at Vladimir and the monastery of Zagorsk.

All the time, cultural contacts with the west remained surprisingly scant. In so far as they existed at all, they largely took place in the 'intercultures' created by the presence of, especially, Genoa and Venice in Byzantium, where, across the Golden Horn, the 'Frankish' commercial communities of Galata and Pera provided a gate between east and west; of lesser influence were the European merchants in the scales of the Levant itself, from Antioch to Alexandria. Significantly, a Venetian scholar raised in the Byzantine Empire and settled in present-day Hungary engaged upon the translation of one of the most important philosophical works of late Antiquity, John of Damascus' *Fountain of Wisdom*, from Greek into Latin. Thus, he provided one of the basic elements for Thomas Aquinas' famous *Summa Theologica*, which would influence western culture for centuries to come. Yet the most important contributions of Ancient Greek culture to Europe were not made through the medium of Byzantium, but through the texts produced by the other heir of the Graeco-Roman world, Islam.

A far corner of the earth: Roman, catholic Christendom

Certainly from the seventh century onwards, educated people in the west wanted their world, their Christian community, the source of their norms, values and ideas, to coincide as much as possible with the geographical concept of Europe. This was partly boosted by the division, gradually more marked, between the Roman Church which called itself the 'catholic', that is to say 'universal' one, and the eastern or Orthodox Church. Both sides felt, but also wanted, this division mainly for reasons of politics, whereby the popes in Rome and the patriarchs in Constantinople marked out their mutual spheres of influence.

Paradoxically, this division brought new unity to people in the west; *Christianitas* (Christendom) and Europe now became synonymous, even if the latter term was still not used frequently, just as the Islamic world also did not describe itself geographically but rather culturally and religiously – *Dar ul-Islam* (the House of Islam).

Besides rivalry with its eastern Christian neighbours, Islam was another factor in the unification of Europe. Under Muhammad's successors, a conflict over power between the Islamic caliphate in the south-east, the Frankish Empire in the north-west and the Byzantine Empire in the north-east of the Mediterranean was inevitable, for economic, political and religious reasons. As this situation of conflict developed, it also contributed to the nascent unity at least within the catholic Christian world.

In the Christian countries on the north-west coast of the Mediterranean, people like Alkuin, mentioned earlier, gradually became aware that Christianity as they professed it was now actually contained within this part of the world. Charlemagne, praised as the defender of this world, was one of the first rulers who had to determine how to react to the two rivals in the Mediterranean area, both Islam on the southern border of his empire and the Greeks on its eastern flanks.

For the new religion, Islam, was getting dangerously close. Monotheistic like Christianity, it quickly spread by force of arms not only through the Near East but also in North Africa. Christianity had flourished there for centuries, indeed for much longer and more intensely than in Europe. Now, in the eighth and ninth centuries, most Christians in the Levant and North Africa gradually converted to the teachings of Muhammad. Sometimes they were forced to do so, but actually conversion mostly occurred in a natural process of social and cultural adaptation to the norms of a new class of rulers which only few could resist.

Soon, the threat of Islamic expansion was felt on European soil, too. Crossing the Straits of Gibraltar, Islamic armies penetrated into the Iberian peninsula and several times even raided the Carolingian heartland beyond the Pyrenees. The rise to power of Charles Martel, Charlemagne's grandfather, was partly due to his success in raising an army among the Frankish nobles and defeating the 'Saracens' near Poitiers, in AD 732. From North Africa, Islamic troops also reached southern Italy, via the islands of Malta and Sicily. Via Anatolia and the Bosporus, they threatened Byzantium, which the west considered a not altogether bad thing, but also the Balkans, the backyard of the Greek empire disputed by the west.

Yet, for too long the historical picture has been distorted by presenting an image only of an aggressive, Islamic world. In the ninth and tenth centuries, with population in the western part of Europe slowly growing, tensions within the agricultural economy with its strictly limited food production forced the powers in this region to enter on a policy not only of the peaceful reclamation of waste lands but also of aggressive expansion into territories inhabited by people that, if only for that reason, had to be stigmatized as enemies, barbarians. Undoubtedly, Europeans began to put increasing military pressure on the eastern and southern frontiers of their world. However, the contemporaneous extension of the Byzantine and Islamic spheres of influence meant that there were only a few opportunities for expansion. In north-western Spain, Christian potentates sought to extend their domain southward, which led to a process of direct conflict with Islam which was to last for several centuries. In the east and south-east, the advance forces of western Christendom met the frontier garrisons of the orthodox world, aggravating the rivalry between these two Christian 'Europes'. This contributed to the militarization and marginalization of south-east Europe, with results which can still be noticed today.

The forces of western expansion also met the 'heathen' hordes of the Slavs in present-day Hungary, Czechoslovakia, Poland and in the coastal regions of the eastern Baltic. In the process, part of the peoples living in central Europe were Christianized by Rome; also, however, from the German heartland there came to these quarters land-hungry colonists who were to dominate them for a very long time indeed; this, of course, resulted in tensions in every field of economic, political and cultural life. Meanwhile, to the south-east many of the Balkanic peoples as well as the principalities of Russia fell under the influence of Byzantium.

The Crusades: western Christendom versus Islam and eastern Christendom

As the power of Islam spread along the northern coasts of the Mediterranean, thus beginning to co-determine the history of Europe up to the present,[15] a coalition between the Greek and Latin Christians against Islam would have seemed obvious. Yet the political and cultural pretensions of Byzantium, and the dreams of political and cultural domination of Charlemagne and his successors could not be combined. One must also question whether in each empire the nature of Graeco-Roman civilization, even though it was considered an essential characteristic by both, had not already changed long ago as a result of the differing outside influences which had become manifest in the previous four centuries and had gradually merged with the remains of the Roman heritage: in the west, the cultures of central Europe and the further regions of Asia, in the east, the imports from Asia Minor and Egypt.

Be that as it may, it quickly became clear that, in the face of divergent political interests, there could be no talk of a common ideology. Even in the face of the threat of Islam, which lasted seven hundred years for the Christian east and nine hundred for the Christian west, from the eighth to respectively the fifteenth and seventeenth centuries, the two Christian rivals were unable to create any solidarity, either in defence or in aggression. However, this threat did have an evident influence on the development of greater internal cohesion in both worlds, especially in moments of crisis.

This was certainly true of the western world which began to feel like 'Europe'. The seventh-century chronicler Isidore of Seville described as 'Europeënses' the troops who, under King Charles Martel's leadership, stymied the 'Saracens', thus preventing further Islamic penetration into Europe beyond the Pyrenees.

Plate 11 European, Christian pilgrims, both laymen and priests, arriving at their holy city, Jerusalem, from a fifteenth-century fresco cycle in the church at Brancion, France
Source: Centre for Art Historical Documentation, Nijmegen, The Netherlands

Plate 12 The archangel Gabriel appearing to Muhammad to tell him of God's wish that he start his mission of converting the people to a life of penance and charity. From a Turkish miniature in the Topkapi Museum, Istanbul. In the same series, one finds an illustration of the Prophet ascending into Heaven from the centre of the Jewish faith, the Temple Mount, an episode which makes the city of Jerusalem holy to Islam, too
Source: Centre for Art Historical Documentation, Nijmegen, The Netherlands

For nine hundred years, the Church of Rome successfully tried to convince these 'Europeënses' that there was great danger outside their own, safe Christian world. From the pulpit it was proclaimed that everything which that world held dear – the Faith, the Church, their own norms and ways of life – would be destroyed unless everyone formed a united front and prepared to give battle.

Indeed, for the promotion of solidarity nothing was and is more effective than the creation of a common enemy. In the interaction between the Islamic and Christian worlds, such an image was finally created during the Crusades, which were presented as 'holy wars' against the Muslims, just as Islam presented its raids against the Christian world as *jihad*. In the Crusades, Islam was made into Europe's most 'significant other', a world filled with every characteristic that Europeans themselves felt not at ease with. Indeed, Islam was forced to continue to play this role till today and, in turn, proceeded to cast Christianity in a comparable role. The same Crusades, of course, can and should be interpreted, too, as Europe's armed invasions of the Holy Land and, sometimes, of Christian Byzantium.

For two centuries, beginning in 1095, Crusades were undertaken with great regularity.[16] Their aim was, at least according to Christian propaganda, to safeguard the accessibility to Christian pilgrims of the holy places of Christendom, which had been occupied by the Muslims. We now realize that, besides this, power politics and economic motives played a considerable, and, according to some, pre-eminent role as well: the western world sought to expand into the eastern Mediterranean both at the expense of the Byzantine Empire and of the emerging Islamic states. True, the need to recuperate the holy sites was, of course, both a powerful propagandistic weapon and to many an utterly sincere, deep-felt emotion. Yet for the religious elite the chief prize was renewed control over the Orthodox Church while the secular authorities craved control over the trade routes to Central Asia, Europe's source of indispensable silver and thus of economic and political power, and to the Indian Ocean, from where the import of silk and spices satisfied Europe's increasing demand for luxury goods.

CLERMONT, 26 NOVEMBER 1095: POPE URBAN II CALLS FOR A
CRUSADE

In the autumn of 1095, Pope Urban II took advantage of a Church council being held at Clermont in France to express his concern about the situation in the Holy Land. From the reports of his sayings, it becomes clear that at least one thought behind his public announcements was his hope that a common assault on Islam would put an end to the many disputes and wars which ravaged European society and to the social unrest which was caused, for instance, by itinerant robber barons and plundering gangs of dispossessed farmers.

Although the papal words were not set down verbatim, various of those present have given their version of them. Here is the certainly idealized text as recorded by Fulcher of Chartres, who wrote it after the dream of the conquest of Jerusalem had become a fact. It is a text which, though it should be judged against the background of both ignorance and increasing suspicion between the two religions, cannot fail to remind the reader of the danger of any form of religious fundamentalism.

> O children of God, he [i.e. the Pope] said, since you have promised God, more earnestly than usual, to keep the peace among yourselves and faithfully maintain the rights of the Church . . . it is vital that you should make a rapid expedition to help your brothers who live in the east, who need your assistance and have now many times appealed for it. For, as most of you have already been told, they have been invaded as far as the Mediterranean sea . . . by the Turks, a Persian people, who have overrun an increasing amount of Christian territory on the frontiers of Romania [i.e. the Byzantine world] . . . killing or capturing many of them, ruining churches and ravaging the Kingdom of God. . . .
>
> It is not I but the Lord himself who begs and exhorts you, as the heralds of Christ, to persuade all men, be they knights or common soldiers, be they rich or be they poor . . . to devote themselves to helping their fellow Christians like a hurricane, to sweep away this evil race out of our people's country. . . .
>
> Let those who are brigands become soldiers of Christ; let those who have been fighting against their own brothers and kinfolk now fight lawfully against the barbarian; let those who are hired for a few sous now find eternal rewards.
> . . .
> Those who are going must not delay their journey, but lease their property and gather the money they need, and when winter ends and the spring follows, let them set forth eagerly upon the way, with the Lord going before them.[17]

However, even more fuel could be added to the fire. The monk Robert's version is considerably more bloodthirsty:

> A race from the kingdom of Persia, an accursed race, a race utterly alienated from God . . . has invaded the lands of those Christians and has depopulated them by the sword, pillage and fire. . . . They destroy the altars, after having defiled them with their uncleanness. They circumcise the Christians, and the blood of the circumcision they either spread upon the altars or pour into the vases of the baptismal font. When they wish to torture people . . . they perforate their navels, and dragging forth the extremity of the intestines, bind it to a stake. . . .
>
> Let the deeds of your ancestors move you and incite your minds to manly achievements; the glory and greatness of king Charles the Great, and of his son Louis . . . who have destroyed the kingdoms of the pagans, and have extended in these lands the territories of the Holy Church. Let the holy sepulchre of the Lord our saviour, which is possessed by unclean nations, especially incite you. . . .
>
> When Pope Urban had said these and very many similar things . . . he so influenced to one purpose the desires of all who were present, that they cried out: 'It is the will of God!'.[18]

Rallied by this strong language, many Christians in the west felt compelled to 'take the Cross'. Leaving their hearths and their families, they banded together and made their way to the east, to reconquer the holy cities of Christianity. Soon, the first armies succeeded in capturing Jerusalem and the other places where Christ had lived and preached.

Of course, intellectual as well as cultural honesty bid us to look at the situation from the other side. The Islamic historian 'Izz ad-Din ibn al-Athir (1160–1233) thus describes the seizure of Jerusalem by the 'Franks':

> Jerusalem was taken from the north on the morning of Friday 22 Sha'ban 492 [July 15, 1099]. The population was put to the sword by the Franks, who pillaged the area for a week. A band of Muslims barricaded themselves into the oratory of David and fought for several days. They were granted their lives in return for surrendering. The Franks honoured their word, and the group left by night for Ascalon. In the Masjid al-Aqsa [i.e. the great mosque on the Temple Mountain] the Franks slaughtered more than 70,000 people, among them a large number of Imams and Muslim scholars, devout and ascetic men who had left their homelands to live lives of pious seclusion in the Holy Place. The Franks stripped the Dome of the Rock of more than forty silver candelabra, each of them weighing 3,600 drams, and a great silver lamp weighing forty-four Syrian pounds, as well as a hundred and fifty smaller silver candelabra and more than twenty gold ones, and a great deal more booty. Refugees from Syria reached Baghdad in Ramadan, among them the qadi Abu Sa'id al-Hárawi. They told the Caliph's ministers a story that wrung their hearts and brought tears to their eyes.

One of the most lively and illuminating accounts of the Islamic experiences with the Christians who now settled in the 'Crusader kingdoms' comes from the autobiography of Usama ibn Munqidh, lord of Shaizar (1095–1188), a witty, cultured nobleman whose lifespan covered almost the entire first century of the Crusaders' presence in the Near East. These are some of his stories, which show both the possibilities and the limits of cultural *rapprochement*, not least because of the arrogance of the Christians, as is most clearly revealed in the last fragment:

> This is an example of Frankish barbarism, God damn them! When I was in Jerusalem I used to go to the Masjid al-Aqsa, beside which is a small oratory which the Franks have made into a church. Whenever I went into the mosque, which was in the hands of the Templars who were friends of mine, they would put the little oratory at my disposal, so that I could say my prayers there. One day I had gone in . . . when a Frank threw himself on me from behind, lifted me up and turned me so that I was facing east. 'That is the way to pray!', he said. Some Templars at once intervened . . . and took him out of my way, while I resumed my prayer. But the moment they stopped watching me he seized me again and forced me to face east. . . . The Templars intervened and . . . apologized to me. . . .

I paid a visit to the tomb of John the son of Zechariah – God's blessing on both of them! [These two Christian saints are venerated as prophets by Islam]. . . . After saying my prayers, I came out. . . . I found a half-closed gate, opened it and entered a church. Inside were about ten old men, their bare heads as white as combed cotton. They were facing east, and wore . . . on their breasts staves ending in crossbars. . . . They took their oath on this sign, and gave hospitality to those who needed it. The sight of their piety touched my heart, but at the same time it displeased and saddened me, for I had never seen such zeal and devotion among the Muslims.

[Later, a friend takes him to a Muslim monastery, where:] I saw about a hundred prayer-mats, and on each a sufi, his face expressing a peaceful serenity, and his body humble devotion. This was a reassuring sight, and I gave thanks to Almighty God that there were among the Muslims men of even more zealous devotion than those Christian priests.

A very important Frankish knight was staying in the camp of King Fulk. . . . We got to know one another, and became firm friends. He called me 'brother' and an affectionate friendship grew up between us.

When he was due to embark for the return journey he said to me: 'My brother, as I am about to return home, I should be happy if you would send your son with me . . . so that he could meet the noblemen of the realm and learn the arts of politics and chivalry. On his return home he would be a truly cultivated man.'

A truly cultivated man would never be guilty of such a suggestion; my son might as well be taken prisoner as go off into the land of the Franks.[19]

Two centuries of Crusades greatly intensified contacts between the Christian west, the Byzantine Empire and the Islamic Near East, as a result of the constant travelling between Europe and 'Outre Mer' (Beyond the Sea), as the Christian principalities in the Levant between 1096 and 1291 were called. For the first time in their history, many west Europeans were now confronted with the differences and similarities between cultures. But, while the idea of the Crusades continued to be a stimulus to Christian unity even after the Christians had to withdraw from the Holy Land following the fall of the last of the Crusaders' bulwarks, Acre, the possibilities of actual contact decreased in the thirteenth century. Moreover, as people in Europe realized that the popes in Rome mainly continued to propagate the holy war in order to increase their own power in Italy and elsewhere, interest declined even further.[20]

Yet in the mean time, the Crusades had been influential. As a result of the war against a common enemy, the inhabitants of western Europe increasingly felt that they were one community, 'Christendom'. A comparison is inevitable with the situation after the Second World War when 'the West' – of Europe, combined with the United States and Canada – was opposed to 'the Communist world' and again asked, 'What are we', what is Europe?

The English chronicler and monk William of Malmesbury knew the answer. In his report of the address given by Pope Urban II in 1095 at Clermont to convince the assembled council of the need for a crusade, he clearly indicates in which ways Christians distinguish themselves. They are not barbarians but display *virtus*, i.e. they lead civilized lives, cherish a common cultural language and are, simultaneously, detached from culture and the world. Among them arise people 'whose inspired texts will make them immortal as long as anyone cherishes Latin literature'. But they also respond to calls to defend their high ideals. After all:

> Love of one's own hearth must not prevent you, because for the Christian the world is, in a sense, a place of exile, but, on the other hand, the whole world is his country.[21]

Steeped in the learned, Christian culture of his days, William here gives the arguments for a policy of propagating ideals now defined as specific to his world, whether or not under the guise of a necessity to defend common territory or values. The seed of European expansion is sown here.

While the Crusades that William wrote about certainly resulted in some sense of unity, the Europeans involved also gained some insight into those elements of their culture they perceived as different from Islam. Yet it is significant that the image of Islam as the arch-enemy was created more by those who did not make the journey to the Holy Land than by those who did and stayed there for longer periods. Indeed, the latter experienced not only the differences but also the similarities between cultures and people.

However, the Crusades hold another significance. For the first time in European history, large groups of Roman Christians from diverse regions were brought together. They discovered that, besides the defence of high ideals, very different motives played a role as well, that rulers and 'nations' had their own agendas. Moreover, they experienced for themselves how much they differed from each other: the 'arrogant' French, the 'gluttonous' Germans, the 'dishonest' Italians. The chronicles of the Crusades are full of stereotypes in the making. Seen as a supreme moment of religious universalism in which the one world of Christian culture proved its power and might, the Crusades simultaneously awakened many Europeans to existing and increasing differences within that one world.

6 One world, many traditions

Elite culture and popular cultures: cosmopolitan norms and regional variations

Europe's 'feudal' polities

In the course of the ninth century, the Carolingian Empire collapsed, basically for the same reasons that most empires did not survive. It was too big, and due to its reliance on personal power based on personal relationships between central rulers and local magnates, it lacked the kind of formal bureaucracy that could hold it together in a situation wherein, after the death of a strong leader, weak successors were faced with the bids for independence by their subordinates. After several divisions between successive generations of Charlemagne's heirs, the former unity was lost and Carolingian Europe was fragmented into a number of warring principalities.[1]

Wherever large states emerged, mostly based on an agricultural economy, authority nominally rested in the hands of a single ruler. Sometimes, the origins of such power still lay in tribal leadership, based on a mixture of military prowess and divine sanction, as in those parts of Europe where the Germanic tradition was strong. Such power might become greater by the gradual assumption of ever more functions, whether or not with the willing assent of others in the leader's peer group of feudal nobles. Often, power was simply conquered, or acquired through the voluntary or forced cession by a ruler who could or would not try to hold on to his entire territory.

Indeed, initially, states were anything but static and changes occurred incessantly. For although power mostly was or became hereditary in the family of the man who had first 'founded' the state, a person might lose it through force of conquest, or acquire it through inheritance. Hence the importance of alliances, and the value placed on dynastic marriages to safeguard one's rights.

The rather unstable situation at the end of the first millennium of the Christian era was aggravated by the southward migrations of the Norsemen or Vikings, the still largely pagan Germanic inhabitants of Scandinavia. Long pictured as cruel marauders, only, we now know that their background and motives were rather more complex. Admittedly, they had been pirating the Carolingian frontiers since the end of the eighth century and now, seeing their chance and using their marvellous longboats, invaded and plundered all of north-western Europe. But overpopulation, changing climatic conditions and the ensuing agricultural problems, as well as the quest for easy booty and new trade routes may all have contributed to their large-scale move into England, the Netherlands, the German lands and France, where they settled as farmers, craftsmen and merchants; indeed, the Viking trading towns were important centres of cross-European commerce.[2] Both in present-day Normandy and in Sicily, the Vikings created principalities, as they did, too, in Russia, using its great rivers for transcontinental trade. Meanwhile, the south-eastern flank of Europe was attacked by the Magyars who crossed the Danube in the ninth century and wreaked havoc both in the former Carolingian Empire and in the Byzantine territories.

In this situation of declining central authority and hence security, people sought forms of organization which could guarantee their survival. Instead of relying on the emperors and kings who nominally ruled from the ninth and tenth centuries onwards but were increasingly unable to effectively protect them from internal injustice and external aggression, they now turned for protection to regional military leaders, warrior-aristocrats; the latter, based on their own estates, saw a chance to increase their power and holdings by offering safety to the weaker – other aristocrats, the clergy or the peasants – in exchange for personal, mostly military services or goods. The most successful lords acquired not only economic and political-military power, but also judicial authority, thus effectively eliminating the reality and to many even the concept of a central state as the dispenser of justice.

A clear explanation of the way economic, military and political structures were ever more strongly perceived in terms of personal relationships of protection and service, or obedience, was given by a senior clergyman, Fulbert, who was Bishop of Chartres from 1006 until 1028. In a famous letter to William, duke of Aquitaine, he analyses the mutual duties of a lord and his bondsman, his vassal. In this letter the strong personal ties of trust and obedience are formulated which were considered essential to a well-structured sociopolitical life:

> To William, the most glorious Duke of the Acquitanians, Bishop Fulbert offers the aid of his prayers.
>
> Having been told to write something about the nature of fealty, I have briefly noted the following points for you on the authority of the books. A man who swears fealty to his lord ought always to remember these six words: unharmed, safe, honourable, profitable, easy, possible. Unharmed, because he must not do to his lord any physical injury. Safe, because he must not betray his secrets or damage the defences by which his lord can be safe. Honourable, because he must not detract from the lord's jurisdiction or from anything else which pertains to his rank. Profitable, because he must not cause the loss of any of his property. Easy and possible, lest he make it difficult to do the good deed which his lord could otherwise easily perform, or make impossible what would otherwise have been possible. It is right that the vassal [*fidelis*] should beware of doing harm in this way. But he does not earn his fief merely by so restraining himself. . . . He must still loyally aid and advise his lord on the above six points. . . . The lord ought in all

these things to do the same for his vassal. And if he does not do so, he will deserve to be considered a man of bad faith. . . . I would have written to you at greater length had I not been occupied with many other matters, even with the restoration of our city and our church, all of which was burnt down recently in a terrible fire. Although we cannot fail to be somewhat affected by this loss, nevertheless we breathe again in the hope of consolation from God and from you.[3]

The question is, of course, how this ideal worked out in practice. For an answer, one might turn to the so-called 'formulae of Tours', a set of models for all sorts of legal documents dating from the seventh century. In this specific case a model is given for use by a person who feels too weak to survive on his own and offers his services to a stronger man; in doing so, he becomes that man's vassal on condition that he receives protection, clothing and food:

I, A, to the magnificent lord B.
As it is well known to everybody that I have no means of feeding and clothing myself, I have asked you, in your pity, permission to hand over and commend myself to your protection and your goodwill has granted me it. And I have therefore done so, on the understanding that you must aid and comfort me with food and clothing, according as I am able to serve you and deserve well of you; and that, so long as I live, I must extend to you service and obedience of the kind expected of a free man; and throughout my life I shall have no power of withdrawing from your power and protection, but must remain all the days of my life under your power and protection.[4]

This was the basis of the so-called feudal system, which, however, was no system at all. It should be noted that the term 'feudalism' was coined only in the seventeenth century, as a word to describe a complex of economic, military and political relationships that gave structure and cohesion to European society after the demise of Roman authority. Nor did these relationships concern only great noblemen who strove for an alliance with a still mightier ruler; they could equally well involve a simple peasant who sought the protection of a local landowner.

A hierarchy of loyalties evolved, according to which one vassal received his sustenance – whether or not in the form of property, *feudum* – from or was guaranteed its possession by a lord who, in his turn, might be the vassal of someone even more powerful, as can be seen from the agreement reached in 1076 between the count of Hainault and the bishop of Liège who was, himself, a vassal of the Holy Roman Emperor:

In assigning all these allods and fiefs to the church of Liège, and in the liege homage of this great man the Count of Hainault, it was laid down that the Count of Hainault owed his lord the Bishop of Liège service and aid for all purposes and against all men with all the forces of his vassals [*homines*], both infantry and cavalry, and that once the Count was outside the County of Hainault these forces should be maintained at the Bishop's expense. . . . If the lord Bishop summoned the Count of Hainault to his court or to any conference, he had likewise to pay him his expenses. If the lord Emperor of the Romans summoned the Count of Hainault to his court for any reason, the Bishop of Liège ought at his own expense to bring him safely to and from the court and appear on his behalf and answer for him in the court. . . . Should the Count of Hainault lay siege to any fortress which belonged to his own honour . . . the Bishop must at his own expense assist the Count with five hundred soldiers, whilst the Count must provide the Bishop with means to buy victuals at a fair price. If there were grass or other fodder necessary to horses in the fields, the Bishop and his men might take this at the Bishop's choice.[5]

In his turn, the count of Hainault had vassals who did not always fulfil their obligations, as appeared in 1176:

That same year, disputes arose between the Count of Hainault and his vassal and kinsman Jacques d'Avesnes over certain wrongs which said Jacques was doing to the lord Count. Hence the lord Count summoned Jacques to his court and required him to restore the castle of Condé. Jacques . . . eventually refused outright to restore the castle. The lord Count called upon his [other] vassals . . . to decide what was to be done about this. Hence it was judged that Jacques had no further rights in his castle. . . . The Count of Hainault mobilized his army and at Easter 1176 launched a fierce attack. . . . Since Jacques could not withstand the forces of his lord the Count, he begged for mercy, prostrated himself at the foot of the armed Count and restored the castle of Condé to his authority.[6]

Yet despite these multiple dependencies, there were many parts of Europe where rulers remained relatively strong and where most men, noblemen and commoners, while retaining their possessions as allods (i.e. as free, unalienated property) gave military service to the lords of the land not because they were vassals, but because they were subjects of a ruler. However, the bureaucracies that came to take on an ever greater share of government in the stronger states, while devising a new legal system in which to define the ruler-subject relationship, sometimes rewrote existing obligations in such terms that they closely resembled not only those of the 'feudal ideal' but, at the same time, of the real vassalage that existed elsewhere.[7]

The Church and the early states

By the end of the tenth century, Europe slowly began to recover from the political and economic crisis that had begun at the end of the ninth century. The relative cold that had reigned for more than a century came to an end; this, of course, provided a boost to agriculture and thus to population growth. Consequently, trade and industry were stimulated as well. Also, the Norsemen and other invaders either were driven back forcefully or, more often, permanently established themselves in their newly won principalities, marrying into the indigenous population. On the territory of present-day France the dukes of Normandy soon became one of Europe's strongest powers. In the

German lands, King Otto I stopped the advance of the Magyars, who then settled in present-day Hungary.

Even in those regions where strong rulers had been absent for a time, the concept of a society ruled by law that had been one of Ancient Rome's great cultural achievements still had been preserved and, in its way, implemented by the Church, the only great institution surviving both the Roman and the Carolingian Empire. It had kept alive the idea and the ideal of such a structure, if only because the popes, trying to preserve and increase their power, adapted Roman Law for their own use, thus giving birth to Canon Law.

Indeed, this ability of the Church to manage, so to say, whenever strong states structuring civil society were lacking, has been of the greatest advantage to Europe's further development. The Church proved itself able to integrate the community through a policy of legislation that combined secular aims with religiously legitimized rules. It first tried to contribute to a more peaceful climate through the imposition of Sunday as the Lord's Day, on which no one was to attack his enemy. Soon, the increasing number of saints' days to which the same rule applied, coupled to so-called truces of God, helped to create a more peaceful atmosphere as well, as did a ban on fighting on market-days – no mean stimulus to economic growth. Also, the Church successfully tried to keep the more bloody forms of warfare within bounds, though applying different rules of warfare for Christians and infidels. Even more successfully, it managed if not to eradicate at least to curb the ubiquitous blood feuds. Undoubtedly, in the beginning the rules laid down by the Church were but poorly observed. However, new legal systems turned the exercise of blood vengeance into a prerogative, first, of the Church and its courts, and then of the secular authorities; the process was, one might say, a colonization from within.[8] Slowly, a vision was being realized of a legal, civil society, wherein the members of the community could expect to be treated equally, if, most times, only in theory.[9]

Not least important was the Church's policy towards marriage and family matters. It seems that, from the beginning, Christianity has stressed matrimony as something sacred, not only attaching to it great social importance, as, in their way, classical Rome and Greece had done as well, but also investing it with a unique moral, religious value, to the exclusion of other forms of relationship.

Undoubtedly, strengthening the ideal and practice of a priest-sanctioned marriage gave the Church greater control over its flock than otherwise would have been the case. Secular authorities, too, were quick to see the advantages of a regulated, single-system society. Hence, this policy met with considerable success. Of course, for the majority of Europeans, the agricultural poor, procreation was a dire necessity, whatever their inclination: without children to help work the land, the life of a peasant, especially an ageing one, would have been practically unliveable. Also, in a community which valued the transfer of patrimony and privilege along proven bloodlines, the stress upon the sacrality of a union which by and large guaranteed the legitimacy of children definitely was important.

On the other hand, in this as well as other socio-economic groups, same-sex relations certainly were not uncommon, partly because women were not available, partly because they left no possibility of unwed mothers, with all the concomitant problems for the off-spring in an acutely ancestor-and-kinship conscious society. This may have been one of the reasons why, for a long time, homosexuality continued to be widely practised without strong opposition by the Church, and was, according to some historians, sometimes even officially sanctified by it in same-sex unions.[10]

Yet there is abundant evidence that the trend was increasingly towards heterosexual relations and, moreover, towards the expression of sexuality as 'legitimate', as acceptable in the eyes of God only within the sacred marriage bond, with the sole aim of procreation. Indeed, while the Church stressed the fact that man's salvation was best served by celibacy, it could not deny the obvious necessity of the reproduction of the species. Thus, both for men and for women who did not aspire after a monastic life, marriage and parenthood were seen as the only viable destination.[11] Inevitably, the Church itself, although it had tolerated married priests for a long time, in the end became the victim of the order it successfully sought to impose: priests who did not live up to the ideals which, though only partly, were interiorized by the people, became the object of violent persecution.[12]

Meanwhile, an existence in the world certainly brought men more opportunities than women. Of course there were a few, mostly high-born female artists, writers of courtly and mystic poetry, as well as noble ladies who patronized the arts. There were even women scholars.[13] But they were the rare exceptions, rather than the rule. Most women were convinced that their life had to run the course from being a 'clean maid', first, to being a 'true wife': chaste motherhood was their real vocation, following the example of that mother *par excellence*, the Virgin Mary, whose cult was increasingly stimulated.[14] If their husband died, they might, of course, marry again, but preferably they should spend the rest of their life as a steadfast rather than a merry widow.[15]

The growth of a community made up of small nuclei embedded in a family system legitimized both by sacred and secular law loosened whatever there might have been of strong extended kinship networks in the older, tribal societies. However, Church policy in this field was also influenced by the fact that, for several centuries, large parts of Europe lacked strong states. Almost inevitably, strong states would have been predatory organizations, which would have resulted in the insecurity of the tenure of landed property. Now the Church, which neither could nor would adopt such a predatory attitude, tried to ensure the legal possession of property instead. Whether this was for motives of easier cultural, religious control or for economic reasons after all – detaching property, land, from large kinship systems – is not altogether clear. Certainly, self-interest played a role, for the Church received many grants of land in return for the prayers that should enable the donors to comfortably live their lives on earth, assured of a place in heaven. Still, the security of property was a powerful incentive to investment in land, both on the side of the big landowners and of the smaller, freeholding peasants. All this contributed to a growing individualism which, in itself, strengthened the market-orientation of European economic life and, in its turn, the growth of a well-ordered, legally structured society – Church-dominated, of course, but only so for the time being.[16]

Economic and technological change and the early states

Despite increasing trade, both regional and, largely via the Mediterranean and the Baltic, interregional, this economy and this society were still agricultural at heart. Europe was a world of manors and estates with, at the centre of a hamlet or village, the homes of the landowners, castles or fortified houses. These, ranging from simple wattle-and-daub structures scarcely more comfortable than the dwellings of the peasants to magnificent, stone-built fortresses that might be more roomy but, mostly, were equally uncomfortable, formed the one pole of economic, social and political life, with the parish church as its spiritual and cultural counterpart. In this world the peasants lived and worked: the free men, usually fitted into this system of lordship one way or another, and the unfree, the villeins and serfs, who were largely bound to the soil and its owner, a nobleman or knight.

Food supply was dependent on a mixture of climatic and soil conditions on the one, and human technology on the other hand. This, of course, was the same all over the world. In Europe, however, some conditions as well as some inventions allowed for a different development.[17] For its greater part, Europe was a rainfall agriculture, allowing each farmer to work a considerable number of square metres, instead of the rather small plots that could be worked in more arid regions that depended heavily on irrigation. Moreover, an ingenious method of crop rotation was used within the so-called open-field system, wherein at any one time half the land was under cultivation while the other half lay fallow; soon, an even more ingenious system was adopted, the three-field or three-course system, which allowed for summer and winter sowing while the last third of any property was left to recuperate. Such sources of energy as the watermill – known to the Romans but not widely used by them because they had a dependent (indeed a slave) peasantry to do the work and were loath to invest in this rather costly piece of engineering – were used all over Europe from the sixth century onwards, and from the twelfth century windmills were introduced as well, greatly facilitating such actions as fulling and sawing.

This brings us to the topic of technology, an integral part of cultural history. As, in this context, we have to view the relationship between Europe and Asia, we touch upon the problematic question of the diffusion of knowledge and technology between civilizations as opposed to parallel, indigenous inventions.

It will be obvious that non-European inventions would not have been adopted in Europe if Europeans had not already had the skills necessary to modify, adapt and develop them to suit their own use. Also, one has to realize that the very early indigenous invention or adaptation of non-human energy, mostly in the form of water and, later, wind, in a certain way made Europe equal to the civilizations of China and Islam. The fact that windmills were used in Europe only from the middle of the twelfth century onwards, and that some scholars hold that they were introduced from Persia or even the Far East does not detract from that statement, for even if they were not a European invention, it seems that at least the change of a vertically shafted mill to a horizontally shafted one was definitely a European improvement.[18] Indeed, the improvements in European technology from as early as the fifth century onwards were such that many historians have argued that, largely because of the use of water-driven machines,[19] by the twelfth century not only the utilization of energy had been drastically changed but also the use of manpower, as water-power had helped to do away with the need for a slave-worked economy.

First introduced in the world of the monastic economies – not, however, for economic motives, but to enable these communities to retain their isolation from the wicked world by assuring a great measure of autarky – water-power was soon adopted by lay entrepreneurs as well; they saw its possibilities for material profit, and inevitably made it the object of extensive investments, and of continuous improvement. Consequently, according to some historians, a veritable 'medieval' industrial revolution took place.[20] By the twelfth century, corn, olives, grapes, wood, iron, leather and paper could all be, and often were processed by water-driven machines with a remarkable range of applications, although for the majority of small-scale operators such machinery was too expensive, and manual production continued to be the norm. This situation has led other historians to argue that though the genius to improve technologies was there, the incentive to actually do so was largely lacking.

Meanwhile, we should realize that although peat and soon coal were used for fuel, and a considerable mining industry developed, water-power continued to remain Europe's main source of energy well into the eighteenth century and that it is no exaggeration to say that the beginnings of the so-called Industrial Revolution were based as much on the water-wheel as on the steam engine. New methods to produce energy were combined with the increase of the production of iron in wind-driven mills, which affected the manufacture of more effective wheel-driven ploughs, with mouldboards and better shares, and the increased use of horses in agriculture – horses, especially second-hand ones, being cheaper than oxen which could be used for meat. All this helps explain how the average agricultural yield in Europe rose considerably between the ninth and the thirteenth centuries. Walter of Henley, who in the thirteenth century composed a widely copied and therefore supposedly also widely read treatise on land husbandry, wrote that for mere survival, a ratio between seed and yield of one to three was necessary. It seems that by this time, an average manor got a yield of one to five.[21] This situation, and the resulting improvement of the diet, which probably was far better than in many other parts of the earth, goes a long way to explain the almost continuous population rise and the further development of the European economy and the changes in European culture in this period.

Still, it cannot be denied that by the twelfth century, the technologies of the worlds of Asia were far broader in scope than those of Europe. In almost every field this had resulted in machinery of a sophistication totally unlike anything so far invented in the west. Consequently, Europe continued to learn from Asia.

Geopolitically, the world of Islam both separated and linked the worlds of further Asia and Europe. Indeed, in one aspect these worlds were terribly united indeed. What has been called the 'microbial unification of the world' became manifest in the great bubonic plagues that spread from Central Asia both to China and to Europe, first ravaging the Islamic Near East and the Byzantine Empire from the sixth century onwards, and then creating havoc all over Eurasia from the twelfth to the fifteenth centuries.

Due to its position, the Mediterranean was the road *par excellence* which connected the two worlds, economically and culturally. In Europe, this was one of the causes for a situation wherein Italy and southern Germany became centres of economic productivity and of cultural, i.e. also technological exchange, change and progress; meanwhile, of course, Spain, though less important economically, had a great influence on the diffusion of an immensely wide variety of ideas; these originated both from ancient Greek science and philosophy, and from ancient and contemporary Asiatic science and technology; these two traditions came to Europe through the filter both of Islamic scholarship and of Mediterranean commercial, largely maritime practice.

Many scientific notions as well as some very practical technical innovations reached Europe by way of Islamic North Africa and Islamic Spain. When Toledo, one of the great Islamic cities, fell to the Christians in 1085, and European scholars were introduced to the enormous stock of knowledge stored there by generations of scientists, they took over Indian medicine and, even more important, Hindu numerals, including the symbol for zero. These numerals and the resulting decimal system, so much easier to work with than the laborious Roman system, helped simplify mathematics to such an extent that they became fit for use in everyday European economic life, which, in a certain sense, was as big a revolution as the introduction of the simplified Phoenician script had been to Mediterranean trade three millennia earlier.

Christian scholars and students who flocked to Toledo also began to study the numerous manuscript books discussing mechanical devices of all sorts; thus, the idea of the weight-driven clock, probably originating in India, entered Europe as well. Among the really important technical devices which came to Europe along the African–Spanish road were pedal-operated looms, which left the weaver's hands free to pass the shuttle backwards and forwards. They were probably introduced into Europe during the twelfth century.

However, by far the most important were the paper-making techniques that employed vegetable fibres pounded in water till a pulp was formed that could be made into paper sheets. The technique was first invented in China and according to some sources entered the Islamic world as early as the eighth century via Central Asia.[22] It was perfected in Baghdad, both through the addition of starch which created a paper suitable for the use of quills or pens, instead of brushes, and through the introduction of a water-driven machine that operated hammers pounding the fibres into pulp. These inventions stimulated the production of books and thus the dissemination of knowledge in a remarkable way. The subsequent westward spread of manuscript books in the ninth and tenth centuries in turn led to the westward spread of the new paper-making techniques as well, resulting in the first paper mill being opened in Spain in 1151.

Actually, the roads connecting the worlds and technologies of further Asia with the Christian west were four. Whereas Islamic Spain seems to have been the main channel through which many important scientific notions and technological devices came to be known to Europe, Islamic Sicily was the first subsidiary one. The use of complex labour-saving reeling machines for the processing of silk thread from the cocoons, which had been in use in China for ages, travelled to Byzantium and the Near East sometime in the eleventh century. A hundred years later, we hear of silk manufacture in northern Italy. Significantly, however, by then the machine had been modified and, indeed, improved into the throwing machine with a circular frame.

At approximately the same time, the Crusades created a second subsidiary link between Europe and the Near East. It allowed such diverse techniques to enter Europe as food-processing for the production of pasta and the making of certain incendiary weapons. The use of the latter was, of course, not only to revolutionize European civilization but also to give it one of its great holds over the rest of the world.

The first real intimation of the possibilities of high-nitrate powder became evident when the Mongols began their expansionist policies in the thirteenth century, thus creating the fourth road that connected East Asia with Europe. We do know, for example, that well into the fourteenth and fifteenth centuries, captives from Mongol armies were brought as slaves to Italy and these may well have introduced various skills developed within the Chinese-Mongol cultural sphere.[23]

Europe, of necessity, soon became very interested in the new superpower of Central Asia, and decided to get to know it better. The popes sent their ambassadors to the great khans. A Franciscan friar, William of Roebroeck, returning from Mongolia in 1257, had learnt about the military use of explosive powder, which the Mongols had taken over from the Chinese – the tale that the Chinese used what we call gunpowder only for innocently artistic fireworks is a fable. A year later, experiments with gunpowder and rockets were made in Cologne, and Roebroeck's friend, the monk Roger Bacon, wrote a tract analysing the new invention for the scientific world of Europe. At the same time, the new weaponry had also become known to Europeans in the Near East; there it had been even further developed as part of the fruitful interaction between the worlds of Islam and those of China; consequently, even more advanced ideas about the military use of gunpowder soon reached Europe as well.

Although we normally associate gunpowder with hand guns, the earliest really useful gunpowder weapon, the bronze-barrelled cannon, seems to have been developed in Manchuria only in the last decades of the thirteenth century; the same holds for the smaller Chinese-Manchurian hand gun. By the beginning of the fourteenth century, these new devices turn up in European drawings and are soon in material evidence as well. The invention had probably reached Europe by way of the Mongol-dominated regions of Russia and, perhaps, by the trade routes connecting these regions with the Baltic: some of the earliest cannons have been unearthed in Sweden.

The case of gunpowder and guns is especially significant because it shows that object diffusion and idea diffusion have coincided here, while at the same time it is obvious that to simply characterize the process as an example of the transfer of technology would be wrong; one should rather explain what happened in terms of a dialectic, a technological dialogue, or an inventive exchange.

Stronger states – stronger rulers?

All the above technological developments, whether indigenous or imported, as well as the socio-legal and ideological structures created or favoured by the Church gradually resulted in the formation of stronger states, both by contributing to their cohesion and military power and through the growth of the economy and, hence, of their fiscal capacity.

For a long time, such princes as there were shared their sovereign authority with numerous other lords. A centralized state, with a nonlineage-based structure and a bureaucracy that would ensure some sort of rational govern-ment as well as a revenue for public purposes and that held power over all subjects within its territory, yet had to evolve. Yet this was what many monarchs wanted and, indeed, actively strove to create; of course, their wish resulted in continuous strife with their neighbours as well as with the magnates who did not want to give up their independence and their income from a growing economy that, besides profiting from improved agriculture, now began to have its base in trade as well. Slowly, however, some rulers were successful in acquiring a more than equal share of sovereign power.

In England, during the invasions of the Norsemen, the local chieftains had gradually come to accept the authority of one king who eventually ruled over the seven former Anglo-Saxon kings. It was King Alfred of Wessex, named 'the Great' (849–99) – whose life was written by the bishop of Winchester, Asser – who was counted with this feat.[24] Indeed, he gained a status in English history near to the mythical Arthur, who was supposed to have united the country in the period when Roman authority disappeared. Soon, Anglo-Saxons and Vikings intermarried, even producing a new dynasty, and a slow process of administrative and fiscal unification started. This formed the basis on which William 'the Conqueror', the Viking-descended duke of Normandy who crossed the Channel in 1066, bringing not only an army but also an already proven system of central government, could start enlarging the royal power in England.

The territory of present-day France was divided between many independent rulers although a number of them nominally recognized the sovereignty of the King who, in fact, held real power only over his own domain, the region of Paris. Yet through war, marriage, inheritance and diplomacy, the successive 'kings of France' succeeded in acquiring ever more territories. Though they left regional customs well alone, they employed a complex bureaucracy to secure a fiscal efficiency that significantly enlarged their financial and military possibilities. From the thirteenth century onwards, an important additional element made itself felt. As large parts of western France were controlled by the kings of England, the rulers of France began to exploit anti-English sentiments among the population to create an embryonic 'national feeling', asking the feudal lords of France as well as the common people to unite and fight under their banner.[25]

In Germany, a system had evolved wherein numerous ecclesiastical and lay lords, while ruling their own principalities, elected one of their group to the kingship – a man who usually received the imperial title afterwards, as the heir of Charlemagne's tradition and hence of Rome and all it implied. However, the actual power of this Holy Roman Emperor was but small, depending mainly on the extent and wealth of his own domains.

Thus, in most regions of Europe, states emerged in the eleventh and twelfth centuries, in Sweden as well as in Denmark, in Poland as well as in Hungary and, of course, in the Iberian peninsula, where a wealthy kingdom developed in Aragon, around Barcelona, largely based on profitable trading across the Mediterranean. Still, by and large the sovereigns had but little power because their functions were restricted and hence their subjects' inclination to pay was limited as well. With the Church performing most services now considered within the public sphere – education, the care of the sick, the orphaned and the ageing – the kings, except in times of real danger to the state, were not very successful in extracting money from their subjects; the common people realized that the revenue was mostly used to finance wars that brought them only misery, whereas the aristocracy knew that the kings would use their armies to curb their power to compete.

However, most people did see the advantages of a peaceful, structured society wherein the use of arms was not each and everybody's privilege and wherein legal transactions of any kind were binding under a superior authority. This is what gave most aspiring monarchs a real chance to increase their power. To set themselves up as the state's supreme judicial authority, to guarantee everybody's property and security if not yet everybody's equality before the law was a service that made them increasingly popular. Working towards their own aims, these princes could rely on the foundation of equality of all citizens stipulated by Christianity. This equality, however theoretical in most cases, allowed for the slow growth of a climate of agreement and consensus, of competititon and contractual relationships, both in the field of economics or of politics.[26] This was to prove highly important to the further development of European society. Developing a uniform system of rules, mostly derived from the basic tenets of Roman Law, often via the papal Canon Law, all over Europe princes furthered the acceptance of their dominion by projecting themselves as the keepers of the 'community', and demanding, in return, payment of taxes and submission to their 'absolute' authority;[27] thus they were beginning truly to build a state.

Even though the regional magnates gradually lost out in their competition for power, they continued to defend their independence *vis-à-vis* growing state authority. In trying to retain some of their influence, they often felt forced to compromise with the monarch; accepting the latter's ultimate sovereignty, they would demand that the ruler acknowledged their right to be his first advisers and to have a big say in government. This happened in England in 1215, when the great barons forced the reigning king to accept the *Magna Carta*, the 'Great Document' that, in listing a number of fundamental rights of the English people, basically proclaimed that everyone, including the monarch, had to obey the law. Comparable developments took place all over Europe.

The towns and the early states

Into this society came a new element, or rather an old element that acquired a new importance. The genesis and development of the towns that were to play such an essential role in the economic, political and cultural life of Europe has not been a uniform process. Actually, the nuclei around which urban structures evolved were quite varied.[28]

In those parts of Europe where the Romans had created their administrative and military centres – they, too, often building upon pre-existing settlements – urban traditions continued even in the ages wherein the European economy was, by and large, an agricultural one. Thus, we find a continuity of city life all over Italy, where the battles between popes and emperors had actually resulted in a power vacuum,[29] as well as in southern France and parts of Spain, but also in such former Roman frontier colonies as Cologne, Trier and Vienna. But these *civitates* that, after the gradual disappearance of Roman or romanized civic rule in the fourth and fifth centuries, were often ruled by a Christian bishop – e.g. Winchester in England – were not really different from the surrounding countryside; mostly, they had a distributive, rather than an industrial function for agricultural products and farm-produced manufactures.

Other pre-urban nuclei developed as a *portus* (a port town) – like the important and extensive eighth-century settlement of Dorestad on the lower reaches of the Rhine – or a *vicus* or *wike*, a street of houses outside but under the immediate protection of a castle or a monastery. However, many of these towns did not survive the period of crisis of the ninth and tenth centuries.

Yet when peace and stability returned in the eleventh century, and the economy revived, a number of old cities re-established themselves, like the great episcopal towns along the Rhine. Some communities developed on commercially suitable spots, whether a ford where people crossed a river or the intersection of two or more trade routes. The Anglo-Saxon kings founded new centres on a large scale. Also, once more, towns evolved around the religious cores of Christendom – the monasteries which commanded huge estates and needed a central market – as well as around the more important strongholds of regional magnates trying to dominate a greater area. Thus abbeys and castles became regional centres, to which peasants flocked to sell their products, and where merchants settled to ply their trade. Artisans might then join the community, and the typical traits of a town would begin to show.

From the eleventh century, when the population of Europe began to grow again, in the urban centres in particular a surplus of labour became available that could turn to large-scale manufacture for an expanding regional market. Merchants and money lenders became an ever more visible group who gladly fostered such efforts. Banking was soon dominated by the Jews; they were a literate community in the midst of a largely illiterate society and, as they were forbidden to own land, applied themselves successfully to this complicated but lucrative business although it made them even more vulnerable to the periodic outbursts of anti-semitism of which they were the victim.

Besides trade, the mainstay of most urban economies became some kind of proto-industry, with textiles easily being the major sector. Indeed, many towns started producing, first linen and later fine woollen cloth, as did Ghent, in Flanders. The need to provide the looms with supplies of high-quality wool stimulated trade between such industrial centres and the regions producing wool, as is shown by the trade links that were established between north-eastern England and the continent, especially the north of France, Flanders and Holland. In northern Italy, silk manufacture stimulated trade with the Levant and the production of ironware led to transalpine trade; both generated great prosperity.

As factory-organized production did not really exist as yet, the household itself was the basic economic as well as social unit. For most townspeople, the house was both a dwelling and a workplace, often open to the street during day time.[30] The owners, whether they were artisans-and-shopkeepers, or bankers, merchants and tradesmen, usually employed not only members of their own family, including their wives, but also unmarried apprentices and salaried workers. As the latter mostly lived in, we should not think of these groups in terms of a 'nuclear' family; the concept of 'household' would more accurately describe the situation. This, of course, influenced the lives of all involved in a variety of fields. Urban lower and middle-class women, rather than being restricted only to the house, participated in economic and hence public life to a considerable extent. Children were often reared by elderly relatives. And with many people sharing restricted space, modern ideas of privacy simply did not apply.

Whatever their origin or specific characteristics, whenever a town became sufficiently important it would try to gain some sort of independence. As trade, from the eleventh century onward, became the mainstay of Europe's economic and financial development, the leaders of the towns, who often based their wealth on financial or mercantile transactions, would try to exploit their political usefulness; this particularly concerned the rulers who based the day-to-day exercise of their power mainly on the money made available by urban financiers, who often acted as tax-farmers; advancing lump sums to the state, the latter grew rich in the fiscal business. Of necessity, this mutual dependency had to result in a political *modus vivendi*. However, in the highly personalized power relationships of these centuries, the position of a collective structure such as a town was not unproblematic. New kinds of relationships had to be devised. This was the origin of the so-called town charters, which were used to guarantee the liberties or privileges granted to city dwellers by the rulers.

The right to hold a market and certain guarantees for undisturbed trade was, of course, considered basic. Often, regional potentates would gladly grant market charters, realizing their importance for the economy and thus for their own power. So did the German kings who wanted to revitalize trade with the Balkans and the Middle East through their border regions in central Europe. To further develop these market functions, towns were also given a lord's special protection.[31]

Another important privilege was that living in a city for 'a year and a day' liberated a former serf from his obligations towards the lord of the land to which he had been tied, giving him the status of a free man. This obviously attracted many a person; besides contributing to the growth of towns, it also changed the structure of society. In 1188 King Philip Augustus of France granted such rights to the community of Pontoise:

> In the name of the holy and indivisible Trinity, Amen.
> Philip, by the grace of God King of the French. All men, present and future, shall know that we have established a commune at Pontoise, reserving fealty to us and our successors and saving all customs, in this wise:
> That all who dwell in the parishes of Pontoise and St Martin shall by perpetual right be free and immune from every unjust tallage, from unjustified arrest, from unfair use of the right to purchase their goods, and from all unreasonable exactions. . . . If anyone brings within the walls somebody who has unwittingly done wrong to a member of this community, and if that person can prove upon oath that he did this in ignorance, he shall . . . be allowed to go free and in peace. . . .
> Anyone who comes to market within the walls shall be allowed to come and go in peace. . . .
> Traders who are in transit or who dwell in Pontoise shall at all times be left in peace. . . .
> If anyone living outside the walls has committed any offence against the community, and has refused to make amends on being summoned to do so, the community may punish him for it in whatever way it can. . . .
> All the men shall as a community provide for common needs, such as the watch, the prisons and the moats and all things pertaining to the defence and security.[32]

In the towns that were ruled by a local or regional secular or religious prince, forms of co-government often developed; the inhabitants organized themselves to negotiate with their lord for a number of other rights. Mostly, the towns-people tried to gain jurisdiction to deal first with commercial matters, but gradually with every other aspect of town life and government. Thus, many towns managed to ensure a certain degree of self-government, either with or without the supervision of a lord's representative. In this way, political struc-tures developed whereby the entire community could operate independently, instead of individuals being confronted with other individuals.[33]

Indeed, the urge to gain greater independence was increased by the high degree of united action that characterized town life, as can be witnessed in the guilds. These organizations of artisans and merchants specializing in a specific branch of industry or trade fostered a definite sense of self-sufficiency. Women, operating independently, played an important part especially in the crafts' guilds, making up a large minority of its members in many towns.

These guilds soon developed a sense of social and cultural solidarity, as well as a sense of power. This became obvious in such manifestations as the care they took of their sick and ageing members, their willingness to help save the souls of their deceased brethren by spending freely on masses for the dead, the construction of special chapels in churches and the magnificent guild halls they erected.

Most European towns were actually ruled by small groups, consisting either of persons from the landowning nobility who had interests in the towns as well – as was the case in Spain and Germany, and especially in Italy – or of wealthy merchants, as, for example, in most towns of the southern and northern Netherlands. Depending upon the town's major economic function, both groups might have a stake in its rule; quite often, the two would merge into one single oligarchy. For most town governments definitely were oligarchic; the members of the ruling elite held the major administrative positions and dominated the city council even where this was composed through some sort of election by a larger portion of the inhabitants.

From the eleventh century onwards, in western Europe towns became a major influence, both in economic and in political life. Aware of their unique position, and of the advantages it gave them, they sometimes tried to organize even across state borders. In the twelfth century, the Hanseatic League emerged, a network of trading cities that covered a large part of north-western Europe, facilitating the movement not only of goods but also of ideas, commercial, technical and artistic.[34]

After several centuries, cities and their ruling elites were a power factor which could not be disregarded anymore, and they knew it. In 1458, an anony-mous merchant in Naples recorded his thoughts on his profession. The text evinces a highly developed self-awareness, based on an ideal-type vision of the merchants' importance to the economy, society and culture. Strikingly, he saw trade not only as an essential motor for the economy, ensuring prosperity along with the agricultural sector, but also as the essential factor in the proper functioning of the state, since bureaucracy and taxation depended on it.

Moreover, he presented the merchant as the 'ideal' citizen. The Neapolitan reasoned as follows:

> The dignity and office of merchants is great and exalted in many respects, and most particularly in four. First, with respect to the common weal. For the advancement of public welfare is a very honourable purpose, as Cicero states. . . . The advancement, the comfort, and the health of republics to a large extent proceed from merchants. . . . Through trade . . . sterile countries are provided with food and supplies and also enjoy many strange things which are imported from places where other commodities are lacking. Merchants also bring about an abundance of money, jewels, gold, silver, and all kinds of various crafts. Hence, cities and countries are driven to cultivate the land, to enlarge the herds, and to exploit the incomes and rents. And merchants through their activity enable the poor to live; through their initiative in tax farming they promote the activity of administrators; through their exports and imports of merchandise they cause the customs and excises of the lords and republics to expand and consequently they enlarge the public and common treasury.
>
> [A merchant is] sparing, temperate, solid, and upright . . . ; no professional man understands or has ever understood the monarchies of this world and the states in regard to management of money upon which all human states depend as does a good and learned merchant.[35]

In the centuries following the decline of the Roman Empire, political organization in Europe sometimes had developed along republican lines, with final sovereignty over a certain territory being exercised by a small elite, as, for example, in the great merchant republics of Venice and Genoa, or the powerful towns of Hamburg, Bremen, Lübeck and Danzig in northern Germany. For a long time, these town-states managed to resist incorporation in the territorial monarchies that became the European norm. For all over the west, the common tendency was towards princely rule.

With the rise of the towns within these princely states, their roles multiplied. Economically speaking the role of towns for Europe's growing prosperity has been essential. Also, the specific way of life that developed in urban conditions contributed to a slow but gradual change from an agricultural society and culture to an artisanal and proto-industrial one, which at least partly held different values. Finally, the towns' political structure became of major importance for the further development of the European states. In the traditional struggle between monarchs trying to increase their power and nobles trying to retain as much of it as possible, the towns, if only through the revenue they generated, became an ally whose favour was sought by both parties. Mostly the princes, conferring ever more privileges on the urban communities, succeeded in tying them to their interest, while yet, inexorably, introducing an element that finally would alter the concept of absolute princely power.

For as the towns, or rather the urban elites, acquired a stake in the preservation of central power for their own aims, their demands as to participation in state government inevitably increased. Most princes realized that they could not but admit them or their representatives to the consultative assemblies that came into existence all over Europe as a result of the complicated play for power between the various power groups in society. In England, a 'parliament' which included the representatives of towns was first convened in 1295; a decade later, in France, King Philip IV called for the assembly of the 'États-généraux' when he needed his realm's support in his struggle against the power of the Pope.

Thus, in most states, eventually a balance was struck between kings, nobles and towns – with, of course, the Church as a fourth factor.[36] While each group tried to realize its own particular goals, they yet knew it was in their own interest to preserve the state that was increasingly seen as a common responsibility, a guarantee against chaos, war and poverty. Depending upon the quality of the balance, a state could be strong or weak; but it could not survive anymore without the active or at least passive participation of the cities and their elites.

A Christian world or a world of Christian nations?

The dream of a new empire coinciding with the territory of (western) Europe, which had seemed to materialize in the realm of Charlemagne, had evaporated after the emperor's death. The political fragmentation which characterized the west after the collapse of the Carolingian Empire in the ninth century had, by the tenth century, already led to the creation of states which frequently centred around particular ethnolinguistic unities. Soon, the division between those parts of Europe where the Romance languages were spoken, and the part where 'thios', 'diutsch', 'deutsch' (i.e. German) was the basis of the languages was widely felt.[37] By degrees, the various states acquired their own character despite the unity of religion and, at least in the upper classes, of culture that still seemed to bind them to a larger concept. Yet many did not want to accept this new situation and argued for a continued universal hegemony, either papal or imperial.

Three men whose stories present a view of their world can help to understand better the history of this period. In the last decades of the twelfth century, a learned and witty cleric named Walter Map wrote his *De Nugis Curialium* (On Courtiers' Trifles), a fascinating series of mostly satirical stories about his own times. This Welshman, having grown rich in the service of King and Church, had studied in Paris and been one of the English representatives at the third Lateran Council in Rome. About France, which he knew well – after all, a large part of it still belonged to the English Crown – he was short: it was the 'the mother of all mischief'. The Greeks were dealt with at somewhat greater length; they were 'soft and womanly', 'voluble and deceitful' and 'of no constancy or valour against an enemy'. Rome, via one of his storytellers, was curtly characterized indeed: ROMA stands for '*r*adix *o*mnium *m*alorum *a*varicia' – the root of all evil is avarice. But with a definite note of self-confident self-mockery, Map says that his compatriots, the Welsh, are 'wholly unfaithful to everybody – to each other as well as to strangers'.[38]

In about 1200, a well-travelled, anonymous clergyman from Saxony wrote a text which is the oldest chronicle of the world known in German. Starting with God's creation, the story quite quickly reaches the early Christian era. Constantine's reign is, of course, an essential marker:

> Do he do cristen wart, do wart gehoget over all de werelt de cristenlike name . . . di hilege ecclesia gewan grote sekerheit unde grote vrede.[39]

> As he became a Christian, the name of Christ was exalted all over the world . . . and Holy Church created safety and peace.

A little further on in the text he tells us 'de Engelsaxen gewonnen Brittanniam unde besaten dat lant wante an disen dach, dat is nu Engelant' (the English conquered Brittany and possess it up till the present day; it is now England). Other states are also named; the framework within which they function is 'de Cristenheit' (Christendom).

Of course, he brings up the rise of Muhammad, presented as a false prophet who misled the witless masses with a promise of a heaven full of eating, drinking and fornication. Contrast this then with Charlemagne:

> Der keiser Karl . . . mit deme quam dat rike an de Vranken, unde darna an de Dudischen herren . . . was an godes dieneste vlitich, wande he was wol geleret; he san oc selven mit sinen kapellanen. . . . He merede de Dudische sprake mit der Walschen . . . de keiser Karl let sine kindere alle leren.

> The Emperor Charles, with whom the empire fell to the Franks, and afterwards to the German lords, served the Lord with great fervour, for he was well educated; he also sang [during mass] with his chaplains. He added Latin to the German tongue; the Emperor Charles caused all his children to study.

This is the intellectual speaking, the man who attaches importance to showing how literate this exemplary emperor was. In Anglo-Saxon England, the king who had introduced unity and Christianity, Alfred the Great, was put forward as an example for the people in a similar way. It is the intellectual speaking, the man who, significantly, indicates that the vernacular can be enriched by additions from the standard cultural languages, the 'Walsch' ones, i.e. the languages derived from Latin, mostly Italian and French. It is the intellectual speaking, the man who indicates what the distinguishing criteria are in contemporary culture and society: reading and preferably writing, although it is known that Charlemagne for one hardly mastered the latter art. It is, in short, the intellectual who, like his clerical colleagues all over Europe, is actively creating a socio-cultural and thus psychological dividing line between *literatus* and *illiteratus*, a dividing line which also separated the powerful from the powerless.[40]

The world-view presented by a Viennese burgher is different but just as intriguing. In about 1276, one Jansen Enikel wrote a gigantic rhymed chronicle of world history, 27,000 stanzas long; it is in the vernacular as well, but much juicier than the lines of the anonymous author of the Saxon world history.[41] Enikel's story, too, begins with the creation and then quickly moves on to Noah and his sons:

> der ein was Sem genant/des tugent zieret wol ein lant/der ander hiez Japhet zwar/der was an tugen gezieret gar/des dritter sones nam was genant Cham/und war der tumbist under in.

> the one was named Sem, whose virtue adorned a land; the other was called Japhet, who possessed great virtue; the third son was called Cham, and he was the most stupid of them all.

A prejudice with long-lasting and far-reaching results had been born: black Africa was dismissed as dumb.

Jansen attaches great importance to the founding of Rome, and to the history of the ancient emperors and of the popes which was seamlessly attached to this. He does not once use the word Europe. *Orient* and *Occident* are the two parts of the world, until Constantine the Great appears on the scene, after which 'Kristenheit' is the order of the day, clearly as a geographical-cultural-religious concept. But for Jansen this 'Kristenheit' is divided into separate countries: 'Frankenlant, Engellant, Yspaniënlant, Italië, Oesterreich', or peoples: the 'Beier, Lamparten, Sahsen, Ungern'.

It is noteworthy that he later specifies his divisions in the form of an overview of the twelve languages – the number is symbolical – which are spoken in his world with, it goes without saying, German in the first place. Curiously enough, the Greeks are the fifth group of languages named, and the Armenians are the ninth, perhaps because both still belonged to the 'Kristenheit'? What is definitely surprising is that the Moors form the tenth group: perhaps because they live in Spain and are therefore included in a geographically defined Europe?

Significantly, Jansen adds something extra to each language group, often an apparently long-standing prejudice about the national character of those concerned but also something about their diet – we must not forget that in these centuries food was central to most people's thinking precisely because it was such a scarce commodity:

> Beiern is ein diutsch lant/daz ist mir wol bekant/daz sint gûtig liute . . . [And] ze Tyrol in dem lande/da lebt man an schande/und ze Görz ist ir vil . . . Die Kernder auch diutsch kunnen/der ern muoz man in gunnen . . . hirsbrin ist ir spis.[42]

> Bavaria is a German land – that I know well; the people who live there are good people. In the land of Tyrolia, people live without honour . . . and they have a lot of corn. The Carinthians also know German, I have to admit; they eat wheat porridge.

Clearly something in the way people thought about Europe was changing. At the beginning of the fourteenth century, the senior official Alexander von Roes wrote:

> It is now appropriate for me to describe the borders of Europe, and the different habits of the diverse peoples and groups. After all, Europe has four important empires, namely, the Greek in the east, the Spanish in the west, the Roman in the south and the Frankish in the north, while there are still more small kingdoms on the borders.[43]

The text contains two striking elements. Von Roes, like Jansen, includes the Greek Christians as part of a world he calls Europe but unlike him he does not once describe European unity in terms of the *Christianitas*-idea. Europe is simply made up of different political entities, each with its own culture.

Indeed, most states were building some sort of collective identity, to give themselves greater cohesion. In a Christian culture, no better way than to make the national heroes into saints, or the saints into national heroes. Thus, for example in France, the cults of St Clovis, St Denis, St Louis and St Michel gave those who were ruled by the French king a rallying point, to be used, specifically, when wars had to be fought against encroaching neighbours.[44]

The new idea of Europe certainly reflects the fact that by now Church and State, which both considered themselves universal, were actually unable to cooperate. This had become manifestly clear when they started fighting each other continuously in the tenth, eleventh and twelfth centuries. Struggling for sole or at least supreme power, popes and emperors each called on what was, however, in terms of content, a very different 'renovation' of the old Roman hegemony. In their fighting they greatly damaged what there was of cultural and political unity in 'Europe',[45] eroding the *Christianitas*-concept, the main base of their power claims. While the popes had great moral authority, and a very efficient bureaucracy, also in fiscal affairs, they had no army to really wield power; the emperors on the other hand, lacked a proper bureaucracy and, indeed, beyond their own domains, a manageable territory to draw power from – the 'German Empire' actually stretched from the Baltic to Brindisi and from The Hague to the lands beyond Vienna, and was already subdividing into a multitude of smaller states that only nominally accepted imperial suzerainty.

No wonder, then, that different thinkers were intent on finding different ways to heal the rift which threatened Europe. In 1310, the Florentine poet Dante Alighieri proposed in his tract *De Monarchia* that the spheres of State and Church finally should be separated: the emperor, using the law, was to give human society on earth an ideal form, while the Pope, with the help of God's revelation, was to lead mankind to its ultimate destination, heaven.[46]

At almost the same time, the French writer Pierre Dubois formulated a statement about the Pope, designating him the 'universal' authority while establishing that the emperor could not have a similar hegemony. However, despite the Pope's spiritual power, according to Dubois the guarantee of the law actually rested with the various sovereign kings who ruled over the independent states of which the Christian world was in fact comprised. Instead of an imperial hegemony in secular matters, Dubois anticipated a sort of assembly of states or a 'council', in which the Christian world, which he does not call Europe, is united.[47]

In the stormy discussions between the popes in Rome and the various rulers of Christian Europe, with the emperor in the lead, about whether there was a supreme Roman authority in spiritual as well as in secular matters, innumerable arguments for and against were put forward, often referring to the texts of such classical writers on politics as Aristotle and Plato which, though not available in their entirety, were avidly read and commented upon.

The Italian, Marsiglio of Padua (*c.*1275–*c.*1342), doctor, philosopher and rector of the Sorbonne in Paris, took a very daring stand in his work *Defensor Pacis* (1324), demanding absolute autonomy for every political unity – city-state, principality, kingdom and empire. He also advocated the establishment of a 'Christian council' that should deal with general problems concerning all believers and, thus, states. It is true that papal censorship tried to prevent the text being read or spread. Yet Marsiglio's words, certainly when seen retrospectively, were a great moment in the development of ideas about the position of man as a citizen, and of the body of citizens as the basis of all authority; thus, they certainly have had a great influence on political and, indeed, ecclesiastical thought in Europe:

> [I, 15.2] Let us say, in accordance with the truth and the doctrine of Aristotle . . . that the efficient power to establish or elect the ruler belongs to the legislator or the whole body of citizens, just as does the power to make laws. . . . And to the legislator similarly belongs the power to make any correction of the ruler and even to depose him, if this be expedient for the common benefit. For this is one of the more important matters in the polity; and such matters pertain to the entire multitude of the citizens. . . .
>
> The method of coming together to effect the aforesaid establishment or election of the ruler may perhaps vary according to the variety of provinces. But in whatever way it may differ, this must be observed in each case, that such election or establishment is always to be made by the authority of the legislator who, as we have very frequently said, is the whole body of the citizens, or the weightier part thereof. . . .
>
> [II, 20.2] And now I am going to show that the principal authority, direct or indirect, for such determination of doubtful questions belongs only to a general council composed of all Christians or of the weightier part of them, or to those persons who have been granted such authority by the whole body of Christian believers. . . . Let all the notable provinces or communities of the world, in accordance with the determination of their human legislators whether one or many, and according to their proportion in quantity or quality of persons, elect faithful men, first priests and then non-priests, suitable persons of the most blameless lives and the greatest experience in divine law.[48]

Still, if one travelled through Europe in these ages, many signs would have marked its continuing cultural unity under the tutelage of the Church, however disputed its political power might be.

Each city of some importance would announce itself in the landscape with the spires of its many churches. Entering the gates, one would often find, dominating the central square, a cathedral, whether of romanesque style, with heavy walls and small windows with rounded arches, or in the newer fashion – which only later was called 'Gothic' – characterized by soaring vaults, pointed arches and huge windows, as in the famous cathedrals of France, like Chartres and Lâon, or England, like Salisbury and Winchester. Indeed, the daring inventiveness of the architects of these ages seemed to know no bounds, as is shown by the breathtaking perpendicular fan-vaults and the almost completely stained-glass window-walls of the chapel of King's College, in Cambridge. Cathedrals, far from being separate, self-sufficient entities, were the living heart of an episcopal town, structures where many people found employment, and where both individual religion and civic pride found its expression in daily devotion, magnificent feasts and great works of art.[49]

The portals of these great churches as well as of the less important ones that arose in every city were decked with sculpted visions of hell and heaven, of the devils that lived in the realm of eternal damnation, where no true Christian ever hoped to end, and of the saints floating in paradise. Inside these churches, which were not sterilely white as we often see them nowadays, but very brightly painted with biblical and hagiographic scenes, one could make the round of the many side-chapels and chantries with their altars and altar-pieces, painted or sculpted in stone or wood, while, in the apse, the high altar might present a supreme vision of life on earth and in heaven. In the papal capital and in the wealthy towns of Tuscany, religious painting – commissioned not only by cardinals and prelates, religious orders and nobles, but also by rich burghers and civic fraternities – now began to show traces of a new 'realism'. Around 1300, Pietro Cavallini, in his fresco cycles for the great papal basilicas in Rome and, slightly later, Giotto di Bondone in the churches and chapels of Assisi, Florence and Padua depicted men and women as real people, rather than idealized types. Such religious art flowered all over Europe. In the grand retable made by Veit Stoss for one of Cracow's main churches, sculpture and painting are united in one stupendous vision of a deeply religious world.

And then of course, dotting the countryside, there were the monasteries, both big and small, many of them already centuries old, other ones the manifestation of the constantly new inspiration and vigour in the monastic movement. Everywhere one found the offspring of the great foundation at Cluny; this abbey, first built in 909, through its 'reformation' had become the example to many others for a more strict observance of the rules in monasteries all over Europe; this network now contributed to Cluny's vast wealth. At the end of the eleventh and the beginning of the twelfth century, a new call for monastic austerity and purity was heard, this time from the monks at Citeaux, led by St Bernard. Their movement, too, found followers everywhere; they established several hundred monasteries all over Christendom, engaging in agricultural and industrial business,[50] and, all the while, functioning and acting as the centres of an all-pervading religious culture.

Elite culture and popular cultures: cosmopolitan norms and regional variations

After the decline of the old romanized elites in the fourth, fifth and sixth centuries, almost without exception those who held power in the Church, the monks and the priests, were the only ones in Europe who could read and write. As writing (or rather literacy) is an essential means of exercising power in every complex society, with the rise of the Frankish Empire and other kingdoms in Europe from the eighth century onwards, the clergy came to hold great power in the secular world as well.

Besides at the rulers' courts, the Christianization of civilization occurred mainly in the writing rooms of monasteries and the classrooms of cathedral schools.[51] There, the clergy raised its pupils, who were the sons of the nobility, often trained for military and administrative functions in the State or for senior positions in the Church, as well as the sons of commoners, who were almost always educated for an ecclesiastical career. In this milieu, the clergy preserved and commented on a tradition of knowledge based on those elements of classical culture which the Church was prepared to take over – to the extent, that is, that they did not conflict with the biblical and other authoritative arguments put forward by Rome.[52]

In a process of sifting and selecting, the clergy expanded the corpus of knowledge which educated people were allowed to digest and which they could use to exercise power.[53] Although the artistic, philosophical and scientific way of thinking in which Christian theology and the classical tradition slowly merged, remained the culture of an elite, both spiritual and secular,[54] gradually something did emerge which we now recognize and define as 'European culture', even though no one yet used this term.

In the mean time, as a result of the political discord following Charlemagne's death, in the minds of the educated, the 'guardians of tradition', his empire, the revived Roman Empire, became more and more like a dream and his reign was increasingly idealized as a 'golden era'. A Europe dreamt of in this way can be found in the works of influential historians like Notker Balbulus and Nithard;[55] they gave further shape to the 'myth' of Europe, often elaborating on the Church of Rome's wish for the borders of the religious and political worlds to coincide, to form one unified culture over which it claimed power.

Although the Church did not actually succeed in realizing this vision, it did create a unity which was the more substantial because it survived many political changes, devastating wars and grave economic crises. The Christian world was one, in belief, liturgy and institutions. The laws of the Church, or Canon Law, evolved out of Roman law, contributed to a way of thinking on the legal relations between the individual and state government which soon was proclaimed to be universal, transcending all local customs. The Christian calendar, structuring the year around the major feastdays of the Church, the many saints' days and the accompanying rituals, regulated everyone's daily life.

All this has been termed the 'small tradition', a framework for the whole of western and central Europe within which everyone arranged their lives.[56] Yet this common basis did not result in a common feeling, at least not for the vast majority of people, most of them somehow tied to the soil, almost all of them illiterate. Their horizon was, in fact, limited to their own locality; their habits and lifestyles mostly took form within the confines of their self-enclosed farming communities, frequently attached to a nobleman's manor, with a castle and perhaps a village as its secular centre.

Churches and chapels were the religious centres, where most people's ideas of the world were shaped. It was there that the clergy proclaimed the message central to the lives of many Europeans as Christians: this life is only temporary; do not attach too much importance to it; accept suffering as a result of man's imperfection, of his fundamental state of sinfulness; man will regain his perfection in the hereafter; God's mercy will help him to reach this goal.[57]

Thus, although the majority of Europeans thought essentially the same, they did not experience these thoughts as a common culture. On the contrary, anyone who came from beyond the horizon was seen as foreign and different. Yet this local awareness was not absolute. From all layers of society people went beyond the horizon at least once in their lives; they were the pilgrims who, like their fellow believers in the Islamic world, considered that a pilgrimage to the holy cities was essential for their salvation. As Dante Alighieri (1265–1321) indicates in the introduction to the fortieth sonnet, 'O pilgrims', of his *Vita Nuova*:

> Those who travel over seas are called palmers,
> as they often bring back palms;
> Those who go to St. James' shrine in Galicia are called pilgrims,
> because the burial place of St. James was further away from his country than
>   that of any other apostle;
> And Romeos are those who go to Rome,
> which is where those whom I call pilgrims were going.[58]

By sea or over land, often following the highways which had been constructed centuries earlier by the Roman legions, the pilgrims journeyed from the west, north or east to the south, to the cradle of Christianity.[59] On the way they met other people, whose languages and ways of life were different; yet all shared the same belief, all needed to reach the same sanctuaries, all held on to the same expectations of the hereafter, all eagerly anticipated paradise in heaven. The fact that in the phenomenon of pilgrimage, devotion and trade often went together only strengthened its influence on Christian culture.

Pilgrims' routes were the routes to Jerusalem, by ship from Venice or another Mediterranean port, or overland through the foreign and very dangerous Balkans. The *Pieterpad* or 'St Peter's Way' led from Scandinavia through the Netherlands to Rome, to the graves of the apostles Peter and Paul and so many other saints and martyrs. The *Camiño de Santiago* from every corner of Europe directed the faithful to the shrine of St James at Santiago, in Galicia, the north-west of present-day Spain.[60] These were 'roads of civilization', along which all sorts of major and minor forms of culture spread over the entire Christian world: the sculpted shell pattern associated with Compostela, the expressive forms of early romanesque architecture and sculpture, a vision of the remnants of ancient Rome whose ruins rose around the Christian shrines, the elements from dialects and languages, European as well as Semitic, which crept into the pilgrims' parlance. Of course, one should realize that pilgrimages took place on a regional and interregional level, too. From the whole of north-west Europe people travelled to Canterbury, in England, where St Augustine was buried – later, Thomas à Becket was venerated there as well – or they made a somewhat more modest but still considerable journey within their own region as, for instance, in the Netherlands to the grave of St Servaas in Maastricht.

All these journeys, often difficult, undertaken not only by members of the elite but also by numerous persons from the uneducated classes, led to new visions of the world; yet it remains doubtful whether they contributed much to a further articulation of a feeling of fundamental European unity. After all, people also learnt about each other's peculiarities, about the habits and morals which had developed so differently precisely as a result of local or regional isolation and which frequently led to mutual irritation or, even worse, derision. Judgements quickly became prejudices – and condemnations. The twelfth-century *Liber Sancti Jacobi*, part of which for hundreds of years served as the travel guide for pilgrims going to Santiago, called the Gascons 'braggarts and lecherous drunkards', and the Spaniards 'uncivilized'. Similar texts warned the traveller against the dirty tricks played on one with double-bottomed beakers containing far less beer than bargained for, or against people who saw no problem in sexually assaulting man and animal alike. On the other hand, Dante noted that most pilgrims were hardly interested in what they saw and experienced during their journeys:

> Ye pilgrim-folk, advancing pensively
> As if in thought of distant things, I pray
> Is your own land indeed so far away –
> As by your aspect it would seem to be –
> That nothing of our grief comes over ye
> Though passing through the mournful town midway;
> Like unto men that understand to-day
> Nothing at all of her great misery?[61]

Monks and priests, warriors and courtiers and, increasingly, the wealthier townspeople, even if they largely lived according to the same premises as the peasants, nevertheless experienced the influence of a wider world.

Educated, to a minor or major extent, in a literate or even scholarly tradition, they were confronted with ways of thinking, with problems and questions that, seen from the perspective of the 'ordinary people', must have seemed to belong to and deal with another world. For them, philosophy, art, theology and

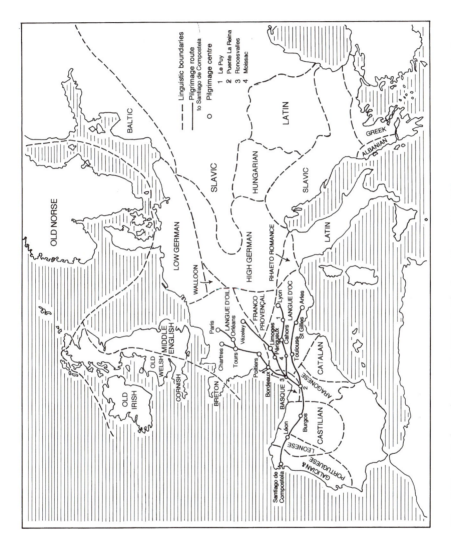

Map 4 Linguistic boundaries, *c.*AD 1200 (with eleventh- and twelfth-century pilgrimage routes)

Plate 13 A teacher, in his cap and gown which mark him as a university graduate, follows his (male) pupils' exercises. From a mid-fifteenth-century manuscript on alchemy in the University Library of Prague
Source: Centre for Art Historical Documentation, Nijmegen, The Netherlands

Plate 14 The teaching of theology at the Sorbonne, from a fifteenth-century French manuscript
Source: Centre for Art Historical Documentation, Nijmegen, The Netherlands

science could become the means to shape their ideas and express their creative urge. And, of course, they expressed themselves in literature. Their way of life has been called the 'great tradition'.

―――――――――

LONDON, AD 1378: GEOFFREY CHAUCER DESCRIBES HIS WORLD

In his *Canterbury Tales*, written between 1378 and 1400, Geoffrey Chaucer (1342–1400), an English civil servant who travelled widely on the continent, has left a vivid picture of life and culture during these years, presented in the stories of a number of persons from all walks of life making their pilgrimage to the shrine of St Thomas à Becket, in Canterbury. Characteristically, the first person we meet is a knight, whom Chaucer portrays in a highly stylized and idealized way, stressing the true knightly values: he is a gentle, noble man, not arrogant but modest; he does not offend others, he defends the frontiers of Christendom, and he goes out to combat the Infidel:

> There was a Knight, a most distinguished man,
> Who from the day on which he first began
> To ride abroad had followed chivalry,
> Truth, honour, generousness and courtesy,
> He had done nobly in his sovereign's war
> And ridden into battle, no man more,
> As well in Christian as in heathen places,
> And ever honoured for his noble graces.
> When we took Alexandria, he was there,
> He often sat at table in the chair
> Of honour, above all nations, when in Prussia.
> In Lithuania he had ridden, and Russia,
> No Christian man so often, of his rank.
> When, in Granada, Algeciras sank
> Under assault, he had been there, and in
> North Africa, raiding Benamarin;
> In Anatolia he had been as well
> And fought when Ayas and Attalia fell,
> For all along the Mediterranean coast
> He had embarked with many a noble host.
> In fifteen mortal battles he had been
> And jousted for our faith at Tramissene:
> Thrice in the lists, and always killed his man. . . .
> He was of sovereign value in all eyes.
> And though so much distinguished, he was wise
> And in his bearing modest as a maid.
> He never yet a boorish thing had said
> In all his life to any, come what might;
> He was a true, a perfect gentle-knight.[62]

―――――――――

Plate 15 Builders constructing the Tower of Babel, a miniature in King Wenceslas' Bible, written and illustrated *c.*1389–1400, in the National Library, Vienna. It shows the remarkable building techniques of fourteenth–century Europe
Source: Centre for Art Historical Documentation, Nijmegen, The Netherlands

Chaucer's *Canterbury Tales* are a rather late reflection on Europe's 'age of chivalry' and the role of the knight in it, with his indefatigable valour and courageous deeds, and also his modesty and good manners which distinguish him from the boors and the peasants. One should really quote such earlier knightly tales as the *Chanson de Roland*, the most influential example of the genre of the heroic poems, originally composed in old French but translated into English, German and Dutch as well.

Plate 16 A water-driven flour-mill on the bank of the River Vltava at Prague, in a colour-wash, pen-drawing by the Dutch artist Roelant Savery, *c.*1610
Source: Centre for Art Historical Documentation, Nijmegen, The Netherlands

These *chansons de geste* probably went back to a very old, oral tradition but continued to be sung or chanted, perhaps accompanied by one or more instruments, to a noble audience. They were first written down in the eleventh century. A mixture of fact and fantasy, they illustrate the values held by and the struggles within the European warrior class,[63] telling about noble heroes who live for loyalty and the dignity of war, especially war for their lord and against the Infidel. 'Roland's Song' describes in vivid detail the battle of Charlemagne and his paladins against the 'Saracens' – who were probably Basque warriors living in the Pyrenees.[64] Often, these poems were meant to function as a warcry to incite the world of Christendom against those whom it felt to be its enemies. Unlike 'Roland's Song', whose protagonist cannot be easily identified anymore, the 'Poem of my Cid' – typically, Cid was taken from the Arab word *Sidi* (lord) – was based on the life of the historical hero Rodrigo Diaz de Vivar, who had led Castilian troops against Muslim Valencia. The poem enjoyed great popularity.[65] In later ages, its theme was reworked by the French seventeenth-century playwright Pierre Corneille (1606–84), and set to music by numerous eighteenth- and nineteenth-century composers.

Besides the *chansons de geste*, these ages saw the rise and development of the poetry of courtly love, possibly influenced by comparable genres in the Islamic world of Spain; beginning with simple, lyric statements, it culminated in the *Romance of the Rose*, which explores the psychological depths of a situation wherein a lover, a knight, completely abases himself for his beloved. In a certain sense this is adulterous poetry, for the beloved is always a married woman, un-reachable, the wife of the knight's lord, who will decide over his advancement, and whose favour, in a way, he seeks by paying court to his lady. Often, this lyricism of illicit love, with its barely veiled sensuousness, was frowned upon by the Church, which sought to redirect the nobles' amorous fervour towards a more spiritual goal, the Virgin Mary. In both forms, this poetry and its thematic continue to inspire writers up till the present day. However, as the *chansons de geste*, courtly poetry, too, gave an idealized vision of an old world, the world of 'the knight', failing to indicate the multifaceted social and cultural reality of these centuries.[66]

Chaucer's stories also give us a glimpse of a more complex society, in which the old power structure, the idealized rather than factual three-tiered order of Church, aristocracy and peasantry,[67] was rapidly changing under the influence of the towns. As well as describing priests and knights, and a feminist *avant la lettre*, the garrulous but strong-willed 'wife of Bath', Chaucer tells tales of merchants and lawyers, the representatives of a commercial, town-centred society. The 'new' world, represented by the thriving urban culture of northern and central Italy, was even more vividly depicted in a series of a hundred tales-within-a-tale under the title *Decameron* (1353), the masterpiece of the Florentine writer Giovanni Boccaccio (1313–75). Boccaccio's Florence is peopled by well-to-do burghers and wealthy patricians. It is a world of close-knit families, living within close-knit neighbourhoods. While they have a lot on their mind, what with their city being under threat by the Plague, fear and the concomitant turning to religion are remarkably absent; rather, the stories which the protagonists tell one another to while away the time in the seclusion of a hillside villa are about man and his foibles, seemingly taken from contemporary daily life; while the intrigues sometimes revolve around the use one can make in urban society of a well-turned phrase or a clever repartee, they mostly dwell on sex; they portray, often wittily, a world of hen-pecked husbands and cuckolding wives, of fornicating priests, even.

Though the 'great' tradition of which men like Chaucer and Boccaccio were part, was firmly embedded in the Christian culture of Europe, those who were part of it surmounted the local limitations of the 'small tradition' precisely because of the influence of writing, which can disseminate ideas, and precisely because their different economic and social position meant that they did move around more, meeting others and exchanging ideas.

Warriors and courtiers travelled, as Chaucer's knight amply illustrates, if only to join a fighting band of mercenary knights or to participate in a big tournament, to attend a dynastic marriage with a great show of power and might, or to finish some business at an important administrative conference.

A Burgundian nobleman like Guillebert de Lannoy (1386–1462) journeyed to eastern Europe several times. Because of the wars between the Brandenburg or Teutonic knights against the Slav tribes who, living along the Baltic coast and in western Russia, were felt to live beyond the edge of civilization and hence to be 'barbaric', this region was seen for a long time as a desirable 'field of honour', as Chaucer describes it for his ideal knight. Lannoy also attended jousts in Castile and, with what could be called a mixture of duty and pleasure, fought the Moors twice on the Christian-Islamic border in central Spain, another region where fame could be earned. Some time later he visited the Nasrid sultan's palace in Granada, almost as a tourist. But he also travelled on a diplomatic-military mission (read: as a spy) to the nascent Turkish Empire. And finally, he went to the Holy Land, as a pilgrim.[68]

Merchants travelled, though, at this time, really transcontinental business trips were not yet customary. Still, they might journey beyond the rivers and mountains that bounded their own region; even when establishing their own permanent communities in far-away cities, as Italians did in Flanders, creating a home away from home, they could not but experience the otherness of a strange environment, Christian and yet different.

Monks and priests travelled, if only to the neighbouring bishop's town or, of course, to Rome, where the Pope resided. Increasingly, however, they took the road to go and study at some famous cathedral school in another part of Europe. Indeed, in the course of the eleventh century, the first universities developed, mostly in towns, where cathedral schools had paved the way for a tradition of higher education that now, with the increase of population and the growing need of well-trained men for the service of Church and State, found a new outlet.[69] Many of the new urban academies quickly achieved a supra-regional fame and function, such as the one at Bologna, known all over Europe for the excellence of its teaching of Roman Law.

The importance of the universities

From far and wide students and teachers began to pour into the universities. From the eleventh century onwards, this phenomenon clearly contributed to the formation of a Christian, elite culture as an integrated, European culture.[70] The meeting of minds from different backgrounds and regions influenced a way of critical thinking, a creative mentality that, despite the stultifying and in-bred atmosphere that often characterized these institutes of learning, proved of great importance to the development of Europe.

In order to ameliorate the conditions under which an intelligentsia could develop, in November 1158, the Holy Roman Emperor Frederic I issued a decree to all his dominions which, among other things, ordered a safe-conduct to be given to all students and teachers who travelled for the sake of education:

> Bishops, abbots, dukes and all the judges and most eminent men of our sacred palace having diligently considered the matter, we grant this favour of our dutiful love to all scholars who are travelling for the sake of their studies, and especially to teachers of the divine and sacred laws: that they and their representatives may safely come to the places in which letters are studied and live safely in them.
>
> For we consider it fitting . . . that we should with a certain particular love defend from all harm all those by whose knowledge the world is enlightened and the lives of subjects are moulded into obedience to God and to us, his servants. They all excite compassion, for they have made themselves exiles for love of knowledge.[71]

Once they were studying at a university, students could follow the method set out by the famous 'scholastic' Petrus Abelardus or Peter Abelard (1079–1142). Just after 1120 he had prepared a syllabus in which he juxtaposed conflicting passages taken from the works of the Church Fathers. In the foreword to this text, known as *Sic et Non*, Abelard explains how a real scholar ought to work critically:

> We should . . . take great care that we are not being deceived by a false attribution or by corruption of the text itself. For a great many apocryphal writings were headed with the names of saints, that they might carry authority; and some even of the texts of the Holy Testaments were corrupted through the fault of the copyists. . . . Let us simply say that it is written in Matthew and John that the lord was sacrificed at the sixth hour, but Mark says the third hour. This was an error of the copyists, and 'the sixth hour' was originally written in Mark, but many thought the Greek letter was a gamma. . . . So if perchance there appears to be something in the writings of the saints which is not in harmony with truth . . . either we should suppose that that portion of the text is not faithfully translated or is corrupt, or we should confess that we do not understand it. . . .
>
> When different things are said about the same matter, it is necessary to discuss thoroughly what is intended as a binding precept and what as a dispensation relaxing the law or an exhortation to perfection, so that we may seek to resolve the conflict by taking into account the difference of intentions. . . . We can easily resolve a great many disputes if we can maintain that the same words have been used with different meanings by different authors. . . . If it happens that there is such an obvious conflict that it cannot be resolved by any argument, then the authorities must be compared, and the one whose testimony is more robust and more fully confirmed should be preferred. . . .
>
> The outstanding canonical authority of the Old and New Testaments is in a different category from the books of later writers. If anything in the Bible strikes you as absurd, it is not permissible to say 'The author of this book did not uphold the truth', but that either the manuscript is false, or the translator made a mistake, or that you do not understand it. But if the little works of later men which are contained in innumerable books are thought to diverge from the truth (perhaps because they are not understood in the original sense), then the reader or listener is free to judge, and to approve what he likes and condemn what he dislikes and anything of that kind, unless the argument or account in the book is supported by sure reasons.[72]

This rationalistically logical, almost experimental way of looking at the world and everything in it, may well have been stimulated by the contacts between Christian scholars and the Islamic universities of the Iberian peninsula. Indeed, it has been argued that the European universities themselves, as well as the structure of their curricula, originated in or were heavily influenced by the Islamic colleges or *madrassas* and their teaching methods.[73] Though this may be overstating the case, the importance of Europe's cultural contacts with the Islamic world in this field, too, certainly should not be underestimated.

Since the eleventh century, a process of cultural fusion, already long in the making, was intensified. It occurred when the island of Sicily was 'reconquered' from the Islamic Berber rulers. Now dominated by Norman rulers who cleverly played the Christian against the Islamic world, it was the University of Salerno that served as a window through which Europe catched a glimpse of a culture, especially a scientific culture, that was far in advance of developments in peninsular Italy and elsewhere. Through Salerno, medical research, based on the Islamic elaboration of the ideas of the Greek physicist Galen, came to Europe where such notions as the circulation of blood or the empirical treatment of women's diseases, though received with deep distrust by traditional practitioners, did not fail to slowly influence the vision of man and his body.

Meanwhile, on the Iberian peninsula, Islamic kingdoms had flourished since the eighth century, ruling most of what is now Spain. Learning also thrived there, in a way not yet manifest in Christian Europe. The eleventh-century jurist Said al-Andalusi, active in Toledo, in his description of the world ascertained that the Christians, whom he placed in the lowest of the three classes of human beings, were stupid. He attributed this partly to the fact that they did not study physics and the other exact sciences.[74] He was, of course, not entirely wrong; during these centuries, perhaps due to the Koran's admonition that the faithful should study Allah's creation in all its manifold aspects, the empirical strain in Islamic thinking was definitely stronger than in Christian thought.

The cultural situation had become more complicated when Christian princelings from the mountains of northern Spain started very slowly to 'reconquer' the peninsula.[75] Soon, several Christian kingdoms occupied the entire northern half of Spain. In 1492, the last Islamic kingdom, of Granada in Andalusia, was conquered by Ferdinand of Aragon and Isabella of Castile, the heirs of two long lines of Christian-Iberian princes, whose earlier marriage had laid the basis for the future Spanish state. With the fall of Granada, 'Europe' as a geographical entity again appeared to be a Christian world. It is true that the conquerors added force to the idea of Europe as a Christian continent, working, albeit not always consciously so, towards a 'territorial rounding off' of a Europe which increasingly defined itself as Christian. Yet in the process of the *Reconquista*, Europe not only had been absorbing a body of classical thought via the 'heathenish world' of Islam, but also had imbibed part of that Islamic culture itself. The Islamic-Greek influence had so fundamentally confronted Christian civilization with its origins, the classical tradition, that at least the educated culture of Europe, the intellectual or 'great' tradition, was no longer the same.[76]

With the gradual establishment of Christian rule over the Islamic parts of Spain, the great centres of learning had come into the power of Christian rulers and, of course, of the Christian clergy. Often, bigotry led to the destruction of irreplaceable cultural treasures. Luckily, however, some Spanish princes were aware of the unique opportunity to broaden their horizon.

Among them was King Alfonso X of Castile (1221–84), rightly called 'el Sabio' (the Learned). A gifted poet himself, who left a great collection of song texts, written in Galician, the poetical language of the time, he also protected and propagated the work of the so-called 'Toledo School of Translators'. This was a group of scholars who spent their lives translating the Arabic and Hebrew texts they had found in the conquered cities. Often consulting with their Islamic and Jewish colleagues – the Jews had been made as welcome in the Islamic world as they had been oppressed in Christian Europe – they produced a great number of translations, both in Latin and in Spanish, which King Alfonso made the state language; thus, all kinds of new knowledge were now revealed to Christian Europe.

Also, the fame of the libraries of the renowned Islamic universities soon attracted students and scholars from all over the Christian world. For about three hundred years, from the twelfth to the fifteenth centuries, as the Spaniards pushed their frontier to the south, they flocked to Toledo, Cordoba and Granada to study the translations now produced of the Arabic versions of classical Greek texts on law, philosophy and the sciences, texts which had disappeared in Europe or which the Church had deliberately 'forgotten' because they conflicted with Christian doctrine. Of course, they also read those texts in which the Islamic scholars themselves had commented and elaborated on the Greek tradition.

Returning to Europe, to their monasteries and universities, these scholars contributed to the wider acceptance of the Ptolemaic world-view, which presented the world as a globe; thus disappeared gradually the notion of a flat earth which had, until then, been held by most, albeit not all Europeans. New ideas in the fields of astronomy and mathematics were spread as well. Most important perhaps, the idea that the only purpose of man's existence on earth lay in preparing him for a life after death, in the world of heaven, which was, after all, the basis of Church doctrine, this idea, too, began to fade under the influence of the classical cosmology, which centred more on man and his role in this world.

The resulting confrontation between the traditional scholastic culture of the Church and the many new ideas in all fields of scholarship and science greatly intensified the old tension between the classical heritage and Christian theology; it was a tension that had to be resolved somehow. Thomas Aquinas (1225–74), reflecting on what Augustine had already worked out in the fourth and fifth centuries during that much earlier confrontation between belief and reason, created a synthesis. He wanted to reconcile, on the one hand, the Church's interpretation of the Bible and, on the other hand, Aristotle's thinking about man and nature, society and learning, as now understood through the texts of such Islamic scholars as Ibn Sinna (980–1037) and Ibn Rushd (1126–98), known in Europe as Avicenna and Averroës. Ibn Sinna wrote important texts on medicine, which, combining Greek and Indian learning with many practical insights, greatly influenced Jewish doctors, almost the only scholarly practitioners in this field in all of Europe. He was also a philosopher, arguing that the 'forms' – souls – flowing from God became manifest in matter, which exists eternally with God, who is the 'unmoved mover'. Ibn Rushd elaborated on this idea. For him, religion was the 'visible' presentation of that which can be reasoned about philosophically, aiming primarily at all those who could not simply follow this reasoning, namely the majority of people.

Thomas Aquinas now proposed that man is endowed with an insubstantial, immortal soul. One of the most important aspects of the soul is reason, so that even 'the humanity of man flows from his participation in reason.' Reason enables man to achieve knowledge. Thus, man can know all that has been created: nature. That which apparently cannot be reasoned about, God, will nevertheless be accepted by man as true, from the deepest part of his being. Thomas therefore wrote, among other things, that:

> Because it transcends understanding, our belief cannot be proven by intellectual reasoning. However, because it is true and thus does not conflict with reason, it also cannot in any way be toppled by oppressively rational arguments.[77]

However, the tension which Thomas had hoped to resolve remained inherent in Christian culture, if only because the process of assimilating classical elements into that culture was pursued on more and more fronts.

Meanwhile, one certainly should not think of European universities, where old and new were taught, where Thomas's thoughts flourished but heterodox sounds could be heard as well, as being quiet havens of learning and research, only. What life in the academies was like in practice can be inferred from the writings of Jacques de Vitry (c.1180–c.1240), a prominent clergyman. The picture he paints of Paris, where the Sorbonne counted as one of the foremost academies of Christendom, is rather less than elevating.

De Vitry makes clear not only that teachers' standards are not very high but also that many students are studying for the wrong reasons. Moreover, he observes the important role played even then by national rivalry and prejudice and the harm they do to the ideal of the university. All sorts of cultural stereotypes seem to be in circulation, some already very old, such as remarks on the uncouth behaviour of Germans during feasts: we have seen these in Tacitus and other Roman authors who wrote about the Celts and Germans. Notice how clearly the author shows that in the lands we now call France and Italy many and very different 'nationalities' were distinguished at that time, corresponding with political unities since dismantled, such as the county of Poitou, the duchy of Burgundy, the Lombardy region, and so on:

> Almost all the students at Paris, foreigners and natives, did absolutely nothing except learn or hear something new. Some studied merely to acquire knowledge, which is curiosity. Others to acquire fame, which is vanity. Others still for the sake of gain, which is cupidity and the vice of simony. Very few studied for their own edification, or that of others. They wrangled and disputed not merely about the various sects or about some discussions; but the differences between the countries also caused dissensions, hatreds and virulent animosities among them, and they impudently uttered all kinds of affronts and insults against one another.

They affirmed that the English were drunkards and had tails. The sons of France proud, effeminate and carefully adorned like women. They said that the Germans were furious and obscene at their feasts. The Normans, vain and boastful. The Poitevins, traitors and always adventurers. The Burgundians they considered vulgar and stupid. The Bretons were reputed to be fickle and changeable. . . . The Longobards were called avaricious, vicious and cowardly. The Romans, seditious, turbulent and slanderous. . . . After such insults from words, they often came to blows.

I will not speak of those logicians before whose eyes flitted constantly 'the lice of Egypt', that is to say, all the sophistic subtleties, so that no one could comprehend their eloquent discourses in which, as says Isaiah, 'there is no wisdom'. As to the doctors of theology, 'seated in Moses' seat', they were swollen with learning, but their charity was not edifying. Teaching and not practicing, they have become 'as sounding brass or a tinkling cymbal', or like a canal of stone, always dry, which ought to carry water to 'the bed of spices'. They not only hated one another, but by their flatteries they enticed away the students of others; each one seeking his own glory, but caring not a whit about the welfare of souls.[78]

No wonder Pope Gregory IX considered it necessary to interfere. On 13 April 1231, he issued a bull dealing with teaching and the management of university institutions, but also laying down the law on the contents of science and scholarship:

Bishop Gregory, servant of the servants of God, to his beloved sons, all the masters and scholars of Paris, greeting and the apostolic blessing.

May Paris, the mother of sciences, be famous in her riches. . . . Since untidiness can easily creep in where there is no order, we grant you the power to make prudent statutes and ordinances concerning the time and the manner of lecturing and disputing; on the regulation dress; on the burial of the dead; and on who of the bachelors must lecture, and when and on what subject they must do so. . . .

We further ordain that masters of art shall always give one lecture on Priscian and shall lecture on one book after another in an orderly fashion. They shall not use at Paris those books of natural philosophy which have on sure grounds been prohibited at a provincial council until they have been examined and cleansed of every suspicion of error. Masters and students of theology shall strive to employ themselves in the faculty which they profess, and shall not parade as philosophers. . . .

They shall not speak in the language of the people, nor confound the sacred language with the profane, but shall discuss in the schools only those questions which can be determined by means of theological books and the treatises of the Holy Fathers.[79]

Language, of course, always has been and will remain an important cultural factor, not only in communication but also in defining different groups within society. At this time, it could be divisive, as was the Latin used by the Church and by scholars, that was not understood by the great majority of the European faithful, or the Norman French, the language of the conquerors that was imposed upon Anglo-Saxon-speaking England.[80] But using the same Latin as the *lingua franca*, or through personal multilingualism, often in some of the many forms of German or French, or even something in between, people like the bureaucrat Chaucer and the nobleman De Lannoy as well as the many anonymous students travelling all over Europe to study at the best universities were able to communicate with their peers. Such multilingualism existed not only in the great European capitals and centres of learning but also on the periphery, for instance at the count of Holland's court in The Hague.[81] So, among the Europeans, there was division in unity, and unity in division, starting with such a basic cultural phenomenon as language.

A certain feeling of community gradually emerged, most markedly among the people who were part of the 'great tradition', which ever more clearly became the basis of an 'idea of Europe', though one must admit that despite these people's greater 'cultural competence', they, too, did not always manage to avoid judgements, prejudices and condemnations.

However elitist the new notions might be, they yet developed along the roads worn into the landscape of Europe by the two largest groups of travellers, the anonymous armies using the highways constructed by the Roman legions, and the pilgrims who trod the routes linking northern and central Europe to the south-east and the south-west from the time Christianity had been introduced. Indeed, a network of trajects developed along which, largely unintentionally, unconsciously, from monastery to monastery, from town to town, from university to university, forms of culture were being transferred.[82]

Interlude

The worlds of Europe, *c*.1400–1800

Writing about Europe poses the central question whether and, if so, to what extent there was a European awareness among the 'Europeans'? Was there a common culture which bound together regions and countries, states and nationalities across all sorts of natural and artificial borders? On an even more fundamental level one must ask how those who inhabited the continent in the past did actually live, and whether, from their cultural condition, they knew about the different regions and, on the basis of this knowledge, understood and valued each other's ideas and lifestyles?

In the previous chapters the many and radical changes which economy, society and culture went through in the course of the thirteenth, fourteenth and fifteenth centuries have been outlined. However, it is vitally important to establish that for the great majority of the population many of these changes and, indeed, the subsequent technological innovations were hardly noticeable, if at all. Indeed, one must be aware that up till *c*.1800, Europe actually consisted of 'two nations': on the one hand, the agricultural population who lived their lives according to a rhythm fixed largely by nature and which remained fairly constant until the end of the eighteenth century;[1] on the other hand, since the eleventh and twelfth centuries, were the people of the cities, which in many respects remained distinct from their rural hinterlands; there, trade, banking and incipient industry flourished; there, political life had its centre;[2] there, new ideas were formulated and discussed in schools and universities.

Of course, there was a measure of interaction between these two worlds: economically they were increasingly dependent upon one another, and culturally they shared a number of characteristics. The relationship was stronger in Europe's more urbanized regions, such as northern and central Italy, parts of France, southern and Rhinelandic Germany, Flanders, Holland and southern England. Here, many new notions and inventions were developed and intro-duced into the countryside from the towns where they were first formulated or practised – increasingly from the sixteenth century onwards.[3] However, the larger part of rural Europe experienced little or no such influences up till the late eighteenth and even early nineteenth centuries.

Consequently, it has to be maintained that in the majority of cases, towns and countryside largely had their own cultures: whereas western Europe may have had some 20,000 towns, it had some 160,000 villages, where the majority of Europeans lived.[4]

A world of villages

From the beginnings of agriculture in Europe, in the centuries between 10,000 and 5000 BC, until the eighteenth century AD, between 70 and 80 per cent of Europe's population were farmers or, to be more precise, survived on the basis of agricultural labour. People worked their own farms or tenanted other people's property, always employing their next of kin, both females and children, for the farming economy was very much a family economy. If one were born without property, one would seek employment as an agricultural labourer on big rural estates. Thus, people spent their lives tied to the soil, sometimes legally but always materially. In large parts of Europe, especially the central and eastern regions, it was not even possible for people to leave the land they tilled because they were, to a greater or lesser extent, bound to their landlord in some form of serfhood.

Fundamentally, a farmer's life was determined by the need to cultivate the soil in order to provide that most basic commodity, food. Not surprisingly, the one and only material supplication in the most important prayer of the Christian world, the 'Our Father', was: 'give us this day our daily bread'. But the Old Testament told believers they had to earn this bread with their own sweat. Their success determined whether they could keep going on the right side of the line which separated survival from death by starvation, the very thin line which in our time is still so horribly obvious in the 'Third World'.[5]

Farming life took place according to a simple, iron regularity. Getting up with the sun to plough, to sow or to harvest, and to tend the cattle, and going to bed when dusk fell. There was usually no money for lighting the houses during the evening hours. Thus, people did not get around to what are now normal forms of after work relaxation. Moreover, working as a farmer was tough; one needed all one's strength and therefore all the sleep one could get – and that was not much between sunset and sunrise. On top of that, the majority of the farming population were not very strong. The composition of the daily diet was limited and, by our standards, unhealthy. Such things as an endemic illness caused by certain worms accounted for a general weakness among hundreds of thousands of farming people.[6] Health care was not available to many, as most qualified doctors lived and worked only in towns. Generally speaking, people's physical condition left much to be desired. In short, most people lacked the time, the money and indeed the energy to spend on sports or play. As to other forms of culture, reading and studying, for example, these were almost totally absent in peasant societies.

This brings us to the question concerning which means of communication would have enabled Europeans to become acquainted with each other's ways of life. Before the range and depth of communication extended, first with the gradual penetration of print culture in the sixteenth century, but, effectively, only with the advance of mass communication in the late nineteenth century, there really were only two channels to transmit information: oral and hand-written communication and, to a lesser extent, the visual messages of paintings and frescos and, again, from the sixteenth century onwards, printed images. However, a more detailed consideration immediately shows the limitations of even those media.

Until the nineteenth century, Europe's farming population was largely illiterate.[7] Apart from the expense involved in education, for most people a formal training was totally irrelevant. Reading, writing and arithmetic were of no conceivable use when handling a plough or a hayfork was the most important technique. And, moreover, where were farmers' children to find the time to learn? As soon as they could walk they were expected to give a helping hand on the farm. There simply was no time or money to go to school. Admittedly, in winter farming partly came to a standstill. Children could have attended school then. But for most the question of how to get there would have presented a huge problem. Only rich farmers possessed a donkey or horse, but such traction animals were too valuable for agricultural work to carry children to school every day. Of course, children could have walked. But not every village had its own school – actually, these were located only in the larger rural centres or in cities of some size. Thus, a walk to school would have meant a journey of ten or more kilometres on average every day for most farmers' children. Therefore, school attendance and, consequently, learning to read and write largely were precluded, except for those who overcame all these problems and, at least in winter time when their labour was not needed, sought some basic education. And even those who were sent to school after all, went there not really to learn how to read and write, but to be taught a certain discipline and some notions as to how to behave[8]. This meant that for most people the transfer of culture through the written word was barred.

Other forms of large-scale communication were also lacking in the agrarian communities which comprised the larger part of Europe. For people engaged in agriculture, travel, certainly travel for pleasure, was an unknown concept. Any trip cost time and money, precisely the two things which farmers did not have. For the majority of people a visit to the weekly market was the only connection between life on the farm and in the neighbouring village, and the outside world. That world began in the city.

For the countryside in Europe, the city was friend and foe, nearby and yet far away, a separation, a cultural division which in many regions lasted until the nineteenth century. Entering the city gates, countryfolk were confronted with different habits and morals, with people who often looked down on farmers as rustics or outsiders, because they had a different culture which was considered less sophisticated and less civilized: they could not read or write, they lived in and with wild nature, and in many of their traditions reflected the untamed, dangerous elements of that nature. A mixture of disdain and fear frequently characterized the attitude of city dwellers towards countryfolk who, in their turn, were inclined to distrust city dwellers as stuck-up cheats.[9]

Yet to country people, going to the weekly market, while an economic necessity, also meant having an outing, seeing other folk, hearing the stories of travelling salesmen and pedlars, and listening to actors and singers, who opened a window on the world, on life outside their own little village communities. But the market was a serious business: people had to sell their wares and to buy the necessities not available in the village. There was little time left to relax in the tavern or just strolling along the street to listen to the latest news. At the most, people heard some strange tales, told in bits and pieces, without grasping the details.

People from the countryside had to leave the city before dark, primarily because the gates were shut and those who did not live within the walls were expected to remove themselves. Moreover, it was not advisable to travel the Lord's roads after night had fallen. Until late in the eighteenth century, large parts of the countryside were perilous indeed. Few people left the safety of their own surroundings for pleasure, simply because travelling was not free of danger. One should not forget that great stretches of land were not cultivated but consisted of huge moors and dark forests. Highwaymen could rob you of the profits of a week's or even a long year's hard work, not to mention worse things. Besides roving bands of professional robbers you might encounter plundering soldiers 'living off the land' to improve their meagre pay or farmers who had become penniless and rebellious through failed harvests or other economic disasters; they all made the countryside very unsafe indeed, the more so as a regular police force was still unheard of there. Besides, the roads were mostly unmetalled, unlit and not signposted. Hence, manifold dangers persisted in the rural areas of the Netherlands and England certainly until the eighteenth century, and in the vast, but remote and sparsely populated parts of Scandinavia, France, Germany, Italy and Spain, as well as in central and eastern Europe well into the nineteenth century.

But it was not only people who made life difficult for the traveller. There were ghosts and spirits, who had all sorts of nasty plans up their sleeves. There were even devils, like the wicked Moenen, who meets the girl Mariken, in the play *Mariken van Nieumeghen*, written around the year 1500 in the eastern Netherlands. This is a gripping, even fascinating play and, moreover, a historical source which has much to tell us about the culture and mentality of 'ordinary' people in these centuries of transition.

On market day, the girl Mariken, who keeps house for her uncle, a priest, walks to Nijmegen to do her shopping. She has to cover a considerable distance and in the evening, after an exhausting day and an unsettling experience with a distant relative, she also has to return again. On the way back, as darkness falls, she realizes she will not be able to get home in time and starts looking for shelter in the roadside woods. There, the devil Moenen confronts her. With promises of plentiful and delicious food, of wealth and of knowledge, he seduces her. She decides to accompany him to the big city, Antwerp, at that time the trading metropolis not only of the Netherlands but also of north-western Europe. The life they embark on there is filled with all the sins known to man in the late fifteenth century: excessive food and wine, whoring and, moreover, too much seeking after knowledge of heaven and earth – a privilege not of man but of God. In presenting these pleasures, the play actually contains a series of morals and warnings, which the spectators would have understood from their own experiences. One of the messages was: do not travel, certainly not by night – it leads only to misery.

Thus people did not travel unless it was absolutely necessary. As they could not read, either, the two most obvious and influential means of communication and information were lacking: contact with other people and ideas through meeting them in the flesh, and contact with other people and ideas through the written word. In short, the culture and mentality of most who lived in Europe's agricultural communities were severely limited. By material limitations: a lack of money. By spatial limitations: distances which were too great. And by mental limitations: the lack of communication.

As a result, the factual and mental horizon of most Europeans reached only as far as they could see: to the end of the fields, to the edges of the village. Every community was largely closed in on itself, with its own local culture which, despite its riches of orally transmitted ideas, of social organization and custom, was only slightly and slowly influenced by external factors of change. Life revolved around work, interrupted only by such moments of relaxation as the annual harvest festival – the origin of the village fair – and the many days which the Catholic Church had marked as special, such as Christmas, Easter, the feast of the patron saint of the local church and a number of other holy days. On those days, if no famine reigned, villagers would feast on beer and meat, there would be dance and music, as well as games, and itinerant musicians and players would perform.

Let us pause for a moment to reflect on the role of the Catholic Church, the Church of Rome. It called itself universal as, indeed, it was in about 1500 because all people in western and central Europe were still Catholic. This Church actually tried to govern the very essence of the lives of Europeans, their actions but, even more important, for guiding those actions, their deepest thoughts. Every community had a church as its visual anchor, its social and cultural centre. The local priest, besides being a shepherd of souls, frequently doubled as a doctor, a village arbiter and, if possible, a schoolmaster, though the supposedly literate clergy often verged on the edge of illiteracy. The Church taught people to love their neighbours and to obey the ecclesiastical and secular authorities as well as telling them about the existence of heaven, hell and purgatory, which would harbour them after death. Above all loomed the constant presence of a severe and yet good God.

Here, we come up against an apparent contradiction. For centuries, the priests of the Church were the pre-eminent guardians of a long tradition of knowledge which was passed on from generation to generation in manuscript texts. Yet their flock, the faithful, unable to read, could participate only with eye and ear in the culture which these priests controlled. Nor did the Church really want to provide extensive instruction to the masses. As an institution, it actually considered knowledge of and insight into the great problems of theology and cosmology superfluous and even dangerous for ordinary man. It would only keep him from his daily work, or, worse, tempt him to a life of sin, as Mariken experienced.

Because the clergy, at least partly, were the 'information caste', they wanted to preserve their exclusiveness. In fact, they derived their position from an almost magical power. Ideally, they could read and write, which already resembled magic in the eyes of many people; they knew and understood more than most others; they could explain or even predict simple natural phenomena that so terrified most people. Not surprisingly, they wanted to retain this position of power. If only, therefore, knowledge was not shared with as many people as possible; on the contrary, it was monopolized by the monks in their monasteries and by the representatives of the Church, who were often the only educated persons in Europe's village world.

Whatever the Church chose to teach to the masses was mainly taught through the spoken word, from the pulpit, and through images, visual representations: statues and paintings. On the façades and portals of churches and chapels, on their walls and ceilings, stories from the Bible and edifying scenes from the saints' lives were depicted for all those believers who could not read. After the coming of printing, crude printed images were used as well.

A world of villages, and of villagers. Were they Europeans? Word and image had ensured that in the period beginning with the time that Christianity first became established, i.e. in the fifth and sixth centuries, and ending *c.*1500, all Europeans up to the invisible dividing line from the Baltic to the Balkans still recognized the Pope in Rome as the head of their Church. When Mariken, by Divine Providence, was brought to repent of her sins, she travelled to Rome to crave forgiveness. Everyone felt Christian in the Catholic sense. Yet what this meant in the daily routine of those who dwelt on the other side of mountains and rivers was something most people never asked themselves. Christianity created a common culture whose solidarity seldom could or had to be tested in practice.

Thus the mental world of Europeans, of farming communities in particular, differed greatly from what we can imagine today. What occupied the common people in Europe? In any case, few or none of the things we fill our lives with. There was no television, no film, no radio. There were no newspapers and, for most people, no books. Sport did not exist as an organized leisure activity, or as passive entertainment. Indeed, outside the circles of the aristocracy and the well-to-do urban middle classes, leisure was not a concept.[10] Politics hardly played a role, at least, not in the sense of national or world politics, if only because there was virtually no information about this. Moreover, parties, programmes, all the things which nowadays stimulate political awareness or discussion did not exist. It was only in the big cities that there was any sort of political consciousness.

Of course, people knew about wars, but mainly as something which occurred in their own surroundings: until the end of the seventeenth century all over Europe small or great wars were waged somewhere every year. But people hardly realized what were the larger issues behind them. There were no news analyses and commentaries. War was simply a part of daily life, incomprehensible, as was so much. It was certainly not an intellectual or moral problem.

What did actually occupy people historians have tried to infer from the stories which they told each other, the songs they sang, and the poems they recited. In the evenings, especially in winter, the villagers gathered to listen to storytellers and singers – local people or travelling ones – who were the preservers of the complex collective memory of the village community, circumscribing a world at once local and cosmic, through tradition and myth. Stories, songs and poems were passed on orally, from generation to generation. It was not until the eighteenth and nineteenth centuries that assiduous scholars began to collect and record them. Charles Perrault, in France, and the brothers Grimm, in Germany, carried out pioneering work in this field; they, and a host of other scholars who studied folklore gave us a chance to look back into the past through those stories, to the lives and minds of those who did not normally record their ideas and feelings. Although, of course, these tales are heavily filtered by time, by centuries of oral transmission, by the writing of their final recorders, the other sources which document the life of ordinary people certainly are as biased, if not more so. For though secular and ecclesiastical records yield fascinating insights, too, they nearly always represent the culture of people's daily life through the eyes of educated middlemen – clerks and chroniclers, for whom written words were a specific world, into which the world of 'others' had to be fitted.[11] Combining all available sources, and using the visual and material evidence as well, historians nowadays venture to present an image of what went on in that largely oral culture.[12]

People were mainly occupied by what conditioned their daily lives. Therefore, eating dominates many stories: the misery caused by a lack of food and the joy when there was plenty for a change can be sensed in almost all texts. Sexuality was also important, without, however, being unrestrained.[13] Especially in the country, people enjoyed sex rather freely until the nineteenth century, when a large-scale civilizing campaign staged by the Churches and the urban middle class made many things taboo, which they came out of again only in the 1960s and 1970s. Moreover, from a psychological perspective entirely different from ours, sexuality was probably much more essential than we can imagine now. Not only was it necessary that many children be born in order to guarantee the reproduction of the species and ensure that adults would have someone to take care of them as they aged, since society made no provisions for this, but also, according to the psychologists, sexuality, letting go of oneself, was actually the only way to escape the fear of transitoriness or of death.

Death, for the average European, was uncomfortably close. Infant mortality was appallingly high and of those who survived, many still died between the ages of 30 and 40. And then, of course, there were wars; whether great or small, they seemed to be there continuously. With everyone having some experience of them in their own lives, they were spoken and sung about a great deal, if only as a sort of defiance.

Finally, natural phenomena, such as lightning and thunder, comets and solar or lunar eclipses, played a very important role in tales, poems and songs, threatening everyday life, and yet not understood. Hence the many ghosts and spirits and also the witches and wizards who appear in all sorts of stories. The former were the manifestations of the incomprehensible, of all those things for which no simple remedy could be found and the latter, if properly managed, the potential helpers in the ongoing struggle with this other world which presented itself as a continuation of daily life. Indeed, fear in the face of a world which, rather than orderly, presented itself as chaotic and unruly, was perhaps a central emotion in this Europe. To master this fear, people devised all sorts of means which were entirely rational within their mental paradigm. Not surprisingly, the supreme vision of an ordered world, where there was no fear, no want, no suffering, was paradise, a garden as unlike actual nature as possible; an 'enclosed garden' where every valley had been made plain, everything crooked straight.[14]

The one organization that helped people create order was, of course, the Church, the keeper of a faith that can be interpreted as Europe's collective attempt to bring man and nature into a balance, to make comprehensible, acceptable and liveable what was incomprehensible, unacceptable and unliveable without the help of God and the promise of heaven: the misery of every new day, the pain of life, with its many illnesses, its unavoidable death, and the question of what the purpose of it all was. Yet precisely because much of what the Church tried to teach was relatively complicated, people needed concrete help, and sought refuge with those same wizards and witches, and with sayings and charms. Most of these forms of culture, albeit denounced as superstition by the Church, in fact were the forms which that same Church had not absorbed already into its own arsenal of ritualistic action devised to make life controllable.[15] Indeed, the priests themselves often acted within and made use of a complex scenario of ways and means which definitely were not accepted by the small group who defined right speaking and acting within the Church. This situation has caused some historians to ask to what extent this culture really was Christian at all, in its ideal sense, rather than the complex survival, under different names, of more ancient beliefs branded as 'paganism' by the same Church.[16]

A world of towns

The majority of city dwellers consisted of salaried labourers and free artisans, with a 'middle class' made up of entrepreneurs in various fields of trade and industry, as well as of professional people who served the needs of these groups in so far as they necessitated producing written records: lawyers, public notaries and town officials. This, in turn, presupposed a group of people, of teachers at various levels, who were capable of instructing all these men in the arts of literacy and numeracy. For apart from reading and writing, arithmetic had become ever more essential, especially to urban society. What with book-keeping, handling an abacus, trying to account for constantly shifting exchange rates between the hundreds of different monetary systems, measuring the contents of ships and carts, of tuns and bales, Europe, urban Europe, was becoming a rational, measured society.[17]

Whereas these teachers might be some of the many priests or monks who constituted a considerable proportion of the population in almost every European city up till the sixteenth century – indeed, even the physical city itself was often dominated by the sometimes huge, walled properties of churches and monasteries – this situation changed when the influence of the Church decreased; in the course of the sixteenth century, secular, professional teachers began to set up schools as well.

The ruling elite or the urban patriciate might consist either of the wealthiest entrepreneurs or of a mixture – sometimes through intermarriage – of this group and of nobles from the surrounding countryside. The latter, however, might themselves be descended from traders or bankers who, in earlier generations, had acquired landed estates and sometimes even titles of nobility. For the distinctions between classes, especially in those regions where trade and industry became important, certainly were not as rigid as often seems.[18] Nobles would invest or even actively participate in banking and trading, and wealthy tradespeople would retire to the country to enjoy a more 'noble' life, building luxurious houses, collecting books and paintings, if only of faked ancestors and, invoking that most aristocratic of privileges, going out to hunt.

Economic life, in the city, was of a different nature than in the countryside. Artisanal production could be family-centred, as of old, with both women and children being integral parts of a 'family economy', but often developed into big enterprise, employing dozens or even hundreds of labourers, sometimes under one roof in a system of proto-industrial manufacture.

Trade, too, could be small-scale, specialized and local, or cover many products and regions, involving the set-up of networks of 'counting' houses all over Europe. Normally, entrepreneurs would like to staff these offices with family members, as being the most trustworthy, for the ties of kinship, even outside the conjugal family, were felt strongly, as still is common business practice in eastern Asia. However, when more capital was invested, the need to expand, to specialize, to attract the most capable soon resulted in the employment of non-relatives as well.

Meanwhile, increasing competition in the urban economy, especially in times of crisis, as, for example, in the late sixteenth and early seventeenth centuries, resulted in a growing tendency to prevent women from taking an active role in the production process. All over Europe, the corporations or guilds in which production was mostly organized, adopted rules which forced women who had set up business for themselves, or had inherited it from their deceased husband, to either remarry, choosing a male member of their guild, or to sell out to such a person. This is not to say that women did not work. The poorer ones most certainly did, especially in the bigger cities, where they would be likely to make up most of the marketing population, or else serve in the more affluent households.[19]

With changing labour relations, especially among the prosperous trading classes, a shift in gender roles came about as well. Men who tried to emulate the elite would prefer their womenfolk not to work. Those families who could afford to exempt their womenfolk from participation in the labour process often did so, aping the wealthier groups in society, especially the aristocracy who still functioned as the cultural role model. As in the aristocracy, the main role of a prosperous bourgeois woman was to provide her husband, and his family, with preferably male children to continue the line and to inherit the property, but she should not interfere in business or encroach on other male domains.[20] For aristocratic women normally did not work. In the upper reaches of the nobility, they would lead a life of luxury, participating in court society, showing off the status of their husband's family. At most, such noble ladies would supervise a big household. This might entail very practical work as well, as is evident from that fascinating cache of documents called the 'Paston Papers', which have revealed the life of a well-to-do English landowning family at the end of the fifteenth century[21]. Indeed, Margaret Paston often acted as her husband John's steward during his absence, managing his estates, advising him on his business and legal affairs, taking decisions, even. But even though the Pastons owned manor houses and castles, Margaret's lifestyle would seem to have been more bourgeois than aristocratic.

Running a large household was what many women from the affluent middle class came to do. Increasingly, this led to new ideals about femininity. A good woman was a good mother, first, and a good housewife, second. Yet it has to be said that while women in this group generally retreated from active participation in public life, their hold over their families increased, and with it their power to shape the conduct of all involved.[22]

This became more evident as economic specialization, greater wealth and the desire to demonstrate that wealth and the way of life that went with it all resulted in a situation wherein such traditional practices as using the house as an office, a shop and a warehouse at the same time were discontinued. With the separation between work and home among the more prosperous urban groups came an awareness of the home as a private place where, within the intimacy of the family, presided over by the mother, people lived a life different from the façade they presented to the public.[23]

What life was like in these bourgeois households, where there was both leisure time and money to spend on a comfortable, hospitable interior, on good food, on lighting in the evening, and so on, is shown by contemporary painting, especially from such a quintessentially urban, bourgeois society as that of the Dutch province of Holland – even though these paintings may have had some moralistic purpose, depicting desired instead of actual behaviour. They show mothers supervising their children while they prepare dinner, as well as, in the evening, people sitting around the table, playing cards or singing together, or reading by themselves – as the old burgher with his glasses, who has fallen asleep over his book.

With growing wealth and, consequently, bigger houses, notions of privacy not only separated the house from the office or the shop, but also came to extend to the spheres of parents on the one hand, and children on the other. This seems specifically to have affected the experience of sexuality as something which belonged to the adult domain of married life. Still, various bodily functions and, indeed, the body itself were not yet surrounded with the notions of intimacy, shame or taboo they were to acquire in the nineteenth century: in sixteenth- and seventeenth-century paintings, while women publicly would give their children their bare breast to suck, one sees men pissing in public, although this latter behaviour was already becoming associated with rustic boors rather than with refined urbanites.

All this, in turn, also contributed to the construction of childhood among the more well-to-do people. After infanthood, the period of being cared for by their mother, young boys and girls, though they might be physically able to participate in the work process as, indeed, their counterparts in the labouring classes both in the countryside and in towns were forced to do, entered into a period of childhood, of growing up, of further education in relative freedom.[24] Still, we should realize that the moment these children were considered to have reached adulthood occurred in their mid-teens rather than, as nowadays, in their early twenties.

Though most educated people theoretically would defend the position that man and woman were created equal, at the same time women increasingly were seen as docile, subservient even. In many countries, women's legal rights were limited; in parts of Germany, women could not even stand trial because, *de iure*, they were considered to be like children, who could not be held responsible for a crime. Indeed, if they failed to comply with the new ideals, they might be branded as 'different', as bad women. Some scholars have seen this as the birth of the evil witch, who was to become a disciplining warning to European women till the end of the eighteenth century, when the last witches were burned. Of course, the phenomenon of the witch was more complex, involving the psychology of closely knit communities, with their need to define insiders and outsiders and, equally, the need to project tensions onto specific persons.[25] In their turn, men were impressed with the notion that they were chosen to take on a double responsibility: as the *pater familias*, they were both the provider for their household, their family, as well as its public face.

The institution of marriage was the ideal basis for such ideas. However, in the thirteenth, fourteenth and fifteenth centuries, a great variety of forms of concubinage had come into use, condoned and indeed often sanctioned by the Church. Thus, it had become quite common for a couple to enter upon an engagement at the church door and then to return home and live together till the wife became pregnant; when this proof of the viability of the marriage had been obtained, the couple would return to church for the final vows at the chancel steps and then proceed to the altar for the Eucharist. Thus, in paintings of French weddings, the bride radiantly shows her pregnancy. However, numerous undesirable constructions had been devised, as witnessed by Chaucer's 'Wife of Bath', who married five times at the church door without finalizing her vows. All kinds of secular relationship rituals existed as well as, for example, when prospective partners sealed their intention to live together by jumping over a broom in front of witnesses.

While the Church was losing control over marriage and sexuality, the State became increasingly concerned about an ordered society, preferably one in which working males, the majority of tax-paying subjects, could be held responsible for the rest of the population, their families. Hence, in the late fifteenth and early sixteenth centuries, the two powers joined forces, trying to once more legalize and sacralize marriage as the only institution in which sexuality could be expressed and out of which legitimate offspring could be borne, and the family or household as the fiscal basis of society, its legal microcosmos; in both, the father ruled supreme.[26]

Much like the countryside, towns, too, whether great or small, were not quaint, idyllic communities, as nineteenth-century romantic writers or twentieth-century conservationists sometimes would have it. Admittedly, some research indicates that neighbourhoods were seemingly comfortable, closely knit groups, where the quarrels that occurred were solved through the intercession of the neighbourhood's representative, where people attended each other's funerals, even paying a penalty if they failed to turn up, and where annual gatherings were organized in the form of huge drinking and eating parties to physically and symbolically stress group harmony.[27] But other case-studies tell of poisoned letters, of abuse and defamation, of violent quarrels ending in murder and of people trying to kill their neighbours using black magic.[28]

Increasingly, the wealthy tended to congregate in a safe, comparatively spacious and clean centre, while the poor would live on the periphery. As urban populations grew to overspill the area protected by the city walls – most European cities were walled till the middle of the nineteenth century – they would live in new, often very squalid quarters which, if only for that reason, were disdainfully looked upon by the more affluent burghers. Houses here would be built of wood, and have straw roofs well into the nineteenth century. In most cities, the majority of streets were often unpaved, and mostly unlit at night. Closed sewage systems were absent. Consequently, all kinds of illnesses spread easily, creating havoc among the population, especially those who lived in cramped surroundings. Crime in violent forms was quite normal, even in the bigger cities, where there was some kind of police system. Prostitution, too, showed itself quite openly; it was not morally frowned upon, and heavily punished only when it brought syphilis into the armies.[29]

Both phenomena are amply attested in such a major town as seventeenth-century papal Rome, where a prominent citizen, Giacinto Gigli, fills his diary with notes of murders, rapes and, indeed, rampant superstition, as well as the vain efforts of the papal government to increase the moral tone of this capital of Catholic Christendom. He also notes the ways in which the authorities reacted to many kinds of undesirable behaviour, setting the stage for death – for serious crimes, till the end of the eighteenth century, were harshly dealt with; criminals were burned at the stake, hanged or quartered; such public executions were meant to show what the norms of society were, and impress upon the onlookers that order would always be restored.[30] The people would flock to these theatrically presented occasions, sometimes giving in to an almost orgiastic celebration of sin and redemption.[31]

Two worlds?

The above survey is, necessarily, very general. It synthesizes innumerable details about the equally innumerable local, self-centred and enclosed communities which comprised rural Europe; it juxtaposes these communities to the often dissimilar economic, social and cultural reality of towns. Obviously, such a representation can be invalidated by citing individual cases wherein the differences between town and countryside seem less extreme. Especially in the field of culture, towns, especially smaller ones, much resembled villages, in that there, too, one would encounter widespread illiteracy, the predominance of oral traditions, little proof of communication with the wider world and the many manifestations of what the Church called superstition.

Yet if one looks at Europe from about the fifteenth to the eighteenth centuries, bearing in mind all the details presented so far, one must conclude that there existed a deep chasm in European society. It was a chasm which was not only economic and social but primarily cultural in nature.

The mass of the peasants, living in their communities limited by the horizon, with no appreciable means of communication, had a restricted world-view. Consequently, most people also lived in great fear of everything that was not familiar and hence different. People or things that were 'different' were easily seen as alien, even as dangerous.[32] Nor were the local cultural forms consciously experienced as part of a communal European tradition. After all, education, if it reached people at all, reached most of them only as an attempt to learn to read and write. Even if they succeeded, a version of the Bible, frequently simplified in allegories and metaphors, was often their only frame of reference. The culture of Greek and Roman Antiquity was a closed book to them and many of the finer points – some historians would even argue that the essence – of Christianity often remained in the dark. Travel, unless professionally necessary, was a senseless and useless action. From itinerant preachers and pedlars they might have heard, but vaguely at most, about the Mediterranean, about the worlds of Byzantium and Islam, and probably even less about the worlds beyond the wide seas. The past consisted of stories about the village and the village community in earlier times and of folk tales and legends which put everything strange and incomprehensible in its place in a largely magical context. In short, most people lacked every reference which could give 'Europe' existence, and make it into a living concept; at most, it was just a meaningless word.

Crossing a 'border', as for example a river or a mountain, people arrived in communities with different social codes, different habits and different tongues. Hence the concept of solidarity was applied only to the limited surroundings of a person's own village or city. People were attached first and foremost to their *patria*, their *Heimat* or their native soil. Some, but certainly not all, felt themselves part of the region which had absorbed the village or city in days of old: farmers' sons who, as soldiers, served a regional leader, or village administrators who visited the regional capital with any regularity.

Regional leaders themselves – low or high ranking nobles and city administrators – equally held to their particularistic outlooks. This was certainly the case when they had to defend their power against an increasingly mighty central elite: the nobility at a princely court and the senior administrators who were the main instruments of state formation in the capital cities. In view of this complex situation, it was long before people finally began to feel part of the new, larger political structures which slowly were being formed.

Let us also remember that at least the 'ordinary man' frequently could not even talk with his 'fellow countrymen' from another region. After all, in most countries there still was no single language, taught to and spoken by everyone. Until the fourteenth century the English elite spoke French and therefore experienced difficulties communicating with the English-speaking population at large, while the Norwegian elite used Danish for much longer. In Spain the inhabitants of Catalonia or of the old kingdom around Valencia, vexed by their subjection to the Castilians, foreign oppressors from the region around Madrid who did not even speak their language, emphatically tried not to use Castilian, if only to express their deep-rooted opposition. In France the majority of the inhabitants of Provence or Brittany thought of themselves as a nation which unfortunately had not been strong enough to withstand the imperialism of the kings from the region around Paris. If only for that reason, Bretons and Provençals did not master the language which was now called French. They usually could not understand the officials who ruled them in the name of the government in the capital. Thus, communication between, for example, city officials in Gascony and the Parisian bureaucrats was possible only through an interpreter.[33] Indeed, until the nineteenth century, many 'French' people spoke only languages or dialects which their fellow countrymen could hardly understand, if at all.[34]

Central governments here and there did make attempts to codify one of the languages as the 'national' language and to impose this, by force if necessary, on the entire population of their state, yet it was a process which, due to the prevalent illiteracy, did not yield large-scale success until the introduction of general education in the nineteenth century. Only then did the farming population in the more isolated parts of France feel themselves to be French citizens.[35] And in the Northern Netherlands? Reading the minutes of the Nijmegen city council in the seventeenth century one could be forgiven for thinking that they were written in one of the varieties of the Low German that even nowadays is spoken in the Rhineland and Westphalia; it little resembled the Standard Dutch that is now the country's language. Indeed, people did not feel Dutch but rather identified themselves as Frisians, Gueldersmen or Hollanders, if they were given at all to what was, for most of them, a futile form of reflection.[36]

For the masses the 'great tradition', culture as a system of ideas and ideals articulated in the whole of Europe, was not a part of their thought and life. Obviously there was an idea of 'Europe', at least for the few who had any knowledge of the earth's shape and for whom a map was not an unreadable document. Yet for most of these it remained only a geographical notion. Europe as a dream of cultural unity continued to function in and for the small circle who had invented it: the intellectuals, the scholars and others who had had the benefit of education and who travelled – in a nutshell, the elite. They were 'the people with history', members of an ever more self-conscious, cosmopolitan and to a very large extent urban society.

By the fifteenth and sixteenth centuries, the European elite had slowly changed both in composition and in outlook, growing ever more complex. Besides the monks and warriors, merchants had been acquiring increasing economic power since the twelfth century. In the succeeding centuries, this power was also translated into political terms. Thus, the elite was by no means a closed circle any more. There were the leaders of the First Estate, the lords spiritual, the clergy with their Christian and thus, according to their own definition, universal culture embracing the whole of Europe. There also were the leaders of the Second Estate, the lords temporal or the nobility, who, it is true, had participated in that culture since the eighth and ninth centuries but who had begun to think more and more 'nationally' within the framework of the various budding states.

But increasingly in evidence was a Third Estate, made up largely of wealthy entrepreneurs and professionals, the most powerful group in the urban middle class. Their bases were the often independent cities which made them feel that, unlike warriors and the clergy, they did not fit into such large unities as State and Church, which transcended local borders. Partly as a result, they formed values which were different, at least to a certain extent. Even though they often had an international economic outlook, politically and culturally they had only a local orientation. And even though they might model their material culture on the example of the older elite, many aristocratic values, especially those associated with knightly culture, remained alien to them. Looking for economic and political power, they sponsored both education and the sciences, if only for utilitarian motives. They were also an important factor in the development of controlled tolerance, but, yet again, largely for pragmatic reasons; for tolerance or, to give the idea a larger context, the idea of a civil society, regulated by rules of law which applied to each and everyone indistinctly, proved an essential prerequisite for the expansion and power of this group.

Regardless of their socio-economic complexity, at the same time this elite remained unequivocally a cultural upper class because of its common background. After all, it consisted of people who accepted the ideology of Christianity because they were raised in Christian doctrine from childhood. They also shared common norms of civilized behaviour, which came into existence precisely during these centuries as a result of the increasingly literate interaction between classical Antiquity and Church teaching, an interaction particularly expressed in formal further education. Thus, together, these groups were the main agents of various new developments that began to influence Europe.

Part III

Continuity and change

New ways of looking at man and the world

7 A new society
Europe's changing views of man

The survival of classical culture and the beginnings of Humanism

It is worth bearing in mind that a resurgence of interest in the culture of the classical Greek and Roman worlds occurred at the court of Charlemagne, and can be noted even more markedly from the twelfth century onwards and not, as is so often written, only as late as the fifteenth and sixteenth centuries. Indeed, it is probably more correct to observe that this interest had always been present since the decline of the Roman Empire in the third and fourth centuries. Though many classical texts were deliberately destroyed or simply lost in the course of time, the Catholic Church had assiduously retained all those elements of classical civilization of which the underlying ideas did not conflict with Christian doctrine, and had passed these on through the manuscript texts which were the primary carriers of information. Thus, the 'great tradition' continued, for the cultured elite always had access to, and communicated with the culture of the ancient Mediterranean.

A man like Dante Alighieri was a prime example of this 'great tradition'.[1] Fully versed in classical and later Latin, as well as in the poetical traditions of Provence – such as the *Romance of the Rose* – and the north of France, looking at the painter Giotto's efforts to bring new life into his pictures but also gazing at the Graeco-Byzantine frescos of Ravenna which told of an old tradition, this descendant of a crusading knight also lived the life of a Florentine citizen; he observed the world of popes and emperors, listening to their political and theological arguments about power and salvation, as well as participating in the party strife of his own town. With this background, one can see how his masterpiece, the *Divine Comedy*, which he finished in the year of his death, 1321, could chart the totality of history as it was known to him. It narrates the author's trip through time and space, where he meets with figures historical and mythical. It culminates in his visit to heaven, where he lovingly contemplates the perfection of Creation; for in doing so, man can begin to understand the *lieto fautore* (joyful Creator), who gave him his soul and thus the possibility to enjoy this very creation. It is in this very insistence on the essential importance of belief for man's total experience of life and death that Dante is a typical representative of a Christian world-view. But in other ways he was the precursor of a group of men, urban middle-class laymen rather than clergy or landed nobles or gentlemen, who in the following decades would distinguish themselves by a new way of looking at things, who created a culture that would later be designated as 'humanist'.

Due to the capital generated by Mediterranean trade and a flourishing manufacturing sector, Italy was certainly Europe's wealthiest region during the thirteenth, fourteenth and fifteenth centuries. The many city-states and principalities, with Florence and Venice, Mantua and Urbino and papal Rome in the lead, were governed politically and culturally by enormously wealthy merchants and bankers, counts and dukes, by the pope and cardinals, who all lived in magnificent palaces and villas. They enjoyed all the good and beautiful things their money could buy. Their attitude to life gradually became more secular, that is to say, more centred on man and the here and now than on God and the hereafter. This attitude was confirmed by reading the classical texts in which the same mentality, centred on a creative concept of life, was abundantly evident.

As, during these centuries, in many Italian cities learning and learned art acquired more and more prestige, among the wealthy interested in these forms of culture and influenced by the artists and scholars with whom they often surrounded themselves for reasons of status, a more individualistic view of man was systematically developed and conceptualized. They no longer saw man as an anonymous member of the mass of God's obedient creatures, but as a unique being, supreme in his rational and creative capacities which marked him as an individual. Though men had lived the 'I' in previous centuries, the thinkers of these times made the 'I' the centre of their spiritual credo, as it were, and thus also suggested that the optimal development of the individual should be the central aim and value of life.[2] People began to think that every person had special qualities, given to him because God willed it; man would honour God most by making the best of all his possibilities, his qualities.

To develop these qualities, however, one had to study more specifically the *studium humanitatis*;[3] these were a number of academic subjects, namely grammar, rhetoric, poetry, history and moral philosophy; they by no means embraced all disciplines then taught at the universities, but their study was now seen to defeat the rather narrow aims of scholastic education, with its stress on a sophistical analysis of concepts which many found irrelevant. More important, however, these studies were deemed to help a man to realize his innate human, creative potential, which was summed up in the concept of *virtù*. By using his *virtù* man could lead a life that was as full as possible here on earth, within the community he was supposed to serve, and thus fulfil an essential moral obligation. Thus he would realize the richness of creation as God had intended it. Without losing their belief in the basic tenets of Christianity, the outlook of many of these humanist thinkers and writers, artists and musicians, besides becoming more individualistic, also became decidedly more secular.

The study of the humanities called for texts which would help man better to understand these ideals; not the texts produced by the Church and its musty, restricting scholastic tradition but, preferably, classical texts, giving a glimpse of the culture of ancient Rome that, once more, was seen as the touchstone of civilization. Humanists therefore started searching for such texts, and found them in abundance – most often in the manuscript repositories of the very churches and monasteries they despised as centres of old-fashioned lore, and, moreover, many from the transalpine countries that were not held in great respect. Thus, from southern Germany came unknown works by Cicero, Petronius and the *Institutes of Oratory* of Quintilian, which taught a man how to speak in public, an important asset in view of the fact that the humanists wanted their *virtù* to express itself in service to the community, to their town.

In the thirteenth, fourteenth and fifteenth centuries, new information about that classical, humanistic culture also came to Europe from areas which had not been controlled by the Catholic Church. During those centuries Europe completed a process which, more forcefully than ever, integrated the non-Christian, classical, Graeco-Roman part of its past with its own culture;[4] remarkably, once more this happened to a large extent through, or at least with the help of, Islam. Indeed, following the earlier contacts with the Islamic world on the Iberian peninsula, it now was the Graeco-Byzantine civilization of Europe's orthodox Christian south-east which gave new impulses to the culture of the Christian world in the west.

The loss of Byzantium – the gain of Europe: the further development of Humanism in Italy

Despite the growing power of rulers who tried to maintain their claims to sovereignty, by steering a middle course between the Church, the landed aristocracy and the increasingly powerful elites of the cities, the urge for a central ideal that might give them a hold in troubled times developed among many people, especially but not only intellectuals. One of the reasons was, of course, that the budding national states were frequently involved in long-lasting conflicts causing chaos in the lives of each and all. But the need for more unity increased further when the threat from outside again became tangible in the course of the fifteenth century.

Word had spread of the growing might of the Turks, a militant tribe who, while originating in Central Asia, after moving into Anatolia in the twelfth century had converted to Islam and quickly developed into a regional superpower. Now, the Turkish sultans' overt pretensions directed at the last remnants of the Byzantine Empire and, thus, at the borders of Catholic Europe, created a fear which again fanned the flames of the centuries-old feud between the Christian and Islamic worlds. Europe trembled. This not only led to frantic attempts to settle mutual divisions within the world of western Christendom, as had happened so often in European history – the Council of Constance

(1414–18) already had been a sign of this – but also led to a resolve to try for common action.

The advance of the Turks into the homeland of Greek culture reached a dramatic climax for the Christian world when the Ottomans conquered Constantinople in 1453. Subsequently, a situation developed in which this eastern part of the area now defined as Europe seemed to definitely lose not only its Christian fundament – their claim to it already being disputed by many westerners – but also, in western eyes, its 'European' status precisely because Islam was established there. Therefore it is hardly surprising that, in view of the imminent fall of Byzantium, Pope Pius II launched an appeal for a crusade, but with a different slant. For Pius was also Aeneas Silvius Piccolomini (1405–64), a scholar well-versed in the classics.

As Pope, he was pragmatic and realistic enough to know that the multiplicity of states was an irreversible fact. He wrote this in as many words, deliberately paying attention to the historical and cultural diversity of peoples in Europe.[5] He realized that the universal power of the emperor continued to exist only on paper. And perhaps he even admitted to himself that Rome's leadership of the Church was no longer undisputed.[6] This was precisely why a new ideology was called for which would help to create unity at home as well as stimulate powerful action abroad. Instead of a geographical-religious area, *Christianitas*, ruled by the universal Church with or without the support of an all-powerful emperor in the secular sphere, Pius talked of *Europe*, described politically in rather vague terms indeed but yet defined as a general cultural category in which religion, Christianity, naturally continued to play a central role in every-day life. In the words of this Pope, Europe became 'our home', and being a European meant, simply, being a Christian.[7]

But Pius also wrote:

> Greece is now broken and ravaged – you all know what a cultural loss this is for us; after all, you know that the whole civilization of the Latin world stems from Greek sources.[8]

It is equally significant that Pius believed that eastern Europe, that is the world of Greek Christendom, had to be reconquered in order to reintegrate Europe culturally.[9] Even if he, like his immediate predecessors, probably did have ulterior motives in wanting to heal the rift between Catholic and Orthodox Christians and thus increase his own papal power, his interest in Greek culture was entirely genuine. As the true scholar he was, he had been part of the development of the *studium humanitatis*; and all humanists knew that the Latin culture they were delving into had its roots in the civilization of ancient Greece.

Meanwhile, the renewed acquaintance with classical culture was intensified greatly when many members of the cultural elite of the Byzantine Empire fled the Balkans and ancient Greece in the face of the Turkish threat. The Byzantine scholars and artists who took to Europe principally sought safety on the Italian peninsula. To their refuge they brought their Christian tradition, coloured by the influence of classical Greek civilization to a far greater extent than in the west.[10] In their luggage, the exiles from Byzantium carried many manuscripts, which preserved the thoughts of the great Greek thinkers and other writers hardly known in the west. The *Iliad* and the *Odyssey*, the great poems attributed to Homer, could now be read; also, better or even entirely new versions of Aristotle's and Plato's reflections on man and society became available, as well as Dioscurides's survey of the plant and animal worlds, to name but a few.

Already in 1396, the leading Byzantine scholar Manuel Chrysoleras had been asked by the government of Florence to come and teach at the university, which he did, creating a generation of humanists who began to study and translate Greek texts. In the 1430s, the Greek philosopher Pletho had taught a course on the difference between the Aristotelian and Platonic systems; the latter, less tainted by adoption and interpretation by the Church, was deemed by some to offer an attractive alternative to the former. In his wake, a group of scholars, the so-called *Accademia Platonica* – founded in 1475 with the support of the vastly wealthy Florentine maecenas, Cosimo de' Medici – tried to reach a new synthesis; particularly Marsilio Ficino (1433–99) sought to reconcile a renewed Platonism with Christianity.[11] Also, Florence had been the town where, in 1438, a council was organized to bring the Greek and Roman Churches closer towards one another.

Thus, the necessity for a reconquest of the Greek cultural world now considered vital from a political and religious as well as a cultural point of view by intellectuals like Pius II was an almost logical consequence of the virtually continuous interaction mentioned earlier between the two cores of Christian civilization, the religious values of the Bible, and the more secular cultural elements of Mediterranean Antiquity. It was an interaction which had first peaked in the third and fourth, and once more in the eighth and ninth centuries, and which had intensified from the twelfth century onwards. Hence, even though Greece was liberated only in the early nineteenth century, since the fifteenth century Europe tried to intellectually reconquer the Mediterranean world, which had indeed been one of the most important elements in its cultural formation. It was a reconquest which certainly contributed to European supremacy in 'science and every branch of learning',[12] as the Pope had promised, defining Europe's cultural character in precisely the terms which one might expect to hear from an intellectual.

Understandably, the combined enthusiasm for the ideas of the ancient Greeks and Romans was paralleled by an interest in the languages in which the classical scholars had written. Classical Greek and Latin were now seen as so much more elegant and lucid than the Latin which had been used in previous centuries by the Church and in Church-dominated scholarship. Latin now included many corrupted words and, moreover, had absorbed all sorts of new words. Therefore, it had to be purified. A language which was as precise as possible, preferably the Latin used by the Roman rhetorician Cicero, was to serve as the model for the new Latin. This was to be the medium for a logical expression of ideas that would allow man to articulate his new questions and insights about himself and the world.

In the century following the death of Thomas Aquinas, the study of classical texts and the new attitude towards man and the world that emerged increasingly had led to questions, and doubts which had already existed in the background now acquired a new urgency. What exactly was the relation between man and God? Was the Bible the only source of knowledge about creation, as the Roman Church preferred to present it? Or could man himself, by perceiving the world around him, fathom nature and his own place in it, as the Greek thinkers had asserted? Could man thus acquire knowledge of the order of the cosmos and God's intentions for it?

At least one man thought along quite different lines than most of his contemporaries did. He was Nicholas Chrypffs, 'the crayfish', better known as Nicholas Cusanus, bishop of Brixen and cardinal of the Holy Roman Church (1401–64).[13] Combining his training as a theologian with his interest in mathematics and in astronomy, he went on to speculate about the cosmos and its Creator. He concluded not only that the geocentric model was untenable, but also that the universe knew no bounds and was filled with many planets probably not unlike the earth. It had been willed by God, a being who was the absolutely infinite, centre and circumference, beginning and end, the synthesis of all opposites, the *coincidentia oppositorum*. Writing about God, Cusa used mathematics as well, musing that one might imagine God by thinking of the radius of a circle as infinite, which then would cause the circumference of the circle to coincide with a straight line. With these and other speculations, he was far ahead of his times. That he was able to do so at all shows the relative openness of the Church in matters concerning doctrine and learning – although, of course, the authorities must have realized there was little danger of ordinary people being corrupted by such abstruse thoughts, formulated in Latin and written in manuscript texts.

Far less speculative were those who, following men like Abelard, asked themselves whether the Bible and the texts from the first years of the Christian Church had not been corrupted by 1,500 years of use? Was it not possible that much of what was actually considered incomprehensible or unreasonable in the ideas of the Church was only the result of texts which had been copied incorrectly? Was it possible that the Bible and other fundamental texts of the Church had been worded rather differently at the moment of their origin?

From the Byzantine world now came the old Greek version of Holy Scripture. When compared with the younger, Latin text traditionally used in the west, exciting and even shocking discoveries were made: in the course of time many errors had indeed entered the standard Latin version. On the one hand, this led to new, better editions of the Bible, especially when Hebrew and Aramaic texts were brought in for comparison as well. In consequence, in the sixteenth and seventeenth centuries a number of so-called Polyglot Bibles were produced, which published the holy texts in six, seven or even eight languages in parallel, so that the similarities and differences in language and time became very clear.

On the other hand, it was precisely these scientific analyses of Holy Scripture which undermined belief in its absolute value. The Bible now appeared to be the product of history, a man-made creation. As a result, the authority of the Church, which had, after all, based its claim to absolute power on the absolute, timeless truth of the Bible, was to a certain extent affected. Not surprisingly, even nowadays the unchangeableness of the Koran is being hammered home in the Islamic world. If Islamic clergymen would not do this, their power would decline considerably. A comparable process began in Christian Europe in the late fifteenth century. It quickly led to fierce differences between the traditional religious and cultural establishment, the Roman Catholic Church, and those who pleaded for a new culture. Their position was made abundantly clear in a text by one of their protagonists, the Dutch-born scholar, Desiderius Erasmus (*c*.1465–1536).[14]

Probably because he critically read the old texts, Erasmus began to disapprove of institutions like the Catholic Church which asked the believers to unquestioningly accept those texts as literally and eternally true. In his later years he showed a growing aversion of the power structures in that Church which, in his opinion, could not always withstand the test of intellectual analysis. Yet he did not become a real reformer, though he did cleanse the Old and especially the New Testament of all sorts of incorrect readings and outright mistakes. He also published the texts of important Church scholars from the first centuries of Christianity.

In his *Anti-Barbari*, Erasmus vehemently attacked contemporary culture, especially the way it was served by the Roman Catholic clergy, who dominated most of the primary and secondary schools in Europe. He accused them of hypocrisy and ignorance because of their refusal to base education on a sound study of the secular literature of the ancients, the *bonae litterae*. Instead of striving to raise the level of culture through the advancement of knowledge and learning, they did their best, according to Erasmus, to keep the people ignorant and hence unhappy. Elsewhere, Erasmus observed that at least part of the religious establishment was, indeed, loath to lose its comfortable position as the keeper of tradition; they would not relinquish the power they held through their monopolization of magic, ritual and science, the keys to the world of incomprehensible nature, of God. In a letter he wrote:

> These people see only too plainly, that their own authority will fall to the ground, if we have the Sacred Books accessible in an amended form, and seek their meaning at the fountain-head. And so high a value do they set upon their own importance, that they had rather have many things unknown, many things mis-read and cited amiss from the Divine Books, than appear ignorant themselves of any point.[15]

And yet, in spite of Erasmus's rather over-pessimistic sketch, European civilization was changing rapidly. The fifteenth and sixteenth centuries once again became a period of heightened tension between its two components. The intellectual tradition which had developed from the twelfth century in an effort to reconcile the Bible and the Church Fathers with the Greek philosophical and scholarly body of thought handed on by Islamic culture no longer appeared to be a convincing framework for thought and action for many intellectuals, precisely as a result of their increasingly intense acquaintance with classical civilization in their own time. To them, what was presented as culture in Europe was no longer an actual reproduction of classical values, including the language, Latin, or the original Christian principles. A new analysis and synthesis were needed, which had to result in a true 'rebirth' of both traditions in the purest forms of the past.

From Poland to Portugal, from Sweden to Switzerland, people wrote and painted and built, aiming to bring European, Christian civilization to a new flowering by confronting it with its roots, by a return to its sources. These activities took place within institutional frameworks comparable with those of Italy, namely in the palaces of the rulers, in academies sponsored by princes or nobles, but also in the universities they founded.

In Bohemia, the Emperor Charles IV (r. 1346–78) encouraged both the latinization of his court, and the purification of German; in 1348, he also gave his realm its first university, at Prague, basing it on the example of Bologna and Paris. At his great castle of Karlstejn, frescos were painted in the style of Giotto. Meanwhile, his friend, the Polish King Casimir III (r. 1353–70) followed the same policy, establishing a university at the capital, Cracow, in 1364. And at Visegrád, in Hungary, the kings built a huge palace that became the centre of a court culture that was also a learned culture.

At the same time, learned culture continued to flourish in the oldest centres, the monasteries and their libraries, but now also was pursued in new milieux, the townhouses of the urban elites.

From Humanism to the Renaissance in Italy

Gradually, in the fifteenth and sixteenth centuries, the scholars, the artists, the architects, the musicians and the writers, in short all those who shaped the culture of Humanism, began to experience a more general sense that their society had entered upon a new age, an age reborn after the 'darkness' of the preceding centuries: the 'Renaissance'. While this interpretation of history was a definite exaggeration of the actual newness of the ideas that these men and, increasingly, women professed and the material culture they produced, it was yet undeniable that a new vision of man was being created. The 'new man' was considered sovereign in the world and, with his reason and creative powers, able to penetrate any secret, make anything he invented.

Even physically, a new vision of man was presented by artists. For the material remains of classical culture were now sought as assiduously as the surviving ancient texts: the fifteenth and sixteenth centuries saw the birth of archaeology. Numerous works of art were discovered in the ruins of ancient

Rome, and the finds reinforced the new view of man that had been developing in the previous century. More specifically, the idea that a perfect culture, which had produced the great texts, could not but be the product of perfect men and women induced many artists to produce works based on such revealing examples of classical art as the Roman copies of Greek originals like the 'spearbearer' and the 'wounded amazon'. A multitude of paintings and sculptures of 'perfectly' proportioned men and women were the result. A new, ideal-type human being was created, which has held western man captive ever since: in the twentieth century, it influenced not only the state-controlled breeding programmes of Nazi Germany but also the Hollywood star cult and the fashion industry.[16]

Besides incorporating the secularist and individualist aspects of Humanism, the reborn age or Renaissance should be called realistic as well. In painting, serious attempts were made to represent everything as it appeared. Though not totally absent in the previous ages, if one looks at the marvellously minute renderings of beasts and plants and even people in illuminated manuscripts, one can certainly maintain that for many centuries realism had been relatively unimportant, since the religious idea and the intention behind it determined both the message and the form in which it was cast, the painterly depiction. Already in the fourteenth and fifteenth centuries, during the first phases of humanist culture, painters increasingly attempted to reproduce reality, casting off preconceived ideas about what was morally or religiously acceptable. Increasingly, what the eye could measure or observe – distance, depth, colour and even ugliness – was portrayed. For good reason, this is the time when perspective made its appearance in European art.

In sculpture, too, people were individualized, with recognizable faces, whereas the art of the preceding centuries had mainly depicted types. For more than a thousand years most sculpture had been a component of an architectural background – reliefs more than free-standing figures; now, we see how sculpted images present man according to his newly-won vision of himself as independent, moving, walking, running and fighting if necessary, but free and recognizable as an individual.

There is, too, a pride in the beauty of the body, both the male and, in view of the conventions of the preceding age rather more surprisingly, the female. Whereas woman for a long time had been stereotyped as either an unapproachable saint or an untouchable whore, due to the limits imposed upon her roles by the Church, she now seemed to regain some stature as an individual person, in whose body the perfection of God's creation was made as visible as in the male.

However, one should remember that new ideals always tend to become fashionable. The same individuals who had themselves depicted 'true to life' also wanted to conform to the new ideal. The Florentine ruler, Lorenzo de'Medici, patron of painters and writers and himself a poet and thinker of some merit, allowed his face to be modelled from life but Michelangelo, who was the sculptor, cast his body into the mould of an 'ideally' proportioned

Plates 17 A new combination of mind and body. A Roman mosaic allegedly depicting Plato's academy, showing a number of scholars engaged in discussion, at the National Museum of Naples. It was this academy which inspired the humanist, neo-Platonist group around Marsilio Ficino working at Florence in the fifteenth century. Many humanists realized that the body, too, was God's gift.
Source: Centre for Art Historical Documentation, Nijmegen, The Netherlands

Greek god. Therefore, one must be wary not to exaggerate, as European art historians tended to do in the first decades of the twentieth century. There certainly is more and also more conscious realism in Renaissance art than in the preceding period. But both sculpture and painting were subject to rules and ideals, different from but no less compulsive than the mainly religious conventions of the preceding age. Thus, everything was generally represented more harmoniously than it really was, precisely because harmony and geometric proportions were seen as ideal and, hence, as characteristics of great art: in that area, nature, which was imitated, could, in the opinion of many, be improved.

Nor should we forget that by far the majority of paintings and sculptures still served religious purposes, and were composed in such a way that they aroused

Plate 18 A drawing of a group of bathing soldiers, just before the Battle of Cascina, attributed to Aristotele da Sangallo, 1542, exhibits the delight Renaissance painters began to have in depicting man in all his natural physical beauty; at the same time, they created an idealized version of the human body which, often, has become constrictive.
Source: Earl of Leicester's collection, Holkham, England

an appropriate devotional reaction in the viewers, whether these were private owners contemplating a picture of the Madonna and her child by the Italian painter Raphael in the solitude of their bedroom, or the flocks of the faithful who attended mass and looked up at the huge frescos, mosaics and statues that adorned walls and ceilings and cupolas in an angel-crowded vision of heaven.

ROME, AD 1538: MICHELANGELO TALKS ABOUT ITALIAN ART

In the year 1538, the Portuguese miniature painter Francesco de Hollanda was present at several conversations in which Michelangelo took part as well. The notes which De Hollanda took of the artist's sayings are among our more precious testimonies of the painter's ideas. Though, at first, one might think that Michelangelo is taking a rather narrow, chauvinistic stance, in the end it is clear that what he defends is actually a style, in fact the only style, to wit of ancient Greek painting preserved and resurrected in Italy.

Elsewhere, De Hollanda specifically records Michelangelo's words about Flemish painting, revealing the master's opinions not only on the 'sublime' rather than realistic characteristics of true, i.e. Italian painting, but also about the relationship between certain aspects of taste and aesthetics and persons of a specific class or sex.

Only works which are done in Italy can be called true painting, and therefore we call good painting Italian, just as if it were done so well in another country, we should give it the name of that country or province. As for the good painting of this country, there is nothing more noble or devout, for with wise persons nothing causes devotion to be remembered, or to arise, more than the difficulty of the perfection which unites itself with and joins God; because good painting is nothing else but a copy of the perfections of God and a reminder of His painting. Finally, good painting is a music and a melody which intellect only can appreciate, and with great difficulty. . . .

And I further say . . . that of all climates or countries lighted by the sun and the moon, in no other can one paint well but in the kingdom; and it is a thing which is nearly impossibly to do well except here, even though there were more talented men in the other provinces, if there could be such, and this for reasons which we will give you.

Take a great man from another kingdom, and tell him to paint whatever he likes and can do best, and let him do it; and take a bad Italian apprentice and order him to make a drawing. . . . You will find, if you understand it well, that the drawing of that apprentice, as regards art, has more substance than that of the other master. . . . Order a great master, who is not an Italian, even though it be Albrecht [i.e. Dürer], a man delicate in his manner, in order to deceive me . . . and I assure You that it will be immediately recognized that the work was not done in Italy, nor by the hand of an Italian. I likewise affirm that no nation or person (I except one or two Spaniards) can perfectly satisfy or imitate the Italian manner of painting (which is the old Greek manner) without his being immediately recognized as a foreigner. . . . And if by some great miracle such a foreigner should succeed in painting well . . . it will be said that he painted like an Italian. Thus it is that all painting done in Italy is not called Italian painting, but all that is good and direct is, for in this country works of illustrious painting are done in a more masterly and more serious manner than in any other place. We call good painting Italian, which painting, even though it be done in Flanders or in Spain (which approaches us most) if it be good, will be Italian painting, for this noble science does not belong to any country, as it came from heaven; but even from ancient times it remained in our Italy more than in any other kingdom in the world, and I think that it will end in it. . . .

The painting of Flanders will generally satisfy any devout person more than the painting of Italy, which will never cause him to drop a single tear, but that of Flanders will cause him to shed many; this is not owing to the vigour and goodness of that painting, but to the goodness of such devout person; women will like it, especially very old ones, or very young ones. It will likewise please friars and nuns, and also some noble persons who have no ear for true harmony. They paint in Flanders only to deceive the external eye, things that gladden you and of which you cannot speak ill, and saints and prophets. Their painting is of stuffs, bricks and mortar, the grass of the fields, the shadows of trees, and bridges and rivers, which they call landscapes, and little figures here and there; and all this, although it may appear good to some eyes, is in truth done without reasonableness or art, without symmetry or proportion, without care in selecting or rejecting, and finally without any substance or nerve.[17]

Increasingly, the *studium humanitatis* and the general cultural climate of the Renaissance produced texts which showed this deepening interest in the essence of what made man a more civilized, humane being and which were therefore called *litterae humaniores*. Mostly, these were the texts of classical writers written in Greek or Latin. However, texts which Europeans now wrote themselves were also designated as such, whether they were composed in the purified Latin of the fifteenth and sixteenth centuries or in the second European cultural language, the Italian of Tuscany, the language in which Petrarch (1304–74) had written, the writer who was considered a real humanist, famous for his beautiful sonnets immortalizing his beloved Laura.

The subject matter of a text was actually not important, as long as a writer showed that he could see what man was and could do, both as an individual and as a member of society. This led to very diverse works. The autobiography, in which a person tells his own, unique lifestory, was born in humanist circles. A splendid example are the hundreds of pages which the famous goldsmith and sculptor, Benvenuto Cellini (1500–71), began to write in 1558, telling the story of his own life; it is a secular, individual and realistic work *par excellence*. His 'I' is central: everything is seen and described from his perspective; his readers are forced to see the world around him through his eyes, not according to all sorts of idealizations which Church or State required of people, but realistically, with all the deception and filth which he found in the world but also with everything beautiful, mostly made by man himself, that exists in it.

Thus, Cellini writes of the necessity to record one's deeds, analyses his own character, unwittingly lets us know that, being a city man, he had no idea of the geographical layout of the surrounding countryside, tells of the ancient monuments that inspired him, gives an idea of the sense of life and movement in Michelangelo's work, graphically describes his quarrels with his competitors, and so on:

> No matter what sort he is, everyone who has to his credit what are or really seem great achievements, if he cares for truth and goodness, ought to write the story of his own life in his own hand; but no one should venture on such a splendid undertaking before he is over forty. [. . .]
>
> Like the raw young man I was I answered my poor, distressed father back, and, taking the few wretched clothes and the odd couple of coins that I had left, went out of the house and began walking towards one of the city gates. I had no idea which gate was the one for Rome, and I ended up at Lucca, and from Lucca I went on to Pisa. I went to see the Campo Santo while I was at Pisa, and there I discovered many beautiful antiques, that is, marble sarcophagi. In various other parts of Pisa I came across many other ancient works, and I used to study them assiduously whenever I had time off from work. [. . .]
>
> [Michelangelo] depicted a number of infantrymen who because of the summer heat had gone down to bathe in the river Arno: he caught in his drawing the moment when the alarm is sounded and the naked soldiers rush for their arms. He showed all their actions and gestures so wonderfully that no ancient or modern artist has ever reached such a high standard. [. . .]

> I grew so angry that I was utterly determined to make mischief, and anyway I am rather hot-blooded by nature. . . . I left . . . fuming with rage and rushed back to my workshop. There I seized hold of a stiletto and hurried round to where those enemies of mine lived. I found them sitting down at dinner, in their home above the shop, and as soon as I appeared that young Gherardo who had started the quarrel hurled himself on me. I stabbed him in the chest, piercing his doublet and jacket right through to the shirt . . . and I shouted out: 'You traitors, today I'm going to kill the whole bunch of you'.[18]

At the other end of the spectrum of humanist writers one finds, for instance, Niccolò Machiavelli (1469–1527), a Florentine scholar, who, in his famous 1513 tract *Il Principe* (*The Prince*), describes the role of man in that segment of society which is called politics. Machiavelli, too, is secular and a realist; he shows that the will to power is a dominant principle; though often couched and cloaked in nice words of a religious, ethical or social nature, upon a closer look it reveals itself in all its nakedness as pure self-interest:

> Everyone perceives how praiseworthy a king is who keeps to his word and is candid instead of sly in political actions. Yet the experience of our time teaches us that those rulers who gave their word easily have come far, who knew how to deceive people with their sly tricks and, finally, they have gained the upper hand over those who lived honestly. . . .
>
> It is therefore clear that a sensible ruler cannot and may not stick to his word if this is to his disadvantage and if the reasons why he gave his word are no longer valid. . . . A ruler therefore does not necessarily have to have all the good qualities which I outlined earlier; he only has to give the impression that he has them. . . . He must appear sympathetic, trustworthy, without guile, and pious, and actually be like that. But at the same time his character and nature must be such that, if he has to be the opposite, he can also behave that way. . . . He must be flexible, following fate and circumstance. In short, he must not deviate from the way of goodness, as long as that is sensible, but he must know how to be bad when necessary.

The culture of the fourteenth, fifteenth and sixteenth centuries shows a renewed and intensified form of the 'great tradition'. Renaissance in general and Humanism in particular are the terms we use to characterize this culture of the learned, who communicated in Latin, who read and often wrote books mostly in Latin as well.

Education was among the most important institutions through which this renewed tradition was transmitted. In a letter to one of his pupils, the humanist scholar Leonardo Bruni (1370–1444) explained the essence of a good education:

> Devote Yourself to two kinds of study. In the first place, acquire a knowledge of letters, not the common run of it, but the more searching and profound kind in which I very much want You to shine. Secondly, acquaint Yourself with what

pertains to life and manners – those things that are called humane studies because they perfect and adorn man. In this kind of study Your knowledge should be wide, varied, and taken from every sort of experience, leaving out nothing that might seem to contribute to the conduct of Your life, to honour and to fame. I shall advise You to read authors who can help You not only by their matter but also by the splendour of their style and their skill in writing; that is to say, the works of Cicero and of any who may possibly approach his level. If You will listen to me, You will thoroughly explore the fundamental and systematic treatment of those matters in Aristotle; as for beauty of expression, a rounded style, and all the wealth of words and speech, skill in these things You, if I may so put it, borrow from Cicero . . . for I would wish an outstanding man to be both abundantly learned and capable of giving elegant expression to his learning. . . .

What riches will compare with the rewards of these studies? Perhaps the study of law will more easily get You a job, but it is a long way behind those others in utility and dignity. For they combine to produce a good man than which nothing can be thought more useful; the law does nothing of the sort.[19]

Inevitably, trade and travel, military conquest and diplomatic contacts linked the new culture of the Italian towns and courts with the world beyond. The new culture was admired and imitated all over Europe although, of course, by the better educated and the wealthy, only. For both south and north of the Alps, Humanism and the Renaissance were elite phenomena. Only very few of the new ideas and thoughts filtered down to the ordinary man who, after all, could not read or write the *bonae litterae* and, if only therefore, in the eyes of this elite lacked the means to realize his *virtù*.

Humanism and the Renaissance: Italy and beyond

The fifteenth century saw the peak of the Renaissance and Humanism in Italy, but at the end of the century a complex of factors resulted in cracks beginning to appear in the material basis of this cultural outburst. The lucrative cross-Mediterranean trade, which the prosperity of many Italian cities was based on, gradually collapsed as a result of long-lasting conflicts between the major powers of the Islamic Near East. Also, for a long time already, many Mediterranean trading cities had cast longing looks at the rich trade and the even more promising gold that seemed for the taking in the Maghrebine port towns. Now, partly as a result of the discovery of America and of alternative routes to Asia, around the Cape of Good Hope, the economic centre of Europe slowly but definitely shifted from the Mediterranean to the Atlantic Ocean, where, of course, great wealth had been accumulated already by the French, Flemish and Dutch towns through commerce and industry. The latter, moreover, were able to produce the consumer goods Europe sought at more competitive prices than Italian artisans could.

At the same time, the Italian peninsula became the most important pawn in the fight for political hegemony in Europe between the Habsburgs, who ruled in Spain, Austria, Germany and the Netherlands, and the kings of France.

In 1494, French soldiers invaded Italy and caused havoc. A horde of German mercenaries followed in 1527, destroying Rome, the symbolic centre of Italian and indeed European culture, the papal capital, the 'eternal city'.

Yet, although some historians disagree, Italy, or rather the new forms of culture that had developed there, did survive these blows.[20] In the course of the sixteenth and early seventeenth centuries, Italian artistic culture still became manifest in notable products, especially in the so-called baroque period, up till *c.*1660. Michelangelo Buonarotti, besides being a great painter and sculptor, was the architect who contributed to the design for a new St Peter's that replaced the great basilica erected by the Emperor Constantine over the reputed site of the Apostle Peter's grave. With its mighty cupola and its new-fashioned architecture in the classical vein, it provided Christianity with an effective symbol of power precisely at a time wherein criticism of the Church's teaching was more openly voiced. Giovanni Pierluigi da Palestrina composed his beautiful masses to be sung in the papal chapel. The writer Torquato Tasso produced such great epic poems as *Gerusalemme Liberata* (Jerusalem delivered), which took their inspiration from the stories of magic and knightly chivalry generated by the Crusades. Claudio Monteverdi, court composer at Mantua, delighted his audiences with his madrigals extolling both earthly and divine love. And the first opera was composed by a group of humanists in Florence, who wanted to revive the classical Greek ideal of tragedy combined with music.

Nevertheless, Italy gradually lost the pre-eminently active role it had played in earlier times, even though the whole of Europe continued to look to and admire the peninsula not only as the cradle of European civilization but also as the place where it had been born again after ages of darkness.

In the sixteenth century, Renaissance and Humanism increasingly seemed to become manifest also to the north of the Alps. This can be explained. Spain became enormously wealthy through its new American colonies. In the German states the economy prospered through the distributive trades which connected central Europe with the large trading cities along the North Sea, and in England and the Netherlands the economies were given a new impulse from the textile industry and grain trade which had to feed and clothe Europe's population, which was growing again after the great economic and demographic crisis of the fourteenth century. Thus, the material conditions for a cultural flowering were abundantly present in these countries. The effects of this were soon felt, the more so because in transalpine European thought, too, there had been a change of ideas about the relations between man, the world and God.

From the late fourteenth century, the Church authorities had had to stand by and watch as some of the more intellectual and spiritual of their flock, both men and women, no longer entered the closed existence of the monastery but chose to live an exemplary Christian life in the world. Their thoughts about man's own individual relationship with God, and man's own religious and therefore also social responsibility in the world, were now less controllable; no longer safely confined within the monastic walls, they began to spread. One such movement, significantly called the *Devotio Moderna* (Modern Devotion), became quite influential, especially in the Netherlands and the neighbouring German states.[21] One of the most powerful writers in this context was Thomas Haemerken, better known as Thomas à Kempis (*c.*1380–1471), whose text *De Imitatione Christi* (On the imitation of Christ), offered many believers a new, more simple and personally intense view of Christianity – it became Europe's most popular book after the Bible. Precisely because this group expressly aimed to raise people's awareness and because they chose education as the most effective means of communication, it posed an outright threat to established culture. Indeed, the Church considered the members of such groups to be much more dangerous than the scientists with their complex arguments who might sow the seeds of doubt but who, after all, reached only a handful of colleagues.

In the fifteenth and early sixteenth centuries, the educational institutions of the Modern Devotion produced many humanists. Like their Italian colleagues, north of the Alps the learned, too, began to focus on the classical Greek and Roman texts and on the accuracy of the holy book of the Christians. Desiderius Erasmus, mentioned earlier, was easily the most famous of these north European humanists;[22] in a series of treatises, he tried to lay down the rules for an educational system that, while devoutly Christian, was imbued with the critical spirit of Humanism. Indeed, one should not forget that, contrary to what often has been suggested, most people living the culture of Renaissance and Humanism did not display a 'heathenish', pagan spirit but remained firmly tied to a view of man and the world as, essentially, redeemable only by God. When we look at Hieronymus Bosch's painting of the Prodigal Son, probably finished in 1510, we see how the painter depicts man – the prodigal son – as a free agent who, while looking back on scenes of a past life of waste and sin, yet turns towards the future, the possibility of salvation through the cross, that is the painting's centrepiece.

The Church was fully aware that the new spirit of criticism and free will which was abroad in Europe had indeed created a new concept of man and thus contributed to the genesis of a new man. As long as the new view of man and the world, of man and God, obtruded only on the elite, via texts, pictures and illustrations, the danger was small. But changing perceptions of man can also change large groups of people if the appropriate means and channels of communication are available. It was precisely in this field that the real danger for the Church was lurking.

8 A new society

Europe as a wider world

Economic and technological change and the definitive formation of the 'modern' state

In the course of the fifteenth century, Europe underwent momentous economic changes, after a period of prolonged depression. In the twelfth and thirteenth centuries, a serious crisis had developed partly because the temperature on earth dropped slightly – the phenomenon of the 'small ice age'. The climate had become cooler and wetter, with a sharp dip in the fourteenth century. The abandonment of settlements and the inundation of coastal plains were but a few of the visible manifestations. Then a succession of very wet years resulted in poor harvests, in famine and, soon, in widespread disease. All this caused long-term chaos in the still largely agricultural economy. In a spiral of under-nourishment, child mortality and a lower birthrate, a demographic decline set in, not least because in this situation the Black Death and other epidemics caused hundreds of thousands of deaths.[1]

But when the climate had recovered in the fourteenth century and the economic and social disruption had been overcome by the beginning of the fifteenth century, western Europe in particular began to experience a period of spectacular economic growth. The agricultural sector expanded, the population increased, and surplus production resulted in an extension of regional and interregional trade; in consequence of all this, the fiscal base of governments was considerably broadened. The complex structures of expanding states needed to be managed. Fiscal systems were organized on the basis of mathematical calculations, armies and navies were built like perfect machines in which soldiers functioned according to rules of combat that were planned mathematically as well. Besides, more and more, learning, science and technology were used to maximize commercial and thus state income.

Many of the craftsmen and scientists who could realize all the state's new needs put themselves at their prince's service. These were people who began to think about quantifiable results first, and about the old, religious-metaphysical questions second, if at all. Slowly, a chasm began to emerge between those for whom knowledge and wisdom were forms of speculation about the relation of man to nature and the supernatural and those who sought only the controllability of man and nature. It was a split which in the seventeenth-century debate on the quality of culture was translated in terms like 'old' and 'new', 'ancient' and 'modern'. Actually, the 'reasonable', rational explanations seemed to hold the future, in view of the fact that they were so obviously successful in the creation of power and wealth. The branches of knowledge which produced these explanations therefore meant 'cultural capital' for those whose profession it was, providing them with an entrance to the world of power, to a position in society which otherwise could only be attained by those with money or of noble birth.

During the fifteenth and sixteenth centuries, states in Europe, building on the foundations laid from the twelfth century onwards, definitively acquired the structure which still characterizes them. In a process of, alternatingly, violent and bloody interaction or peaceful negotiation between the rulers, the various aristocratic power groups and the patrician elites of the major towns, most states developed into complex, centralized, bureaucracies, as much a 'work of art' created by human hands as the artistic and literary products of the Renaissance.

If only because the process of state formation was often so painful, many learned Europeans increasingly stressed the necessity for a rational, uniform legal system and for a clear description of state power. They based this belief on their reading of classical texts on political theory as well as on an empirical consideration of the reality surrounding them, a reality of states eager to extend their power internally and externally. Hence, Roman Law was elaborated as a system guaranteeing the state's subjects at least some minimal, inviolable rights while at the same time stressing the supreme authority of the monarch, and complex ideologies appeared that sought to legitimize a prince's right to rule while yet safeguarding the liberties of the subjects; mostly, this was done through reference to the divine origin of princely power but, increasingly, secular contract law was called upon to enhance the legality of the relationship between the state, embodied in the prince, and the subjects.

In the sixteenth century, Niccolò Machiavelli already expressed as his opinion that it was precisely the many relatively small states into which Europe was divided that gave this part of the world its *virtù*.[2] These states proved to be stronger whenever the old ruling elites − clergy and nobility, as well as state bureaucracy − realized that a properly functioning economy was the necessary basis of power, that a relatively strong middle class was the principal bearer of this, and that it must therefore be allowed a certain say in public matters and even in politics. These ideas surfaced more and more in political analyses. The extent to which they were realized in the various states of Europe had a far-reaching influence not only on the development of political institutions but also on culture, separately in each state but also in Europe at large.

Two centuries later, in 1752, François-Marie Arouet, also known as Voltaire, looked back upon the history of Europe in the seventeenth century and wrote his *Le Siècle de Louis XIV*, (The Age of Louis XIV) noting that:

all [states] resemble each other. They all have the same religious foundation, even if it is divided into different denominations. They all employ the same principles of public law and policy, which are unknown elsewhere in the world.[3]

Such of Voltaire's contemporaries as, for example, Charles de Montesquieu and Adam Smith, looking at the past of their world, went even deeper trying to explain the way Europe functioned and exercised its power. They, too, noted the fact of these comparatively small states, with their rapidly evolving production systems, which they ascribed to their continuous competition but also to their inevitable, creative communication. They saw Europe as a world unified by Christianity, but with religion not over-powerful. Nor, for that matter, was this world dominated only by one secular ruler, indeed, the princes themselves who embodied the various states were not all-powerful, either. Though these intellectuals were critical of the situation in many European states, they especially admired the balance which had been achieved in the Dutch Republic and in England, where liberty, equality and wealth, the main elements of a 'virtuous' state, contributed to a prominent position both in Europe and in the wider world.

By and large, later historians have supported these analyses and have named the phenomenon of the centralized, competitive states and the elaboration of public law as some of the most important formative elements in the establishment of the 'wonder' that was Europe.[4]

All these developments were enhanced if not made possible in the first place by far-reaching technological inventions which had far-reaching economical, political and cultural results. Their significance is made clear in a revealing statement by the famous English statesman, philosopher and scientist, Sir Francis Bacon (1561–1626). In 1620, he published his *Novum Organum*, (The New Instrument), referring to Aristotle's celebrated work on the nature of science, the 'Organon'. In his introduction, Bacon says:

> We should note the force, effect and consequences of inventions, which are nowhere more conspicuous than in those . . . which were unknown to the Ancients, namely, printing, gunpowder, and the compass. For these . . . have changed the appearance and state of the whole world.[5]

Bacon not only ascertains which inventions or rather instruments Europe had found to bring about cultural and social changes, but also establishes that these instruments were unknown in the ancient world and that they are therefore the achievements of contemporary Europe. In this he implicitly distances himself from the widely held belief of the humanists that no further progress would be possible once the level of civilization of the ancient Greeks and Romans had again been reached.

From manuscript to typescript

Indisputably, Christian Europe changed radically through the influence of two adjoining cultures, the Islamic and the Byzantine, which both referred back to the ancient Graeco-Roman culture from which all three had originated. The classical tradition, not only the norms and values but also the outward forms of the culture of Greece and Rome certainly became more dominant in the fourteenth and fifteenth centuries, both among the monks and the warriors, the two traditional 'orders' which still formed the basis of Europe's cultural elite. Yet the cultural forms which we now class under the terms Renaissance and Humanism would never have acquired their enduring significance if another development had not taken place.

Culture exists thanks to communication and even is, to a large extent, communication. If people do not share their thoughts with others, they will not endure. They would never be shaped or become manifest as recognizable utterances, which mark people as belonging to a group with common characteristics.

Of course, the spoken word is a carrier of communication, but what is said is transient, and does not make a lasting impression. That which is written more easily survives the situation in which it arose. It leads its own life, becoming transferable information, and moreover the basis for recognizing common thoughts and behaviour. That which is written also may turn into knowledge which is passed on from generation to generation and thus continues to exist. This situation was acutely felt by the Graeco-Byzantine scholar, Johannes Bessarion (1403–72) who had fled to Italy and became a formative influence on humanist culture. In 1468, he presented his enormous collection of manuscripts to the city of Venice, on condition that they be made available to the public. In the letter offering his library to the Doge, he writes of his books:

> They live, they converse with us, they teach us, they form us, they comfort us, they point us to that which we have forgotten. . . . So great is the power of books, their value, their glory, yes, even their divine force, that we would all be awkward and ignorant if books did not exist; there would be no knowledge of the past, no examples, no learning about divine and human things. The tombstone which covers the body of man would also cover up his name. . . . After the fall of Greece and the lamentable captivity of Byzantium, I, with unprecedented intensity, used all my strength, all my care, all my material possibilities to trace Greek texts. . . . And so I have collected all the books of the Greek philosophers, especially the rare ones, which are difficult to find.[6]

Bessarion's letter not only indicates the importance of texts as carriers of culture, but also makes clear that in his time 'books' were rare. Until late in the fifteenth century, the handwritten book was the only vehicle of textual information. Moreover, as manuscripts were not only rare but also expensive – written by hand on hides turned into the costly material, vellum – the group which based its knowledge on them was necessarily small, an elite. Such texts were initially produced in the *scriptoria* of monasteries. From the twelfth century onwards, the universities began to cater to the demand for textbooks of both professors and students. At a slightly later time, professional workshops were set up to meet the wishes of private collectors, bibliophiles, who ordered luxury manuscripts that were mainly if not solely valued for their beautiful illustrations. Thus, by its very economic and social context as well as by its nature, for centuries both the amount and the communication value of handwritten texts was severely limited.[7]

To give an example, in the relatively poor region which the Northern Netherlands was before *c.*1400, not more than a few texts were produced.[8] In the Southern Netherlands and present-day northern France the situation was somewhat better until the economy declined there.[9] In wealthy Sicily the biggest number of books in the hands of any private person in the late fourteenth and early fifteenth centuries amounted to only twenty.[10] Indeed, in about 1450, when Europe had approximately 100 million inhabitants, the number of manuscript books kept in the libraries of cathedrals, monasteries, palaces and castles probably ran only to several tens of thousands. Private citizens, regardless of their wealth and prominence – kings, nobles, senior clergy, the great merchants and bankers – seldom owned more than a few manuscripts. If they bought books at all, these tended to be illuminated bibles, prayer-books and missals, treatises dealing with the art of living as a nobleman or the management of great estates, and, perhaps, one or two courtly romances.

Therefore, any technique which made possible the exact reproduction of a particular text in great numbers would be revolutionary from every point of view. It would reduce the time and cost of repeatedly copying a particular text by hand; it would greatly increase the amount of copies of a particular text; and it would remove the many errors which occurred when a text was copied, and which meant, in the manuscript culture, that after several generations the essential points of a particular text sometimes were so mutilated that the original meaning had partly or completely disappeared, as was painfully obvious in connection with the Bible.

In China, this central communication problem had been solved before the beginning of the Christian era by using blockprinting or xylography; the cutting of texts into wooden blocks had been combined with another invention, paper, on which the ink-covered blocks were impressed. Already before the year 1000 AD, blockprinting helped to produce and spread not only the 150-odd volume edition of the works of Confucius, the founding father of Chinese social and political philosophy – which in its turn spawned a veritable Chinese Renaissance – but also the more than 5,000 volumes in which the Buddhist canon, the *Tripitaka*, was divulged.[11]

In the twelfth century, the Koreans developed and used the technique of individual signs cast in metal, which was also introduced into China. However, the fact that the Koreans do, but the Chinese do not have a phonetic alphabet meant that in China some 30,000 separate characters were needed to print a scholarly text. With manual labour being cheap, for the time being the Korean invention was not taken up in China.

It is certain that Europe knew about Chinese printing methods as early as the late thirteenth century, if only through the tales of the Venetian traveller Marco Polo. Also, news may have reached Europe about type-casting developments in twelfth-century Korea and in the realm of the Uigur Turks, bordering on the Islamic world, who started using wooden letters at roughly the same time.[12] Indeed, blockprinting was in evidence in Europe from the fourteenth century onwards, in the production of playing cards as well as religious prints; it certainly occurred in the Rhineland around the 1370s and probably had been introduced there from the Islamic world. Yet, it is still impossible to determine if, in the case of the early-fifteenth-century efforts at type-casting in the Netherlands and of the subsequent, more successful efforts of Johann Gutenberg (*c.*1400–67) – in the Rhineland, again – we are dealing with independent invention, or, at least, with idea diffusion.

Whatever the answer to this question, from the late fifteenth century onwards, the west continued along the path of typography, whereas China held on to its xylographic tradition. For a long time, the two were compatible at least in the sense that the amount of time and expense it took to found and set the type for a western-style book page was the same as the amount of time necessary to produce a carved page for a xylographically reproduced book. Only in the late nineteenth century, when labour in China became much more expensive, and the technics of typographic or European printing were greatly improved with the introduction of the rotation press, could the west begin to successfully introduce its own system in the land of origin, where understandably it had been discarded as less than practical a millennium earlier.

In Europe, the fame for realizing the great leap from a manuscript to a print culture is traditionally given to the German Johann Gutenberg. He experimented with separate, raised letters of uniform height and width cast in metal; he fiddled around with ink, manufactured on the basis of oil paint; he developed a press which printed the letters, set in line as words and sentences in wooden frames, onto paper, instead of placing the paper on the woodcut letters, as in China.

Between 1438 and 1452, Gutenberg, besieged by industrial spies, developed his technique, shrouding his experiments in secrecy. He operated on the basis of borrowed capital. In the course of the year 1453, the Fust firm, one of Gutenberg's backers, demanded its money. Gutenberg could not pay and therefore had to hand over his materials, just when he was ready to test his invention in practice. In the same year, the first book appeared, printed according to the technique we still know. Significantly, it was a Bible. It was a monument to what was quickly called the *Ars artificialiter scribendi*, 'the art of artificial writing'. 'The Gutenberg Bible', as this book is referred to, was a splendid, clear print in a number of exactly identical copies. Nowadays, a single Gutenberg Bible cannot be bought for millions of pounds.

Gutenberg's inventions led to a veritable revolution in European society: economic, technical and cultural. One might even argue that it was the beginning of the most important cultural revolution which western man had experienced in many thousands of years.[13] Printers, who were simultaneously publishers and booksellers, quickly appeared in all big European cities. Book production now became an economic factor and an industry. In the world of manuscripts a copy was usually made because an individual client had asked for it. Now that books could be printed in larger numbers, and presses, which were of course expensive, should preferably be kept running, a printer-publisher had to investigate and sometimes even create a market. He did this by, among other things, advertising his product, which he offered to customers who did not yet know that they needed it. He advertised a still unknown text by a classical Greek or Latin writer, an even better version of the Bible, yet another hymnbook. But publishers also worked to create a market, e.g. for a new cookery book, a new treatise on the education of children or a new series of erotic or even pornographic stories, complete with revealing pictures. The new medium literally created new texts, which previously had not existed because there was no market for them. Precisely because all sorts of texts could be produced properly and cheaply they were now written and printed. As a result, life in Europe changed fundamentally.

The price of books dropped dramatically, both because it was possible to offer so many identical copies and because paper was used instead of the much more expensive parchment. The technique of manufacturing paper, also developed by the Chinese, had become known in Europe in the thirteenth and fourteenth centuries, again via the Arab-Islamic world of Spain. Because of all this, the transcriber's or copyist's profession virtually disappeared during the sixteenth century.

The new technique was soon perfected. All sorts of typefaces were developed, intended to guarantee greater precision in printing, also for small format books, which now quickly appeared. Gutenberg's Bible had been an enormous, unwieldy tome. In the sixteenth century, the Venetian printer-publisher Aldus Manutius developed more convenient texts, pocket-size books, as an answer to a growing need, which was also a sign of the demand for the product; the Chinese literati, of course, had had them for ages, calling them sleeve-books.

Gunpowder and compass

Undeniably, the instruments named by Bacon have been of central importance for the development of Europe since the fifteenth century up to today. It is therefore necessary to pause and consider their role. The cases of the printing press, the gun and the compass are also illustrative of a situation which contributed to significant developments in the entire field of European technology and, consequently, of the European states but also of Europe's position in the wider world.

Though printing may be considered a European invention, developed independently from, although far later than in China, neither gunpowder nor the compass were European discoveries. Yet Europe applied both instruments in ways that had not been thought of or elaborated elsewhere. It is one of the fascinating aspects of human history that certain inventions, while causing little or no change in a given culture, can bring around a revolution in a different setting.

The very fact that Europe was made up of a great number of small, increasingly competitive political entities may well have been one of the main reasons for the progress made in creatively modifying techniques that arrived from Asia; in later periods, this competition continued to stimulate indigenous inventions.

In view of their demographic expansion, Europe's many polities were forced to exploit to the utmost their meagre resources. But this very division into small states may also have helped it to overcome the depressing effects of the global agricultural and economic crisis of the fourteenth century and its accompanying 'pandemic'. Europe's population, decreasing from *c.*80 million to *c.*60 million between 1300 and 1400, started rising again in the fifteenth century; indeed, Europe entered upon a phase of great expansion in every field. In China, however, a population which had numbered *c.*115 million in 1200 dropped to 85 million in 1300 and to 75 million in 1400. There, this very crisis seems to have been one of the causes which heralded a prolonged period of relative stagnation, which may be explained from a growing tendency to conservatism in the upper echelons of the huge, monolithically ruled empire.[14] Thus, for the first time in history, the technological and consequently economic balance between the two civilizations was reversed.

Nevertheless, the combination of a discernible resurgence of conservative, agriculturally orientated ideologies in China and, though less so, in Japan and India, from the fifteenth century onwards, and the increased interest in technical innovations in Europe cannot entirely explain the technological gap that grew between the west and the east. For while China surprisingly decided to give up maritime expansion after the great and evidently successful expeditions of Admiral Cheng Ho in the early fifteenth century, it still continued to produce inventions, as, for example, the three-spindle spinning wheel and the calendering roller in the textile industry. Nor is it sufficient to note the fact that food prices and, consequently, wages seem to have been higher in Europe than in Asia, which at the European side of the globe stimulated the introduction and perfection of machines in most fields of production.

Rather, it seems that the main cause for the growing gap between east and west lay in the notion, propagated by such men as Sir Francis Bacon, that science should be studied systematically, through the collection, classification, analysis and interpretation of ever greater amounts of empirical data and, moreover, that such scientific work should be strictly organized. Such positivist ideas certainly had their origins in the earlier method of philological empiricism developed from the thirteenth century onwards to deal with biblical and classical texts. Of course, the slow spreading of this mental attitude, contributing to the growth of the habit of abstract thought, was greatly strengthened by the availability of information through printing – the invention of which coincided with the first age of maritime expansion. Printing, besides the numerous other cultural changes it brought about, was certainly immensely important too in facilitating, broadening and speeding up the development of new technology in Europe.

Regarding scientific developments in sixteenth-century Europe, one may assume that thinking in terms of systematic organization and operation developed from the mental absorption of the processes of early machinery; among these, the clock was probably the most influential, both in providing a vision of order and in imposing a sense of regulated time, which, when introduced into economic life, also began changing people's attitudes towards work and leisure.[15] In its turn, this way of thinking was translated to various fields of human endeavour. In the long run all this must have facilitated a mental and organizational change in general industrial production, too, from a craft-orientated attitude to an assembly line mode.[16] In the short run, two sectors of public life were drastically changed.

After its introduction in the fourteenth century, gunpowder in Europe was soon used not only to fire heavy cannon, but also to provide ammunition for light arms to be carried and used by single men operating on foot rather than on horseback. This new application led to a major change in European society, affecting life far beyond the military sphere.

Small, inefficient armies of knights riding expensive heavily armoured horses were replaced with increasingly large armies, consisting mainly of cheap foot soldiers equipped with firearms. The phenomenon of the arms' industry was born, but so was the arms' race; increasingly large masses of troops were deployed, and military technology as well as investments in it came to play a more essential role. New types of weaponry were developed, new ways of protecting cities against the volleys of far-reaching guns and cannons had to be devised. While wars became bloodier, they also became costlier. Even in times of peace, armies continued to demand their toll. Soldiers, when not sent home but retained in garrisons, had to be paid, fed and clothed.

The reforms in military organization in particular, such as the arms drill in marching and the use of weapons practised by Prince Maurice of Nassau in the Northern Netherlands and King Gustavus Wasa in Sweden, were highly influential in creating a mentality tuned to the systematic division of labour. So was the need of early modern armies for the production of food, clothing and weaponry along uniform lines and in great amounts. But thinking about the state in general was influenced by a more technical, machine-influenced image. The state, too, could be seen as a clock, a complex mechanism made up of numerous people all doing their part. The prince, of course, if not the actual clock-maker, was still the person who wound it.

From the sixteenth century onwards, a steadily growing proportion of the

Plate 19 From the 'age of manuscripts': in his study, the scholar-scribe Master Hildebert teaches his pupil Everwin, depicted in a hand-written copy of St Augustine's *De Civitate Dei*, made for Heinrich Zdík, Bishop of Olomouc, *c.*1136–7, preserved in the Library of the Chapter of St Vitus Cathedral, Prague

Plate 20 From the 'age of printing': printer's mark showing a simple printing press, used by Petrus Caesar of Ghent, one of the earliest printers, working in the 1470s

Source: *Gravures sur bois, tirées des livres français de XVe siècle*, Paris 1868

national revenue went to the military. Therefore, the European states needed to increase their income. To the extent that their own fiscal capacity did not suffice, foreign expansion could offer a solution. When a certain balance of power had been reached in Europe, expansion outside Europe continued out of necessity, as it were. This is one of the reasons why Europeans, who for a thousand years had hardly gone beyond the borders of their own world, now began to leave their safe territory in ever-increasing numbers, heading for unknown lands and, even more, waters: individually, they may have sought adventure, fame and wealth, collectively, they looked for opportunities for economic expansion that would be the basis for greater power, abroad but more importantly at home.

In this context, the compass acquired its importance. European sailors, acquainted with it in the thirteenth or fourteenth century, now ventured onto the open seas making use of the new instrument. When new geographical notions attracted Europe's interest following the rediscovery of such ancient writers as Ptolemy and Strabo, they now even dared to cross the oceans, hoping, and later knowing, that the earth was, indeed, round, that each journey outward could also be a homeward journey. So began the voyages of discovery. So began European colonialism: the compass provided the assurance of direction and certainty at sea, and firearms provided certainty and ascendancy in the newly discovered lands. Europe spread its wings and began conquering large parts of the world. But the men who did so acted for the European states, beginning with Vasco da Gama and Christopher Columbus, employed by the Portuguese and Spanish crowns respectively.

═══════════════

THE HAGUE, AD 1625: HUGO GROTIUS EXPOUNDS 'THE LAW OF NATIONS'

In 1625, the famous Dutch legal theorist and lawyer Hugo de Groot (1583–1645) published his *De Iure belli ac pacis* (On the right of war and peace), a systematic account of all legal thinking relevant to the relationship between individual states which, in their development towards formalized and centralized structures, had also become increasingly competitive; the need to regularize this often bloody competition induced Grotius to think thoroughly about the problems involved. In these excerpts, Grotius' concern about the conflict between practice and theory, power politics and the rights of human dignity, becomes clear:

> Many have endeavoured to write explanatory commentaries or concise surveys of the municipal law, for instance, of Rome or of a man's own country. Few, however, have attempted the law which applies to the relations of several nations or of their rulers, whether it be derived from nature itself or instituted by custom or tacit contract, and no one so far has treated it completely and systematically. Yet mankind has a concern that this be done. . . .

True, man is an animal, but of a very superior kind, a great deal more removed from the others than their species differ from another; many activities peculiar to the human race show this. Among the special characteristics of mankind is a desire for society, that is for a life in common lived not anyhow but in tranquillity and (to satisfy one's intellect) arranged with men of one's own kind. So the supposition that every animal naturally seeks its own advantage is true of other animals, but of man only before he has achieved the employment of his peculiarly human qualities. . . .

That preference for society . . . of which I have already spoken is the source of *ius* properly so called. It involves abstention from another's property, its restitution to him if we do happen to possess it, reparation of damage done by fault, and an admission that punishment may be applied among men. . . .

It is quite wrong to suppose, as some imagine, that in war all laws cease to apply; indeed, war should never be engaged in except to obtain lawful ends, nor once engaged in should it be waged except within the bounds of law and good faith. Demosthenes was right to argue that war is an action directed against those who cannot be constrained by process of law. . . .

Holding it thus firmly established that there exists among nations a common law with force for and in wars, I had many and weighty reasons for writing a book about it. Throughout Christendom I saw a readiness to make war of which even barbarians might be ashamed. Men take up arms for light causes or none at all, and once at war they discard all respect for the laws of God and men. . . . The sight of such atrocities has induced a good many truly reputable writers to forbid Christian men all recourse to arms since it is their special duty to love all men. . . .

[Concluding that this situation is irrealistic, Grotius continues to ponder about the regulation of war.] Touching those who are truly enemy subjects, that is from a permanent condition, the law of nations permits them to be injured, as to their persons, in any place. When war is declared against anyone it is simultaneously declared against the men of his people. . . . We may therefore lawfully kill them on our own soil, on enemy soil, or on soil belonging to no one, or on the high seas. It is not permitted to kill them on [neutral] territory remaining at peace. . . .

How widely this liberty extends may be seen from the fact that the killing of children and women is held to be lawful and included in this law of war. . . . Not even prisoners are exempt. . . .

The violation of women is variously regarded as permitted or not. Those who allow it consider only the injury done to the person, which they hold it agreable to the law of arms to inflict on anything belonging to the enemy. The other opinion is better: it takes into account not only the injury but also the act of unbridled lust and concludes that something pertaining to neither safety nor punishment should be no more lawful in war than in peace. This latter view is not the law of all nations, but it is the law of the more respectable ones.[17]

━━━━━━━━━━━━

Whether or not they heeded the law of nations, it was these states which, from the fifteenth century onwards, wondered what kind of Europe they wanted. What they definitely did not want anymore was a situation in which one hegemonic system limited their sovereignty, the more so because the only remaining organization with such pretensions, the Catholic Church, partly derived its authority from its power over the incomprehensible, the magical, through ritual and sacrifice. Most people in Europe continued to be deeply influenced by this kind of power. The Church's might being based on it still made it potentially all-embracing. Thus, it was all the more frustrating for rulers and their bureaucrats, who were striving to attain absolute power over the people they now considered primarily as the subjects of their states.

Church and State: the break-up of religious unity

Until the fifteenth century, the Catholic Church was the only bearer of a religion confessed everywhere in Europe. It was an institution which, transcending the borders of manors, counties, duchies and kingdoms, had created a common religion with a number of values derived from it, and a common cultural awareness, at least among the elite. In the tenth, eleventh, and subsequently the fourteenth and fifteenth centuries, under the influence of the repeated revival of the crusading idea, the habit had developed of equating the term *Christianitas*, which defined the world of Christianity as opposed to the world of Islam, with geographical 'Europe', suggesting that the latter represented a certain cultural unity as well.

However, in the fifteenth and early sixteenth centuries, the Church of Rome lost its monopoly of power in the Christian West. Criticism of the Church's teachings and of its political and moral pretences had been growing in the preceding centuries, but the Church's structure, though crumbling some-what, had largely remained intact. The 'final blow' came from the German theologian, Martin Luther (1483–1546).

From the 1520s onwards, a very successful movement for religious reform developed in Luther's name. Other theologians as, for example, John Calvin, who taught in Geneva, quickly proclaimed their own views of theology and Church organization. Besides addressing doctrinal and theological issues, Luther and his fellow critics were vociferous in condemning a variety of ecclesiastical practices that had developed over the centuries. There was the hotly debated question of the Church tithes and of the sale of indulgences, that channelled much of the wealth of the faithful into the coffers of Rome. There also was the often disappointingly low intellectual and spiritual level of the clergy, who, largely uneducated themselves, kept their flock ignorant of even the most basic tenets of Christian belief.

Before Luther and his like, calls for reform had been made by critical members of the clergy at various Church councils in the fifteenth century. The new demand would have been as ineffective as the earlier ones if it had not been for two important factors. Of course, one of them was the influence of printing, which greatly facilitated the spreading of new ideas. Equally important however, was that the calls for reform were taken up by a number of Europe's reigning princes. Some of them were honestly concerned about the many malpractices affecting their people through the Church, but many just felt that the power wielded by Rome and its regional representatives impinged rather too much upon their own authority, politically and economically, which, precisely in this period, they tried to increase. Thus, they eagerly seized upon this opportunity, using the prevailing climate of protest either to force Rome into a number of concessions, mostly of a financial and political nature, that gave them greater independence in the affairs of the Church in their own realm, or to sever altogether the ties that had bound them to the papacy for almost a thousand years.

The kings of France and Spain, for example, while remaining staunch Roman Catholics, yet greatly reduced Rome's influence in their states, whereas the king of England, followed by the monarchs of Denmark and Sweden and a number of German princes, went over to the Reformation, as the entire movement came to be called although, due to circumstances that varied from state to state, it eventually took different shapes both in north-west and in central Europe.

Basically, the actions of Luther and the other reformers created a fundamental split into what there had been of European unity. They caused the one Church that had given Europe cultural coherence for more than a thousand years to become divided into many religious denominations, all, true enough, Christian, yet quickly developing very different concepts and cultures. The Reformation divided Europeans into Catholics, who remained loyal to Rome, and thus, to Latin as the language of worship and culture, and Protestants of all sorts who translated the Bible and the liturgy in the vernacular and in doing so made a considerable contribution to further linguistic and hence cultural nationalism.

During the Council of Trent, the Catholic Church showed its resilience, formulating standpoints which were intended to buttress anew the might of what was still called the Universal Church. Probably more radically than ever before, this restored Roman Church did indeed influence virtually all areas of culture through religion. On the central level, the Congregation of the Inquisition, a court judging the (im)propriety of doctrine, became an instrument to ensure orthodoxy; obviously, it could also be used to stifle any form of critical thinking remotely affecting, or threatening to affect the teaching and thus the power of the Church. However, one has to realize that it was not very effective outside the Italian states and the Spanish kingdoms. Indeed, despite all its efforts, the papacy did not succeed in making its reformed version of Christianity 'universal' once more.

Due to the political background and backing of the Reformation, in most of the 'reformed' parts of Europe State-dominated Protestant Churches came into existence, controlled by secular and spiritual authorities in an often uneasy balance. For though the reformers had to thank the princes and their bureaucracies for effective support in introducing the new doctrine, they would have preferred to be left free to run their own religious communities. Instead, the states used them to introduce and impose their own views even in the field of doctrine, very much as the Church of Rome had always done and still did in Catholic Europe.

Despite this tendency towards uniformity, the reformers' insistence on the individual's primary obligation and responsibility *vis-à-vis* his Maker may have contributed to or even resulted in a situation wherein alternative thinking, both in matters religious and in matters social and political, slowly began to take roots more easily in the Protestant states of north-west Europe than in the south-eastern regions still dominated by the Roman Church.

However, by and large, the influence of religion in society remained undiminished whether in Protestant or in Catholic Europe. Following the adage 'cuius regio, illius et religio' (who dominates the land also decides upon its religion), most princes continued to use religion both as a channel for propaganda and, in many cases, as an instrument to enforce cultural cohesion in their state, with the sole aim of increasing their own power. To the extent that the states of Europe still felt the need to capture their subjects by ritual and sacrament, the kings were increasingly presented as rulers sent and sanctioned by God. They were or became the embodiment of the state or the nation.

Once again it was the intellectual elite who helped shape this ideology. An elite, as always, of scholars and even, by now, of 'intellectuals', of men who while making the accumulation and transfer of knowledge their profession,[18] set out to influence society through the power they held over the word and through the ways in which they used and manipulated images and symbols. They were writers of chronicles and histories, political theorists and propagandists. However, they were no longer, as in the time of Charlemagne, recruited exclusively from the ranks of the Church which, at that time, had still supported the State. Instead, they were increasingly laymen, servants of the State, often even hostile to every claim the Churches still dared to make, and certainly enemies of the one Church which did so by calling on its unique function as the protector of Europe's unity.

The rise of the Reformation and the growing opposition to papal authority, even in Catholic circles, meant that in the sixteenth century there was neither place for a common European front based on a common religious foundation, for instance against Islam, nor for the accompanying sense of identity. 'Rather Turkish than popish' was a slogan often heard. Perhaps precisely because many people rejected the papacy, which underpinned its claims to supremacy by calling on a universal Christianity which was presented as identical with Europe, more and more people also rejected the one-thousand-year-old identification of *Europe* with *Christendom*. In short, as a result of all sorts of developments, the notion of *Christianitas* was gradually forgotten and the concept of *Europe* became firmly established. But even though most educated people may have thought in these terms, yet they saw Europe exclusively as a composition, a context of interaction, perhaps, between independent sovereign nations, whose task it was to realize peace and prosperity by maintaining the balance.[19]

Printing, reading and the schools: education for the masses?

Until the fifteenth century, education had been restricted largely to the elite. In schools directed by monks or other clergymen and attached to monasteries and cathedrals, the sons of the upper classes received a rudimentary education in which reading and writing were central. Future knights and administrators did not actually need much more.

Someone desiring a career in the ranks of the Church naturally needed other skills – Latin, theology and philosophy. Moreover, a career in the Church was the only chance for a decent education for boys from other milieux, since the Church did not make any social distinction when recruiting clergymen, although the highest positions in the hierarchy were increasingly given to those who not only boasted a good education but also the family background that gave them easy access to patronage and power.

It was precisely this better education that meant that clergymen were frequently asked to fulfil all sorts of functions in secular politics; we regularly come across them as advisers to kings, who often preferred unmarried priests to members of the aristocracy, who, after all, wanted to enlarge their own power and that of their offspring, often at the monarch's expense.

In the fifteenth and sixteenth centuries, when princes began to expand their power through, among other things, a policy of administrative centralization, they were aware of the need for an effective bureaucratic apparatus. They knew that a powerful state can exist only if it is based on a large, well-organized civil service.

This required many well-educated people who not only were able to read and write but also were at home with the principles of taxation and public finance. Besides this, they had to be especially well acquainted with the foundations of Roman law. Whether or not Roman Law was mixed to varying degrees with the 'Germanic' legal tradition, it was considered by virtually all of Europe as the basis of political-administrative thought and of the legal system, the pre-eminent factor ensuring the uniformity and homogeneity that were necessary to a powerful state. A better education also became important for economic activities: growing international trade and banking naturally required different skills from running the corner shop.

The need for more and better education thus was felt all over Europe. But it was only printing which finally realized it. After all, without the printed word, education on a large scale would have been virtually impossible. Now, textbooks about all areas of learning were printed at prices affordable for parents from the middle class and not just the social elite. For precisely the well-to-do burghers were the people who wanted to give their sons the chance to climb the social ladder through careers in all the new sectors – the swelling government bureaucracy, banking, commerce, overseas trade and beginning industrialization.

Indeed, in the fifteenth, sixteenth and seventeenth centuries, the number of schools increased significantly; thus education indisputably became one of the 'basic structures of culture' in Europe.[20] For instance, in England there was a definite trend towards more schools with education for more people as the fifteenth century drew to a close, which became more intense in the following centuries. This was helped by the fact that English slowly replaced French as the spoken language of the elite and as the written language of government, a development stimulated by growing political differences between England and France.[21] As education apart from the three 'R's' consisted mainly of religious teaching, the choice by the English Reformation for the vernacular as the language of worship and the emphasis on independent reading of the Bible in the translated, so-called King James version (1611) was an influential one. For the same reasons the Dutch so-called 'State Authorized Version' (*Statenvertaling*) (1637), had an effect on the standardization of Dutch and the reading ability and language use of people in the Dutch Republic, both those who attended school and those who were confronted with it only at home.

Yet the effects of education based on the new print culture differed greatly in Europe, according to region and especially social group, and were not felt as quickly everywhere. Considering the lowest level of education, that is, reading and writing in own's one language, it has been established that literacy slowly increased. However, it is worth pointing out that in most research the ability to write one's signature often served as the only proof of this development. Measured in this way, illiteracy dropped to 80 per cent for men and 95 per cent for women in the England of Queen Elizabeth I. Still as high as that in about 1600, the figures dropped to 70–90 per cent in about 1650, 55–75 per cent in about 1700 and 40–60 per cent in about 1750. Then a stagnation set in, lasting well into the nineteenth century.[22] In France, using the same gauge, 70 per cent of men and 90 per cent of women were still illiterate even by about 1700, a situation which hardly improved in the next one-and-a-half centuries.[23]

While this may not be an impressive performance, we should not be surprised by this low level of literacy, if only because in large parts of Catholic Europe badly educated clergymen were the sole teachers. When in 1671 a new bishop, Monseigneur Le Camus, made a tour of inspection in his new diocese, Grenoble – the first which had taken place for two hundred years – he came across some devoted and cultured parish priests, but the majority were alcoholic, fornicating and almost illiterate, and one of them had never even heard of the New Testament.[24] What were the peasants supposed to learn from such men? Nor was the situation any better in the 'reformed' parts of Europe. Reading the autobiography of the seventeenth-century English theologian Richard Baxter, one still feels his dissatisfaction with a youth not nourished by well-educated, high-principled clergymen:

> We lived in a country that had but little preaching at all. In the village where I was born there were four readers successively in six years time, ignorant men, and two of them immoral in their lives. . . . the clerck could not read well. . . . Within a few miles about us were near a dozen ministers that . . . never preached . . . ; poor, ignorant.[25]

However, historians have long argued that the level of literacy in Protestant countries, where, after all, the Bible had been translated into the vernacular and the reading of it was encouraged, was certainly higher than in Catholic states; there, the decrees of the Council of Trent (1545–63) had forbidden translations of Holy Scripture, thus making it impossible for most people to read it, so that the clergy continued to form the only 'information caste'. This impression appears to be wrong: in those German states which had embraced the Reformation the people were confronted only with very simple excerpts from the Bible and it seems that they could hardly understand even these. There has also been great enthusiasm about how in Sweden, especially through the efforts of the Lutheran Church, the reading proficiency of large groups in the population was already high by the seventeenth century. Yet here, too, scattered indicators point to the fact that this reading ability, largely limited to Holy Scripture, in no way meant that people actually understood what they were reading.

Meanwhile, in Rome the spiritual authorities did try to use cheap prints to promote different forms of popular piety to enhance the vision of the Church as they saw it, a situation which, of course, printers eagerly took advantage of.[26] But on the whole, both the Catholic Church and the Protestant Churches seem to have pursued a fairly restrictive policy with regard to the extent to which they wanted their believers to become independent thinkers through the printed word.[27]

Many who learned to read and write did not learn anything else. By far the majority of people in Europe attended only 'vernacular schools', where both dictation, the didactic method most popular in the fourteenth and fifteenth centuries, and the few new teaching methods developed in their own times, remained in use for the following centuries.[28] When debate about improving these schools began in the eighteenth century, it appeared that in France, which called itself 'enlightened', most thinkers, for reasons of economic and social expediency, did not consider it wise to burden pupils from the masses with anything more than reading, writing and arithmetic: grand ideas would lead only to political and social criticism and dissatisfaction.[29]

From a 'primary school' one could go on to the Latin School, as it had always been called, because the language of instruction was Latin. From the fifteenth century onwards, all over Europe education at these schools was deeply influenced by the *Studium Humanitatis*. In this, the classical texts, reconstructed to be as close to the original as possible, were central and Cicero became the model for elegant prose. Overall, the same subjects were taught at the 'Latin Schools' as, till the middle of the twentieth century, were characteristic of the traditional 'gymnasium', 'lyceum' or grammar school: these subjects emphasized the value of the classical tradition, presented in a framework which established the norms which Christianity imposed on everyone from early childhood.

Certainly, education at these Latin Schools and at the academies or universities which a small group of boys attended afterwards was authoritarian and, moreover, imitative rather than creative.[30] Only one person seems to really have tried to improve the system. He was Johann Amos Komensky, or Comenius (1592–1670).[31] Born in Moravia, he became a priest and a poet – in his native Czech – as well as a scholar and a didactician. He advocated ecumenicism among the religions, and the need for Christian pacifism. He wrote about the necessity to create an international legal order and a universal language. While living in Poland, he composed his *Didactica magna*; in it, he stressed the importance of studying creation and all its *realia* besides the Bible and the *litterae humaniores*; he also suggested that only the inclusion of sports and other forms of play would result in a proper curriculum; finally, he proposed that boys and girls be educated together. In Sweden, he was allowed to introduce some of his ideas in the school system; in Hungary, he set up a school entirely along his own lines. While in Comenius' ideals we recognize much that has contributed to modern notions of education, by and large his ideas proved too much in advance of his age and only very slowly gained recognition. Thus, for a long time girls were excluded from public schools beyond the primary level. If they received any further education at all, this was done at home or, in the Catholic world, in monastic establishments; it was only in the late seventeenth century that private, secular boarding schools for girls developed in the Protestant world.

Yet despite the didactic and intellectual, the economic and social and, indeed, the gender restrictions of most Latin schools, they must be considered a major pillar of European civilization. The forms of classical Antiquity which had slowly merged with the values of Christianity, for centuries gave a footing to those who would create the more articulate manifestations of culture of their own time and who could thus be called, with some rhetorical exaggeration, the 'bearers' of European civilization.

From the Latin School talented or wealthy male pupils would go on to university. Whereas in earlier centuries universities had mostly originated in cathedral and monastery schools, in the fifteenth and sixteenth centuries the number of new, secular foundations grew explosively. The new states promoted secondary and higher education from understandable self-interest, especially to create a reservoir of highly educated people from which an administrative elite could be recruited. Also, a university was considered to lend prestige to a city or state. Finally, the Reformation caused the creation of new academies for the academic training of Protestant theologians; many of these institutions quickly acquired a more general university function as, for example, Strasbourg (1538) and Leiden (1575).

But always, this was education for an elite and scholarship carried out by an elite, even though these elites did not entirely overlap, socio-economically speaking. Though the number of students rose considerably, secondary and higher education were definitely not available to all. Moreover, certainly at university level, the choice of study was strongly influenced by financial factors; for example, the study of medicine was expensive and thus beyond the reach of most people.

Yet the great expansion of academic education in the sixteenth century meant that the percentage of the European population which could participate in it grew,[32] significantly changing the cultural character of Europe in the centuries that followed. However, at the end of the seventeenth century a slowly increasing elitism appeared;[33] the attendance percentage dropped again.[34] Partly as a result, the social and mental openness which had been created in Europe by, among other things, the universities, seems to have decreased at the end of the eighteenth century. It was not until the twentieth century that the percentage of those participating in higher education again reached the same levels as in the sixteenth and early seventeenth centuries.

The educated European, who had gone from primary school to Latin School and perhaps even on to university, wanted to understand his place in the world in all its facets. The fifteenth and sixteenth centuries were precisely the period in which the world became vastly more complex. The first overseas discoveries, the new medium of printing and the increased possibilities to acquire an education meant that a flood of information now reached a wider public than had ever been the case. In a world which was getting bigger every day, people tried to fit the multitude of new data and ideas which became available into traditional but inevitably slowly changing frames of reference. As a result of all these factors, educated, reading individuals had to redefine their position both in relation to their fellows and society and in relation to their Creator. A changing culture led to stimulating questions but frequently also to nagging doubts.[35]

The interaction between the norms and values taken from classical Antiquity and from Christianity was reinforced by the challenge which an increasingly complex world presented. Together they determined secondary and higher education as well as the world of learning. The two concepts Renaissance and Humanism capture these developments. Together they describe a cultural ideal which for a long time has been an enduring form of European thought and, in a changed, adapted form, perhaps still is.

One might object that the religious differences which ravaged Europe in the sixteenth century – the rupture in the universal Catholic Church, the split between Rome, Wittenberg and Geneva – preclude a general pronouncement on the 'European character' of education and learning. Yet it should be borne in mind that, despite many differences, to a certain extent the same questions arose in both the Catholic and Reformed worlds. People discussed the same issues and, even if they did not discuss these together, they shared a number of educational ideals and practices. Thus, the pedagogical concepts of the Protestant humanist Jacob Sturm (1507–89), who lived in Strasbourg and all his life strove for unity in the Christian world, greatly influenced the *ratio studiorum*, the curriculum of the Jesuits; all over Catholic Europe, in their boarding schools the latter moulded innumerable generations of boys who came from or entered into the cultural, largely also sociopolitical, elite.

Reflecting on the common ground between the religiously defined cultures in Europe, one recalls the theological discussion among both Catholics and Protestants about the text and substance not only of the gospels but also of the entire Bible, as well as about the normative function of the early Christian

Church. Both camps also struggled with questions concerning the core concept of grace, as well as the increasing tension between belief and reason, between perceptible nature and the question about the place of man and God therein. Nor should we forget that there were innumerable areas where religious differences were less pressing, where people of opposing religious views yet could actively discuss them with each other, the more so because communication still flowed reasonably easily as, for the time being, Latin remained the common language of traditional learned culture, and mathematics, a universal symbolic language, became the vehicle for the new sciences.

All over Europe, education and learning, which had been given such an enormous boost by the invention of printing, did indeed share many fundamental characteristics which made them truly 'European'.

Unity and diversity: printing as a cultural revolution

The most important, largely unforeseen results of the invention and introduction of the art of printing were cultural in the widest sense. Indeed, there were actually no areas of European life, even for those who could not read or write, which were not somehow influenced by the coming of the printed word. But it is precisely because we can hardly imagine a society without it which makes it so difficult for us to appreciate the cultural revolution which in fact took place.

It was of course obvious that the effects of printing would first become manifest in scholarship, where the need for communication was probably felt most acutely. In the time of manuscript communication, scholars could usually learn of other people's ideas in their field of research only with the greatest difficulty, if at all. Of many important texts often only one or at most a few copies were available. There was, therefore, hardly any continuous and widespread accumulation of knowledge. New notions might develop in a particular region but did not spread easily and swiftly to contribute to discussion and an increase of knowledge elsewhere.

This quickly changed under the influence of the art of printing. When, in Venice, Aldus Manutius began a systematic edition of classical Greek texts, based partly on the manuscripts introduced by Greek-Byzantine refugee scholars like Bessarion, Europe acquired the *Iliad* and the *Odyssey* and, thus, the subject matter of many a learned debate of a philological and historical nature. When well-researched and complete editions of Aristotle and Plato appeared for the first time, European philosophers could not believe their luck. And (as discussed above) the text of the Greek Bible, showing the incompleteness of the Latin version used by the Catholic Church, set Roman theologians and philologists to work on a new edition and also led to vehement discussions with repercussions in various domains, including Church politics.[36] Thus, the seemingly simple but essentially scholarly, scientific work of establishing a 'correct' text and making it public through the art of printing contributed greatly to the sense of community among Europe's learned elite − as it had done in such other cultures which had developed this art, namely China, Japan and Korea.

One of the most important aspects of the printed word is that it gives those who have power over it the opportunity to exercise or increase their power through its use. The two main components of the European elite, the leaders of State and Church, were the first groups who appropriated the new instrument.

In 1539, King François I of France issued the edict of Villiers-Cotterets, in which he made it known that from then on the dialect of Paris, French, would be the official language of the entire kingdom. Presenting all official documents in this one unequivocal language – the laws and regulations printed in Paris and spread as pamphlets or broadsheets all over France – the King could really expect to reach the mass of his subjects. Of course, he meant to buttress his authority and extend his possibilities to exercise it on essential points. After all, the many regional languages spoken in France – as in Spain, England, the German states and in fact the whole of Europe – prevented the various peoples of his state from understanding each other. This severely limited the power of central government in Paris. Under these circumstances, a real feeling of 'we, Frenchmen', a 'national awareness' could never develop; it also meant that the different parts of the state of France retained their own cultural identity, and were therefore better able to resist the often unwelcome intrusion in regional and local government by royal officials from Paris. The same situation also caused great practical difficulties. The collection of taxes and the administration of justice did not function properly because the officials and the citizens literally did not speak the same language. By making one language compulsory, King François hoped to clear up all these problems. He knew that the printing press was the principal, indeed the only means to give this provision effect. For without educating his entire realm in this one language, he would not succeed. And, without cheap texts in this one language, or, in other words, printed texts, large-scale education could not function. With the help of the printed word, however, he could expect to greatly enlarge his royal power.

In language itself, printing led to crucial developments. How were children to be taught the one, 'national' language, the language, therefore, of the elite? How did the dialect of Paris become French, or the dialect of Holland, Dutch?

Books establishing the rules of grammar appeared. And, as mentioned before, in the Protestant countries, bibles were translated and printed in that specific variety of the vernacular which now became the national language. As the Bible was the most important story on which children were fed from an early age, the language in which it was read was bound to become one of the most influential factors in shaping the 'national' language. However, those languages which were not promoted and codified in this way – as was the case in France with many 'regional' languages – became 'mere' dialects, spoken still but not written or printed anymore. They also withdrew, as it were, because they lost their status. People who wanted to be part of the establishment, political or cultural, had to start learning French instead of Breton or Provençal, English instead of Gaelic, Dutch instead of Guelders. In this way, language became a characteristic of national unity. But it also meant that language became an instrument for central government, for princes and their bureaucracies.

Through incipient mass education, based on printed textbooks, uniform, 'national' languages were now formed in France and in other European countries. Central government began to express and impose regulations and ordinances in these languages, which came to be understood in the same way by every educated citizen. In France, in the early seventeenth century, Louis XIII even decided to found an official newspaper to make his government's opinions known to as many of the public as possible.

These developments had their reverse side as well. Those who disagreed with the government also began using the weapon of print. Thus, the sixteenth century was the first to see large-scale propaganda and anti-propaganda, through an official and a clandestine press. Moreover, governments introduced a weapon that until then had hardly been necessary – censorship, under which all printed material first had to be officially approved.[37] However, the clandestine press refused to be silenced; subversive texts were printed in secret or abroad, and distributed underground.

Through the printing press, propaganda acquired other forms and uses than the printed word. The public display of power by kings, which most people never saw because they did not travel and therefore never went to the capital, was now depicted in printed pictures which could be sold cheaply and in large quantities, as, for example, in the royal almanacs which were spread all over France in the seventeenth century, to proclaim the glories of Louis XIV, and of France; coronations, court celebrations and parades for military victories could all now be seen, as it were; the state's power, symbolized by and in the King, was thus brought closer to the people. Even the King himself, who was certainly considered unique by the ordinary people, inhabiting a sphere somewhere between heaven and earth, could now be 'seen' by them as he was made visible, too. Engraved portraits showed people what their ruler looked like and, understandably, princes ensured that they presented themselves as impressively as possible, with all the pomp of their dignity and power.

That other government, the Church, also used the printed word to divulge its ideas and wishes and to impose and enforce these as uniformly as possible. Already in the late fifteenth century, the Catholic Church had realized that the printing press was an excellent means of spreading its dogmas and rules to strengthen its power and to enforce uniform behaviour among as many people as possible and under as closely controlled circumstances as possible. Rome even proclaimed that the invention of printing was excellent proof of the superiority of Christian civilization. The argument was heard again in the first great political campaign ever directed with the help of the press: the call to mobilize Europe against the Turks in the late fifteenth and early sixteenth centuries, when the sultan's soldiers, having already seized Byzantium, stormed the Balkans and even came to threaten the walls of Vienna.

Yet Rome did not want the press to spread alternative opinions, to encourage the individualistic interpretations of the man–God–world relation increasingly voiced by those schooled in the views of Renaissance culture and humanist thinking. Therefore, the Roman Catholic Church tried to introduce censorship in the form of the so-called *Index*, a list of banned books, of publications that proper Catholics were forbidden to read – a form of censorship that could be expected of an organization trying to hold on to its power in an increasingly literate culture. However, here too one has to admit that its power was limited, as it relied largely on the reader's moral acceptance of Rome's bans. More effective was the demand made of printers in the Catholic states to obtain permission of the Church authorities before publishing a text, though this prescript, too, was frequently disregarded. Indeed, it seems that the efforts of the secular authorities to create an effective censorial system as a weapon against political criticism were, for the most, far more successful, as is proven by the example of France.

Criticism of the Church's views and practices, or rather of papal authority in Rome, increased significantly at the end of the fifteenth century. Of course, there had been criticism before. In the fourteenth and fifteenth centuries men like the Englishman John Wycliffe and the Czech Jan Hus had clearly expressed their dissatisfaction. Yet their influence had remained regionally limited. After all, they could spread their ideas only by oral or handwritten means. It was therefore impossible for them to mobilize multitudes of followers in large parts of Europe. Now, at the beginning of the sixteenth century, the situation was considerably changed. The German theologian Martin Luther (1483–1546) is an excellent case in point. When he decided that discussion of the conclusions he had reached on the basis of his study of the Bible and other important texts from early Christianity was necessary if only because the Catholic Church's practices were found wanting, he took the course normal in the scholarly world. He formulated his ideas in a number of propositions and advertised them in public – in this case by nailing his handwritten theses to the door of the church at Wittenberg. It was then 31 October 1517.

Raised in the humanist tradition, Luther finally broke with the traditions of the Church of Rome in all those areas wherein, according to him, they were no longer founded on the oldest Christian texts. Central to the many doctrines which Luther derived from his thorough study of the sources of Christianity was the idea that the core of God's revelation is found only in Holy Scripture. He questioned the value of several of the seven sacraments because in his opinion they had not been established by Christ and, moreover, they had become mere acts without any content. Indeed, Luther observed that many Christians had absolutely no notion whatsoever of the norms and values presented in the Bible, simply accepting, uncritically and superstitiously, as salutary the magic of all sorts of actions performed by priests. Hence, he wrote:

> Thus it is not baptism that justifies or benefits anyone, but it is faith in that word of promise to which baptism is added. This faith justifies and fulfils that which baptism signifies. . . . It cannot be true, therefore, that there is contained in the sacraments a power efficacious for justification, or that they are 'effective signs' of

grace. . . . For if the sacrament confers grace on me because I receive it, then indeed I receive grace by virtue of my work, and not by faith; and I gain not the promise in the sacrament but only the sign. . . . Therefore let us open our eyes and learn to pay heed more to the word than to the sign, more to faith than to the work or use of the sign.[38]

More fundamentally, Luther disputed free will: man himself does not determine whether, as a result of his way of life, he will be blessed with salvation. God has already predetermined this. Only a person's belief, also given him by the mercy of God in the beginning, can still save him from damnation if he shows his belief. Luther proves himself to be a real humanist here. After all, this doctrine of providence is clearly derived from the study of early Christian ideas which in their turn had been influenced by Greek Stoicism and Persian Manicheism.

In a debate with Erasmus, who fiercely defended the doctrine of free will as central to Catholic theology, Luther wrote a rejoinder in his *De servo Arbitrio* (On the bondage of the will), published in 1520:

It is then fundamentally necessary and wholesome for Christians to know that God foreknows nothing contingently, but that He foresees, purposes, and does all things according to His own, immutable, eternal and infallible will.

. . . the will of God is effective and cannot be impeded, since power belongs to God's nature; and His wisdom is such that He cannot be deceived. Since, then, His will is not impeded, what is done cannot but be done where, when, how, as far as, and by whom He foresees and wills. . . .

I frankly confess that, for myself, even if it could be, I should not want 'free-will' to be given me, nor anything to be left in my own hands to enable me to endeavour after salvation; not merely because in the face of so many dangers, and adversities, and assaults of devils, I could not stand my ground . . . but because . . . I should still be forced to labour with no guarantee of success, and beat my fists at the air. If I lived and worked to all eternity, my conscience would never reach comfortable certainty as to how much it must do to satisfy God.[39]

The introduction of such ideas effectuated a profound change in the traditional views of man and the world and, as a result, in all sorts of cultural forms. While many derived a pious optimism from Luther's teachings, hoping they might develop a more personal relation with God, also through a life of good works, many others were steeped in sombre thoughts of doom and gloom, in apathetic pessimism.

Instead of relying only on traditional methods of dissemination, Luther's friends and followers saw the opportunity for a much greater debate which the new print culture offered.[40] Not only did they take care that Luther's propositions were printed, but they also had them distributed. One way of doing this was through the travelling bookseller, a recent phenomenon; he journeyed from city to city and especially from village to village to provide with reading material those who could read but had no regular access to bookshops. It is known that in 1517, 1518 and 1519 many booksellers in the German states were paid by Luther's followers to stock themselves with only one sort of text, Luther's publications, instead of their usual selection. Many customers, either curious or simply for the love of reading, bought and read Luther's works and were frequently affected by his ideas.

Between 1517 and 1520 no fewer than 300,000 copies of Luther's works were sold in this and other ways. Thus his ideas became the basis for a real religious reformation, while the equally radical alternatives which had been proclaimed in earlier years had never had this effect. Luther himself said, with good reason, that the invention of the art of printing had been 'God's greatest mercy'. Soon, in Germany illustrated broadsheets and picture books provided visual propaganda for the illiterate and the semi-literate, exploiting popular belief as well as producing it.[41] In England, too, the new visions about man's relationship with God were widely popularized through broadsides combining catchy music − godly tunes − with religious pictures to instruct those who could barely read, or not at all.[42]

The Catholic Church's reaction to the actions of Luther and other reformers has been called the Counter-Reformation − a nineteenth-century term − or the Catholic Reformation; in fact, Rome's approach to the many issues which had presented themselves since the late fifteenth century was mainly formulated during the nearly twenty years that the Church's main representatives sat in council, albeit intermittently, in the Italian town of Trent; the council was one of a millennial tradition of councils that were convened whenever the Church's local and regional spokesmen rather than the Curia and the popes in Rome itself felt the need to deliberate on internal and external problems and re-establish unity. To a considerable extent, the so-called Tridentine reforms became a success thanks to the printing press. From 1530 onwards, Rome increasingly used the printed word to make known its answer to Luther and the other reformers. Religious uniformity was imposed and enforced through all sorts of books. The *catechism* comprehensively summarized the central points of Catholic doctrine for the general public; the *breviary* and the *missals* made the liturgy the same all over the Catholic world; sermon books instructed priests on the best, psychologically most effective ways to approach the faithful.

Among the many instruments devised by the Church of Rome to effect social control and discipline, the reform and strengthening of the sacrament of confession was, perhaps, most profoundly successful. Trent's new stress upon confession as a central sacrament and the subsequent policy of educating priests to actually introduce and enforce it in their parishes, aided by printed confession books, resulted in a moral and indeed cultural conformity at the deepest level, that of people's innermost thinking in terms of what was accepted behaviour and what not, in the eyes of God, of the Church and of society. Speaking about one's sins, about the ways in which one had not obeyed the rules of the Church, to a priest who was the representative of that Church, in due time created a complex psychological and social interaction between a set of rules imposed from above and their acceptance both by individuals and groups who increasingly began to live according to these precepts.

The introduction of the tenets reformulated or newly conceived by Trent was greatly facilitated by the foundation of new religious orders, among which the Society of Jesus was the most conspicuous; the Jesuits and their like especially concentrated on education, trying to create a truly Roman Catholic elite by recruiting pupils from the urban middle and upper classes, who eagerly flocked to their colleges because of their reputation for an intellectually rigorous, superior education.

Moreover, as Rome embarked upon a new missionary campaign using all available propagandistic means, vast parts of Catholic Europe, especially in the more remote agricultural areas, were now properly Christianized for the first time. What with all these new or revitalized policies, and the impact of print that now helped to spread them, it is perhaps permissible to say that for the first time in a thousand years Christianity actually became a vital force, even though, at the same time, its institutional unity was disrupted; where there had been many local varieties of Catholicism during the first millennium of European Christianity, the religious culture of Catholic Europe and, with it, the code of norms and conventions, now became much more uniform.

In their own ways, the Reformed Churches, too, succeeded in creating greater uniformity. Of course, the stress on the importance of reading and following Scripture seemed to lay primary responsibility with the individual believer. However, the locally organized Churches, with their ministers and, in Calvinist countries, their elders elected from the local community, did not fail to influence the behaviour of the faithful through a regiment of religious and social control. They, too, used the printed word, in its form of moral and pious tracts, to drive home their notions of proper conduct.

Thus, the art of printing, used as a new and powerful instrument of government in both Church and State, greatly contributed to the standardization and uniformity of culture and thought. Moreover, this occurred not only in language and religion but also in many other areas of life where earlier there had been considerable variety. Thus, in 1520, the first 'Manual for Tailors' appeared in Seville, establishing, as it were, the prevailing Spanish dress habits. Through the distribution of this text via the press it was now possible to become acquainted with Spanish clothing conventions in other parts of Europe. Because Spain was also looked upon as a culturally pre-eminent country, as a result of the wealth it had acquired from its colonies and its consequent European power policy, its customs were emulated by many. Without books like the Seville guide, tailors could never have stimulated and satisfied their clients' demands.

Printing therefore contributed to something essentially cultural like clothing being spread internationally. But at the same time, this led to a growing uniformity, with regional variants often coming off worst, just as had been the case with language. Publicizing prevalent dress conventions through printing also led to more rapid changes, resulting in what now became 'fashion', a phenomenon that we can observe from the beginning of the sixteenth century. It is clear that this altered man's consumption patterns and also, as a result, the economy. The same happened when the first cookery books were published: in food culture, too, habits from a particular region or social group now spread more quickly and became 'fashionable'.

Indeed, more and more people discovered the possibilities of the printed word. People with ideas about better methods of education, better codes of behaviour for young men and women who were courting, or better ways to build houses could now all try to impress their ideas and views on as many readers as possible. Treatises on horsemanship and fencing,[43] on the theory and practice of dancing and music, on painting and the theatre appeared in bewildering numbers. Architecture is a good case in point. Both in building and in urban construction and layout, the virtues of 'classical' forms, that is the forms thought to be advocated by the great architect of ancient Rome, Vitruvius, were extolled in texts by such Italian Renaissance architects – practising ones or only theorists – as Andrea Palladio and Sebastiano Serlio; this changed the way public buildings and towns in Europe looked for the following four centuries, and still influences modern or rather 'post-modern' architecture, that, from the 1980s onwards, has been eclectically referring to it.

Also, many of the less obvious 'cultural' forms which, nevertheless, are often far more deeply engrained as codes of behaviour in Europe stem from the first period of the influence of printing. Don't eat with your mouth open, don't grab food with your hands, use a knife and fork, don't blow your nose with your fingers and then flick off the snot, but use a handkerchief, don't start fighting another person for the first insult he offers you – these are all concepts which were first adopted by particular, often powerful cultural groups for reasons of social distinction. More specifically, if people with new ideas received the support of government or of one of the sociocultural elites, the concepts propagated in their texts helped to establish norms, as well as their material manifestations, if only because many people wanted to ape those who acted out this behaviour because it connotated high sociocultural standing.

In short, a variety of manners and ideas acquired wide and sometimes even general application, both through the printed word and through the education made possible by it. Thus was inaugurated a development towards collective and indeed individual behavioural self-restraint which went on till well into the twentieth century. All over Europe uniformity – although perhaps in manners more than in ideas – increased while at the same time printing contributed to changes in what was 'in' and 'out' occurring faster and on a wider scale than ever before. It must be clear, however, that this process, which somewhat misleadingly has been called the 'civilizing process',[44] has not necessarily made European man more civilized if the latter term is used as the equivalent of intrinsically humane, as often seems the implication.

Thus, culture in Europe underwent a gradual but definite transformation. For many, a new perception of reality developed. The 'literal' truth, the truth of the written word, became increasingly central, especially in the Protestant world, where through Luther Holy Scripture, as the word of God, was presented as the only source of authority, a situation which then led many believers to actually see all authoritative words as 'true'. Furthermore, people everywhere started to 'live according to the book', their thoughts and actions now becoming more uniform. However, at the same time, the need to escape from this compulsion and the restrictions it brought increased as well, because the individual 'I', whose development since the fifteenth century had been put forward as educated man's goal in life, wanted to manifest itself. Standardization provoked reaction.

Many elements inherent in the culture of print as a new medium of communication are illustrated by one of its fascinating and successful products. In 1605, the Spaniard Miguel de Cervantes Saavedra (1547–1616), published a book. He intended it to be a comic novel about a man called Don Quixote, a man who had read too much and, moreover, believed everything he read to be true. Don Quixote's passion were novels of courtly love, in which knights errant went out on a complicated quest of honourable fighting to gain the hand of their beloved. Such novels had proliferated in the early years of printing, bringing an already old genre popular in the manuscript culture of the preceding centuries to a new, larger public. Cervantes himself had travelled to Italy, and had fought both at Lepanto and at Algiers in two of Christian Europe's bloody battles with Islam, before returning to an unprofitable career in Spain; he soon became bitterly disappointed at the discrepancy between the courtly ideal held up to so many readers in novels and other texts, and the social reality of his own times. In his *El ingenioso hidalgo Don Quijote de la Mancha* (The ingenious nobleman Don Quixote from la Mancha), the protagonist, accompanied by his servant Sancho Panza, sets out on a long journey, prepared to give chivalrous battle to injustice wherever he meets it. Increasingly dejected by his experiences, Don Quixote gradually loses his idealism. Sancho Panza, on the other hand, the embodiment of an agricultural, down-to-earth, no nonsense society, though very sceptical when he set out with his master, is becoming increasingly convinced of the essential value of the knightly ideals. In his *Don Quixote*, Cervantes created one of the first 'modern' literary texts, a text that explores the psychology of its characters and even shows their development.[45] Due to the very fact of printing, the novel was soon famous all over Spain. Translations were made in English, French and German, and numerous seventeenth- and eighteenth-century writers all over Europe were influenced by it. It was illustrated by well-known artists. In the nineteenth and twentieth centuries, Salvador Dali and Gustave Doré were inspired by it, as were such composers as Jules Massenet, Manuel de Falla and Richard Strauss.[46]

From the beginning of the sixteenth century onwards, more than ever before, daily life in Europe became embedded in a body of common rules; man created and became subject to a collective morality, which was spread and propagated more easily and intensively through the printed word. All over

Europe, the orally presented power of traditional, individually and often locally recognizable authorities, the 'interpreters of information' or cultural inter-mediaries, became more dependent on texts put together by mainly anonymous creators of norms. Power itself, both religious and secular, increased though it became more anonymous precisely because the printed word distanced it further from its subjects. Orders which for centuries had been given orally by authorities who, even if only for that reason, were close to the people, were now imposed in writing by the mainly invisible 'powers that be'. This also explains why many of those who could not read often saw printing as a threat, the secret instrument of power of the 'high-up'. The 'culture brokers', both the 'official' ones, the members of the various elites like the clergy and the bureaucracy, and the unofficial ones, like quacks and colporteurs, in short all those who contributed to the formation of established, standard codes of behaviour, of 'ritual repertories', now were living the tension which arose between the ambiguous space which for so long they had been able to exploit to their own use and advantage and an official, normative, increasingly enforceable and controllable printed culture.

The illiterate, besides experiencing the new administrative pressure, were influenced, too, by the encoding in writing and in print of standardized norms because the written message was frequently imposed on them through the filter of some of the most effective media in a culture that to many still remained largely oral. Both songs, which were sung in the market-place and street, inn or pub,[47] and the various kinds of drama. The latter was – and, until the nineteenth century, remained – one of the most influential means of com-munication, with its combination of word, image and emotive act. New notions of what was civilized and uncivilized were expounded in plays: consider how from the sixteenth century onwards peasants were frequently portrayed as rough and wild, as characters who defecated, gorged themselves and copulated in public, all things which were no longer deemed acceptable, civilized; thus, new standards were being imposed through printed material by those who held power, both the nobility and the influential urban middle class, for the simple reason that they thought that 'different' also meant 'uncontrollable'.

A striking example of the way the educated, written, printed culture penetrated the oral culture of enacted word and song is the play *Mariken van Nieumeghen*, which was also translated into English and German. When she is considering going to live with the Devil, Mariken asks him:

> Eer ghi met mi sult versamen in ionsten,
> suldi mi leeren di seven vrije consten,
> Want in alle dingen te leeren verfray ick.
> Ghi sullet mi all leeren, suldi?[48]

> Before you will couple with me,
> you will teach me the seven liberal arts,
> for I very much want to learn everything and become a more rounded person.
> You will teach me everything, won't you?

The Devil agrees: 'Noyt vrouwe en leefde op eerde so abel also ic u maken sal' (Never, my lady, there was on earth one so learned as I will make thee). Not surprisingly, from the sixteenth century onwards a central element in the call for women to be given more equality was often the demand for better education, voiced under the influence of the Renaissance concept of man,[49] and the diffusion of this concept in print. A severely patriarchal culture still had problems in accepting these claims. Only by a hair's breadth does Mariken escape from temptation, and from the worst fate, her union with the Devil, by once more seeking communion with the Church. An essential part of the message was that knowledge should not be sought by each and everybody. After all, learned circles all over Europe feared that the number of people who could read and write might become too numerous. They would undermine the monopoly of power implicit in the monopoly of knowledge. If only for this reason, the Catholic Church forbade the reading of the Bible in the vernacular. So, while the story acknowledges that knowledge is power, its moral is that the learned aspirations of a woman cannot go unpunished if society is to remain stable or unchaotic. Indeed, what was probably the most important cultural factor in the division of the sexes in Europe, the educational disadvantage of the 'second sex', was deliberately upheld by Europe's mainly male-dominated society until late in the nineteenth century.

As printing began to revolutionize life and culture in Europe in all its aspects, contemporaries, mostly intellectuals and politicians, voiced their concern: might not the common people, given the chance to acquire new ideas and test them against their own opinions of their present position, come to voice their criticism?[50] The printed word that interpreted the world would also mobilize it. It was feared that it might lead to revolutions in the centuries to come, as indeed it did.

Europe and its frontiers: nation-feeling and cultural self-definition

The same *studia humanitatis* which led to a clearer view of the classical and Christian roots of European culture by calling for a careful analysis of the Greek and Latin texts on which the learned tradition rested also led, in the sixteenth century, to research into and a greater appreciation of all that was valuable and had been written in the vernacular. In this way, people began to understand more clearly the past of their own communities, which had been formed in interaction with but to a certain extent also in tension with the 'myth' of Europe as upheld by the Catholic Church. Humanism, despite its cosmopolitan nature, also promoted the genesis of a gradually more 'national' culture. Europe was becoming rather a unity of varieties. Surviving and, if possible, expanding their own power gradually became the most important aim for the majority of states.

Indeed, it is not surprising that the earliest 'national' poems had developed in the regions where the threat was greatest: the Iberian peninsula and the

Balkans. There, a typical 'frontier' mentality of constant alertness underlined the importance of propaganda.[51] The wide variety of ideological material available was plundered for those elements which could most effectively strengthen and motivate those involved in a constant fight to survive, to help them establish or maintain their own identity. That material usually originated both in the *Christianitas* concept and in an often idealized past of shared emotions and actions, strengthened by a sense of linguistically proven togetherness.

At an early stage, south of the Pyrenees the confrontation between Christendom and Islam had led to self-reflection and, thus, to 'border poems' written to bolster up regional identities: in the eleventh and twelfth centuries, on the frontier between the Christian and the Muslim world, the *Chanson de Roland* and the *Poema del mio Cid* were created, epic poems which expressed first the Frankish and later the Castilian 'frontier feeling' with regard to the Islamic enemy. In the late fifteenth century, that same border feeling, now combined with a new front of contact and confrontation between Portugal and the rediscovered world of Asia, was expressed in Luis de Camoes's *Os Lusiadas*, which articulated Lusitanian nationalism.[52]

On Europe's other frontier, in the Byzantine Empire, before the fall of Constantinople, the threat of Islam produced the 'Akritic Songs' as a species of frontier poetry, wherein the Greek-Christian girl marries a Saracen, Islamic man who then converts to Christianity.[53] Further north, in Split on the Balkans, around 1500 Marko Marulić wrote his epic *Judita*,[54] and the Serb Ivan Gunduliç published his *Osman*, both works aimed against the advancing Turkish forces. But the religious and in a broader sense cultural sensitivity which underlay these poems could not prevent the region's capture by the sultan's janissaries.

All these texts point to a slowly growing feeling of national identity, especially in regions where this served an obvious need against an enemy. It is a feeling which can also be observed in the increasing use of the 'vernacular' both in such cultural expressions as literature and in government administration, education and so on. Indeed, the purity of the 'national' language became a symbol for the purity, the one-ness of the nation. Thus, Juan de Valdes, writing about the history of the Spaniards in 1535, noted that:

> This conquest . . . lasted until 1492 when the Catholic Kings, of glorious memory, took the kingdom of Granada and expelled the tyrannical Moors from Spain. But during this time, the Spaniards were unable to keep the purity of their language and stop it from mixing with the Arab one, for even though they recovered kingdoms and cities, towns and other places, as many Moors stayed living in them, their language also stayed; and things remained like this until a few years ago the Emperor [i.e. Charles V] ordered that they become Christians or leave Spain. But speaking with them, many of their words have stuck to us.[55]

In Spain, the demand for the purity of language was soon combined with demands for religious and even racial purity. Although not all European states were to employ the extreme measures used in Spain – after the Moors had been forced to convert or were expelled, the Jews were treated in the same way – many were embarking upon some kind of policy to safeguard that purity.

Meanwhile, comparison, especially between the more obvious 'national' texts, shows that the virtues which now were attributed to a people's own culture not infrequently conformed with those of other nations, rooted as they ultimately were in that Christianity which was so often put first and foremost, and in that contact with classical civilization that often was the touchstone. Thus, an increasingly diverse 'Europe' still defined itself in these dual, even if by now somewhat hidden component parts.

9 A new society

Europe and the wider world
since the fifteenth century

The 'old' world and the 'older' world

Even before the genesis of Christendom, some of the peoples living in 'Europe' had been aware of their debts to 'Asia'. The Greek revered the wisdom of Egypt and Mesopotamia and, indeed, received a considerable part of their culture from the civilizations of the Near East, of Persia and of India. From the age of Alexander the Great onwards, the links with Central Asia, with China and the Indian subcontinent remained strong, even though contacts were almost always indirect, by means of intermediaries, as for example the merchants who travelled along the so-called 'silk road', the chain of trading routes connecting the Chinese and the Mediterranean economies.[1] Rome, too, continued to be aware of the powers and the products of the east. Admittedly, in the centuries following the decline of the Roman Empire, the ties grew weaker, and Asia became more of a fantasy land, for the role of its silver in the resurgence of the European economy under the Carolingians was understood only dimly, if at all, by even the most knowledgeable of politicians and traders.

The connotation of riches and wonder which came to be attached to Asia undoubtedly increased because of Christianity's roots in the Near East, which brought many a pilgrim to the Holy Land, where they were told stories about the fabulous wealth of the world beyond the Arabian desert. The very fact that the Bible told the Christians that God had created the world in its original, sublime form in a garden 'in Eden', and that this garden still existed somewhere in the east, greatly contributed to the magic of Asia. Thus, the lands beyond the Levant continued to attract Europeans, even though few ever reached them.[2] At one time, the popes thought that they might conclude an alliance with the Mongol emperors to combat Islam, and monks were sent to the Great Khan's court at Karakoroum; although nothing came of their efforts, the monks returned with wondrous tales that did not fail to fire the imagination. The travels undertaken by the members of the Venetian merchant family of Polo at the end of the thirteenth century were certainly inspired by them.

Although the fact of Marco Polo's presence in China has been doubted from the moment he returned to tell his story to an attentive but disbelieving audience – his tale became one of the greatest bestsellers both of the last century of manuscript books and of the first age of printing – it seems that he definitely was where he told his amazed and unbelieving friends he had been: in Cathay.[3] There, paper money was used, because one could trust the state that issued the bills; there, the streets of the big cities were paved and lit; there, people travelled in safety; there, an emperor ruled with a might as great as the Roman rulers of old. There, in short, one could find a civilization which in all respects was equal to Europe, if not superior to it. For indeed, even the absence of any trace of Christianity did not prevent it from being a humane society which held values that in Europe, too, were deemed sacred.

Soon, Asia, India, China or the east – all terms were used indiscriminately to denote the world beyond the world of Islam – not only was coveted for its wealth but also admired for its culture that might even induce Europeans to think twice about their own achievements. Indeed, for all the changes characterizing scientific and technical developments in Europe from the sixteenth century onwards, Europe continued to learn from the east. However, from the sixteenth century onwards, the process definitely became less one-sided in the technological sphere, but rather more marked in a general, perhaps even philosophical sense. Gradually, Europeans began to wonder whether, perhaps, Asia was the land of origins: the origins of knowledge – for, after all, man had had amazing knowledge in the garden of Eden, before he had wanted to know too much – but also the origins of language; and, perhaps, even the origins of religion.

Of course, travel, the possibility to broaden one's horizons, had always been part of European culture in several ways. Undeniably, however, from the fifteenth and sixteenth centuries onwards, Europeans increasingly left their own, trusted world; had not Arab tracts about seamanship and cosmography and maps drawn by Jewish cartographers shown them the way both in the Mediterranean and beyond? Perhaps partly through a growing self-awareness, partly through the promises of development which the many new ideas brought, the Europeans became more independent-minded, daring to confront the challenge which the unknown always presents. The genesis of the 'modern' state can be given as an additional explanation for the overseas expansion which would bring Europe economic and political mastery over large parts of the world from the late fifteenth to the early twentieth centuries. For it was these states which had to vie with each other over what was, after all, a limited territory, and which were thus forced to use all their resources, material and human, as inventively as possible.

Already in the fourteenth and fifteenth centuries, traders, discoverers, adventurers and missionaries – a few or even all roles sometimes united in one and the same person – crossed the Mediterranean with increasing frequency to travel to the Middle and Far East and the coasts of North Africa. However, from the late fifteenth century onwards, the balance of power in the Mediterranean area, especially in the eastern part, started to change. The struggle between the two regional superpowers, the Ottoman Empire and the Persian kingdom, severely decreased the profitability of the caravan and shipping routes which, through the deserts of the Near East and over the Mediterranean, linked the European market with the Indian Ocean and the production centres in Asia. Europeans now wanted to find their own routes to the east. Thus, when the Portuguese started to sail the Atlantic Ocean, searching for gold and slaves in the interior of West Africa, they were also searching for the wealth of Asia, for allies in the fight against Islam, and even for a strategic southern detour to the Holy Land. In the last years of the fifteenth century, still somewhat anxiously keeping to the African coastline, they discovered an alternative route to the fabulous Orient, via the Cape of Good Hope and the Indian Ocean.

It is one of the ironies of history not only that some of the most important technical phenomena which were instrumental in Europe's 'take-off' in the fifteenth century had been part of the technology transfer from Asia to Europe, but also that these phenomena enabled Europe eventually to bypass the Islamic world in its search for the riches of the east. For both the development of shipbuilding and of the entire array of nautical instruments such as the magnetic compass originated in the body of knowledge that had reached the Christian West in the previous centuries via the Islamic Mediterranean.

The vicissitudes of the compass present us with another problematic case of technology transfer. We know that it originated in ancient Chinese religion, more specifically in divination techniques, wherein a board combining representations of earth and heaven and a magnetite pointer were used. Well before the year AD 1000, this had developed into various measuring instruments. Yet we do not know how it reached Europe, where it was first mentioned in 1198. It may have come over land, through Central Asia and the Islamic world, as a surveying instrument. It may also have reached Europe by the Indian Ocean, with Chinese and Arab mariners who used it in its compass form.[4]

As to shipbuilding itself, it is obvious that during the fourteenth and fifteenth centuries, construction techniques, for example on the Iberian peninsula, realized a level of sophistication that explains, at least partly, the success of Portugal's subsequent enterprises in the Indian Ocean. Yet the building of the light, three-masted Iberian ships may well have been influenced by illustrations of multiple-masted Chinese junks represented on late-fourteenth- and early-fifteenth-century European world maps and in the tales of Marco Polo. Once again, the process of transfer may have taken place at the meeting point of east and west in the eastern Mediterranean. As early as the 1420s, the Jewish and Arab sailors and savants at Sagres, the base of Prince Henry the Navigator, combined the Douro *caravela* with the Arab *caravo* to construct a ship that could confidently expect to return home even by sailing against the wind, now it was rigged with its lateen sails common on the Egypt coast and the Indian Ocean.

Once the first Europeans had arrived in Asian waters, new, direct technological transfer between Europe and Asia could develop. Already after rounding the Cape in the 1490s, Vasco da Gama learned new navigational techniques from his Arab pilot, the famous Ibn Majid, author of the monumental encyclopedia of navigation and nautical technology, *Kitab al-Fawa'id* (1490).

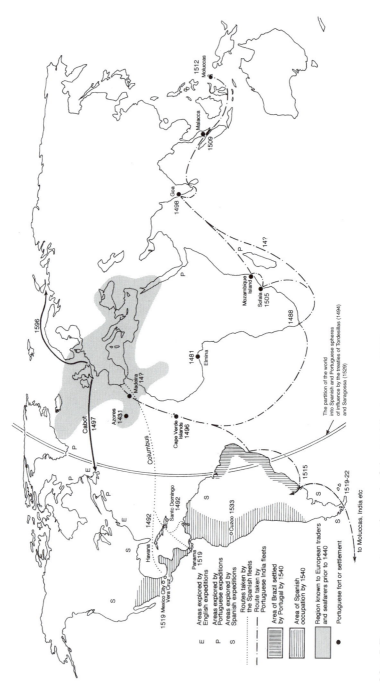

Map 5 European expansion at the end of the Middle Ages to *c.*1540

After their arrival on the Indian coasts, the Portuguese and later the British soon learned how to use local shipbuilding techniques, also employing local materials, a process that continued until the eighteenth century. At that time, for example, the English East India Company adopted the rabet work of Surat, with its sealing of the joints with cotton and tar, finding that it produced more durable ships and reduced construction costs by almost a half.

Another irony of history was that the use of guns and cannon helped to underpin the Europeans' bid for power in the east. Although in both India and China, to name but two of the Europeans' main economic and military targets, the arms' industry had continued to flourish since the period when the earliest technology in this field had begun on its slow road to Europe, developments in Europe had taken on a momentum that by the late fifteenth century was lacking in Asia; consequently, in the sixteenth and early seventeenth centuries, the Portuguese, on arriving in China, could profit from their ability to help the warring factions in the Chinese empire with their by now superior technology. In Japan, the shogunal authorities who gained power after the great civil wars of the sixteenth century retained the knowledge of gunpowder and cannon; yet they relied on the weapons of the Dutch, who arrived in the early years of the seventeenth century, to help them suppress the revolt of the Christian peasants of Shimabara in 1638. In subsequent years, the Japanese government's enforced return to sword and bow, hallowed by ancient samurai tradition, became all but complete. Hence, it was only with the coming of the westerners in the nineteenth century that Japan once more regained a gunpowder concept of warfare.[5]

Meanwhile, one may ask what happened to the world of Islam, which for centuries had been the essential intermediary between Asia and Europe. Admittedly, many scholars would hold that culturally, and more specifically intellectually, the world of Islam belonged to the Mediterranean-European *oikoumenè* rather than to the civilizations of Asia, if only because of its great indebtedness to ancient Greek science and philosophy. Hence, it would seem that the Islamic cultural sphere could not but have participated in and made use of the numerous highly important inventions which it transferred to the Christian world and which enabled Europe to start upon its road to economic, technological and political power.

By the late fifteenth century, however, the Islamic world had entered into a period of stagnation, especially in the field of technology, while Europe continued to develop. This is not the place to explore in detail the reasons for this process. They are manifold, and the debate on them is still ongoing. Most of the reasons belong to the same complex of causes which also changed the technological, and consequently economic, political and cultural balance between Europe and Asia, as sketched above. Some factors, however, can be singled out.

Such elements as fruitful competition between states disappeared in the wake of the rise to hegemony of the Ottoman Empire, which tended to become ever more conservative. Also, one may point to the use (or rather non-use) made in the world of Islam of a major technology like the art of printing. This was one of the technologies that, in Europe, greatly contributed to the development of learning in general, and of education, scholarship and intellectual exchange in particular, consequently contributing to further technological and material progress. Yet for various reasons, mainly of a religious and more broadly cultural nature, this technology was not really introduced in the Islamic world, with lasting negative results if one judges developments only from the economic perspective.

Undeniably, with Europe's discovery and subsequent domination of the sea route to Asia, not only did the importance of the Islamic world and the Mediterranean as the main road to the riches of Asia decline, so did its role as a receiver and transmitter of technology. Also, because of political strife in the Islamic region, the costs of transport and hence of trade in the Levant rose considerably, which negatively influenced the use that Europeans made of the camel roads through the deserts of the Middle East. Therefore, it is difficult to determine whether the decline of the Mediterranean as a region of commercial and hence cultural exchange was a consequence of the general cultural, political and economic decline of the Islamic world, or one of its causes, robbing the Islamic world of its function as an intermediary and thereby reducing its vitality – for it seems undeniable that in the long run most cultures benefit from interaction rather than from seclusion.

In the course of the fifteenth and sixteenth centuries, as commercial and industrial activity in Europe acquired new centres, shifting away from the Mediterranean coasts and concentrating on the Atlantic, Europeans discovered their own roads to Asia. The cultural exchange that, from times immemorial, had developed along the maritime and overland routes through the Near East and Central Asia now mainly, though not exclusively, took the ocean routes via the Cape. Inevitably, the organizations that dominated these routes became the main agents of cultural exchange including the transfer of technologies from Asia to Europe. These were the great maritime-commercial companies of the northern European states, and the spiritual companies of the Church of Rome, more specifically the Company of Jesus: merchants and missionaries became the main contacts between the old world and the older world. When a Swedish East India trader brought news of technical innovations in Chinese agriculture, his text was soon translated all over Europe;[6] and when a Jesuit priest first told Europe about the secret of porcelain manufacture, Europe was quick to take the cue. But precisely because these groups were forever looking for new and easier roads towards this older world, they also came to play an important role when Europe discovered an entirely new world.

For while the Portuguese were trying to find their way to India, succeeding when Vasco da Gama reached Calicut in 1498, the Spanish were navigating the dangerous western seas in Columbus's wake, sailing to the most distant corners of the earth. In doing so they discovered a new world. Subsequently, posing itself between Asia and America, Europe definitely fared well. International trade, which now became a permanent element of European commerce, acted as the pre-eminent booster for the European economy: commercial capitalism first really peaked in the late fifteenth and sixteenth centuries.

The 'old' world and the 'new'

Nowadays most Europeans take for granted the potato, the coffee bean and tobacco. Yet it is worth remembering that Europeans, when they talk about European culture, are talking about a culture which is based on and also expressed in such simple things as the daily diet. Although according to some statistics the use of tobacco has been decreasing in recent years – as is well known, statistics lie – potato consumption and the daily cup of coffee are still essential elements of the European eating pattern.

One should realize that this pattern partly goes back to what happened in 1492 – or, to put it less romantically but more precisely, to the Spanish conquest of the Caribbean area, of Mexico and Peru, and to the Portuguese colonization of Brazil during the sixteenth century. Because this is where those products came from, just like the cocoa bean which produces the chocolate to which many people in the western world are just as addicted as alcohol. Reflecting on this theme, one quickly reaches the conclusion that the discovery of the 'new world' not only had a great influence on the 'old world' but even substantially changed European culture.[7]

Why did Europeans actually head in a westerly direction, charting a sea which for most was still threatening because they lost sight of the safe coast, sailing towards the horizon without knowing where they would end up?[8] Was it from a longing for adventure or a desire for fame, from religious fervour or fanaticism, or, simply, from profit seeking? For some it was a dream in which all these elements coincided, the dream of a paradise that offered both the promise of innocence and the fulfilment of earthly longings of material plenty. We should not forget that for Europeans in the fifteenth and sixteenth centuries, starvation was terribly real and any notion of paradise had to be a material one as well, including an easy abundance of food. The Genoese Cristóbal Cólon or Christopher Columbus was one of them.[9]

The log he kept on his first westward journey in 1492 is revealing. It is true that the original was lost in the sixteenth century, yet much of it was preserved in a transcription and arrangement by the monk Bartolomé de las Casas, who saw the original text. Columbus regularly talks about gold and pearls and about the lucrative commercial contacts with China and Japan, the countries in the east which, after all, he thinks he is going to reach by sailing in a westerly direction. Navigating from island to island in the Caribbean, Columbus repeatedly notes that he will soon arrive in Cipangu or Cathay – Japan and China – and thus be able to hand the letters of credential which the Spanish kings had given him to the Great Khan,[10] the ruler of the Far East, whom Europe knew about only from the fabled and garbled stories of thirteenth-century monks and of Marco Polo. Columbus had read Marco Polo's travel story, using the first printed text of Polo's story – printed in 1492 by a

Dutchman, the Gouda printer Gerard Leeu; in his copy he had noted just those places where the Venetian talked about a sea east of China beating the shore of hurricane-swept islands.

Yet the thing that strikes most in the many pages Columbus devoted to the Caribbean islands which he finally discovered is his continuously expressed amazement about a country and people more beautiful than he has ever seen, about a climate so mild, a harvest so abundant, the likes of which cannot be found in Europe. Of course, there was a propagandistic purpose behind these eulogies, as Columbus needed further support for his enterprises. Still, his rapture seems genuine enough. Peace reigns here, arms and laws are unknown here, everyone understands each other, and belief in God, although not formalized in religion, can be observed everywhere. Only at the end of his story does Columbus use the term 'paradise', yet it is clear from his descriptions that he actually thought from the beginning that he had discovered a paradise or, as Las Casas writes, 'He told that he felt like wanting to stay there forever',[11] in a state like that before the Fall and the confusion of languages, in a landscape as glorious as that in the garden of Eden.

Others were less obviously intrigued and moved. Bernal Díaz del Castillo, companion of the Spaniard Hernán Cortés who was the first European to set foot in Aztec Mexico in 1519, articulated his ideas briefly but forcefully when, on anchoring at the place they christened Vera Cruz (the True Cross), he noted that 'we came here to serve God and the King, and to become rich.'

The first generation of Europeans who crossed the Atlantic Ocean actually thought they had reached 'India', by which name they used to refer to Asia beyond the Indus, where they expected to find the fabulous wealth that had spilled from the stories about the Orient for centuries. With Columbus in the lead they thought that they had landed on the coasts of Asia; they hoped to obtain part of the mythical riches of an old continent: silk, spices, pearls and gems, the things that had formerly reached them only via the complicated trade routes of the Mediterranean and the Near and Middle East.

But, as slowly became clear, the supposed riches of 'India' were not to be found in the western lands reached by the Europeans. This could be explained only when people realized that the first Spaniards to cross the Atlantic had not landed in 'India', in Asia, at all, but in a new world. A certain disappointment came over the conquerors and the first colonists, continuing until it appeared that this new world offered its own, unexpected treasures: new stimulants and nourishing plants and, besides these, gold and silver in seeming abundance.

For the Europeans who trod this American soil in the wake of Columbus, men like Cortés and Pizarro, who conquered the empires of the Aztecs and the Incas, many of the cultural elements which they came across were surprising indeed. Thus Hernán Cólon, son of the discoverer, writes in his report about his father's arrival in Cuba:

> On the way they met many people who had a fire with them to light a certain herb of which they inhaled the smoke; they also used it to lit the fire on which

they roasted the roots, which they gave to the Christians to eat and which were their main nourishment.[12]

Tobacco and the potato. But there was more. In his account of the first meeting between Cortés and the Aztec emperor Montezuma, when the Spaniards observed the ruler while he ate, Bernal Díaz says that: 'Sometimes they brought him, in cups of pure gold, a drink made of the cocoa plant which, according to them, he always drank before he went to visit his wives'.[13] Further on he noted that

> they also put three pipes on his table, painted and gilded, into which they poured fluid amber mixed with herbs called tobacco. After eating, Montezuma inhaled the smoke from the pipes. He only had a little, and then fell asleep.[14]

These elements of native America's material culture quickly became common property in Europe. Already in about 1520, the first tobacco seeds arrived in Portugal from Brazil. The French ambassador in Lisbon then took them to France: his name was Jean Nicot de Villemain.[15] 'Nicotine' began its conquest of the world. Is lung cancer native America's delayed revenge on Europe?

In the 1550s, the potato was first introduced into Spain from Peru where, in the mean time, Spain had defeated the Incas and now governed it in the form of a vice-kingdom.[16] It was not a success: the berries were poisonous and, at first, it was thought that the tubers were, too. However, the plant went from Spain to Austria. There, people learnt how to prepare the potato for human consumption. Gradually it became popular, although not until the seventeenth and eighteenth centuries. Some enlightened souls saw the value of the potato tuber as a staple food for the great mass of Europeans, for whom grains had formed the basis of their diet during the previous millennia. King Frederick the Great of Prussia wanted his soldiers, whose physical strength he needed for his armies, to start eating the nourishing and cheap potatoes. The soldiers, often farmers' sons, stubbornly refused. The King then decided – at least, this is how the story goes – to assemble his troops at Breslau. He had a splendidly laid table placed on the balcony of the palace, with only one dish on it: a bowl of steaming potatoes. He made certain to overtly enjoy his meal, and thus set an example to his fighters.

In the course of the seventeenth and eighteenth centuries the cultivation and consumption of potatoes increasingly spread across Europe. It was in poorer regions that the tuber became the main part of the diet. As a result, in some areas the cultivation of grain virtually disappeared. This was the case in, for example, seventeenth-century Ireland, where the potato first served as cheap rations for the English occupation army and where, subsequently, the local population became completely dependent on it.

Unfortunately, the contemporary state of botany was unable to prevent such plant sicknesses as potato mould. Whenever this occurred, the harvest of one or even several successive years completely failed. In Ireland, this happened regularly. The disaster of 1847 and 1848 in particular is remembered there even today. A terrible famine broke out, hundreds of thousands of Irish people died, and hundreds of thousands left hearth and home. Ironically, they sought refuge in America, from where the cause of their misery had come three centuries earlier. The Irish were followed by thousands of Dutch, and by much larger groups of people from the German states, central Europe and Scandinavia, for there, too, devastating potato epidemics occurred in the nineteenth century.

The massive depopulation which had taken place among the Indians in America in the first decades of the sixteenth century largely resulted from such illnesses as influenza, measles, mumps, smallpox and tuberculosis which the Europeans had brought with them and which wreaked havoc among the Indians, as the native Americans had no resistance to them. The innumerable emigrants who settled in the new world, especially in the nineteenth and twentieth centuries, unknowingly corrected the balance.

The import of food from the new world was not limited to tobacco and potatoes.[17] Cocoa and coffee quickly became popular as luxury drinks among more prosperous Europeans. Moreover, the 'sweetening' of European taste buds soon followed the import of sugar from Brazil and the Caribbean area.[18] Also, the first 'peppers' arrived from America, which were greatly valued in the fairly uninteresting European cuisine because of their piquant and even sharp taste. Being imported through Spain, they were called 'Spanish peppers'. Europeans, in their turn, transported these plants to Asia, where they had a very real influence on culinary habits in the East Indies and China. From there, they returned to the west in the twentieth century, as part of an orientalized food culture.

Likewise, in the sixteenth century, a new phenomenon appeared in Italian culture: the *pomo d'oro* (golden apple), as the new delicacy, the tomato, was quickly called. Already centuries before the arrival of the Europeans, the Aztecs had discovered that the weed which grew between their corncobs and which they called *tomat* in Nahuatl, could be improved into a food crop. When the Spanish came, the Aztecs had already created many varieties, and had written instructions on how to grow them. In Europe the tomato was initially a 'love apple' or aphrodisiac. Only as the centuries passed did this fruit become a colourful part of Europe's vitamin-obsessed diet.

The 'Columbian exchange'

In the wake of Columbus, thousands and, later on, hundreds of thousands of Europeans migrated to America. Spaniards and Portuguese went to escape poverty and hunger in their own country, dreaming of untold riches in the new world. Thus, Central and South America were colonized by the Iberians.

Undeniably, the experience was a brutal one for the native Americans. Millions of them died: a minority were killed in the bloody wars that were waged between the conquerors and the continent's first inhabitants, but by far the most perished because of the illnesses that the Europeans, unwittingly, introduced. In the process, most native cultures were profoundly modified and some totally destroyed, not least because the new, colonial authorities, both the secular and the religious ones, wanted to create a political system and a society along European lines, with the true, Christian religion as the main instrument of cultural cohesion. Especially the material remains of Indian culture disappeared, as, for example, most indigenous texts were burned. But the imposition of new languages, too, both Latin and Spanish, contributed to a loss of collective memory, and to the gradual genesis of a new, hybrid culture, a fusion of native American and European.[19]

To the Caribbean and to North America came a rather greater variety of immigrants, from a rather greater variety of motives. At the end of the sixteenth century, Jews settled there after their forceful expulsion from the Iberian kingdoms of Philip II of Spain. And by the beginning of the seventeenth century, Englishmen started crossing the sea to the east coast of North America, in search of the gold and silver that reportedly had brought fabulous wealth to Spain. They did not find these precious metals; but they found fertile soil, suitable for all kinds of highly profitable agricultural ventures; soon, they had established plantations where black slaves, bought in and brought from Africa, toiled to produce another kind of wealth, based on tobacco, cotton and sugar. Other Englishmen fled their country because they felt they could not freely express their religious and political opinions; both 'puritan' Protestants and Roman Catholics, maltreated at home, founded colonies to create their own 'promised land'. Meanwhile, Dutchmen and Swedes, as well as Germans and Frenchmen established settlements, too, sometimes to escape poverty or persecution in their homelands, sometimes because their governments encouraged them to create overseas bases for profitable expansion.

To this new world, each group brought its own customs and ideas; but each group also brought back or sent back some of the products of the new world, thus establishing an exchange that, however unequal in many ways, has been of prime importance to the history of Europe and, indeed, of the world. Yet it was not only precious metals and fruitful, nourishing products which the Spanish, the first to return from America, imported into Europe. Without people realizing it, the first 'Columbian exchange' also brought death. For the Indians who participated in the victory parade to welcome Columbus in Barcelona in 1493 did not only carry gold and colourful parrots. They also carried a latent sickness which they themselves were immune to. After the first sexual contacts between Indians and Europeans, syphilis was introduced into the old world.[20] For about one hundred years, until late in the sixteenth century, this sickness did its often devastating work among Europe's population. It was spread, in particular, by the armies which were continually on the move during the sixteenth century. They brought the disease to the most remote parts of the European continent, with the French calling it the 'Italian sickness', while the English called it the 'French malady'. Worse still, in their turn, European seamen, traders and soldiers brought this venereal disease to Asia and Africa. In 1498, just six years after the discovery of America, the first Portuguese to set foot in India introduced syphilis there.

However, there are scholars, mainly biologists, who hold another theory. They propose that forms of syphilis had always been present across the whole earth and that Columbus therefore did not bring anything new and terrible back from America. There is little evidence to support that proposition. For the present, the Columbian theory seems the more convincing, if only because the first great syphilis epidemics in Europe did not break out until after 1492.

Meanwhile, the cultural consequences of syphilis, whatever its origin, were both surprising and devastating.[21] Prostitution, which until then had been a more or less accepted phenomenon, came to be severely frowned upon in the early sixteenth century. Partly as a result of this, bathing in public bathhouses quickly disappeared from European culture. Authorities started to close the 'stews' as these places were called, rightly assuming that they were mostly brothels. But also the kiss, until then such a normal sign of friendship and emotion, suddenly became suspect. Shakespeare hinted at this in his play *Henry V* (1600), in which a soldier's departure is described and a warning is given to those who want to say goodbye to him in this way.

All manner of medical treatments were now also viewed with an almost psychotic anxiety. Erasmus, an important chronicler of his times, sums up the dominant hysteria in one of the dialogues in his *Colloquia*; from this it appears that even the barber, who wields the knife and hangs above open mouths and noses, is advised to wear a cloth over his face and also to protect himself in other ways. The striking and disconcerting parallel with the great fear that surrounded Aids in the 1980s and 1990s is obvious. Public reaction in those decades was often as unpredictable and cruel as it was five centuries earlier. Against this background, the question might well be asked whether Europeans over the past five hundred years have become much more civilized.

Apart from all sorts of fascinating foodstuffs, which lessened the initial disappointment about the absence of the highly prized spices, Central and South America provided the Spanish and later the Portuguese with apparently inexhaustible supplies of precious metals: gold and silver. In retrospect, this discovery has been decisive not only for the further development of European culture, but also for its economic and political position in the world, so triumphantly established in the period between the fifteenth and twentieth centuries.

Europe's deposits of precious metals had always been negligible.[22] This was why gold and silver had such great value until the discovery of America. With the recovery of trade in Carolingian Europe during the eighth century, these precious metals had quickly become indispensable as payment for all sorts of products in interregional trade. Gold and silver were even more important in later centuries when a flourishing trade with North Africa and the Near East was re-established. It was the trade which formed one of the fundaments of the slowly developing European capitalism in the twelfth and thirteenth centuries.

It was the trade on which Europe's growing prosperity and, partly, its cultural flowering rested.

In the fourteenth and fifteenth centuries, Europeans themselves travelled beyond the Mediterranean Sea for the first time. The Middle East and East Asia increasingly became suppliers of greatly desired luxury items such as spices, silk, porcelain and so on. But the Asian traders wanted cash payments. They did not care for bartering what were, in their eyes, inferior European products. They demanded cash: gold and silver.

During the fifteenth century, this led to serious financial and economic problems in Europe. The amount of precious metals that merchants knew how to lay hands on was simply not enough to pay for this foreign trade and keep the economy running on its course of expansion. Therefore, the discovery of large quantities of gold and silver in the new world at the beginning of the sixteenth century was nothing short of a godsend. It saved the European economy from threatening stagnation and from a subsequent slow but certain decline. But that discovery did more: it gave economic life a stimulus which for many centuries – indeed, until the middle of the twentieth century – made it the strongest in the world.[23]

The gold and silver mines in Mexico and Peru, opened by the Spanish, were worked very energetically from the 1520s and 1530s, even though the native Americans were soon seen to be physically unfit for this kind of hard labour. It was one of the main reasons why black people started being imported as slaves from Africa. Admittedly, there the phenomenon of slavery had been endemic for many centuries. But now Christians, Europeans, became the main slave traders, even using religious, biblical arguments to justify their trade. American precious metal, increasingly the motor behind Europe's trade with Asia, now also began to involve sub-Saharan Africa in the ever closer network of 'the European world economy'. From those years until the end of the sixteenth century, when the approaching exhaustion of the ore deposits first became manifest, an enormous quantity of bullion flowed from America to Europe. Until 1540, it was mainly gold; later, most of it was silver.

The annual gold and silver fleet, heavily protected by convoys, brought the precious metal into the Spanish economy through the Spanish monopoly port of Seville. However, that economy was not a specifically Spanish affair: after all, the Spanish kings Charles V and Philip II, of the Austrian Habsburg family, also ruled other parts of Europe, both in Italy and to the north of the Pyrenees and the Alps. Thus, gold and silver poured in there, too. It enabled Spanish nobles, prelates and private citizens to pay for the services of the hundreds of Dutch artists and artisans who flocked to Spain in the early decades of the sixteenth century, to build and decorate cathedrals, monasteries and palaces; they soon integrated in Spanish society. It also enabled the Spanish government to pay the soldiers who protected the Habsburgs' wide-ranging political interests. In the Dutch rebellion against Philip II, which became increasingly violent in the late 1560s, the mercenaries who fought for the Spanish against the rebels in the Netherlands were paid with American silver. Many of these soldiers stayed on as well, marrying local girls. Thus, the American bullion indirectly stimulated European migration.

One can safely say that the Spanish kings could not have engaged in international politics and in expensive wars if the American colonies had not contributed to the royal fisc in this way. Indeed, if a gold or silver fleet failed to arrive in Seville at the end of summer, because of head winds or because of pirates' activities – the Dutch like to recall Piet Heyn, while the English think of Francis Drake and Walter Raleigh as national heroes who robbed the Spaniards of their ill-gotten wealth – the paymasters of the Spanish army faced empty coffers and the hirelings engaged by the Spanish in Flanders or in the German states stopped fighting immediately, sometimes even taking to plunder or rising in instant mutiny.

But the money did not only benefit Spain and Spanish power politics. To finance its wars, the Spanish government had negotiated gigantic loans, especially with Portuguese, Italian and Flemish financiers and with the Fugger banking family of Augsburg. The precious metal of America was used to pay off Spain's national debts. As a result, these financial circuits invested their American gold and silver in the economy of the whole of Europe. This influenced European society in three essential ways.

First, this financial infusion substantially contributed to the further extension of European trade with Asia, which started to grow from the second half of the sixteenth century. This revival and intensification of an age-old contact also proved to be fundamentally significant precisely for the image Europe had of itself, as it had to measure itself against the great civilizations of the east.

Second, this infusion influenced government finance in the European states largely because of its broad economic radiance. The many new enterprises which were now founded ultimately also generated a larger taxation volume, especially in Spain, France, England and the Netherlands. This tax income became the foundation for the government bureaucracies which were expanding enormously in the sixteenth century. Thus, the basis was laid for the great power which the state came to hold over society through its officials – a power we still know and feel.

Plates 21 and 22 A sixteenth-century engraving, showing Francisco Pizarro, the Spanish adventurer who conquered the Inca Empire, watching the last emperor, Atahualpa, collecting his treasures to serve as a ransom in 1535; the emperor was murdered nevertheless. Meanwhile, another Indian is being baptized. In other parts of the world, too, Europeans tried to introduce Christianity. Travelling to Asia, they were especially fascinated by China. Though trading with the Celestial Empire was not made easy to European merchants, the Chinese authorities did allow the Jesuits to establish a mission in Peking – mainly, however, to allow them to teach China their technological skills, especially in the field of astronomical research, which they pursued in their observatory, here shown with all its measuring instruments in an eighteenth-century engraving.
Source: Centre for Art Historical Documentation, Nijmegen, The Netherlands

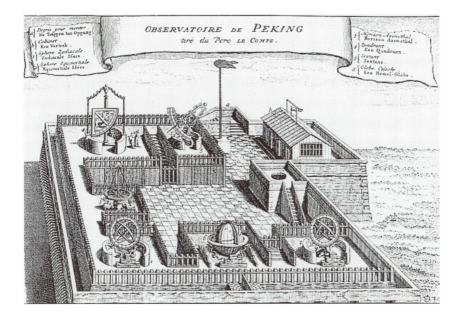

A third result of the tidal wave of precious metal which flooded Europe for roughly eighty years was certainly negative for the average European. Galloping inflation affected all but the most wealthy.[24] For the sudden and uncontrollable increase in the money supply was not immediately absorbed by a simultaneous growth in production. As a result, prices rose sharply everywhere; those who had a fixed income experienced the greatest difficulties. Nor did this affect only the lower income groups. Big landowners, for instance, were also victims. As many of them had let their lands on long-term leases, rising prices which could not be translated in new contracts reduced their purchasing power. These nobles often became discontented and, moreover, showed it, certainly when their power was threatened in other ways as well. This was the case in this very period. For long, princely governments had been trying to reduce the competition of the old aristocracy and to strip it of its military and administrative functions. Now, the changing economic climate, which slowly brought princes more income from taxation, gave them the possibility to struggle free of the nobility by replacing them with paid bureaucrats and mercenaries. Of the local or even national noble revolts which occurred in most European countries during the second half of the sixteenth century and in the early seventeenth century, most had their origin in this situation. In France, during the *frondes*, dissatisfied nobles, sometimes seeking an alliance with disgruntled urban elites, warred against an increasingly oppressive central authority which was blamed for everything. In sixteenth- and early seventeenth-century England, struggles continually flared up between sections of the aristocracy, many of whom felt restricted in their power and status by the changing economic and political situation. The protestant 'water beggars' who, in 1566, presented the Spanish governor of the Netherlands with their famous petition, in which they expressed their grievances requesting an adjustment of royal policy on, among other things, religious freedom, included members of the nobility who had been adversely affected by the prevailing economic situation. It was one of the crises that led to the Dutch Revolt and the subsequent independence of the Netherlands.

Thus, one must conclude that the influx of American precious metal was definitely not a blessing for everyone in Europe. On the contrary, for many it was more like a malediction, just as, in another context, syphilis and, later, dependence on the potato would prove to be a curse.

EUROPE, THE EARLY SIXTEENTH CENTURY: OPINIONS ON THE CONQUEST OF AMERICA AND ITS CONSEQUENCES

Contemporaries had a clear view of what happened when America came within Europe's power range. Spanish American gold and silver heightened the creditworthiness of the House of Habsburg enabling Charles V, with the aid of loans provided by the Fuggers, the Augsburg banking firm, to purchase the imperial crown, since he managed to outbid his rival François I of France.

In 1523, old Jacob Fugger hastened to remind the emperor of his obligations, with a frankness indicating the position of power such bankers now enjoyed:

> Your Imperial Majesty doubtless knows how I and my kinsmen have ever hitherto been disposed to serve the House of Austria in all loyalty to the furtherance of its well-being and prosperity; wherefore, in order to be pleasing to Your Majesty's Grandsire, the late Emperor Maximilian, and to gain for Your Majesty the Roman Crown, we have held ourselves bounded to engage ourselves towards divers princes who placed their trust and reliance upon myself and perchance on no man besides. We have, moreover, advanced to Your Majesty's agents for the same end a great sum of money, of which we ourselves had to raise a large part from our friends. It is well known that Your Imperial Majesty could not have gained the Roman Crown save with mine aid, and I can prove the same by the writings of Your Majesty's agents given by their own hands. In this matter I have not studied mine own profit. For had I left the House of Austria and had been minded to further France, I had obtained much money and property, such as was then offered to me.[25]

Old Jacob's words did not go unheeded. Among the things with which Charles V paid back his loans from the Fuggers were lucrative mining concessions in Peru and a number of hugely profitable monopolies in the various states of the far-flung Habsburg Empire.

For a few decades, American precious metals flowed into Europe, until the first ore deposits had been exhausted. European politicians watched the situation carefully. In 1559, the Venetian envoy to the Spanish court, Michele Soriano, wrote a cool and revealing assessment of the entire colonial situation for the benefit of his masters, the rulers of the Republic of St Mark:

> From New Spain are obtained gold and silver, cochineal – little insects like flies from which crimson dye is made – leather, cotton, sugar and other things; but from Peru nothing is obtained except minerals. The fifth part of all that is produced goes to the king, but since the gold and silver is brought to Spain and he has a tenth part of that which goes to the mint and is refined and coined, he eventually gets one-fourth of the whole sum, which fourth does not exceed in all four or five hundred thousand ducats. . . . Nor is it likely that it will long remain at this figure, because great quantities of gold and silver are no longer found upon the surface of the earth, as they have been in past years; and to penetrate into the bowels of the earth requires greater effort, skill and outlay, and the Spaniards are not willing to do the work themselves, and the natives cannot be forced to do so, because the Emperor has freed them from all obligation of service as soon as they accept the Christian religion. Wherefore it is necessary to acquire negro slaves, who are brought from the coasts of Africa, both within and without the Straits, and these are selling dearer every day, because on account of their natural lack of strength and the change of climate, added to the lack of discretion upon the part of their masters in making them work too hard and giving them too little to eat, they fall sick and the greater part of them die.[26]

The Frenchman Jean Bodin (1530–96), one of the most outstanding political analysts of his day, theorized about the consequences of the new situation

– basing himself on solid historical and statistical research, which shows the pervasiveness of a new scientific spirit. In 1568 he wrote:

> I find that the dearness we observe comes from four or five causes. The principal and almost the only one (to which no one has heretofore referred) is the abundance of gold and silver, which is much greater in this kingdom today than it was four hundred years ago. I do not go further back since the extracts of the registers of the court and of the chamber which I have do not go beyond four hundred years. The rest has to be drawn from old histories with little certainty.
>
> The second cause of dearness comes in part from monopolies. The third is scarcity, which is caused as much by exports as by waste. The fourth is the pleasure of kings and great nobles, who raise the prices of the things they like. The fifth is the price of money, debased from its old valuation.[27]

Images of America and mirrors of Europe

Though the analysis of Europe's relationship with America may seem rather materialistic so far, it is worth bearing in mind that on an empty stomach man rarely arrives at great thoughts of a philosophical or religious nature. And without money no churches or palaces are built, no splendid paintings painted, no magnificent operas composed or produced. A healthy financial basis is necessary for every form of artistic or scientific production.

In this respect, the discovery of America greatly strengthened the material basis of European culture. Indeed, from the sixteenth century onwards European culture showed a new blossoming in many areas. Moreover, in that culture, the 'experience of America' became an intrinsic element too, a source of inspiration. In the European mind the discovery of America led to a fundamental change in many fields. First and foremost because the prevailing world-view had to be adjusted as existing geographical notions changed almost daily.[28]

Until late in the sixteenth century, far and away the majority of Europeans still adhered to Kosmas' notion of the earth as a flat surface surrounded by a finite stretch of water embedded in nothingness which led to death. These same Europeans had no idea of the actual vastness of that water and of the contours of that land. Nor did it greatly interest them, landbound as they were. What did they care about the wider world?

Only a tiny minority of Europeans, the ones influenced by the new knowledge gained by the contacts with Islam and, through it, ancient Greek science, had a completely different world-view; this was based on the spherical conception of the classical geographer Ptolemy. One of these Europeans was Columbus. But his dream of reaching 'India' – that is to say, East Asia – already indicates that he was not completely aware of the actual dimensions of the globe.[29]

In 1492, the same year that Columbus set sail, Martin Behaim of Nuremberg constructed a globe, according to many the first of its kind. Coincidence? Not really. Behaim came from the same Portuguese-Spanish maritime milieu as Columbus. Behaim had lived in the Flemish merchant colony on the recently discovered Azores. This Bavarian therefore knew of the geographical details which the expeditions of the Portuguese along the west coast of Africa had produced. He also knew the Florentine scholar Paolo Toscanelli (1397–1492) and his world map and theories about the possibility of reaching the east coast of 'India' by travelling westwards from Europe; Columbus also had corresponded with Toscanelli.

One does not as yet see a 'new world' on Behaim's globe. He positioned an enormous ocean between Europe and Asia – containing only a small island, the mythical land of St Brendan, the Irish monk who was said to have gone to sea long ago in order to discover a new world. True, Behaim does indicate the position of China and Japan for the first time. Yet everything else on his globe is as wrong as could be from a present-day perspective. One must therefore conclude that, although the world opened up for Europe, most Europeans barely knew what it looked like. But that the world was a globe slowly became clear to more people. It was shown by the globes now being manufactured in increasing numbers, though they were very expensive. But maps, too, could convey this new notion and even though their reliability was as yet minimal, they could be reproduced for a larger public because of the recent invention of printing.

Meanwhile, ever more energy was expended on improving cartographic reliability. The European economy, which was receiving an enormous boost from the discoveries, was thirsting after scientifically based, but first and foremost applicable knowledge, certainly in such fields as cartography. Map making soon became an industry, not so much fuelled by the disinterested intellectual pursuit of scientific accuracy and objectivity as by the awareness that progress and the success of Europe's international trade and politics depended on it; indeed, maps soon came to show the economic and political agenda of rulers and governments both within Europe but, far more importantly for all those who now started on their path to riches and domination, in the world at large.[30]

During the first decades of the sixteenth century, in the wake of Columbus's expeditions, more and more new details came pouring in almost every day. In 1513, Spaniards crossing the Isthmus of Panama in Central America discovered that on the other side another great ocean stretched out: it now became absolutely clear that Columbus had been mistaken in his conviction that he had reached the east coast of Asia. But the disappointment created a new challenge: in the years 1519–21, the Portuguese Ferdinand Magellan (c.1480–1521), rounding the stormy capes of South America, circumnavigated the world for the first time.

A first requirement now was to position this 'new world' geographically. The way the globe was filled in had to be reconsidered as 'America' had to be accommodated. Already in 1507 Martin Waldseemüller had provisionally charted the east coast of the new continent, naming it after the Florentine navigator Amerigo Vespucci (1451–1512) whose claim to have first reached the mainland on his voyage of 1497 or 1499 he accepted – whether rightly or wrongly is not certain even now. Meanwhile the American west coast remained a sketchy, straight line. A thousand years after Kosmas' *Kosmographia*, Waldseemüller wrote:

> It is clear from astronomical demonstrations that the whole earth is a point in comparison with the entire extent of the heavens. . . . There is about a fourth part of . . . the world . . . inhabited by living beings like ourselves. Hitherto it has been divided into three parts, Europe, Africa and Asia.
>
> Europe is bounded on the west by the Atlantic Ocean, on the north by the British Ocean, on the east by the River Tanais [i.e. the Don], Lake Maeotis [i.e. the Sea of Azov], and the Black Sea, and on the south by the Mediterranean Sea. Europe is so called after Europa, the daughter of King Agenor [i.e. the king of Phoenicia, in the Near East]. While with a girl's enthusiasm she was playing on the sea-shore accompanied by her Tyrian maidens and was gathering flowers in baskets, she is believed to have been carried off by Jupiter, who assumed the form of a snow-white bull, and after being brought over the seas to Crete seated upon his back to have given her name to the land lying opposite. . . .
>
> Africa is bounded on the west by the Atlantic Ocean, on the south by the Ethiopian Ocean, on the north by the Mediterranean Sea, and on the east by the River Nile. . . . It is called Africa because it is free from the severity of the cold. . . .
>
> Asia . . . far surpasses the other divisions in size and in resources. . . . Asia is so called after a queen of that name. . . .
>
> Now . . . a fourth part has been discovered by Amerigo Vespucci. Inasmuch as both Europe and Asia received their names from women, I see no reason why any one should justly object to calling this part Amerige, i.e. the land of Amerigo, or America, after Amerigo, its discoverer, a man of great ability.[31]

The honour of giving America a really adequate place on the map should, according to many, be given to Gerard Mercator (1512–94). After having studied the humanities at Louvain, Mercator continued his education there with the famous mathematician Gemma Frisius, to prepare for a career as a constructor of mathematical instruments. In 1536, together with his master, he made the first celestial globe and, with a Louvain goldsmith, the second terrestrial globe. In the following years, Mercator drew and published maps of the Holy Land based on existing data – naturally a 'must' from a cultural point of view, in a Christian society and, moreover, of commercial interest for the pilgrim industry. Mercator quickly gained a good reputation: Emperor Charles V ordered him to manufacture astronomical instruments.

In 1579, roughly three–quarters of a century after Behaim, Mercator published a world map *ad usum navigatorum* (for the use of navigators). On his map he established his interpretation of the earth's outlines using a cylinder projection based upon straight lines of longitude and latitude intersecting at right angles. Mercator combined Ptolemy's data and ideas with those which were more recent – Marco Polo's, regardless of how controversial they still were – and with those which were almost contemporary, the discoveries of the Portuguese and Spanish navigators. The map also incorporated America. However, basing himself on all sorts of information brought to Europe by navigators and land surveyors, Mercator did draw South America much too large and the barely known North America much too small. Moreover, he also added two large polar continents.

In the mean time, cartography had become a subject of evident scientific and economic importance, as can be seen from the large number of maps produced by Mercator after his map of the world; all of these, however magnificent and costly their editions, were commercially successful.

Interestingly, for a man like Mercator the world was still one. He integrated theoretical notions and practical research and application in one Christian cosmological context which encompassed the earth and the heavens, as became apparent after his death when, in 1596, the first part was published of what he considered the synthesis of his work, his own *Cosmographia*. Edited by his son, it consisted of five parts. The first part was called *Atlas*. In his 'Foreword to the Atlas', Mercator clearly suggests that the really wise person attempts to harmonize his knowledge of heaven and earth. The print on the title page shows the mythical Atlas with the celestial globe on his knee and, at his feet, the terrestrial globe, with America on it, too. In this first so-called atlas, Mercator discusses creation. He analyses the book of Genesis and the four Gospels. This section is followed by a new edition in four parts of map collections of various parts of Europe and the other known continents which had been published earlier.

The complete 'Cosmography' was published in Amsterdam. As the centre of the European economy had shifted from the Mediterranean to the boards of the Atlantic in the early decades of the sixteenth century, by the end of the century it moved from the main commercial metropolis, Antwerp, to the harbours of Holland, partly because the Dutch, in their revolt against Spain, decided to permanently blockade the River Scheldt. Map and instrument makers now established themselves in the Dutch port towns, applying the results of empirical research to produce new technology and thus contributing greatly to the success and growth of international trade. Holland was also the place where the most important printers and publishers in Europe settled, trying to market the knowledge about the new worlds. Pouring out travel stories and novels, encyclopedias and atlases, they spread knowledge about the rediscovered older world and the new world in the old world, where, initially, a disbelieving astonishment and, subsequently, a centuries-long curiosity continued to ensure a lively demand for new texts and pictures.

Money is power. As Europe became richer, the size of armies which rulers sent into battle and the fleets which sailed the seas also increased; more and more areas outside Europe were actively made to submit to European states. Power leads to a sense of superiority. Travelling Europeans observed that they were stronger than others, 'better' than Asians, Africans and Americans. First and foremost, they were superior militarily, with their use of gunpowder. Naturally, they wondered why this was so. The answer they found was simple, as the answer for mainly simple and believing people had to be: it was because Europeans were Christians, supported by the one, true God. The more educated employed a somewhat more complex reasoning. For Jean Bodin it was clear that Europe towered above the rest of the world precisely because European culture not only had its unique basis in the fundamental achievements of Greek civilization, but also had managed to surpass many of these.[32]

This growing self-awareness was also reflected in geographical representation. On maps, Europe was now shown as a region which dominated the world instead of as a remote corner of the great Eurasian land mass. Sometimes, even, the geographical contours were so transformed that the western corner of the continent was given the shape of a triumphant queen, as on the famous map in Sebastian Münster's *Cosmographia universalis*, published in Basle in 1588. Soon, this sense of superiority turned expansion into a 'mission', which created its own legitimacy, thus providing the arguments for further expansion, for new conquests.

A worldview naturally does not exist only on a globe or map. It is also a way of thinking. The new world had to be fitted into the European mind. As America was a world inhabited, according to the stories, by people with completely different physical features and habits, a world where animals and plants existed which did not appear in traditional biological manuals, for Europeans its discovery was an enormous culture shock.[33]

For many Europeans the reports about the new world were so astonishing, certainly in the first decades after Columbus's voyages, that they thought that, after centuries of searching, the Earthly Paradise had at last been discovered: the place where people still lived as God had created them, not spoilt by the Fall.[34] The belief was strong among the first missionaries who departed for Mexico in 1524, the Franciscans. They tried their best to convert the Mexican Indians. However, they wanted to protect the new believers at any cost from contact with the, in their eyes, godless Spanish colonists. Besides concentrating power over the new Christians in their own hands, in pursuing this policy they also hoped to realize God's kingdom on earth with these Indians, his innocent children.

Something of that (for today's reader) naive belief in the continued existence of a terrestrial paradise or the possibility of its human re-creation somewhere on earth can be found in many literary texts. Such a well-known writer as the English poet Andrew Marvell (1621–78), in a poem called 'Bermudas', praised God who had brought the English to:

> . . . an isle so long unknown,
> And yet far kinder than our own.
> He lands us on a grassy stage,
> Safe from the storms, and prelate's rage
> He gave us this eternal spring
> Which here enamels everything.[35]

An island, therefore, where the English could live in an atmosphere they no longer had at home, an atmosphere of freedom – of religion among other things – in a paradisical context. A few decades later George Berkeley (1685–1753) wrote his 'Verses on the Prospect of Planting Arts and Learning in America':

> The Muse, disgusted at an age and clime,
> Barren of every glorious theme,
> In distant lands now waits a better time,
> Producing subjects worthy of fame . . .
> There shall be sung another golden age,
> The rise of empire and of arts . . .
> Not such as Europe breeds in her decay:
> Such as she bred when fresh and young.[36]

The poem voices another theme which would recur for several centuries: the old world, Europe, is decaying; in the new world, Europeans can realize that which has no nourishing soil there any more. For Berkeley actually wanted to transplant what most eighteenth-century Europeans still considered to be the essence of Europe: arts and learning, showing that, essentially, Europe's self-definition had not changed since the same notions had been voiced in the fourteenth and fifteenth centuries, or even earlier.

A comparable, in some ways even more idyllic vision of the new world as the garden of Eden, and of the Indian as the 'Noble Savage', the uncorrupted man living in nature as created by God, can be found in many sixteenth- and seventeenth-century prints and paintings – by Albrecht Dürer and Jan Mostaert to name only two examples.[37] Yet many Europeans would hold that Indian societies were not civilized societies. Judged by humanist norms of civilization, wherein communication developed along the lines of public oratory and eloquence, denoting an ordered, regulated polity, or by Christian norms of civilization, wherein the belief in the one, true, unseen God denoted the same, they had to be educated, to be raised to the level of Europe. Nor was actual contact with the Indians as peaceful as the more idealistic images would have us believe. On the contrary, European connections with America were, if anything, often calculating and equally often cruel, even by contemporary standards.

The traces of this contact turned conflict can be found in another of Shakespeare's plays, *The Tempest*, about a group of Europeans headed by the exiled Prospero who find themselves stranded on a strange island. The playwright is known to have been inspired by stories of Europeans who were shipwrecked in foreign parts. Yet this play is more than a poetic fabrication of such travel stories. It is an allegory of the way Europeans behaved towards their new fellow men. *The Tempest* can therefore be read as follows. At first, the natives, represented by the wild Caliban, are friendly and show the foreigners their treasures and secrets if only because in return they are taught some of Europe's arts:

> When thou camest first,
> Thou strokedst me and made much of me; wouldst give me
> Water with berries in't; and teach me how
> To name the bigger light, and how the less,
> That burn by day, and night; and then I loved thee
> And showed thee all the qualities o' the isle,
> The fresh springs, brine-pits, barren place and fertile.[38]

Then these foreigners, the Europeans, turn away from the natives because they find them uncivilized. The Indians react correspondingly. The Europeans now start using their superior technology, symbolized in the play by the magic of Prospero; they use it to enslave the natives. The latter try to defend themselves by setting up newly arrived foreigners against their masters, and Caliban calls out:

> I'll show thee the best springs; I'll pluck thee berries . . .
> A plague upon the tyrant that I serve!
> I'll bear him no more sticks but follow thee,
> Thou wondrous man.[39]

But their fate is sealed; they become only more dependent. Moreover, they are now branded as bloodthirsty monsters.[40]

In the first decades of the seventeenth century, when in North America, too, Europeans and Indians entered in more frequent contact, the fight for land began. Many colonists, born and raised in the strict traditions of Protestantism, strengthened their moral position and defended their actions by using biblical arguments. In dozens of sermons and tracts the image is used of an elite corps of believers whom God has placed in this 'wildernesse', as a test, just as had once happened with the people of Israel in the desert. But the promised land is around the corner, 'a garden enclosed, a fountain sealed', and with God's help 'Jerusalem shall be inhabitable without walls', just as the Bible says.[41]

Yet no Jerusalem without a struggle. Outright war between the settlers and the natives soon followed. In 1637, this occurred on a large scale for the first time; the tribe of the Pequot was exterminated completely. Some colonists questioned whether all this bloodshed could somehow be justified. An anonymous minister's answer was:

> I would refer you to David's war. When a People is grown to such a height of blood and sin against God and man . . . sometimes the Scripture declareth women and children must perish with their parents.[42]

Among the many texts which propose to conquer the new world as the Jews once did their promised land, that is with Old Testament violence, one is relieved to sometimes find a somewhat more nuanced judgement, like that of Robert Beverly, who concluded his 1705 outline of Indian society with the words:

Thus I think I have given a succinct account of the Indians; happy, I think, in their simple State of Nature, and in their enjoyment of Plenty without the Curse of Labour. They have on several counts reasons to lament the arrival of the Europeans, by whose means they seem to have lost their Felicity, as well as their Innocence.[43]

Another colonist went one step further when, in 1708, he realized that:

We neither give Allowance for their Natural Disposition, nor the Sylvan Education and strange Customs (uncouth to us) they lie under and have ever been trained up to; these are false Measures for Christians to take, and indeed no man can be reckoned a Moralist only, who will not make choice and use better Rules to walk and act by.[44]

Until well into the eighteenth century some European Americans and many more Europeans indulged in an uncritical idealization of the 'Noble Savage'. Yet careful analysis of the writings of most of these thinkers shows that they are always addressing the European who must improve himself, if necessary by recognizing his own failings from the contrast with original, still uncorrupted worlds and beings. Seldom does one find a plea for an acceptance of 'the Other' as intrinsically different, and thus as his own self. Indeed, as far as the problem of the relationship is addressed at all, what dominates is the image of the dependence of non-European man on the European. In the early eighteenth century it was codified in Daniel Defoe's famous story *Robinson Crusoe*, which created archetypes of the relation between the European and 'the Other'; that in this case the other was black instead of red is unimportant: it shows that the discovery of America, of new worlds, and the meeting with 'the Other' substantially influenced the way Europeans viewed themselves. They began to see themselves as superior, as natural leaders.

Further cultural consequences of expansion

Undeniably, the process of contact and conquest in which Europe came to dominate a large part of the world, has caused great suffering all over the globe.[45] Obviously, historiography is not the forum to make moral judgements on those periods and people of the past which often held values so different from our own. Yet one may conclude that colonialism and imperialism, though practised by many civilizations all over the world during known history, in their European form and by Europe's very technological possibilities, often transgressed even the norms of the time itself.

However, surveying European history, one cannot fail to note also that the rediscovery of Asia and the discovery of America have been decisive factors in the creation of numerous, and lasting forms of culture: of artistic masterpieces still visible all over Europe, of lifestyles and luxuries but, perhaps more important, of ideas and attitudes which shaped the European mind for centuries to come and, in their turn, influenced the wider world.

A family of Florentine bankers like the Medici, in whose coffers huge heaps of the gold and silver from Asia and America ended up, were Michelangelo's first patrons.[46] The new St Peter's which rose in Rome in the course of the sixteenth century – it took more than a hundred years to build – was constructed in part thanks to the ecclesiastical taxes which flowed in from Spain and Portugal and, hence, from their gold and silver mines in Iberian America. In the seventeenth century, in that same Rome, on the Piazza Navona, Gianlorenzo Bernini created the dream-like 'Fountain of the Four Rivers', one of which symbolized the Rio de la Plata, the River of Silver, while all four rivers supported an obelisk, seen as the representation of the oldest culture of the world, Egypt, but that one, in its turn, topped by the Christian cross.

On the Iberian peninsula itself, the bullion that came from the Americas resulted in sumptuous buildings, among them Philip II's church-monastery-palace of the Escurial, in the mountains above Madrid, in commissions for music to be played and sung in churches, monasteries and palaces alike, and in a wide demand for emotionally evocative baroque paintings and sculpture to adorn these buildings.

In the far north, in Amsterdam, Jacob van Campen's palatial townhall with its statues by Flemish sculptors, the proud symbol of the foremost mercantile city of the seventeenth century glorified the Dutch trading metropolis as 'mistress of the world'. Significantly, the façade of the building was crowned with a gigantic Atlas-figure shouldering the globe. For good reason, two enormous world maps were represented in the many-coloured marble pavement of the great hall. That globe and those maps certainly served to remind visitors and passers-by of the colonies the Dutch had conquered on the Portuguese in Brazil, of the 'New Amsterdam' which Dutch traders and settlers had founded on the banks of the Hudson, and of the even vaster colonial empire they had built in the east.

The same satisfaction surfaced in a poem in which the Dutch poet Joost van den Vondel referred to Amsterdam's position of power in the old and in the new world. In the more than one thousand lines in which he provided the inauguration of the new townhall with an allegorical-ideological context, one reads that Amsterdam, which knows all 'shores', including gold-filled America's, is, by right, the ruler of the earth; by Vondel's time, the Dutch East India Company, the world's first multinational, had firmly established its hold over South Africa, parts of the coasts of India, Ceylon and present-day Indonesia, while they were the only Europeans allowed to enter the magic island empire of Japan.

In France, at the end of the seventeenth century, sumptuous tapestries were hung in the pompous palace of Versailles. For some of the series, representations were derived from paintings made by Dutch artists in Dutch Brazil.[47] Other paintings were used as the basis for the engraved illustrations of several successful travel stories published in the Netherlands in the seventeenth century: Caspar Barlaeus's 1647 history of the Dutch conquest of Brazil, and the still more famous *Brasiliaensche Land-en Seereise* (Brazilian Land and Sea

Journey), written in 1672 by Johan Nieuhof, servant of the Dutch West Indies Company, the global trade organization which focused, in particular, on the Americas.[48] But France, of course, longed to dominate the world all by itself. In 1662, young Louis XIV, for whom his first minister even had sought the imperial crown, entered the Place du Carroussel for a festive procession to mark the birth of the Dauphin. He was dressed as a Roman emperor, and served by his brother and his first nobles, who typified the Persians, the Turks, the peoples of India and the Americans; it was, of course, an act of political propaganda, as almost all the later Sun King's fêtes.[49]

In the first decades of the eighteenth century, magnificent ceiling frescos were painted by Giovanni Battista Tiepolo for the vaulted staircase of the prince-bishop's baroque residence in Würzburg and at the prince-bishop's new summer palace Weissenstein, in nearby Pommersfelden. Representing the different parts of the world in colourful allegories, they depict Europe as 'queen of the continents', implying that she rules the earth.[50] The palaces of the Habsburg emperors and their noble courtiers, as well as of other German courts in the eighteenth century, were adorned with pictures of America, too.[51] At those courts, one might hear an opera by the composer Karl-Heinrich Graun whose theme was the tragic fate suffered by the Aztec Emperor Montezuma through the Spanish conquerors; the same story was also set to music by the Venetian composer Antonio Vivaldi. Indeed, these were only a few of the many compositions in which the Indies, America, formed the location of the action, and the Indians were the characters. By this time, in a more 'enlightened' Europe the 'wild' Indian had become 'noble' again and it was possible to take a more nuanced view of his destiny at the hands of rapacious Europeans.

In England, the nobility's craze for the layout of huge gardens received a new impulse when, at the beginning of the eighteenth century, engravings depicting the gardens at Jehol, the Chinese emperor's summer palace, were published by a Jesuit returning from the Far East; he had been part of a group of Christian missionaries staying at the imperial court, the fourth generation to do so since the beginning of the sixteenth century. Chinese pagodas began to crop up in English vales while Chinese-style furniture started to fill the country houses. Indeed, a wave of 'chinoiserie' swept over Europe, not only to satisfy the need for a new fashion, but also because the Jesuits in their travel tales had succeeded in portraying China as a powerful state with a civilization that, perhaps the only one in the world, did actually match that of Europe.

In short, many of Europe's works of art would not have been created without the material contribution the worlds of Asia and America were forced to give, nor, for that matter, without the inspiration which the wonders of this new, foreign and to many dreamlike world had given to the European mind.

At an early stage, Europe had first become independent in the Greek self-definition as voiced, largely, in Hellas's opposition to Asia. The definition had been further articulated when Europe felt the need to form a common front against Islam, to actually cooperate in the Crusades. Now, in the fifteenth, sixteenth and seventeenth centuries, the definition was elaborated once more as the result of a clash with other cultures, not only those of Asia, the older world, but also those of America, the new world.

Vondel's poem cited above was a glorification not only of Amsterdam. It also described Europe as the continent where the 'burgher', the citizen was the centre of society, the politically free individual, who continues the tradition of the ancient Greek city states. But these burghers now drank coffee and tea imported from Asia, and sat down to dinner at tables laden with china ware, sometimes decorated in patterns specifically requested by them, to end a pleasant evening smoking a cigar made of American tobacco – undoubtedly unaware of or comfortably ignoring the fact that the tobacco was grown on plantations worked by black slaves from Africa, that the china was produced in ever more complex factories on the Chinese mainland, that the cultivation of tea and coffee was slowly disrupting traditional Asian economies and that much of their luxuries were bought with the profits they themselves made from the opium trade.

In their gardens they often grew plants from seedlings brought all the way from India or Indonesia by the ships of the Dutch East India Company. Some of the wealthiest burghers owned private zoos, where privileged visitors were allowed to gape at exotic animals gathered from all over the globe. Such visitors were also invited to enter the luxurious townhouses that lined the Amsterdam canals, in order to view, or even to study the collections of strange objects brought from overseas: minerals and manuscripts, coins and other curios. Indeed, all over Europe such collections were being formed by the curious and wealthy, to indicate culture and status, or for reasons of genuine learning and scholarship. In England, the German-born court physician Sir Hans Sloane bequeathed his extensive collection of artefacts, books and manuscripts to the nation of his adoptive country on the condition that it be publicly displayed, thus laying the foundation for the British Museum and its library.

These objects, as well as the animals and the plants, documented a world that, though new discoveries filled in the blanks on its map, yet grew ever more complex, and hence asked to be interpreted, to be understood. The new and the strange could either be explained as being superficially different, but essentially the same as European things, and thus controllable, not dangerous, or as radically different and consequently dangerous, a challenge to be met, a world to be conquered in order to remove the threat of its uncontrolled otherness.

The fact that some of these cultures, like the Chinese and the Japanese, appeared to be highly developed themselves, even according to the criteria posed by Europe, only increased the necessity to underline Europe's own identity as a Christian and hence superior civilization. How else could one justify the use of guns and cannon in the many attempts to conquer other cultures for the purpose of expanding Europe's economic and military power?

Only by maintaining that in its very essence every other civilization lagged behind Europe's, with its roots in Christianity and the Classics, only by believing and proclaiming that for that very reason every other culture contentedly had to accept European supremacy and its resulting economic and political dominance, Europeans could legitimize their efforts to establish overseas colonies and empires, phenomena which both appeared from the sixteenth century onwards. Economically, politically, religiously and culturally, large parts of the non-European world were gradually incorporated in what slowly became a 'European world system'.

From this time on those Europeans who thought about their own world, about Europe, would always be influenced by dreams about other worlds. For the first time leaving the security of home in large numbers, Europeans were also forced for the first time to account for the fears and desires in their deepest heart, emotions which could not so easily be given free rein at home, if only because people had to preserve the relative stability of their own environment being endangered. What forms of culture were to be preserved, defended and even disseminated, regardless of the cost? What new, 'foreign' things should be understood, accepted?

Those who had made distant journeys now were better informed about what was 'own' and what was 'other' and thus contributed to the development of European self-awareness. In 1544, the cartographer Sebastian Münster proclaimed that Europe, although the smallest of the known continents – something which now could and had to be recognized – was yet the most fertile, the most densely populated and consequently the strongest.[52] The English minister Samuel Purchas, always taking notes while listening to the seamen who told their tales on returning from their journeys, collected a large number of travel stories which he published in 1625. He wrote that 'The Qualitie of Europe exceeds her Quantitie, in this the least, in that the Best of the world.' After all:

> If I speake of Arts and Inventions (which are Man's properest goods, immortall Inheritance to our mortalitie) what have the rest of the world comparable? First the Liberall Arts are most liberall to us, having long since forsaken their Seminaries in Asia and Afrike, and here erected Colleges and Universities. And if one Athens in the east (the antient Europaean glory) now by Turkish Barbarisme be infected, how many Christian Athenses have wee in the west for it. As for Mechanicall Sciences, I could reckon . . . the many artificiall Mazes and Labyrinths in our watches, the great heavenly Orbes and motions installed in so small a modell. What eares but European have heard so many Musicall Inventions for the Chamber, the Field, the Church?

This very revealing panegyric which enumerates many phenomena even now considered by many to constitute Europe's unique cultural heritage, continues for several paragraphs, until Purchas poses the question:

> And is this all? Is Europe onely a fruitfull Field, a well watered garden, a pleasant Paradise in Nature? A continued Citie for habitation? Queene of the World for power? A Schoole of Arts Liberall, Shop of Mechanicall, Tents of Military, Arsenall of Weapons and Shipping?

Garden, paradise, city, the very locations of civilization, the archetypical images of which had been grafted onto Christian thought by the first books of the Old Testament. What blossomed there? Besides music and instrument making, art, technology, commerce, all of them creating power in the widest sense. It is fascinating to see how Purchas establishes an almost essential relationship between these things. For him not only the arts and sciences, but also the nascent commercial-industrial society of Europe itself is a cultural phenomenon. It was a notion that slowly gained acceptance in wider circles until, in the nineteenth century, it had become the very basis of Europe's self-esteem, in all cultural and scholarly circles.[53]

Purchas's question naturally required an answer, and he provided one, in equally enthusiastic prose:

> Nay, these are the least of Her praises, or His rather, who hath given Europe more than Eagle's wings, and lifted her up above the Starres . . . Europe is taught the way to scale Heaven, not by Mathematicall principles, but by Divine veritie. Jesus Christ is their way, their truth, their life; who hath long since given a Bill of Divorce to ingrateful Asia where hee was borne, and Africa the place of his flight and refuge, and is become almost wholly and onely Europaean.[54]

Once more, the Bible provided the historical arguments which served to belittle the significance of the other old continents. But on top of this, Purchas explicitly noted that Europe had discovered and conquered the world; its cultural qualities are not restricted to its religion, political structures and military might, to its arts and sciences, but include its capacity for expansion. After all:

> Who ever tooke possession of the huge Ocean, and made procession round about the vast Earth? Who ever discovered new Constellations, saluted the Frozen Poles, subjected the Burning Zones?[55]

Here, indeed, Purchas touches upon an important point. For it has to be admitted that no civilization but the European had ever undertaken such large-scale travel; the spirit of adventure and discovery and, consequently, the will to expand one's horizons and one's power seem to be, if not specific European, characteristics that Europe, more than any other culture, could claim to have translated into real actions. Or should one term them Christian characteristics? After all, Christianity was a religion which, as Purchas himself indicated, was aware of the fact that its roots did not lay in the region where it actually had become dominant; consequently, it almost forced its believers to travel, the more so as the Christian belief in a paradise on earth as well as in a promised land proved an additional, perhaps even more powerful stimulus to engage in travel, however perilous.

Europe's often discordant contacts with other parts of the world and the resulting reflection did not only lead to a broadening of the definition of that which was considered to constitute its essence. Many began to contemplate Europe's failings and to consider how to remedy these. Significantly, from the late fifteenth century onwards, time and again plans were devised for the establishment of a better society. These plans offered an intriguing view both of the reality and the ideals of the period in which they were formulated. Mostly, they centred around four elements. A happy society nearly always was presented as a city, an idea for which the Europeans certainly were indebted to the Greeks. It also implied the notion that nature, essentially uncontrollable, had to be tamed. In this city, health-care was optimal: obviously, the fear of death played a crucial role in the European, Christian view of man. Also, education – of the middle class, the ruler, and the learned – is given a high priority. Last but not least, prosperity is divided according to principles of justice. The fact that the opportunity to publish and distribute one's collected works is sometimes a fifth characteristic of these ideal societies betrays their origin in the minds of intellectuals and scholars who were concerned about their future reputation.[56]

Even though, of course, none of these ideal societies were ever realized, they did influence the European self-image. In consequence, reality, both in Europe but more often abroad, in regions that still could be dreamt of as unspoilt by the negative aspects of society at home, was frequently sketched as if it were ideal already. Besides, these ideals were often included in the political and social demands which individuals or groups made of reality, dissatisfied as they were with it; thus they did help to slowly change that reality.

The process can be traced from the visions on man and society in Thomas More's *Utopia* (London 1516) and Tommaso Campanella's (1568–1639) *Città del Sole*, 'Sun City' (1603), via Johann Valentin Andreae and his 'Description of a Christian Republic' (Nuremberg 1619), to the German philosophers Leibniz and Herder in the eighteenth century, and to the 'utopian' socialists of England and France in the nineteenth century. One aspect is particularly striking. A utopia really needs a virgin land. Many of the early utopians located the world of their dreams not in their own world, or in the older world of fabulous Asia but in the newly discovered America, as yet untainted by civilization.

In retrospect one can see the fifteenth and sixteenth centuries as a period of change; in many fields of culture old values and systems disappeared and, mainly because of the communications' revolution in Europe itself, new norms and institutions were born. In the mean time, education and the increasing dissemination of texts ensured that the notion of a wider world – Europe itself, but also the worlds beyond, and both of them mentally as well as geographically perceived – filtered down to ever more people. Through their contacts with these worlds a more complete, also more secular vision of self took shape.

The poet Philip Freneau, fed on the often superficial, for largely uninformed, cultural relativism that took root in intellectual circles in the Atlantic world in the latter decades of the eighteenth century, in his 'The American Village' of 1772 described his world as the place where:

> Renowned sachems once their empire rais'd
> On wholesome laws; and sacrifices blaz'd.
> The gen'rous soul inspir'd the honest breast
> And to be free, was doubly to be blest.

Yet, after this idealistic representation of Indian society as a community of noble, free, self-governing men, reflecting a yearning for a life no longer possible in the civilized west, the same Freneau, in another poem called 'The Rising Glory of America', observed:

> How much obscur'd is human nature here!
> Shut from the light of science and of truth.[57]

Unavoidably, and despite his dream of a romantically simple society, he shows himself to be rooted in European values which, precisely in the eighteenth century, increasingly considered science to be the basic norm of truth and progress.

10 A new society
Migration, travel and the diffusion and integration of culture in Europe

Migration, travel and culture

People sometimes wonder whether travel and the ensuing encounter with other cultures is, indeed, a factor of cultural integration. It is true that someone who travels does move to locations where people live and behave according to different norms, creating a different culture. But do not most travellers carry only themselves, namely their own identity and their own prejudices which are, consequently and sometimes even agreeably, confirmed by confrontation with the other? Often, travel does not seem to lead to positive interaction, let alone integration.

Yet this chapter will try to establish that travelling, outside but, more importantly, also within Europe, did lead to cultural changes. For example, long periods of actual domination apart, various forms of travel, especially trade, continued to result in linguistic interchange, contributing words and ideas to Europe's languages; Spain, of course, had its hundreds of Arabic words after seven hundred years of Islamic domination; but so had England, through its far shorter contacts with France. Italy absorbed a fair share of Turkish words through trade, and in the golden age of its commercial and technical superiority, Dutch shipping terms entered many a language, including Russian. Also, travel resulted in greater knowledge about such fields as the geography, economics, politics and the morals and customs of other regions, both for the individual traveller but also, as a result of a cumulative process, within the groups who were the main culture makers in the regional cultures of which Europe was, in fact, comprised. Finally, travel was an important element in the formation of a cosmopolitan culture which increasingly tied together the elites of the various countries at a European level.

This process was, of course, not exclusively determined by the phenomenon of travel. Other factors were the invention of printing and the subsequent developments in education, which led to a slow but nevertheless important diffusion of culture in the sixteenth century, as well as the new phenomenon of correspondence networks and cultural periodicals which further promoted this spread. After all, without knowledge and information the books could not have been written which, from the sixteenth century onwards, led an expanding reading public to new ideas. But without travel and epistolary contacts that knowledge and information certainly would not have been amassed on such a large scale that one can, without exaggeration, call the period from the early sixteenth century onwards a period of growing cultural complexity. Precisely through the interaction between elements which, partly traditional, partly new, now functioned together, the centuries between *c.*1500 and 1800 acquired a particularly 'European' character.

Non-voluntary travel: the cultural significance of migrations

In view of the land-bound character of the great majority of Europeans, until the early nineteenth century most people travelled rarely or not at all; the few who did, did not do so for motives which really opened up the possibility for cultural communication. While considerable numbers of people from all kinds of social groups have always been forced either professionally or by unpleasant circumstances to travel or even migrate, this type of travel, though of un-mistakable cultural significance for Europe, did not lead to a growing feeling of solidarity, to a concept of 'Europe'. Moreover, we know little about the collective or individual experiences of the vast majority of the people who travelled, especially those who did so involuntarily, mainly because they rarely recorded their experiences. Thus, the lack of the most important sources for the study of past travel experiences and of the ensuing reflections – letters and travel reports[1] – inevitably leads to a somewhat scanty picture.

Of the numerically really large groups who travelled there was only one that was not more or less forced to do so: the group of pilgrims who annually went to the innumerable locally venerated shrines and to the few universally revered holy sites of the Christian world, among which Rome and Santiago de Compostela were the two outstanding destinations – Jerusalem being too far and too expensive for most people. Making themselves recognizable with staff and scarf, the pilgrims travelled, often on foot, to the holy places. We know something about what went on not only from the pilgrims' manuals but also from such literary texts as Chaucer's *Canterbury Tales*, which was successful pre-cisely because of its recognizable stories.[2] People did not just go on pilgrimage whenever they felt the urge to do so, not least because pilgrimages were bound to the seasons, undertaken only after the cold of winter had disappeared and before the new snow made the passes in the Alps and the Pyrenees impassable again. Thus, Chaucer begins his story with the famous words:

> Whan that Aprille with his shoures soote
> The droghte of March hat perced to the roote
> . . . Thanne longen folke to goon on pilgrimages
> And palmeres for to seken straunge strondes.[3]

The number of people who went on pilgrimage was gigantic. The figures for the period before the sixteenth century are frequently unreliable but, fortunately, in Rome, careful counting took place. Thus, in the Holy Year 1600, according to estimates, at least half a million pilgrims arrived from all over Europe, in a city which at that time had only 100,000 inhabitants. The atmosphere on these trips was less pious than one might perhaps expect: it was the atmosphere of an outing. For this is how most pilgrims – except penitents sent on a punitive pilgrimage by secular or religious judges – naturally experienced it: as a unique moment in a person's life, the only sanctioned, long-lasting interruption of a routine which was, for the most part, determined by work and sleep.

Little is known about the individual experiences of pilgrims. Most of them were illiterate, unable to express their impressions and emotions on paper. We do not know how they reacted to the people they met, the villages and cities they saw, the different eating habits and other forms of behaviour they experienced on the way. Yet they must have come home with many, sometimes wild stories. Quite likely they influenced those who had stayed at home and, consequently, unconsciously altered their view of the world beyond the horizon; but quite likely they also confirmed existing prejudices.

Plate 23 Religion and travel: from all over Europe, each year tens of thousands of pilgrims travelled to Rome, to visit the seven main basilicas – here on a sixteenth-century map – which were the most important among the city's hundreds of churches and sanctuaries. The final destination was St Peter's, shown at the bottom, the nave and Michelangelo's cupola still unfinished in their intended form
Photo: P.J.A.N. Rietbergen

Equally doubtful is the positive impact of the involuntary travels of the many poor wretches who, compelled by all manner of economic and social misery, left hearth and home for often long periods of time, signing up as mercenaries in the new states' armies or swelling the crews of the big trading fleets. From the sixteenth century onwards, in most European states both the military themselves and their lifestyle became definitely international.

Between the late sixteenth and the early nineteenth centuries, Spanish soldiers' letters from the period of the Eighty Years' War[4] and Dutch soldiers' letters written at the time of the Napoleonic campaigns[5] tell us about the world of those living the harsh life of the army, forced to leave their native soil, often never to return. Huge numbers of them were killed in battlefields where, as a result of their actions, the map of Europe was continually drawn anew. Yet reading their records supports the assumption that while all this 'travelling' may have led to a growth in knowledge, it certainly did not result in large-scale mutual understanding, in any form of 'European thinking' *avant la lettre*.

It is equally difficult really to gauge the effects on the dissemination and integration of culture of the economically and socially vital group of itinerant workers or of the fascinating phenomenon of the *fahrende Leute* (the travelling people), the often large groups of tramps who frequently crossed state borders.[6] And also, although they did not travel in the strict sense of the word, it is certainly worth noting the large group of migrants who left their homes and moved around until, sometimes after long periods, they settled down again, either at home or, frequently, elsewhere. One thinks first and foremost of the mainly forced migrations of religious refugees, who abandoned their native soil and settled in more liberal climes. They brought their own culture, their own world of ideas and lifestyles; often adapting themselves with difficulty, they had to find a place in the new world of the receiving culture.

Of course, the clearest example are the Jews. After the Romans had conquered Israel at the beginning of the Christian era, they had subdued various Jewish rebellions. During one of these, they destroyed Jerusalem. Many Jews then fled and settled around the Mediterranean as well as in central Europe. For centuries, they were forced to live marginal lives on the border of an increasingly Christian and, to them, increasingly hostile world. Whenever local or regional problems occurred, they were often treated as scapegoats, branded as magicians, murderers of Christ, and so on. Obviously, one of the underlying reasons for this attitude was jealousy of the prosperity of many Jews: Jewish bankers and merchants were often very visible in European economic life, to which they contributed greatly. Additional reasons were, precisely, their otherness in such forms of culture as religion and language.

For a long time, in the Islamic world of the Iberian peninsula their lot had been relatively easy. However, after the Christians reconquered Spain, and the Spanish kings sought to create a unified, homogenic state, also in the religious-cultural sense, hundreds of thousands of Jews were expelled in the late sixteenth century.[7] Later, large groups felt forced to migrate from the states of eastern

Europe to safer areas because of the bloody persecutions or pogroms that hit them – a phenomenon that went on for several centuries until well into the nineteenth century. Moving, and moving again, in their new worlds the Jews often lived in more or less official ghettos, which limited their cultural influence. Yet there was a certain dialogue with the mainstream Christian culture, especially in the scholarly world.[8] The mysticism of the Jewish Kabbala as well as Jewish theological speculation within the rabbinical tradition inspired many Christian scientists and scholars until the nineteenth century; moreover, the discussions about Hebrew and the other languages relating to the Bible contributed to the revival of European interest in the cultures of the Near East since the sixteenth century.

Another example of religious refugees are the protestant Waldensians and Huguenots, who, as a result of the centralizing religious policy of Louis XIV and also in consequence of their obvious economic power, in the last decades of the seventeenth century were forced to flee France and north-west Italy and to settle elsewhere. The French protestants mainly sought refuge in the German states, the Dutch Republic and in England.[9] They gave an economic and technological boost to the budding manufacture in all these countries, as had done the Jews;[10] specifically the Huguenot intellectuals contributed to the growing influence of 'French' culture in many European cities, despite the fact that the horrific stories about the tragic lot of the Huguenots and Waldensians frequently fed the hostile vision of France that already existed all over western Europe because of Louis XIV's aggressive foreign policy.

Three types of cultural travel

What sort of travel can be distinguished within the group of literate people who were in a position to actually communicate with their foreign surroundings? Which group cultures gained a more international character and gave Europe a more marked cultural unity?

In view of the economic and social preconditions of background and education, such travel by and large was limited to the landowning aristocracy, the urban patriciate and the affluent upper-middle class. Travel in these centuries was thus also principally, although not exclusively, an elite phenomenon which cannot be compared with the mass tourism which began with the creation of mass transport in the late nineteenth century. Because of the elite background of most travellers, their experience initially contributed to the formation, consolidation and change of culture only within the elite.

The business trip: merchants and bankers

From days of old, business trips by merchants who operated on a European scale had been important. Even before Roman times, there had been trans-European trade contacts. In the period from the fourth to the seventh centuries

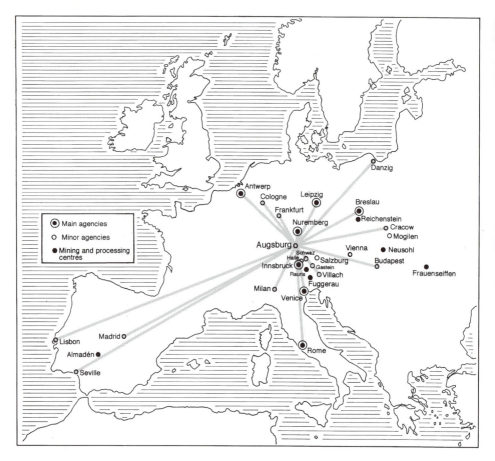

Map 6 Agencies and commercial interests of the Fugger trading and banking house, *c.*1500

Plate 22 Trade and travel: Jacob Fugger, the Augsburg banker, and his chief accountant, Matthäus Schwarz, depicted in the Fugger's headquarters with the filing cupboard labelled with the various branch offices that formed the Fugger empire, and between which the Fugger factors journeyed to conduct their variegated business. From a coloured drawing dated 1516
Source: Centre for Art Historical Documentation, Nijmegen, The Netherlands

of the Christian era – tumultuous centuries because of mass migration, population decline, economic malaise and political crisis – commercial travel decreased considerably. As a result of Charlemagne's economic policies, from the eighth century onwards one can observe a revival which, with interruptions, lasted until the crisis of the fourteenth century.

In the fifteenth century, Europe's economic life substantially intensified. Until then, leaving aside exceptions such as the Hanseatic network and transalpine and Mediterranean commerce, trade and industry often had been orientated locally. Now national and even international trade began to develop, stimulated by more intense contacts with Asia, America and, finally, Africa. However, one should realize that for thousands of years such contacts were often maintained not by a single person travelling over long distances but through a chain of merchants, each of whom travelled only regionally.

Yet the extent to which merchants became part of the changing Europe can be seen from the large number of travel guides which were published specially for this category by eager printers keen to serve this market; one study counted almost a thousand different titles for the period between 1500 and 1600.[11] These guides were mainly of a very practical nature and intention. They gave the most accessible and safest travel routes, but also information about local and regional currencies, which because of their huge variety necessitated conversion tables. Useful advice concerning market times and reasonable hotels was given as well. Some guides even contained short vocabularies to help people to make themselves understood in different European languages.[12] Yet even though these guides greatly facilitated travel, they also emphasized that elsewhere everything was different.

In this commercial world, which was so much more spacious than the agrarian world of the farming population, one meets the agents of the international trade and banking house of the Fugger family, the backers of the Emperor Charles V (1500–57), the first ruler since Charlemagne who really did operate supranationally. In their turn, the Fuggers and their clerks operated supranationally as well, from a network of offices that stretched from Warsaw to Lisbon, from Rome to Antwerp. Their thinking became international. In their letters, national borders seem to fade and an awareness at least of common economic problems, of factors that determine global trade was growing.[13] The big entrepreneurs and their travelling personnel certainly thought on a European scale.

Yet the question remains if this sense of growing economic dependence and unity also influenced other aspects of their world-view? Once more, their letters give us a clue. Besides the 'German' Fuggers and Welsers, there were other merchants and financiers working on a European scale, as the Portinaris and Della Failles, who hailed from Italy but soon established themselves in the new economic centre of Europe, the Southern Netherlands, as well as the Burlamacchis, who came from Lucca to Amsterdam, but also the Portuguese Jews like the Suassos. The correspondence of these entrepreneurs shows that they were thoroughly aware of the cultural peculiarities of Europe's different trading regions. This certainly caused them to put the interests of states and their small political problems in their proper perspective.

The growth of a more cosmopolitan, 'European' way of thinking in these circles also depended on the level of education. It was certainly stimulated by the frequent practice of sending abroad the younger members of the family firm – for this remained the basic organizational unit; staying with foreign business relations, they could not only learn the basics of their trade but also acquire a sense of what was different in the international economy. In his youth, Heinrich Floris Schopenhauer (1747–1805), father of the famous philosopher Arthur Schopenhauer and himself descended from a dynasty of Danzig wholesalers as well as the son of a Dutch merchant's daughter, spent several years in France and England. On his return, he accustomed himself to reading *The Times* every day; his library contained the works of French writers like Rousseau and Voltaire. Schopenhauer's wife Johanna Trosiener, nineteen years his junior, whom he married in 1758, had grown up in the same atmosphere and spoke both English and French; her most trusted friend was a Scottish doctor practising in Danzig.[14] In such cosmopolitan mercantile milieux, which existed from Gothenburg to Seville, from Amsterdam to Narva, some sort of 'European' thinking was normal indeed.

The diplomatic trip: ambassadors and politicians

Another group who travelled extensively were the diplomats. It was not only a fairly new group, coming into existence in the fifteenth and sixteenth centuries, with the rise of self-conscious states. It was also a group which was much bigger then than it is now, mainly because the ambassadors to the various European capitals usually kept a retinue of dozens, and on special occasions even hundreds of people, ranging from a suite of noblemen to a host of servants. Consequently, their significance for the 'Europeanization' of Europe certainly could be as great as that of the merchants.

The European royal courts, where these diplomats were accredited, were pre-eminent locations where culture was expressed in many ways. As a result of alliances between the various royal houses, courts were, by definition, the milieu where at least two, and often even more, 'national' cultures continually mixed – or would it be better to talk of 'regional' cultures in a period when nations were only slowly starting to take shape?

At first, contacts between Italy and France became frequent. Partly as a result of the struggle for power over Italy between the French kings and the Habsburg rulers of Spain and Austria, in the sixteenth century people often travelled from France to the peninsula. This led to cultural relations with the Italian courts and to a perceptible change of French court culture. In the wake of, among others, Maria de' Medici, daughter of the Florentine banking family turned dukes who, decked with gold, was married to the heir of France, Italian customs reached the French court at the end of the century. Many Frenchmen quickly found fault with this preposterous foreign culture, if only because it presented itself as superior. At the same time, however, they adjusted to it, in the visual arts, in science, in music, in food, in short, in all expressions of elite culture.

Several decades later, in the retinue of Henrietta Maria of Bourbon, who had been given in marriage to Charles I of England, French culture travelled to the capital of the island kingdom. The famous diarist and chronicler of London life, Samuel Pepys (1633–1703), noted both its pleasant and its to some, if not to him, less attractive aspects: French influences on drama and music and even on food, but also on sexual mores.[15]

The presence of large contingents of diplomatic actors and spectators on these royal stages further increased the international, cosmopolitan character of these courts. In most European countries elite people began to realize that their education was not complete unless they had travelled on a diplomatic mission at least once. In the instructions set up for the education of royal children and young members of the aristocracy, such journeys were soon mentioned as a necessity.[16]

Through this form of travel, a relatively large part of the future leadership came into contact with various aspects of foreign court culture. Norms, ways of behaving and other cultural expressions were observed abroad and sub-sequently, consciously or unconsciously, taken over, at least if they were sufficiently attractive and dominant. In the late sixteenth and early seventeenth centuries this meant a growing ascendancy of first Italian and, later, Spanish culture in Europe's higher circles. In 1637, an imperial ambassador, Johann Fürst Eggenbergh, who went from Vienna to Rome to offer Pope Urban VIII the obedience of his master, the newly elected 'King of the Romans' Ferdinand III, was received in regal fashion. The city and the papal court still considered themselves as the trend-setters and arbiters of culture which, it went without saying – and thus usually remained unsaid – was to be understood as both Christian and European.

We do not know which of his Roman experiences impressed Eggenbergh most. However, it is certain that the banquets which Francesco Cardinal Barberini, Secretary of State and Cardinal-nephew to the reigning Pope, and many other high-placed inhabitants of Rome offered their guest were in the most luxurious and fashionable taste. Table culture at Italian courts was an important cultural element *tout court*. The 'ingredients' of this culinary culture – presentation, etiquette and the food itself – were both native, Spanish and international.[17]

North of the Alps civilized people felt that they had not reached the same degree of refinement, yet. In a process comparable with what had happened through the Italo-French connection, in the wake of ambassadors like Eggenbergh, the Italian norm, naturally experienced as Roman by the Romans, was slowly imposed on northern Europe. Continuing the influence of the Renaissance, dance and diet, fashion and music, literary and artistic conventions, all these cultural forms 'travelled' in the wake of diplomats. Consequently, for almost the entire sixteenth century, in many areas of culture the Italian example remained the European norm.

In the second half of the seventeenth century, French court culture became the dominant factor in Europe, to remain so till the end of the eighteenth century. France had developed into Europe's most powerful country, both economically and politically. The French king was the embodiment of this power. Especially Louis XIV, who ruled during the greater part of the century's second half, tried to emphasize and enhance his prestige through a sophisticated propaganda policy. Its central instrument was his court, which became a 'theatre of power', where everything was 'conspicuous consumption' in the prince's service.[18]

To realize his goal, Louis willed the palace of Versailles, a new creation, far from Paris, the cramped and politically troublesome capital.[19] When the building was finished, it contained hundreds of rooms and galleries and vestibules. In all rooms, the curtains and the tapestries covering walls and furniture were changed twice a year: in winter, green and red velvet were used, in summer silk embroidered with gold and silver.

The palace had two nuclei. First, the great *Gallerie des Glaces*, where seventeen huge mirrors covered the wall, each of them worked on by several artisans for many years. On the ceiling, the frescos exalted Louis's military triumphs and the glory of France: it was the room where the King received the representatives of his foreign rivals, and where he fêted his court. The second centre was the royal bedroom. There, on a dais, stood the splendidly canopied royal bed. There, each royal day began and ended with the elaborate ritual of the *lever* and the *coucher du roi*. Each morning, France's most illustrious nobles assembled around Louis's bed to watch His Majesty rise. A happy few of the princes and dukes were chosen to help the King take off his night shirt and then some hundred people were allowed in to watch while another select group assisted the royal dressing. One by one they reverently handed the King his clothes: shirt, breeches, socks, shoes, rapier, mantle, feathered hat and so on. These ceremonies were called the 'little' and the 'grand' *lever*. People fought for the honour to be present. Huge bribes were given to be included in the group who handled the royal garments. At night, the entire ritual was repeated in reverse order. Between these two moments, the King's day ran according to an iron routine, described by the Duke of St Simon, one of the inner circle of court nobles, as 'the machine of Versailles', referring to the world of the theatre where stage machinery produced the desired effects![20]

At each and every act of the King, tens or even hundreds of nobles and commoners were present: as he ate, played at cards, walked, went to chapel or danced – Louis often was the centre of great ballets and operas set to stately music by such composers as Jean-Baptiste Lully that celebrated him as the Sun.[21] On this splendid stage, the King acted as a demi-god, whose most simple action was presented as holding extraordinary significance. That, of course, was the very aim of this theatre: the noble courtiers, the humble servants, the haughty foreign diplomats, all of them had to be impressed, to be persuaded that this king's power was absolute, that everything depended on him. To the untrained eye this was, indeed, the case: the King dispensed the most influential functions in government, the top military posts, the most lucrative bishoprics. Through royal favour, a person could reach the peaks of power; incurring the royal disgrace meant, to many, that life had become lacklustre, not to say useless.

The French example was followed all over Europe. Every prince wanted a palace as splendid as Versailles, a court as magnificent as the one that displayed itself there; the cities and countryside of Germany which, at that time, was still divided in numerous small states, even now afford many examples of the beautiful but, of course, costly results of this desire for emulation. Indeed, in one way or another, all European nobles strove to emulate their French colleagues: in England and Poland, in Sweden and Spain they started building country palaces and town mansions after the French manner, filled them with treasures after the French example, dressed according to the fashions dictated by France, ate as was prescribed in the manuals produced by the French cuisiniers.[22] They even behaved as the French nobles did, aping the intricate court manners of Versailles, in the way they walked, waved their hands, bowed their heads, and so on. French was the fashion in everything, even in pornography and whoring.

Consequently, whether people visited the palaces of the rulers in the many minor German states or the luxurious residences of the nobility in Swedish Skane or in Austrian Styria, the signs of French culture could be seen everywhere, partly as a result of the owners' experiences while on diplomatic missions. Even in a middle-class society like that of The Hague in the seventeenth century, Dutch culture was heavily influenced by French examples, also because of the influence of the diplomatic, largely aristocratic milieux on the local bourgeois elite.[23]

In short, over these centuries, elite culture slowly changed. Interaction between the Christian values which the Church had proclaimed as universal since the eighth century, and the even older regional or popular cultures, had resulted in the birth of 'national' elite cultures from the ninth and tenth centuries onwards. Since the fifteenth century, as a result of contacts with the courts in Italy and with French culture, that is, the culture of the French kings, these national cultures, while retaining their own character, yet acquired a more 'European' aspect as well. Reading the travel notes of that fascinating eighteenth-century Englishwoman, Lady Mary Wortley Montagu, one notices how easily this diplomat's wife moved among her class and sort when travelling around Italy and France;[24] travellers, belonging to a specific national elite, quickly felt at home in their own circle elsewhere in Europe.

Yet another factor played an important role in the development of this cosmopolitan court culture. Due to the invention of printing, those who travelled only within their books could read all manner of reports about court life, first oriented mainly towards Italy and Spain and subsequently towards France. Particularly influential was the idealized picture of court culture given in novels like Honoré d'Urfé's *L'Astrée* (1627) or Madame de la Fayette's *La Princesse de Clèves* (1678), the latter a moving and to many aristocrats, especially aristocratic women, recognizable psychological sketch of a woman's struggle between passion and reason that resulted from the stifling norms imposed by court society on its members. Indeed, in the seventeenth century, a flourishing and intriguing genre of what can be called 'court novels' developed, often of as little literary value as the sentimental novelettes of our own time yet certainly of great significance for the development of new norms, behaviour and expectations among their aristocratic and other readers.

The educational trip: students, scholars and artists

A third group of cultural travellers, formed by students, scholars and artists, was undoubtedly the most important for the formation and transmission of culture. In the form of the written and printed word or of visual representation, their work had an important communicative function, far more penetrating than can be imagined in a time of electronic mass communication.

One would be mistaken in thinking that the travels of this group had a less directly professional character than the travel of merchants and diplomats – that, rather, this travelling was anchored in the ideal world of 'culture'. For many in this group – a considerable number of the students and besides them the scholars and the artists – the world of high culture also was or would be their professional world. Theirs was the world of printed texts that would bring them jobs in education, in bookshops or with publishing firms, or the world of art, in which the word, the 'theory' and the 'explanation', played an increasingly important role in the reception and understanding of the visual product.

For this group there existed systems of education, scholarship and science whose basic characteristics were 'European'. These systems had centres of excellence: certain universities, for example, Bologna, Heidelberg, Leiden, Orléans, Oxford, Paris and Salamanca enjoyed European fame, while others had a more limited but still respectable supraregional attraction.

Depending on their place of origin and their financial possibilities, students for whom a good education was a career necessity or a sociocultural requirement, travelled to the nearest or to the most famous academies. Swedes went to Heidelberg, Leiden or Utrecht if they were not happy with Åbo, Lund or Uppsala. The Dutch, depending on their religious background, travelled either to the catholic universities of Louvain or Orléans, or to protestant Heidelberg, Geneva or Saumur.[25] The French travelled to Pisa or Bologna. Young Greeks from the Orthodox East flocked to the famous academy at Padua, the university of Venice, before taking up positions in the formerly Christian parts of the Ottoman Empire, or even in Ottoman imperial bureaucracy. Thus, Padua, from the sixteenth to the eighteenth centuries, became the gate to western learning for the south-east periphery of Europe. Bohemian students, 90 per cent of whom were from the urban middle class, sought places at academies all over the German Reich and in Switzerland. Of the latter we also know how old they were when they departed on their international journeys: usually 12 or 13 years of age.[26] That should remind us that the notions of 'child' and 'adolescent', in so far as they existed at the time, were interpreted quite differently and were actually experienced differently, emotionally and maybe even physically and biologically. It was not until the eighteenth century that the age at which most people in Europe started their university study reached the present-day 'norm' of 18.[27]

Established scholars travelled the same roads as students. Then, as now, state borders were of less importance to them, although religious differences sometimes imposed limits on their choice of destination. They followed the call of lucrative salaries, accepted prestigious professorships at famous universities or took up promises of good research possibilities.

In this way the *peregrinatio academica* (academic pilgrimage), became a permanent part of university education, at least for those students who could afford such a trip. Many Dutch students, future government servants, doctors, lawyers, Church ministers and university professors, followed a 'German route' or a 'French route' to study abroad for a shorter or longer period, while between 1575 and 1814 some 5,000 foreigners studied in the Republic – usually opting for medicine or law.[28]

The value of studying abroad was impressed on everyone as early as the first decades of the sixteenth century, when Erasmus wrote about it. However, the most influential text was a much-read and translated one by the Flemish humanist Justus Lipsius (1547–1606). In his *Epistolarum . . . centurio prima*, a 'collection of hundred letters' published in Antwerp in 1586, he made an impassioned as well as practical plea for the academic journey. Lipsius' text, which went through many editions until well into the eighteenth century, greatly influenced the educated European public through the way it stressed travel as one of the most important elements in the development of human knowledge and understanding, the way to a truly civilized life and behaviour – the very reason why Lipsius' contemporary, King Philip II of Spain, fearing his subjects might get the wrong ideas, forbade Spanish students to travel abroad. It also emphasized the significance of Italy as the cradle of civilization. Lipsius did, of course, refer only to men. Girls, if they travelled at all, did so only to accompany their husband or father as his wife or daughter.

Besides Lipsius' treatise, other manuals soon appeared which gave more detailed information about academic travel for specific career preparations. Thus, there were travel guides specifically for lawyers and doctors, both those who were still studying and those who were already established.[29]

Artists had comparable reasons for travelling though, for the completion of their training, they did not go to a university but rather to the studios of famous colleagues or to professional academies. Most times they combined this with a visit to old and new monuments, sketchbook in hand. Just like the students, their travels almost always ended in Italy, which, until late in the eighteenth century, was seen as one of Europe's most authoritative artistic centres. When they had finally succeeded in making a name for themselves, the same was true for artists as for many scholars: they did not have deeply felt ties with a 'national' culture. They established themselves where their clients lived, at the royal courts in the capital cities of the various European states or at the homes of the great aristocrats who wanted to express their power and status through their patronage.

In the early sixteenth century, painters travelled from Antwerp and Bruges, from Haarlem and Utrecht to Italy, to Rome, where they sold their work to cardinals and Curia officials – they introduced perspective into the realism of Italian landscape painting. On the other hand, they learned from Italy as well, especially from its by now long tradition of anatomically correct representations of the human body: the quality of Albrecht Dürer's painting differed considerably before and after his stay in Italy. For some artists, travelling became a cultural must, for others a professional necessity. In 1521, the famous master Jan van Scorel even travelled to Jerusalem, afterwards incorporating his idealized impressions of the Holy Land in his paintings. In the same century, choristers and other musicians travelled from Burgundy and Flanders to the courts in Munich and Burgos, in Venice and Cracow, in Mantua, Florence and Rome, to sing in royal or papal chapels and to compose their masses and madrigals; some stayed for a year, others for the rest of their lives.

This is how, as a 12-year-old chorister, Roland de Lattre (1532–94), born in Bergen, or Mons in the Low Countries, went with the viceroy of Sicily to Naples and Palermo, where he was called Orlando di Lasso. At the age of 20 he became the choirmaster of the cathedral of St John Lateran in Rome. Subsequently he worked in Antwerp where the publisher Tilman Susato saw that money could be made from his music; its publication made Lasso famous all over Europe. In 1556, he left for the ducal court of Bavaria at Munich, where he first became a singer and, after eight years, Master of the Duke's Music. To hire singers he travelled back to the Netherlands and once again visited Italy. The Pope knighted him and the Bavarian duke raised him to the nobility.

In their turn, painters and other artists from Italy travelled northwards. In the sixteenth century, the Florentines Leonardo da Vinci and Benvenuto Cellini went to the court of François I of France at Fontainebleau, the one to paint, the other to make his astonishing pieces of silverwork. In the seventeenth century, the Roman architect-sculptor Gianlorenzo Bernini temporarily established himself in Paris in order to design palaces and statues that tickled the vanity of Louis XIV. In the eighteenth century, the Venetian Giovanni Battista Tiepolo worked for the prince-bishop of Würzburg's 'Residenz'. Many of his compatriots found employment in the creation and decoration of the sumptuous churches and monasteries that began to adorn the towns and the countryside of southern Germany – although they were soon supplanted by immensely talented native artists, such as the five architects from the Dientzenhofer family, who built cathedrals, abbeys and palaces all over Franconia and Moravia.[30]

In the same period, generations of Italian architects erected the golden towers which rose against the steely blue sky of the new tsarist capital, St Petersburg. Meanwhile, in the London opera houses Italian sopranos, tenors and castratos sang the virtuoso arias of Georg Friedrich Handel (1685–1759), English court composer of German origin; they were arias written in a style which Handel had made his own during his stay in Italy where, for several years, he had been employed by Italian aristocrats. In the same years, two of Handel's colleagues and contemporaries, the Italian composers Domenico and Giovanni Locatelli – no relatives – travelled crisscross through central Europe, seeking and finding employment at various German courts, both in catholic and Protestant milieux, and even in Russia; the former ended his career in Kassel, the latter in Moscow. The great Johann Sebastian Bach (1685–1750) moved around, too, composing his cantatas for the services in Leipzig's St Thomas Church, but producing his Brandenburg Concertos for the electoral court at Ansbach; his numerous musical sons and other relatives worked all over Germany.

And, finally, Mozart (1756–91). As a boy, Wolfgang Amadeus was toured all around Europe by a proud but also penny-conscious father, performing in Paris, London and The Hague. And while he began his career as court composer to the prince-archbishop of Salzburg, he went on to Vienna to make a name for himself in the imperial service as well as providing compositions to the great aristocrats of the Habsburg states. For the coronation of Leopold II in 1791, he travelled to Prague, where his beautiful opera *La Clemenza di Tito*, praising the new emperor's forgiveness of his enemies, paid witness to the influence not only of Italian musical style but also of the impact of classical themes on contemporary political propaganda-through-music.

A particularly good example of the phenomenon of the growing exchange of cultural forms and ideas is seventeenth-century Sweden. In the 1640s, Magnus Gabriel de la Gardie, favourite of Queen Christina and later chancellor of the realm, undertook several ambassadorial trips to the Dutch Republic and France. He subsequently arranged for Swedish nobles and artists to study there; thus, David Klocker Ehrenstrahl, after having studied in the Netherlands and having married a Dutch wife, became the foremost painter of the Swedish baroque, decking, for example, the ceiling of the new, classically styled Riddarhus in Stockholm with a painting of Svea, the goddess allegorically representing this proud nation. Foreign artists and scholars, too, were offered attractive conditions by De la Gardie to establish themselves in Sweden, at court or at the universities of Uppsala and Lund, which he patronized generously, also enriching their libraries with foreign acquisitions.

His colleague in the kingdom's government, Carl-Gustav Wrangel, a war commander who had become immensely wealthy as a result of the Swedish conquests on the eastern shores of the Baltic, did not lag behind in building sumptuous dwellings, confiscating works of art on his military campaigns – partly through plunder in imperial Germany – or buying them from all over Europe through a network of agents. His Renaissance dream palace of Skokloster, a classically symmetrical structure in glistening white stone, was the jewel box for his magnificent collection. He also formed a splendid library there. In consequence of the patronage of such magnates, in a few decades Swedish culture began to show a humanist-Renaissance face, with obvious Dutch and French features especially in architecture and interior decoration.[31]

Business trips, diplomatic trips, educational trips – three types of travel which not infrequently appeared in some sort of combination.[32] Businessmen were often asked to carry out diplomatic missions as, occasionally, did artists like the famous Flemish painter Peter-Paul Rubens who was sent to England by his Spanish masters. Young members of the nobility or the sons of wealthy middle-class citizens regularly combined a trip as a member of an ambassador's retinue with a period of study at one or more universities and a visit to the most important sights.[33]

During the seventeenth and eighteenth centuries, the combination of the diplomatic and educational trip developed into a phenomenon that could be called a European cultural constant: the Grand Tour.[34] This was understood as a grand trip, in view of the fact that it was meant to influence the education of the European elite in a cosmopolitan-cultural sense. But it was also a trip which, certainly when seen from a north-west European perspective, was grand because it had to include Italy and in the seventeenth and eighteenth centuries often France as well. Indeed, for most Europeans, the 'Grand Tour' showed a clear southerly gravitation. It was based on an 'Italy feeling'[35] that, until the eighteenth century, seems to have existed among most cultured Europeans, including the already culturally chauvinistic French.[36] One might even term this emotion a 'Mediterranean passion',[37] a *Drang nach dem Süden*, which, in different guises, has continued to direct the European urge to travel until our own times.

Significantly, travel in the northern direction was far less frequent. Admittedly, the Italians and French travelled to those bleak regions when the occasion arose, with the Dutch Republic among their principal destinations.[38] In the seventeenth century, its policy of tolerance, driven by financial pragmatism and fundamental principle, had made the country a European centre of education, science and publishing. For the same reasons the Northern Netherlands held an irresistible attraction for people in central and east Europe. After the Republic, England and the German states were good second choices in the travel routes of those who came from the south and east. And yet, though sufficient quantitative data are lacking, the impression remains that the south–north movement was far less important than the north–south movement.

This should not really surprise us. After all, the roots of both classical civilization and Christianity, the two components of the cultural tradition which the elite cherished most, both could be found in Italy. Moreover, as the material manifestations of that glorious past could be admired in Rome's ruins, more recent cultural products inspired by it could be seen in the contemporary city; both the classical and the modern monuments and other artistic expressions were viewed as a collective heritage which people wanted to recreate in order to participate in that tradition.

ROME, WINTER 1644–5: JOHN EVELYN VISITS THE ETERNAL CITY

In May 1641, John Evelyn (1620–1706), a young Englishman from a comfortable background and with a somewhat lazy, pleasure-loving and yet inquisitive disposition, set out on a journey through Europe that was to last for nearly nine years, bringing him to the Netherlands, Germany, Italy, Spain and France, before he returned to England and settled down to a long life mainly devoted to leisure and amateur scholarship. He has left an extensive and delightful diary covering the larger part of his life and affording precious insights both into his way of thinking and into the culture of his time.

The following selections account of his visit to Rome and illustrate some of the characteristics of travel, of daily life in an urban context, of the position of Jews, besides the extent of a cultured visitor's interest in what to most Europeans still was the 'Eternal City'.

> I came to Rome on the fourth of November 1644, about five at night ... November 6, I began to be very pragmatic. In the first place, our sights-man (for so they name certain persons here who get their living by leading strangers around

to see the city) went to the Palace Farnese, a magnificent square structure, built by Michel Angelo, of the three orders of columns after the ancient manner, and when architecture was but newly recovered from the Gothic barbarity.

[. . . eighth November] We visited the Jesuits' church, the front whereof is esteemed a noble piece of architecture, the design of Jacomo della Porta and the famous Vignola. In this church lies the body of their renowned Ignatius Loyola, an arm of Xaverius, their other Apostle; and, at the right end of their high altar, their champion, Cardinal Bellarmine. Here Father Kircher (professor of Mathematics and the oriental tongues) showed us many singular courtesies, leading us into their refectory, dispensatory, laboratory, gardens, and, finally (through a hall hung round with pictures of such of their order as had been executed for their pragmatical and busy adventures) into his own study, where, with Dutch patience [to Englishmen, Dutch and German were and often still are the same], he showed us his perpetual motions, catoptrics, magnetical experiments, models, and a thousand other crotchets and devices, most of them since published by himself.

[. . . nineteenth November] I visited St. Peter's, that most stupendous and incomparable Basilica, far surpassing anything now extant in the world, and perhaps, Solomon's Temple excepted, any that was ever built.

[. . . 21st November] I was carried to see a great virtuoso, Cavaliere Pozzo, who showed us a rare collection of all kind of antiquities, and a choice library, over which are the effigies of most of our late men of polite literature. He had a great collection of the antique basso-relievos about Rome, which this curious man had caused to be designed in several folios.

[. . . fifteenth January] The *zitelle*, or young wenches, which are to have portions given to them by the Pope, being poor, and to marry them, walked in procession to St. Peter's, where the Veronica [i.e. the cloth with the imprint of Christ's face] was showed.

I went to the Ghetto, where the Jews dwell as in a suburb by themselves; being invited by a Jew of my acquaintance to see a circumcision. I passed by the Piazza Judea, where their seraglio begins; for, being environed with walls, they are locked up every night.

[. . . eighteenth January] From thence, through a very long gallery (longer, I think, than the French Kings' at the Louvre), but only of bare walls, we were brought into the Vatican Library. This passage now was full of poor people, to each of whom, in his passage to St. Peter's, the Pope gave a mezzo grosso. I believe they were in number near 1500 or 2000 persons. This library is the most nobly built, furnished, and beautified of any in the world; ample, stately, light and cheerful, looking into a most pleasant garden. . . . The largest room is 100 paces long; at the end is the gallery of printed books; then the gallery of the Duke of Urbino's library, in which are MSS. of remarkable miniature, and divers China, Mexican, Samaritan, Abyssinian, and other oriental books.

[. . . After a trip to Naples] Thus, about the seventh of February, we set out on our return to Rome by the same way we came, not daring to adventure by sea, as some of our company were inclined to do, for fear of Turkish pirates hovering on that coast.

[. . .] On the thirteenth of February, we were again invited to Signor Angeloni's study, where with greater leisure we surveyed the rarities, as his cabinet and medals especially, esteemed one of the best collections of them in Europe. He showed us two antique lamps, one of them dedicated to Pallas, the other Laribus Sacrum, as appeared by their inscriptions; some old Roman rings and keys; the Egyptian Isis, cast in iron; sundry rare basso-relievos; good pieces of painting, principally the Christ of Correggio, with the painter's own face admirably done by himself; divers of both the Bassanos; a great number of pieces by Titian.

[. . .] The next day, we went to the once famous Circus Caracalla, in the midst of which there now lay prostrate one of the most stately and ancient obelisks, full of Egyptian hieroglyphics. It was broken into four pieces, when overthrown by the Barbarians, and would have been purchased and transported into England by the magnificent Thomas Earl of Arundel, could it have been well removed to the sea. This is since set together and placed on the stupendous artificial rock made by Innocent X, and serving for a fountain in Piazza Navona, the work of Bernini, the Pope's architect . . . Hence, to a small oratory, named *Domine, quo vadis?*, where the tradition is, that our Blessed Saviour met St. Peter as he fled, and turned him back again'.[39]

The impressions gained on the Grand Tour led, in the whole of Europe, to a creative interaction between well-travelled clients and well-travelled or travelling artists, so that churches, palaces, country and town houses were built and paintings and sculptures were created according to aesthetic principles accepted in the whole of Europe. All these cultural expressions – paintings and buildings, but also literary and scientific works and music – referred to the 'universal', classical and Christian values, yet they increasingly had a double reference: they also sang the praises of the excellence of their own state and nation, of the men who commissioned and the men who executed them. Consequently, a general 'style' developed which despite its national varieties was immediately recognizable everywhere in Europe.

Business trips, diplomatic trips, educational trips – three types. Was there yet a fourth, that we could simply call 'tourism', travel for the sake of travelling and sightseeing, for the sake of experiences without an ulterior motive? There certainly was. Beginning in the seventeenth century but especially during the eighteenth century, people, influenced by a new, more positive, perhaps even 'romantic' perception of nature, started going on pleasure trips. However, as opposed to the trips mentioned earlier, these trips rarely went far, were usually short and, finally, contributed little to the cultural integration of Europe.

The practice of travel

For travellers of our time, accustomed to travel agencies and fast transport, it is difficult to imagine how laborious travel was until the beginning of the nineteenth century. How did the traveller tackle the limitations associated with it and the difficulties that accompanied it?[40] Travellers thoroughly prepared themselves for their trips, certainly when these were to last many months and sometimes even several years, as was often the case with the 'Grand Tour'. Besides the pattern of expectations shaped by upbringing and education, intensive reading formed a basis on which the actual experiences would grow. Published travel stories and travel guides were important not only because people could briefly inform themselves about what should be seen but also because they contained many useful tips, for instance, about where to eat and, naturally, what.

Many future travellers were also instructed by family members, friends, acquaintances, teachers or colleagues as to which people should be visited: local dignitaries, famous scholars or collectors with interesting collections of antiquities or curios, artists whose ateliers were open to passers-by, and so on.

In his youth, a man like the famous French bibliophile, researcher and collector Nicholas Fabri de Peiresc (1580–1637) travelled and studied in Italy for more than a year; he also travelled to England in the retinue of a French ambassador and, subsequently, went to the Netherlands all on his own in order to talk to the leading scholars. At the beginning of the seventeenth century he enjoyed an international reputation because of the many contacts which he maintained by letter with men of letters all over Europe. He regularly helped his younger friends and acquaintances with lists indicating how they could make the most of a trip to England or Italy.[41] What to see, whom to talk to, which things to buy – Peiresc was able to indicate all this from his rich, much-travelled experience.

It was advisable for people to arm themselves with letters of recommendation to this and that person so that one did not appear somewhere unintroduced and thus unexpected and, perhaps, unwelcome. Passports and escorts were also very important in view of the fact that there was always a war going on somewhere in Europe. And people's financial affairs naturally had to be settled as well. Taking cash money was dangerous; bills of exchange, which could be cashed with bankers or merchants en route, could prevent serious problems.

Travellers embarked on a long journey. Only for the very rich the experience was a really comfortable one, although even they cannot have enjoyed the jolting of carriages without adequate suspension on often unpaved roads. However, many more had to make do without their own carriage and travelled by stage coach,[42] by horse or, if the opportunity arose, by barge or sailing boat. For poor students or artists, as well as for pilgrims, walking often was quite normal, as appears from the useful guide that G. Grutarolus had published in Basle as early as 1561, called *De Regimine iter agentium vel equitum, vel peditum, vel navi, vel carru, seu rheda . . . utilissimi libri duo* (Two very useful books including a guideline for those who travel by horse, by foot, by ship, or with a two- or four-wheeled carriage). Many simply had to use whatever means of transport were available and affordable at a given place and time.

Because streets were not normally lit and sailing vessels and carriages often did not carry lanterns, as well as for reasons of safety, it was wise to travel only during daylight. Hence one had to get up very early and end the day's travel in time to start searching for a place to stay the night. It was then that travellers were waylaid by cheeky youths who, on the instructions of rival innkeepers, loudly praised the qualities of their accommodation, qualities which not infrequently turned out to be complete fantasies. Inns where a night's rest was not spoilt by lice in a bed that, moreover, had to be shared with two or three other guests, were expensive and thus, for many, such as travelling students or artists, an unaffordable luxury. In short, the hostelry offered most travellers little rest. In his *Colloquia*, Erasmus, an experienced traveller, fulminated against the poor quality of inns, mainly German ones.[43] And yet frequent stops were unavoidable, for the tempo of travel was slow. Travelling by coach, it might be possible to cover 50 kilometres a day, but on foot this was obviously unthinkable.

Travellers looked around. The central question is what directed their gaze and what did they see? Admittedly, we know little about the process. As already indicated, to a certain extent people were prepared for their 'Grand Tour', not only by the expectations created by their Christian-humanist education but also by reading works of a general historical and cultural nature as well as special travel guides. However, once they reached their destination, most travellers frequently showed themselves very dependent, unquestioningly following the directions of professional guides who were either employed for the occasion or travelled as permanent escorts – there were people who made a career of accompanying young members of the aristocracy on their tours.[44] Others decided on a route and a sightseeing schedule themselves but in doing so often used a printed guide as well.

Much of what we know about travel experiences in this period stems from the diaries which people kept, mindful of the adage of, among others, Francis Bacon, one of England's leading scholars and intellectuals. In his essay 'On Travel', he wrote: 'Let diaries therefore be brought into use',[45] since any experience gained and any knowledge acquired had to be set down systematically in order to be profitable. A comparative study of the printed guides with the experiences that travellers chronicled in their letters and diaries results in striking although perhaps not unexpected conclusions. Many travellers saw only what their travel guides prescribed. Noting their impressions, whether on the spot or later, as they sat down to recall their memories, they frequently recorded not so much their own views as those which the book, which they often had at hand, taught them. And as far as their emotions were concerned, sometimes a suspicious similarity shows between the admiring commentaries, programmed, as it were, by the printed travel guides and the feelings expressed by travellers in their own writings with such an ostensible air of originality.

Travellers met people. Or at least, they should do so if they remembered the advice in Bacon's essay: 'Let him [i.e. the traveller] sequester himself from the company of his countrymen and diet in such places where there is good company of the nation where he travelleth'.[46] Of course one may ask whether most travellers really were inquisitive and, if so, what were the possibilities for actual contact? Francis Bacon also wrote: 'He that travelleth into a country before he hath some entrance into the language, goeth to school and not to travel'.[47] Indeed, language was an essential means of communication, but it was frequently an insurmountable barrier as well. Those who, numerically, were the most important group, the pilgrims, often spoke only their own language, trusting a small group of leaders to arrange everything for them. They travelled in and with their own world, outside of which another was visible yet incomprehensible – not unlike the majority of modern tourists travelling within the semi-closed context of their operated tour.

Language was far less of a problem for the elite. They had learnt Latin at an early age. Moreover, in the sixteenth and early seventeenth centuries, Italian was a 'European' language, a function which the French acquired in the seventeenth and eighteenth centuries. Thus, it was possible to establish contact in one of these three languages with those who moved in the same privileged circle, who shared the same social and educational background. Reading contemporary travel letters and diaries, it seems German or English aristocrats felt rather more at ease with the luxurious life of a Frenchman or an Italian of their own social class than with the drudgery of a labourer in their native country; they simply understood each other better, even on the level of language.

To travel or not to travel?

Travel in Europe clearly acquired a wider scope and frequency from the sixteenth century onwards. This can be seen already from the enormous increase in publications which aimed specifically at the travel market and which, either by presenting practical information or by emphasizing the moral and educational aspects, intended to serve an apparently growing public. The boom in this flow of books occurred in the last decades of the sixteenth and in the early years of the seventeenth century and, subsequently, in the last years of the seventeenth and the first decades of the eighteenth century.[48]

Many apparently were of the opinion articulated by the Englishman William Bourne. In his *A Booke called the Treasure for Travailers . . . contaynyng very necessary matters, for all sortes of Travailers, eyther by Sea or by Lande*, published in London in 1578, he writes: 'it is a playne case, that Travailers into other Countreies doo much profyte the common weale.' He underlines the need for contact with other countries, and, although he does not pose this explicitly, with other cultures, arguing that if people do not travel, 'in process of time wee should become barbarous and savage.' As seen above, it was precisely for fear of such outside influences that Spaniards in the sixteenth and seventeenth centuries were forbidden to embark on educational travel. And elsewhere, too, there were those who were less than certain that travelling was indeed a worthwhile experience. On the contrary, early in the seventeenth century one already finds commentators who judged the phenomenon negatively. By no means all parents and educators were convinced of the value of a southward trip, heading for Italy. All too often, young travellers passed the time eating and drinking, playing cards and roulette and, not infrequently, indulging in sex which, if things went wrong, affected one's purse as well as one's health.

Other objections were raised as well. In his tract *Quo Vadis? A just Censure of Travell*, published in London in 1671, the Englishman John Hall wondered whether all those young members of the English nobility who said they simply had to travel to the continent and, especially, to France and Italy, would not get bad ideas, whether, in short, travelling would not lead to 'private and publicke mischiefe'? And the German Johannes Thomasius, in his tract called *Programma XLII de peregrinationis usu et abusu*, 'a programme of 42 points on the sense and nonsense of travelling' published in Halle in 1693, argued that travel had actually become unnecessary now that books could be obtained so easily. He added that one of the dangers of travel lurked in the uncritical acceptance of what people came across elsewhere, pointing in particular to the risk that travelling might dilute proper Protestantism – Thomasius, being a protestant pietist, clearly referred to the dangers of Popery.

Such statements give cause for reflection. Other morals and customs, even if people encountered them in Europe, in the Christian world, apparently did not by definition evoke feelings of cultural solidarity. Besides, one may observe a certain fear in such men as Thomasius and Hall of the propagandistic, even corrupting power of Catholicism which, after all, was showing all its post-Tridentine baroque splendour to the many travellers who visited southern Germany, France and especially Italy. It is a fear that for centuries has characterized European anti-Popery, stemming from the opposition between Catholicism and Protestantism which had created such a fundamental schism in Christian unity.

For different reasons, the English philosopher and pedagogue John Locke (1632–1704) was not completely convinced of the usefulness of the 'Grand Tour'. He wondered whether a person would not benefit more from a foreign stay when he had grown to manhood; he would, then, be less easily influenced.[49] The famous Swedish biologist Carl Linnaeus (1707–78) used another argument when, in 1741, he gave his inaugural address as professor at the university of Uppsala. He regretted the wanderlust of many young Swedes who travelled to distant lands yet knew their own country hardly, if at all. With some pride he pointed to his own practice; after all, as a young man he had joined one of the first scientific expeditions to Swedish Lapland; he now considered that a similar experience with the unknown regions and cultures of a person's own country could be salutary.[50] However, in later years this opinion did not stop Linnaeus from sending his students on overseas expeditions which even explored the remotest corners of the earth.

Those who did not heed such warnings, but yet were seldom if ever able to actually travel themselves could, of course, indulge in 'armchair tourism'. Sitting by the hearth or at their desk, they enjoyed the products of what was quickly becoming one of the more successful genres in European book production, travel literature. Special books were even written for them. In 1600, the Englishman Samuel Lewkenor published a work in London with the telling title, *A Discourse not altogether unprofitable, nor unpleasant for such as are desirous to know the situation and customs of forraine cities without travelling to see them*.

Clearly, the craving for the exotic, the need to escape from everyday routine, greatly popularized precisely those travel stories in which a completely different and thus mainly non-European world was described, a world where Europeans could still project their dreams of an earthly paradise or a promised land. Yet travel stories of journeys in Europe also enjoyed considerable success. After having completed his studies, the Guelders country squire Thomas Walraven van Arkel, who in the seventeenth century led a quiet life at his castle of Ammerzoden in the Betuwe area, rarely travelled. However, the inventory of his rich library – he owned approximately 2,000 titles – seems to prove that he read a great deal, especially travel stories, as well as, not surprisingly in view of his origins and status, many court novels of the genre described above. In this way, he and, as is shown by numerous other inventories, many members of his class in the rural backwaters of Europe kept up with the latest developments in a lifestyle which they considered theirs, which, perhaps in their youth, they had 'sniffed' during a diplomatic or educational trip, and which they still experienced as normative, even if they could only partly live it out in their own lives.[51]

Travel as an element in growing cosmopolitanism and cultural integration

Travel letters, travel diaries, published travel reports – do they allow for the conclusion that besides growing cosmopolitanism, travel in the period from the late fifteenth century onwards caused or promoted some form of supraregional solidarity, a concept of 'Europe'? The answer is twofold.

Although many travellers certainly gained some knowledge about other countries and peoples, most of them but little understood or valued the different, 'national' or regional cultures in the other European countries or states. Reading their recorded experiences reveals the existence of prejudices which were hardly, if at all, removed by travelling; on the contrary, they frequently appear to have been confirmed by it. Maybe this was only to be expected; after all, the manuals that prepared the traveller for his new experience abounded with warnings regarding certain habits, certain patterns of behaviour characteristic of the various European nations. Even the largely impartial Lipsius could not refrain to enumerate them: French vanity, Italian degeneracy, German gluttony and *nota bene*, Spanish 'Africanness' – for, indeed, by many Europeans Spain was seen as non-European, for the very reasons that made it so recognizable to the Moroccan ambassadors who, when visiting Madrid, travelled through Andalusia and were proud to note that in this otherwise dismal country Arab culture had survived, to become one of its few redeeming points.[52]

Thus, there were definite limits to the Europe which the traveller got to know. Particularly in their appreciation of the various aspects of daily life – the 'low' culture of the 'small' tradition – travellers frequently showed their irritation. Without batting an eyelid, a mainly tolerant, relatively cosmopolitan traveller like John Evelyn describes an incident as being 'after a true *trecherous* Italian guise.'[53]

For many travellers the contemporary society of the countries they travelled in held little or no fascination. On the contrary, travellers seem annoyed by foreign customs, by codes of behaviour which were often considered bizarre and sometimes ill-mannered. Remarkably enough, in central and northern Europe this negative appreciation is expressed precisely about the countries of the south: the vision of a glorious, all too idealized past, hoped for but certainly not always found, that was the basis of 'high' culture, of the 'great' tradition, inevitably clashed with the realities of daily life, of contemporary culture in that very region, a reality which, especially for many protestants, was so evidently catholic, superstitious and, moreover, often somewhat seedy in its street-lived openness.

Nevertheless, certain forms of culture were profoundly influenced by the phenomenon of travel, becoming characteristic of a larger Europe as a result. Returning home, travellers did not only look back upon their stay abroad as an enjoyable conclusion of their relatively carefree youth, a chapter closed before the beginning of a responsible career. For many, the memory remained a life-enhancing experience, a factor which somehow determined their future thoughts and actions. An increasingly close interaction between travel and other forms of educated communication altered the elite vision of European culture.

11 A new society

The 'Republic of Letters' as a virtual and virtuous world against a divided world

The Republic of Letters: a quest for harmony

The political and religious divisions of Europe, which reinforced each other from the sixteenth century onwards because disputes on the one front were often fought out with arguments from the other domain, resulted in almost uninterrupted discord, in a general feeling of insecurity. Not only did all states actually fight each other, but they also felt that their own identity, which was judged increasingly important, would be lost if a single state were to achieve hegemony.

In the sixteenth century, this fear centred around the imperial aspirations of the House of Habsburg, reflected in an ideology and a propaganda policy which linked this family, who had borne the imperial crown for several centuries, backwards to Charlemagne, to the early German and Roman Empires, and even further to Japhet and Adam, while its acquisition, through marriage, of the Spanish crowns of Aragon and Castile and, consequently, of the dominion over parts of the Mediterranean, and of America, Africa and Asia was seen as proof positive of the Habsburg right to rule the entire world. In the seventeenth century, Europe feared the equally megalomaniac concepts of Louis XIV of France which continually threatened the quest for peace and quiet that now determined the foreign policies particularly of smaller states, admittedly rather more from pure necessity than out of any idealism. Reactions to this situation, which regularly led to devastating military crises, were two-fold. Both can be interpreted as attempts to reach a more precise definition of 'Europe' and thus limit the results of war and dissension as much as possible.

First of all, one senses that, at least among the European elite, thinking and acting were to a large extent intensified by experiences gained during diplomatic and educational travels. A cosmopolitan culture recognizable in the whole of Europe developed which, though limited to the upper classes, in the long run did not fail to have a more widespread influence on very diverse areas of life. Obviously, many lived this culture only as a superficial lifestyle, but specifically the intellectual elite began to direct itself to the values which appeared to guarantee the more fundamental ideals of unity, civilization and, it was hoped, the resulting peace: Christianity in its original, universal form and classical culture. These values became internalized through common educational norms and practices and therefore were considered Europe's collective inheritance even if, depending upon the specific philosophy and the world-view of those involved, this was now felt to be Christian-European, European-Christian or perhaps just European, without any clear religious connotation.

Because unity, civilization and peace offered the possibility of escaping from the political and religious differences which so cruelly influenced or even disrupted the everyday lives of many, people made attempts to contact and stay in contact with each other across the very borders of the states which increasingly thought in 'national' terms, thus fuelling that very discord. The frequent travels undertaken by the elite to complete their cultural formation by university study elsewhere, by visits to art collections and classical ruins and by contacts with scholars and other famous figures clearly did not in themselves alone create a fundamental sense of solidarity. Other means of communication, too, contributed to the genesis of a culture and, finally, a mentality in which it was possible to believe that the consequences of political and religious conflicts could, as it were, be transcended by emphasizing what was of essential importance, what should bind everyone: the belief in individual freedom and the chances for creative development, the improvement of the human mind, and all this – at least for the majority – in relation to the challenges presented by the great miracle of God's creation. These ideals, which transcended and partly even had to deny the borders of a person's own region and state, were given shape in what was very significantly called the *Respublica Literaria* – a concept frequently, but as time went by decreasingly defined by the additional *Christiana*.[1] From the late fifteenth century, the Republic of Letters was felt to be a non-institutionalized community based on commonly experienced norms such as brotherhood and tolerance and on a common aim like the advancement of knowledge in order to become more human. This ideal and its background are strikingly articulated in a poem by the sixteenth-century Englishman Samuel Daniel, who writes:

> It be'ing the proportion of a happie Pen,
> Not to b'invassal'd to one Monarchie,
> But dwell with all the better world of men,
> Whose spirits are of one communitie;
> Whom neither Ocean, Desarts, Rockes nor Sands
> Can keepe from th' Intertraffique of the minde,
> But that it vents her treasure in all lands,
> And doth a most secure commencement finde.[2]

The Republic of Letters and the ideal of tolerance: theory and practice

However, this ideal, which implied a view of man and the world, of a tolerant fraternity remained only a dream, voiced in the conscious and unconscious

Plate 25 Religion and the practice of intolerance: people watching heretics and witches being burned in a straw hut, depicted in a text on criminal law and procedure, the *Cautio Criminalis* of 1632
Source: Centre for Art Historical Documentation, Nijmegen, The Netherlands

propaganda of its bearers; indeed, later historiography which, after all, has often been the product of people who had their roots in this tradition gave the concept of the *Respublica Literaria* more status as an achieved European cultural unity than contemporary reality warranted. The expectations which people cherished of the humanizing, civilizing influence of a brotherhood of all those who wanted to advance the *bonae litterae* contributed to this image.

CHATEAU MONTAIGNE, NEAR BORDEAUX, AD 1580: MICHEL DE MONTAIGNE ON EUROPE AND 'THE OTHER'

In 1580, Michel de Montaigne (1533–92), a French intellectual and one of the sharpest minds of his age, published a number of highly perspicacious essays, covering a great many aspects of contemporary culture in a spirit of criticism, not to say scepticism. In the *Essais*, he showed himself to be an example *par excellence* of undogmatic, cosmopolitan thinking, of the Humanism that had grown in the previous centuries. Later thinkers, from the seventeenth, eighteenth and nineteenth centuries, like Pierre Bayle and John Locke, Jean-Jacques Rousseau and Friedrich Nietzsche were influenced by him. With his

Plate 26 Religion and the hope of tolerance: imaginary conversation, probably on the question of Holy Eucharist, between the Pope, a Protestant minister and a Jesuit, before Christ, on a French engraving from the seventeenth century. Proceedings are eagerly watched by the princes of Europe, whose peoples' lives were greatly influenced by religious discord and warfare
Source: Centre for Art Historical Documentation, Nijmegen, The Netherlands

essay 'On the cannibals', Montaigne joined one of the most fundamental debates of the Republic of Letters, indeed of Europe, the debate on tolerance. Reflecting on the 'otherness' of the newly discovered American Indians, he actually voiced a critique of the situation in Europe. On the basis of travel literature he sketches an idealized version of Indian culture and society: not hierarchical, not determined by birth and wealth. In this society, man lives 'in the wild', in a state of nature and, therefore, nobly, for in a way as intended by creation:

> The discovery of an enormous continent deserves consideration. I do not know that I can be sure that some other may not hereafter be added, seeing that so many great men have been deceived in this. . . .
>
> I find . . . that there is nothing barbarous or savage about that people, as far as I have been able to learn, except that everybody will call anything barbarous that does not agree with what he is used to. Admittedly, we have no other test of truth and reason except the example and model of the notions and customs of our own country: the perfect religion, the perfect society, the perfect and complete employment of all things are natural here. Those others are savages, just as we call

those fruits wild which nature produces unassisted and by its ordinary processes; whereas by rights we ought to apply the term to those which we by our science have changed and perverted from their proper state. . . .

Those people, therefore, seem barbarous to me because they have received very little conditioning by the human mind and are still close to their original simplicity. The laws of nature, but little bastardized by ours, still govern them, and in such pure form that I am sometimes distressed by the thought that the knowledge of all this did not come sooner, at a time when there were men who could have brought greater insight to the matter than we can. I am sorry Lycurgus and Plato knew nothing of this; for it seems to me that what we have learned about those people there exceeds not only all images with which poetry has embellished the golden age and all the fanciful inventions about a happy state for man, but also the arguments and even desires of philosophers. These could not imagine so pure and simple a lack of artificiality as we now see before our eyes; they could not believe that our society could maintain itself with so little contrivance and human sweat.

Those peoples, I would tell Plato, have no knowledge of trade or letters, no science of numbers, not the name even of a magistrate, no superiors to rule them; no use of services, of wealth or poverty; no contracts, no inheritance, no property rights, no occupations except those of leisure; no respect for ancestry except that which they all share, no clothes, no agriculture, no metal, no use of wine or wheat. The very words signifying lies, treason, deceit, avarice, envy, slander, pardon – all unheard of! How far would he find that his imaginary republic differs from such perfection? . . .

[But they are] ignorant how dear their acquaintance with our corruption will one day cost their peace and happiness, and how this intercourse will bring about their ruin.[3]

Can one interpret Montaigne's sketch as European self-criticism, as a 'dream of Europe'? One certainly can. Does it imply a plea for tolerance of 'the other'? It obviously does. But yet, the Indians whom Montaigne glorifies lived far way. Had he chosen to portray the 'Moors', the Muslims, who lived nearby, on the Balkans, and for many Europeans constituted the real danger, the message would have been rather more poignant, or more difficult to swallow – as is shown by the reality of Europe's reactions to those neighbours. Osmin, one of the main characters in Mozart's opera *Die Entführung aus dem Serail* (The Escape from the Seraglio) (1782), was ridiculed by the Austrian composer's librettist; it is one of the possibilities to ward off the danger of the nearby 'other', the foreigner who is seen as a threat. Monostatos, too, the 'Moor' in *Die Zauberflöte* (The Magic Flute) (1791), the Mozart opera in which white and black, light and darkness, good and evil are so child-like and yet so profoundly contrasted with each other, is clearly 'the enemy'. Both operas, based on texts in the vernacular, were very popular: real crowd-pullers, instead of elite events, only. They undoubtedly had the effect of confirming prejudices.

Still, one may maintain that Montaigne had tried to counter precisely such feelings. Nevertheless, his text shows that even he could not avoid to explicitly derive the norms and terms he used to describe and analyse 'the Indians' from

Europe's ideal model of civilization, classical Greece. Nevertheless, one cannot simply interpret Montaigne's thinking as 'cultural imperialism'. Maybe, people can accept 'the foreigner' only when they are able to describe the potential 'enemy' as an ideal self.

———————————

For centuries, Europe, as most other cultures on earth, had wrestled with the problem of insiders and outsiders, the problem of tolerance. It became a central problem in its understanding of itself as a unity, certainly as the normative function of Christianity began to lose its force. It remained a problem both in theory and in practice. John Locke and Pierre Bayle (1647–1705), two of the many intellectuals who participated in the tolerance debate in the last decades of the seventeenth century, brought about a gradual change in the description of the concept through their writings, from a resigned tolerance of that which could not be changed to the peaceful acceptance of other opinions – and behaviour? – which one did not necessarily approve of oneself.

But this still left the practical problems all but unresolved. Indeed, it was an intellectual debate, mostly, in a context in which the actual contrasts to be tolerated were, moreover, not very big. Yet the growing conceptual consensus within the intellectual elite in no way guaranteed that people – those who moved in less comfortable positions but also intellectuals themselves, men of letters – now accepted, in everyday practice, those of their fellow men who were clearly different culturally; it was the more difficult when that acceptance had to be proven in an economic situation which did not favour tolerance. The situation in seventeenth-century France provides a telling example. In 1589, King Henry IV had proclaimed the Edict of Nantes, according a measure of safety and even liberty to the French protestants, a religious minority living in an overwhelmingly catholic world. For a century, they had been able to enjoy this tolerance which, though it did not extend throughout the realm, yet had resulted in a powerful economic and cultural presence of these so-called Huguenots in French society. This irked Henry's most famous, or infamous successor, Louis XIV. In 1685, in the same period that the debate on tolerance was carried on, the protestants were given the choice either to convert or to leave their possessions and their native France; victim to the religious intolerance of the Sun King, in their hundreds of thousands they went into exile, giving up their culture.

Many European countries allowed them in, either moved by sincere sympathy, or because the host countries saw them as potentially profitable immigrant workers. Yet not all exiles proved easily employable. Many were and remained poor; appealing to social funds, they were soon seen as a threat to local social stability. It was only then that tolerance was – and still is – really tested. Many Huguenots realized that far-reaching assimilation and giving up their own dreams were the best, indeed the only protection against the resentment and spite with which many now treated them.

This in no way detracts from the fact that many Europeans genuinely tried to put all sorts of high-minded thoughts into practice. From the end of the sixteenth century onwards, in learned circles the most grandiose projects for 'eternal peace' were devised with increasing regularity. Mostly, they pleaded for some sort of federal political organization which would guarantee that violence and other miserable consequences of the perverted use of power and intolerance be banished from Europe. Besides the creation of the *Respublica Literaria*, these projects constituted the second attempt to realize some unity in a situation that so often threatened to take on the proportions of a crisis.[4] However, even more than the Republic of Letters, these plans remained only paper ideals, though they contain many elements which, from the late nineteenth century onwards, were proposed for the unification of Europe.

The Englishman William Penn, leader of a protestant sect nicknamed Quakers, published his *Essay towards the present and future Peace of Europe* in 1693. It is a peculiar text that successfully avoids the usual long-winded references to the Bible or the classics, and hardly uses baroque or classical figures of speech. It is also a short text. It proposes a 'European parliament' in which all participating states are represented by a number of delegates – that number to be determined on the basis of their economic strength! The German Empire holds pride of place, with twelve seats; France and Spain are next, with ten votes each. Writing from his cultural, religious background of pacifism and tolerance, Penn argues:

> And if the Turks and Muscovites are also admitted, which is only just and right, then two times ten representatives will also be added.

Thus, a political constellation is created which, it is true, covers only:

> a quarter, but still the best and richest, part of the known world, where religion and education, civilization and art have their place.[5]

It is noteworthy that while Penn's definition of the elements that constitute European civilization unmistakably refers to a long tradition, he does include the two cultures which most of his contemporaries would have excluded, even emphatically so. Fascinating also, from a present-day perspective, is Penn's awareness of the tensions that will inevitably develop between sovereign states and a 'parliament' of representatives.

One of the most significant aspects of Penn's plan is that while he does not attempt to achieve a traditional Christian world order, yet his inspiration was in its deepest essence biblical. However, economic and utilitarian considerations play a clear role, too, undoubtedly because the formation of his theory was partly based on the works of such 'common sense' thinkers as his contemporary John Locke.

In Penn's outline of a civilized society, the concept of 'freedom' stands explicit and central; not a single person must live in fear. As a result, 'justice', or controlled 'violence', is the basis of a state, and freedom of conscience is the logical consequence. Penn implicitly proposes that true Christianity lies in the acceptance of others, if only they, too, accept justice and freedom. Finally, education is an obvious necessity.

It is characteristic of the problematic nature of Penn's idealistic vision that ten years earlier he had sought to realize his plans in the new world, on the other side of the ocean, where many readers had situated Thomas More's *Utopia* and where so many people had actually attempted to make their dreams come true. Pennsylvania and Philadelphia – 'Penn's colony in the woods', in an Eden-like garden, and the 'city of brotherly love' – were the outcome of William's ideas on the ideal state and the ideal city. Yet, where he advocated equality of Indians and Europeans, on the condition that civilizing work could be carried out – to be understood as Christian mission – his followers quickly proved unable to reconcile the requirements of practice with the ideals of theory.[6] Penn's utopian society soon became a European colony using and even exploiting both Indian territory and the Indians themselves.

The Republic of Letters and its enemies: national cultural policies, or the political uses of culture

Plans like those of Penn not only revealed the notion that many intellectuals held of Europe's ideal self, but also made clear that in this same Europe people seriously took into account the reality which had slowly become more perceptible from the sixteenth century onwards, the reality of increasingly powerful national states; they formed the framework in which Europe's cultural self-awareness was articulated and shaped. Let us read how the French publicist Louis le Roy looks back on the past in his *De la vicissitude ou variété des choses de l'univers* (Paris 1575):

> We in the west have, during the past 200 years, regained the value of knowledge and learning and have restored to honour the different branches of science which for so long appeared to be extinct. The constant dedication of many scholars led to so many successes that today our time can measure itself with the best that ever was. . . . The rulers who have done the most for the recovery of culture are Pope Nicholas V and King Alfonso of Naples, who welcomed those who offered them the Latin translations of Greek books with tributes and royal support. The King of France, François I, paid the salaries of professors in Paris and had a splendid library assembled at Fontainebleau. Without the support and generosity of the kings of Castile and Portugal the discovery of new countries and the journey to the Indies would never have taken place. The Medici lords of Florence, Cosimo and Lorenzo, also gained many merits because they received scholars from all over the world and supported their work.

At the end of the sixteenth century and in the early seventeenth century Europe's cultural elites were obviously well aware that society and culture had undergone great changes in the preceding two hundred years.

While at the beginning of the period which Le Roy described, the aim of many Europeans had been to revive and relive the culture of the ancient Greeks and Romans, according to him people now, two centuries later, no longer considered this the only worthwhile goal. Indeed, the development of knowledge and of the arts in Europe had been so stormy that classical civilization had been overtaken already.

It is also clear that the state, in the person of the ruler, played an important role in the advancement of the arts and sciences. The reason for this was, of course, not always the innate civilization of princes but rather the cultural prestige and the propagandistic value which this patronage brought with it. Equally important was the consideration that many of the products of culture and, especially, science, could be of eminently practical use, for example for the development of education and thus the training of a well-informed bureaucracy but also for all kinds of technological improvements, not least in military matters.

Because state governments, growing powerful, started using all sorts of cultural forms to yet increase their power, the freedom to form and exchange ideas slowly became limited precisely because culture was now embedded in official structures. Royal academies of science and fine arts were founded and educational institutions, especially at university level, were used to support royal prestige which, of course, was the prestige of the state, the nation.[7] This is most clearly shown in the writing of history, whether it be in the royal biographies commissioned from well-known authors via the system of 'gratifications' in France, or in the so-called *Pragmatische Geschichte* produced in the German states from the sixteenth century onwards, or in the descriptions glorifying the past and present cultural and political achievements of a people, as e.g. the *Italia Illustrata*.[8] In Spain, Juan de Mariana, linking his nation's fame to its military and colonial expansion, wrote:

> The name and valor of Spain, known to few and confined within the narrow limits of Spain, was in a short time, and with great glory, spread abroad, not only through Italy and through France and Barbary, but to the very ends of the earth.[9]

Indeed, until late in the eighteenth century those expressions of culture principally produced for and dominated by the elite – the visual arts, literature, music – could exist only within the limiting framework of patron–client relationships. Thereby, the leaders of State or Church, princes, nobles and prelates acted as patrons. For the artists involved, this was not always a pleasant situation. Thus, in 1508, in a letter to a friend the painter Raphaello Santi lamented: 'You yourself have several times experienced what it means to be robbed of one's freedom and to live under the yoke of a patron'.[10]

By now, only the Catholic Church could still maintain that its manifestations of grand culture actually underpinned a universal cause. Most states had developed distinctly 'national' varieties of culture. In France, the powerful ministers Richelieu, Mazarin and Colbert used culture to enhance the glory of the monarch, the embodiment of the state, harnessing prose writers, playwrights and historians, but also architects, musicians and painters into a bureaucracy of the arts hitherto unknown in European history. The creation of scientific academies (the *Académie Française* was founded in 1635), libraries and museums further strengthened government control over a culture that had to be 'national'. In the German principalities, too, culture increasingly became a concern of the state, a matter of national prestige. In 1700, the Prussian Academy of Sciences was founded in Berlin, directed by the famous philosopher Gottfried Wilhelm Leibniz (1646–1716).

As all over Europe, in England, too, classical architecture was highly valued; yet the designs attributed to the famous Roman master builder Vitruvius but actually based on sixteenth- and seventeenth-century interpretations of him were published under the telling title *Vitruvius Britannicus*, adapted to English needs and the English climate. And while Italian and French music may have delighted English ears, yet new melodies were catchily presented in a guise both classical and national, as in *Orpheus Britannicus*, two volumes of songs published by the widow of the great composer Henry Purcell in 1698 and 1707, and in *Amphion Anglus*, in which John Blow collected his music in 1700. Indeed, the music itself was by now often unabashedly national, as shows Purcell's delightful music to the very chauvinistic air 'Fairest Isle, all isles excelling', from the equally chauvinistic masque 'King Arthur' written by the poet John Dryden in praise of England as the ideal island, a society where no worries exist anymore but those of man's sensual pleasures.

In Russia, which attempted to come out of its isolation in these centuries, the process of interaction between cosmopolitan and national culture was even more complex. The full panoply of Byzantine coronation rituals, which, in a way, had survived in the west through the complex ceremonial of the papal court, was introduced in Russia in the late sixteenth century. Meanwhile, Italian Renaissance forms began to structure the great cathedrals built inside the Moscow Kremlin, the churches of St Michael the Archangel and of the Dormition of the Virgin. Yet the famous Cathedral of St Basil, dominating the great square outside the palace with its many-coloured façade and its bulbous domes, was built to show a visibly different style, that was considered less European, more national and 'Russian'.[11] From the end of the seventeenth century onwards, Tsar Peter not only ordered a great literacy campaign but also decreed the setting up of an imperial academy and a university – all following the European example but decidedly intended to serve Russia's national fame and prosperity,[12] as were the large-scale scientific expeditions to central and east Asia organized by the Imperial Academy from the 1720s, that helped Russia to map, literally, its growing empire in that region. Peter's successors continued his policy of western-style education and the advancement of modern, i.e. European learning, but it has to be stressed that it was successful only among the nobility and the bourgeois elites of a few cities. When, in 1767, Tsarina Catharine declared in one of her famous decrees, 'Russia is a European state',[13] she showed she was by birth a German princess and, moreover, a woman whose will though it often became law nevertheless revealed more about her wishes than about Russia's cultural reality.

The development of national cultures all over Europe is, perhaps, best represented in one characteristic moment. In 1700, at the book fair in Frankfurt, which had become Europe's largest in the late fifteenth century and has remained so ever since despite a decline in the eighteenth century,[14] only 4 per cent of the titles available were in Latin, that one-time cosmopolitan language. European books were now published largely in the various national languages, as is eloquently shown in the fair's catalogues.[15]

The Republic of Letters, or how to communicate in an invisible institution

The community that transcended the state, which the *Respublica Litteraria* intended to be, was repeatedly formed anew by travel and its resulting personal contacts, but in everyday practice it mainly continued by the writing and, thus, reading of letters. On this point, too, Bacon had clearly expressed himself in his essay on travel: 'When a traveller returneth home, let him . . . maintain a correspondence by letters with those of his acquaintance which are of most worth'.[16]

Unlike today, the letter was the privileged means not only of personal but also of professional communication. Naturally, the printed word was influential. Its role in European society gained considerable importance during the sixteenth and seventeenth centuries because the need for information on all fronts of life and culture grew continually. Yet for daily communication the handwritten word, the letter, remained for a long time a primary carrier of information.

All over Europe people, while working in their often relatively closed milieux, were inspired by the vision of a larger world, held together by a network of correspondents which they, along with thousands of others, belonged to. Many who regularly corresponded with each other also knew each other, even if only as a result of a few meetings during the trip they had made to round off their education. Yet some who wrote to each other for years never actually met but stayed in contact through their letters. To all of them, correspondence was one of the most important possibilities to keep up with the latest news, whether personal or political, religious or scientific. The world of learning in particular was largely dependent on contacts by letter. Thus, a man like Erasmus relied on more than a hundred more or less regular correspondents, mostly in the Netherlands, England, France, Italy and the German countries, while a century later the French *érudit* Peiresc exchanged letters with more than two hundred friends, domiciled in the same area.[17] Of course, the kind of letter involved was not a 'private' one. The addressee frequently shared the scholarly contents of an epistle with a wide circle of like-minded people who gathered at his house with the specific aim of hearing the latest news. Despite the postal problems caused by climatological or political circumstances, it was possible to get around such uncertainties by sending several copies of a letter. This was less feasible, and far more expensive with heavy loads of printed texts, whose postal distribution was equally difficult as a result of commercial, financial and political limitations.

Yet printing indisputably caused a momentous increase in the diffusion of knowledge, both in a quantitative and a qualitative sense. After the invention of printing, which in Europe coincided with the beginning of a century of unheard-of economic expansion and increased purchasing power, only some small technical and, in the case of very ambitious publishing enterprises, somewhat bigger financial problems still limited the distribution of the book and, thus, the further expansion of communication and the spread of knowledge. While there had been people trading in manuscript copies of mostly learned and devotional texts in the fourteenth and fifteenth centuries, as well as marketing such bestsellers as Marco Polo's tale, or the famous romances, the sixteenth and seventeenth centuries really saw the beginning of the mass distribution of texts.

The age of the printers and publishers had arrived, of people who saw a market for their products. Sometimes, they were actually interested in the promotion of culture, but mostly they were in it only for reasons of profit. Besides the few famous 'scholar-publishers' – Aldus Manutius in Italy,[18] Johann Amerbach and Johann Frobenius, the printer-publishers and friends of Erasmus in Basle, Christoffel Plantijn in Antwerp – there were innumerable less scholarly and idealistic entrepreneurs who simply saw money in the nascent information culture. Playing on improving education, on the widening group of readers, and taking into account the change from one, universal language, Latin, to the many national languages, they adapted to the market or even took the lead. They introduced cheaper books which were also less awkward to handle than the heavy folio and quarto volumes which had dominated in the sixteenth century. The supply of titles in the various national languages grew expansively, as did the texts providing general information or entertainment; slowly, literary prose and poetry, historiography and, especially, travel stories[19] became more popular than theological or scientific treatises.

In the first years of printing, book production had concentrated mainly in Italy, the land of many courts, the land of Rome and the papacy, the cradle of Humanism and of the Renaissance. Especially Venice, where publishers could use a long-established trade network and where the demand for Greek classical texts could be most easily met was a major centre. As an important cultural consequence, the Orthodox Christians of the Balkans, who were deprived of the benefits of printing by Ottoman rule, were now educated mainly through the products of the Venetian presses, that provided not only classical learning, but also started publishing a religious and popular literature in Greek, later enriched with works of modern science; this contributed considerably to the reintegration into Europe of the Orthodox Christian intelligentsia of the south-east.

By the beginning of the sixteenth century, book production moved to the north. There, first Antwerp and subsequently, in the seventeenth century, the cities of the Dutch province of Holland, with Amsterdam and Leiden in the lead, ran the show internationally.[20] The arrival of the Huguenots, mentioned earlier, certainly contributed to Holland's increasingly important function as an intellectual entrepôt; the Huguenots hoped to make money with books, not least because they rightly reasoned that the country from which they had been banished represented an enormous market which, as a result of the French kings' censorship, could be served more profitably from abroad. The fact that part of their fellow believers had ended up in the German states and in England increased the ease with which they could establish international contacts.[21] Thus, the eighteenth-century Leiden printer, publisher and publicist Elie Luzac, a Huguenot, cooperated with the secretary of the Prussian Academy of Sciences in Berlin, Samuel Formey, a Huguenot, on the publication of a periodical whose title, *Bibliothèque Impartiale*, clearly indicated the contemporary ideal of tolerant but yet critical knowledge.[22]

While travelling cost time and money, so did reading books. Already in the seventeenth and eighteenth centuries it became too expensive for many. Nevertheless, information was important to those who wanted to keep up professionally or were interested in new developments in all fields of culture. At the same time, the flow of information had become tempestuous, even uncontrollable. European publishers quickly thought up a solution for people who, for whatever reason, could or would not buy new titles by the dozen. A new phenomenon, the periodical, appeared on the European cultural scene in the 1660s. Within a few years' time, political, literary and scientific journals acquired a central function, spreading knowledge and new ideas among people who seldom if ever travelled, and had little money to buy expensive books. More than all kinds of serious scientific studies, these periodicals disseminated the ideas of the Republic of Letters precisely because they reached an increasingly large readership. After all, they were not primarily directed at specialist scholars who had their books and letters, but rather at a broader circle of educated people who wanted to keep up with the latest in a variety of fields: theology, philosophy, political theory and literature.[23]

Those periodicals which specialized in general information or commented on recent events satisfied an increasing demand; still more popular were the periodicals filled with summaries of new titles, preferably providing extensive, critical excerpts or reviews. Until the late eighteenth century, the market for these journals was mainly supplied by Dutch publishers. They were often written in French, the role of which as a *lingua franca* had already been confirmed by diplomacy and was now reinforced.

Yet even the regular perusal of periodicals can be too much. An even more concise, preferably critically acceptable form of collected knowledge was thought to offer a solution. Publishers soon realized they had to provide for that situation as well. The encyclopedia, in itself a very old phenomenon, now appeared on the European market. It is difficult to judge whether stories about the printing of gigantic encyclopedias by the Chinese emperors, which became known in seventeenth-century Europe through the reports of the Jesuits and other travellers, contributed to its introduction. The fact is that in the second half of the seventeenth century, the first 'libraries without walls' appeared: Louis Moreri's *Dictionnaire* was published in 1674, followed in 1697 by Pierre Bayle's *Dictionnaire Historique et Critique*, which was talked about and read for decades.[24] The latter was an excellent example of 'literature of recollection', a text which was, as it were, to be the memory of that European culture which Bayle had become acquainted with in his reading and which he wanted to understand and interpret as grown historically but to be considered critically.

The Republic of Letters and the 'intertraffic of the mind': three examples

At the end of the seventeenth century, the Dutch envoy in Stockholm, Christian Constantijn Rumph (1633–1706), maintained contacts with the major representatives of Sweden's political and cultural elite. Also, for twenty-five years he corresponded virtually every month with Gisbert Cuper (1644–1716), a Deventer professor of classical languages but also mayor of his native city and member of the Dutch States-General.[25] His contacts with the learned Cuper made Rumph a godsend for his Swedish friends and acquaintances who frequently gathered at his house, among whom many professors from Uppsala who had studied in the Dutch Republic in their youth and who retained the best memories of those years. With Rumph's help, these Swedes obtained the books and periodicals discussed in the Republic of Letters but which could not be easily acquired, if at all, in their own country. Cuper, the 'insider', was also able to supply them with the latest political and cultural news.

Through these letters, Cuper's Swedish contacts also prepared the publication of their scientific work in the Dutch Republic since as yet there were no up-to-date printing facilities in Sweden. Only for the finishing touches did they have to undertake the difficult journey to Amsterdam – difficult because, as a result of the many destructive wars in these decades, the Baltic and North Seas were anything but peaceful waters. When their books were finally published, Swedish knowledge of the geography of northern Europe and central Asia, of the origins of the Goths and so on could be discussed in learned Europe.

In his turn, Cuper corresponded regularly with dozens of men from all parts of Europe, ranging from Cardinal Noris of the Roman Curia and the Florentine librarian Magliabecchi to the English, Anglican theologian and historian Burnet and the German, Lutheran philosopher Leibniz. News of all kinds from Italy thus ended up in Amsterdam and the Netherlands and, subsequently, in Berlin and in Prussia, as well as in Sweden.

One of Cuper's best friends was the Amsterdam merchant and politician Nicolaas Witsen (1641–1717), one of the richest and most powerful men in the Dutch Republic and director of the Dutch East India Company. Both in his palatial canal house and in his country place he kept an enormous library and filled the rooms with collections of the most valuable and exotic rarities. In his gardens grew choice shrubs from the east – he offered the coffee plant to the city's botanic gardens – and his zoo was famous, too. Travellers from all over Europe who visited Amsterdam asked permission to visit him.

Almost every month, Cuper sent Witsen a six or seven pages-long letter and duly received a reply.[26] A considerable part of the Cuper–Witsen letters concerned questions which they, both fanatical readers of travel stories, asked in the margins of the multifarious information which their reading matter offered: what was the origin of languages? Had Asia and America once been linked? Was Chinese Confucianism a pre-Christian form of Christianity? And so on. Witsen supplied Cuper with data from China, Japan and India, but also from Brazil and Canada. Cuper again informed his German and Swedish acquaintances, introducing Witsen to Leibniz, who asked him for material on the globe's innumerable tongues. Much of the information which was spread in this manner eventually found its way into the scientific and other publications or periodicals which came from these circles.

As opposed to his correspondent, Witsen had travelled a great deal, as far as Russia. He regularly exchanged letters with a number of distinguished Russians but, besides this, also with French Jesuits and with members of the Royal Society in England. Frequently, his letters contained requests for more detailed information concerning the data which he obtained from his scientific reading and from the travel stories which he devoured. In the discussions which followed, carried on by letter, one sees how Witsen's world-view, his concept of culture, gradually changed, how he came to think of the world as fundamentally a unity, a single creation under a veneer of cultural diversity that, on closer inspection, revealed surprising similarities.

Such networks spanning all Europe enabled people to exchange ideas; this led to an intensification of intellectual curiosity and resulted in a form of dynamic cosmopolitanism in educated circles. In the 1720s, following the years wherein Rumph, Cuper and Witsen established a complex epistolar north–south axis, the Phanariote Greek Nicholas Mavrocordatos kept up a correspondence with the Amsterdam Huguenot scholar and magazine director Jean Le Clerc. Mavrocordatos, scion of an intellectual Greek family, whose father had studied medicine at Padua and had published several books, was appointed by the Ottoman sultan prince of Moldavia and Walachia, the Balkan border regions between the Christian and the Islamic world. Not only did Le Clerc supply him with recent maps of central Europe and the eastern Mediterranean; also, answering Mavrocordatos's incessant requests for information about new developments in the world of arts and letters, he sent him the books of recent western learning that Nicholas asked for. Thus, Mavrocordatos enriched his library with the works of Newton and other scientists, and with John Locke's *Two Treatises of Civil Government* (1690), a highly influential tract about a more balanced political system in which royal absolutism was mitigated by representative institutions. Mavrocordatos's intellectual interests fully appear in his novel *Les Loisirs de Philothé*, which was the first text to introduce the names of Bacon and Hobbes into Greek culture and to declare that if Aristotle were alive he would gladly become a pupil of the Moderns[27] – those who held that contemporary culture had, indeed, surpassed classical civilization.

At the end of the eighteenth century, the wealthy bibliophile Gerard Meerman (1722–71), former Pensionary of Rotterdam and former Dutch ambassador to England, lived in The Hague. He had travelled extensively – starting with a Grand Tour that lasted for three years and brought him to Germany, France, Switzerland and Italy. His luxurious house was crammed full with an enormous collection of books, manuscripts, coins and antiquities which he generously opened to people provided with a proper introduction. By letter, Meerman remained in contact with all of Europe, including, among other correspondents, the erudite Spaniard Gregorio Mayans y Siscar (1691–1781).[28]

Meerman and Mayans never met. However, their letters, over a period of more than twenty years, totalled several hundreds, each often three or four pages long. They served to transmit a treasure of information in many fields. Mayans, one of the most important figures in Spanish culture in the eighteenth century, benefited from this in the many works he wrote and in which he pleaded for a more modern view of science and society to achieve the cultural regeneration of Spain. These were partly published abroad, including in the Dutch Republic, where Meerman, instructed by Mayans's letters, bestowed essential assistance. In his turn, Mayans acted as intermediary in the purchase of Spanish books and manuscripts and supplied Meerman with the details for a number of his publications, especially concerning the history of the invention of printing, which Meerman considered one of Europe's central cultural feats and which he wanted to ascribe to a Dutchman, Laurens Janszn Coster.

The letters also reveal how Mayans and Meerman tried to practise what they felt was their duty as 'men of letters': to gather and critically test knowledge. However, at least as important is the fact that their epistolary exchange shows how much both correspondents were aware of the political and religious structures and traditions which separated their countries. Consequently, they expressed the need for tolerance and mutual understanding to demolish these barriers and to serve the interests of what they never specifically named but clearly did experience: Europe's 'common culture' and, through it, their own humanity.

Contacts with like-minded people from other nations provided the basis for the very exclusiveness of the members of the Republic of Letters, of Europe's cosmopolitan elite. During these centuries, these men – the Republic being a predominantly male affair – were not yet heavily pressured to make their country's rather than their own intellectual, cultural choices. Undeniably, however, many of these people, too, were profoundly prejudiced against representatives of other nations, especially when the latter remained anonymous and definitely when they did not belong to the same sociocultural group though, as soon as they got to know each other personally, or through letters, prejudices would often disappear.

Of course one should ask if the ideal of the Republic of Letters was a limited and elitist one? I think it was. Certainly it was easier to pay lip-service to an abstract concept in letters, books and periodicals, to propose tolerance and even understanding on paper, than to be confronted in one's daily life or on trips abroad with other people's regional or national cultural peculiarities. Yet the indisputable limitation both of the ideal and of the various elite groups who were its bearer did not make the idea behind it less functional or valuable. Despite a growing nationalization of culture, in the Republic of Letters Europe enjoyed a form of communication, a form of culture which, *de facto*, created a certain unity that was almost completely lacking in other fields. This situation lasted for almost three centuries. Only by the beginning of the nineteenth century did it start to alter.

12 A new society

From Humanism to the Enlightenment

Humanism and empiricism between 'ratio' and 'revelatio'

The critical attitude towards all kinds of scriptural knowledge shown by such men as Abelard and Erasmus was shared by many others. This became increasingly obvious from the late fifteenth century onwards, as printing and epistolary networks intensified the dissemination of knowledge and the ensuing debate. It is frequently suggested that the emphasis on texts, originating from or based on the classical tradition, combined with the great influence of the Churches on education, hindered the development of the modern, more experimental sciences. However, this is not the case. The interaction between the empirical research methods of philology as used in the study of religious and literary texts and the fundamental problems which philosophy continued to formulate with regard to the nature of man and the cosmos actually stimulated experimental scrutiny in other areas, for instance, in the natural sciences.[1] Thus, the Venetian Daniele Barbaro translated the work of Dioscurides which codified Greek botanical thought, yet to this text, which was not based much on empiricism, he added many a contemporary observation. Indeed, in these years, a way of thinking developed in Europe that more than ever before raised profound questions concerning perceptible reality but which also, in the long run, created a growing gulf between the real, that is to say physical world, which people now thought could be understood and explained rationally, and the world of the invisible, whose existence was acceptable only on the basis of arguments of authority and belief. The lives and works of the Polish astronomer Nicolaus Copernicus (1473–1543) and the Italian astronomer and physicist Galileo Galilei (1564–1642) show what happened.

Niklas Koppernigk, born in the Polish city of Torun, studied at the great university of Cracow, specializing in both philosophy and medicine, and astronomy and mathematics. He travelled to the Italian universities of Bologna, Ferrara and Padua, to continue his studies there, finally returning to his homeland to take up the practice of medicine. Afterwards, he entered the administration of the bishopric of Frauenburg. Always continuing his studies, Copernicus, in 1543, shortly before his death, took the risk of publishing his principal work, *De Revolutione Orbium Coelestium* (On the revolution of the heavenly spheres).[2]

It is a work that bears witness to great intellectual courage because it went against everything that the sixteenth-century Church and State saw as the established order of man and God, of earth and heaven. It is a work that laid the foundation for the modern, western world-view. A few notions from it can make clear how revolutionary Copernicus's concepts were. In the foreword, addressed to Pope Paul III, it is said:

> After long research I am finally convinced:
> That the sun is a fixed star, surrounded by planets which turn around it and of which it is the centre and the torch.
> That besides the major planets there are planets of the second order which circle around these major ones like satelites, and, all of them together, around the sun.
> That the sun is a major planet, subject to threefold movement.
> That all the phenomena of these daily and annual movements, such as the periodic return of the seasons, all the vicissitudes of light and the temperature of the atmosphere which accompany these movements, are the result of the rotation of the earth and its periodic revolution around the sun.
> That the seeming orbit of the stars is nothing but an optical illusion, the product of the actual movement of the earth and the oscillations of its axis.
> I do not doubt that the mathematicians will agree with me, if they will take the trouble to study, not superficially, but in a sound manner, the proofs I will give in this work.
> If some people, of a superficial and ignorant mind, want to use some passages of Holy Scripture against me, distorting their sense, I reject their attacks: mathematical truths can only be judged by mathematicians.[3]

The text clearly shows the author prepared for criticism from those who, appealing to the Bible, wanted to reject empirical considerations as irrelevant or even godless. Actually, Copernicus called into question the Bible's authority only as a book from which scientific knowledge can be deduced. Moreover, he maintained there are certain forms of science which the uninitiated cannot judge: the ability to do so rests with those who have mastered mathematics. In this text, the growing division between an old and a new world-view becomes apparent, with the development of mathematics as a 'new language', a medium of communication that made the more technical sciences unknown territory for the ordinary intelligent person and which thus, in the long run, divided the culture of Europe. In 1623, a century later, this was echoed by the Italian astronomer Galileo Galilei, who wrote:

> Philosophy is written in the big book, the universe. But one cannot understand the book unless one first learns the language and the signs in which it is written. It is written in the language of mathematics, and the signs in which it is written are: triangles, circles and other geometric figures; without knowledge of these, a person cannot understand anything about the universe; without knowledge of these, one wanders lost, as in a dark maze.

Consciously or unconsciously repeating the words of Ibn Rushd, Galilei was also convinced that the Bible itself, however revered, was only an allegory, meant for those who could not read that other book.[4]

Instead of trying to discover the secrets of the heavens, other scientists delved into the earth in order to discover the chemical basis of life. The sixteenth century saw the rise of mineralogy, of research into the secrets of caves and fossils, but also an increased interest in alchemy, the quest for the elixir of life, and for the Stone of Wisdom which was thought to disclose all knowledge. Moreover, well into the seventeenth century, the belief in sorcery and witchcraft, in black magic and the stars, which, to the present-day mind, smacks of pseudo-science or sheer deception, was strongly present in the very same cultured and even scholarly environments and, indeed, people who showed the greatest interest in the new, empirical sciences. Thus, life at the court of Emperor Rudolph II, of Pope Urban VIII and of King Louis XIV was profoundly influenced by people claiming insight and power from these sources.

The contradiction hidden in the fusion which men like Augustine and Thomas had hoped to create between the rational views of the world and man as developed in Antiquity, and Christian revelation and cosmology became ever more apparent. In the long run, the new view of nature as a complex but understandable machine of which man was only a small part led to conflicts with institutionalized religion. Admittedly, up till the 1630s, the papal court in Rome was a centre of the new sciences, where research in every field was welcomed. It was only when the catholic authorities realized which doubts would result from Galilei's speculations on the nature of matter, which touched upon the central doctrine of transsubstantiation, rather than from his ideas about the universe, that he was silenced – and perhaps then only because the reigning Pope himself, Urban VIII, who had protected the Florentine scientist, felt unable any longer to manoeuvre between the Church's major religious orders which were warring about power issues rather than about scientific theories.[5]

Meanwhile, Galilei's predecessors Nicolaus Copernicus and Johannes Kepler (1571–1630) had been squarely condemned by the protestant leaders. Martin Luther, confronted with Copernicus's heliocentric views, had called the Polish scholar 'an ass who wants to pervert the whole art of astronomy and deny what is said in the book of Joshua [i.e. one of the books of the Old Testament], only to make a show of ingenuity and attract attention'; with his theologian, Philip Melanchton, he vehemently defended the geocentric model as the only one that conformed to the Bible, whose literal truth could not be questioned.[6]

For even though Copernicus, Galilei and Kepler advocated the study of the 'book of nature' as being just as pleasing to God as the reading of the Bible, arguing that it was nature which revealed God's greatness, the new science and the new language of 'numbers and figures', incomprehensible to ever larger groups within the intellectual elite but which Galilei yet considered necessary, endangered the Christian tradition. To many it seemed as if God and his saving grace had completely lost their power and significance.

Not surprisingly, besides these thinkers whose influence continues up to the present, others made themselves heard who wanted to again give man a central role in God's creation. In this period, Giordano Bruno (1548–1600) and Jacob Boehme (1575–1624) represented positions which returned to earlier attempts to narrow the abyss between belief and reason.

Bruno replaced the Platonic and Christian view of a transcendent God who, as Creator, stood outside the universe, with the conception that the universe it-self is a living being, the soul of which is God; to him, God and nature are almost inseparable. It took the gentlemen of the Inquisition of the Catholic Church, which, because of its dogmas, could never accept these pantheistic proposals, eight years of deliberations before they condemned Bruno to death at the stake, an indication that these judges were not without intellectual scruples.

The south German cobbler Jacob Boehme argued in innumerable tracts that heaven and hell, good and evil, light and darkness are the essential charac-teristics of nature, of God, and of man who, after all, is the manifestation of God. All this came into existence in a 'Nothingness' where space and, thus, time are absent. Substance, nature grew in this:

> We understand that without nature there is only an eternal immobility and stillness, that is to say, Nothingness; and then we understand that in the Nothing-ness an eternal Will exists, which wants to form the Nothingness into Something, because the Will can know, feel and behold itself.[7]

In this way God, man, the other organic creatures and the inorganic things come into existence. Good and evil are the two options open to man because they are 'Will to Something' and 'Will to Nothing'.[8]

Although the influence of these thinkers for whom the *virtù* of man, his creative capacity, became united with nature, with God, was much weaker than that of their empiricist contemporaries who enjoyed the added prestige of technological success, it is still recognizable as an undercurrent today. More-over, in the course of the following centuries it did not leave untouched the great philosophers who remained part of the western canon.

From scientific empiricism to new visions of man and society

Most scholars tried to carry out their research without openly asking whether they were acting in conformity with the basic values propagated by the Churches, without subordinating their scientific thought to the problem of the relation between God, man and the world. The Englishman Francis Bacon (1561–1626) and the Frenchman René Descartes (1596–1650) embodied developments in which, in the course of the seventeenth century, the way of thinking of men like Copernicus and Galilei was carried on.

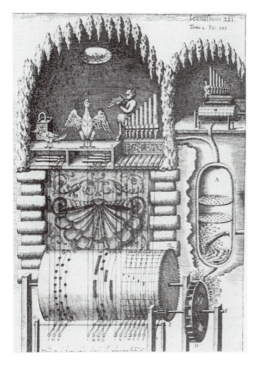

Plates 27 and 28 Europe enters an era of expanding technology, between dream and reality. The spirit of the age is well illustrated by the enormous number of mechanical gadgets one encounters in contemporary publications; some of them were actually realized, such as the water-driven organ–cum–automata devised by the learned Jesuit Athanasius Kircher (1602–80), from A. Kircher, *Iconismus*, Rome, vol. II, f. 343. To many, the new ideas seemed far-fetched and impractical, as is shown in an eighteenth-century print making fun of science, in a vision of an air-borne world
Source: Centre for Art Historical Documentation, Nijmegen, The Netherlands

EUROPE, THE EARLY SEVENTEENTH CENTURY: VIEWS ON THE
SCIENTIFIC METHOD OF FRANCIS BACON AND RENÉ DESCARTES

Sir Francis Bacon, scholar and statesman, contributed to the development of
modern scientific thought with a number of wide-ranging discussions. In
particular, he propagated the essential value of the inductive method:

XIV A syllogism consists of propositions, propositions consist of words, words
are tokens for ideas. If therefore the ideas themselves (the foundation of the
matter) are confused and rashly deduced from things, there is no sort of firmness
in the superstructure. Therefore, the only true hope lies in *induction*.

XVIII All that has so far been discovered in the sciences pretty well remains
subject to vulgar notions; if we are to penetrate to the heart and limits of nature,
we shall have to find a more certain and better fortified way of inferring both ideas
and axioms from things. Altogether, a better and more certain method of
reasoning will have to be brought into use.

XIX There are, and can only be, two methods of enquiry and the discovery of
truth. One flies upward from the sense-data and particulars to extremely general
axioms and causes, and discovers from these principles and their unchanging truth
the intermediate axioms; this is the method now in use. The other deduces axioms
from sense-data and particulars by steadily and gradually climbing higher, coming
at last to the most universal generalisations; this is the true method, but one not yet
tried.

XXI The intellect, left to itself, in a sober, patient and serious condition
(especially if not impeded by received teaching), tends markedly towards the
second and right way, but at a very slow rate of progress; since the intellect, unless
directed and assisted, is an inadequate weapon and altogether unable to overcome
the obscurity of things.

XXII Both methods begin with sense-data and particulars, and culminate in
generalisations of a universal order, but they nevertheless differ enormously. For
the one only just touches on experiment and the particular, while the other
employs these properly and by rote; the one from the first posits certain abstract
and useless generalisations, while the other by stages arrives at the truly knowable
aspects of nature.

XXVIII Anticipation [Bacon's word for hypothesis] is not the least more useful
for the establishment of agreed facts than is interpretation [of phenomena].
Gathered from a few facts – and those as a rule the ones that occur familiarly – it
only dazzles the intellect and stimulates the fancy. Interpretation, on the other
hand, gathered all over the place from very varied and far separated data, cannot
strike the mind with such sudden force; the facts must be treated, like opinions, as
hard and discordant, not unlike the mysteries of the faith.

XCV All practitioners of science have been either empiricists or dogmatists.
Empiricists, like ants, only collect and put to use; dogmatic reasoners, like spiders,
spin webs from within themselves. The bee's is the middle way: it extracts matter
from the flowers of garden and field, but, using its own faculties, converts and
digests it. The true operation of philosophy is not unlike this. It neither relies

exclusively on the powers of the mind, nor simply deposits untouched in the memory the material provided by natural history and physical experiment. Rather it transforms and works on this material intellectually. Therefore we may have hopes of great results from an alliance so far unconcluded, between the experimental and rational methods.[9]

Against Bacon's proposition that only the experimental method can lead to valid knowledge, the Frenchman René Descartes proposed a mathematic but deductive style of argumentation as the basis of all science. The resulting 'Cartesianism' subsequently influenced the western way of thinking for centuries, even if the actual results of Descartes's own scientific thought, for example in physics, were quickly overshadowed by empirical research and other theories. Descartes tells about his quest for the perfect method in an autobiographical way:

> When I was younger, I had devoted a little study to logic, among philosophical matters, and to geometric analysis and to algebra, among mathematical matters – three arts or sciences which, it seemed, ought to be able to contribute something to my design.
>
> But on examining them I noticed that the syllogisms of logic and the greater part of the rest of its teachings serve rather for explaining to other people the things we already know, or even . . . for speaking without judgement of things we know not, than for instructing us of them. . . . as to the analysis of the ancients and the algebra of the moderns, besides that they extend only to extremely abstract matters and appear to have no other use, the first is always so restricted to the consideration of figures that it cannot exercise the understanding without greatly fatiguing the imagination, and in the other one is so bound down to certain rules and ciphers that is has been made a confused and obscure art which embarrasses the mind, instead of a science which cultivates it.
>
> This made me think that some other method must be sought, which, while combining the advantages of these three, should be free from their defects. . . . I believed that I should find the following four [precepts] sufficient, provided that I made a firm and constant resolve not once to omit to observe them.
>
> The first was, never to accept anything as true when I did not recognize it clearly to be so, that is to say, to carefully avoid precipitation and prejudice, and to include in my opinions nothing beyond that which should present itself so clearly and so distinctly to my mind that I might have no occasion to doubt it.
>
> The second was, to divide each of the difficulties which I should examine into as many portions as were possible, and as should be required for its better solution.
>
> The third was, to conduct my thoughts in order, by beginning with the simplest objects, and those most easy to know, so as to mount little by little, as if by steps to the most complex knowledge, and even assuming an order amongst those which do not naturally precede one another.
>
> And the last was, to make everywhere enumerations so complete, and surveys so wide, that I should be sure of omitting nothing.
>
> The long chains of perfectly simple and easy reasons which geometers are accustomed to employ in order to arrive at their most difficult demonstrations had given me reason to believe that all things which can fall under the knowledge of man succeed each other in the same way, and that provided we only abstain from

receiving as true any opinions which are not true, and always observe the necessary order in deducing one from the other, there can be none so remote that they may not be reached, or so hidden that they may not be discovered. . . . What satisfied me most with this method, was that by it I was assured of always using my reason, if not perfectly, at least to the best of my power.[10]

In fact, in his *Discours sur la Méthode*, Descartes studied his own thought processes; he concluded that man frequently starts from the wrong suppositions because he does not look systematically at all the factors which influence a thought, perception or action. Descartes therefore introduced the concept of fundamental doubt: before one departs from a particular point, which one wants to assume as a relative certainty, one must examine one's own thoughts about it as thoroughly and impartially as possible. However, Descartes still left open the possibility that it is God who instils these particular references in man, his creature. So, while he had to erode the function of all authority that could not be made acceptable on the basis of reasonable arguments, God remained as unquestionable for him as for Augustine.

John Locke went one step further than Descartes, without acknowledging or denying God. In his *Essay concerning Human Understanding* (1690) he reasons, among other things, on the basis of the observation of children, that man has no inborn ideas or principles; everything that he thinks and does during his life comes forth from or builds on ideas and principles that he has learnt or which are passed on to him within his cultural context; man is not ruled by 'universal ideas'. In the same years, the 'journalist' and cultural commentator Pierre Bayle, in his *Dictionnaire Historique et Critique*, further spread the Cartesian attitude of radical doubt which, in his view, ought inevitably to lead to tolerance.

Meanwhile, the debate about the spectacular findings of the 'new science', experimental physics, increasingly influenced all issues of belief and religion. The invention of the microscope in the 1620s had opened up an 'invisible world' that showed the gradual development of many life forms from eggs or semen. Some argued that putting a slice of nature under the microscope would hardly contribute to a greater understanding of such a complex whole – and in a way they were right. Others, however, rejoiced in the idea that now the realities of nature could be seen beneath the surface of nature, which gave them a powerful weapon against the occultists who, for so many centuries, had used the book of nature only as a text full of secret signs.[11]

By the later decades of the seventeenth century, the concepts of the empiricists, whose thought was guided by the study of the cosmos, of the visible world, had become a new philosophy.[12] This was most clearly manifested in the writings of the physicist Isaac Newton (1642–1727), first a professor at Cambridge and later master of the Royal Mint of England.[13]

In 1704, Newton published his great work *Opticks*, or the 'Optica'. In this he explains the true method to attain knowledge and insight, the right way to look at man and the world:

analysis consists in making experiments and observations, and admitting of no objections against the conclusions but such as are taken from experiments or other certain truths. For hypotheses are not to be regarded in experimental philosophy, and although the arguing from experiments and observations by induction be no demonstration of general conclusion, yet it is the best way of arguing which the nature of things admits of, and may be looked upon as so much the stronger by how much the induction is more general. And if no exception occurs from phenomena, the conclusion may be pronounced generally.

The way of thinking of Newton and his generation shows both a Baconian trust in the value of empirical research and the use of Descartes's method of 'fundamental doubt', resulting, for many, in a clear optimism with regard to the human capacity to know the world and even the universe. People now began to assume that the cosmos was governed by general laws which one could penetrate by careful observation. This epistemology was codified, as it were, in Newton's *Philosophiae naturalis Principia mathematica*, published in 1687 with the support of the Royal Society. The book unleashed a revolution precisely because, as the title indicates, it was more than a treatise on physics. Let Newton speak for himself:

> I offer this work as the mathematical principles of philosophy, because the whole content of philosophy seems to exist in this – from the phenomenon of movement to the study of natural forces, and from these forces to the demonstration of other phenomena. . . . I am induced by many reasons to suspect that (the phenomena of nature may) all depend upon certain forces by which the particles of bodies, by some causes hitherto unknown, are either mutually impelled towards each other and cohere in regular figures, or are repelled and recede from each other; which forces being unknown, philosophers have hitherto attempted the search of nature in vain. But I hope the principles here laid down will afford some light either to that or some truer method of philosophy.[14]

Elaborating on the speculations concerning the movement of the planets by Copernicus, Kepler and others, Newton wanted to present a sound system based on quantitative, physical arguments. To this end he used the integral and differential calculus through which it was possible to establish the position of a body at a particular moment if the relation between the position and the speed of the body or the change in speed at another time were known. When Newton subsequently reflected on the existing concepts concerning gravitation in his general study of gravitation, he was able to describe the cosmos mathematically as a system in which the celestial bodies moved eternally in set positions which were determined by the relative gravitational force of sun, earth and planets.

The consequences were profound, for there now resulted a definite break with the Aristotelian cosmology of the Christian world, in which the Creator always had to be present as the prime mover because movement supposed the constant exercise of force. According to Newton, creation, built up of atoms, was, once God had brought it into existence, a dynamic mechanism that worked in accordance with a simple law of nature. Newton confirmed what many had already suspected, or feared: God does not continuously interfere in man's life.

More than he could ever have suspected, man was now thrown back on himself. The Frenchman Blaise Pascal (1623–62), who formulated such striking thoughts on many questions in his *Pensées*, voiced the 'angst' which this insecurity evoked, writing:

> When I consider the brief span of my life absorbed into the eternity which comes before and after – as the remembrance of a guest that tarrieth but a day – the small space I occupy and which I see swallowed up in the immensity of spaces of which I know nothing and which know nothing of me, I take fright and am amazed to see myself here rather than there: there is no reason for me to be here rather than there, now rather than then. Who put me here? By whose command and act were this time and place allotted to me? . . . the eternal silence of these infinite spaces fills me with dread.[15]

Many still feel that fear. Nevertheless, many others, especially those who experienced the power and authority of the Churches as a hindrance to a more rational world-view, rejoiced; to them, with Newton, Europe seemed at last to have seen the light: the universal explanation of the universe had been found. The fact that science now became a power system, too, demonstrating its use through the public presentation of all kinds of experiments with, preferably, spectacular instruments, gave it increased standing in society.

However, empirical, rational observation not only began to dominate research in the natural sciences, which slowly became more important in the European economy and society; it now began to direct the way people thought about themselves and about their position in the cosmos as well. Newtonian physics and other scientific concepts soon gained considerable influence on various non-physical domains of human thought, varying from practical aspects such as time and distance measurements on land and at sea to economic and political philosophies about man as an individual citizen, as an individual entrepreneur. Indeed, the new sciences began to change the way people observed their environment and interpreted the nature, the organization and functioning of society and politics.[16]

Thus, the political philosopher Thomas Hobbes (1588–1679) analysed and described society as if it were a physical phenomenon. In his famous work *Leviathan, or the Matter, Form and Power of a Commonwealth, Ecclesiastical and Civil* (1651), he established that all citizens are only individual entities, swirling particles which try to avoid collisions as much as possible; as a result of this necessity, they set up the state as an instrument to avoid calamity and to realize the highest attainable good for the greatest number of people.

From Humanism to Enlightenment: a long dawn

The growing confidence in the results of man's capacity to know himself and his world, which was widely felt throughout the Republic of Letters, became a characteristic of European learned culture in the late seventeenth and early eighteenth centuries. Many people considered themselves and their time as 'enlightened', namely by the light of healthy common sense, which observes and only then concludes. Many educated Europeans felt less and less inclined to accept as truths those ideas which could not be reduced to empirical observations.

Doubts arose with regard to all claims to authority and power which were not founded on logically reasoned and thus acceptable principles. People threw off the shackles of tradition. They argued that man could live without being paralysed by the past, by the authoritarian but unreasoned ways in which Church and State used to impose their power. Specifically religion as preached by the Churches was thought to obfuscate the very qualities in man which must be the basis of his thinking and acting, namely, reason and tolerance. In short, people's attitude towards life became critical, sceptical even, and they judged the world around them accordingly. A more empirical, individual and secular way of thinking, which had begun in the Renaissance, now achieved its provisional completion in a way of looking at man and the world which has been called the Enlightenment, because its main champions were convinced the world finally was ready to be illumined by the light of reason.

This enlightened century was characterized by concepts which, though sometimes centuries-old, once more were instrumental in distancing man from the traditional vision of God and his presence in creation, in the universe. For some, as for the French author La Mettrie, who wrote a widely discussed and, to many, abhorrent tract called *L'Homme machine* (The Machine-Man) (1747), the universe contained no God, but physical, moving bodies only; the most complex body ever evolved was man, a self-regulating machine whose functioning or dysfunctioning depended upon its fuel, food.[17] Such thoughts were naturally fed by the growing influence of technology and the technical sciences.

Yet in the long run a mainly Christian 'enlightened' thinking was the most successful, affecting the minds of educated persons well into the twentieth century, specifically when and where it became structural in cultural institutions – for instance, in institutions for education and science. Everywhere, this Christian Enlightenment was to a large extent an urban phenomenon that became manifest in such cities as late-eighteenth-century Edinburgh, the town where, in the late seventeenth century, the presbyterian ministers had roamed the streets on Sundays, to make sure that everyone attended divine service, if necessary by force, and, of course, both in the morning and the afternoon; the town where, at that time, witches were still being burned. A comparable change was noticeable in eighteenth-century Amsterdam and Middelburg, but also in 'enlightened' circles in Madrid and Valencia under the reign of Charles III and in the bourgeois milieux of north Italian cities like Milan. In Great Britain, this 'Enlightenment' was embodied in scholars like George Berkeley (1684–1753) and David Hume (1711–76). In the German states, it found expression in the works of Gotthold Ephraim Lessing (1729–81) and, perhaps most of all, in Gottfried Wilhelm Leibniz.

He has rightly been called the last 'universal scholar'. Admittedly, he never developed the all-embracing scientific system he longed for, with a language to match it, based on the irrevocable logic of mathematics – with Newton he shares the honour of having developed differential calculus; yet he contributed seminal ideas to a wide variety of fields, ranging from linguistics to philosphy, from library science to political theory. His cosmology has influenced people till the present. It was built on the notion of the 'monad' as the essential, basic, conscious element of the universe, matter and spirit in one, on which all more complex structures are built, including, somewhere in the range of complexity, man himself, but culminating in the all-encompassing structure that is God.[18]

Indeed, the problem of God weighed heavily on the enlightened spirits. To a greater or lesser degree, most thinkers wrestled with the relation between knowable nature and unknowable supernature and with the relation between matter and spirit. Already in the seventeenth century, the Jewish-Dutch philosopher Baruch de Spinoza had decided that man, in this age and time, needed a scientitific proof of God's existence, and had proceeded to give it. In his *Tractatus Theologico-Politicus* (Amsterdam 1670), he had created an image of God very unlike the personal God essential to Jews and Christians for thousands of years. Spinoza's God was a primeval force, of which all men, indeed all creatures were, in a way, part. But to be able to conceive of such a God, Spinoza stipulated freedom; to him, liberty was the essential precondition both for public peace and for private piety, and both were conditional to a humane society.[19]

Ultimately, the major minds of the eighteenth century, too, could not really distance themselves from some sort of vision of God as an uncreated substance, as creator outside and above the world. Even the German philosopher Immanuel Kant (1724–1804) was unable to do so. Admittedly, in his *Kritik der reinen Vernunft* (Critique of Pure Reason) (1781), he reasoned that all experience was realized only in rational categories and that ideas such as the soul, the world and God could certainly be thought but were not provable with reason, nor, moreover, were they refutable, so that the world of belief lies outside the borders of theoretical reason. Yet in his *Kritik der praktischen Vernunft* (Critique of Practical Reason) (1788), he argued for an acceptance of religion on ethical grounds, as a human and social necessity which, of course, implied some notion of belief as well.

Kant's discussion with the Swedish mining specialist and thinker Emmanuel Swedenborg (1688–1772) in the 1760s is fascinating because it clearly articulated the eternal tension in European-Christian thought. In a series of works, of which the *Arcana Coelestia* (The Celestial Secrets) of 1749–56, and *De*

Coelo et Inferno (On Heaven and Hell), were the most important, Swedenborg had developed a vision of man and the universe which made Kant his opponent but won him many adherents even in our own age. For the Swede, attempting to prove God's existence, the spirit is a substantial, organic whole in which man and God coincide in its successive stages of awakening. Churches and religions are irrelevant for him, and he unhesitatingly rejects the universal claims of Christianity: 'Everyone whose heart is enlightened can see that not a single person was born for hell' and 'the Church of the Lord is spread over the whole world and is therefore universal: all are members of it who live a life of brotherly love, in accordance with their own religion'.[20]

For others, the world and everything in it were only projections of the human spirit. So it was for Arthur Schopenhauer (1788–1860). In his *Die Welt als Wille und Vorstellung* (The World as Will and Idea) (1819) he accepted that man can acquire knowledge through experience but he questioned what man can say about the nature of things. His answer was: not much, for each man is an object, a body, 'an idea', and at the same time, a subject, self-awareness, 'will'. To survive in this world, each man assumes that the same counts for all other humans:

> Wenn also die Körperwelt noch etwas mehr seyn soll, als bloss unsere Vorstellung, so müssen wir sagen, dass sie äusser der Vorstellung, also an sich und ihrem innersten Wesen nach, Das sei, was wir in uns selbst unmittelbar als Willen finden.

> Therefore, if we want to maintain that the material world is more than merely our idea of it, we must conclude that beyond idea it is, in its essence and according to its own innermost self, that which we, in ourselves, immediately will it to be.

Schopenhauer concludes that a world of sorts does exist but that, actually, though we have the illusion of its manifoldness, it is nothing but the projection of one essence: 'Jeder erkennt nur *ein* Wesen ganz unmittelbar: seinen eigenen Willen, im Selbstbewustseyn' ('Everybody is able to know only one essence immediately: his own will, in his own consciousness of it').[21]

Among the countries of continental Europe, eighteenth-century France was, perhaps, most open to 'enlightenment'.[22] French society was characterized by innovation and diffusion, by production and distribution, by circulation and mobility. Books and ideas acted on social mores, practices and artefacts, and together they were interwoven in an ever tighter network of communication, indeed, of change.[23] Enlightened thinkers like Voltaire (1694–1778), reasoned that if their principles were widely disseminated – by making knowledge accessible in dictionaries and encyclopedias, through education and reading, by displaying nature and culture in museums and visualizing it in experiments – they could actively set society on a course of progress.

Consequently, many concepts considered characteristic of the Enlightenment evolved mainly in France; though some of them might be very old already, they were now described and advocated more convincingly than ever. In his *Du Contrat Social* (On the Social Contract) (1762), Jean-Jacques

Rousseau (1712–78) reasoned his way towards revolutionary ideas about freedom, equality and fraternity. However much his notion of popular sovereignty was based on his experiences of a small city-state – his native city Geneva – and was difficult to apply in larger societies, Rousseau's ideals of political and social change impassioned many; it was precisely their inconsistency that allowed everyone to interpret them as they pleased. However, few French *philosophes* were as radical as he was: many sought a middle course between existing economic and social structures and the necessity to effect change gradually, especially through politics.[24]

In all of educated Europe, French writers were read and commented on,[25] even if their more extreme concepts were only partly applied. In many countries, people saw greater advantage in a moderate version, in which earlier humanist and cosmopolitan thinking was accentuated by growing tolerance, especially regarding freedom of expression, and an increasing confidence in the civilizing value of reason.[26]

Though precisely the non- or even anti-religious aspect of 'enlightened' thinking was not shared by the majority of educated Europeans, both the Enlightenment itself and the many debates that were of its essence inevitably contributed to a quickening erosion of Christianity as the all-powerful normative framework of European man. This reinforced the process which gradually robbed Europe of a way of thinking, a world-view that, regardless of one's judgement of its morals and practices, had formed its most fundamental claim to unity.

Meanwhile, cosmopolitan thinking not only became less Christian, but also became more of a vision which pretended to comprehend the entire world rather than only Europe. The belief in the power of reason increasingly led to ideas about man and society which heavily emphasized a universal, globally recognizable morality that, if applied in its pure form would of itself result in such values as a sense of public responsibility and the search for beauty.[27] The knowledge relating to or influenced by the non-European world which had grown so tempestuously in the two preceding centuries had laid the foundation for this mentality. Ethnology and the cultural relativism it had engendered had entered European thought about man and the world, about Europeans and others.[28] Yet, of course, the universal values now envisaged were the result of a European vision of humankind.

In this vision, a book pretending to encompass all knowledge played a central role. First, in 1728, the English *Cyclopaedia* by Chambers and, subsequently, the much more radical and influential French *Encyclopédie*, which was published in twenty-eight volumes between 1751 and 1772,[29] became the basic repositories of Enlightenment culture. It is, however, characteristic that Paris knew nothing of the German enterprise of J.M. Zedler, who published his *Grosses Vollständiges Universal-Lexicon aller Wissenschaften und Künste* (Great and Complete Universal Dictionary of all Sciences and Arts) from 1732 onwards; it indicates the limits of communication between the regional languages now that Latin had lost its position as Europe's communal tongue.

Enlightenment and Romanticism: poles apart?

Paradoxically, the process in which a mainly moderate, Christian version of the Enlightenment filtered down to wide circles of the educated population of Europe at the end of the eighteenth and in the first decades of the nineteenth century was reinforced through the considerable criticism of some of the more far-reaching 'enlightened' concepts, the more so when these became connected to political and social revolution. This happened when, all over Europe, people outside the circle of those who called themselves progressive – first and foremost French-orientated intellectuals – reacted negatively to the 'spirit' of the political and social revolution that shook France from 1789 onwards, resulting in the fall of the monarchy and the institution of a dictatorship. According to them, the blatant secularity and the bloody chaos that characterized French politics in this period had been the inevitable outcome of those aspects of the Enlightenment which, to them, embodied materialism, unbelief and inhumanity; at the same time these very developments proved to them that they were right in rejecting the Enlightenment altogether. They were strengthened in their conviction by General Bonaparte, later the Emperor Napoleon, and his large-scale attempt to unite the whole of Europe politically, at first with the help of the youthful elan of the French revolutionaries but soon by means of destructive wars.

In this situation, from the late 1780s onward many educated Europeans developed a new way of thinking about culture, their culture. In the complicated process of cultural transmission and borrowing between different social groups a symbiosis grew in which the culture of Humanism which had gained a new stimulus in the enlightened institutions of the Republic of Letters – a cosmopolitan but also elite culture in its origins and essence – now acquired a far broader social base.

Meanwhile, this culture had been fitted into a more national way of thinking,[30] the more so as the European states tried to use it for their own goals, especially in its scientific, technological achievements. It was made clear to the middle classes, who increasingly carried this culture, that service to the state was to be their prime objective. Though all over Europe people continued to admire classical civilization, in the many reading circles and debating clubs which became hotbeds of bourgeois cultural life, the counterpart of the aristocratic salons,[31] the cult of the nation's own past assumed a central position as a focus for thought and action.

This tendency, already visible in the later decades of the eighteenth century, became much stronger in the aftermath of the French Revolution. Indeed, a widespread aversion developed to all those ideas and other forms of culture that, in the wake of the Enlightenment, had been presented as generally valid, unless they now could be fitted into more traditional, controllable frameworks. Many shifted the emphasis in their thinking, or learnt to shift it. Instead of relying on the universal, which was threatening in its vagueness and offered little hold, people fell back on the trusted particularities of their own country, as its religion, language, customs and morals, which were more easily recognizable as anchors of identity than the high-flung, so-called universal philosophical principles.

In those countries where French culture in its eighteenth-century, strongly secular form had been less influential – parts of the German Empire, the Netherlands and Scotland but also Spain and Italy – traditional religious concepts fused with the new scientific views, influenced by although not always acknowledged as of the Enlightenment. A more personal belief, frequently of a pietistic nature, and a moderate form of progressive thinking interacted fruitfully with growing pride in the achievements of one's own state. Although all over Europe certain forms of communal thinking had a long tradition already, now the search for common roots became more crystallized, evolving into a well-defined national feeling.

What remained was the admiration for the great achievements of Europe's classical civilization, which were experienced, at least by the more educated, as part of their identity, indeed, as their own roots. It was an emotion that was greatly reinforced by the spectacular discovery and subsequent excavation (1738–48) from the ash and lava of Mount Vesuvius of the splendours of the Roman cities of Herculaneum and Pompeii. At the same time, the undeniable Afro-Asian components of that classical civilization were gradually written out of ancient Greek and indeed European history by the guardians of tradition, the scholars, precisely to ensure that this tradition could be presented as uniquely 'European'.[32] With the French Revolution and, even more, the politics of Napoleon, many European states experienced a growing disapproval of imperial aspirations; consequently, the admiration for ancient Rome decreased, while that for classical Greece grew. Greece, idealized as the cradle of democracy, Greece, where the intellectual had been able to claim a far more powerful position than in imperial Rome, that Greece was very popular until the end of the nineteenth century, both in the German states and in England,[33] both of which claimed to be the true heirs of that ideal. Meanwhile, in Greece itself, for several hundred years a backward province of the Ottoman Empire, as was the greater part of the Balkans, the ideas of the Enlightenment had taken hold as well, if only among a small urban elite. An intellectual like Iosipos Moisiodax (*c.*1725–1800) boldly came forward to claim that the Balkan societies should remodel themselves along European 'enlightened' lines; one of the instruments in that process should be a reorganization of education, wherein vernacular Greek should be the medium.[34]

Against a European background that in itself was slowly being nationalized could be discerned a growing appreciation for that part of the past that more convincingly could help to underline and explain the nature and indeed singularity of one's own state and society. Trends which had been set in the late seventeenth century now became more pronounced.

In England, James Macpherson, in his *Ossian Poems* of 1761, sang the praises of Celtic culture as an element in the formation of Britain. In the previous decade, the composer Thomas Arne had produced a masque to be acted before the crown prince's court called *King Alfred* – with Arthur, he was one of Britain's near-mythical founders – which contained the rousingly nationalistic song 'Rule Britannia'. In the German states, Johann Wolfgang von Goethe (1749–1832) and Friedrich Schiller (1759–1805) drew their inspiration from both classical Greece and their own Germanic-German past. In Spain, intellectuals like the monks Benito Feíjoo and Martin Sarmiento pointed to the influence of Islamic civilization on Spanish culture and, more generally, glorified Spain's *Siglo de Oro*, the 'golden' sixteenth century.

As if to prove that such appreciation of the past need not result in stultifying conservatism but could be a creative influence, many of these men also strongly voiced the need for change, to recapture the erstwhile grandeur of the nation. Even in Spain, considered by many northern, often protestant Europeans almost as backward as the Balkans if only because it was judged to be 'priest-ridden', enlightened monks and other thinkers, often from the provincial bourgeoisie, contributed to a climate wherein, for the first time in more than a hundred years, part of the ruling elite did indeed consider and even implement new policies; in the economic and educational sectors, ideas from England and France were discussed and adopted.[35] The same occurred in Italy, especially in Milan and the other towns of Lombardy, where the rule of the Church was less oppressive than in the papal states. Intellectuals from the clergy as well as from the secular bourgeoisie, and innovative entrepreneurs discussed both the past and the future, proposing reforms to restore Italy's ancient cultural and economic pre-eminence; in doing so, they created a situation wherein, by the end of the eighteenth century, northern Italy was on its road to become one of Europe's most prosperous areas

Besides the tendency to reduce the space of meaningful experience to one's own nation, and to glorify it, also in its past greatness, the elevation of spontaneous feeling as well as the cult of a harmoniously growing – though in the new fashion of garden architecture artfully arranged – nature became elements of a new awareness, a new sense of life. Instead of the mathematically cold lines of classicist architecture, of a totally controlled society and environment as epitomized in the denatured gardens of Versailles, people stressed the value of organic growth, both in art and architecture and in society and nature; significantly, the woods, once the abode of the uncivilized, the wild, and of the old, pagan gods, now became the natural habitat of a man at ease in communication with his roots and with the cosmos, regardless of the question whether this cosmos was ruled by a personal, omnipotent God or was the ultimate force of life itself. This cultivation both of nature and of the past, indeed, of a society grown 'naturally' through the ages, with time thus nurturing it and hallowing its results, this sentiment has been termed romantic.

The new views had a wide resonance. In the imperial capital, Vienna, Franz Joseph Haydn (1732–1809) was avidly reading the works of contemporary philosophers and other scholars.[36] He also travelled, to England among other places. Going there in 1791 and again in 1794, his music was greatly appreciated. While in London, he acquainted himself with Handel's great choral works that inspired in him the wish to create something comparable. Back home, Baron Van Swieten, one of the Empress Maria Theresa's courtiers and her librarian, presented Haydn with the text of the Englishman John Milton's poem *Paradise Lost* (1658–67), on man's creation and life in paradise, which he had translated and adapted. Haydn set it to music in 1798. But paradise was not lost to these eighteenth-century musicians and thinkers. From an intriguing nexus of cultural lines reaching through time and space, the oratorio *The Creation* became a paean of praise to God's work, a joyous song about the variety and sheer life of nature; it is a vocal résumé both of European man's Christian vision of his origins and further development, and of his optimism over his future achievements as ruler of the earth.

Yet, even in a vision like Haydn's, which, with so many others, can be labelled romantic, the communality of Europe inevitably receded into the background. Perhaps that is one of the most important elements which differentiated the cultural form called Enlightenment from this other cultural form called Romanticism.

Even while enlightened thinking had been gaining a firm foothold all over Europe by the end of the eighteenth century, reactions against it already started appearing, denouncing its so-called dehumanizing tendencies. Especially in Germany, in the milieu of Jena University, a new or rather an old philosophy using new terms and ideas was preached. This 'Naturphilosophie', embodied in Friedrich-Wilhelm Schelling (1775–1854) but strongly present in the scientific and the poetic writings of Goethe and other romantic authors as well, sought to reunite nature and culture. To do so it developed dynamic and even organic explanations for natural phenomena using both chemics and mathematics and applying such concepts as polarity and complementarity, metamorphosis and identity. Although this philosophy did not go in for experiment, it did, in fact, generate important scientific results, precisely because such concepts as unity and polarity led to discoveries in the fields of contact-electricity and electro-magnetism. In the end, the largely deductive character of this approach was felt to be unproductive and in the 1830s even resulted in a very positivistic, inductive view of science that eschewed any relationship with philosophical reflection. Yet the idea of a more holistic interpretation of nature lingered on, resurfacing every now and then, as, for example, in Germany itself, where, at the end of the nineteenth century, a new call was heard: 'zurück zu Goethe' ('back to a humanizing science'). It was a call that is heard up till the present, pointing to what has been termed 'the unfinished business of our times';[37] a call heard by all those who, whether scientists or other educated people, think that a purely positivistic and moreover technological bias would be damaging to human culture.

Indeed, from the late eighteenth century onwards, many have found problems choosing between the poles of positivism and poetry. In these years, Goethe conceived his greatest play, *Faust*, a 'scholar's tragedy' in which he, through Faust, empirical thinker and doubter, articulated weighty questions about the limits of knowledge and thus about the position and purpose of man in the world. Not surprisingly, both in Germany and, for example, in the Netherlands, Baruch de Spinoza, was rediscovered, by some as the anti-Christian, atheistic philosopher of a scientific, secular culture, but by others as the prophet of a convincing pantheism.

It is necessary to consider these developments precisely because criticism of the Enlightenment and its consequences has echoed loudly in the last years of the twentieth century. Depending on the extent to which one experiences the effects of that which initially developed in the Enlightenment as positive or negative, one will consider this period as a blessed or a cursed phase in European history.

In retrospect, many have judged the period between *c.*1680 and 1820, in which the Enlightenment slowly became manifest and, subsequently, triumphant, a period of decreasing belief in authority which, especially in the area of religion, led to secularization and even to scepticism and unbelief. We also might say this period can be considered as a time of growing human awareness, and increasing rationalism. Between them, these phenomena signalled a definite break with the 'harmonious universe' that most intellectuals had tried to maintain one way or the other since the union of the classical and Christian world-views sought in the previous centuries. Together, these forms of humanism and rationalism greatly contributed to the decline of a European culture determined by institutionalized religion and marked the transition to a more secular view of man and the world. To many contemporaries as well as to many present-day observers, the problem was aggravated precisely because the organic world-view had been supplanted by a mechanistic vision that was to hold an almost absolute sway over Europe till the middle of the twentieth century.

It is beyond doubt that the Enlightenment led to developments which, even if they at first only affected a small group of intellectuals and the better educated, also began to influence the middle class during the nineteenth century and then became a basis of European thought about man and the world in the twentieth century.

However, this process could happen precisely because the Enlightenment certainly was not as diametrically opposed to Romanticism as is often argued. The Enlightenment glorified empiricism, but it was an empiricism not only of reason but also of the senses! Thus it bore the fruit of which the seeds already had been sown in early Humanism and the subsequent Renaissance. The difference mainly became manifest in the more secular character of the Enlightenment; yet we have come to realize that in this very period innumerable creative combinations of reason and religion remained or even came into existence: from the esotericism of such secretive and indeed secret societies as the Rosecrucians and the Free Masons, to the catholic 'Aufklärung'.[38] In particular, the moderate, bourgeois version of Romanticism kept asking many of the questions which people in the Christian Enlightenment had asked too, even though these questions were now clothed in other words. Maybe one must conclude that only the extent to which the answers to a number of fundamental questions betrayed a clear return to a more religious, metaphysical view of the world really differentiated Romanticism from the Enlightenment. Indeed, the two often seem to have fused, especially in the first decades of the nineteenth century.

Part IV

Continuity and change

New forms of consumption
and communication

13 Europe's revolutions

Freedom and consumption for all?

Material culture and conspicuous consumption: a process of consumer change till the end of the eighteenth century

Until well into the eighteenth century and, in some areas of Europe, up till the end of the nineteenth century, most families, especially in the countryside, possessed little more than a dozen household goods, the ones that were absolutely necessary: some simple stools, a plank table, some cooking utensils, perhaps two or three beds and mattresses, and a few blankets. The fact is borne out by an investigation organized in the German countryside at the end of the nineteenth century. In the survey we read:

> The bed was a wooden plank with a straw mattress; there was a cupboard, a rough-hewn wooden table, a few stools, all of which a carpenter could make in a few hours. In my youth the first stoves were introduced; before, we only had an open fire with a kettle hanging above it. Around 1860/1870 my father bought such a stove. . . . In the old house . . . we had an oven, which my parents had purchased when they married, a pump, and a sofa. We ate and lived in the kitchen, with its wooden floors, its scrubbed table, its settee and cupboard, all made by Father . . . The few clothes we had were hung on pegs, maybe behind a curtain. Mostly, two children shared a bed.[1]

To know whether this situation prevailed all over Europe and, moreover, whether it did apply to the non-agrarian population as well, a cultural historian must delve into the archives. For the answers are, at least partly, given by the inventories enumerating the possessions of citizens and farmers in towns and villages. Research into the material culture of Europe is a fairly recent branch of scholarship. Formerly, most historians were more interested in the traces left by the great thinkers and artists, the ramifications of political intrigues and dynastic affairs, the mechanisms of social processes. But these certainly do not suffice to write cultural history. We also want to know how ordinary people lived, what their houses looked like, what they ate and how they dressed: in their daily lives European culture was shaped fundamentally, in its basic material conditions.

One of the first results of this new type of research has been that we now know that all over western Europe the average number of household items gradually increased between the late fifteenth and the late eighteenth centuries. In the same period material possessions were perceptibly if slowly more evenly spread over the social classes. Both developments undoubtedly were caused by the economic changes produced, especially, by trade and industry.

Up till the end of the eighteenth century, only one social group lived a life resembling our modern consumer society; only one social group was always well fed, able to buy even the luxury food it did not need and, moreover, able to buy any amount of material objects which were completely useless for the purpose of survival. This, of course, was the elite, comprised both of the old nobility who based their wealth largely on landed income, and of a small number of top bureaucrats grown rich in the service of the state as well as of plutocrats who had amassed their fortunes in trade and banking. What did their material culture look like?

Their houses were big, even very big, boasting an amount of space far and above what was needed to give simple shelter: it was space which proclaimed that these people had the money to buy 'superfluous' room, room that was luxury and thus gave status to its possessor; it showed wealth and the kind of social position usually associated with some kind of power. The rooms in these houses were filled with objects which were useless as well: sculpted wooden chests, big armoires, tapestries, paintings. In the chests and cupboards rich clothes were stored, and caskets full of jewellery and plate. All these objects shared the function of the space they occupied: they displayed wealth, gave status to their possessor, referred to his power.

But the thought behind it all went deeper: the wealth of the elite, all the money that was available without it having to be spent on life's bare necessities, was yet put to good use. Building or buying the splendid mansions, castles and palaces, commissioning the beautiful and costly objects that filled them meant that the elite cared for culture and showed that the society of which they were the leaders was a truly civilized society. This way of reasoning was prevalent already in the sixteenth and seventeenth centuries. The mentality of which it was an expression has been described as the need of 'conspicuous consumption'. The function of spending money on luxury was to underline the privileged position of the possessors. Of course, the phenomenon included not only luxury goods, but also leisure, for that, too, showed everyone that one did not have to work to stay alive. Hence, leisure was luxury as well, a consumer good that gave status.

The nobles and high officials of France, England and Sweden, of the Burgundian and the Spanish-Habsburg courts frequently organized hunt parties and tournaments that lasted for days; dressed in splendid clothes they attended princely or aristocratic weddings that were often celebrated with week-long festivities. They were the guests at banquets which took an entire day, where more than a hundred different dishes were served. All that was 'conspicuous consumption', both of money and of time, the more so as these festivities and dinners were being held in public, to ensure, as it were, maximum visibility for the common people who watched the display.

These aristocrats wore costly garments of velvet and silk, threaded with gold and silver and stitched with pearls and gems, as is shown on the portraits painted by François Clouet, Hans Holbein and Titian (Tiziano Vecelli), the painters of fifteenth- and sixteenth-century princes and nobles. The dishes they ate were composed of the most exotic and therefore obviously expensive ingredients like peacock tongues and salmon cheeks. The food was served on tables groaning under the weight of gold and silver vessels, crystal goblets and plate cutlery. While fountains spouted wine, musicians and dancers entertained the guests.

In royal processions, splendidly decorated floats passed under triumphal arches richly painted with all kinds of classical or mythological scenes, usually presenting a political and dynastic message. It was all a display of money and power. And it reproduced power: through these manifestations of power, the public was strengthened in its belief that the existing order was, indeed, the natural one. Even such a cynical and critical observer as the Scotsman James Boswell wrote in the diary of his 1763 London sojourn:

> This day being the Queen's birthday, I was amused by seeing multitudes of rich-dressed people driving in their splendid equipages to Court. Really, it must be confessed that a court is a fine thing. It is the cause of so much show and splendour that people are kept gay and spirited.[2]

Indeed, for a long time the courts of the European princes were the centres and even the motors of this 'system'.

The French court at Versailles in particular was a place not only where the power of France was concentrated, but also a theatre where immense wealth and opulence were displayed and where especially the aristocracy was strangled in a continuous orgy of feasts.[3] Some 3,000 to 4,000 nobles attended the court; together, they made up approximately 1 per cent of the *c.*400,000 people who constituted the nobility of France; in their turn, these were only 2 per cent of the country's population of some 20 million souls. Surrounding them were, of course, armies of servants, but also the French state's top bureaucrats, for the palace was the government's central ministry as well.

The court nobles lived in a sphere of fierce competition; they all wanted to obtain the King's favour, for the power and the riches it brought. Emulating the King's example, everybody wanted to show himself in as favourable a light as possible. Man and wife dressed luxuriously, following the fashions set by the King and the Queen, or rather the King's official mistress. One felt forced to spend fortunes on festivities, hoping the King might deign to attend. One decorated one's own house as a little Versailles. Indeed, one did everything possible to show that one knew what it meant to be a courtier, to impress the world with the fact that one belonged to the centre of power. No wonder the Duke of St Simon, who in his diaries left a surprisingly cynical description of life at court and of the 'Sun' who reigned over Versailles, writes that Louis deliberately urged his nobles to spend, making luxury into a matter of honour, crippling them with debts and, thus, increasing their dependence on him.[4]

To judge by the many descriptions of foreign visitors, in the last quarter of the seventeenth century, Versailles became Europe's foremost stage where 'conspicuous consumption' was enacted, precisely by the costly and time-consuming ceremonies and rituals that served to display and cement the power of royalty and aristocracy. The message was that people who could live this kind of life, spend so much money on futile things and futile pastimes, lived well and above the solid burgher, the industrious artisan and the hard-working farmer. Those who lived in this way belonged to the political, social and cultural elite.

Because the court aristocracy were the leaders of society in most parts of Europe, other people who were seeking status, who wanted to climb the ladder of social and political success, tried to live as the aristocrats did. Indeed, Saint-Simon had already indicated as much, concluding that the 'vice' of overspending spread from Versailles to Paris, and finally infected the general public. More specifically the wealthy members of the bourgeoisie, who, though not born to this culture, yet had reached positions of considerable economic power by virtue of their industry began to imitate the court nobility. Their number was increasing in the course of the seventeenth and eighteenth centuries; by 1800 they made up some 10 per cent of the European population. Admittedly, most of them could not afford to spend their lives in a continuous *dolce far niente*, as did the leading nobles; yet they tried to emulate the aristocratic lifestyle by demonstrating as much leisure as they could afford to, and, moreover, by surrounding themselves with all the trappings of riches and power, with as many luxury goods as possible. Thus, the upper echelons of the bourgeoisie aped the example of the aristocracy precisely through 'conspicuous consumption'.[5]

Inevitably, there were those who condemned these developments. Many even voiced moral objections to increasing consumption as *luxuria*, a sin destroying harmony because it made people want to break the restrictions posed upon them by the Divine, by Nature and by Society. They maintained that all this luxury was but waste, turning people away from the real values of life and, hence, resulting in moral decadence. At least from the fifteenth century onwards, governments, mostly using moral arguments but also trying to preserve class boundaries and, thus, the traditional order of society, had repeatedly proclaimed so-called sumptuary laws, forbidding those of the middle and lower classes who were so inclined to indulge in the various forms of luxury. Bourgeois women were not to dress in costly velvets or furs, and the ever-longer tips of shoes, which sometimes had to be tied to the knee to prevent a man from tripping over them, were denied to non-noblemen; the number of attendants at funeral processions was regulated in accordance with one's position in society, and so was the number of chimneys that one's house could boast. Still, such laws were hardly ever successful, if only because many governments also found it expedient to incite their subjects to spend as much as possible, in order to profit from the taxes on production and consumption.[6]

Indeed, a clear-minded, non-moralizing philosopher like the Frenchman Voltaire, and a clear-minded, non-moralizing economic theorist like the Anglo-Dutchman Bernard Mandeville tried to counter the moral arguments. They argued that 'conspicuous consumption', though perhaps decadent from a moral point of view, nevertheless did contribute to economic and social progress; without this powerful stimulus, the European economy would have no motor, and Europe's progress would come to a standstill. Mandeville's was the most incisive comment. In his *Fable of the Bees: Private Vices and Public Benefits* (London 1714), which, essentially, is a debate on the morality of capitalism and consumerism, he showed that both the European economy and, in a specific sense at least, European society thrived on the unbridled spending of certain groups, even though people continued to condemn the way of life of the spendthrifts as utterly sinful.[7]

Production and reproduction: a process of economic and demographic change till the end of the eighteenth century

Well until the seventeenth century, in western Europe the 'normal' structure of the basic unit of social organization, the family, was not that of the so-called 'extended family' or clan, of several generations living together under the authority of a patriarch or matriarch; indeed, in this part of Europe such clans probably never were the common type of family at all, unlike in other regions of the world. Instead, the conjugal family was well established. When children married, they went to live by themselves, creating their own household. They might take in one or more of their parents or elderly relatives when advanced age made them unfit to provide and care for themselves anymore, and in this way the image of a three-generation household became common, but its nucleus was still the couple with its children.[8]

Outside the aristocracy, the one group in which marriage ties were often forged at an early age to secure the preservation of power and wealth for the next generation, people married rather late: well into adulthood, i.e. in their late twenties. Also, many persons never married at all. For marriage depended heavily on a future couple's possibility to support themselves; in Europe's largely agricultural society, this meant that both had to work before they could acquire a farm of their own. In trade and industry, too, people had to work for a long time before they were able to start their own business. As most boys and young men went out to work if not employed in the family business, so did the girls, even though their opportunities were fewer. By far the most common job for a girl was to serve in another household, whether in the country or in town. There, it has to be said, their plight often was not easy, what with beating and sexual attacks by their mistresses and masters. Normally, if they got pregnant, they had to leave the house. Often they had no alternative but to become a prostitute. They, as well as those who freely entered the profession, or were forced to do so by sheer destitution, account for the enormous amount of whores who populated the European cities, up to the many thousands in such capitals as London, Paris and Vienna.

Meanwhile, all kinds of sexual intercourse were practised both before and outside the marriage, as is shown by the many rules surrounding mating behaviour, reflected in all kinds of popular customs connected with courtship; these indicate a rather daunting measure of social control especially in this field. Although lawful wedlock was propagated both by the Churches and by the State, we certainly should not look upon this society as anything as sexually restricted and, indeed, priggish as a glance at the ideals developed and enforced in the nineteenth century might make us think it had been. Thus, for example, the sexual allusions used in the very popular catches of seventeenth- and eighteenth-century England were of the very broadest. Samuel Ives made his public sing along lustily on such texts as the following:

> Come pretty wenches more nimble than eels,
> and buy my fine boxes, my stones and my steels;
> let me touch but your tinder and you would admire
> how quickly my steel and my stones will give fire . . .
> take my steel in your hand, wench, and try but a blow:
> i'faith I dare warrant 'tis true touch and go.[9]

The sexual fulfilment of women, as well as of men, was openly discussed – a situation that would begin to change only by the end of the eighteenth century when, once more, the Churches undertook to make marriage the only venue for sex, and procreation its sole justification.

Once married, birth control was, if not uncommon, not very effective, due to the lack of foolproof contraceptive devices; the most common practice was *coitus interruptus*, the withdrawal of the penis before ejaculation. Abortion flourished, though the methods used were highly primitive and, consequently, the deathrate among the mothers appallingly high; it was, however, illegal and, moreover, condemned as a mortal sin, especially by the Churches.

While both Church and State tried to control marriage as the tie that bound the family as a moral and legal unit, they also tried to refrain especially the poor from marrying at all, as this would result in too many children being abandoned, too many paupers roaming and ravaging the countryside, and too much money being needed to spend on poor relief.

It is not unlikely that the pattern of marriage and family which characterized Europe during these centuries contributed to a mentality that differed considerably from the pattern common in other cultures. At least in western Europe, couples of mature men and women formed the essential basis of society, persons with a spirit of self-reliance and self-responsibility, that may have translated itself in forms of creativity both in the individual and in the community.

By the middle of the eighteenth century, a number of factors began to work together to effect profound demographic and resultingly cultural changes. A 'rural revolution' took place when the three-course system was abandoned and the farmers started working their entire property, expanding the yield through new systems of crop-rotation and the use of new fertilizers. In the same period, economic behaviour was influenced by the increased opportunities offered by the cottage industry and, later, of more complex forms of industrialization. Especially in the more industrialized regions, marriages were now concluded earlier and, what is more, no longer dictated only by economic reasons but by sentiment. However, the number of illegitimate children rose sharply as well, especially in the urban areas. This indicates a sexual, indeed, a cultural transformation, that ties in with the greater mobility of life in Europe in general and with the declining social control of closed communities in particular. It can also be explained from a general dissatisfaction with prevailing living conditions, against economic restrictions, against a society wherein legal separations divided the classes, against laws that forbade the poor to marry at all.

This coincided with an exceptionally long period of peace between 1763 and the end of the century, as well as with improving hygienic conditions – such things as the paving of streets and the collection of refuse were now introduced in the main towns of western Europe, and some of the more devastating illnesses finally found a cure as, for example, when smallpox vaccination was introduced in 1796. With the deathrate considerably reduced, these changes resulted in a new situation that has been stamped 'the demographic transition'.

Yet life expectancy of newly born children remained dismal. Infant mortality was still very high: one in five children died before its first birthday, mostly from infectious diseases. The practice of breast feeding – by the natural mother in the lower classes, by a wet nurse among the bourgeoisie and the aristocracy – did at least provide babies with a good diet. It also helped to reduce the birthrate, as it interfered with ovulation. Nevertheless, the practice of wet-nursing was, necessarily, a bad one. Not because of the commonly held belief, spread in many folk tales, that a woman employed to suckle a babe might change its character for the bad or even be inclined to kill the new-born left to her care to be able to take the money for another one, but because it was a business after all, and most children tended to receive less care than they needed.

While the Christian Church at a very early stage of its existence had declared criminal one of the common practices of Antiquity, infanticide, which was made punishable by death, people, mostly for economic reasons, continued to kill their offspring. Leaving children on the doorstep of a church was a less cruel solution, taken by numerous parents. The number of foundlings in a major city ran into many thousands a year. Mostly, either the Churches or, increasingly, private charities or the state began to take care of these children as well as of the many orphans, the result of the high deathrate among the adult population. Life inside these foundling hospitals and orphanages was less than healthy, for all their sometimes palatial external splendour, still visible in the huge buildings erected in London, Paris, Venice or Rome. Malnutrition, illnesses and only the most sketchy of medical care led to an appalling mortality in these institutions, especially in times of economic or political crisis in the outside world.

Children who survived faced a hard world. As to parental attitudes towards their children before the cult of the family became common in the bourgeois world of the nineteenth century, historians differ greatly in their judgement.[10] True, some of the visual evidence – especially the more intimate conversation pieces produced by Jan Steen and other Dutch painters of the seventeenth century, the 'Golden Age' of Dutch painting, or by that accomplished Frenchman Jean-Baptiste Chardin in the eighteenth century – seem to suggest harmonious family lives with well-fed infants playing contentedly with their toys or pet animals. Yet mostly, life for children in all socio-economic groups was emotionally harsh from a present-day point of view, even though their material circumstances could differ considerably.

A process of social and cultural change: the convergence of elites till the end of the eighteenth century

The growing influence of and interaction between the various means of communication, especially the printing press and travel, reinforced the cosmopolitan tendency which in the late fifteenth and in the sixteenth centuries was, on the one hand, observable in European court culture and, on the other hand, perceptible in the thinking of educated people, whose background in humanist education was now strengthened by the continual stimuli of contemporary culture. In a civilization process that, viewed chronologically, showed influences from Italian, Spanish and French court culture and the humanist culture which developed partly within and partly outside these circles, a distinct European elite culture had evolved.[11]

Yet well into the sixteenth century, the Europeans who participated in this culture – the 'great tradition' – still belonged to two socially rather separate groups. A more intellectual, scholarly elite, stemming increasingly from the middle class, from people who, partly through the professionalization of learning, sought to improve their position. And an elite which largely coincided with the property-owning nobility on the one hand and the 'bourgeois' urban patriciate on the other, together constituting an upper class which everywhere in Europe occupied leadership positions in society; its members did not look upon culture as a career opportunity but as an element of distinction, of status.

From the sixteenth century onwards, a complex integration took place. The 'court culture', lived in the milieux of king and nobility, inevitably also penetrated into other social milieux, especially the highest reaches of the well-to-do middle class. The 'notables' or 'patricians', who had been slowly gaining influence and wealth both in the service of the state – more specifically in state bureaucracy and the military – and in the free professions, as well as in trade and industry, came to form a distinct, largely urban elite.[12] Indeed, in the whole of western Europe this group began to play a more important role in society, both economically and politically. Yet socially and culturally it continued to reflect, at least in part, the norms and values of the traditional upper class, the nobility, assimilating many of that group's cultural expressions.

However, in the course of the sixteenth and seventeenth centuries, it emerged that the old aristocracy could no longer be the principal carrier of the 'new', bureaucratic, centralized states, which needed new means of power for the effective exercise of that power. The connection between growing state power and an economy increasingly tied to the state was reflected in the fact that both successful entrepreneurs and powerful government officials now mainly came from the middle class. As it became obvious that 'knowledge' actually meant 'power', it was mainly the well-off bourgeoisie which underpinned and consolidated its economic and political power and the social advancement associated with it through increased emphasis on education and knowledge. These were considered useful as well as 'dignified' because they were effective in helping to achieve position and wealth.

Thus, inevitably, members of the old aristocracy, too, realized that service to the state with its 'modern', bureaucratic-technical government was the means to maintain their economic, political and social position. For them, too, education, specialization even, became necessary. Culture, especially in the form of useful science, gained universal value.

One of the places where this process became visible were the 'salons' of seventeenth-century Paris; there, the sceptre more and more often was waved by daughters of the rich middle class who had been able to marry into the aristocracy on the strength of their dowries and who now received artists and scientists from the middle class in their homes, mixing them with the lords from the court nobility of Versailles.[13] Places where the process was visible as well were the innumerable courts in the German states; in a cosmopolitan milieu like eighteenth-century Weimar, on winter evenings the reigning duchess and her courtiers could be observed sitting at table with their learned advisers, among whom was Johann Wolfgang von Goethe – a commoner raised to the nobility, since the aristocracy remained, socially, the most desirable order – and with educated citizens from the town.

Slowly, middle-class norms and values started filtering through to the aristocracy who, in order to maintain their position economically and politically, increasingly took up people from other social groups; as a result, this group's composition, character and culture started changing. Even though the two groups never became completely one, they increasingly came to share a common lifestyle and a cosmopolitan attitude, on the basis of which the English politician and thinker Edmund Burke could observe at the end of the eighteenth century that 'No European can feel completely like an exile anywhere in Europe'.[14] But of course he was talking about an elite, about those who could read, write and travel.

Perhaps the collision as well as the fusion of aristocratic and bourgeois elite cultures can best be observed in the periodicals. In the first years, these principally aimed to further the 'correspondence' between scholars[15] or to help the economic-political elite to reach an informed opinion of the issues of the day. However, by the end of the seventeenth century, periodicals were published which intended to popularize all manner of information and know-ledge, also because, instead of employing the languages of the scholars, Latin and French, the vernacular was used: German, English, Dutch. A new reading public devoured such new periodicals as the 'European Library' or *Boekzaal van Europe*, which first appeared in the Dutch Republic in 1692.[16] The *Spectator* was influential both in and outside England from 1712, and the fascinating *Biedermann* was widely read in the German-speaking areas. In the eighteenth century, the number of journals increased spectacularly: in the German states alone there were approximately one thousand periodicals in 1780. In many of these one detects signs which indicate that people wanted to change or even abolish certain norms and traditions too closely associated with the old aristocracy. The *Spectator* fulminated against the waste of money and time displayed by the aristocracy, and *Biedermann* asked its readers whether children raised by servants instead of by their own mothers could ever become worthy citizens, referring, of course, to the absentee parenthood practised by the aristocracy.

Rather than listen to the elevated but to many unrealistic and outdated aristocratic conflicts between honour, love and duty articulated in the tragedies of seventeenth-century French playwrights like Pierre Corneille and Jean Racine and given musical expression in the allegorical and mythological operas of such eighteenth-century composers as André Campra and Jean-Philippe Rameau, people read novels that dealt with the vicissitudes of 'real' men and women in comfortable bourgeois households. By disseminating the principles of the happy family, of a sober, virtuous life, through education and reading, through utilitarian science, these weekly papers wanted to civilize society on the basis of middle-class rather than aristocratic values.[17] This 'civilizing offensive' was quite successful.

All over Europe, members of the bourgeoisie wished to search for knowledge, for truth, in a sociable way, that is, in a more or less closed group with other reasonable, well-educated people. Indeed, this was experienced as a road to virtue by more and more members not only of the affluent middle class but also of the aristocracy;[18] sociability in salon or café, or in a reading circle, if only to lighten the financial burden of the costs of reading material, became a characteristic of the cosmopolitan culture of the eighteenth-century European elites, though their behaviour often was very divergent on many other points.

The single most important factor in the process that shaped an increasingly dominant 'middle class' self-consciousness was, perhaps, the amount of volun-tary associations, in which the burghers started organizing themselves and where they talked freely, that is, irrespective of rank, wealth or even their legally circumscribed position in society. These associations became a kind of 'subscriber democracy'.[19] The many hundreds of clubs that were founded for all kinds of civic or cultural purposes soon developed into miniature civil societies, characterized by self-government through their constitutions, elections and representatives; constituting part of the growing power of bourgeois culture, they also became a hotbed of new ideas about social and political organization, and turned into the training ground for practices people now thought they might want to introduce in society at large, as well.[20]

Two 'revolutions': one political, one economic, both cultural

All over Europe, the control over political power always had been an issue that threatened the stability cherished by the rulers and the ruling elites alike.

In the seventeenth and eighteenth centuries, in many countries the inevitable reaction to the growing power of the princes and their top bureaucrats, which tended to emarginate the consultative role which had been claimed by the 'estates' since the twelfth century, took the form of constitutionalism. This certainly was not democracy in the present sense of representational government based on universal suffrage, in which the franchise, or right to vote, is given to all adults. Yet it was one more step in its direction. Many people experienced growing revulsion against the princes' claims to 'absolute' power – power that, theoretically at least, was not restricted by other laws than those made by the sovereigns themselves, and the general, 'natural' laws which God had instilled in his creation. They felt that there should be some balance of power, between government on the one hand, embodied in the sovereign, and the rights of subjects on the other, especially of those subjects who visibly contributed to the continued prosperity of the state, as did, to their own idea, the cities and, of course, the nobles.

In many states, exploring the limits of the balance between King and Country, factions tried to force the rulers to accept some kind of constitution that would bind them to laws made, preferably, by the representative assemblies rather than by the prince, only.

But where these assemblies became, in their turn, instruments of power coteries, other socio-economic groups, who had acquired power in new sectors of the economy and felt their stake in the state's economy warranted greater participation in its government, made themselves heard as well, sometimes aided by those of the older elites who were dissatisfied by the distribution of power. They tried to influence the balance, playing the ruling aristocracy against the sovereign. Consequently, as elites never were unified groups, others, primarily the wealthy representatives of the business and entrepreneurial classes in the European towns, manoeuvred themselves into positions allowing them to either establish their own power – with different results according to the economic and political situation in the various European polities – or, if this seemed politically more viable, to seek alliances with dissatisfied sections of the ruling elite and of the populace, expecting, of course, to hold the balance themselves. Thus, in several states a more broadly based political system was achieved. But changes came only slowly. Much depended on the willingness or necessity experienced by princes and ruling elites to alter the political and social system. Not everyone agreed that traditional society, largely organized along the lines of the 'three estates', was obsolete. Indeed, most monarchs only sought to increase their own power.

In England, the Stuart monarchs' bid for 'absolute' power in the seventeenth century was checked. Instrumental in this was an uneasy alliance between part of the nobility, who largely dominated the country's constituencies and, thus, the majority of the seats in the House of Lords and in the House of Commons, and part of the non-noble elite, both land-based and town-based, the latter the representatives of the influential banking and mercantile interests of the London City and other commercial towns.

In 1688, a *coup d'état* was staged, called the Glorious Revolution by the winners. Its importance lay in the fact that a new monarch was put on the throne – the Dutch stadholder William III of Orange – who, ruling with his wife Mary, the daughter of the deposed king, accepted a number of restrictions on royal authority, while the successful alliance accepted its responsibility for the state, mainly because in allowing government to tax their wealth they began to bear a considerable part of the increasingly burdensome state expenditure. The novelty and the advantages of this system were soon discussed all over Europe. One should realize, however, that post-1688 England was far from democratic. Indeed, the new political system was definitely oligarchic. However, the fusion of old and new elites did help to prevent serious social and political unrest for more than a century to come. Also, it assured considerable tolerance especially for those who held alternative religious opinions.

One who was influenced by the apparent advantages of the English situation and, consequently, wrote convincingly on the need to create a greater equilibrium between the various functions of the state *vis-à-vis* the citizen was the French nobleman Charles de Montesquieu (1689–1759). After having travelled extensively in various European countries, he published his *De l'esprit des lois* (1748). In it, he proposed that at least the powers of the judiciary should be separated from those of the legislature and the executive, to prevent the concentration of power in a few hands, as this would lead only to its corruption and abuse. His text was avidly read and commented upon in political circles in Europe as well as in the more liberal milieux of the English and even the Iberian colonies on the other side of the Atlantic Ocean.

A prince who did think that change was necessary and might even be possible without, perhaps, conceding too many of his own rights, was King Frederick II of Brandenburg-Prussia, who ruled from 1740 to 1786. He wanted to create a more modern, efficient state which could rely on the support of all its citizens, instead of precariously navigating between hostile socio-economic groups. He greatly favoured agricultural innovations and experiments, as witnessed by the introduction of the potato,[21] but also furthered the various branches of industry. As a fervent friend of Voltaire's – one of the most outspoken advocates of a more 'enlightened' society that would create equality of all before the law, a more rational, and humane system of criminal justice, etc. – the King decided to act accordingly. In 1740, he declared:

> His Royal Majesty in Prussia has, for weighty reasons, decided that in His States torture will be totally abolished in the Inquisition, except in cases of Crimen Laesae Majestatis and high treason, as well as in murder cases which involve the death of many people, and when it is deemed necessary to determine the accomplices of serious delinquents. In all other cases, criminals will be punished according to the law, after hearing the strongest possible evidence of reliable witnesses, even if they do not confess of their own free will.[22]

Frederick II also resolved to strongly punish those landowners and government officials who ill-treated the taxpayers – mostly farmers. In 1750 he wrote:

> As up till now various officials have ill-treated the farmers by having them beaten with sticks, and We cannot possibly tolerate such tyranny against Our subjects, We declare it to be Our will that when it can be proven that someone has beaten a farmer with a stick, he will immediately, and without any possibility of reprieve be imprisoned for six years, even if such an official were well in advance with paying the farm of his taxes.[23]

Noblemen and noblewomen who maltreated their servants were to be thus punished as well. But while things changed in England and Prussia, albeit in very different settings and with different intentions, it has to be admitted that few princes in western Europe entered into politics as enlightened and as forcefully as Frederick did.

In monarchic states like France, Spain and Sweden, but also in the Dutch Republic, to name but a few, traditional views lingered on considerably longer. That may have been one of the reasons why tensions built up, eventually exploding in revolutions of varying violence that created great upheaval in European society in the decades from 1770 onward.

The case of France must be cited specifically, not only because it represented to the full the economic, social and political problems that characterized most European states, but also because the revolution that was the answer to these problems greatly influenced developments elsewhere in Europe. In France, the clergy and the nobility, the first two of the three traditional estates, were 'privileged' if only in the sense that they paid little or no taxes, thus virtually refusing to help bear the financial burden of the state. The price they paid for this freedom was that, though individually they might rise to positions of great power, especially if they loyally served the King at Versailles, as a group they could not determine the course of government. Actually, the French kings retained the almost absolute authority they had won during the sixteenth and seventeenth centuries in their continuous struggles with the nobility, the Church and the towns. In the end, this situation proved the undoing of the *ancien régime*.

In the later decades of eighteenth century, it became obvious that France lacked a sound financial base, provided by a fiscal system that could tap the entire nation's wealth instead of mainly taxing the peasantry and the towns. In the 1780s, a grave financial crisis induced the advisers of King Louis XVI to suggest fundamental fiscal changes. The King let himself be persuaded but the nobility fiercely resisted. To be able to introduce reforms after all, Louis then felt forced to convene the States-General, the body of the representatives of the three orders that had not met since 1614. It was then that both the countryside and the townspeople rose to the opportunity to make themselves heard. Especially their leaders, who mainly hailed from the educated rural and urban middle classes, had been profoundly influenced by the often critical texts about the position of man in political society, and their trust in the words of authority as spoken by the state and, even more, the Church had greatly diminished.[24] Now, they demanded that the representative system be changed drastically. Instead of convening and voting in the estates which actually left out the great majority of the French people, general elections should be held, to result in a convention of true representatives, each with one vote, each voicing his own opinions according to his own responsibility to those who had elected him. These demands resulted, from 1789 onwards, in a veritable revolution, that in the following years took on a momentum of its own, resulting in fundamental political but soon also socio-economic changes.

The French Revolution articulated a number of principles in the form of a 'credo' that, with adaptations suiting other situations, did lead to a gradual restructuring of society in many countries of Europe in the period between 1790 and 1850. In these decades, all over western Europe slowly but inexorably the power of the old elites, the first and second 'estates', was broken, at least in its legally privileged sense. Slowly, in most countries every citizen – that is to say the educated, taxpaying male citizen – was given a vote and legal barriers between social classes were demolished. Thus, the process of individualization which had become increasingly manifest in thinking about man from the Renaissance onwards was now translated into the political, social and economic spheres, at least for the well-to-do male part of the population. Women, of whatever social class, had no such rights as yet – it would take a hundred years or more before the first states were ready to introduce female suffrage. Nor, it has to be added, did the revolutions help women acquire full legal rights in other fields; in most countries, their fathers and, if they married, their husbands continued to administer whatever property they might have well into the nineteenth century.

PARIS, 27 AUGUST 1789: THE CULTURAL IMPORTANCE OF THE 'DÉCLARATION DES DROITS DE L'HOMME ET DU CITOYEN'

On 27 August 1789, the members of the newly elected French *Assemblé Nationale* voted to adopt the so-called 'Declaration of the Rights of Man and

Plates 29 and 30 A broadsheet containing the 1789 'Declaration of the Rights of Man and the Citizen', with allegorical illustrations including God's all-seeing eye. One of the features of the 'new Europe', where the chains that had fettered man for so long and in so many ways had been finally broken, was its far greater freedom of movement. This, of course, was greatly boosted when the first railways were constructed. The first German railway, between Nuremberg and Fürth, was inaugurated in 1835
Source: Centre for Art Historical Documentation, Nijmegen, The Netherlands

Citizen'. Not only did they hope to end centuries of what they thought of as the oppression of the French people at the hands of the aristocrats, but also they hoped to rally all well-intended Frenchmen behind a new vision of society. The text of the declaration, though originating in a European and, moreover, very specific sociopolitical situation, presents man as the possessor of inalienable rights that still resound in any discussion about the relationship between state and individual from a democratic point of view. If only therefore, the Declaration is a major monument of European culture. It reads as follows:

> The representatives of the French people, organized in National Assembly, considering that ignorance, forgetfulness, or contempt of the rights of man are the sole causes of public misfortunes and of the corruption of governments, have resolved to set forth in a solemn declaration the natural, inalienable, and sacred rights of man, in order that such declaration, continually before all members of the social body, may be a perpetual reminder of their rights and duties; in order that the acts of the legislative power and those of the executive power may be constantly compared with the aim of every political institution and may accordingly be more respected; in order that the demands of the citizens, founded henceforth upon simple and incontestable principles, may always be directed towards the maintenance of the Constitution and the welfare of all.
>
> Accordingly, the National Assembly recognizes and proclaims, in the presence and under the auspices of the Supreme Being, the following rights of man and citizen:

> 1 Men are born and remain free and equal in rights; social distinctions may be based only upon general usefulness.
> 2 The aim of every political association is the preservation of the natural and inalienable rights of man; these rights are liberty, property, security, and resistance to oppression.
> 3 The source of all sovereignty resides essentially in the nation; no group, no individual may exercise authority not emanating expressly therefrom.
> 4 Liberty consists of the power to do whatever is not injurious to others; thus the enjoyment of the natural rights of every man has for its limits only those that assure other members of society the enjoyment of those same rights; such limits may be determined only by law.
> 5 The law has the right to forbid only actions which are injurious to society. Whatever is not forbidden by law may not be prevented, and no one may be constrained to do what it does not prescribe.
> 6 Law is the expression of the general will; all citizens have the right to concur personally, or through their representatives, in its formation; it must be the same for all, whether it protects or punishes. All citizens, being equal before it, are equally admissible to all public offices, positions, and employments, according to their capacity, and without other distinction than that of virtue and talents.
> 7 No man may be accused, arrested, or detained except in the cases determined by law, and according to the forms prescribed thereby. Whoever solicit, expedite, or execute arbitrary orders, or have them executed, must be

punished; but every citizen summoned or apprehended in pursuance of the law must obey immediately; he renders himself culpable by resistance.

8   The law is to establish only penalties that are absolutely and obviously necessary; and no one may be punished except by virtue of a law established and promulgated prior to the offence and legally applied.

9   Since every man is presumed innocent until declared guilty, if arrest be deemed indispensable, all unnecessary severity for securing the person of the accused must be severely repressed by law.

10 No one is to be disquieted because of his opinions, even religious, provided their manifestation does not disturb the public order established by law.

11 Free communication of ideas and opinions is one of the most precious of the rights of man. Consequently, every citizen may speak, write, and print freely, subject to responsibility for the abuse of such liberty in the cases determined by law.

12 The guarantee of the rights of man and citizen necessitates a public force; such a force, therefore, is instituted for the advantage of all and not for the particular benefit of those to whom it is entrusted.

13 For the maintenance of the public force and for the expenses of administration, a common tax is indispensable; it must be assessed equally on all citizens in proportion to their means.

14 Citizens have the right to ascertain, by themselves or through their representatives, the necessity of the public tax, to consent to it freely, to supervise its use, and to determine its quota, assessment, payment, and duration.

15 Society has the right to require of every public agent an accounting of his adminstration.

16 Every society in which the guarantee of rights is not assured or the separation of powers not determined has no constitution at all.

17 Since property is a sacred and inviolable right, no one may be deprived thereof unless a legally established public necessity obviously requires it, and upon condition of a just and previous indemnity.

In the course of the late eighteenth century, and with increasing speed during the early years of the nineteenth century, European society changed rapidly and drastically. Many of the traditional political, economic and social structures that had conditioned life in Europe for centuries now swiftly disappeared. For between 1750 and 1850, the political changes that culminated in the French Revolution and its successor movements had gone hand in hand with an equally fundamental Industrial Revolution. Together, they inaugurated a veritable and almost complete transformation of European culture.

Of course, one should not think of the Industrial Revolution as if, over night, a dramatic reversal occurred in the European economy. What actually happened was a very slow process wherein in some regions of Europe the existing, mainly agricultural communities turned into a mainly industrial society.[25]

The process had its roots in the beginnings of commercial capitalism and, therefore, was fundamentally related to Europe's ever-more important economic relations with Asia, the Americas and Africa. However, it was accelerated when agricultural prices started falling in the seventeenth century as related to industrial prices. Especially from the 1650s onwards, the demand for industrial goods increased and the cottage industry together with domestic commerce, rather than foreign trade, sustained an expansion of manufacture in those regions where people had easy access to markets: England, the Dutch Republic, northern France, parts of Germany and so on. It was a complex interaction between a supply creating its own demand and a demand-initiated growth process. Essentially, in these regions households changed their labour attitude, starting to specialize: men, but increasingly also women and children, filled a growing number of hours per day, and days per year with work instead of leisure; significantly, this was the period when the great number of Christian holidays was progressively reduced to raise the number of working days.

Self-exploitation as well as a marked rise in output per worker increased the household income and altered the demand pattern in the direction of manufacture. The growing money income was spent on consumption, on a market supplying both goods and services. This resulted in an 'industrial revolution' *avant la lettre*. It also resulted in a gradual and complex sociocultural change: more and more, women obtained a strategic position in the household economy, taking on the role of consumers, spending money on clothing and the home, in short on consumer goods.

The first country to properly industrialize was England. There, the surplus wealth created in agriculture, the cottage industry and trade during the early eighteenth century, sought an outlet in new investments. Also, the surplus labour that resulted from increased agricultural productivity because a smaller percentage of farm labourers was now sufficient to realize a greater yield, freed men and women for other kinds of work. If only because there were often not sufficient jobs in agriculture and the closely related industries any more, people became more mobile, moving to places where they could more easily earn their wage, even if this meant they were forced to work and live in miserable conditions.

Spinning and weaving, which had been part of the small-scale, agriculture-related industry for a very long time, now became increasingly profitable alternatives, especially so when various technical improvements were introduced, such as the fly shuttle that facilitated the operation of a loom, and the spinning jenny, a kind of mechanized spinning wheel. The revolution was made complete when, in the 1780s, Richard Arkwright started using the steam engine to drive his wheels. Soon, the new technology was applied in manufacture everywhere where fuel – especially coal – and infrastucture – especially water-ways – encouraged people to invest their money in factories: the Southern Netherlands and northern France, the Rhineland area of Germany and northern Italy.

These developments took several decades to mature and resulted in the Industrial Revolution proper, a mainly organizational and technological restructuring of production in the factory system. Its effects were to be deeply felt in the period *c.*1780–1830. Of course, coal and iron mining themselves, to answer a growing demand, expanded into large, mechanized industries as well, providing employment to many.

At the beginning of the nineteenth century, the cultural consequences of both revolutions, the political-legal and the industrial, began to really show themselves, first of all in their material aspects. A letter written in the 1830s by the German aristocrat Prince von Pückler-Muskau to his wife, in which he narrates the events of his trip through England, is quite revealing:

> Birmingham is one of the most prominent and at the same time most ugly towns of England. It numbers 120,000 inhabitants, two-thirds of whom must be factory workers; indeed, it looks like one huge workshop.
>
> Immediately after breakfast I went to the factory of Mr. Thomasson, our consul, the second largest as to size and extent; for the biggest, where a 1,000 labourers are at work each day and where a steam engine with a strength of eighty horses produces an infinite amount of products, including buttons and needles, has been hermetically closed to all foreigners since the visit of the Austrian prince (some of whose suite are told to have stolen some important secrets). Here, I spent a number of hours, albeit in horrible, filthy and smelling holes serving as work rooms, and was mighty interested; I even made a button. . . . On the ground floor, in the better rooms, all products made by the factory are exhibited: things made of gold, silver, bronze, sheffield plate, lacquer (which even surpasses the Chinese originals), steel of every sort, et cetera, to a number, and of an elegance which really astonish. . . . Here, I got to know a great number of new and pleasant luxuries, both small and big.[26]

In a nutshell, this letter summarizes many of the characteristics of the new industrial society and its culture. The increase in population which cities like Birmingham experienced was the result both of greatly improved hygiene and the discovery of simple but effective remedies against some of the most destructive illnesses; in turn, the population increase resulted in a rapid growth of the old towns, and in the foundation, in the industrially profitable areas, of new ones that fast became populous and wealthy, too. In these industrial centres, the factories settled their labourers, initially recruited from the mass of the agricultural poor but soon from the urban proletariat itself. The very different circumstances of town life and factory labour influenced the reproductive patterns of the industrial parts of European society; especially sexual mores became less strict and marriages were concluded earlier, now; this, in its turn, led not only to further population growth but also to different attitudes in the field of family relationships. The economic and social ties that had given cohesion to a mainly peasant society became loosened or were severed altogether.

Soon, many Europeans became the dependants of the machine that enslaved them within the horrible working conditions of the industrial centres, where new forms of solidarity were called for. Factory workers started organizing themselves in fraternities to plead their rights with the owners – if necessary enforcing these pleas with strikes. Both in England, that had the advantage of a quick start and, initially, drowned the continent with its products, and in other parts of industrialized Europe, people raised their voice in protest against the new developments, using both economic and socio-ethical arguments. The *Kölnische Zeitung* of 1818 published an article that argued along the following lines:

> A steam engine often renders a thousand people jobless, and brings the profit which otherwise would be divided between all labourers into the hands of one person. Each new perfection introduced into a machine robs new families of their daily bread; each new-built steam engine increases the number of beggars, and one may expect that soon all money will be in the hands of a few thousand families, and that the rest of the population will be begging to serve them.

Soon, people started to protest against what they saw as a huge plot to rob them of their labour, blaming the new machines for all evil in European society. Soon, too, new ideologies were being formulated, voicing the demands of those who now depended on the jobs provided by factories, precisely because working conditions were often dismal. Meanwhile, the market economy came to rely increasingly on technological progress. Industrial espionage developed as factories realized the importance of new inventions. Technical colleges were founded and laboratories established, funds were given and prizes offered. Indeed, the technical sciences gained an ever more central position in society and culture.

It was a culture that, for the first time in history, at least in its material aspects and, consequently, in its social outlook, began to level the differences between the various groups in European society, without, however, necessarily altering the real power balance between these groups. One of the most influential long-term consequences of industrialization was the production of ever more consumer goods, rightly described by Pückler-Muskau as luxury. The first ones to profit were the bourgeoisie: the industrial economy gave them not only wealth and power, but also numerous products that enhanced and facilitated life: all kinds of household goods and knick-knacks, patent medicines and preserved foodstuffs that contributed to their comfort; also the agricultural machinery that helped to provision their towns and the trains that brought them from their quiet, not-yet polluted residential neighbourhoods to their shops and offices, or to their holiday destinations; and, of course, the weaponry that helped them win the wars that ensured their colonial possessions, from which they extracted the raw materials for their factories and to which they exported part of their products. All this could be seen when, preceded and indeed inspired by a number of comparable, very successful French ventures, in 1851 the British government staged London's Great Exhibition, almost entirely a celebration of the machine age.

The steam-driven machine that caused both a significant reduction in production time, and thus in wages, and an enormous increase in production volume, soon resulted in a markedly wider distribution of consumer goods over the various income groups. Just as the invention of printing, through the cheap, mass produced texts, had resulted in the spreading of knowledge within groups previously denied access to it, the mechanization that allowed for mass production in all kinds of fields now made a wide range of cheap consumer goods available to an ever wider public.[27]

It was not long before the machine was able to execute a number of techniques that gave its products a highly refined appearance. Machines made furniture adorned with scrolls and flourishes closely resembling pieces made at far greater cost by the slow and judicious use of a hand-operated lathe; mass-produced pottery was artistically decorated with intricate patterns that were stencilled instead of painstakingly painted by hand; new chemical processes enabled the factories at Sheffield and Solingen to turn out cutlery and other luxury metalwork that resembled hand-made silverware in everything but its price. In short, many products had an aristocratic air, exuding status, and nevertheless were within the reach of many. Luxury was democratized.

Developments in other fields contributed to the process as well. Precisely because the political upheaval in France, preceded and followed by comparable changes elsewhere, was closely linked to, not to say caused by the Industrial Revolution – historians do not agree on this – the old society, which people now denounced as feudal, began to crumble. Most visibly, the old aristocracy had lost its constitutionally or otherwise legally guaranteed power. Although the right to vote was still restricted, being tied to a person's ability to pay taxes, with the advance of democracy, the way to the top and to power was now open to practically all. Not surprisingly, the great entrepreneurs, who dominated the mercantile and now also industrial economy, hastened to ensure that they would also dominate politics. Thus, once more, a new elite came into being. The older elites, desperately trying to hold on to their position, were now joined by a new upper class formed by these entrepreneurs: bankers, factory-, ship- and railway-owners, men engaged in international trade. As all of them tried to show off and enhance their new-found status, they followed the example set by the older elites: to demonstrate their wealth and their power and to acquire the social and cultural position that went with it, they surrounded themselves with its outward symbols, luxury consumer goods. The more luxury objects, manifestly useless, one could show, the more people would think, or know that one 'belonged' – as a personage in Oscar Wilde's novel *The Picture of Dorian Gray* (1891) says: 'We live in an age when unnecessary things are our only necessities'. But in other ways, too, this new, industrial elite aped the lifestyle of the older aristocracy – for, as the same Oscar Wilde told his readers: 'the middle classes are not modern'.[28]

For example, as one of the consequences of the sociopolitical revolutions, the master cuisiniers and couturiers who had worked for princely courts and aristocratic households had lost their patrons, and, if not exactly out of work, did feel the new situation in their purse. They now entered the market. Thus, one sees, at the beginning of the nineteenth century, the genesis of the fashionable restaurants and the great fashion shops; competing with one another for the favour of a new clientele, they offered the trappings of a luxurious lifestyle to a public that was quite willing to pay handsomely, but perhaps not as extravagantly as the old nobles had been. The food, the clothes, the furniture once reserved for the happy few could now be enjoyed by the new rich as well.

The revolutions also resulted in the abolition of the guilds, that were deemed to have imposed unacceptable restrictions on the free play of economic forces, limiting progress and continuing inequality. People were now free to establish their business wherever they wanted, and to engage in competition as best they could; thus, well-trained artisans vied with one another for customers, creating a new market, more free and less expensive than before; indeed, many products whose prices had once been kept artificially high now came within the reach of a far greater group of customers, consumers.

In the course of the nineteenth century, both through continuing industrialization and through the enormous increase of state bureaucracy, a considerable group of well-to-do families came into existence; through lack of inherited wealth, they could not aspire to the upper-class status of the old aristocracy, nor were they as wealthy as the new, industrial elite; nevertheless, through solid education and solid, well-salaried jobs, they came to form a distinct middle class.

This group increasingly adopted many elements from the lifestyle of those they considered their social superiors. Hence, the culture of the aristocracy that had been democratized by wealthy traders and entrepreneurs in the seventeenth and eighteenth centuries, and by the new industrialists in the early nineteenth century, now found an even broader diffusion among a growing middle class.

Urban, industrial culture: the regulation and consumption of time

Increasingly, the Industrial Revolution brought visible changes to Europe. Most visible were, perhaps, the consequences of the massive trek from the countryside to the towns, where a growing number of Europeans now came to live and work: Paris, for example, which had some 600,000 inhabitants at the end of the eighteenth century, grew to a population of 1 million in 1851, and of 2.7 million in 1900.

The French painter Eugène Delacroix (1798–1863) saw it all happening. He watched as numerous Frenchmen left their fields and villages to work in the factories and live in the towns. Describing the process in his diary, he painted a very gloomy, sometimes one-sided picture. Yet his concern was shared by many all over Europe; they too easily forgot that agrarian life was far from a rustic idyll and that many farmers followed the call to a new life simply because it seemed better than their present conditions could ever be. Indeed, most of these cultural commentators were intellectuals, who had never handled a spade. In 1853, Delacroix noted in his diary:

> Will steam stop before churches and cemeteries? And will the Frenchman, returning to his fatherland after some years, be reduced to asking where it was that his village stood, and where the grave of his forebears was? For villages will be useless as the rest: villagers are those who cultivate the soil, for they have to stay in the place where their care is required at every moment. It will be necessary to build cities big enough to harbour this workless and disinherited mass of people, who will no longer find anything to do in the fields; it will be necessary to construct for them immense barracks where they will lodge pell-mell. And when they are there, the Fleming beside the man from Marseilles, the man from Normandy besides the man from the Alsace, what will they have to do but read the quotations in the newspaper, not to see if, in their region, on their beloved fields, the harvest has been good, whether they can advantageously sell their wheat, their hay, or their grapes, but to see whether their stocks in the unanimous universal property are going up or down? They will have paper instead of land! They will go to the billiard-rooms to gamble with this paper against their unknown neighbours, different in customs and in speech. . . .
>
> O unworthy philanthropists! O philosophers without heart and without imagination. You think that man is a machine, like your other machines. You degrade him from his most sacred rights. . . . Instead of transforming the human race into a vile herd, let it retain its true heritage – its attachment, its devotion even to the soil. . . . And then, when new invasions of barbarians threaten what they still call their fatherland, they will rise with joy to defend it. They will not fight to defend the property of the machines. . . .
>
> Alas, poor peasants, poor villagers. . . . They are already abandoning the work of the field in haphazard fashion and with the most ill-founded hopes; they are rushing headlong into the cities, where nothing but disappointment awaits them . . . there, they complete the perversion of those feelings of dignity offered by the labour of love, and the more your machines feed them, the more they will become degraded! What a noble spectacle in this best of centuries – human cattle fattened by the philosophers.[29]

Quite obviously, Delacroix's fears concern the decline of the old, regional cultures with their agrarian economy, their separate customs and their own linguistic identity. It was a process of two worlds, the rural and the urban, finally merging through the joined influence of continuing industrialization and the cultural integration brought about by the nation-state, which, in its turn, would not have succeeded without the wealth brought by that very industrialization.[30]

In the process, both European culture and Europe's way of thinking were deeply changed. Many Europeans now traded a life in the country, conditioned by the static work in the fields, by the rhythm of day and night and the change of the seasons, for a job in town. It would be a job in a factory, or in one of the growing number of shops that catered to new consumer demands. Provided one had received some education, it might be an office job, one of many in the ever-growing bureaucracy that had to help the state to control this increasingly complex society. It might also be a job in one of the numerous affluent bourgeois households, for the middle classes, aping the aristocracy, hired more and more servants. A well-to-do family of five or six easily employed an equal number of staff, and the really wealthy would be surrounded by a multiple. In a town like London, around the year 1800 some 30 per cent of the population was made up of those who served in the houses of the richest citizens, who comprised less than 20 per cent. A very considerable part of these domestic servants would be unmarried young females, coming in from the rural areas.

The townspeople no longer reckoned their days from sunrise to sunset. The houses, the factories, the shops and the offices were artificially lit. Moreover, to remind people that time was money, clocks were introduced everywhere. In the towns, the biorythm of the Europeans started changing as the traditional sense of time slowly disappeared.[31] Soon, the clock reigned supreme, regulating work in both factories and offices, dictating the long hours – ten, eleven, twelve, far more than were ever worked on a farm – now put in by men, women and children under conditions that were, often, horrific. Women especially came to make up a huge, flexible workforce: underpaid, fired without any warning, they often had to leave their children, their ageing or sick parents and other relatives unattended to go out to work. For to survive in the city, everybody had to work, both harder and duller than in the country. Everything became routine, conditioned by the motions and the speed demanded by the clock-working machines.

The firm of Krupp, one of the oldest and biggest industrial groups of Germany, in 1838 set its workers the following rules:

> Each workman has to be faithful and unquestioningly loyal, behave himself decently both within and outside the factory, keep, exactly, the hours set for his task, and show by his diligence that he intends to work for the common good of the factory. In so acting, he may expect to be paid according to the value of his labour. Whosoever unintentionally or consciously forgets his duties, will be punished. Drinking spirits on the premises is not tolerated. Who spoils a piece of goods, or an instrument, will have to pay for it. Who arrives at the job 5 minutes after the bell has sounded, will lose ¼ day; who of his own desire stays away for ¼ day, will lose ½ day; for ½ day, ¾ will be subtracted from his wages, et cetera.[32]

Slowly, the outlook of the European towns changed. The division between rich and poor neighbourhoods became more visible than ever. The outskirts of most towns, like the northern fringe of Paris, became the areas of poverty, immorality and vice. Often, the police did not dare enter there when riots broke out. People living in these quarters were termed the 'dangerous classes'. For the well-to-do, propertied classes, a visit to these parts of town was like going into another world. Or, as a French politician claimed:

Plates 31 and 32 A view of the Krupp firm's factories at Essen, Germany, in a (coloured) engraving of *c*.1860. Living conditions in the industrial centres were often appalling. To many, the smog- and soot-covered slums of London, here depicted in one of the famous prints by the French artist Gustave Doré, from his *London, a Pilgrimage* (London 1872), came to symbolize this situation
Source: Centre for Art Historical Documentation, Nijmegen, The Netherlands

> Workers are outside political life, outside the city. They are the barbarians of modern society. They should enter this society, but be admitted to it only after passing through the novitiate of owning property.[33]

Property, of course, was the very thing most people did not have. And it was precisely the reason why that other world encroached upon the more affluent neighbourhoods as well, as witnessed by the huge numbers of beggars, and the many unlicensed prostitutes roaming the streets day and night; for prostitution greatly increased with the massive influx of labour from the provinces, with the poverty that prevented men and women to contract marriage, and with the need, for women, to make ends meet, or even to literally survive.[34] As in the eighteenth century, when a child was born, infanticide was an option. Of course, many women could not persuade themselves to that course. One of them said, presenting her baby to an orphanage:

> Why do I send this little child to the [foundling] hospital? Because I am without any resources . . . but I don't want him to be lost for good. . . . I beg you to have the kindness to keep him there, so I can see him again when I can, because I am not married.[35]

In most towns, for those who had little to spend on food, the diet was considerably less varied than in the country. Despite the hygienic and sanitary improvements of the late eighteenth century, illnesses increased, not only because of insufficient or bad nutrition, but also because of the insufficiency of other living conditions. In the nineteenth century, towns, especially the regional and national capitals and the industrial centres, evolved into a huge cluster of mostly filthy tenements where five, six or seven people often were packed into one small room totally lacking in sanitary conveniences; both outside and inside, everything was soaked in the soot produced by the coals that were the fuel of progress. The French artist Gustave Doré captured the soot-covered slums of nineteenth-century London in a series of harrowing images. The English novelist Charles Dickens evoked the misery of the poor who lived there. But though England was the first nation to fully show the effects of industrialization, all over Europe its consequences were experienced, providing inspiration to artists and writers, philosophers and politicians to reflect on both the positive and the negative aspects of this new world.

14 Progress and its discontents

Nationalism, economic growth
and the question of cultural
certainties

The revolutions and their aftermath

The industrial and the political revolutions had complex consequences, principally in western Europe, though changes made themselves felt in central and eastern Europe as well. Ideologically, conservatives and liberals in particular became the main opposition groups within the newly created constitutional, partly democratic political systems. The former, those who regretted the consequences of the revolutions in their entirety, preferred to see the old power structures maintained or restored as much as possible; they also advocated a vigorous government. The latter were of the view that social progress was best served by as free a play of the social forces as was possible, implying a reserved attitude of the government in economic, social and certainly cultural affairs.

Meanwhile, a third ideology opposed to both conservatism and liberalism increasingly came to the fore, that of socialism, most visibly born of the great European revolutions, principally the industrial one. But although its birth as a political force would not have occurred without the changes of the late eighteenth and early nineteenth centuries, its roots were much older, composed of such diverse strands as guild solidarity in the cities of the twelfth and thirteenth centuries, the growing individualism of Renaissance and Reformation culture, the organizational structures of the Enlightenment clubs and romantic notions of the value of labour and the artisan.[1]

Most socialists did not want to undo the recent political-economic changes but mainly wanted to combat what they saw as their negative consequences. The evident problems which large parts of the working population faced, required, in socialist opinion, a steering of society – through a government that would truly care for all its people – such that prosperity and welfare could be adequately guaranteed to each and everybody.[2]

In the 1820s, the French author and social critic Henri, count of Saint-Simon, provided an interesting mix of the three by arguing that:

> At the outset, I wish to state that the only way to bring sustenance to people is through employment. The government has to be controlled by the heads of industrial enterprises. These men are the true leaders of the people, whom they

direct in their daily labour. Therefore, directly and in their own interests, the heads of industrial enterprises will use their authority to expand business as much as possible. From this will result the greatest increase in economic activity, leading to larger employment.

Yet while there is a strongly paternalistic tendency in Saint-Simon's society, he apparently did hope for a mitigating – or only a disciplining? – influence when he wrote:

> I now come to another question. What is the best education for people, and in what ways should it be given? The education that people need most, and that will enable them to work best, should be based on the subjects of geometry, physics, chemistry, and hygiene . . . , incontestably the most useful as a preparation for life work. The scholars in the physical and mathematical sciences are the only ones fit to establish a good system of education.[3]

Of all the ideologies that were, more or less, elicited by the new, industrial society, Saint-Simon's has perhaps been the most prophetic as to the direction actually taken by western capitalism, especially in the late twentieth century.

Already in the decades during which Saint-Simon contemplated his world, the success of the 'modern' sciences, especially the success of technology and industrialization which for the first time in history proved able to offer many people a certain prosperity, greatly influenced culture and society. Due to the demands of the mechanization of industry, the nineteenth century brought an increasingly far-reaching division of labour; this contributed to the genesis of many parallel, but by and large separate sociocultural networks and thus ultimately furthered the advancing process of individualization. At the same time, standardization led to both the expansion and the internationalization of production. The consumer culture that developed increasingly crossed the borders of states, nations and their traditions, creating a first phase of 'globalization'.

However contradictory it may seem, the national state yet proved itself, even increasingly so, the most adequate framework for all these progressive developments. Nationalism was – and perhaps is – both a component of and a reaction to the 'processes of modernization' which the economic and political revolutions expressed, processes which should more appropriately be called 'processes of change', since both 'modernization' and 'progress' are to a large extent immeasurable phenomena, mainly moral and, thus, subjective categories.

On the one hand, old certainties were lost, on the other, a strong state was clearly an advantage in growing international competition. Hence, from the late eighteenth century onwards, cultural notions were increasingly linked with politics in an attempt to achieve a sense of identity and thus of unity that, soon, acquired rather extreme dimensions. Nationalism became an ideological instrument used not only to reconcile the disparate and often conflicting sociocultural elements and regional identities that made up the European states but also to buttress these states' expansionist politics.

The development of nationalism in late-eighteenth- and early-nineteenth-century Europe was greatly strengthened by Europe's recent experience of a supranational dictatorship. In the wake of the French Revolution of 1789, Napoleon Bonaparte had tried and for a short time succeeded to unite the whole of Europe, up to the borders of the tsarist empire, excepting, of course, the British isles; to do so, he had employed not only military means but also the same appeals to hegemony which in earlier centuries so many others had voiced: unity, even if that unity could be achieved only by force of arms, would prevent division and its destructive consequences. Admittedly, Napoleon's policy brought about a heightened awareness of common problems in and between various European countries. It also introduced or helped speed up a number of reforms of vital importance to the creation of a structured, economically free and legally more egalitarian society: legislative unification culminating in the famous Napoleonic Code (1804), the slow admittance, in great parts of continental Europe, of a metric system, of standard weights, of a standard coinage, in short, a number of structures which greatly facilitated the further development of the European economy as well as of sociopolitical change.[4]

Nevertheless, opposition to Napoleon's conquests arose in many states; in that opposition there was, from the political and propagandistic point of view, no room for the more idealistic arguments for European unity, for a culture presented as a European culture; after all, the dictator had used these very arguments. England, Sweden and, at a later stage, also the Netherlands and parts of southern Europe joined against Napoleon. And so did the many states which had been united since Charlemagne in the 'Holy Roman Empire of the German Nation', an empire which Napoleon had abolished.

In 1805, Napoleon had defeated the Prussians and imposed severe conditions on their country. In 1813, the Prussian king, Friedrich Wilhelm, decided to enter the alliance against the French emperor. In an impassioned pamphlet he appealed to his subjects to fight. In his words, the various cultural elements of nationalism can easily be recognized. The common past as well as the achievements which people had fought for earlier were put forward as arguments. However, at a closer look one may discern that those civilized and civilizing elements Europe for long had prided itself on culturally, were named as well, but now as characteristics of a national culture: freedom of conscience, industry and science stand beside honour and independence.

To my people

There is as little need to explain to My loyal people as to the Germans the causes of the war which is now beginning. They are clear for undeluded Europe to see. We succumbed to the superior power of France . . . The lifeblood of the country was sucked away, the principal fortresses remained occupied by the enemy, agriculture was crippled, as were the once-prosperous industries of our cities. Freedom of commerce was impeded, thus choking off the sources of profit and prosperity

... I hoped to make things easier for My people and finally convince the French emperor that it was to his own advantage to leave Prussia its independence. But my wholly innocent intentions were rendered useless by his arrogance and faithlessness . . . Brandenburgers, Prussians, Silesians, Pomeranians, Lithuanians! You know what you have endured for seven years, you know what tragic fate will be yours if we do not end with honour the fight which now begins. Remember the past, the Great Elector, the great Frederick. Keep in mind the benefits which our forefathers won under them in bloody battle: freedom of conscience, honour, independence, commerce, industry and science. Think of the great example of our mighty allies, the Russians; think of the Spaniards, the Portuguese. Even smaller nations have joined battle with mightier foes for such benefits and have triumphed. Remember the heroic Swiss and Dutch. . . . No matter what sacrifices may be demanded of individuals, they do not balance the holy boons for which we make them, for the sake of which we struggle and must triumph, if we do not wish to cease to be Prussians and Germans. . . . You will go forward boldly . . . because a Prussian and a German cannot live without honour. But we must have complete confidence: God and our firm will shall bring victory to our just cause, and with it a secure and glorious peace and the return of better times.

Friedrich Wilhelm, Breslau, March 17, 1813

The arguments offered by the Prussian king essentially were the same as the rhetoric used in other countries by those politicians who now posed as national leaders in the growing opposition to the French dictator. Sometimes, these leaders were the bodily or ideological heirs of the old princes, sometimes they were new arrivals who tried to cement their power with an appeal to old traditions, now increasingly presented as national values.

Elements of nationalism: the political culture of the nineteenth century

Even if the images which, at the end of the eighteenth century, began to give shape to a 'Europe of nations' were a limited selection from the wide-ranging cultural heritage, these inventions, as the earlier, more universal dreams, formed an ideology which, more than ever before, was propagated by all means possible by governments and ruling elites in order to advance solidarity. It was the nation which was now represented as a unique and essential unity, the living body of its citizens; its idea was consciously constructed by the state through a wide range of cultural manifestations that amounted to a deliberate policy.

All over Europe, traditions were 'invented' to give the citizen a feeling of a centuries-old solidarity.[5] All over Europe, history was rewritten or written anew from the point of view of the state as the natural structure in which the nation and the community expressed itself politically. This new past was then glorified by governments as a uniting factor by emphasizing the importance and results of commonly fought battles, the role of great men – rarely women – and the glorious feats of the past, now presented as a 'national' past of the nation's shared heroism. Everywhere, emphatically historicizing education programmes contributed to this end.

So did the arts. All over Europe splendid monuments arose, to celebrate the nation's greatness. In Rome, itself the outstanding monument to the past and present of a millennial Church with universal pretensions, the very nationalistic and anti-clerical Roman republic, the outcome of the Napoleonic conquest of Italy, decided that secular culture should be remembered as well. In the Pincio Gardens, on a terrace overlooking the old town, dozens and dozens of marble busts were placed, honouring Italy's great sons and, admittedly, a few of its daughters as well; the policy was continued when, after a temporary return to political division, Italy was finally united in the 1860s. The guide book to this 'remembrance park' was used as a prize gift in nineteenth-century Italian schools.[6] The Bavarian kings built a classical Greek temple on a ridge overlooking the Danube, yet calling it the Valhalla, after the heavenly seat of the ancient gods of the German tribes; thus indicating the dual inspiration of contemporary German culture, they filled it with monuments glorifying the great men of Germany. But old buildings and other places of historic interest, too, were now restored, as 'sites of memory';[7] they were made the object of secular pilgrimages, where the nation's past could be experienced as a living influence.

All over Europe, literature served the national ideal as well, in poems that evoked a past distant or recent, but always decidedly romanticized, in plays that re-enacted the great moments of the nation's history, and in a genre that was relatively new but particularly effective: the historical novel. Leo Tolstoy's monumental epic *War and Peace* (1863–9), referring to Russia's heroic battle against Napoleon, greatly helped to create a sense of the Russian nation's greatness through establishing its identity and destiny. In the person of the simple farmer-soldier Platon Karatayev, Tolstoy created the embodiment of the uncontaminated pure soul of the Russian people, whose example imbued the novel's noble protagonist, the aristocrat Pierre Bezuhov with a sense of individual and collective suffering that helped him gain spiritual freedom.

And, of course, one could create literary 'sites of memory', if only by cultivating the places where the literary giants who were identified with national culture had lived. The English had been doing so in the Shakespeare-cult staged at Stratford-upon-Avon since the middle of the eighteenth century, and in Germany, Goethe's Weimar became a place of pilgrimage. It was also possible to bring the literary heritage of the nation to the people's own homes, as witnessed by the decision of the publishing house of Macmillan to create its very successful *English Men of Letters* series in the 1870s; it was a veritable exercise in popular, national education,[8] as was, in a slightly more elitist way, the creation of the 'Pleiade'-series, the printed pantheon of the authors who were deemed to form the literary canon of France.

Last, but not least, all over Europe music was instrumental in inciting feelings of national pride, especially in the form of grand opera, both romantic and patriotic. In Brussels, in 1830, such an opera, *La Muette de Portici*, fuelled the already heated feelings of the 'Belgians' who were dissatisfied with Dutch rule; in due course, Belgium gained its independence as a nation from the

Netherlands. During the political fragmentation of the Italian peninsula, the very name of the composer Giuseppe Verdi (1813–1901) came to be a rallying cry for those seeking to finally abolish both feudal and clerical authority and create a unified, national state under a new king, 'Vittorio Emmanuele Re d'Italia' – the composer's name could be read as the King of Sardinia's acronym. In Germany, the musical dramas of Richard Wagner such as the famous *Nibelungen*-cycle evoked the image of a mythical, Germanic past that served as a stimulus for action in the present, too. Wagner hoped that the German people would flock to his new opera house on the green hill at Bayreuth and, like the Greeks of ancient Athens in their theatres, be incited by the message encoded and enacted in the drama they saw and heard and thus become better citizens of the German nation that soon would be a state as well.

For in this climate of nationalism, new states were born to give political expression to the expectations and hopes of peoples who, instigated by the rhetoric of political and cultural leaders alike, felt that a state that was a veritable unity, encapsulating all who spoke the same language and shared the same traditions, would be a guarantee for a better life. In the course of the nineteenth century, the numerous German principalities were united under the aegis of Brandenburg-Prussia, as was Italy under the aegis of Savoy-Piemonte. On the other hand, existing multicultural states, such as the old, far-flung Habsburg empire, increasingly felt the centrifugal power of nationalism which, in the early twentieth century, led to its final disbandment.

Frequently, in the process of nationalistic state formation, older, regional cultures were subordinated to and sometimes even violently forced to conform to the new ideal. All over Europe, language became an instrument of power that was used to help create the unity of the state. All over Europe, national governments attempted to make the populations within their country's borders speak the same language, a policy which often evoked outbursts of regional particularism. Regional cultures now became nationalized. For the time being, such peoples as the Irish, the Baltic and the Finnish lost their cultural autonomy. Cruel campaigns of Anglofication, Russification and Swedification superimposed the languages and frequently also the religions of the ruling elites on, or forcefully put them in the place of those who had not succeeded in retaining their power. Indeed, the terrible policy which came to be called 'ethnic cleansing' at the end of the twentieth century, really had started with such campaigns as the ones waged by the English against the catholics in Ireland from the times of Elizabeth I onwards until the nineteenth century. In consequence, all over Europe groups who were now put in the position of 'minorities' tended increasingly to cherish their own traditions. Secretly or openly they tried to defend their identity, defining it in cultural, including religious terms, as well as on ethnic and political grounds, but always with linguistic arguments, too.

The ultimate reason for these nationalizing campaigns was that unity was required to secure internal cohesion and peace, necessary to pursue well-founded foreign policies and to maintain a leading position in the increasingly

expanding world market. What states needed was a general feeling of community among the people that would support the rulers' claims to sovereignty and
the pretensions to power of those who led 'the nation'. Governability requires
controllability. It was assumed that controllability was most easily achieved if
a single system of norms and values were imposed on society. It was thought to
be even more effective if it caused people in such a community to feel that
those norms and values really formed their own specific identity, bound them
together, making them strong against everyone who presented himself as
an enemy – or who was presented to them as such. In the nineteenth century,
to a greater or lesser extent virtually all European powers were each other's
enemies, fighting for limited natural resources in order to make their
economies as strong as possible and thus buttress their positions of power. It is
one of the reasons why science, especially in its applied forms, interacting with
the advance of industrialization, became increasingly a pre-eminent manifestation of national culture, proudly presented as an expression of the national
'genius'. Thus, the great 'world exhibitions' such as the 1851 Londone one,
despite their stress on the 'universality' of industrial and technological progress,
were mainly windows for the display of national entries.[9]

New elites, new mechanisms of cultural diffusion, new manifestations of culture

The group which mainly carried the national ideology was described succinctly
by the nineteenth-century Hamburg publicist Johann Curio who wrote:

> Wir haben keinen Adel, keine Patrizier, keine Sklaven, ja selbst nicht einmal
> Untertanen. Alle wirklichen Hamburger kennen und haben nur einen einzigen
> Stand, den Stand eines Bürgers. Bürger sind wir alle, nicht mehr und nicht
> weniger.[10]

> We have no nobility, no patricians, no slaves, no, not even subjects. All real
> Hamburgers know and have only one class, the class of burghers. Citizens we are,
> nothing more and nothing less.

As a result of the economic and political changes, by the 1840s it was mainly
people from the affluent industrial and professional classes, partly new,
'self-made' men, partly descendants from the old urban notables, who pre-
dominated in many fields. Everywhere, their power grew, not only in the
financial-economic world but also in politics, even if only because officials who
kept the wheels of state running were increasingly recruited from their ranks;[11]
consequently, they began to control cultural life as well. The new elite was
formed, intellectually and, in a broader sense, culturally, within and through an
extensive and complex set of mechanisms of cultural diffusion.

States striving to achieve a heightened sense of national identity were helped
in their endeavour by better communication; the construction of roads and
railways facilitated the mobility of people who for ages had been tied to their

villages; increased migration as part of the process of industrialization was another factor, and so was the recruitment of soldiers from the remotest corners of the country and from the whole population to serve in a 'national' army.[12]

Yet it was principally the enormous growth of education that contributed to the spreading all sorts of ideas and traditions. To supply the needs of a growing technical-industrial economy, primary schools were founded on a grand scale and basic education was often made compulsory; consequently, the literacy rate in Europe quickly rose, although this varied greatly from country to country.[13] In the industrialized parts of Germany, the number of illiterate between 1870 and 1900 – measured among recruits for the army and among people who had to sign a marriage certificate – dropped from the remaining 2 per cent to nil. In a still largely rural Italy, the percentage dropped from a high 59 to 33 per cent, and among women, from 78 to 48 per cent.[14]

Education, especially at the secondary and tertiary levels, was now no longer limited to the old and new elites, but began to reach large sections of the moderately well-to-do middle class as well; yet it was still an education whose structure and content were largely based on the practices and concepts developed in the late fifteenth and early sixteenth centuries.

An authoritative 'educational philosopher' like the Englishman Matthew Arnold (1822–88) succinctly articulated the problem in his essay *Culture and Anarchy* (1869).[15] Arnold argued that good education is the basis of any society which claims the epithets 'civilized' and 'humane'. He wanted, first of all, to reform the public schools where boys from the well-off middle class and the aristocracy in England were educated. However, in his plans he referred explicitly to the situation in the German states.[16] There, Wilhelm von Humboldt (1776–1835) had voiced new ideas about secondary and tertiary education which, in his view, should be realized through deliberate, government-controlled policies, instead of, as was usual in nearly the whole of Europe, being left to the Church and other private institutions.

For Arnold, 'Hebraism' and 'Hellenism' were the two pillars of European culture. The 'desire for reason' attributed to the latter combined with 'the will of God' inherent in the former produced those forms of culture which were worth propagating: 'the best that is known and thought in the world'.[17] There was every reason to propagate precisely this culture for, as Arnold wrote in 1848: 'I see a wave of more than American vulgarity, moral, intellectual and social, preparing to break over us'.[18]

However, like Von Humboldt, Arnold noted a growing and dangerous divergence between 'the strictness of conscience' that Christianity imposed on European man and 'the spontaneity of consciousness' that classical antiquity had fostered. He wrote: 'neither of them is the law of human development, as their admirers are prone to make them; they are, each of them, contributions to human development'.[19] Yet, reading between the lines, his deepest inclination obviously was to Hellenism, or rather to 'the habit of fixing our mind upon the intelligible law of things . . . [that] makes us see that the only absolute good . . . is the progress towards perfection, – our own progress towards it and the progress of humanity'.[20]

For some of Arnold's critics, this cultural ideal smacked of paganism; moreover, for many it was definitely too elitist. Henry Sidgwick wrote that any culture worth propagating should:

> learn 'to call nothing common or unclean'. It can only propagate itself shedding the light of its sympathy liberally; by learning to love common people and common things, to feel common interests. Make people feel that their own poor life is ever so little beautiful and poetical; then they will begin to turn and seek after the treasures of beauty and poetry outside and above it.[21]

The influence of education was strongly reinforced by the culture of reading that was transformed by new techniques of printing and illustrating that made mass publishing far cheaper than before.[22] Since the end of the eighteenth century, all sizeable European cities boasted of reading rooms and lending libraries where newspapers, periodicals and books could be consulted. Yet, if one were to ask what the visitors of these establishments actually read, the answer, as far as it is possible to give one, is disappointing.

Analysis of inventories and loan records shows that in the eighteenth century relatively large numbers of informative, general publications were read but that, partly as a result of the censorship imposed all over Europe on these kinds of institutions in the years during and following the French Revolution in the whole of Europe, reading patterns changed in the early nineteenth century.[23] People still read many daily papers and periodicals but they mainly read novels.[24] The 'fiction industry', already in evidence at the end of the eighteenth century, now went to its first boom, precisely through an interaction between reading clubs and lending libraries;[25] when, in the course of the nineteenth century, general primary education became the norm in many European countries, this development continued to an even higher degree, especially when cheap magazines began to serialize the fiction both of hack writers and of more serious authors, influencing audiences hitherto unreached.

Novels, in so nationalistic a culture, often had as their theme their own society in the present or past. Yet novelists did not escape articulating, even if in a glorifying national context, the many Christian values that had been considered characteristic of Europe for so long and which, in the mean time, had been made middle-class and secular. Nor were novels entirely uncritical; indeed, they often vented opinions – be they popularized and 'filtered' – which had been expressed much more forcefully by cultural commentators but not heard by the general public, yet.

Meanwhile, the continuing disadvantaged position of women, economically, socially as well as politically, robbed culture and society of many positive influences. Even Alfred, Lord Tennyson (1809–92), Queen Victoria's 'bestselling' Poet Laureate, realized this. Admittedly, his very popular poetry, exalting the ideal of the middle-class family, contributed to the consolidation of male–female relations in which the woman was denied virtually every right and even feeling. Not allowed to vote or to enrol in university, largely restricted to their roles as wife and mother, and, hence, confined to the house, bourgeois women were increasingly dissatisfied. Yet society, and a cultural pattern that had been shaped over the past centuries and of which both women and men were prisoners, was not easily changed by the protests of a few courageous females, who were widely condemned as radical feminists and unwomenly women. Nevertheless, Tennyson at one time succumbed to the temptation to write a poem which not only made clear which spheres of cultural life women were excluded from but also in the introduction showed that he himself experienced the 'spirit' of his own time as restrictive and, hence, unproductive:

> At last
> She rose upon a wind of prophecy
> Dilating on the future: everywhere
> Two heads in council, two beside the hearth
> Two in the tangled business of the world,
> Two in the liberal offices of life,
> Two plummets dropt for one to sound the abyss
> Of science, and the secrets of the mind;
> Musician, painter, sculptor, critic, more;
> And everywhere the broad and bounteous Earth
> Should bear a double growth of those rare souls,
> Poets, whose thoughts enrich the blood of the world.[26]

Indeed, the early decades of the nineteenth century saw the coming of age of a new species, the female novelist. All over Europe, women took the opportunity which the medium of mass printing offered. Some of them did so to make a living on the basis of the new market; others enjoyed writing as an outlet for pent-up creative urges; often combining the two, some also used the novel to voice, hesitantly or radically, opinions about the position of women in an oppressively patriarchal society. Thus, the largely female readership of the greater part of the popular novels were slowly acquainted with new opinions on the relationship between men and women, which heralded the first step towards the movement that claimed liberty and equality for women. In England, Mary Ann Evans, writing as George Eliot, in her great novel *Middlemarch* (1872), explored the socio-economic and psychological boundaries which restricted both men and women.

Criticism of a society that was still essentially class-ridden emerged as well. The German novelist and journalist Theodore Fontane, for example, in the exquisite novel *Effie Briest* (1895), set in late-nineteenth-century Berlin and the surrounding Brandenburg countryside, painted a vivid portrait of the constraints which an aristocratic society set on its members, male and female alike; in France and Spain, Gustave Flaubert's *Madame Bovary* (1857) and Clarin's *La Reggenta* (1884) depicted life in provincial towns, where the customary power of the Church and the local notables stifled any expression of individual emotion that threatened the borders of propriety set by tradition.[27] Meanwhile, it is worth noting that three of the most famous novels about the situation of nineteenth-century women were written by men.

Another point of sociocultural criticism effectively expressed in novels concerned the threats posed to the poor by increasing industrialization. It was most eloquently voiced in England by Charles Dickens (1812–70), the more effectively because his stories were usually serialized in the periodicals first, thus reaching that part of the public which could not afford to buy his novels. Criticism did not fail to awaken the authorities to the need for actual social reforms.

Yet the danger of potentially more radical cultural changes, such as the growing significance of the machine for man, was taken less seriously. The unknown possibilities which, since the last decades of the eighteenth century, the sciences, especially mechanics and chemistry, had appeared to offer, had also revived fears about 'the mechanical human' in a stream of books.[28] Mary Godwin Shelley's gripping novel *Frankenstein, or The Modern Prometheus* (1817) is one of the most important works in the genre precisely because she shows to which extent man, the maker of machines, can always choose to use them for his own good or evil. Towards the end of the first 'machine age', the English novelist Samuel Butler (1835–1902) published his satire *Erewhon* (1872), in which he contrasted the England of his time with a society which had consciously distanced itself from all sorts of 'modern' conveniences precisely because of fear of the machine, noting that:

> The largest machines will probably greatly diminish in size. . . . a day will come when . . . its language shall have developed from the cry of animals to a speech as intricate as our own . . . Man's very soul is due to the machines.[29]

The characters in Butler's novel articulate a perennial fear – the stronger because at the same time it voiced a desire? – which already had been expressed in the Roman version of the Greek Prometheus story, in which the hero, breathing life into a clay figure and, thus, god-like, making life out of inane matter, subsequently loses control over it. The central question was, of course, the extent to which man could and should interfere in the process of creation.

The new 'bourgeois' elite, frequently educated within the culture outlined above, had yet been raised in more limited financial and cultural circumstances than the earlier, aristocratic elite. Moreover, they were firmly persuaded that their power and prosperity were principally bound to the destiny of their own national economy. Had they not been prepared to sacrifice money and life for their country, for example in the fight against Napoleon? Had they not subsequently forged a closer bond between nation and state because they had made a case for some form of popular representation? And was this process, which in many west European states had created at least the formal framework for democracy, not proof that they, these nations, Europe, essentially distinguished themselves from the greater part of the world, politically, institutionally, morally even? The German novelist Gustav Freytag depicted the new society, with its civic-national values and aspirations in his famous novel *Soll und Haben* (Assets and Liabilities) (1855), in which he pitted the bourgeoisie, educated, thrifty, idealistic, concerned both about its own prosperity and the nation's progress, against a self-seeking aristocracy, and against the financial manipulations of Jewish bankers; for like so many other European novelists, he, too, openly voiced the growing, increasingly virulent anti-semitism of the age, a sentiment that was certainly not tempered by growing nationalism and even expressed itself in the construction of global Jewish conspiracies. While in Freytag's novel the latter groups lost out, the former, of course, triumphed.[30]

This atmosphere of triumphant middle-class nationalism seemed almost to suffocate a more Europe-centred spirit, precisely because nationalist thinking was so closely intertwined with the radical economic changes which had started to reshape large parts of Europe since the end of the eighteenth century. Even among the traditional elites the old cultural ideal – the dream of Europe – largely disappeared. By now, these elites, too, had to identify as much as possible with their own state and nation. Following the expansive growth of the European economy in the Industrial Revolution and in world-wide imperialism, following the political and social changes which the revolutions of the last decades of the eighteenth century had brought, these elites were no longer the same as they had been for centuries. According to many historians, the beginnings of a cosmopolitan culture, felt and experienced all over Europe at royal courts and in the residences of the aristocracy, had slowly disappeared; or, one should rather say, it been translated by the new power groups in society, into forms which could be more nationally experienced.

Of course, artists and scholars continued to read, write and travel, and many individual members of this principally intellectual part of the elite still cherished a sense of community. Yet two phenomena began to undermine this cosmopolitanism. On the one hand, from the end of the eighteenth century, but certainly during the nineteenth century, the study and dissemination of classical culture increasingly became the domain of a professional class of 'career intellectuals' who gradually ensconced themselves in the ivory towers of universities and other academic institutions: the 'demolition' of the influence of the classical heritage in European society in a broad sense had begun.[31] On the other hand, most of those who were now, for the first time, able to look over their own fences and who did so by travelling and reading – the solid, proud bourgeois – frequently did so from another mentality than the Grand Tour-travellers of earlier times.

Admittedly, the new elite continued to look upon Mediterranean Europe as the region of classical culture. They travelled to Italy, which became a unified state in 1861. They also travelled to Greece, which in the mean time had fought itself free of Turkish domination – helped by cultural enthusiasts from all over Europe as well as by European governments who wanted to increase their economic and political influence in the Ottoman provinces of the eastern Mediterranean – and now entered Europe's sphere of influence. But Europe's upper middle class no longer journeyed *en masse* to German universities or to the French court, with the aim of ending their trip and completing their education in Italy, and of turning themselves into members of a cosmopolitan elite whose representatives, recognizable across state borders by their common behaviour, shared certain norms and values. Increasingly, most of those who now went abroad did so only for pleasure, to enjoy themselves, preferably in an atmosphere in which an exotic landscape and a pleasant climate coincided with an interesting, status-enhancing cultural experience. The 'Grand Tour' was giving way to consumer tourism, for which the middle class's increased prosperity created the economic conditions. Improved means of transport – the steamship, the train – made it technically possible. And the cultural context made it into a mental, psychological imperative. Indeed, travelling or taking a holiday became fashionable and, as a result, quickly a necessity as well, for a much bigger group than ever before – a group also that, inevitably, had different wishes and expectations.

Details for a reconstruction of the new mentality are supplied by newspaper articles and propaganda material supplied by the first travel organizations and travel guides like the German *Baedekers* and the English *Murray's*, which were written for the incipient mass tourism of the 1830s and 1840s; they seem to aim at a group who, despite their education, had a different attitude towards culture and towards Europe. Equally fascinating are the many travel stories for which special magazines were created; a good example is the magazine *Le Tour du Monde* (Around the Earth), which was translated into many languages and eagerly read by the bourgeoisie. Both the travel guides and these illustrated periodicals covered not only the exotic parts of the non-European world but also Europe itself, which was now represented as a region made up of different, national cultures. As most travellers were west Europeans, their views of central and eastern Europe are particularly revealing. There was a marked increase in the interest in Russia; but inasmuch as the world outside the imperial capital, St Petersburg, did not resemble the changed – meaning technologically and politically improved – conditions in western Europe, 'at home', most travellers and commentators tended to negatively judge the tsarist empire as part of 'barbaric' Asia rather than of 'civilized' Europe.

Searching such sources for the prevailing concepts of culture, national or European, one must conclude that the 'sense of Europe' was little developed. Indeed, they point to what was perhaps a growing gap between 'us' and the 'others', even within Europe, resulting by and large from the nationalism which now formed most people's political and cultural context, determining their thoughts and actions.

The predominant feeling among most educated Europeans was a fascination with their own nation's past, which was glorified in literature and the visual arts and all remains of which were cherished. The centuries which at first had been denigratingly described as the 'Middle Ages', the period between the end of the classical world in the fifth century and its 'rebirth' in the fifteenth, were now glorified: after all, it was precisely in those ages that most of Europe's nations had set their first steps on the road towards the formation of the sovereign, territorial states which now, in the nineteenth century, gave them such power and glory.

Already at the end of the eighteenth century, the German poet Friedrich von Hardenberg (1772–1801), better known as Novalis, had proclaimed that the ghost of nationalism and the horror of revolution would disappear only if Europe once more drank from the source from which the inspiration for unity and civilization had once come, Christianity. However, though Novalis's mystic poetry was much admired, he did not find a large audience with his impressive and impassionate essay *Die Christenheit oder Europa* (Christendom or Europe) (1799). He preached a message of an all-encompassing humanity, based on democracy and the fruitful interaction between nature – mastered for man's progress by science and technology – and culture, as a system of values inspiring man's actions; thus he hoped to bridge the fundamentally threatening gap between an all too elitist humanistic vision of culture and an all too populist mechanistic, physical world-view. He also hoped to undo the results of a narrow-minded Eurocentrism. While Novalis certainly did not lapse into shallow cultural relativism and even less in reactionary traditionalism – he was far from preaching a romantic-medieval Christianity – his ideas were misunderstood, wilfully or not, by many,[32] and not surprisingly so. After all, the nations of Europe, instead of searching for unity, continued to struggle for hegemony.

Plates 33 and 34 While many Europeans eagerly entered the 'age of consumption', symbolized by the new phenomenon of the great department stores, such as the Parisian Au Bon Marché, here depicted as it was *c.*1870, others harked back to times they thought more ennobling. Around 1800, the painter Tischbein had shown the German poet J.W. von Goethe wistfully contemplating the Roman countryside, with its ruins of ancient grandeur. (Städelsches Kunstinstitut, Frankfurt). All during the nineteenth century, Europeans would travel south in Goethe's wake, trying, nostalgically, to recapture the greatness of Europe's past – while, of course, glad that the new technologies enabled them to travel in much greater comfort
Sources: Centre for Art Historical Documentation, Nijmegen, The Netherlands and Städelsches Kunstinstitut, Frankfurt, Germany

BASLE, THE MIDDLE OF THE NINETEENTH CENTURY: JACOB
BURCKHARDT (1818–97) CRITICIZES CONTEMPORARY CULTURE

Ever wider grew the gap between those who gloried in the measurability of nature, in the 'makeableness' of everything that man could need, and those who maintained that this could not be the only, and certainly not the ultimate, concern of man. The Swiss historian Jakob Burckhardt became famous all over Europe with his masterly analysis of the culture of the Renaissance. In his *Die Kultur der Renaissance in Italien* (1860) he virtually created the image of that period for many generations to come. However, his vision of the Renaissance was a highly positive one; indeed, perhaps a too positive one, not least, one suspects, because in representing the past in a way suited to his feelings about the present this 'aristocrat of the mind' tried to find some sort of spiritual refuge from the many unpleasant aspects which he discovered in his own society and culture. Some fifty years later, the famous Dutch historian Johan Huizinga fell for the same temptation with his powerful but equally one-sided recreation of the later Middle Ages.

Burckhardt's private opinions – some of them clearly dated, some of them still relevant, most of them fascinating – can be gleaned from his many letters. He was writing to his friend Hermann Schauenburg in the fateful years 1848 and 1849, when revolutions occurred all over Europe because the new elites wanted more power and asked for more democratic rights for themselves, while the common people sought and hoped for improvement of their wretched living conditions in industrial society. These were also the years wherein Karl Marx's *Communist Manifesto* (1848) was widely read and discussed. Burckhardt, betraying the continued fascination with the classical cultures of the Mediterranean that characterized Europe's intellectuals, noted:

> I think I can detect a look of silent reproach in your eyes, because I am off so light-heartedly in search of southern debauchery, in the form of art and antiquity, while in Poland everything is going to pieces and the messengers of the Socialist Day of Judgement are at the gates. Good heavens, I can't after all alter things, and before universal barbarism breaks in (and for the moment I can foresee nothing else) I want to debauch myself with a real eyeful of aristocratic culture, so that, when the social revolution has exhausted itself for the moment, I shall be able to take an active part in the inevitable restoration . . . Just you wait and you will see the sort of spirits that are going to rise out of the ground during the next twenty years! Those that now hop about in front of the curtain, the communist poets and painters and their like, are mere *bajazzi* [clowns, PR], just preparing the public. You none of you know as yet what the people are, and how easily they turn into a barbarian horde . . . We may all perish; but at least I want to discover the interest for which I am to perish, namely, the old culture of Europe. . .
>
> I hope for nothing from the future . . . for I am of the opinion that democrats and proletarians, even though they make most furious efforts, will have to yield to an increasingly violent despotism, for our charming century is made for anything rather than for real democracy.

Some twenty years later, when, in the 1870s, Europe was, indeed, once more in turmoil as a result of the terrible war between France and Germany, Burckhardt wrote to his friend Friedrich von Preen:

> The two great intellectual peoples of the continent are in the process of completely sloughing their culture, and a quite enormous amount of all that delighted and interested a man before 1870 will hardly touch the man of 1871. . . . The worst of all is not the present war, but the era of wars upon which we have entered, and to this the new mentality will have to adapt itself. O, how much the cultured will have to throw overboard as a spiritual luxury that they have come

to love! And how very different from us the coming generation will be. . . . Anything that has to live on must contain a goodly portion of the eternal. And if anything lasting is to be created, it can only be through an overwhelmingly powerful effort of real poetry. To me, as a teacher of history, a very curious phenomenon has become clear: the sudden devaluation of all mere 'events' in the past. From now on in my lectures, I shall only emphasize cultural history . . .

Those who arranged those things [i.e. the Franco-German war] could all read, write and even compose newspaper articles and other literature. And the ones in Germany . . . are no less educated. But just look at England, bursting with wealth, and secretly kept in a state of siege by analogous elements! Up till now, for two hundred years, people in England have imagined that every problem could be solved through freedom, and that one could let opposites correct one another in the free interplay of argument. But what now? The great harm was begun in the last century, mainly through Rousseau, with his doctrine of the goodness of human nature. Out of this, plebs and educated alike distilled the doctrine of the golden age that was to come quite infallibly, provided people were left alone. The result, as every child knows, was the complete disintegration of the idea of authority in the heads of mortals, whereupon, of course, we periodically fall victim to sheer power. In the meanwhile, the idea of the natural goodness of man had turned, among the intelligent strata of Europe, into the idea of progress, i.e., undisturbed money-making and modern comforts, with philanthropy as a sop to conscience. . . . The only conceivable salvation would be for this insane optimism, in great and small, to disappear from people's brains. But then our present-day Christianity is not equal to the task; it has gone in for and it got mixed up with optimism for the last two hundred years. . . .

One of the principal phenomena which you emphasize reveals itself as clearly as can be in Switzerland: a flight from the risks of business into the arms of the salary-paying state is manifest in the fact that the moment farming is in a bad way the numbers who want to enter classes for teachers increases. But where on earth is it to end . . . Here in Basel we are now faced again with disbursements of two millions for new schools buildings! It's a single chain of related facts: free instruction, compulsory education, a maximum of thirty per class, a minimum of so and so many cubic metres per child, too many subjects taught, teachers obliged to have a superficial knowledge of too many subjects, etc. And, naturally, as a result: everyone dissatisfied with everything, a scramble for higher positions, which are of course very limited in number. Not to mention the absolutely insane insistence upon scholarship that goes on in girls' schools. . . . It may even be that the present educational system has reached its peak, and is approaching its decline.[33]

Inevitably, all over Europe urban life became more complicated, an assault on man's senses: the crowdedness and filth of the smog-infested cities, where proper sewage systems were often lacking, which meant that such epidemics as cholera claimed huge numbers of victims because of the mingling of human waste with drinking water; the rampant prostitution and the consequent effects of venereal disease; the insecurity of the job market and the sense of a society constantly changing and on the move.[34]

By the end of the nineteenth century, in the more industrialized regions of Europe, the elite's well-informed self-interest slowly, indeed, very slowly, resulted in improved working conditions in the factories as well as in better housing. Also, both the hospital and the medical service were now reorganized and extended. Large-scale vaccination campaigns were launched against such epidemic diseases as smallpox; initially, they aroused emotional, political and religious reactions revealing the widespread revulsion against the ways government and science increasingly invaded man's private life; indeed, it must be admitted that such policies did contribute to the growth of the power both of governments and of the medical profession, while, in retrospect, the health effects of the campaigns were debatable.

Some kinds of insurance against illness, accidents and old age were introduced, in Germany already as early as the end of the nineteenth century. This and other, related, developments marked the final transformation of a society based on charity as a voluntary act to a 'social state', where the right to a minimal level of material comfort was guaranteed to every citizen. It was, perhaps, the major development which, at that time, came to distinguish European societies from those in the other worlds.[35] Of course, the industrial elite did not always decide upon these changes of their own volition. Indeed, the influence of the labour movement on the process should not be underestimated.[36]

One of the results of industrial action was that holidays were introduced for the labouring classes – a few days a year. People started to save some of their hard-earned money for an outing. They wanted to leave the overcrowded towns for the fresh air, deemed beneficial even if taken only for those few days. Fresh air became a symbol of escape from real and imagined illnesses, caused not only by the filth of factory towns and the terribly unhygienic living conditions, but also by stress, although the word had not yet been invented. Increasing numbers travelled to the mountains or the seaside.[37] Only those who were better off could afford to be pampered by doctors and nurses in health resorts, mostly watering places that offered cures for each and every disease: Europe is still dotted with spas, the monuments to a bourgeois society's concern with its illnesses, real and imagined.

A new, far more positive sense of nature developed, in which the erstwhile disdain for and fear of the countryside as something wild, untamed and uncontrollable was replaced by the feeling that only here the real life could still be lived, that only here man's real inspiration for great deeds could be gained.[38] It was a notion especially made visible in landscape painting, which now presented man in the context of a sublime nature. Among the more daring and artistic, walking holidays, unheard of till that time and still looked upon with amazement by the working classes, became fashionable.

Even though for most Europeans a real vacation was still limited to one or two day-trips a year, the more affluent citizens already took their holidays for two or three weeks. It was the wheel that turned this leisure revolution: both the wheels of the steam train, which permitted mass travel over long distances from the 1840s onwards and, by the end of the nineteenth century, the introduction of a safe and manageable bicycle which gave people greater mobility within their more immediate surroundings.

Everywhere, people came to think of leisure as both a symbol of status and a necessity of life: from the end of the eighteenth century onwards, consumer demands and the consumption pattern more and more came to turn around free time, a commodity both scarce and expensive. The more leisure one was able to show, the more one moved away from the working poor, the lowest group on the social scale.[39]

However, leisure time had to be filled and even regulated. If people became bored, they would only be tempted to start drinking or indulge in promiscuous sexuality or in wild games, all of which would lead to social unrest and chaos, specifically among the working classes: the culture of the people meant disorder. That, at least, was the reasoning of the mainly bourgeois political and social leaders who now controlled Europe's cities.[40] This resulted in a number of new cultural phenomena.

The well-to-do citizens – the men but also their wives, who were considered the natural keepers of civilized life – began to stage all kinds of activities to civilize and discipline the 'lower classes'. Temperance societies were formed to combat the demon of drink. Cookery classes taught women from these lower classes to be proper housewives according to the bourgeois model; it would help them to provide a welcoming home both for their husbands, who would be less inclined to go from the factory directly to the pub and drown their hard-earned wages in drink, and for their children, who would be reared in more congenial surroundings, and be taught to be proper citizens.

Obviously, all these activities were meant to help to keep a tight rein on the large group of underpaid labourers who were suspected of the most shocking behaviour, which made them a potential danger both to the social and the political order. In 1825, the Prefect of the Rhône department wrote:

> I learned that men and women were sitting around a table in a separate upper room and . . . said indecent things and sang songs no less obscene. At dessert, everyone undressed completely. Paired off in couples, they proceeded to simulate the ceremony of marriage. One of them dressed in certain derisive garments . . . and married a couple in a parody of the religious ceremony of the Church. After . . . a sermon, the couple went into an adjacent room to consummate 'their marriage'. Afterwards they returned to wipe each other off. These ceremonies, as shocking as they are sacrilegious, continued as many times as there were couples to be joined in this scandalous manner.[41]

Concern for such and other forms of disorderly and indecent behaviour led civil and ecclesiastical authorities to collaborate in the transformation of all kinds of traditional popular pastimes. Thus, they tackled the phenomenon of the annual fairs and carnivals, which, according to bourgeois observers, always occasioned public drunkenness and, worse, the open manifestation of sexual acts; particularly these two phenomena were felt to destabilize the family bond, the basic value of order that authorities held in high esteem. Therefore, sometimes such manifestations as fairs and kermisses were banned completely, as was the case in many Dutch towns at the end of the nineteenth century. Often, however, the 'pillars of society', recognizing the need for popular relaxation, sought to give these feasts another, more controllable slant, focusing on religious processions and on such elevating activities as amateur theatricals, musical contests, flower shows and so on.[42]

Hence, also, the importance which was now attached to organized sports. They, too, could help to keep this 'mob' from the streets and out of the pubs where they would only create mischief. Moreover, participating in sports would imbue them with team spirit and, generally, incline them to a healthy way of living and thinking. The nineteenth century being the 'age of nationalism', celebrating the glory of 'King and Country', of *la Patrie* or of the *Vaterland*, in most countries the State, aided by the Churches, demanded the obedience of its subjects, if necessary to the point that they would be willing to give their lives for it. Social discipline was considered a basic civic virtue – and sport an excellent means to that end. Soccer especially soon became popular, not least among factory workers. Yet the game soon turned into an outlet for all kinds of suppressed aggression. Berlin's most authoritative newspaper around the turn of the century, the *Vossische Zeitung*, warningly writing on the situation in Britain, reported on 23 April 1895:

> The losses of the football season 1894/5 during the past six months already amount to no less than 20 people killed, as well as several hundred badly wounded. However, it seems that only 10 per cent of the actual mishaps has been reported.
> . . .
>
> Quite deplorable is the custom, increasingly normal, to attack the umpire with bricks and iron bars when his decisions elicit the anger of the competing teams. Often, the public readily joins in, which means that the police, who are present at each match, cannot restore order. I know of English firms whose employees, on being hired, have to promise not to spend their leisure time playing football, as the number of accidents after the matches prevents the regular conduct of business.[43]

The more well-to-do enjoyed sports as well, but more often than not these were not the same ones as those played by the labouring poor. Like all forms of culture, sports, too, have a specific status and specific cultural value. In the eighteenth century, boxing was, to a certain extent, an elite sport, because aristocrats enjoyed watching it, often employing the contestants and at times even joining in themselves; in the nineteenth century, it became one of the common sports. In the first decades of the nineteenth century, football was an elite sport, mainly played by the boys of English public – i.e. private, elite – schools; at the end of the century, it became another common sport. In the first decades of the twentieth century, tennis was an elite sport, but after the Second World War, 'everybody' entered the courts.

In the fast changing industrial society, the status of cultural forms changed equally fast, with the various social groups trying to find new ways of distinguishing themselves as older forms of culture were appropriated by other groups. Indeed, all forms of culture that filled the free hours of the nineteenth century provided status and showed differences of status.

Factory workers and other blue-collar people flocked to those theatres which, besides offering music hall and vaudeville with bawdy songs and risqué scenes, provided the highly popular melodramas, packed with emotional conflicts in often improbable intrigues and with often equally improbable happy endings, that were judged sentimental and, worse, even morally corrupting by the bourgeoisie who were highly suspicious of these forms of 'low brow' culture.[44] They, in their turn, participated in those forms of public entertainment that provided status through their association with upper-class culture. Thus, 'high-brow' theatre continued to flourish, as did public reading rooms and the public lectures provided by scientific societies – a phenomenon that significantly contributed to the popularization of science, reinforcing the belief that this was, indeed, an era of progress. Indeed, it was this science that endorsed such physical notions as high brow and low brow in the first place and made them into stigmatizing characteristics – the high forehead being associated with intelligence or culture, because the upper classes were considered to have experienced a different development from the labouring poor with their low, almost animal-like foreheads.

Important developments took place in musical culture, too. Music had been part of European civilization for ages, both the 'popular' music of the fairs and taverns, and the drawing-room music performed and enjoyed by the bourgeoisie and the aristocracy, besides, of course, the oldest music, the music for the Church. The distinction between the three was far less than the present-day cult of classical music might lead one to presume. Indeed, aristocratic opera and Church music were often constructed on the basis of popular, profane tunes, and court songs were whistled in the streets. However, although there were public concert halls in most European capitals – the seventeenth-century English diarist Samuel Pepys is forever telling us what he heard and saw in the London playhouses where music was given as well – their size was relatively small.

With the revolutions of the late eighteenth century, many court musicians, used to composing and performing for princes or wealthy private patrons – Joseph Haydn was employed by successive heads of the Eszterhazy-family, one of the Habsburg empire's most powerful dynasties – had to find new means of earning a living.[45] As the bourgeoisie, growing in number and with cultural aspirations of their own, were keen on good music, too, the step from the court theatre or court opera to the grand concert hall open to an increasingly numerous general public was not a big one. Indeed, it is around the turn of the eighteenth to the nineteenth century that the first grand concert halls were built. Not incidentally, they revolutionized European music: the size of the audiences necessitated composing on a grander scale, resulting in an increase both of the size of the orchestra and of the reach and pitch of the various instruments. Thus, Beethoven's symphonies were composed for and heard by a larger public than, for example, Mozart's.

It was a public that often enjoyed what it was offered but never forgot that attending these occasions gave status, too, showing that one was a culturally minded person. Audiences started to listen in silence. Having paid for the pleasure, they thought one should treat it as something special. And, in contrast to the aristocracy, who had considered musicians no better than servants, and music a *divertissement*, which should not interrupt polite conversation, the bourgeoisie, less secure, were afraid to speak. But the main change was that people increasingly looked upon music as an art, even as a religion, rather than an entertainment.[46]

In the bourgeois cult of domesticity, the drawing room became the actual as well as the symbolic shrine of a culture whose specific task it was to instil the household and the family with the norms and values of this class, to which music, like reading, provides interesting clues. Studying, for example, the hundreds of 'romantic' poems set to music mostly for the drawing room by Franz Schubert (1797–1828), one of the most gifted composers of the early nineteenth century, one detects the hopes and fears of this bourgeois society. A longing for love and a happy marriage, and a craving for solitude; the need to escape from the bustle of urban life into the fields and mountains, and the joy or melancholy born from a union with nature, with a God sometimes still manifestly present, but at other times unrecognizably hidden in the vastness of the cosmos.[47]

But besides this inward-looking romanticism, music, especially vocal music, was often the medium to express the values of a society not only bourgeois but also nationalistic: satisfied with its economic and political progress, in operas, cantatas and songs it often extolled the nation's glorious past in rousing melodies or obliquely commented upon Europe's superiority *vis-à-vis* the other worlds.[48]

One of the major questions raised by the changes of the nineteenth century is how the values of an urban middle class came to dominate the majority of the population. Between the early decades of the nineteenth and the early decades of the twentieth centuries, the transformation of parts of Europe from a rural into an industrial society and, moreover, into an urban or rather middle-class culture was inaugurated by the massive move of people from a slowly emptying countryside to fastly growing and even overflowing towns. For several generations, increasing numbers of Europeans were confronted with and bombarded by the norms and notions held by the bourgeoisie, whose affluence was the powerful stimulant for all those who sought to escape from poverty.

Great changes were brought about by the various civilizing, disciplining cultural policies pursued by the elite as well as by people's yielding to the lures of the consumer economy of the towns. But subconsciously, worlds were merging as well, introducing the predominance of bourgeois morality in ever wider circles of European society. Undoubtedly the huge groups of male and, even more, female domestic servants were one of the main channels through which bourgeois family values slowly trickled down into the labouring classes, values epitomized in the image of the non-working, mothering wife. Servants were also confronted with the growing taboo of sexuality in these middle-class households, where everything connected with intercourse and the child-bearing process was becoming shrouded in secrecy. Besides the connotation of animal-like and thus non-human, i.e. non-civilized behaviour, the assumption behind it was that the seductions of sexuality, outside the restrictions of the marriage bond, were a disruptive force, in the male and even more in the female. J.J. Virey, a widely read French medical publicist of the 1860s, revealingly wrote of the ideal coupling as one between:

> the most female woman and the most virile man, when a dark, hairy, dry, hot and impetuous male finds the other sex delicate, moist, smooth and white, timid and modest. The one must give in and the other is constituted to receive . . . to welcome, to absorb, out of a sort of need and feeling of deficit, the overflow of the other.[49]

Men were allowed their evenings 'on the town', their drinking and smoking societies, and their liaisons, albeit reluctantly, for the notion of the 'double standard' was certainly not as universally accepted as has been suggested. Women, however, had no such distractions. In the often intensely religious middle classes, it was held that their only respectable outing was the daily walk to church. Also, they were increasingly desexualized. As the guarantors of procreation and thus of the sacred family, they were idolized as worldly innocent, self-effacing wives and mothers, the natural keepers of the house. Slowly, such notions, too, were introduced in and interiorized by the working classes of Europe's urban, industrial regions.

Money and time, goods and leisure: towards a consumer culture

Besides the increasing need for leisure – which became both a status symbol and a psychological craving – the culture of things remained a powerful expression of status through highly visible possessions. Never before the nineteenth century had so many houses been packed with so many useless objects.[50]

Not surprisingly, this was the century of the department store; these showcases of consumer culture proclaimed that, now, luxury goods were within everybody's reach.[51] In 1883, the famous French author Emile Zola (1840–1902) published his *Au Bonheur des Dames*, one of a series of novels in which he aimed to provide a sociologically correct picture of the conditions of contemporary life. He had actually carried out research in one of Paris's grand new shops, the Bon Marché. The technicalities of retailing which he discovered and described seem as pertinent today as they were at the end of the nineteenth century. Probably because its subject matter struck a chord in the people inhabiting the changing townscape of England, too, it was the first of Zola's novels to be translated into English, as *The Ladies' Paradise* (1883). The novel opens with a scene showing a young girl and her two brothers who have left the country for the big city, Paris, wandering around, overwhelmed by the bustle of the metropolis. They try to find their uncle's house. Suddenly, they come upon a palace-like building, all encased in glass, attracting the eye to all kinds of goods that lure the people inside. One of the windows shows, artistically presented, dozens of silk umbrellas, another luxurious ladies' wear. The youngsters gape at this unaccustomed spectacle. Through an avalanche description of consumer goods, Zola goes on to show how, at this moment, the girl must have decided to try and 'make' it in Paris, so that she will be able to enter this megastore as a customer. She had been sold to consumer culture, as had been her brothers:

> Denise had walked from the Saint-Lazare railway station, where a Cherbourg train had landed her and her two brothers ... all three fatigued after the journey, frightened and lost in this vast Paris. . . .
>
> But on arriving in the Place Gaillon, the young girl stopped short, astonished.
> – 'Oh! look there, Jean,', said she . . . 'that *is* a shop!'
> They were at the corner of the Rue de la Michodière and the Rue Neuve-Saint-Augustin, in front of a department store whose windows shone with bright colours, in the soft October light. . . .
> This, to her, enormous place, made her heart swell, and kept her excited, interested and oblivious of everything else. The high plate-glass door, facing the Place Gaillon, reached the first floor, amidst a complication of gilded ornaments. Two allegorical figures, representing two laughing, bare-breasted women, unrolled a scroll bearing the sign 'The Ladies' Paradise'. . . . The establishment comprised, beside the corner house, four others. . . . It seemed to her an endless extension, with its display on the ground floor, and the plate-glass windows, through which could be seen the whole length of the counters. . . .
> Denise was absorbed by the display at the principal entrance. There she saw, in the open street, on the very pavement, a mountain of cheap goods – bargains, placed there to tempt the passers-by, and attract attention . . . the establishment seemed bursting with goods, blocking up the pavement with the surplus.
> . . . following the shop windows and stopping at each fresh display . . . they were captivated by a complicated arrangement . . . an exhibition of silks, satins and velvets, arranged so as to produce, by a skilful artistic management of colours, the most delicious shades imaginable.
> . . . just as she was entering the street, Denise was attracted by a window in which ladies' dresses were displayed . . . and the dresses were in this sort of chapel raised to the worship of woman's beauty and grace. . .
> 'How stunning they are,' murmured Jean, finding no other words to express his emotion. . . . All this female luxury turned him rosy with pleasure.

Essentially, since the beginning of industrialization proper at the end of the eighteenth century, cultural critics have discerned two situations, creating two basic problems for European civilization. After more than two centuries, these problems have lost nothing of their topicality.

On the one hand, some theorists reasoned that as the higher wages made possible by increasing employment and production would enable people to meet basic needs, the demand for leisure could increase and, moreover, be fulfilled; but this posed the moral problem of the anarchy of undisciplined time. On the other hand, the emulative desire that many observers deemed structural in Europe and that was stirred by increased luxury would spur additional effort; but this would lead to a wholly work-driven society, largely based on false needs.[52]

At the end of the eighteenth century, Jean-Jacques Rousseau, as always reasoning within the, ultimately false, premises which he set by positing his small-scale *république* as man's normal political and social context, had prophesied that the problems would be solved by communal discipline.[53] The Scottish philosopher David Hume meanwhile had pleaded for individual self-control.[54] In the mid-nineteenth century, John Stuart Mill argued that the affluence brought by industrialization would lead to a democratic culture of leisure;[55] many other thinkers, both liberal and socialist, followed him, differing only in their selection of the agency that would help achieve this goal: the state or the individual himself. The polarity between these two posed problems of balance that became manifest in other fields of culture as well, has occupied the attention of both politicians and social and cultural critics up till now.

15 Europe and the other worlds

Europe and its expanding world

Although the notion of 'the Columbian exchange' seems to suggest that in the wake of Columbus's 'discovery' momentous developments took place only on both sides of the Atlantic Ocean, because of the interaction between Europe and the new world of the Americas, the continued but increasing interaction with Asia produced changes in the Eurasian world as well.[1]

From the sixteenth century onwards, the European maritime merchants who established trading posts all around the Indian and Chinese seas both satisfied and stimulated a European demand for Asian products such as china-ware, silk and spices. In the process, they slowly began to influence production and, consequently, the way of life of the producers in India, Indonesia and Ceylon. For in order to improve their control of supplies, they tried either to conquer or otherwise to dominate the producing areas or, indeed, decided to transfer production to such regions as were under their power; from the seventeenth century onwards, one finds the Dutch, English and French colonial companies shipping seeds all over Asia, planting them where they could be profitably grown. An unintentional but sometimes devastating process of ecological change set in.

It found its perhaps most poignant expression when, after their discovery in the 1770s, the islands of the Pacific Ocean were colonized; whereas the first European visitors had described them as the last paradise, the true garden of Eden, the next generation turned these delicately balanced ecosystems into plantation societies with the sole function of producing fruit for the western market. Obviously, the introduction of these monocultures had serious social implications as well, changing power relations and all the values that went with them.

From the early seventeenth century onwards, something comparable happened in a region that, for long, remained at the margin of Europe's con-tacts with the wider world. The Russian tsars and their entrepreneurs, while turning to the west for its culture, started an eastward expansion to provide their realm with an economic base outside agriculture. The vast steppes which stretched from the Ural mountains to the China Sea produced the furs which, as a form of black gold, gave the rulers of Muscovy their wealth. In a series of colonizing waves, sometimes prepared by the explorations of well organized scientific expeditions, the Russians extended their power over this region, till in the 1720s they reached the Bering Straits, named after the Dane Vitus Bering, one of the explorers. They then crossed the Straits − as, some 30,000 years earlier, the Asian ancestors of the American Indians had first done − hoping to be able to colonize not only Alaska but also the entire coastal region of the North American Pacific. In this effort they were thwarted by the competition of the British and the Spaniards. Meanwhile, however, by toeing the line which separated their growing empire from the northern borders of China, and by playing the scattered tribes which inhabited the sparsely populated region of Siberia against each other, using their gunpowder superiority, the Russians succeeded in subjugating the region, politically and economically. To help them do so they convinced themselves, as so many other European nations did, too, that they had a mission, that civilizing Siberia was their manifest destiny.[2] They turned it into a colony which, besides furs, now began to yield its enormous mineral riches as well. In the process, which often was as cruel as any of the European conquests in the South and North Americas, slowly but inexorably, traditional society disappeared.

Still, it would be unhistorical to blame European expansion for all evil that befell the world, as many environmentalist campaigners would have it. Thus, for example, the great famines which devastated many of the world's tropic regions from the sixteenth to the end of the eighteenth centuries were caused by the occurrence of a so-called 'little draught age', in consequence of the oceanic movements that control fluctuations in the global climate.[3]

Europe and Latin America: a severed relationship?

For two centuries, the Spanish and Portuguese governments had succeeded in protecting their overseas territories against their European rivals in the colonial market, relatively easily at first, later only at great military expense which, towards the middle of the eighteenth century, no longer balanced the profits. The Iberian governments, moreover, were afraid that the indigenous population, especially in the peripheral areas of the empire, where Spanish and Portuguese power was barely effective, would unite itself with their European competitors, especially England and France: such crucial areas as Florida and, indeed, the entire Pacific coast could not really be defended. Therefore, by the mid-1750s, Spain in particular embarked upon a new phase of expansion.

This time, however, policy-makers in Madrid decided that costly military campaigns and the ensuing need to maintain expensive garrisons would not realize its aims. Looking at the colonial policies of the other European nations, which accomplished great results through commerce rather than conquest, men like the powerful minister Campomanes and the Viceroy Galves hoped for a peaceful incorporation of these territories. Trade with the Indians, accustoming them to all kinds of goods, among which especially alcohol, would soon bring them within the colonial consumer market and ensure their cooperation. Also, in the spirit of the Enlightenment which now penetrated part of Spain's governing elite, it was thought that it was more humane and, indeed, propagandistically opportune if the Indian nations should ally themselves freely to a civilized, enlightened empire which offered to protect them against possible enemies and which, now almost as an afterthought, would also bring them Christianity. In the ensuing process, many Indian tribes settled down to agriculture and trade, and their territories were eventually incorporated, while, of course, their culture was deeply affected.

All this meant a marked departure from Spain's earlier colonial policy, but it still came too late. It did not really solve Spain's grave financial and military problems. Nor did it lessen the pressure which European commercial competition, especially from England, put on the Iberian colonies. Finally, Spain and, if less so, Portugal, also had to counter the growing protests of the descendants of the original settlers of Central and Latin America, the erstwhile emigrants. The latter now considered the colonies their 'own' country, theirs to rule and enjoy. Indeed, they began to resent being administered and taxed by Madrid and Lisbon and, like the European-descended elites of Britain's thirteen North American dependencies, began to voice definite ideas about self-governement. For in all American colonies, among the educated classes the political notions of the Enlightenment had perhaps been studied even more eagerly than by the reformers in Madrid and Lisbon, or, for that matter, in London. This contributed to a climate in which the long-standing links between European centres and their colonial peripheries seemed decidedly less stable than they had been in the preceding centuries.

Consequently, the 'Atlantic revolutions' of the period between the 1770s and the 1830s which, among other things, resulted in the birth of the United States, were also felt in Central and South America. Virtually all former Spanish and Portuguese colonies fought for or were reluctantly given their freedom. During the seventeenth and eighteenth centuries, the protectionist-imperialist policy had considerably weakened the economic and cultural contacts between the Iberian part of the new world and the non-Iberian parts of Europe, with the consequence that Europe had largely lost its interest in the region. Now the newly independent countries availed themselves of the possibility to open up to economic and cultural influences from non-Iberian Europe. Yet at first there was no marked increase in European emigration on a scale as great as that to North America. The main reason was that the new states soon proved to be no sensational economic successes, while the new political structures did not inspire much confidence, either.[4] The hot and humid climate also failed to attract the many potential emigrants who, after all, mainly stemmed from the somewhat cooler north and west of Europe. Finally, they found the dominant role of the Catholic Church in these areas equally unattractive.

But even Roman Catholics, for instance from the Dutch and Belgian provinces of Brabant and Limburg which began to supply an amazing number of priests, monks and nuns to the world-wide missionary efforts of the Roman Church, were not stimulated by the often unexciting reports from the missionaries who had gone to Latin America in the 1820s and 1830s to strengthen the Christian belief among the Indians and black Africans in the Dutch territories, especially when the slave trade was finally abolished. As, in the same period, Dutch and Flemish priests did report with great enthusiasm about the freedom and hope held by the wide prairies of the American north, the choice for prospective missionaries was not a difficult one.[5]

In the course of the nineteenth century and in the first decades of the twentieth century, emigration to Central and South America did increase, especially from the poor regions of Europe's Catholic south hit by the effects of overpopulation and non-industrialization. But for the time being this did not result in a renewed fascination with and a resulting cultural influence of that part of the new world on the elites of the old. It was only the new wave of exoticism which swept Europe in the second half of the twentieth century that created a market for the mainly literary products of the intriguing cultural blend which had developed in Latin America from the fusion of European-Christian, Indian and African elements into a civilization of blacks, reds and whites; the works of authors like the Argentinian Jorge Luis Borges (1899–1986) and the Columbian Gabriel José García Márquez (1928–) were especially popular. The former often explored the intricate workings of a culture's memory; the latter, for example in his *Cien años de soledad* (*One Hundred Years of Solitude*) (1967, 1970) that became a world-wide bestseller, gave an almost mystic picture of this mixed culture. Thus, these writers, descending from European colonists but the actual voices of a new, complex cultural tradition, were creating the new as well as undoing the old mythologies necessary to structure their, and indeed any society, as had been their colleagues in the American north.

The 'old' world and the 'new': North America as a vision of freedom

In 1776, the revolt of Britain's North American colonies against the government in London and the independence which followed gave the former colonists a new self-awareness. Moreover, they were also liberated from the restrictions posed by a number of rules established by Parliament, including those which had attempted to stop their westward expansion into protected Indian territory beyond the demarcation line established in 1763 in the Ohio valley. The endless, still largely unknown interior was now open to European settlers hungry for land, and all ideals which people like Benjamin Franklin had projected onto the pretended empty space now appeared realizable. Echoing the biblically motivated ideology of expansion voiced by the seventeenth-century immigrants, in 1792, General Benjamin Lincoln declared that:

> When I take a view of this extensive country . . . I cannot persuade myself that it
> will remain long in so uncultivated a state; especially, when I consider that to
> people fully this earth was in the original plan of the benevolent Deity . . . if the
> savages cannot be civilized . . . the whole race shall become extinct.[6]

The new nation's self-awareness became the more manifest when it appeared
that, in the upheavals which drastically changed the political and economic
situation in large parts of western Europe between 1790 and 1830, the ideology
legitimizing the political revolutions had grown partly out of a sincere though
sometimes uncritical admiration for the actions and ideas that had shaped the
foundation of the United States. For the sake of convenience, people forgot,
just like the leading Americans themselves liked to do, that the American form
of government of the first decades after the declaration of independence of
1776 was, in fact, aristocratic-oligarchic rather than democratic.

Meanwhile, the ideas of freedom and space, of unlimited possibilities, of
escape from the restrictions of the old continent still too closely associated
with mouldering tradition and rigid structures became alluring to more and
more Europeans. For while Europe became richer as a result of fast-paced
industrialization, the process frequently brought great misery to the lowest
strata of its growing population.

Many if not all of the above elements were described in the *Letters from an
American Farmer*, which, first published in London in 1782, soon after its
translation into other European languages became very influential in creating
an idealized image of North America. In his dedication the author, Hector
St John, writes: 'You viewed these provinces of North America in their true
light, as the asylum of freedom; as the cradle of future nations, and the refuge
of distressed Europeans'.[7]

Besides very realistic elements, St John's description of life in the former
colonies, which had recently begun their existence as an independent nation,
resounds with a clearly arcadian undertone presenting the dream of Eden, or
its recreation as a new, perfect world, to all those European readers whose
enthusiasm made the work into a 'bestseller'. A few quotations illustrate the
image:

> we convert huge forests into pleasing fields, and exhibit through these thirteen
> provinces so singular a display of easy subsistence and political felicity. . . . Here
> nature opens her broad lap to receive the perpetual accession of new comers, and
> to supply them with food. . . . Here we have in some measure regained the
> ancient dignity of our species; our laws are simple and just, we are a race of
> cultivators, our cultivation is unrestrained, and therefore everything is prosperous
> and flourishing.[8]

Elsewhere, St John explains the reasons why most Europeans have made and
continue to make the crossing:

> The instant I enter on my own land, the bright idea of property, of exclusive right,
> of independence exalts my mind. . . . No wonder we should thus cherish its

possession, no wonder that so many Europeans who have never been able to say that such portion of land was theirs, cross the Atlantic to realize that happiness.

However, with a prophetic glance, he indicates why the arguments for emigration could well change in the near future, as in the United States, too, the industrial economy will gradually eclipse the agrarian, rustic, noble way of life:

> As it is from the surface of the ground which we till that we have gathered the wealth we possess, the surface of that ground is therefore the only thing that has hitherto been known. It will require the industry of subsequent ages, the energy of future generations, ere mankind will have leisure and abilities to penetrate deep, and, in the bowels of this continent, search for the subterranean riches it no doubt contains.

Equally prophetic is another pronouncement:

> Many ages will not see the shores of our great lakes replenished with inland nations, nor the unknown bounds of North America entirely peopled. Who can tell how far it extends? Who can tell the millions of men it will feed and contain? For no European foot has as yet travelled half the extent of this mighty continent.

However, the inhabitants of the old continent will always be happier in the new:

> In this great American asylum, the poor of Europe have by some means met together. . . . Everything has tended to regenerate them; new laws, a new mode of living, a new social system; here they are become men: in Europe they were as many useless plants . . . and were mowed down by want, hunger and war.

In short, America gives man, the European, the intensely longed for perfection: 'Americans are the western pilgrims, who are carrying along with them that great mass of arts, sciences, vigour, and industry which began long since in the east; they will finish the great circle'.

In a simpler form, this eloquently articulated message, the verbal depiction of the American or, rather, the European dream of discovery, exploration and conquest occurs in the enthusiastic stories told by many other emigrants. Since the late eighteenth century, the dream spurred more and more inhabitants from the old world to try their luck in the new. 'There are always dreamers on the frontier', wrote the American novelist Willa Cather in *O Pioneers!*(1904),[9] her famous evocation of the life built up by Swedish migrants in the new world. It was these European emigrants who actually gave the United States its present contours. It was they who, in wave after wave, flooded across America, often in conjunction with economic calamities, political unrest or religious disputes in Europe. It was they who slowly shifted the frontier of the United States westwards, until in the 1860s even the Rocky Mountains were no longer a hindrance and the coast of the Pacific Ocean could now be conquered, too, on the Spanish, English and Russian merchants, soldiers and farmers who had settled there in the preceding century.[10]

In the latter decades of the nineteenth century, the flow of immigrants reached gigantic proportions. For many European countries emigration to North America was a phenomenon of great economic and cultural significance, although this was not appreciated for a long time.[11] It is splendidly articulated in Vilhelm Moberg's four-part epic *Romanen om Utvandrarna* (The novel about the migrants), in which he sketches, on the basis of extensive research of the sources, the historical and psychological circumstances behind this process as it took shape in late-nineteenth-century Sweden. He probes into the tension between the lack of freedom in the old and the very real freedom in the new land – a freedom, however, which also poses existential choices: individual development or the welfare of society?[12]

Capitalism and consumerism: freedom or slavery, progress or decadence?

By about 1870, the United States had acquired its present extent and enormous parts of the country, certainly in the mid-west, had indeed been re-created in an agrarian 'paradise' in accordance with the vision of Hector St John and so many others, though some five decades later the dream of Eden, at the hands of the new settlers themselves turned into the nightmare of the over-farmed plains turned into a barren dust bowl.

Meanwhile, on the east coast industrialization had started at such a rate that America quickly became an economic giant on a scale that was hardly equalled in Europe. For the ever increasing flow of emigrants, among whom were a growing number of farmers' sons from central and eastern Europe, there were no jobs in agriculture any more. They had to content themselves with low-paid industrial work: in the iron, steel and meat factories, in the coalmines and in the construction of railways. The same held for the numerous Jewish emigrants, who fled the region between Warsaw and Odessa where they had been 'parked' by the Russian Empress Catherine in the eighteenth century. From the mid-nineteenth century onwards, when they became the victims of new waves of the still widely prevailing anti-semitism, in the form of gruesome pogroms, they left the bleakness of life in the old world hoping to find their promised country in the new world as well.

The same factors which contributed to the tempestuous expansion of American industry – a very liberal fiscal system and very liberal legislation – contributed to a situation wherein there was hardly any protection for the labouring poor. For countless people, the dream they cherished as they boarded the badly equipped ships which were to transport them across the ocean, whether or not persuaded to do so under false pretences by unscrupulous 'dealers in human beings', quickly became a nightmare after their arrival in the promised land.

The reports which the nineteenth-century immigrants sent home to the old world and which, often sentimentalized, began to fill popular magazines as well as the popular drama in which 'the rich uncle from America' or the destiny of emigrants quickly became favourite themes, certainly did not always reflect their true feelings concerning the situation they found themselves in. Many were ashamed to confess they had not been able to realize their dream, or still clung to the hope they might yet improve their situation.

Often, novelists succeed in vividly depicting the atmosphere of a certain period where other contemporaries fail to do so. The American writer Upton Sinclair, after sound research and partly on the basis of interviews, wrote a fierce and to his readers entirely convincing indictment of the inhuman conditions in Chicago's meat-processing industry, where so many who had recently arrived from Europe had accepted a job in order not to die of starvation. In *The Jungle*, published in 1906, the hero, a farmer's son from Lithuania called Jurgis, considers 'that he would go to America and marry, and be a rich man in the bargain. In that country, rich or poor, a man was free, it was said'.[13] But the cruel fact soon appeared that:

> it was a land of high prices, and that in it the poor man was almost as poor as in any other corner of the earth; and so there vanished in a night all the wonderful dreams of wealth that had been haunting Jurgis.[14]

Chicago, 'Packingtown' in the novel, is a cold, damp and poisonous hell, where some thirty thousand people, including children, toil in the meat factories, often for more than ten hours a day, for seven days a week, wading in the blood of the thousands of slaughtered, frequently diseased animals which, in the most horrifyingly unhygienic conditions, are processed into food that will subsequently endanger the health of countless consumers.

Hundreds of thousands directly or indirectly depend on this work. They are exploited, just like Jurgis and his family, by unscrupulous landlords, corrupt police officers and cunning tradesmen who tamper with the food they sold for high prices. If people become ill they are dismissed without mercy and, if things become worse, they die of hunger and cold. Consumption, as well as alcohol, claim their victims. When Jurgis, sick of it all, decides to improve his lot by joining a labour union he quickly notices that he becomes only a tool, in the hands of unscrupulous politicians. It is not long before he is among the many who hate the city 'with an all-inclusive hatred, bitter and fierce'. He also observes how one wave of emigrants after the other only stir up mutual intolerance instead of creating solidarity. One evening, returning home after being forced to participate in a successful attempt to deceive a group of factory inspectors, he realizes 'how those might be right who had laughed at him for his faith in America'.

And yet, despite the often wretched circumstances which many immigrants had to live in, for countless people in Europe 'America' remained a magic word, the land *par excellence* where that which could not be reached at home

Plates 35 and 36 In his famous painting from the mid-1850s entitled *The Last of England*, Ford Maddox Brown showed a family leaving their native soil for an uncertain, but hopefully better future in the new world.

Meanwhile, Europeans were penetrating the 'heart of darkness', the interior of Africa, as shown in this engraving of Livingstone crossing the continent (1853–6) on his white ox Sindbad – after the archetypal traveller from the *Thousand-and-One-Nights*? Sources: Centre for Art Historical Documentation, Nijmegen, The Netherlands, and *Life and Explorations of Dr. Livingstone* (London 1878)

could, apparently, be realized: prosperity and freedom. Thus, continued misery in the old world, as well as continued idealizing reports about the new world, combined with often consciously misleading propaganda on the part of the American government and private entrepreneurs did much, if not everything, to convince people to risk the crossing.

NEW YORK, 1909: HERBERT CROLY (1869–1930) INTERPRETS 'THE PROMISE OF AMERICAN LIFE'

In 1909, Herbert Croly, an American journalist and the founder-editor of the influential periodical *The New Republic*, published a widely read pamphlet which he called 'The Promise of American Life'. In this tract, he voiced both his criticism of the state of contemporary culture and society in the United States and the hopes he yet held for the future if the dangers of excessive individualism, consumerism and, yes, even democracy were adequately met. Precisely because comparable developments took place in Europe, too, the text has a significance which transcends the American experience.

All the conditions of American life have tended to encourage an easy, generous, and irresponsible optimism. As compared to Europeans, Americans have been very much favoured by circumstances. Had it not been for the Atlantic Ocean and the virgin wilderness, the United States would never have been the Land of Promise. The European Powers have been obliged from the very conditions of their existence to be more circumspect and less confident of the future. They are always by way of fighting for their national security and integrity. With possible or actual enemies on their several frontiers, and with their land fully occupied by their own population, they need above all to be strong, to be cautious, to be united, and to be opportune in their policy and behaviour. . . . We were for the most part freed from alien interference, and could, so far as we dared, experiment with political and social ideals. The land was unoccupied, and its settlement offered an unprecedented area and abundance of economic opportunity. . . .

The moral and social aspiration proper to American life is, of course, the aspiration vaguely described by the word democratic; and the actual achievement of the American nation points towards an adequate and fruitful definition of the democratic ideal. Americans are usually satisfied by a most inadequate verbal description of democracy, but their national achievement implies one which is much more comprehensive and formative. In order to be true to their past, the increasing comfort and economic independence of an ever increasing proportion of the population must be secured, and it must be secured by a combination of individual effort and proper political organization. Above all, however, this economic and political system must be made to secure results of moral and social value. It is the seeking of such results which converts democracy from a political system into a constructive social ideal; and the more the ideal significance of the American national promise is asserted and emphasized, the greater will become the importance of securing these moral and social benefits. The fault in the vision of our national future . . . consists in the expectation that the familiar benefits will continue to accumulate automatically. . . . But this is no longer the case. Economic conditions have been profoundly modified, and the American political and social problems have been modified with them. The promise of American life must depend less than it did upon the virgin wilderness and the Atlantic Ocean, for the virgin wilderness has disappeared, and the Atlantic Ocean has become merely a big channel. The same results can no longer be achieved by the same easy methods. . . .

If the fulfilment of our national promise can no longer be considered inevitable, if it must be considered as equivalent to a conscious national purpose instead of an inexorable national destiny, the implication necessarily is that the trust exposed in individual self-interest has been in some measure betrayed. No preestablished harmony can then exist between the free and abundant satisfaction of private needs and the accomplishment of a morally and socially desirable result. The promise of American life is to be fulfilled – not merely by a maximum amount of economic freedom, but by a certain measure of discipline; not merely by the abundant satisfaction of individual desires, but by a large measure of individual subordination and self-denial. . . . The traditional American confidence in individual freedom has resulted in a morally and socially undesirable distribution of wealth. . . . The existing concentration of wealth and financial power in the hands of a few irresponsible men is the inevitable outcome of the chaotic individualism of our political and economic organization, while at the same time it is inimical to democracy. . . . A more highly socialized democracy is the only practical substitute on the part of convinced democrats for an excessively individualized democracy. . . . Democracy may prove to be the most important moral and social enterprise as yet undertaken by mankind; but it is still a very young enterprise, whose meaning and promise is by no means clearly understood.[15]

Europe and 'America': a cultural symbiosis or, the growth of the 'western world'

Already in the colonial period the more prosperous colonists and their descendants sailed to the old world, i.e. mainly to England, frequently to complete their schooling there. However, at the end of the eighteenth century a valued destination besides England – which, in the mean time, had become greatly mistrusted – was France, with its 'enlightened' intellectuals: Paris was seen as the centre of European civilization, a town not to be missed if one wanted to count in the colonial world.

In the course of the nineteenth centur in the United States, too, a prosperous middle class developed on the basis of successful industrialization, which now received the benefit of a cultural formation in the same tradition which for centuries had formed the European elite; a trip to Europe, now including Italy as well, became a sort of 'Grand Tour' for many Americans, the rounding off of their education. In the tale of his travels, the well-known writer Washington Irving (1783–1859) sighs:

Europe held forth the charms of storied and poetical association. There were to be seen the masterpieces of art, the refinements of highly cultivated society, the quaint peculiarities of ancient and local custom. My native country was full of youthful promise: Europe was rich in the accumulated treasures of age. Her very ruins told the history of times gone by, and every mouldering stone was a chronicle.[16]

Irving was not the first and certainly not the last thus to enthuse over the old world. As emigration from Europe increased, for more and more emigrants and especially for their descendants Europe became the land of the past; despite the often unhappy memories attached to it for the first generation, the following generations often wanted to visit it, as being the land where their roots lay. Besides this, especially American intellectuals experienced the vision of a Europe associated with a millennial tradition of culture as a challenge to their creativity. Moreover, depending on the extent that they felt their own society to be constricted by Puritan norms, they saw Europe as the land of freedom – a fascinating complement to the way of thinking which for centuries caused so many European emigrants to make the crossing.

Many American artists and writers began to seek their inspiration in the old world, such as Henry James, who actually chronicled the mutual fascination and antagonism of Europeans and Americans. Both they and the self-made billionaires who, like the Carnegies, the Morgans and the Rockefellers, spent fortunes buying European art and antiques, were criticized or even ridiculed by many on both sides of the ocean, albeit for different reasons: Americans themselves rebuked them for failing to make an effort to create a true, indigenous culture rather than ape the old world, whereas Europeans mocked them for their manners and their crass belief in the power of money. And yet the phenomenon did contribute to a growing cultural *rapprochement* between the two worlds. The numerous affluent and educated Americans who, since the second half of the nineteenth century, made a long or short trip to Europe, contributed to the formation of a positive image of the United States as well.

Against this background, with the wealth shown by a number of sometimes only recently arrived immigrants, and the position of power which the new state quickly achieved, by the end of the nineteenth century America presented a challenge to Europe more than ever before.

For those in the old world for whom progress in particular was measured in economic terms, America was the pre-eminent example, held out to public opinion in many (pseudo-) scientific and popular publications as being worthy of emulation. For them, America had a positive mirror function – the ideal state which paired regulated spiritual freedom with high material development and thus also with civilization.

This admiration and the increasing economic interaction between North America and (western) Europe slowly led to a situation in which, in a number of fields, both cultures began to show great similarities and viewed each other as being closely related, democratic societies which, essentially, strove for the same values. The coastal regions of the North Atlantic now formed a continuum that for many was a cultural as well as an economic unity: the western world.

To the 'heart of darkness': Europe and Africa

Well into the seventeenth century, Europe's knowledge of sub-Saharan Africa had been restricted to the information which it could obtain in the coastal forts built in order that slave-traders, merchants looking for gold and missionaries might do their work, barely daring into the unknown, unhealthy interior. The slaves, mostly procured by indigenous rulers specializing in this 'commodity', and then sold to European companies, were sent to the Americas;[17] the gold went into financing Europe's increasing trade with Asia; and according to the missionaries, the souls of those who converted to Christianity went to heaven. Otherwise, European ships hopping from Portuguese fort to Dutch port on the so-called Gold and Slave coasts of Africa's western half, the Dutch colony at the Cape of Good Hope and the Portuguese towns on east-coast Mozambique, saw Africa only as the inhospitable continent they passed on their way to the riches of the east.

Plates 37, 38 and 39 Explorers such as Speke and Grant, who were mapping Africa (1857–9), also tried to teach the Bible to indigenous rulers such as King Kamrasi of Nyoro (from J. Speke's *Journal of the Discovery of the Source of the Nile*, 1863). Meanwhile, in Europe people were wondering what, if any, were the differences between apes – and also black people, whom many considered to be but little different from the apes – and European man, with all his marvellous accomplishments. To many, Darwin had robbed man of his unique dignity, as is shown by the satirical print opposite of the scientist as and with an ape; both serious and mock debates, as the one in the illustrated journal *Punch* of 1861, discussed the question whether Darwin and his followers were right and, if so, what were the consequences?
Sources: J. Speke, *Journal of the Discovery of the Source of the Nile* (London 1863) and Centre for Art Historical Documentation, Nijmegen, The Netherlands

By the end of the eighteenth century, this situation changed. On the one hand, the European economy became aware of the possibilities of Africa both as a producer of primary goods for and as a market for the finished products of European industry. At the same time, the slave trade, which had transported many millions of black Africans to the plantations of the Caribbean as well as of the American continent, came under increasing attack. Both 'enlightened' humanists and Church-related groups, especially in protestant Europe, now started condemning a practice which caused such indescribable misery. Soon, campaigns were staged to provide public support for a Europe-wide effort to root out the problem. This, however, meant that the situation in Africa's interior would have to be explored, to provide the data which the abolitionists needed to convince their governments that action should be taken. Many governments eagerly assented to officially support expeditions, partly for humanitarian reasons, partly because they saw this as a marvellous opportunity to get to know the continent better and thus create possibilities for extending their economic power.

The slave trade and, later, slavery itself, were abolished in the nineteenth century. But in the process, mission and trading posts had been established along Africa's rivers; the two were often complementary, for, like in South America two centuries earlier, many missionaries realized that the ways of Christ did not necessarily run parallel to the ways of the Mammon, and, therefore, started protecting 'their' negroes from the corruptive influences of soldiers and traders. It was not long before, in an outright 'scramble for Africa', full-fledged colonies were staked out by the major European powers. These now included imperial Germany which, after its political unification in 1870, decided it should be a colonial player as well; indeed, as the other industrializing nations, it increasingly needed the African markets as much as the German missionaries, both protestant and catholic, needed the African souls.[18]

Yet it would be altogether too simple to present Africa as the silent victim of Europe's predatory politics. Much like in those regions of Asia and the Americas where Europeans had succeeded in establishing colonial rule in the seventeenth and eighteenth centuries, in Africa, too, they were successful only because local rulers often used the colonizing agencies as much as the other way round, trying to implicate them and their superior weapons in their age-old power games. The small group of Europeans who for barely more than a century ruled large parts of Africa were able to survive only because local elites, for manifold reasons of their own, cooperated. Nevertheless, the upheaval caused by European colonial rule was enormous, both economic and social and, of course, cultural. European notions of clock-regulated time, of decent behaviour, beginning with decent clothes, and of labour discipline were introduced to make Africans into willing workers and subjects, as well as into Christians.

Meanwhile, in Europe, many who would never visit Africa nor, perhaps, knew that many of the things they ate or wore were made of the materials produced by Africans, once more had to adapt their view of the world, to include yet another world. They were informed, first, by the tales told by missionaries and widely published to serve as propaganda for the conversion policy of the Churches. Soon, scientific studies especially in the newly defined branch of anthropology were popularized, catering to Europe's desire for the exotic; they painted a picture of a world full of creatures which might or might not be entirely human – were they not, perhaps, the embodiment of some stage between ape and man? As many missionaries in their eagerness to get to know the region acquired a vast amount of information, in a way that made them resemble an ethnographer or anthropologist, the resulting images were often mixed, creating a complex vision of the so-called Dark Continent.[19]

For a long time, many Europeans continued to hold extreme views. In 1864, the Anthropological Society of London debated the desirability of the extermination of the lower races, especially the African ones; when, in 1897, the German anthropologist Friedrich Ratzel published his *Politische Geographie*, it contained the same ideas, which were later eagerly adopted by the leaders of Nazi Germany.[20] Indeed, the advance of evolutionist theories, from the 1860s onwards, had helped to strengthen such views.

Finally, by the end of the nineteenth century, the notion of black Africans being some sort of wild animal was discarded by the more enlightened Europeans; nevertheless native civilizations were still depicted as 'primitive' – sometimes with the connotation of innocence that once had adhered to native America. The late nineteenth and early twentieth centuries then discussed the opinion that evolution, instead of being interpreted negatively as indicating that the backward species had no place in progressive society, should be helped by education which, of course, meant Christianization; others, for various reasons, did not want to embark upon such schemes, if only because educated Africans might come to resent European colonial rule. Often, those cultures of Africa which had been Islamicized were judged rather more negatively than the regions where animism reigned, the latter being seen as more receptive to the preaching of the gospel.

Despite the many instances of individual Europeans working to their heart's content among their 'chosen' Africans, European public opinion often continued to stigmatize the native population as stupid, lazy, addicted to alcohol and indulging in open sexuality. Perhaps even more than had been the case in Europe's perception of the other worlds it had encountered, the peoples of sub-Saharan Africa had come to be the embodiment of emotions and actions which Europeans, precisely because they were now entering upon the 'bourgeois' phase of their culture, came to consider as socially unacceptable and, therefore, morally evil. Consequently, they felt they had to combat these vices, if only to be able to continue believing their own culture was, indeed, superior.

The fact that, at the turn from the nineteenth to the twentieth century, many who belonged to Europe's artistic and musical avant garde developed a decided penchant for the very 'primitivism' of African culture, for its emotionality which they saw as so much more in tune with the essence of being human than the over-refined, restrictive civilization of contemporary Europe, did little to alter the perception of the masses.

The 'old' world and the 'older' world

In the sixteenth and seventeenth centuries, the new world, due mainly to the lack of effective resistance of indigenous societies and the demographic catastrophe that followed the first contacts, had been conquered and became the embodiment of Europe's hope that paradise on earth might yet be found, or that at least the promised land could be built there. Africa was conquered too, in the nineteenth century, but was barely used for the large-scale settlement of European populations. Asia, however, sharing Europe's biological and bacteriological make-up and, moreover, ruled by powerful empires, for a long time resisted any easy conquest.

True, the Dutch had built their empire in the east Indies, replacing the Portuguese, and the Spaniards retained their hold over the Philippines. Further expansion, however, did not prove easy. Japan, still traumatized by the Mongols' efforts at invasion in the twelfth century, had become afraid not only of firearms but also of Christianity as an ideological weapon which might be used by indigenous rebellious magnates – as had actually been the case since their introduction by the Portuguese in the later half of the sixteenth century. Consequently, from the 1640s onwards, the shogunal government of the Tokugawa family closed its islands completely to all foreigners except the Chinese and the Dutch; they, however, were allowed to live only in close confinement on two islands in Nagasaki Bay.[21] Nevertheless, the Dutch managed to see quite a bit of the country, and in a series of important books published in the seventeenth and eighteenth centuries presented its history and culture to a highly appreciative European audience; at the same time, the Japanese used the Dutch to become acquainted with those aspects of European culture they considered useful, such as medicine and some of the new sciences.[22]

China, too, successfully rebuffed any efforts made by European powers to enter the Middle Kingdom beyond the great port of Canton, where china, silk and tea were traded.[23] Only the Christian missionaries, and especially the Jesuits, were allowed to try and convert the Chinese. Their impact was minimal, but in order to gain material and moral support for their policies among the faithful in Europe, they spread highly one-sided, euphoric accounts of China as a society and a civilization uniquely worthy of Europe's attention; it lacked only Christianity to be truly admirable, but the conditions to impose it were favourable, for in the Confucian system of reverence for the gods – perhaps even the one God – and for the well-ordered family and the all-powerful state, China did have its share of proto-Christian ideas and values.[24]

If only for the relative secrecy surrounding these cultures, Europeans, little aware of the actual state of affairs there, tended to idealize Chinese and, to a lesser extent, Japanese culture. Enlightenment intellectuals like Voltaire, highly critical of political and social conditions at home, and not hindered by profound knowledge of the realities of the Chinese political and social system, held it up as an example to the, in their opinion, backward monarchies of Europe.

Also the British, desiring to dominate the huge market of China from their Bengal commercial base, began to force their way into the heavenly empire, among other means by the illegal import of huge quantities of debilitating opium. In the early decades of the nineteenth century, violent controversy arose, resulting in outright wars. Due to the military and technological superiority of the British, the Chinese came out the losers, being forced to accept a series of highly humiliating treaties. From the 1840s onwards, not only did the British and, in their wake, other western powers begin their systematic economic exploitation of China, but also many in the western world lost their former admiration for Chinese civilization.

After being forcefully opened by and to the western world in 1854, Japan, in order to escape such a fate, embarked upon a remarkable policy of agricultural renewal as well as of industrial and technological 'westernization'. It succeeded in keeping its economic and political independence as well as, in a way, earning the reluctant admiration of the western world, precisely because it successfully aped its material achievements. Moreover, many artists of *fin-de-siècle* (turn-of-the-century) Europe, looking for new concepts and ever willing to be lured by the exotic, were inspired especially by its woodblock art and its painting, as can be witnessed from the works of some of the impressionists and expressionists, like Paul Gauguin and Vincent van Gogh;[25] more specifically it was the 'essentialist' tendency which came from the Zen form of Buddhist philosophy that now captured the western imagination.[26]

Perhaps the most amazing episode in the continued interaction between Europe and Asia was the way that Europe and, at a later date, the United States reacted to India. Till the eighteenth century, the vast subcontinent, too, remained largely outside European influence. By then, however, the French and, more successfully, the English began to encroach upon the crumbling Mogul Empire. Meanwhile, ever since the late sixteenth century, Roman Catholic missionaries had tried to convert the Hindus. Confronted with a stubbornly resistant culture, they had found out about the existence and power of the sacred writings of India, the *Vedas*. As these were written in Sanskrit, a language kept secret by the caste of priests, the Brahmins, many Roman priests tried to master it one way or another. Though they partially succeeded in doing so, their results were not widely publicized in northern Europe. At the end of the eighteenth century, the servants of the English and French colonial companies, also confronted with indigenous culture and society, experienced the same desire. Finally, a few managed to learn the language. From the 1780s onwards, the *Vedas*, the *Upanishads* and the ancient Indian

Map 7 Major spheres of European cultural influence, c.1800

Spanish
(Roman Catholic
cultural influence)

Portuguese
(Roman Catholic
cultural influence)

French

Russian

Dutch

English

epics were translated into French, English and German, and created a veritable craze.

At the end of the eighteenth century, Sir William Jones, a senior civil servant in the British colony of Bengal, though certainly not the first to formulate the idea, was the first to publicize the notion of Sanskrit being the oldest language on earth, the mother of all major languages of Eurasia, including Greek, Latin and all the Germanic ones. Being written in the 'oldest' language, the Sanskrit texts were also considered to contain the oldest knowledge of things material and spiritual. Consequently, at many European universities professorships of Indology were established, studying the philology and the literature of India, as well as its religion and philosophy. Soon, the idea of a common linguistic origin was further elaborated in the systematization of Indo-European languages – including Persian and Sanskrit – which assumed them to be the offspring of one 'proto' Indo-European language. Also, Indian culture was interpreted as the oldest known civilization whence European culture had originated and, moreover, a civilization that had kept its childlike innocence, surely another sign of its great antiquity.

These theories, from the late nineteenth century onwards, were at least partly confirmed by archaeological research indicating the diffusion of culture into Europe and western Asia from a region covering parts of present-day Iran, Afghanistan, northern India and Asian Russia. It was not long before the notion of an ancient 'Aryan' people who had been the creators of all the major civilizations of the world – emphatically excluding the world of Islam – entered the European conscience; it was highly popular in England as well as in Germany, but also found adherents in other countries. In retrospect, one must conclude that the 'Indian Renaissance' was, in large part, an enchantment with origins, European society's romantic and revealing search for roots.

The second part of the nineteenth century shows elements of Indian culture being introduced into western literature and music, often shallowly but sometimes creatively. Of greater importance was the way in which Hinduist Indian philosophical notions – and in their wake also Buddhist and specifically Zen ideas – about the essentials of man's self and his relation to the cosmos crept into European philosophy. Thus, for example, Arthur Schopenhauer, using Indian philosophical concepts, came to maintain that all human reality was *maya* (illusion) only, the projection of man's mind, the one reality, *brahman*; yet he also reasoned that this individual essence was part of the world-soul, *atman*.

To many, the culture of India, sometimes indiscriminately mixed with other oriental civilizations, was seen as less one-sidedly rationalistic than 'the European mind'; thus, it fed their craving for a new spiritual dimension, which in their opinion Christianity could provide no longer: the foundation, in 1875, of the Theosophical Society, which tried to reconcile western scientific thought and eastern holistic visions is but one of its many manifestations; in their own way, the 'hippy movement' of the 1960s and the New Age ideas of the 1980s showed the continued attraction of these influences.

By the early nineteenth century, the Islamic Near East had become an area of actual European expansion as well, for the first time since the Crusades. Though 'God's Shadow on Earth', the sultan at Istanbul, still claimed to rule it as the Prophet's heir, his authority had become only nominal, steadily eroded by regional potentates since the seventeenth century. Internal weakness had come along external pressure. For in the same period, the Ottoman Empire had grown important to European trade; indeed, by the eighteenth century, its economy was partly run by Dutch, English and French firms, aided by Greek Christian middlemen. The reason the Ottoman world started acquiring even greater importance in the early nineteenth century was, of course, that through it ran a number of the vital overland routes linking Europe to its Asian colonies. Moreover, its Balkan provinces were becoming the battleground of two major expansionist European powers, the Austro-Hungarian monarchy and tsarist Russia; the latter not only was creating its eastern empire, but also strove for ice-free harbours in the Mediterranean. Consequently, all European powers which had a stake in south-eastern Europe, the Levant or central Asia were now interested in further weakening the sultan's power.

This economic and political interest ran parallel to and was often reinforced by a twofold cultural factor. On the one hand, the Christian Churches from the early nineteenth century onwards experienced a revived interest in the Holy Land as the region of its origin and, perhaps, its fulfilment – might not Christ return there on the Day of Judgement? Partly connected with this movement, biblical scholarship, increasingly influenced by positivistic scientific thinking, sought to prove the holy book's literal truth by engaging in extensive archaeological research.[27] On the other hand, parallel to the discovery of India, the notion that perhaps Europe's culture was not based only on Graeco-Roman antecedents created a new fascination with the world of the ancient Near East; its languages and its literatures now became widely studied, often in combination with the newly discovered languages of central and eastern Asia. The first scholarly periodical devoted to oriental studies was founded in Vienna, in 1808, by the 'father' of Ottoman studies, Joseph von Hammer-Purgstall.

While, undeniably, many scholars were deeply fascinated by the new worlds that opened up for them, such learned journals as *Fundgruben des Orients* as well as the slightly later French venture, *Journal Asiatique*, also show the growing interrelationship between oriental studies and the colonial policies of Europe's states: not surprisingly, Russia concentrated on the languages and cultures of central Asia, while England almost exclusively studied those of India; French scholars developed a specialism in Near Eastern and Indo-Chinese studies, still hoping to create an oriental empire there, after having lost their Indian possessions to Britain.

The spreading of the new knowledge about the cultures of Asia and the other continents was not confined only to the world of learning. It was helped considerably by the greatly increased number of travellers who, aided by modern technology but still often braving very primitive conditions in those regions where this was not available, gained the far ends of the earth. By the end of the nineteenth and the first decades of the twentieth centuries, for the first time in history Europeans could boast that they had 'discovered' the entire earth. From the impenetrable rain forests of the Amazon to the unscalable peaks of the Himalayas, Europeans, whether economic adventurers, empire builders, expedition leaders, journalists or just more than normally enterprising tourists brought home their tales.

Also for the first time in history, a sizeable group of these travellers were women. Often they went to escape the restrictions of genteel life as an un-married 'maid' or, worse, a divorced wife in Europe, travelling either on the basis of some slender private means or even trying to finance their expeditions by publishing the stories of their experiences, catering to the ever-growing market for exotic stories. Whatever their background or motives, they, too, contributed to Europe's growing knowledge of the world while at the same time creating an alternative vision of European womanhood, suggesting that a woman could, after all, do the things that only men were supposed to do.[28]

Thus, it was not only Henry Stanley who travelled to the heart of Africa, or the Swede Sven Hedin who crossed the Gobi Desert; the intrepid Scots-woman Isabella Bird journeyed along 'unbeaten tracks' to the northernmost parts of Japan and became one of the first Europeans ever to live among the Ainu tribes; the Dutch noblewoman Alexandrine Tinne first ventured into the Sudan and then moved among the Touaregs; French-Danish Alexandra David-Neel claimed to be the first woman to have entered Lhasa, Tibet's forbidden city on the 'Roof of the World', where no Europeans had set foot after a handful of Jesuit and Capuchin missionaries who, without much success, had tried to bring Christianity there in the eighteenth century.

Irrespective of the gender of their authors, the majority of travel tales, both literary and scholarly, reflected European attitudes and values and stressed the superiority of European culture in all its respects, often sketching the world of the 'others' as timeless, or even stagnant and backward.[29] The sketching should be taken literally as well, for the nineteenth century was the first period in European history wherein considerable numbers of artists left their own world to travel; the few painters who had gone to Dutch Brazil in the seventeenth century, and who had accompanied Captain James Cook on his epochal voyages of discovery in the Pacific Ocean in the 1770s, had been the exception rather than the rule; moreover, in these early ventures artistic and scientific observations were clearly mixed.[30] Now, many artists left on extended trips, concentrating, however, on the Near and Far East. A wave of orientalist painting showed the new fascination for the brilliant light and, consequently, the equally brilliant colours created by the Orient's glaring sun; in the themes they chose, these painters also showed the dreams they and their buyers had, and which Europe's increasingly industrialized, regulated society could not satisfy anymore: dreams of a world lost, of a simpler life, of greater passions and of unrestricted sexuality.

Undeniably, such texts and, also, such paintings, idealizing and objectifying the Orient and all of Europe's worlds gave further ground to all those who were of the opinion that the east was neither modern nor progressive, and that Europe had a civilizing mission towards the rest of mankind. Yet a minority showed not only an increased interest in but also a growing awareness of the fact that these cultures might be superficially different but still be, somehow, equal and even fundamentally the same. Friedrich Schlegel, for a few years the driving force behind a journal called *Europa*, in his *Ueber die Sprache und Weisheit der Indier* (On the Language and Wisdom of India) (1808), was one of the first scholars to alert Europe to the culture of India. He wrote:

> Now that in the history of peoples Europeans and Asians form one big family, Asia and Europe one inseparable area, we should try to see the literatures of all civilized peoples as a continuing cultural development, one tightly constructed building; this will allow us to view everything in its unity; many one-sided, restricted views will disappear, and, acknowledging the many interdependencies, we will come to understand things and see them in a new light.

And yet, Europe was forever creating new boundaries, in order to be able to define itself. One of the most fateful was also the nearest. For in the eighteenth century, notions about the 'difference' of the central and eastern part of Europe were ever more strongly voiced. True, already in 1647, a book published by the German traveller Abraham Olearius on the culture of Muscovy had given Europe damning proof of its barbarism:

> If one were to judge the Russians by their character, customs and life-styles, it would be just to number them among the barbarians. . . . For the Russians do not love the arts and the sciences, nor have they any desire to get acquainted with them . . . Consequently, they remain unlearned and rude.[31]

Once more, Europe expressed itself as the embodiment of civilization, through its cultural accomplishments, especially in the arts and sciences. Translated in almost all western languages, Olearius' text was used by other travellers to Russia in the late seventeenth and early eighteenth centuries, who always wrote in confirmation of his views.[32] Since the mid-eighteenth century, these views were being expressed rather more forcefully, and even began to include the whole of central and eastern Europe, from Russia to the Balkan.

Now, the entire region was described as 'oriental', being part of the strange world of Asia rather than of Europe. In European public opinion, a deliberate cultivation of the region's backwardness took place, enabling Enlightenment thinkers – Voltaire being one among many to air these views, despite his profitable relationship with the Russian Empress Catherine – to present their own Europe more effectively as the model of civilization. When Mozart, not normally given to reflection on such issues, went from Vienna to Prague, he felt that he entered another world, a Slav world, an oriental world.[33]

Of course, the fact that parts of central and eastern Europe were only marginally involved in the feverish economic development of the western region, and that Russia was hardly involved in it at all, made the differences seem the more obvious.[34] Even Poland, whose contribution to Humanism and the Renaissance had long been recognized, and which, being Roman Catholic rather than Orthodox, strongly felt part of the western, Christian world, now fell victim to the new view – not least, one suspects, because of the ease with which, at the end of the eighteenth century, the Polish kingdom was divided between contending neighbours; thus, it lost a characteristic which 'Europe' had come to think of as vital to any civilization, its independence and its sovereignty.

Still, the German philosoper Johann Gottfried Herder, reflecting on the course of world history in 1791, did ask himself whether eastern Europe and, more specifically, Russia, might not eventually emerge from this backwardness. Though according to him the Slav peoples seemed born to servitude, no doubt because they had been subjected for so many centuries, they did have the potential to imbibe the best elements of European culture; in doing so, might they not, at one time, follow the course of the United States, which had thrown off its colonial shackles to become a major power?[35]

16 The 'Decline of the Occident' – the loss of a dream?

From the nineteenth to the twentieth century

The sciences: positivism and increasing relativism

The tension between a humanistic view of man and society and a more physical vision of the world which was felt from the fifteenth century onwards heightened in the second half of the nineteenth and the early decades of the twentieth century. A way of thinking mainly couched in terms of the concept of progress, that already in the eighteenth century had started to reflect a rosy vision of the development of European culture and that was adopted by philosophers around the turn of the century, now seemed to acquire an empirical, scientific basis.

In particular in the exact sciences and applied technology each decade brought new discoveries, which sometimes could be put to immediate practical use, making life easier and more comfortable not only for the old elites but for the masses as well; the fact that still not everyone could and did profit from them equally does not detract from their importance.

The list of new ideas and new techniques is long indeed. Suffice it to give a few examples. In biology, Remak discovered cell division in 1852, and Mendel's theory of heredity appeared in 1865. In medicine, Morton developed the ether anaesthetic in 1846, while in 1861 Semmelweiss showed how puerperal fever could be combated; Koch discovered the tuberculosis bacteria in 1882, and in 1883 Behring developed the diphtheria serum. In physics, Fresnel startled the world with the theory of lightwaves in 1815, while Faraday developed electric induction in 1831 and electrolysis in 1833; in 1888, Hertz wrote about electromagnetic waves and in 1895 Röntgen gave the world x-rays. Siemens introduced the dynamo in 1867 and the electric train in 1879, and Otto developed the four-stroke engine in 1876. In 1884, Daimler patented the gasoline motor, and in 1885 he brought out the first car.

From the 1820s onward, Nièpce, Talbot and Daguerre had developed photography; in 1839, a proud French government bought Daguerre's formula, presenting it as 'a gift to mankind'. But the breathtaking inventions of one generation were the old fashions of the next; the exact likenesses captured in the photograph soon seemed outmoded when film made images actually move. A new mass medium was born in 1897, that was to deeply influence

European and indeed western society.[1] For many Europeans, life acquired a new speed, an almost breathless quality, not least because, for the first time in history, they could now look at themselves as they really were.

BERLIN, 1877: HEINRICH STEPHAN REJOICES IN THE FIRST GERMAN TELEPHONE SERVICE

In November 1877, the German postmaster-general Heinrich Stephan wrote the following letter to Fürst Bismarck, chancellor of the newly formed German empire, in which he outlined the general physical principles of the telephone, the history of its development and the possibilities of its use:

> Your Grace knows that moving a piece of steel or iron within the reach of a magnet will induce an electric current that lasts while the movement of the iron or steel lasts. If one projects one's voice against a sheet of steel or iron so thin as to enable the human voice to make it tremble, and if a magnet, within a coil, is near, there will be electric vibrations in this coil which completely match the sound waves induced by the voice. The coil is connected to a normal telegraph cable, and through it the currents are transmitted to the receiving station. There, a similar instrument is connected to thin sheets of iron, through which the electric currents once more are transformed into air currents, and consequently into sound. . . .
>
> On the above, the theory of the telephone is based. Only a century ago, people first conceived of the relationship between electricity and magnetism, when a stroke of lightning caused the magnetic pole of a compass to reverse. Fifty-eight years ago, Oerstedt established the principles of electromagnetism, and Ampère, only three years later, proved that magetism was the consequence of electric vibrations. Nowadays, this research, combined with the principles of accoustics, which have been known for some time, has resulted in the invention of the telephone, which, I am convinced, will have a great future in the realm of human communication.
>
> As far as is known today, in 1861, Philipp Reis, a Frankfurt school teacher, has been the first to have constructed a telephone capable of transmitting musical sound. Afterwards, the Americans have got hold of the idea, and Messers Bell, Edison and Gray have constructed various telephones to transmit human speech. As far as I can see, the most practical one is Bell's machine, which has served as the model for a number of telephones which I have ordered from the firm of Siemens and Halske. During the last weeks of October, we have first tried them out, to start with from my central office in the Leipziger Strasse to the General Telegraph Office in the Französischen Strasse. As these experiments were totally satisfactory . . . we started transmitting to Potsdam on the same day. With Potsdam, too, perfect communication has been established.[2]

Undeniably, these developments greatly helped to improve the material quality of life, facilitating not only transport and communication but also the movement of goods, thus, for example, contributing to a more varied and better diet; moreover, through increased medical knowledge, the chemical industry, which developed in the wake of mechanical industrialization, by the mass production of patent medicine could help to increase life expectancy and reduce the deathrate from all kinds of illnesses, though it also unscrupulously exploited people's fear of sickness and death for commercial purposes.

In a subtle and complex way, these new discoveries not only changed people's material life but also their perception of themselves and of their relationship to nature. Understandably, most of these developments were hailed as triumphs of science and technology, of the genius that more and more seemed to characterize Europe, giving it its unique position in the world – to many, 'Europe' and 'progress' became almost synonymous. Yet the results of research in other fields, where the spiritual rather than the physical person and the material world was involved, were less unequivocally positive, not to say rather unsettling, especially to those who were convinced the Christian Bible was the fount of all truth.

Already around the turn of the eighteenth to the nineteenth century, French scientists like Buffon and Lamarck wrote about the variability of organic forms and their gradual evolution from monad to man, undermining the concept of the uniqueness of the human species. Meanwhile, geology showed that the earth must have been shaped in the course of several million rather than several thousand years, considerably undermining the ideas proclaimed by the Churches about the age of the world and a creation which was supposed to have been completed in a single week's time.

Partly as a result of these discoveries and speculations, biologists went on asking new questions about the development of life on earth. Already in the 1780s and 1790s, an English country doctor, Erasmus Darwin, had voiced his opinions about the creative force of natural or sexual selection in the origin of new species; though he had carefully couched his ideas in such a way so as not to irritate the religious establishment, he soon found that society was not yet ready to accept the notion that, perhaps, humans stemmed from the apes. Some 60 years later, in 1844, the eccentric Scotsman Robert Chambers produced his *Vestiges of the Natural History of Creation*, presenting an evolutionist view of the genesis of life. He did so anonymously, undoubtedly afraid of adverse reactions within the conservative Christian community. His work was not heeded.

Plates 40 and 41 An engraved representation of the Great Exhibition at Vienna in 1873, showing the German section of the 'Hall of Machines'. Machines, or mechanical and later electrical appliances, not only facilitated production in almost all sectors of the economy, but also entered the family home, being widely advertised as the means to finally free women of their heavy household chores
Source: Centre for Art Historical Documentation, Nijmegen, The Netherlands

Yet by that time, Charles Darwin (1809–82), building on the studies of all these predecessors, including his own grandfather,[3] had started thinking about biology in terms of evolution as well. In 1859, his *On the Origin of Species by means of Natural Selection, or the Preservation of favoured races in the Struggle for Life* convincingly, for scientifically, 'proved' to many that new species developed in a constant process of evolution in which, in accordance with a fixed law of nature, stronger specimens of older species survived by adapting themselves, while the weaker disappeared.[4] When Darwin, although somewhat hesitantly, reached the logical conclusion of his own position and in 1871 published *The Descent of Man*, the human species lost its position at the apex of creation, the sole being created in the image of God. For many, Christianity in all its authoritarian institutional forms began to lose an essential part of its credibility.

Still, the success of Darwin's books, written in an almost novelistic style and, if only for that reason, appealing to a large audience,[5] shows the extent to which the cultural climate had changed during the early decades of the nineteenth century. For though the Churches did react negatively, the scholarly community by and large did not, nor did the general public: Europe had been ready for a 'change of paradigm', for a theory which answered the questions raised by a new society, a world of growing economic and social tensions and of global contrasts. Darwin's concepts were quickly popularized.[6] They flourished in a climate of continuing scepticism in the field of religion and to a large extent reinforced this, precisely because they were marked with the stamp of the increasingly unassailable scientific method.

In these years, too, the human sciences, 'invented' in the late eighteenth century, began to dominate the scientific and cultural debate. Social theory, anthropology and, finally, psychology increasingly found expression both in the world of scholarship and, far more important, in the works of popularization that were influential in restructuring European man's ideas about himself.[7] In the year 1859, in which Darwin first gave his theory to the world, the European view of man and the world was shocked on more fronts. For in the same year Karl Marx (1818–83) published his *Zur Kritik der politischen Oekonomie*. Against the background of the social misery and the political tensions caused by unbridled economic expansion in large parts of industrializing Europe, Marx scientifically showed that, in his view, society developed just as systematically as Darwin said nature did: in a constant fight for the means of production, the stronger became stronger and the weak, the workers, went to the wall.

Indeed science, rather than religion, was on its way to becoming the new faith.[8] For the first time in European history, a notion taken from the natural sciences succeeded in influencing all areas of life in an unprecedentedly short time: not only the other exact sciences but also politics and economics, as well as philosophy and literature, and, indeed, religion itself. A new view of man was born, strongly coloured by biological determinism. Free will as an essential human characteristic seemed to have disappeared. God, providence and deliverance had no place in the Darwinian world. Who could still believe in nature as a harmonious order? Was it not a battlefield, in constant movement as a result of the struggle between the representatives of the diverse species? Good and evil were no meaningful categories anymore: survival and progress were the only criteria.

Notwithstanding such potentially dangerous developments as the monk Mendel's genetic experiments and, indeed, the boost to genetic research given by those who studied the implications of Darwin's ideas, at the end of the technologically highly successful nineteenth century most Europeans were thrilled rather than worried by the prospects of science. Of course, the big majority did not understand the implications of the scientific discussion. If anything, they would rather read the dozens of exciting books written by the Frenchman Jules Verne (1828–1905), who showed how the many applications of the machine – including a number which were 'invented' by him only on paper and not realized by science and technology until well into the twentieth century[9] – would make life for people easier, more pleasant and more exciting.

The nineteenth century being the first 'century of children's books' on a scale to deserve this name, it is a highly significant aspect of European culture that Verne's massive production, translated in all European languages, aimed at an adolescent rather than an adult public; in such books as *Voyage to the Moon* and *Robur the Conqueror*, the belief in the power of science was inculcated in the new generation from an early age onwards. Nor was he the only one to incorporate new ideas. Those British children who read Charles Kingsley's highly popular *The Water Babies* (1863) were given a didactic fairy tale about a poor little chimney sweep who fled his persecutors by drowning himself and lived on in a new, clean, healthy world – a typical image of the age of pollution; moreover, it was a watery world that confidently spelled out the benefits of progress through evolution and the survival of the fittest.

Yet one should note that in this age of triumphant positivism and materialism, the need to escape from reality seemed greater than ever, especially if judged by its manifestation in literature. The past, or at least a time when myth and a village culture, rather than machines and towns, dominated man's life, became a powerful attraction. The first woman to win the Nobel Prize for literature, the Swedish author Selma Lagerlöf (1858–1941), wrote her *Gösta Berling's Saga* in 1891; this tale of the vicissitudes of a Lutheran minister who had fallen from grace was a powerful evocation of the landscape and the culture of her native Värmland, a mixture of realism and phantasy, of folklore and psychology. And in *Nils Holgersons underbara resa genom Sverige* (1907), fairy tale, travel book and *Bildungsroman*, which made her famous all over the world, she successfully tried to teach her youthful readership the history and beauty of the Swedish country. At the same time, both texts evince a kind of metaphysical Darwinism, showing man's evolution in a constant battle between his animal drives and his divine potential.[10]

This past-oriented tendency was dominant in many fields of elite culure. Already in 1859, in 'Darwin's Year', Europe had been given the long melodic lines of Richard Wagner's (1813–83) revolutionary opera *Tristan und Isolde*, in which physical love was openly shown as a passion which governs everything; it now was even coded in notes: Wagner's musical characteristics, the leitmotiv, tried to express the compelling impulses which people experience and which determine their behaviour in the face of rationality and even all other emotions.[11] This and other of Wagner's works were all set in a mythical, German past, though there were many among his audience who thought they could detect messages for the present in his tales of heroes and heroines.

Rather than turning to an idealized or at least romanticized past, Friedrich Nietzsche, one of the many who were influenced by Darwin's thought, had felt compelled to propose what he thought a more realistic analysis of the present, but did so in creating a heroic view of man that had not failed to influence Wagner: 'This world is the will to power – and nothing else! And you yourself are this will to power – and nothing else!'[12] Nietzsche called Christianity the symbol of the complete distortion of precisely all those natural values which help man to survive in this world, the only one he is given:

> It was the sick and dying who despised the body and the earth, and who invented heaven and the saving drops of blood, and they even deprive the body and the earth of that sweet, dark gift.[13]

Thus spoke Zarathustra, the ancient Persian philosopher whom Nietzsche made his mouthpiece. Christianity had made the world into a vale of tears by damning all passions, instead of making optimal use of them as the positive forces that they were. Nietzsche wanted to undo this *Umwertung aller Werten* (The Revaluation of all Values) which had, in his view, negatively directed Europe for centuries.

In the same period, comparative ethnology flourished as never before, especially as a result of the acquaintance with more and more different peoples and cultures which arose from European colonialism and imperialism. It was now slowly given form as a science of man in his cultural environment. One of its first influential practitioners, James Frazer (1854–1941), threw himself into comparative religious history. In his riveting twelve-part analysis of world religions and the myths associated with them, *The Golden Bough* (1890–1915), he set out to show that Christianity in its essence and functioning was definitely not unique, that both its beliefs and its characteristic rituals could also be found in many other religions. He convinced many readers. Yet many felt shocked when they realized this meant that the distinction often made between magic and religion, between the many non-western 'superstitions' and the one, true western religion was built, at least from a scientific point of view, on sand.

To make matters worse for those who continued to cling to traditional beliefs and attitudes, the practitioners of philology, of that textual science which already in the world of humanist learning had cleansed the Bible of all sorts of mistakes, now subjected the life of Jesus to a historical analysis; they did so according to the rules developed by the nineteenth-century study of history, leaning heavily on scientific empiricism. Among others, the highly controversial *Leben Jezu* (1839) by David Friedrich Strauss (1808–74) as well as Ernest Renan's (1823–92) *La Vie de Jesus* (1863) led to violent reactions all over the Christian world: what more was left of the Son of God than an 'incomparable human being' and an inspired rebellion leader?[14]

Consequently, the tendency towards secularization became even stronger. After Copernican physics had robbed the earth of its place as the centre of God's universe in the sixteenth and seventeenth centuries, Darwinian biology now removed man from the pedestal on which he had placed himself as the culmination of God's creation and reduced him to a 'coincidental' winner in the process of evolution, while anthropology gave the Christian religion a place just as lacking in glory, as a culturally 'explainable' phenomenon in the midst of so many other religions. Thus, while many traditional values now became relative, only the belief in science seemed to reign supreme.

Europe in hiding, Europe surviving

While developments in the domain of high culture influenced Europe's intellectual upper crust, much larger groups were affected by the large-scale migration from the countryside to the towns which was connected with industrialization and urbanization, which in most countries became more marked from the 1860s and 1870s onwards.

People became detached from their traditional social and religious institutions, especially the rural community and its centre, the Church, where the clergy still held the population in a forceful grip. Removal to the ever more anonymous environment of the big city meant an erosion of the 'moral economy' of traditional societies; the bonds with the Church but also with the old frameworks of family, village and neighbourhood – were slowly weakened. When this became obvious to the spiritual authorities, a large-scale offensive began to take shape all over Europe, undertaken by the various Churches. They often tried to cooperate with state authorities, who for several decades had already been equally alarmed at the disintegration of society and the political dangers inherent in increasing individualism.

An intriguing situation developed. The very means used by the secular ruling elites from the 1840s onwards to civilize the urban underclass, such as literacy campaigns, organized sports and large-scale community singing in amateur choirs that presented proper patriotic music, aided by the new mass education and the incipient mass media, from the 1860s and 1870s were also used to bring the non-European subjects of these elites into the fold of colonial rule. The Churches, assisting the secular authorities through their global missionary activities, were particularly eager to employ these instruments of mass manipulation. Rome, with renewed vigour, undertook extensive mission campaigns, partly out of fear for the equally energetically undertaken protestant missionary movement which, from the early nineteenth century, had greatly affected the Catholic Church's near-monopoly on the proclamation of Christian,

European values in large parts of the world. But now, by the late nineteenth century, the various Churches also began to look upon the industrialized cities and regions of Europe itself as frontiers, which had to be wrung from the new barbarism of individualism and of liberal or socialist doctrine by the same missionary methods.

Reactions to this religious-cultural offensive differed greatly from country to country, from social group to social group. Protestant communities, especially the less hierarchically organized ones, had obvious difficulty binding their congregations to tradition, whether or not revamped and revitalized. After all, the authority of the clergy in these Churches traditionally had not been very strong and opinions of individual believers had played an important role in shaping religious policy, so that often scepticism could not be held in check by authority.

In the catholic world, Rome's attempts to reinforce its hold over the believers sometimes did result in the strong 'ultramontanism' which it had hoped for: a renewed orientation towards the centre of the Catholic Church, 'beyond the mountains'. In such countries as the Netherlands, Belgium and Austria, a growing 'sectarianism' concentrated all areas of culture in the Catholic communities around religion and the clergy. Sometimes, however, the increasing demands of the Roman hierarchy had the opposite effect, resulting in a slowly more critical attitude and even in a political as well as cultural compromise with more recent movements like liberalism and socialism.[15]

In 1869, during the first Vatican Council, the Catholic Church, trying to keep at least the educated believers, supposed to be the leaders of their communities, within its flock, elevated some of Thomas Aquinas's doctrines to dogma. In a large-scale campaign Rome once more tried to reimpose its traditional views on the relation between man, the world and God. But this so-called neo-Thomism was only a reformulation of old positions, a fresh attempt to eliminate once again the tension which the Church itself had introduced into European culture almost 2,000 years earlier. Yet Rome hoped to rebuild itself as a power bloc which could compete with the national states whose aims often did not run as perfectly parallel with the Church's ideas as had been expected. It wanted to combat and finally destroy those phenomena which it saw as the destructive consequences of Enlightenment and Revolution and which were condemned as 'Modernism' – materialism, dwindling acceptance of authority, and secularization.

Nevertheless, even in such a religious society as the Spanish, the combined forces of industrialization, the adoption of a constitution and the growing power of the bourgeoisie resulted in a new mood; many no longer were willing to accept the domination of the Church in cultural life. Liberal bourgeois leaders like Don Francisco Giner, with his 'Institute of Free Education', founded in 1875, decided that Spain had to be educated anew, preferably not by an undereducated priesthood. His educational reforms inspired a host of collaborators who travelled to the far ends of the country, taking books, paintings and music to teach the new generation, and introducing them to sports and country walks; it produced painters like Pablo Picasso and Salvador Dali, musicians like Isaac Albeniz and Enrique Granados.[16] But with a government unable to find the funds for the large-scale adoption of this experiment, right-wing Catholicism continued its hold over the middle classes, who needed education as a means towards economic and social mobility.

Only a small group continued to hold the conviction that Europe, apart from showing material progress, stood for more profound norms and values which had to be cherished in the fight against the dangers of the increasing aggression between the European nations and of the growing gulf between the humanities and the natural sciences, two developments that would destroy Europe's cultural unity.

Just as in earlier centuries, concern about the outcome of these struggles caused many to devise all sorts of plans and strategies to maintain peace and bring about greater cohesion so that Europe might actually live up to its claim to be a humanistic civilization.[17] But even if people thought in terms of closer cooperation between states – one hears echoes of ideals like those which Dubois, Penn and Novalis had once articulated – the independence of Europe's sovereign nations was seldom discussed.

In this respect, the books written by the Danish state councillor Carl Friedrich von Schmidt-Phiseldek, are intriguing. In 1820 he published his *Europa und Amerika oder die Künftigen Verhältnisse der civilisierten Welt* (Europe and America or the future situation of the civilized world) and in 1821 *Die Europäische Bund* (The European Union), to impress upon his readers the danger that the young United States posed to a divided Europe. In 1859, J. Fröbel was even more terse in his *Amerika, Europa und die politische Gesichtspunkte der Gegenwart* (America, Europe and the political aspects of the present); if Europe did not develop some form of unity it would quickly become a mere stage for the inevitable struggle between America and Russia. In 1867, the French writer Victor Hugo felt forced to point out that Europe was still at least the 'mother country of mother countries'. But three years later, such notions did not prevent a gruesomely bloody war breaking out between France and Germany. With the misery of this war still fresh in his memory, Friedrich Nietzsche yet tried to convince himself, in his 1886 book *Jenseits von Gut und Bösen* (Beyond Good and Evil), that:

> nowadays the most obvious signs are not read, or even wilfully misinterpreted, which show that *Europe will be one*. In all people who, during this century, have looked beyond the surface, this has been the real direction their soul, in its mystical work, has been taking: to prepare the way towards that new *synthesis*.[18]

But deep down he must have realized that this vision would remain only a dream, the dream of a few intellectuals. In the cultural context typified by political and cultural nationalism and socio-economic individualism, it seemed as if the European ideal could no longer be a living force. In Europe itself, only a few still pointed to it as a world with unique, transnational values and norms shaping everybody's thoughts and actions regardless of their social or national background. Only a few felt that all European nations collectively showed common cultural characteristics which gave this part of the world both unity and unicity, distinguishing it from the rest of the world. Only a few translated these notions into a concept of Europe meant to bridge differences or prevent disputes.

Yet seen in retrospect, such characteristics were nevertheless evident, even if only in the domain of elite culture, in which, because of that culture's cosmopolitan character, they had been able to acquire their validity in the first place. A few should be named here.

Many Europeans still admired the two great examples, Greece and Rome, which had so essentially influenced Europe's view of man and had contributed to the formation of Europe's notion of the state. For even though the practice of democracy in the ancient Greek city-states had not at all resembled that which took shape in the constitutional and representative democracies of nineteenth-century Europe, still the idealized inspiration Europeans derived from ancient Greece and from the republican virtues of classical Rome had been strong in shaping political and social ideology from the sixteenth century onwards and, hence, in furthering the spirit of change that characterized the nineteenth century.[19] Another characteristic was Europe's way of empirical, later positivist, scientific thinking which, it is true, was not unique to it – compare the developments in China until the seventeenth century[20] – but which nowhere was carried through as extensively as in Europe. Here, the continuity with Antiquity, though equally idealized, was, actually, far more real than in the domain of political thought. Besides the momentous consequences in the development of the sciences themselves, the ancient Greek notion of the free spirit that is able to know all greatly contributed to the climate of secularization and, hence, of cultural change that characterizes the nineteenth century as well.

Then, of course, there was the unifying role of certain motifs in the visual and literary arts referring to contrasts and tensions apparently experienced everywhere in Europe: one may think of the mythical figure of Prometheus, the 'one who looks forward', one of the Titans, who, disobeying his father, Zeus, brought fire to the earth and thus embodied the spirit of creation and individualism with which Europe liked to identify its culture. But one must link to it the equally mythical figure of Faust, who embodies the ancient tension between the powers of belief and reason: 'Zwar weiss ich viel, ich möchte aber alles wissen' (I do know much, but would like to understand all).

Music by now was really unique among most other musical cultures in the world by its insistence on ever more complex harmonic polyphony, both instrumental and vocal, as well as in the quantity of the instruments and the -performers used for large-scale religious and secular works. True, the intro-duction, in the eleventh century, of a uniform, written musical notation, attributed to the monk Guido of Arezzo (*c.*990–*c.*1050), had led to the gradual loss of an important, orally transmitted musical culture – perhaps Portugal and

Spain are among the few European countries that, with the flamenco and the fado, still have a significant tradition in this field. It also had resulted in a composers' rather than a performers' culture. Finally, in the long run, it resulted in a powerful urge to differ from one's predecessors, in a need for originality that became almost vital to musicians from the eighteenth century onwards.

Yet this musical culture increasingly became a unifying force in European cosmopolitan culture, too. In the middle of the eighteenth century, composers like Christoph Willibald von Gluck (1714–87) left their homelands to work in Paris, developing French modes of their music. At the turn of the nineteenth to the twentieth century, the music of Pyotr Ilich Tchaikovsky (1840–93) and Modest Mussorgsky (1839–81) was brought from St Petersburg to the concert halls of Paris by such culture brokers as Sergei Diaghilev (1872–1929) – a music that breathed a spirit of the exotic, of a Russia that, though trying to retain, or perhaps even find again its own character, yet was approaching western European culture in more than only music.

One might argue that it was an apparent paradox, that in the very nationalistic nineteenth century all these forms of culture developed more strongly than before, perhaps precisely because less emphasis was placed on their common 'European' character and they were presented and experienced as 'genuinely German', 'specifically English' or 'typically French' achievements or expressions. Tennyson, while not creating great poetry when he wrote:

> Not in vain the distance beacons. Forward, forward let us range.
> Let the great world spin forever down the ringing groves of change.
> Thro' the shadow of the globe we sweep into the youngest day:
> Better fifty years of Europe than a cycle of Cathay[21]

clearly indicated how proud England was of its conquests and progress; yet contrasting these achievements of British culture to China, he also presented them as European.

In doing so, his poem, with its reference to the faraway Middle Kingdom which, in these very decades, was increasingly dominated by the English and other European powers economically, politically and militarily, was an expression of what is yet another seeming paradox. Most European states, despite their constant and sometimes bloody competition at home, at the same time manifested themselves abroad spreading certain cultural forms and values as specifically European touchstones of civilization. This was how they justified their hold over the non-European world, which acquired its most trenchant expression in imperialism. Consciously or unconsciously, many European civil servants, merchants, entrepreneurs and missionaries, in short, 'empire builders', experienced the need emotionally and intellectually to justify their participation in a policy of actual economic, political and cultural domination. They needed an ideology to underpin their actions. Sometimes they appealed to 'social Darwinism', a way of thinking in which the principles of Darwin's theory of biological evolution were misleadingly used to scientifically base the cultural, economic and political differences between peoples on racial distinctions. Often, the universal values of the Christian faith were referred to. And sometimes Europe's manifest position of power simply was established as its own justification. Always, Europeans were trying to legitimize what they imposed on and asked of others: conversion to one of the forms of Christianity, acceptance of the capitalist system, a lifestyle according to 'European' norms of civilized behaviour which was supposed to express and to prove that refinement.

This imperial ideology, expressed in Europe's growing periphery, helped to strengthen the cultural cohesion of the metropolis as well. All kinds of visual and printed propaganda, including a massive effort to educate Europeans, especially children, to an awareness of empire and its responsibilities, e.g. through highly romanticizing fiction, drove home the message that the nation and, behind it, Europe, stood for certain ideals, which had to be preserved and spread.[22] Perhaps one of the most astonishing writers in this field was Karl May (1842–1912), in terms of sales easily the most successful German author of all times; he influenced generations of boys and adults in works that were translated into dozens of languages. Though he never left his native country, he not only contributed outstandingly to the new genre of 'westerns', but also almost single-handedly created the genre of 'easterns', writing as convincingly about the noble Indian as about the noble Bedouin. Sincerely outlining the plight of the former at the hand of ruthless land speculators and of the latter in a Near East beset by corrupt Turkish officials, he helped to cement the stereotypes that Europe needed to rationalize its imperial policies. Despite May's criticism of imperialism's rougher edges, always the indigenous protagonist – 'Winnetou, the red Gentleman' being the most famous one – was aided, not to say saved, by the humanity and wisdom of the European hero, who epitomized a utopian vision of individual power directed by a benign, obviously Christian providence.[23]

A growing sense of *fin-de-siècle*: between pessimism and optimism

All over the earth, both those Europeans who travelled and those who ruled presented a front of pleasant, uncritical and even uncompromising faith in the many, in their view positive characteristics and values of the civilization in which they maintained to differ from the cultures they encountered and sought to dominate. Yet in Europe itself the continuous economic and political rivalry that was both the cause of and inherent in the phenomenon of nationalism resulted in increasingly bitter and bloody wars during the later nineteenth century: the machine had brought into use weapons which were vastly more effective and, thus, more destructive than ever before.

For those who seriously analysed contemporary society, the constant threat of war as well as the many changes wrought in society and culture by industrialization – the rise of new elites, of mass education, of mass consumption, the decline of 'old' values and traditions – created a sense of almost inevitable disaster. This feeling was enhanced by the relativism that became a dominant force in European elite culture from the end of the nineteenth century onwards. Despite all changes, the idea of a physical world built on the inalterable atom and the inalterable cosmos, and of man as a rational creature had remained unchallenged for most educated Europeans. But around the year 1900, even those certainties were threatened.

Many poets and philosophers – men such as Boehme and Bruno, Novalis and Goethe,[24] men such as Schopenhauer and Nietzsche – had cherished notions of the subconscious as the realm from which man was actually moved in his thoughts and actions. Now, the Viennese neuro-chemist turned 'psychologist' Sigmund Freud (1856–1939) further developed this concept;[25] he even refused to admit he had read Nietzsche and Schopenhauer, knowing how much his own ideas owed to theirs. In his *Die Traumdeutung* (The Interpretation of Dreams) (1900) he showed how an 'archaeological' survey of the mind through research into man's dreams could reveal the – to many frightening – world of the subconscious. There, rational controls did not rule; on the contrary, deeply embedded anxieties and suppressed lusts seemed to steer man's life. Despite the abundant evidence that Freud doctored much of the data he used to support his theories about man, and despite the fact that his patients, rather than accepting his preferred role as an impersonal investigator, made him into a father-figure, an idealized lover, a saviour even, he nevertheless was a great clinical observer and a great writer. Perhaps more than any other writer, he has altered the way western people in the twentieth century have thought, talked and written about human nature.[26] One may say that the Viennese psychoanalyst stood at the end of a long revolution. It had started when Newton, albeit implicitly, all but denied God's role in the active governance of the macrocosm, of the universe; it had continued to the point where Darwin had robbed God of his role in the development of life on earth; it now found its climax in Freud, who seemed to suggest that even in man's soul God had no role.[27]

It soon became evident that the revolution had not yet reached its final phase. For in physics, too, the turn of the century brought a revolutionary change. Traditional thinking on the structure of the microcosm was challenged and the idea of the unchanging atom was discarded: scientists began to accept that even atoms are unstable and produce energy when they disintegrate. Thus, it was increasingly evident that energy and matter were not separate worlds. Here, too, scientific proof was now presented for ideas that had been developed intuitively in earlier centuries, mostly by alchemists: matter can be altered, it can be changed into energy.

In the year 1900, the patrician American Henry Adams, thoroughly schooled in the humanist tradition of western culture, was in Paris. He wanted to visit the Universal Exposition, the umpteenth in a series that had started a century earlier, in 1798, also in Paris, with Europe's first ever industrial exhibition, a manifestation that had elevated the products of manufacture to the status formerly enjoyed by the products of the 'Arts'. Adams, who had been travelling and studying in Europe from the 1850s onwards, now wrote to his brother Brooke:

> As far as I have guessed the results of this Exposition, the Germans alone show very marked development of energy. But I see no one to give me a general idea of the whole field, and of course no single corner of it has value without the rest. The limit of the great economies may be near or far. Since 1889, the great economy has evidently been electricity. . . . electricity must have altogether altered economical conditions. Looking forward fifty years more, I should say that the superiority in electric energy was going to decide the next development of competition. That superiority depends, in its turn, on geography, geology and race-energy. All these elements have somewhat exact numerical values, and the value of your theory depends on getting the values of these unknown quantities. We should both have gained by knowing a little mathematics. That deficiency, due to the shocking inefficiency of Harvard College, has destroyed half the working value of our minds as trustworthy machines.
>   . . . I can see no reason for expecting any collapse at present, in Europe. . . . We ought to see a long period of rising prices and extensive economies. Apparently, Europe can go on indefinitely as she is, and the future type of England and France may be merely an extension of the Belgian and Dutch experience.[28]

Whereas Adams's political predictions proved false, his observations on economic development and the role of science and technology in it are quite interesting, as is his conclusion that to understand it all he lacks a basic precondition – some knowledge of mathematics, etc.

In the same year, Adams found a friend willing and able to explain to him the implications of the new sciences. From these lessons he proceeded to draw definite conclusions as to his own attitude towards culture, his need to understand and, perhaps, even somehow reconcile the old, Christian-humanist culture and the new sciences. He tells about it in his autobiography, in a chapter which he titled, significantly, 'The Dynamo and the Virgin':

> Until the Great Exposition of 1900 closed its doors in November, Adams haunted it, aching to absorb knowledge, and helpless to find it. . . . While he was thus meditating chaos, Langley came by, and showed it to him . . . Langley threw out of the field every exhibit that did not reveal a new application of force, and naturally threw out, to begin with, almost the whole art exhibition. . . . He taught Adams the astonishing complexities of the new Daimler motor, and of the automobile. . . . Then he showed his scholar the great hall of dynamos, and explained how little he knew about electricity or force of any kind. . . . To Adams, the dynamo became a symbol of infinity. As he grew accustomed to the great gallery of machines, he began to feel the forty-foot dynamos as a moral force, much as the early Christians felt the Cross.
>   . . . the new forces were anarchical. . . . The force was wholly new. . . . In these seven years man had translated himself into a new universe which had no common scale of measurement with the old. He had entered a suprasensual world,

in which he could measure nothing except by chance collisions of movements imperceptible to his senses, perhaps even imperceptible to his instruments, but perceptible to each other, and so to some known ray at the end of the scale. [. . . he] seemed prepared for anything, even for an indeterminable number of universes interfused – physics stark mad in metaphysics.

. . . the rays . . . were a revelation of mysterious energy like that of the Cross; they were what, in terms of mediaeval science, were called immediate modes of the divine substance. . . . Clearly, if he was bound to reduce all these forces to a common value, this common value could have no measure but that of their attraction to his own mind. He must treat them as they had been felt; as convertible, reversible, interchangeable attractions on thought. He made up his mind to venture it; he would risk translating rays into faith. . . . Here opened another totally new education, which promised to be by far the most hazardous of all . . . two kingdoms of force which had nothing in common but attraction.[29]

In view of his attitude towards the role of science in culture and society, Adams's experience may be deemed archetypal of one current of development of European, indeed of western man in the course of the twentieth century, the optimistic strand.

In 1900, the German physicist Max Planck (1858–1947) stipulated that subatomic radiation was not emitted in a steady stream, but rather in uneven little spurts, which he called quanta. He also introduced a new constant in the field of physics, meant to determine the distribution of energy produced by a radiating body. This so-called 'Planck's constant', symbolized as h, soon proved fundamental in the development of a new mechanics of the atom, termed quantum mechanics. This spelled the end of the exclusive dominance of the classical, mechanistic interpretation of physics codified by Newton two hundred years earlier.

Albert Einstein (1879–1955) synthesized many of the new developments in his 'General Theory of Relativity'. After his already revolutionary gravitational research that had upset traditional, Newtonian views, he now claimed, among other things, that time, space and movement should not be seen as absolute entities but, rather, be interpreted as relative in accordance with the position of the observer. Aristotelian logic, Euclidean mathematics and Newtonian physics that together had structured the European vision of the universe now seemed to collapse. And with it a number of non-scientific certainties in the fields of ethics, philosophy and politics that had been loosely based on that structured universe with its fixed laws. No wonder that Einstein's views led to a passionate debate in which theologians, philosophers and historians joined with his scientific colleagues.[30] Surprisingly, the Belgian-born priest-mathematician Georges Lemaître (1894–1966), a member of the papal academy of science, took up Einstein's own mathematics and in 1927 came up with the idea of the primeval atom that was the beginning of life, when the universe was born with a big bang, some 15 billion years ago. He also argued that this universe was anything but static. Einstein himself accepted Lemaître's position only when, in

1931, the two of them got together with the American astronomer Edwin Hubble (1889–1953), who had presented the world with the proof of the existence of other galaxies besides the Milky Way. But despite the meeting of these three great minds, and their final consensus, the discussion about the precise nature of the universe as either contracting or expanding, or even static continues.

Meanwhile, both Einstein and Planck tried to counter the indeterministic world-view that seemed to follow logically from their own arguments and that, moreover, was supported by their fellow physicists Nils Bohr and Werner Heisenberg. They held that a distinction should still be made between man the observer and the object of his observation, the physical universe.[31] But to many this distinction was no longer viable.

The feeling of uncertainty pervading the last decades of the nineteenth century and the first years of the twentieth century, because numerous people perceived their own age as more revolutionary than any before it, was reflected in various forms of culture, as were the new ideas about man and the cosmos that were soon widely popularized. In a kind of wild abandon, a frenzy of creativity that manifested itself in painting and architecture as well as in literature and music, many artists took up an 'avant garde' position; re-examining the languages of the arts and using radically new techniques, they hoped to succeed in creating something worthwhile. Analysing, deconstructing and reconstructing reality as they saw or heard it with such wide-ranging means as atonality and collage, cubism or expressionism, they did, indeed, succeed in their effort.[32] However, much of their creative production was actually of a pessimistic nature.

In the 3,000-odd pages of the great cycle of novels *A la recherche du temps perdu* (Remembrance of Things Past) (1913–27), in which Marcel Proust (1871–22) tried to capture the mystery of time and its relentless workings in man and society, he analysed, specifically, the ways and means of the new leaders, the bourgeoisie, trying to penetrate the bastions of the old aristocracy. In a series of merciless analyses of their individual members, Proust depicted the decline of the latter and the shallow, valueless drive for power and pleasure of the former, manifesting themselves in forms of grotesque social opportunism and hypocrisy. The spirit of the time was also criticized, albeit rather more implicitly, in the works of the great Norwegian playwright Henrik Ibsen (1828–1906). He fathomed the growing conflict between an evermore restrictive society and the individual, between illusion and reality, in a series of haunting plays that, not incidentally, centre around powerful females in whose lives these conflicts are tragically shown; in *Samfundets Stotter*, *Et Dukkehjem* and *Gengangere* – Pillars of Society, The Doll's House and Ghosts – he described dilemmas that, as was shown by their success all over Europe, were felt increasingly by the entire bourgeois world of the west. Pablo Picasso (1881–1973), in the many still-lives he painted in the years between 1910 and 1914, often positioned his glasses and bottles against a background of a newspaper page: in each, something tragic is told – a chauffeur murders a woman, a soldier spits out a bullet, an actress poisons her lover; society is sick from moral decay and physical violence.[33]

Others, while convinced that western civilization was doomed and, worse, that it had called down this doom on its own head, precisely by relinquishing the old norms and values, were optimistic: out of the ashes of the past, if necessary the ashes left by another great war which seemed unavoidable, a new society would rise, not burdened by tradition but free. Thus, in Italy, the philosopher and cultural critic Benedetto Croce (1866–1952) tried to develop an open-ended historicism as an alternative to traditional religion and the culture of science. To him, reality was history: the human world forever grows as a result of the creative answers of individuals. He posed that truth and morality do not dissolve if one denies transcendence and accepts historicity: men will always use these delivering capacities to order the world.[34]

A world between wars

Nevertheless, in 1914, a 'world war' was the almost inevitable outcome of the economic and political tensions that had built up during the preceding decades and that had been translated into military preparations by the three main imperialist nations of Europe, England, France and Germany.

One has to admit that to term this global conflict a 'world war' is, in a way, hypocritical. For it was, first and foremost, a war fought between the states and nations of Europe, for motives and interests entirely their own; the only reason why this struggle came to involve much of the non-European world was the very fact that Europe's economic and political interests had acquired global proportions, influencing even the farthest corners of the earth and the people living there, if only because so many men from French Africa and British India were called to military service in a world which they had never seen before.

Against the background of this 'world on fire', the dream of Europe turned into a nightmare. As often before, part of the intellectual elite rejected their responsibility for the disasters befalling the old world; yet they stated their claim to be once more seen as Europe's cultural conscience, demanding to be involved in building a new one. The Austrian literary critic and writer Hugo von Hofmansthal (1874–1929) wrote, with an acute insight also in the social, mainly urban character of Europe's cultural elite:

> We, we. I know very well that I cannot speak for the entire generation. I speak about several thousand people spread over Europe's big cities. Some of them are famous; some of them write . . . moving and gripping books; some . . . write only letters; . . . some of them leave no traces. . . . And yet these two or three thousand people have a certain significance; . . . they're not necessarily the leaders or the soul of their generation: but they are its conscience.[35]

True, many intellectuals were certain not only that a century had ended, but also that the end of civilization itself had come. This sense of doom was aptly coined in the phrase *Der Untergang des Abendlandes* (The Decline of the West), the title given by the German philosopher Oswald Spengler to the two-volume study he published between 1918 and 1922 – a book which was an instant bestseller. Others, such as the Belgian historian Henri Pirenne in his *Mahomet et Charlemagne* (1937), created a vision of a European civilization that would have continued triumphantly from its ancient origins to its Christian fulfilment were it not for the coming of Islam, that had disrupted the unity still prevailing at the end of the sixth century – as if to alert Europe to the fact that it could define itself only in contrast with other cultures, as if to remind Europe of the central, Christian roots and characteristics of its civilization.[36]

Meanwhile, many of the scientific ideas evolved around the turn of the century, though often misunderstood or not understood at all, became highly influential in other fields of early-twentieth-century culture, precisely because they seemed to support a view of man and his world as unstable and relative. They definitely contributed to the prevailing climate of scepticism as is shown in the work of poets and other writers, such as the Czech author Franz Kafka (1883–1924).[37] On the other hand, these emotions, emphasized by the terrible experience of the millions of deaths that had been the inheritance of the First World War, confronted people with the question of the validity of these scientific ideas and their consequences, and, finally even with the question of the meaning of existence.

The sense of alienation that caught many people was, perhaps, voiced best by the Austrian author Robert Musil (1880–1942), who, like Proust, used the novel to research the conditions of contemporary society; his gigantic, multi-volume *Der Mann ohne Eigenschaften* (The Man without Qualities) (1930–43) in its very construction of hundreds of short pieces showed the fragmentization of life and thought that, to many, seemed to characterize European culture in the first decades of the twentieth century.[38]

In this context, the relationship between Europe and America was reconsidered once more. Opposing those critics of culture, those philosophers and social analysts who, at the end of the nineteenth century and during the first decades of the twentieth century admonished Europe to copy the 'American model', were those who tried to use contemporary American culture and society as a mirror, to hold up to Europe and show it which dangers would arise if this example were indeed followed: human misery and cultural consumerism would be the result of unbridled egoism and unrestricted materialism. They argued that the expectations voiced by Hector St John, that the culture of the old world would find its fulfilment in the new had been proved entirely wrong. On the contrary, America showed what would happen to man if he did not have the benefit of traditions to structure his thoughts and actions.

Meanwhile, the American dream, or nightmare, was soon symbolized by the skyscrapers that seemed to touch the clouds; they were the embodiment of human pride, or of human tragedy, as those who knew their Bible were wont to point out. It was an image eagerly taken up by the European media to signify the United States. The new medium of photography, soon followed by the cinema, gave the skyscraper world-wide notoriety.[39] Moreover, the cinema often combined this image with another one, that of the all-powerful machine. In Fritz Lang's fascinating film *Metropolis*, made in 1926, that had its genesis in the artist's first impression of New York's electrically lit skyline as seen from the ships arriving from Europe, the machine inhabits the mile-high buildings and shows man his diminishing importance; in the end, it threatens to devour man, as a new moloch.[40] This was the very fear Europe had had for the past hundred years; the stormy developments of technology in the United States only increased it.[41] A vision of technology as a dehumanizing influence now combined with a pessimistic view of the equally dehumanizing effects of the metropolis to create a deep-rooted anxiety about the coming end of the individual, that proud, central figure in European culture. Hence, the heroic struggle of man against machine became a recurrent theme in western cinema; as recently as 1988 the very images that made *Metropolis* unforgettable returned in the 'cultfilm' *Blade Runner*.[42]

It is clear that the appreciation of America fluctuated on the waves of Europe's self-image. In the early years of the twentieth century, Franz Kafka devoted the first of his great novels to America as the at-once alienating and yet challenging context in which his protagonist Karl Rossmann comes to know himself, through a series of situations that remind one forcibly of the bitter-sweet atmosphere that colours the movies of Charlie Chaplin, between naive innocence and world-wise cynicism; landing in New York, Rossmann muses: 'Die ersten Tage eines Europäers in Amerika seien ja einer Geburt vergleichbar' (the first days of a European in the United States after all resemble birth).[43]

The negative view of the United States held in European elite culture from the end of the nineteenth century onwards had ended decades of positive propaganda. It certainly was the outcome of growing cultural pessimism, especially in intellectual circles who were profoundly influenced by the horrors of the First World War, when mass destruction ended the life not only of so many irreplaceable humans but also of so many irreplaceable monuments. In the Netherlands, the famous historian and cultural critic Johan Huizinga published his philosophically rather than historically founded opinions of the United States and their influence on the Old World in his *Mensch en menigte in Amerika* (Man and multitude in America) (1918), followed in 1927 by *Amerika levend en denkend* (America as it lives and thinks); in these books he voiced views by then held by many all over Europe, reflecting a certain ambivalence towards the culture of the new world. On the one hand one could not deny that America showed Europe the logical consequences of its own way of thinking and living that had originated in the optimist, progressive attitudes of the eighteenth-century Enlightenment. Consequently, Huizinga, himself the heir of this intellectual tradition, showed a decided admiration of the 'vitalistic attitude' inherent in the American way of life, an attitude of 'Dit, Hier en Straks' (of this, now and soon); Huizinga combined this with an essentially pessimistic vision on the situation of contemporary European culture, that had lost its erstwhile vitality, the will to fight the inevitable decadence.[44] Yet his admiration was mixed with an equally clear aversion of the increasing massification manifest in the culture of the United States.

The issue of decadence was also addressed by one of Germany's and indeed Europe's most creative twentieth-century writers, Thomas Mann (1875–1955).[45] He tried to analyse his world, the world of the first two decades of that century, in a monumental novel, *Der Zauberberg* (The Magic Mountain) (1924). Its hero, Hans Castorp, goes to visit a relative in a Swiss sanatorium; if only by the 'magic', the opaque language and actions of a staff of sinister, in their science incomprehensible but apparently all-powerful doctors and psychologists, he is convinced that he, too, will succumb to the century's most dreaded illness, tuberculosis, if he does not follow their strange prescriptions; he decides to stay. Finally, he comes to know himself as well as the maladies of his age: the conflict between freedom and responsibility, between art that can become anarchy, and civic values that yet can stultify the spirit if not inspired by art; the conflict, he fears, between any form of tyranny, physical or spiritual, and chaos. In a gripping scene, set on the snow-capped mountain top, Castorp thinks about the possibilities of a synthesis between the Apollonian and the Dionysian face of culture, of man: the harmony produced by a spirit of reason and the rapture produced by a spirit of emotion. When the novel ends, with Castorp leaving for the front, he dreams that, after death brought by the war, Europe's fatal disease will be cured and there will be fraternity, a new humanity.

But, during the 1920s and 1930s the lessons of the terrible war of 1914–18 were not heeded, nor did the various forms in which Europe reconsidered the roles of humans and their culture produce the positive effects many, including Mann, had hoped for. That much, at least, was clear when in 1939 a second all-European war seemed imminent; when it erupted it soon proved even more disastrous, also globally speaking, than its predecessor.

The rise of totalitarian modes of thinking, even of totalitarian states, from the 1920s onwards, had been one of the most profound shocks ever felt by those who believed in Europe as a civil society based on certain norms and values, such as democracy, tolerance and responsibility *vis-à-vis* one's fellow human beings, precisely because most people deemed them intrinsically European. Now, new disasters produced a culture that almost denied the value of the individual. Worse, they resulted in the bloodiest war the world had ever seen.

And yet many have argued that the preconditions for this episode in European history lay in the very structure of its culture and society. The more or less liberal nationalism of the nineteenth century had seen the further development of the European states and their constitutional and parliamentary democracies, resulting in as well as being the result of the gradual enlargement of the electorate until, finally, it encompassed all adult males and, by now, even females. Some have argued that despite the hopes raised by democratization, it was the democratic system itself which facilitated the transformation into new, totalitarian policies of the feelings of resentment and vengeance felt by those states which had lost the First World War, or thought they had not gained enough. Both in Italy and, even more, in Germany, these feelings galled from the moment the allied forces settled the reckoning at the 1919 peace congress at Versailles. Now, parliamentary democracy itself, that, to many, seemed unable to prevent the degradation of state and nation, provided an easy ladder to those political leaders who were trying to climb to positions of power, exploiting these feelings of hurt national pride and promising revenge and national glory if only they were given a free hand.

The capitalist economy and the society based on it had, from the late nineteenth century onwards, brought unprecedented wealth to Europe at large and raised the standard of living of the majority of its people to unknown heights. But allowed to develop unchecked, this socio-economic system had been unable to restrict the economic and social consequences resulting from the periodic crises inherent in it. Aggravated by irresponsible financial speculation, such a crisis occurred in the 1920s, resulting in mass poverty all over Europe, not least in defeated Germany. There, as elsewhere, the process combined with a growing lack of faith in democratic institutions and solutions, and propaganda for totalitarian alternatives promising national glory and national wealth. Such a new medium as the movie film was a perfect vehicle to drive the nationalistic message of salvation through strong, heroic leaders home to the masses.

In France, which had a special bureau producing historical films, one of Europe's great cinematographers, Abel Gance (1889–1981), created his greatest work, *Napoléon* (1927), using the most daring of techniques – among other things projecting three different images simultaneously, on three screens, an innovation not taken up at the time and reinvented in the 1950s. In this epic, he illustrated the vital force of the French nation as embodied in the revolutionary hero. In Germany, the Austrian Fritz Lang (1890–1976), a trained architect and painter of large-scale canvases produced *Die Nibelungen* (1927), an impressive as well as oppressive film version of the ancient epic, dedicated 'to the German people'; it seemed to put the force of myth before the power of reason. Like its numerous historical counterparts elsewhere in Europe, it did not so much visualize the past as, more precisely, present the public with an idealized past of strong, even heroic men, and sometimes women, that might help it survive the unpleasant present. The warning message contained in the Dane Carl Dreyer's (1889–1968) moving master-piece, *La Passion de Jeanne d'Arc* (1928), that the past also had been a time of fearful repression of the outspoken individual by powerful systems, Church and State, was definitely less welcome.

Indeed, without the technology that was greatly broadening Europe's perspective both of itself and of the world, the cultural and political con-sequences of social and economic change would not have been as serious as they were. Both the radio and the cinema, two of the most exciting techno-logical manifestations of twentieth-century culture, provided the very means for the propaganda that helped Europe's would-be dictators on their way to power.

Undeniably, the technology that produced the new communications' media was also facilitating people's lives all over the western world, contributing greatly to their material well-being as well as to an easier and healthier life: the mechanical and chemical industries that provided food and medication, public transport and domestic appliances. At the same time, this technology was used to produce weapons which could bring death on a scale and with a thoroughness hitherto unknown. The very wings that in the early years of the century finally realized man's eternal dream of flying and that, through commercial machinations and a public demand for glamorized heroes, almost immediately were represented both in established and in popular culture – through photography, the cinema, and songs[46] – soon brought the bombs to the cities where other dreams of Europe had found their expression, both in magnificent works of 'high' art and in the by now highly improved 'popular' housing estates where many people now lived in reasonable comfort. In the end, experimental physics, based on theories about the atom and the basic structure of matter going back to the ancient Greeks, created forces that could easily destroy the world and the culture that had produced it.

The social, or human sciences, by the end of the nineteenth century had begun to study politics and society and interpret it as a rational and therefore even makable organization; the work of the German scholar Max Weber (1864–1920), to name but one of the most creative spirits in the field, is still monumental in the insights it offers in societal and cultural processes, even though it studied and implicitly judged other cultures such as the Chinese and the Indian by the standards of modernity and progress which Europe had set.[47] With their empirical base in sociohistoric data, and with some success in explaining the problems of contemporary society, these as yet mostly theoretical ideas about 'social engineering' seemed to offer the perfect proof to those who said they were able to liberate the world from its present predicaments and shortcomings: socialist politicians, social-democrat thinkers but equally more totalitarian-minded persons. The modern state, with its efficient bureaucracy, had succeeded in almost eliminating private violence by concentrating the right to legal violence – jurisdiction and punishment, the use of the army – in its own hands. But that state could also be used as the highly accurate instrument it was to enforce whatever policy carried the day in a democracy that lost its sense of human dignity.

In a Europe showing so many possibilities, the egotism of states – both the losers and the winners of the First World War – resulted in their failure to create an acceptable balance, an international order that did not breed dissatisfaction and war. In most states, the narrow interests of various groups could and sometimes did lead to a situation wherein the electorate failed to accept responsibilty for society at large and for the weak in particular. Only slight excuses were needed to break with traditional values now considered ineffective and to take recourse to other ideas, equally part of the European tradition, that promised greater value: where democracy and tolerance disappeared, dictatorship and repression succeeded. Perhaps this occurred more readily in those countries where industrialization, education and democracy still were comparatively recent developments, a thin veneer covering an older, rural, more traditionally hierarchical society.[48]

In Germany, by the end of the nineteenth century in many ways one of Europe's most civilized countries, producing musicians, painters, scientists and writers whose works still inspire European culture, almost all of the above-mentioned preconditions were fulfilled at the same time. This fact helps understand the genesis there of a totalitarian system of unprecedented brutality and effectiveness, the 'Third Reich' and its 'final solution'.[49] The so-called Holocaust – a word meaning sacrifice to the gods and, hence, an inappropriate name for what was plain mass murder or genocide on the most gigantic scale – caused the death of millions of people: not only Jews from all over Europe, but also blacks, gypsies, homosexuals, mentally ill people and others. All of them were slaughtered because the system needed conformity and total obedience, and made scapegoats out of those who could be stigmatized as 'the other'. In a way, the leaders of Nazi Germany exploited a prejudice against 'strangers' that had been part of European culture for more than a thousand years;[50] but in the twentieth century not only were they able to give their racist ideology a pseudo-scientific gloss, but they could also use the instruments of modernity, like advanced technology and the bureaucratic apparatus of the modern state, to implement it.[51]

Yet it is important not to forget that comparable visions had raised their head elsewhere. In Italy, the birthplace of Humanism and the Renaissance, of new visions of man and society, from the early 1920s a fascist dictatorship ruled for more than twenty years, succumbing, if only at the end of Mussolini's era, to the attractions of racist policies as well. Moreover, there were distinct totalitarian tendencies and the ensuing scapegoat ideologies in France and Spain as well, and sometimes, as in France or the countries of central Europe, as explicit in their anti-semitic form. There were groups advocating strong leadership with little or no regard for democratic principles in Belgium, England and the Netherlands and, indeed, in almost all countries of western Europe, as there were in central and eastern Europe, too.

In short, all over Europe a complex culture of 'modernity' had come into being, full of possibilities for good and evil, that goes a far way to explain the origins of dictatorship in democracy, of war and mass murder in a society that, objectively judged, had never been as educated and prosperous.

17 Towards a new Europe?

Science, culture and society

By the first decades of the twentieth century, the dominant cultural forces in Europe were largely the forces generated by an urban, industrial culture, in which the machine or rather technology had become an all-pervading presence, despite large areas remaining rural in their economic and cultural life. The new world was visualized in Walter Ruttmann's memorable movie *Berlin, Symphonie der Großstadt* (Berlin, the symphony of a metropolis) (1927); in the same years the concomitant features of this culture were voiced by the film actress Marlene Dietrich (1901–92), who sang:

> Es liegt in der Luft eine Sachlichkeit, es liegt in der Luft eine Stachlichkeit . . .
> Durch die Lüfte sausen schon Bilder, Radio, Telefon, durch die Luft geht alles
> drahtlos und die Luft wird schon ganz ratlos, Flugzeug, Luftschiff.

> There's business-like rationality in the air, there's stimulation in the air . . .
> already, the air is filled with images, radio, telephone, all is going wireless and the
> air doesn't know how to handle it all: airplane, airship.

This song presents an image of a bewildering and bewildered world that finds itself completely dominated by the products of science and technology. Indeed, many wondered whether there were any limits to what science might produce. But equally many were afraid that, in the end, man might be the victim of the realization of his own dreams.

In 1929, the German composer Paul Hindemith (1895–1963) and his compatriot, the playwright Bertolt Brecht (1898–1956) collaborated in the creation of a fascinating theatre piece, combining an orchestra, a chorus, solo singers, a group of clowns and cinematic projection, which they gave the title *Lehrstück* (Instruction piece), for in accordance with Brecht's idealist-socialist attitudes not only should it be staged and performed by and for the people,[1] but also it should instruct them with its message. It tells of man's aspirations to dominate the world, nature, through technology, which had produced many marvellous machines and yet not realized a society that could prevent people from dying of starvation. In realizing his desire to fly like a bird, man had finally reached the limits of his ability. In the *Lehrstück*, the pilot, proud of his achievement, crashes. When he asks for mercy as he lies dying, the multitude assembled around him denies him any help. On the contrary, they impress upon him the need for humility. Only when the pilot assents to his essential nothingness is he forgiven, and dies in peace.

Seen against the background of the grave economic and social crisis of the 1920s, Brecht's message represented a very negative vision of contemporary culture. One might ask whether it was not born from an increasing ignorance of modern science, from fear, even. And yet the fear was understandable. Within less than twenty years since the beginning of the century, science had come a long way from the British physicist Ernest Rutherford (1871–1937) who had said that physics could be good, only if one could explain it to a barmaid; as someone who had conducted basic research into the structure of the atom and received the 1908 Nobel Prize for chemistry, he may have slightly exaggerated.

For while the age-long gap between two of Europe's worlds, the rural and the urban, was being closed, a new one, in the making since Copernicus, now opened up definitely, dividing a world that could be understood, interpreted by all who had received a decent education from a world whose comprehension required a complex, non-verbal language understood by only a minority. Because the natural sciences speak a single, universal language, that of mathematics, and, by and large, use a single methodology, in the twentieth century the world of science has become, indeed, the World.

At the beginning of the twentieth century, the central field in the natural sciences was physics, and one of the central questions in it the nature of the atom. Further investigating the structure of the atom, so long seen as the stable building block of the physical universe, between 1911 and 1913 men like Rutherford and Bohr discovered its nucleus and the electrons circling around it; they also discovered that a theory of causality relying either on waves or on particles would not suffice to explain its reality. Moreover, Werner Heisenberg (1901– 76) claimed that after a physical observation the object observed always shows a finite change, which would imply that the knowledge claimed of such an object is fundamentally limited as well. He therefore claimed that we are unable to know the position and speed of the individual electrons; therefore, it is impossible to predict their behaviour. All these developments led to the further elaboration of quantum mechanics which discerns a pattern of frequencies in the atom produced by successive quantum states that, putting matters simply, manifest the complementarity of both waves and particles. To accept this, man, even scientific man, had to leave behind most theories held sacred in science for a long time, specifically determinist causality.

As in many fields of culture, the Second World War proved a catalyst in science, too. All contestants had devoted enormous efforts of time and money to research that should produce the technology to win the war. Indeed, 'pure' or theoretical science and 'applied' science, i.e. practical technology, though their union had its basis in the nineteenth century, now effectively joined on a grand scale, never to separate again. Thus, the allied battle against Germany and Japan resulted, first, in the discovery of nuclear fission – the achievement of Otto Hahn (1879–1968), in 1939 – and, after the scientists told the politicians and the soldiers of the possibilities, in nuclear warfare, when a team led by Robert Oppenheimer (1904–67) at Los Alamos, in the desert of New Mexico managed to test an atomic explosion successfully in 1945. Tragically, it had to be actually used before many of the scientists involved started to have second thoughts, realizing the full and dreadful potential of the hydrogen bomb as well as the political use it had been put to by the United States, ostensibly to end the war against 'yellow imperialism' but, as some historians have argued, actually to threaten Soviet Russia not to advance too far either in Asia or in Europe.[2]

At the same time, the possibilities of the Englishman Alan Turing's (1912–54) speculations in mathematical logic, dating from the mid-1930s, had become evident, too. Soon, the machines that were constructed to help to decode enemy (i.e. German) messages evolved into the computers that now regulate many of western people's most routine actions, from reading the bar codes on every piece of supermarket consumer goods to giving access to world-wide telephone services or the electronic highway. Indeed, the moment these computerized systems fail, western society is increasingly faced with its daily dependence on them.

By the end of the twentieth century, science has become the basis of society, of an economy and a culture that cannot exist without the technology it continues to produce, at ever greater speed, with such exciting developments as the reintegration of physics and chemistry.[3] Soon after research in solid-state physics showed the electromagnetic properties of crystals, the transistor revolutionized communication systems. And only some years after F. Crick and J.D. Watson discovered the structure of DNA in 1953 – the deoxyribo-nucleic acid that was known to play a role in heredity but whose capacity for gene-copying and, thus, central function in the actual operation of heredity was as yet unclear – the so-called recombinant DNA techniques revolutionized biology and the life sciences in general;[4] by the 1980s, combining the genes of one species with those of another, biotechnology altered such diverse fields as agriculture and medicine.

These developments, while obviously beneficial in a great number of ways, yet have negative effects as well. In agriculture, the concomitant pollution of the environment, and the many problems caused by foodstuffs containing heavy doses of growth-inducing chemicals and pesticides have become an object of political and, indeed, cultural debate, questioning the dependence of society on what many consider the unnecessary overproduction of irresponsibly doctored food that becomes a burden on the environment as well. In medical biology, the possibility of uncontrolled or uncontrollable genetical manipulation has posed worries, against the background of the increasingly consumerist attitude of many people, who may all too easily think that shopping for an altered or even new body is as much everyone's individual right as is the acquisition of a newly enhanced personal computer.

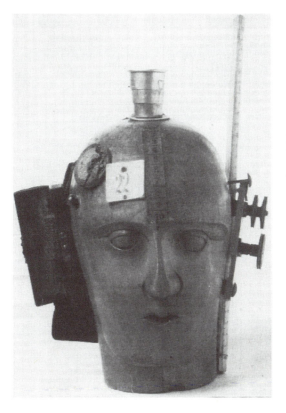

Plates 42 and 43 In *c.*1920, the French artist Raoul Hausmann created an 'assemblage' which he named 'Mechanical Head', to symbolize the 'Spirit of Our Age'. Some forty years later, scientists had gone a long way to uncover the 'mechanical' and even chemical nature of man, opening up a whole new world of research into all human functions and capacities, including those of the brain. One of the major developments was the discovery by James Watson and Francis Crick of the structure of DNA, now universally known through the famous image of the 'double helix'
Source: Centre for Art Historical Documentation, Nijmegen, The Netherlands

Indeed, by the second half of the twentieth century Europe, and the wider world as well, was not yet completely at ease with the fundamental role of science. On the contrary, with its ascendancy, the cultural criticism of its power increased. There was widespread fear, mainly, one must conclude, because to most people science has become incomprehensible and, moreover, its practical and moral consequences unpredictable.

It is hardly accidental that, after the Second World War that had introduced so many deaths through the means of technology, that had given nuclear power, and that seemed to inaugurate an as yet endless period of 'cold war' between the western and the communist world, two men have engaged in a debate that raised the fundamental question of the role of science in a humane society.

C.P. Snow (1905–80) and F.R. Leavis (1895–1978), together, created the famous image of a world of two cultures, defining the course of western civilization as running, continuously, through a field of tension between the 'natural sciences' and 'the humanities'. These two English intellectuals first crossed swords in 1959–61. Snow, nuclear physicist and top bureaucrat, the embodiment of the fusion between the powerful exact sciences and the state that had gained much of its power controlling this field of knowledge, was yet a man from the humanities, the author of a series of novels called *Strangers and Brothers* that tried to paint a picture of the changes in English society between the 1930s and the 1960s. His opponent Leavis, a famous as well as influential literary critic, was a teacher at the old, tradition-hallowed university at Cambridge, to many the embodiment of the 'ivory tower',[5] even though, of course, it was Cambridge itself that was increasingly known for its contributions to modern scientific research.

Snow had voiced his concern about the gap he saw growing between the two cultures; while referring to the traditional rivalry between the humanities and the natural sciences, his main concern was the increasingly obvious inability of the students and practitioners of the one to understand the basic values governing the research and the motives of the others. This, he argued, would be fatal to Europe, indeed to culture in general.

As Leavis did, many have accused Snow of surreptitiously trying to establish the primacy of the sciences for economic development and, consequently, for prosperity, implying that only a technologically powerful and, hence, economically strong society would be able to compete with other ideologies – i.e. the communist one – and that, in doing so, he practically neglected the contribution made by the humanities to the values that many considered central to European civilization.

Yet while Snow certainly had this agenda – many politicians and cultural critics writing and speaking after him have used it as well, one way or the other – one can hardly deny that his analysis went to the core of twentieth-century culture and society. Almost everything people have come to take for granted in the way of physical and material comfort has been the undeniable product of an increasingly complex and powerful science and technology, up to the medical and biological research that not only has prolonged the life of our bodies but also now promises the perfection of our minds as well through genetic manipulation. But taking things for granted implies denying responsibility, and with science that means responsibility both over ourselves and our earth. The release of fluorocarbons – a substantial element in such comfort contrivances as refrigerators and aerosols – may have greatly damaged the ozone layer that ensures liveability on this planet. The advances in molecular biology and the cracking of the genetic code will probably contribute to the elimination of much human suffering; they may also damage future creatures, or allow humans to go further on the path to, first, 'perfect' themselves, at least physically, and then endlessly replicate these perfect beings, a possibility clearly proven by the animal-cloning experiments of the 1990s. In both cases, only well-informed persons with at least some scientific education can expect to participate in and exert some influence on the public debate which sustains a responsible society, a debate over the future of human culture and what we have come to see as its essential humanity; a debate, moreover, not only with the scientists themselves but, equally important, with those who finance and hence at least partly control their work. For it is bureaucrats and politicians who fund and allocate the gigantic amounts of public money that keep science going.

However, while in Europe, in the last decades of the twentieth century, there were some 1 million people actually engaged in scientific research and experimental development,[6] on a total population of some 700 million, few outside their circle did understand even the basic lines along which this research develops. Consequently, average educated individuals, who, morally or otherwise, are concerned about the development of society, have lost their grip on one of society's most creative cultural fields, as well as one of its most powerful tools. In so far as they consciously refuse to interest themselves in these basic lines, they can hardly expect to be able to confront the practitioners of the sciences with the validity of the values that the tradition of the humanities should continue to instil in that same society. People should engage in a debate over the desired course of a civilization dominated by science instead of increasingly turning their back on its fundamental principles and only enjoying its fruits; they should accept science as an essential part of their cultural heritage but, with it, the responsibility to be acquainted with at least the fundamentals of its thinking. They should not become as the sorcerer's apprentice in the eponymous musical composition by Paul Dukas (1897), based on Goethe's *Der Zauberlehrling* (1797), who could not control the forces he unleashed because he refused to learn from his master.

Admittedly, entering the world of science for the layperson is far from easy, as can be shown from the continuing quest for the 'ultimate particle'. In the 1960s it resulted in a proliferation of 'quarks', and later of neutrinos – particles not yet 'seen', but proven, at least to many physicists, by their effects. Their very intangibility is, perhaps, reflected in the fact that the name for the 'quark' is taken from one of James Joyce's most enigmatic novels, *Finnegans Wake* (1939). Not surprisingly, twentieth-century scientists, themselves confronted with confusions and contradictions, have continuously tried to find new ways to describe the wholeness of nature in a single model that would reconcile or even efface all contradictions. Einstein worked on his 'unified field theory' to connect electromagnetism and gravitation. Bohr tried to do so with his idea of complementarity, arguing that the various modes of perceiving and understanding need not be mutually exclusive, indeed, probably somehow will contribute to a final comprehension, to a new unity of the sciences – a fascinating view, even more so if one realizes that he came to this conclusion partly on the basis of reading the American philosopher Wiliam James's *The Principles of Psychology* (1890), a work decidedly not part of the canon of the physical sciences. But then, Bohr was already trying to bridge the gap between the humanities and the sciences.[7]

Efforts by men like Bohr and Einstein, though not always understood, nor, for that matter, accepted by subsequent generations of scientists, seem to represent a basic yearning in creative man when confronted with a nature that, however well explored, still remains a mystery. Indeed, they somehow mirror the emotional needs that had driven the physicists of the German *Naturphilosophie* of the early nineteenth century to try and reconcile the material and the spiritual universe and discover basic structures in each and every manifestation of life. This quest has continued, producing a series of 'solutions' that are still being debated. Meanwhile, discussions in the two scientific fields that seem each others' greatest opposites show how far removed from final answers man still is.

Brain research, though greatly advanced at the end of the twentieth century, has shown an extraordinary lack of consensus as to what a human brain actually is like, still leaving scientists to dispute over the question what, exactly, constitutes man.[8] Some have argued that the brain as being capable of non-computational intuition, can be understood only if a special type of physics, as yet unknown, is developed. Others have explained its functioning merely from the oscillation of our nerve cells. Still, there have been many physicists, like the Nobel Prize winner John Eccles, who have said that understanding the brain will not make us comprehend man any better, because its study leaves out a spiritual soul – a point of view that certainly echoes the mind–body discussions of the ancient Greeks, of Descartes, of La Mettrie and so many others throughout the history of Europe.

Moving from the brain's tiny neurons to the origins of the universe, the most accepted cosmological solution, the so-called Big Bang theory which first emerged in the 1960s, maintains that it all began with a point, a mathematical singularity, some 15 billion years ago – a concept surprisingly made into something of a scientific hit by the British astrophysicist Stephen Hawking (b. 1942) in the 1980s. But for all its exciting vistas through space and time, these theories have not even started to answer the simple question that has perplexed man since he first formulated thoughts about the cosmos: what, then, is the origin of the cosmic seed from which the galaxies and, ultimately, life and mankind are said to stem?[9]

Meanwhile, if anything, developments in the world of science and technology have shown that Europe is not the world's sole leader any more nor, one should admit, is it among the world's most creative and productive regions. True, some of the most influential and unsettling discoveries of the first half of the twentieth century have been made in Europe but since the Second World War the centre of gravity has moved to the United States, not least because in the 1930s so many of Germany's most creative and productive minds were forced to move to the other side of the Atlantic – though others, after working for the Nazi regime, went on to do so for the former Allies.

Yet precisely because science and technology increasingly determine the course of mankind and the world, a Europe that tries to hold up certain values in the interplay between the sciences and that world, and to translate them into liveable realities, can still be a force to the good.

After the Second World War: deconstruction and reconstruction

Both the winners and the losers of the Second World War faced a number of grave problems. After mass destruction, economic reconstruction was, of course, imperative. But moral reconstruction was equally important. Germany had to come to terms not only with having lost another war but with the traumatizing stigma of having produced Nazism and the Holocaust. The allied states not only had to avoid another situation like Versailles and its aftermath, allowing, even helping Germany to recover its erstwhile position among Europe's civilized nations, but also they had to ask themselves why a Europe of civilized nations had not prevented the war in the first place; a witch hunt for those who had collaborated with the German occupiers was the easiest way out, but people soon realized that pointing an accusing finger at the guilt of others was too facile; it certainly was not going to answer the question as to what structural conflicts within European culture and society, indeed within European people might result in such a – temporary? – loss of those values which many had thought to be held as fundamental by everyone alike.

Another effect of the Second World War was the seemingly final division between east and west within geographical Europe. The power of Soviet Russia, that had been growing stronger since the Bolshevik Revolution of 1917 had brought about the downfall of the tsarist empire, had been consolidated between the wars and had reached its apex in the second war; its armies had spread over large parts of eastern and central Europe, overthrowing the existing regimes, some of which had collaborated with or outrightly sold out to the Third Reich. By 1945, the Soviets were firmly entrenched there, establishing a series of satellite states to serve as a buffer zone between the Russian heartland and western Europe.

Last but not least, the Second World War accelerated the process of decolonization, forcing the leading nations of western Europe that had possessed colonial empires – some of them for more than 300 years – to face the fact that they no longer ruled the world. The process was enhanced by the obvious change in world politics brought about by the rise to global power status of the United States, that was accompanied by a growing American preponderance in the economic, cultural and, specifically, scientific fields – Fröbel's predictions had come true after all.

Consequently, the traumas produced by the war and the sombre vision of a continuing conflict with the communist world that might even result in the world's end now that nuclear arms had given man the power of total destruction, induced many western Europeans once again to examine fundamentally their hopes and policies for the future. Was it acceptable that each nation should continue to fight for its own ends, as had been the case for far too many years and with such obviously tragic results? Or was cooperation called for now, at least in the fields of economic and military policies? Would not this be a better answer to the challenges posed by a post-war world to a Europe that wanted to survive?

To avoid the ever-present danger of recurring chauvinism and nationalism and to foster a sense of European unity, as well as to create a bulwark against Bolshevism, a policy of formal economic and political-military cooperation between the states of non-communist Europe did indeed seem the best solution. Thus, western Europe went on its slow way to form a community,[10] following some of the leads provided by the many plans formulated in previous centuries.

It was not, however, easy to eradicate the old, national ways of thinking that, growing to their strongest expression in the nation-states of the nineteenth and early twentieth centuries, had become a set of often oversimplified values inculcated in the minds of each citizen through education and constant propaganda. As the result of much soul-searching by intellectuals and politicians during the Second World War, in the years following various bold and far-ranging forms of economic cooperation were slowly realized – beginning, in 1952, with the Schuman Plan that resulted in the European Coal and Steel Community and ending with the 1957 Treaty of Rome that formed the European Economic Community. But a new ideology was called for as well. However prophetic in their vision, in trying to present a concept of European culture the 'European saints', the post-war founders of the European idea, those who 'rebuilt' the dream, understandably were still bound to their past, perhaps rather too much so.

In a time of crisis Konrad Adenauer, Alcide de Gasperi, Jean Monnet, Robert Schuman and Paul-Henri Spaak – intellectuals or, at least, erudite politicians all of them – attempted, like so many of their predecessors, to formulate an ideal that could at least function as a political-rhetorical instrument. Perhaps not incidentally, most of them belonged to the Roman Catholic Church and pointed to (western) Europe as the geographical-cultural framework in which the classical tradition and Christian thought had become the norm-bearing pillars of European civilization. Indeed, Adenauer, Schuman and Spaak often conversed in German. Perhaps one might even say that something of the spirit of a man like Novalis was still present in them. However, even in their time the values and institutions which had once formed the core and expression of this European dream already had become less self-evident; specifically, the Churches have been losing influence since the 1950s.

Yet in the years after 1945 politicians and also historians have done their best to describe the European past, the achievements which were considered and represented as having evolved in a process lasting for more than two thousand years, in such terms that people's expectations with regard to the present and the future appeared to be substantially based on them. Admittedly, this has proved a difficult task, if only because to many the disadvantages of centralization under the aegis of 'Brussels' soon seemed to outweigh the advantages which were all too quickly forgotten. Indeed, even despite the as yet virtual absence of a clear-cut concept of European identity, a growing number of people have felt forced to take action against what they experience as 'the dangers of the European ideal'. To them, that ideal threatens to demolish the nation-states and, worse, their cultural identity. Obviously, we should ask if that fear and the implied accusations are legitimate?

Looking at the actions of the founders of the 'European dream' after the Second World War, one cannot avoid the impression that at first they were mostly intent on rebuilding their own states on the ruins of post-war Europe: cooperation, starting in the economically and strategically central sectors of coal and steel, was mainly necessary to create the economic conditions for their own recovery.[11] It was this recovery that had to prevent a devastating war waged for ideological or economic reasons breaking out again. Yet since then, with the power of 'the Community' slowly growing, the defence of the nation-state by Euro-pessimists is waged more strongly than ever.

What, exactly, is that 'Community', this 'Union'? Is it, after decades of growth, more than an expensive, to some Kafkaesque and ultimately self-serving bureaucracy with overpaid officials that regulates economic, social and political life for the sake of old and new capitalists – the image often presented in the media and taken over by many Europeans? Or must we accept 'the united Europe' and its admittedly sometimes absurd and often costly consequences as the price we are willing to pay for the hope that the inhumanity of two materially and morally devastating wars in the twentieth century will not occur again, at least, not on the 'Union's' territory? Must we not realize, too, that precisely because of the economic policies pursued under the guidance of 'Brussels', such European countries as Spain and Portugal, which had been virtual dictatorships for several decades, could become more democratic, open societies in the 1960s and 1970s? The post-war, free trade spirit that followed the protectionist policies of the 1930s did at least help to demolish the tariff walls that shielded these countries economically, but also culturally from the rest of Europe. With greater economic freedom, with tourism, too, came, slowly, an exchange of views, a greater spiritual freedom that contributed considerably to the final demise of these regimes.

Still, since the early 1970s, another important question has been asked over and over again. Are the costs of communality the price that states and their citizens will want to pay only if things are going relatively well, yet which they will consider too high if their own economy, as a result, is mixed with the lesser achievements of other countries which comprise or aspire to membership of that 'Union', or if that economy continues to be too attractive to those outside it?

Meanwhile, it seems evident most observers would argue that for the time being the efforts at communality have resulted in a Europe of bureaucratic elites rather than in a Europe of the citizens. Bureaucracy and democracy have certainly not gone hand in hand in the development of European institutions, as the still restricted role of the (incidentally equally costly) European Parliament clearly shows. To counter, if only through a change of practice, the negative feelings this situation causes among many 'Europeans' is one of the challenges the future holds. And yet 'Europe' goes its own way, economically, socially, politically, culturally. Those who express their scepticism about attempts to reach more in-depth integration by defending the elements that, to them, comprise the sovereignty of states may well be fighting a rearguard action.

After all, has not the essential *raison d'être* of states in past centuries been the serving of the *res publica*, the promotion of the welfare of the state's subjects? Well, then, the care for these things to a considerable extent has been entrusted to 'the European Union', even if the results are certainly not yet in complete accordance with its intentions and promises, and the consequences are still difficult to gauge. On the other hand there are those who maintain that, precisely by giving up some of their sovereign rights, the states of Europe over the past decades have been able to maintain a far greater measure of actual independence than otherwise would have been possible.[12]

Also, we should be wary to hold up the nation-state – not a centuries-old but on the contrary a fairly recent construction, a 'created tradition'[13] – as an untouchable ideal that under no condition should be destructed by 'Brussels'. It is quite interesting to note that in many cases the nation-state is not as strong as has been thought and that a much older concept of a mainly regional cultural identity seems to be hidden behind it. Here, too, one might maintain that it is precisely the security which the new Europe offers that enables the states to accept a growing measure of regional independence of a variety of cultures within their national structures. In Germany, the construction of the post-war state has from the beginning acknowledged the importance of regions, also in the field of culture. In Spain, Catalonia among others offers a fine case of the continuous strength of regional culture, as does Scotland in Great Britain. Indeed, the results of the 1997 vote demonstrated the latter region's wish to be formally identified as an independent culture and polity, to demolish, at least in part, a state structure erected nearly two hundred years earlier.

In most instances, a notion of a shared past, however revitalized beyond its erstwhile reality, or even completely invented, sometimes coupled with religion but especially with language, appears to be the powerful basis for regional identity.[14] Perhaps it is true that these older roots have to be cherished, if only because of the argument that only healthy 'provincialism' can lead to any fruitful 'universalism', at least in a cultural sense.

Undeniably, the offensive undertaken by those who are pressing the ideal of European unity to its furthest limits appears, in many states, to be breaking up against the as-yet solid walls of these more concrete structures which have, apparently, influenced and even formed man for longer and more radically than that concept of Europe which, despite all its undeniable practical and ideological purposes, is still a dream. A satisfactory, politically and culturally convincing definition of the essentials and characteristics of European culture has not been presented while the second millennium of what is, by the way, still called the 'Christian era' turns into the third.

Perhaps it would be preferable if a simple concept of European culture were never to be given. After all, such concepts contain the great danger that they can all too easily be manipulated to rouse the masses, the same danger that is presented by the more extreme defences of national or religious identity often based on cultural criteria and characteristics.

From the 1950s onwards, in the context of Europe's search for its own identity, the relationship with America became an issue once more. However powerful the voice of critics like Johan Huizinga, in the Netherlands, and his like in other European countries might have been in intellectual circles, for decades the popular press had continued to publish loudly the success stories of the new world. The new medium, film, which, in its American form, dominated the European market in the years following the First World War because indigenous production had all but collapsed, seemed to stress the truth of what the papers proclaimed: in images that 'could not lie' the Hollywood dream factory triumphantly showed a world of desires come true in every field from consumption to sexuality.

Subsequently, the undeniably crucial role of the United States in the liberation of the greater part of western Europe from fascist dictatorships had greatly strengthened its popularity with the peoples of Europe. But the ambivalence of the relationship remained.[15] A small group who felt themselves to be a cultural elite and did not hesitate to proclaim themselves as such continued to cry out its warnings against the danger of moral, cultural decadence in the old world precisely because of the soulless materialism that reached it from the new world, both in the form of consumer goods and of the messages contained in films and, later, television. And yet the public at large, for all the patronizing words of their self-appointed cultural leaders, continued to enjoy everything the new world had to offer.

In the 1960s and 1970s, as American culture in its commercial expressions of film, fashion and music definitely fastened its hold on the European market, agitation ran high and many people called for a concise, rhetorically effective concept of Europe. Especially France has openly fought against these influences; inevitably, the French, for all their pride in their own, national culture, have fought this battle under the banner of European values and traditions, claiming they needed everyone's support to uphold European civilization.[16] Yet the campaign was rather surprising. The market these Euro-defenders wanted to protect, while not, perhaps, owing its existence to the 1947 Marshall Plan, certainly had been revived and expanded greatly by the gigantic financial injection with which the United States had, only twenty years earlier, contributed to the restoration of the European economy, out of a mixture of understandable self-interest and altruism.

Whatever one's opinions on the merits or validity of this cultural anti-Americanism, the tide of the 'American influence' seems unstemmable. Just as Columbus had portrayed the Indians as the ideal people and in doing so had given the European readers of his journal a vision of a physical perfection that resembled God's image of man, so Hollywood movies since the 1920s, advertising since the 1950s, the Barbie dolls since the 1960s, and video clips since the 1980s have shown many more Europeans a vision of man that, however, is far more forceful: a compelling influence in their own self-perception that in extreme cases results in anorexia or plastic surgery.

As in previous centuries, Europe adopted, and still adopts – though it sometimes also adapted and adapts – American food ways and other fashions, indeed everything money can buy; it also adopts and adapts American ideas that either inspire or are spread by the visual arts, by literature, by music, by the cinema and by television. Thus, it seems as if five hundred years of communal history have only intensified the Euro-American relationship. Both such basic fields of culture as the European diet – from the potato and cocoa to the hamburger and coca-cola – as the rather more complex ways of looking at man and the world have altered in the centuries since Columbus. Europe's dreams and their realization in the images that fill its art and architecture, its literature and music are still being profoundly influenced by America. Ever since the discovery of America, the culture of Europe has shown its presence. What Europe is now, what Europeans are now is, to a large extent, incomprehensible if one does not take into account the economic, political and cultural influence of America, of a process of interaction and integration that began in 1492.

Here too, the fact that people have called for a clear definition of Europe's identity to enable Europe to mount a well-defined cultural offensive against the supposedly pernicious influences of another culture seems the best argument against such a definition: a culture that closes itself off from the outside world is bound to atrophy. Yet many are still searching for a satisfactory definition of what it is that gives Europe its specific value. Among them, obviously, are the politicians and policy-makers who support the ideal of the European community and increasingly need it because their agenda, besides the economic and military cooperation which has been largely realized since the 1970s, now includes the new topic of political cooperation as well. But among those hotly discussing this issue also are many intellectuals who are not bound professionally – at least not overtly so – to European institutions.[17]

Now that a religious foundation of European culture largely appears to have become an anomaly, many are of the view that a more secular definition of what people describe as the essence of European culture is necessary. To find out what material there is for such a definition, we should turn to the culture that has developed since the mid-twentieth century.

Nowadays, an analysis of the manifestations of European culture and the underlying structures and assumptions does not have to rely anymore – at least not solely – on the often one-sided individual testimonies that have helped us to reconstruct the more remote past, however painstakingly collected, and however speaking and valuable these data may still be. The advance of the social sciences and their research methods, combined with improved communications and data-collecting and processing systems, has created the possibility of large-scale investigation, producing extensive surveys that cover the practices and ideas of people across national or even continental borders. A decided but unavoidable disadvantage is that in the telling of the story that is history, the individual experience now tends to disappear behind anonymous categories, and often is even reduced to sheer numbers.

One of these surveys, the so-called 'European values research', which was carried out in the decade between 1980 and 1990 in Europe and North America – working from the assumption that this Atlantic region does indeed form a cultural continuum – has contributed fascinating data for the analysis of late-twentieth-century culture, even though one must be careful when dealing with the results and interpretations of such very global overviews based on random samples.[18]

A culture of time versus money

With the real coming of the mass market and the ensuing democratization of goods at the end of the nineteenth century, scepticism about the cultural consequences became more marked. Intellectuals noticed that capitalism and democracy, together, resulted in both endemic overproduction and the multi-plication of occasions for imitation, rather than creating a rational, cultured society based on clear and limited means. They saw the dangers of competition and conformism in the pursuit of luxury by a crowd whose taste was untrained and who would, in the end, swamp 'high' culture.

Yet the solutions that were proposed remained, by and large, the same as those formulated a century earlier, albeit they were worded differently.[19] In the 1880s, Paul Lafargue denounced the right to work as a false fixation causing a growing dependence on and increasing waste of material things. One of the founding fathers of sociology, Emile Durkheim, asked for some sort of social control of luxury, hoping to find exemplary asceticism in the individual and the genesis of 'social' religion among the population at large.[20]

By the beginning of the twentieth century, mass-production technology promised and delivered an endless quantity of goods. The average purchasing power rose steeply, first in the United States and then in Europe as well. It was assumed that economic growth and increased production would result in free time and in a 'mass leisure society'. Debates about the question how to democratize leisure soon followed, but it has to be admitted that it was rather the liberal-leftist intellectual elite who worried over the issue than the majority of people themselves.[21] Many well-meant experiments were undertaken, especially in the 1920s and 1930s, by intellectuals, cultural educators and social workers to reintegrate those who were considered socially and culturally lost in urban, anonymous mass production society by means of the ordered free time of cultural and sports clubs. However, most capitalists argued strongly against increased leisure as it limited their access to flexible production while many workers were more concerned about job and wage security.[22]

Mostly, the optimists had the day, economic and social theorists who peppered their works, however empirically based, with highly moralistic ideas. The French sociologist Eugène Tarde, who published his 'The Laws of Imitation' in Paris in the year 1890, while admitting that mass-goods society arose from the imitation by the urbanized masses of the models of a creative class, yet voiced the hope that, in the end, the trend would reverse itself and a cultured democracy would emerge in which the masses – educated by now under the system of compulsory primary education that had been introduced by most European states – would operate discriminatingly between the poles of consumer goods and spiritual goods. Some decades later, the English economist John Maynard Keynes touchingly assumed that after the satisfaction of absolute needs people would devote their further energies to non-economic purposes and fill their leisure with the 'art of life itself'.[23]

Meanwhile, the Depression of the 1930s and the Second World War left most Americans and Europeans with an increased craving for material gratification.[24] When the war had ended, women returned to their homes from the factories and offices, by and large resuming their by now dual traditional role, of home-maker and of decision-maker in the spending of the family income. Ideas about the reduction of worktime and leisure planning that were heard in the immediate post-war period were soon deemed obsolete. Full employment and a vision of unlimited consumption were what most people – both politicians and workers – wished to realize; there was wide-ranging acceptance of the ideals of mass production and high wages.

A manipulated need creation on an unprecedented scale soon followed. Thus, after 1945, a 'consumerist consensus' seemed the prevalent attitude.[25] Indeed, consumerism was hailed everywhere. With a rise in the standard of living in accordance with – and, matching, market-wise – an increase in production, everyone would be able to aspire to and eventually acquire the lifestyle of the well-to-do middle-income groups. Social classes would disappear as the United States and Europe reached the 'last stage of economic growth' prophesied by the popular economist W.W. Rostow.[26] In Europe, the adoption of what was called 'the American model' did not encounter great opposition. The French politician Jean-Jacques Servan-Schreiber, in his *Le Défi*

Americain equated liberty with consumer choice and democracy with mass access to consumer goods.[27]

Intellectuals did ponder over the desirability of this situation, but, mostly, they failed to influence decision making.[28] An economist like J.K. Galbraith might point out the cultural, ecological and social consequences of unrestrained growth, in his famous book *The Affluent Society*,[29] and Raymond Aron voiced his fears in an equally famous study of *Les Desillusions du Progrès* but most westerners – both Americans and Europeans – were more optimistic.

Admittedly, by the late 1950s, first in the USA and later in Europe, people began to express some concern as television began to show its influence. The new medium was soon thoroughly commercialized as advertising began to direct programming. Ever more, leisure became consumption as many people began to spend their free time and their hard-won money in increasingly long hours of shopping, induced therein by merchandisers via television;[30] the half-joking, half-critical expression 'shop till you drop' became an adage. Even when not directly sending advertising messages, the home screen still projected lifestyles leading to consumerism through films and the family drama's sponsored by the household detergent industry, the so-called 'soap operas', a genre that continues the highly popular melodramatic theatre so beloved by both lower-middle classes and working population during the nineteenth century. In Britain, the percentage of homes provided with a television set rose from zero to 66 per cent between 1955 and 1959, and to 90 per cent in 1969. By that time, people spent about half of their leisure time in front of the screen and have continued to do so ever since.[31]

The merchandisers' efforts to manipulate the culture industry resulted in a – seemingly conformist – mass culture, mostly led by the needs they discerned among the middle classes, the 'status seekers' so aptly analysed in Vance Packard's classic study of 1959.[32]

Tourism and its cultural connotations provide a fascinating case in point. Travel for pleasure, indicating almost unbounded leisure – albeit legitimized by the consumption of high culture – had been an elite phenomenon till the end of the eighteenth century, culminating in the southbound Grand Tour. In the nineteenth century, increased wealth and transport made it available to the well-to-do bourgeoisie. They were no longer satisfied with a week in the mountains or at the seaside, if only because even the better-off labourers were now going there; also, of course, they were eager to ape the aristocracy in a pattern that enhanced status as well as affording an escape from an industrialized, increasingly stress-ridden world. So, they now took the road southward as well. Innovative entrepreneurs like the firm of Thomas Cook and Sons or the Belgian *Compagnie Internationale des Wagons Lits* soon realized what market there was to further open up and manipulate.

However, most people continued to avoid the summer heat of the Mediterranean, travelling in the relatively mild autumn, winter and early spring periods. When in southern France or in Italy, they protected their faces, shielding under huge parasols. Not only did they come from societies with a strong agricultural component, wherein a fair complexion traditionally distinguished the rich landlords from the poor peasants and, consequently, had become a sign of beauty both in the female and in the male, but also they wanted to stress their difference from the darker-skinned 'locals', whose ancient culture they admired but whose contemporary lifestyle was considered so much less civilized and progressive than the society of the democratic, industrialized north-west. But in the course of the twentieth century, when transport, especially with the coming of the motor car and the airplane, as well as increased income made long-distance travel available to the masses, a tanned face came to denote a holiday in the sun and, hence, a possibility to accentuate status. Soon, of course, marketing strategists were also exploiting the argument that a sun tan equated health. Such is the strength of cultural stereotypes that even though in the 1980s medical research pointed to the increased danger of skin cancer, the majority of European holiday-makers still flocked to the world's sunny beaches.

Already in the 1950s, critics began to doubt the potential of such leisure as there was to be a really liberating force in society, fulfilling the individual; it rather seemed a simple release from the permanent tensions induced by long hours of wage-earning.

By the late 1960s and the early 1970s, a more decided reversal seemed to set in. Largely, the generation that had lived through the Depression of the 1930s and had formulated its material wishes accordingly was dead; by now, the greater part of the European population had been reared from childhood in a world of consumerism. Among them, a 'post-materialist' movement was born. Not only did merchandisers realize that not everybody was willing to share their rose-coloured vision of unlimited consumer demands, but also the sacred tenet of the full-employment economy came under attack, implying a re-evaluation of the work ethic towards a more flexible use of work and leisure time.

This situation has had various, sometimes contradicting, cultural consequences.[33] The 'children of affluence' began to voice consumer demands, asking for participation. The market quickly realized the potential of the increasing number of young consumers who, structurally, rebelled against the more traditional values of their elders. Moreover, many of the current cultural educators no longer were classically-trained humanists with ideas about a 'Hellenist' 'high' culture à la Matthew Arnold or Wilhelm von Humboldt; they were rather people more and more attuned to all kind of forms of popular, 'low' culture.

Meanwhile, intellectuals continued to voice hopes for a society with more free time that would liberate workers from routine and stress, as they had been doing ever since the early 1920s. But their analyses of the present and of the future were – and often are – contradictory and, anyhow, met with great opposition from the circles of economists and political decision makers who, mostly, continued to advocate the ideal of growth.

Also, with real wages rising, the 'cost' of free time rose as well; workers tended to intensify their consumption of leisure and aided it by time-saving devices like camping or gardening, which, however, involve consumer goods which have to be earned: people may long for community and self-expression but goods tend to get in the way of their enjoyment of time and of each other. When questioned, most workers, from the 1960s onwards, have preferred a 40 hours' week and early retirement rather than shorter workdays,[34] although among the economically more priviliged groups the demand for free time is much higher.[35]

With more women entering the workforce, a more equal division of the public and the domestic work sphere between men and women and a re-definition of gender roles seemed possible. Job sharing was advocated as well. Still, it seems illusory to expect radical changes from the realignment of gender. Some theorists and sociopolitical activists have expressed hopes that women, choosing part-time jobs, might effect a new balance between work and leisure. However, with the increasing cost of housing, transport and recreation, in dual income families most women follow a largely male career-centred model; deftly or desperately adjusting their wage and domestic worktime, they try to minimize disruptions in the traditional family sphere.On another level, non-commercial leisure seemed to survive – in 1980, some 40 per cent of the British population joined in participating sports; there was a sharp increase in do-it-yourself activities, while some 80 per cent of the men and 60 per cent of the women belonged to an endless variety of clubs.[36] In France, the same picture emerged, with a sharp increase in cultural activities more narrowly defined like visiting museums and art exhibitions.[37] In the Netherlands, the numbers attending the theatre, concerts of classical music and the opera were increasing as well.[38]

This trend seemed to hold even though in the 1980s economic growth slackened and – as happened in the 1920s and 1930s – the social consequences have been considerable. Once more, there was a confrontation between pressure for further reduction of the work week – which in most European countries had reached 40 hours by 1970 – to *c*.35 hours and prophecies of economic doom as a consequence of it. Indeed, by the 1990s, many employers were still fearing stagnation and increasing competition while a considerable group of economists favoured even raising the 40-hour standard and campaigned for an end to the policies aimed at the lowering of the compulsive retirement age.

Meanwhile, the real danger seems to lie elsewhere. From the 1950s onwards, the 'welfare state' was realized in many countries of western Europe; with its health benefit schemes and old age pensions, its paid holidays and its largely free education it was and is a monument both to economic prosperity and to the democratically expressed will of civic society not only to root out as much human suffering as possible but also to realize as much equality, at least of chances, as possible.

Yet even before it was fully realized in all countries of western Europe, by the end of the 1980s the 'welfare state' seemed unable to sustain its high level of publicly fuelled social services; an increasingly consumerist society that sees its material prosperity threatened tries to reduce or even withdraw its support for the states which have embraced this ideal. With growing unemployment, a possibly fatal gap opens between those who have a job and an income, as well as the position in society that both provide, and those who, though reasonably or even well-educated, remain jobless, and whose children may well remain so, too. Research shows that precisely in these groups, where prospects for the future are bleak, educational performance decreases and criminality rises – in a sphere of forced, largely unstructured 'leisure'. This certainly is a major concern for the future, as is a continued, slavish adherence to a work-and-spend ethic which will certainly create even more tensions between the fully employed and the jobless.

So, on the whole, affluence, while greatly increasing the material wellbeing of the majority of Europeans, does not so far seem to have produced the structural social harmony envisaged by many idealists.

Perhaps the most profound cause of the many predicaments of present-day culture is the continued existence of hierarchy and emulation that makes people seek for 'signs' – whether in the time-leisure or in the money-consumption spheres – to bolster their individual or group confidence, the more so as the security offered by such traditional, primary groups as family and neighbourhood, is disappearing. As these signs tend to be the very consumer goods that can be bought only through the triumph of mass production, time collapses into money.[39] Economic growth does not liberate free time but rather creates affluence and the incentive to work more and harder, and, in so far as it does produce leisure, results rather in private pleasure than in public commitment, especially among the young.

For the majority, free time and spending are happily reconciled both within domestic consumption, largely concentrated in the weekend, and in tourist consumption – the dream of the holiday. Liberty of choice and democracy of leisure seem only intellectual, elitist concepts, which definitely do not figure on the agenda of the population at large. Also, non-profit cultural groups have little influence on the use of public space and time; business and politics mostly control the finance of leisure services, and they tend to be somewhat conservative, channelling 'pleasure' into safe arenas, commodifying free time into such forms that, for many, it has become equivalent to passivity and emptiness.

Utopian schemes to stop what many critics consider cultural and social decline in individual, group or society have been voiced, mostly calling for a break from unlimited, emulative and manipulated consumption and for the formation of non-political, non-market oriented values. However, even if they be humanistic populists, these critical intellectuals have but little power to structurally redirect economic, social and cultural needs and realize alternative forms of individuality and community both in work and in leisure. The dilemma of time versus money will be with Europe and the western world for some time to come.

From 'familyman' to 'salaryman' – from group identity to individual identity?

In Europe, the twentieth century has witnessed the completion of a socio-economic revolution that, especially since the 1950s, has changed its outlook fundamentally.

The first fascinating aspect in which sociocultural change after the Second World War became manifest was that women 'became visible'.[40] The emancipatory movement of the last decades of the nineteenth century, the first so-called 'feminist wave', had brought women the right to enter higher education and, after the First World War, the even more coveted right to vote, which finally made them into citizens. Yet their economic dependency remained appalling. Admittedly, some job sectors had become feminized from the beginning of the century onwards – for instance, secretarial and shop work, and such services as the telephone exchanges. However, most women who were forced to engage in paid labour to enable their families to survive, taking the most menial of jobs, were in grossly underpaid positions. On the other hand, those women who wanted to work were often not allowed to, their sociocultural, bourgeois context practically forbidding them to enter the job market.

After 1945, not only did women from the working classes go out to work in far greater numbers than before, if only to enable their children to have a better eduation; now, educated women from the middle class entered the labour market as well, often not from a wish to add to an already comfortable family budget, but from an urge for freedom and autonomy as well as, of course, equality. Such material changes as the introduction of all kinds of domestic appliances gave them the practical means to do so. Yet far more important was the control that women were winning over their own lives, starting with the growing use of contraceptives in the face of enormous opposition from such traditional, family-centred cultural institutions as the Churches.

Slowly, women began to present themselves as a culturally and politically conscious group, in a striking revival of feminism. One of the most far-reaching consequences can be seen in the field of family law, which, since times immemorial definitely paternalistic, in many European countries was now fundamentally changed for the first time to accommodate such notions as divorce and abortion. Though all over Europe the Churches fought bitterly to counter this movement, women managed not only to claim but also to win the right to decide over their own lives, even in Italy, in the famous referenda of 1974 and 1981. Admittedly, the rates of divorce and subsequent remarriage are still definitely lower in European countries with a Roman Catholic background and their more compelling moralities than in the non-Catholic ones; whereas in Britain, almost one in three marriages ends in divorce, the percentage is lower in Belgium, France and the Netherlands, and even more so in Italy and Spain, but even there the rate is growing quickly.

Hence, as the public roles of women inalterably changed everywhere, so did the 'western family'. Despite its regional and temporal variations, over the ages it had retained its traditional characteristics of a formal, legal marriage, a distinct patriarchal structure and a nuclear aspect, i.e. that its core was a couple of parents and their children, even though there might be other in-living relatives and even though it might function within a larger kin group.

But whereas, from a traditional point of view, the nuclear family may be said to undergo a severe crisis, new forms of relationships have come to exist alongside it. With the relaxation of sexual rules in the sphere of the traditional, heterosexual family has come an acceptance of various other forms of sexuality hitherto considered deviant. Female and male homosexuality have slowly been decriminalized since the 1960s. By the 1990s, same-sex unions have been legalized in a number of European countries, adding as yet non-traditional forms of family-living to the spectrum of European society. Culturally, this seems, by and large, a middle-class phenomenon, as well as an urban one. Apparently, the process of 'coming out', much discussed in the 1970s and 1980s – and, not incidentally, resulting in a massive, sometimes very creative artistic output in the way of film, theatre and literature – was easier in the milieu of the relatively free-thinking, higher educated groups who dominate the cities, and in the socially less restrictive atmosphere that characterizes city life; indeed, urban milieux generally have become the centres of cultural growth in most fields.[41]

Quite another development has surfaced in the post-war years as well, becoming more apparent by the 1980s and 1990s. By that time, in many west European countries the number of one-person households had risen to an average of some 20 per cent – with a much higher rate in the urban centres. To many, the fact that the overwhelming part of these households are formed by single mothers in the lower income bracket is distressing indeed, if only because of the obvious emotional and socio-economic disadvantages this situation creates for future generations.

As many traditional forms of emotional and social allegiance have disappeared, so have, at least superficially, class structures and their distinctions, not only at the bottom of the so-called social pyramid but also at the top. Indeed, the three main, well-defined social classes which emerged in the nineteenth century – working class, middle class and elite – have been eroded. The admittedly slow improvement in social mobility through improved education as well as the slow rise in average income and the coming of consumer culture with its egalitarian tendencies – the democratization of luxury – have largely demolished sociocultural barriers and with them the traditional division between 'popular culture' and 'high culture'.[42]

In a first major change, the peasantry as a distinct socio-economic group and the way of life of the agricultural countryside have all but disappeared, at least in western Europe. Whereas in the 1920s and 1930s farming and fishery still accounted for 25 per cent of the population in countries such as Britain and Belgium, to 50 per cent, as for example in Portugal and Spain, by the

1960s the percentage had fallen below 15 per cent in the latter, and even below 10 per cent in the former countries.[43] In consequence, most people born after the Second World War hardly know what a farm looks like. And yet these countries, which all belong to the group of developed industrial nations, are among the major producers of agricultural goods for the world market, both through an enormous increase in capital-intensive productivity per agriculturist and, in recent years, through the successes of agricultural chemistry, selective breeding and bio-technology, which shows the fundamental influence of science on even the most basic ingredients of daily life.

A second major change was the disappearance, since the 1950s, of a distinct, single working class with an equally distinct consciousness and culture, that had been growing since the end of the nineteenth century.[44] Its way of life – the lack of mobility, the segregation in working-class neighbourhoods with little private space, resulting in a mainly public-centred, group-experienced culture of pubs and clubs, the strong organizations with their socialist or otherwise radical political orientation – has been utterly transformed by the social and economic developments that have taken place after the war, specifically by two decades of almost full employment, the coming-of-age of consumer society and the democratization of education.

Yet it is precisely this group, not yet entirely liberated from its erstwhile restrictions, that has been hit hardest by the unemployment which, since the late 1970s, has been almost endemic in Europe, partly in consequence of the high cost of labour in the industrialized countries, and compounded by the exodus of many industries to low-wage countries in Asia and Africa. Indeed, this situation has resulted in a veritable erosion of the industrial workforce, both numerically and culturally.[45] In this context, too, the problems caused by the new phenomenon of mass immigration – unknown to western Europe for almost 1,500 years – became painfully manifest. From the 1960s onwards, many indigenous Europeans felt threatened by the workers from Turkey and Maghrebine North Africa, competing within the same labour market, especially since they started bringing their families and, hence, their culture.

Whereas a small portion of the working class, the skilled, professional part, has entered the middle class, quite often altering its political allegiance accordingly and even assuming many of the bourgeoisie's largely conservative cultural and political values, the far larger bottom part is increasingly condemned to a life on public welfare that many of their fellows, including those who used to belong to the same group, tend to think of as expensive and, perhaps, over-generous.

While the role of the peasantry and an unskilled urban working class has declined drastically, the importance of jobs demanding secondary or even higher education has risen, both in industry and in the tertiary sector. Especially after the Second World War, industrial and government planners realized that economic reconstruction and the creation of a modern society required a great number of skilled workers and administrators. Since then, helped by a state providing modest student aid, many families, of public officials, who had a long tradition in trying to take care of their offspring's future through good education, but now also of white-collar employees, small business people and even skilled workers, decided it was worth the effort to spend part of the slowly increasing family budget on a longer educational career and, hence, better job perspectives for their children.

Consequently, in most European countries university students amount to some 1.5 to 2.5 per cent of the entire population. Secondary and even tertiary education is now deemed an inalienable right of youth. However, with on the one hand expenditure in this field growing, and on the other hand unemployment seemingly inescapable for a structural percentage of the population,[46] even among the better-educated groups, it is uncertain whether this right can be upheld to the level of the 1970s and 1980s; perhaps the transformation of a 'providential state' to an 'insurance society' will increase the gap between rich and poor, and the increasing cost of education will only intensify the process.[47]

Some would say that all these developments and changes affect the visibly manifest, external appearances of culture more than the remaining traces of, especially, elite power structures and the accompanying mentality, although this varies from country to country. Whereas, for example, Britain is still a definitely class-structured society, where both differences in income and status are extremely visible, the Scandinavian countries, to name but a few, are far less so. However, all over Europe, incomes still vary considerably and the various professions, obviously, carry quite different status connotations, partly depending on the amount of education needed to enter them. Also, the codes of behaviour associated with cultural sub-groups continue to create dividing lines and distinctions. If only for these reasons patterns of spending are anything but uniform and, hence, material consumption both as to quantity and quality is still driven by emulation: difference is still used to shape identity, the meaning or symbolic value of things and action is still used to establish or underline power.[48]

Nevertheless, one may argue that, to a large extent, European society has become one big middle class, not only in its material manifestations but also in sharing the same values and expectations, that can be realized by all those who belong to the species of the 'salaryman'.[49]

Dimensions of identity – culture as communication: towards an 'anonymous mass culture'?

In 1951, the German–Italian scholar Romano Guardini published his *Das Ende der Neuzeit* (The End of the Modern Era), in which he tried to analyse the past course of European history to be able, also, to offer a prognosis of its future.[50] One of his most interesting observations concerned the growing discrepancy between the cultural ideal of the free, autonomous person – an ideal dear to European intellectuals through the ages, but especially cherished since men like Von Humboldt and Arnold incorporated it in their educational philosophies and systems – and a culture of the masses that, according to Guardini, was both imminent and inevitable.

In a society characterized by organizational planning in the service of industry and technology, man is massified, not least because, through the mass media and mass consumption, norms and values are becoming massified as well. And yet this does not necessarily imply that man should become degraded only to a 'homo sociologicus', a bearer of functions. The very possibilities of mass culture could and should be used to make man more free, to save the essence of European civilization. In a way, history since Guardini wrote has proven him right.

But if one wants to judge the culture that has emerged since the 1950s dispassionately, one will have to accept that conformity is one of its main characteristics – indeed, schools and the media are its centralizing agencies,[51] even though, superficially judged, many group cultures and subcultures have developed their 'individualistic' manifestations.

Despite Guardini's plea, anonymity and mass culture are two of the recurring negative characteristics used by the many cultural critics who view the present as a period of decline. Obviously, such a view will always be held by those who fail to see that culture is, intrinsically, a system that changes, not only in its outward appearances but also, though more slowly, in the pattern of its norms and values. The sociological survey cited above outlines some of these changes.

In the second half of the twentieth century, individualization, in the sense of both enlarged 'freedom' of choice in all areas of life and of an appreciation which highlights the individual as the norm for all action, appears to be a characteristic of culture in all European countries.

Religiosity, certainly in the sense of Church-bound orthodoxy, is declining everywhere and secularization is advancing. With the loosening of group allegiances and the increased belief in the power of the sciences, both the intrinsic and the social construction of formal religiosity have been undermined. In the past, belonging to a Church and adhering to religious traditions were often imposed within and through social groups and the pressure they bore upon the individual. With the decline of these structures, institutionalized religion is no longer a central value in any of the countries researched, and certainly not a national characteristic any more. Indeed, in the everyday life of many Europeans the moral guidance of the institutions which the Churches are is only minimally accepted. But it also has been established that many Europeans, though they may not turn to the transcendental for relief in those situations in which, nowadays, the sciences bring many, if not all solutions, they still say they want to rely on 'God' or on a somewhat vaguer 'Higher Power' to give them spiritual guidance.

To cite but a few of the interesting phenomena of the past decades, one might refer to the growing number of people who once more travel along the pilgrim road to Santiago. They may not go as penitents, or to acquire as many indulgences as possible to secure a better place in heaven, but they still seem to be doing it both from a wish to communicate with Europe's past and its cultural remains as from the need to find themselves in the process. Also, the increasing interaction between the various world religions, more specifically between Christianity and Buddhism, is a very interesting development. Though one might point out that most of the insights people try to find in Vedic texts or in Zen could as easily be culled from the Christian mystical tradition – most of the texts written by such authors as Master Eckhart, St Teresa of Avila and St John of the Cross, to name but a few, offering insights specifically stressing the individual's relationship to the divine or the cosmos – the contacts between Europe and Asia cannot but help to create greater mutual understanding. Yet if one wants to avoid a slanted image, one must also realize that such phenomena are confined to the well educated; moreover, one must admit that this interest in non-European cultures is often highly superficial and self-indulgent: only seldom does the desire for 'enlightenment' from non-European sources go hand in hand with respect for the different dynamics of these cultures and their necessarily different sociopolitical value systems.

Whether or not one defines tolerance as an aspect of morality, one cannot argue that in that respect the picture presented by Europe is one only of decline. Despite the problems surrounding the economic and cultural acceptance of the post-war immigrants, in many respects greater tolerance, analysed by many pessimists as mere social and moral indifference, is breaking through. Indeed, acceptance of the singularities of fellow countrymen is growing unmistakably, although it is variable as regards many questions and in relation to the ethno-cultural background of those concerned and the socio-economic position of those whose tolerance is tested.

If the traditional religious and moral norms are no longer central in people's own sense of identity,[52] which elements do still have that function? Asked about their sense of national pride, more than three-quarters of the respondents declared that they did have such a sentiment even though not a single European country equalled the high percentage of national pride found in the United States. The 'fear' of an increasingly united Europe varied from nation to nation, although the number rarely exceeded 30 per cent. However, it is perhaps more significant that the most important dimension of identity that was named was neither Europe nor the nation but rather a person's own city or region. Maybe the English writer G.K. Chesterton was right when he wrote: 'For anything to be real it must be local.' Hence, one would assume that the prevailing outlook of most Europeans would be anything but global. Apparently, however, the two can exist together if one realizes that most manifestations of European culture in the twentieth century are closely, if not intrinsically related to the growth and the growing power of the mass communications media which operate world-wide; these are definitely forces of cultural globalization, not perhaps idealistically so but certainly because their economic basis demands it.[53]

During the last decades of the twentieth century, there has been a tendency to describe and interpret European culture from the 1970s onwards as 'post-modern'. Now, there is a definite lack of conceptual resources behind the term, which makes it unfit to serve as an instrument for historical analysis. However, one may define the prevailing outlook on the world as 'post-modern' if it means characterizing contemporary culture as essentially eclectic, in the sense that it does not seem to be ruled by one given set of values, by one tradition, whether it be that of Christianity, of secularized humanism, of the Enlightenment or even of 'modernity'. It seems that the change in communications and information culture – the two, while not the same, do to a considerable extent overlap – may be at the root of this situation. Within the ever more complex communications landscape, several trends can be discerned, which are shaping culture in ways unknown in the past centuries.

With the coming, first, of the cinema, then of television and video, and also of computerized services, more specifically the personal computer and the internet, with their 'virtual spaces, real histories and living bodies',[54] everyone who has access to these media can delve into the gigantic store of information and pleasure they provide. But control over this store reposes less and less with those groups in society who used to be the guardians and distributors of culture: the State, the Church, the University, the Academy, and the elites who were the often self-serving inhabitants of these cultural strongholds till the end of the nineteenth century. More and more, control over information, knowledge, culture and the communications' media which are instrumental in spreading it is a commercial affair, value-neutral in the sense that it is mainly or even only ruled by the laws of profit and loss although these, of course, represent a system of values in themselves, reflecting a capitalist, consumerist society.

It is too early, yet, to predict whether a situation wherein these media are increasingly available to most Europeans, regardless of their economic and educational background, will result in a democratization of information in the same way that the Industrial Revolution resulted in a democratization of luxury. The same holds for the question whether communication really is being improved by this situation.

Thus, the linking of the internet to television undoubtedly will greatly alter, and perhaps even more democratize information.[55] However, some critics will say that not only will it spell the end of the 'book' as we have known it since the beginning of scripture on clay tablets or palm leaves, but also it will fragmentize knowledge. Others argue that the seemingly free, global exchange of information will only hide a continuing, age-old localism or regionalism. Yet others, while admitting that such a phenomenon as e-mail has greatly facilitated all kind of contacts globe-wide, not only in commercial situations but also in entertainment and infotainment, creating groups of people sharing the same interests, have noted that it reduces face-to-face communication; for example on the work floor, its too immediate and imperative *modus operandi* tends to increase unwanted individuality while decreasing much-needed cooperation.

Both in the communications media and increasingly in the information media as well, there are a number of big, semi-industrial, often multinational companies providing most of the popular fare, a development which really started in cinema after the Second World War. However, more than the cinema, television has become engrained into the daily life of Europe's national cultures, and into the culture of the western world as a whole; if only in view of the many hours a day people in all sociocultural classes and age groups spend watching television, it is now a principal cultural factor.

After the Second World War, a kind of television largely if not only as produced in the United States has come to dominate visual culture. One would not be wrong to assume that, both for financial reasons and because of the west's leadership in consumer and, hence, behaviour fashion, in the end this will greatly reinforce a tendency towards global uniformity.

However, the multiplication of TV channels and the widespread use of home videos from the early 1980s onwards may have opened a possibility for the public's choice to increase, and for independent, small companies to survive on productions not aiming at the whole market, but at segments of it. This is of potentially great value to any society which wants to retain some pluriformity and, which is equally important, values to reflect its multiculturality. Most societies in western Europe will need to do this somehow.[56] Though many cultural critics have feared that all programmes, whether in the audio-visual media or in the computer landscape, would increasingly tend towards a dulling sameness, robbing Europeans of their freedom to choose, of the possibility to retain their own, regional culture, this does not yet seem the case.

Still, there are definite signs of growing uniformity, a development which seems unavoidable in view of the market position of television. This was accentuated as the home screen, even more than the cinema, entered the economically fruitful but for a diversified culture less interesting osmosis between the various agencies that determine the world distribution of images, such as the fashion industry and the pop music business; the latter, with the rise of the video clip, once more stresses the centrality of the eye in western culture.[57] Yet, while television and, indeed, cinema in general show a clear shift from the written word to the visual image, this in turn tends to rely more and more on the message of sound, which sets the mood and marks emotions.

Connected with it, at least in mainstream television, is the importance of the instant recognizibility factor. In a complex interplay between the desires of the audiences and the wishes of producers and their financial backers, many programmes have come to depend on the routines of meaning they conform to in the appreciation of the viewers. They want to be able to recognize types of programmes within seconds of selecting them, as they have developed a need to link broadcast TV to their daily fragmented routines. This has resulted in the phenomenon know as 'zapping' or 'channel hopping', practised by the majority of the audience, which increasingly is made up of young children and adolescents. Moreover, even though cinematographic or even television melodrama still tends to conform to older forms of representation, these genres, too, are being influenced by the fragmentized and stereotyped structure of most television.[58]

By reason of its near-universal availability, television has become a stubborn sociocultural medium. It mostly takes ideas which already have current value and thus more easily regulate the discourse of large groups or even of an entire national society. The images projected by one of the new media's most maligned but also most powerful expressions, the soap opera, provide the attentive observer with an interesting mirror of the values it presupposes in and projects on its public. Relationships are, indeed, central to the genre, but they are constantly changing relationships, reflecting the tension between the almost unlimited autonomy of individual desire and the need for some kind of emotional stability. On yet closer inspection, the genre shows itself to be morally ambiguous, with a subversive potential within the overall framework of middle-class cultural ideals that television in general mediates.[59] Representing general human problems as domestic, personal crises and, moreover, showing the enigmas of life without offering permanent solutions, the soap has a certain ideological neutrality which allows a broad audience to participate and, consequently, view their own life in such terms. Indeed, the very structure of the soap allows for an adaptability by which new ideologies and moral positions can constantly be woven into new episodes or characters. Far from being restricted only to an adult, female, home-bound, marginally educated audience – which for long has been its denigrating image in intellectual circles – the genre's influence is increasing for it now attracts adolescents and adults of both sexes, along a broad socio-economic and cultural spectrum.

Though the visual mass media have become essential institutions in European culture, the question whether their introduction can be termed another cultural revolution in the positive sense is hotly debated. Undeniably, however, they have contributed greatly to some of the major changes in twentieth-century European culture. Among the most important surely is the way they have accelerated and intensified the change from a culture dominated for thousands of years by the wishes of the adult, middle-aged group to a culture dominated by youth.[60]

In the twentieth century, in the countries of the west maximum height has been reached earlier and puberty has been coming earlier than ever before.[61] At the same time, education prolonged the period of puberty. This resulted in a definite age-band that, with the baby boom of the post-war period, became numerous indeed. As adolescents have been used to do as long as we know, the post-war youths, too, defined themselves in opposition to their elders. With the increasing prosperity realized by their parents, as well as by themselves for those who entered the job market immediately after the age of compulsory education, they became an economic factor to be reckoned with, representing a massive purchasing power. For example, in 1990 western Europe, with less than 5 per cent of the world population, accounted for *c*.35 per cent of the world market of personal products such as cosmetics;[62] much of it was bought by the young.

As youth became such an important, even dominant economic force, the images used to seduce it to buy and consume have become younger as well. This has contributed to a general tendency to view youth not as a transitional stage towards a much desired, for independent adulthood, but rather as the most interesting phase of life *par excellence*. Meanwhile, over the past decades, the age of first sexual intercourse has dropped, resulting, among many Europeans, in marriage at a rather earlier age than was customary. Consequently, the adolescents of the 1960s became the still youngish parents and sometimes even grandparents of the 1990s.

The result of these two trends is that youth culture tends to extend over a group which, in former times, would have considered itself middle-aged, accepting the cultural expressions that went with it. Now, many who are in their forties still call themselves young, and try to act accordingly, thus intensifying the hold of youth culture over cultural production in general while at the same time imbuing it with undeniable middle-class elements.

The most obvious characteristic of the youth culture that has emerged in the second half of the twentieth century is its at least material internationalism. It began with the enormous influence of the American film industry on European culture from the early decades of the century onwards; it was an influence that extended to such material aspects as hairstyles, clothing and interior decoration, but also, along with the growing force of advertising in the consumer society, to the physical appearance of men and, even more visibly, of women. The broad-shouldered, slim-hipped male and the round-hipped, full-bosomed or, in a later period, almost anorexic female became standard models both for American and European adolescents.

The record industry has become another vector of the cultural hegemony of the United States or, to be more precise, of the Anglo-Saxon world, for we should, of course, recall the great importance of the Beatles and other British rock bands or pop groups both for the development of new forms of music and for the music industry. Since the 1960s, its reliance on the purchasing power of youth has been almost all-inclusive – some 75 per cent of its output was and still is sold to adolescents.[63]

The world of popular music provides one more clue to contemporary youth culture. The disco dancing of the 1960s and 1970s, and the 'house music' of the 1980s and 1990s are the heirs of a long and exciting tradition of popular music, on which especially the Afro-American element introduced into Europe from the United States from the 1930s onwards has had an enormous impact.

The hours per week spent dancing by adolescents and adults up to the age of 40 represent various aspects of contemporary culture – not a new phenomenon as, certainly since the Renaissance, dancing had come to signify social order and patterned, ritualistic existence. Of course, increased leisure is the basis of the contemporary disco existence. Watching and being watched, moving in, from the crowd onto the floor, individually, as a couple or in a small group, and moving out again, the dancers seem a miniature of their society; there is participation and sharing, there is peer group cohesion, but there is also a strong sense of individual creativity. There is no greater contrast than with the ball-scenes which so tellingly symbolized the social structure of the bourgeois world of the nineteenth and early twentieth century, where the elderly, sitting sedately at the sideline, watched their offspring amuse themselves, meanwhile closely controlling the proper behaviour of the couples or prospective couples that whirled around the room. Such a scene was nowhere better depicted than in the evocative pages devoted to an aristocratic ball in early nineteenth-century Palermo, in Giuseppe Tomasi di Lampedusa's *Il Gattopardo* (The Leopard) (1958), one of the most brilliant novels ever written in Italy, and filmed in 1963 by one of Italy's foremost cinematographers, Luchino Visconti (1906–76); he rightly span out the ball scene beyond the scope of the book, to make it the symbol of a vanishing society.

The new dancing, which was visualized in such 1970s films as *Saturday Night Fever*, also provides western youth with a culturally acceptable form of more openly exhibiting erotic and sexual feelings, based on a strong rhythm that pervades body and mind. Indeed, it reminds one of Igor Stravinsky's (1882–1971) famous ballet of the beginning of the century, *Le Sacre du Printemps* (The Rite of Spring) (1913), in which he broke the code of polite culture with its harmless salon music, calling up an image of a primitive Asian tribe celebrating the rebirth of nature;[64] the ballet, choreographed by the famous dancer Vaslav Nijinsky (1890–1950), sent shock-waves throughout Europe, creating an uproar among an audience who were not yet accustomed to have these aspects of man openly shown. The parents of the children of the post-war period were equally shocked when their offspring first started to show themselves and their feelings in this way.

Seen from a wider perspective, the so-called popular music enjoyed, in all its variety, by millions all over Europe and, indeed, the world, opens up an illuminating view of contemporary culture as well. Apart from its strictly musical creativity, fed also by a profitable eclecticism, the texts of pop songs show the great variety of feelings of adolescents and adults alike. They voice both the more negative, sometimes self-destructive emotions that people have – whether as a result of the problems peculiar to their age or, more often, as an expression of the lack of ideals that structure their lives – and the more positive, that give a clue to the yearning for emotionally satisfactory relationships and for some spiritual values to give guidance in everyday life.

EUROPE, SINCE THE 1960s: POPULAR MUSIC – HIGH CULTURE?

In 1963, John Lennon and Paul McCartney wrote the lyrics and the music for the song *All my Loving*:

Close your eyes and I'll kiss you, tomorrow I'll miss you
remember I'll always be true
And then while I'm away I'll write home every day
and I'll send all my loving to you.
I'll pretend I am kissing the lips I am missing
and hope that my dreams will come true.
And then while I'm away I'll write home every day
and I'll send all my loving to you.
All my loving, I will send to you, all my loving, darling, I'll be true.

Seen in retrospect, the adverse reaction of many adults of the 1950s and 1960s
to the popular music of such groups as The Beatles seems surprising. Judging
by the texts of many of their songs, their message was anything but negative
or even critical. They mainly mused about the age-old theme that has characterized European popular and, indeed, art songs for centuries: love, mostly
unrequited love. Therefore, it must have been the changed context that
brought about the often condemnatory response: the growing self-awareness
of the young, lounging at street corners, riding their motor bikes, dressing
defiantly different – but yet adhering strongly to new group codes – and
dancing, obscenely, as their elders lamented, to the aggressive rhythm of
rock'n'roll.

At the end of the 1960s, and in the course of the following decade, a rather
more markedly critical attitude transpires in the lyrics of many popular songs, a
certain disenchantment with the political tensions that threatened to disrupt
the western world, as well as with the emptiness of consumer society.

For a group like Fischer Z, the world they explored in songs like *Multinationals
Bite* and *Wristcutter's Lullaby* was grim indeed. They showed special concern for
the inhumanity of the division between east and west, and the threat it posed.
On a record they made in 1980, they included the song *Cruise Missiles*:

We share a common destination,
Each person has their time to die.
But men are speeding up our journey,
By seeing what they can destroy with their
Cruise missiles (We're near those)
Cruise missiles (We're looking for those)
Cruise missiles (They're not five years away)

and in *Berlin* they told their audience:

Those sore red eyes explore the room again.
The signed pictures of film stars who stayed here in eras that knew of no wall.
Berlin . . . Berlin . . . Berlin . . . Berlin
Part of the old world lives on this island in Germany
And still out there through the window at six in the morning. The essence
  survives.
Berlin . . . Berlin . . . Berlin . . . Berlin

In the 1980s, the musical landscape showed an ever greater variety, with such fashions as 'punk', 'funk' and 'heavy metal' representing not only the eclecticism of the 'post-modern' day but also a growing wariness in matters political and social, as well as a growing explicitness in matters erotic and sexual, as represented in the million-selling hits of such mega stars like Prince and Madonna, who reinforced their songs with elaborate videoclips feeding on a wide variety of images, some of them overtly harking back to the Christian tradition.

The group Iron Maiden sang a song called *Public Enema Number One* which told its audience about the normlessness of the streets, the corruption of politicians served by a press that looks only for the sensational, and all the while the earth is dying:

> When it all comes down the line / And the lines they turn to greed
> And you race off with you tyres screaming / Rolling Thunder
> And the people choke with poison / Children cry in fear
> But you've got your fast bullet / One way ticket outta here.
>
> [*Chorus*: Fall on your knees today / And pray the world will mend its ways
> get to your feet again / refugees from the heartbreak and the pain]
>
> In the cities in the streets / there's a tension you can feel / Breaking strain is fast
> approaching / Guns and Riots / Politicians gamble and lie to save their skins
> And the Press get fed the scapegoats / Public Enema number one.
>
> [*Chorus*]
>
> A million network slaves / in an advertising new age
> I don't need a crystal ball to sell ya / Your children have more brains
> Than your drug infested remains / California dreaming as the Earth dies
> screaming.

Yet in the later 1980s, the singer Sting voiced both a complete distrust in the 'lessons of the past' and a hope for the ultimate victory of humane reason in a song titled *History will Teach us Nothing*:

> If we seek solace in the prisons of the distant past
> Security in human systems we're told will always last
> Emotions are the sail and blind faith is the mast.
> Without the breath of real freedom we're getting nowhere fast.
> If God is death and the actor plans his part
> His words of fear will find their way to a place in your heart.
> Without the voice of reason every faith is its own curse. Without freedom from
> the past things will only get worse.
> Sooner or later, just like the world's first day
> Sooner or later, we learn to throw the past away
> History will teach us nothing. Our written history is a catalogue of crime.
> The sordid and the powerful, the architects of time,
> The mother of invention, oppression of the mild,
> The constant fear of scarcity, aggression as its child.

Sooner or later convince an enemy, convince him that he's wrong.
To win a bloodless battle where victory is long.
A simple act of faith in reason over might.
To blow up his children will only prove him right.
History will teach us nothing.
Sooner or later, just like the world's first day
Sooner or later, we learn to throw the past away
History will teach us nothing,
Know your human rights,
Be what you come here for.

It has been said that cinema, television and popular music all highlight another aspect of contemporary culture, its 'plebeian' characteristic, a not altogether felicitous term. Admittedly, instead of projecting bourgeois or even elitist, aristocratic lifestyles, norms and values, as had been the case in many forms of popular culture during the preceding centuries, since the turn of the nineteenth to the twentieth century, these forms of communication show a tendency wherein influences generated by and reflecting the lifestyles of the former working class or even the proletariat move systematically upward along the social ladder, while, at the same time, many of the outward manifestations formerly associated with upper-class lifestyles are accepted by ever greater groups. It is this material eclecticism, in the body cult, dress habits, foodways, interior decoration, music and entertainment, but also in such other fields as sexual mores and language codes, and so on, that increasingly creates a mass culture that is, perhaps, better termed a new 'middle-class' culture that actually combines 'high' and 'low' in a way that Europe never has experienced before. At the same time, acknowledging that there is no such thing as an absolutely individual choice, one may argue that all the ensuing forms of at least seemingly individual choices are, of course, made possible by a spectacular rise in average prosperity experienced in most European countries from the 1960s onwards.

Despite the strict codes imposed upon it by a prudish, self-censuring and censured Hollywood from the 1930s to the 1960s and by only slightly less restrictive European censorship organs, the cinema and, to a lesser extent, television began to openly show various aspects of sexuality that, in earlier times, had been visible on the stage in vaudeville theatres and cabarets, only – that is to say in the milieux shunned by the bourgeoisie as decadent or immoral, though, of course, the young, the consciously deviant and the outcasts always sought out this culture, helping to perpetuate it and introducing it, piecemeal, into the very society that rejected it.

One might even suggest that the visual media, precisely in exploring the limits of acceptability and showing the results of new customs and mores in this field, have contributed to behavioural changes all over the world – namely, the popularity of the so-called French kiss, still so repellent to some other cultures in this world.

Meanwhile, music not only introduced many elements from minority cultural traditions and from the social ghettos, it also used a verbal language that to older generations with a background in bourgeois culture was shocking if not definitely obscene. Though pessimists claim that the influence of the media on both language and, worse, behaviour and mentality, especially of children, is pernicious, pleading for (self-)censorship, the resulting fierce debates have not noticeably altered the products of this commercial communication culture.

In the field of fashion, one example is exemplary for the 'plebeian' development in its entirety. It is, of course, the introduction of the blue denim jeans in Europe and, indeed, all over the world, and, moreover, worn by the 'young' up till the age of 50, as well as, in sign of the growing equality between the sexes, by girls and women.

Another form of twentieth-century culture that reveals many aspects of contemporary society is the role of sports and, more specifically, the function of football. Football, too, is an example of the demotic character of modern culture, having evolved from a decidedly lower-class status at the beginning of the century to the position of the number one popular sport; for though it is not, perhaps, among the most popular active pastimes, television has brought it to every living room.[65] Part of this popularity can be explained from the fact that in most European countries it has become a symbol first of lower-class, and also local group identity and then, in the internationalization of sports, of national identity. The victory of one national team over another is celebrated with an intensity that few other national events are able to generate, what with the anonymity of elected heads of state and the increasingly limited emotional appeal of the hereditary dynasts; indeed, both the former and the latter, like their predecessors in earlier times, realize the importance of being seen when their subjects, now no longer knights jousting, give what still is, like the tournaments of old, a mock-battle. Unhappily, football matches often tend to end in massive destruction and physical violence as well, even among those for whom the outcome is victorious. They seem to provide an outlet for emotions that state and society have suppressed for the sake of social order. It reminds us of the fact that celebrations and violence have always gone together, and that, according to some cultural theorists, this is the price we pay for not having blood feuds and wars anymore.[66] But the very case of football excesses confronts European society with an expression of individuality that it probably will not permit itself to tolerate.

The moral individualism that, within an at least materially uniform culture, permeates contemporary Europe and, indeed, the western and westernized world, can be interpreted either as the triumph of the individual over society's strictures or the uprooting of human beings from the cohesion provided by social structures. If one assumes that the seemingly unlimited right to choose is an aspect of human freedom as it has come to be understood in the west during the nineteenth and twentieth centuries, one cannot earnestly condemn the 'new' culture as intrinsically reprehensible. One can only hope that each individual will make good use of this freedom. Europeans, who pride them-selves on some of the most daring experiments in freedom, and have found mythical expressions for them in the figures of Prometheus, Icarus and Faust, should realize that real freedom will exist only in the acceptance of a system that will limit the individual's wish to express itself to still guarantee its essence. Ultimately, democracy cannot be unlimited individual rights; it has to be reflexive rights, incorporating the responsibility element. Indeed, the prevalent liberalism combined with socialism which seems to characterize most western societies, is plagued by contradiction and paradox. For the liberal quest is an essentially unsolvable but entirely necessary and therefore continuous struggle to construct a rational political order under the rule of law, while respecting the ideal prospect of man's 'natural' individuality and equality, in face of the fact that Nature continues producing inequalities.[67] The major question that now has to be answered is, of course, what will be the results of human efforts to reduce or even end these inequalities, in providing prosperity – a consumerist life? – for each individual through the continued exploitation of the earth and in making all individuals equal to the extent that even genetic differences are eliminated. Obviously, it is a question that cannot be answered in and by Europe alone.

Epilogue

Europe – a present with a future

Es irrt der Mensch, so lang er strebt.
Man errs as long as he strives.

God, in the Prologue to Goethe's Faust I[1]

In the prologue, this book was compared to a walking tour. As a walk preferably has an aim, having arrived at this epilogue, I would like to think I have reached a new point of view. Looking back, it seems that this journey through the past has resulted in questions for the present, and thus for the future. When the English historian Robin Collingwood was asked what purpose was served by the study of history, he replied: to bring man to knowledge of himself, and added, 'the only indication of what man can do, is what man has done; . . . the value of history lies in that it teaches what man has done and, thus, who he is.'[2] Indeed, in my view, in their exploration of the past historians ultimately not only depart from questions which fascinate them in the present, but also want to return to a point in that present, even if it has not been fixed beforehand. For that reason, historians' stories can, at most, only boast to a limited extent of general validity. That is also true of the questions and opinions with which this story ends.

In the course of seventeen chapters and an interlude, an attempt has been made to show how, in the long period since the concept of *Europe* was first introduced, people all over Europe have expressed themselves in all kinds of cultural forms which, especially when need arose, were used to define an identity. Some of these forms were, in the course of many centuries, added as normative elements to the set of values which was used to circumscribe that slowly emerging concept, resulting in an increasingly complex and compelling definition which people used to distinguish themselves from others, outside but also within Europe. Christianity and Christian culture together slowly became the norm of all things, the challenging and at the same time restrictive context for ideas and actions; for a long time they were the most influential factors in the process which shaped 'Europe' out of a geographical coincidence, a remote corner of the Eurasian land mass, out of a series of territorial political unities which, in the mean time, sought closer cooperation for reasons both eminently pragmatic and, many like to think, idealistic.

When the history of Europe had run its course to and through the Second World War, a new divisive element quickly became manifest in the climate of liberation and reconstruction, in the demand for peace and unity which followed it: the estrangement between, on the one hand, a number of more or less democratic states in western Europe and, on the other hand, a number of countries in central and eastern Europe which had been brought under the totalitarian power of communist regimes. In that situation a 'dream of Europe' could and perhaps even had to develop anew. In order to win over the states of western Europe and their citizens for what was to most politicians primarily a political-military necessity for which economic reconstruction was a prerequisite, an appeal to old, partly forgotten images and ideas seemed worthwhile.

As in the past, when perceived dangers outside Europe stimulated self-reflection and self-definition within, once more those ideas proved difficult to formulate, and still more difficult to establish as indisputably valid for everyone. Significantly, Jean Monnet, one of the architects of 'modern Europe', at the end of his life is said to have remarked that if he had to start building the 'European House' anew, he would begin with culture instead of economic or political life. We do not know what, exactly, he meant by this. In this epilogue, it might be useful to try and find out what we would like it to mean.

Some pessimists may hold that for the time being every appeal that claims a role for 'Europe' which goes further than that of geographical and economic unity will sound hollow as long as fundamental intolerance has not totally disappeared, as long as equal opportunities for all have not been realized. Some even argue that the so-called 'Age of Reason' or 'the Enlightenment', introducing a specific kind of rational, scientific thinking which analyses, classifies and even judges has introduced inequality, and intolerance in the face of one of Europe's old, Judaeo-Christian tenets, the fundamental equality of all.[3]

Optimists, on the other hand, will plead that one of the essential parts of the European tradition is, precisely, that it has succeeded in creating unity out of diversity, while, at the same time, allowing diversity to continue to exist, and that, though economic inequality has still not been eradicated, yet Europe, and more precisely the European welfare states have realized a degree of prosperity and well-being for the majority of their population which has no precedent in the world's past. They will hold that this is, indeed, Europe's unique contribution to humanity. As always, up to a point, the study of history can prove both groups right.

Many predict that the third millennium of the Christian era will not be 'ours' anymore; with Europe having lost its global preponderance – it symbolically ended in 1997, when Britain and Portugal handed over their former colonies of Hong Kong and Macao to China – they say the third millennium will be 'Asian' or 'Pacific' instead of 'European'.[4] Yet Europe will have a role to play, as the inheritor of a past that cannot but shape the future. It is, obviously, the interpretation and use of that past which will determine the course of that future.

At first, many of the cultural expressions which in the long run gave Europe a certain cohesion were produced and experienced only by a small, powerful, educated group, always its principal bearer. It is true that it was a group which with most other Europeans shared a common religion, even though Christianity from the sixteenth century onwards was fragmented in a multitude of denominations. But it was also a group which, in accordance with but increasingly also in opposition to Christianity, developed ideals and norms which were hardly, if at all, articulated by the majority of Europeans and had little meaning for them. It was a group which expressed its culture in certain institutions which for a long time were dominated by elites and often also reserved for elites. Of these institutions, the Christian Churches and education were perhaps the most important; of this culture, communication through increasingly extended reading and writing, through the arts and the sciences, and through travel was its clearest manifestation.

Far and away the majority of studies which attempt to chart 'the' cultural history of Europe seem to deny the crucial fact that the great majority of Europe's inhabitants in the distant and not so distant past hardly participated in that specific culture, which, though it should be acknowledged as a scholarly and therefore elite culture, is usually characterized as 'the' European tradition *par excellence*. Though this is understandable from a political and propagandistic point of view, it is highly questionable from a scholarly perspective. Moreover, the assumption implicit in it creates expectations which are not always fulfilled by the actual cultural praxis.

For most of the past millennia, Europeans were not confronted through education, reading, travel or otherwise with the historical roots and the many manifestations of that elite culture, with the ideas and values which were called its expression and were frequently propagated as universally applicable.

It is true that all Europeans through their religion, spread by one of the many Churches within Christianity, did become acquainted with at least a few core concepts, perhaps the most important of which was the equality of every person before God in heaven and the ensuing idea of the equality under law of all people – also on earth. The apostle Paul had argued: there are neither Jews nor Greeks, men nor women, masters nor slaves – for the Eternal One, all are equal. Nor did a number of values – however vague – derived from this, such as 'social justice', fail to exercise great influence on the expectations of many in Europe, if only at a political-rhetorical level.

The expansion of education from the second half of the nineteenth century onwards certainly confronted most Europeans with values considered essential by governments, by educated elites, values either directly derived from or developed out of the Christian stock of ideas. But let us not forget one thing. Even if that education in the years since the end of the nineteenth century became available to increasingly large groups, for most Europeans until the Second World War it was only primary education, with a very limited content and scope, regardless even of the great educational differences between north-west, central, east and south Europe.

Meanwhile, the influence of Christianity, both as a religion and as a cultural tradition, has been slowly ebbing. This has become manifest in the actual experience of beliefs and, as a result, in everyday life and, *a fortiori*, in education. With the knowledge of classical Antiquity and its traditions declining as well, what many people seem to retain is some sort of belief that is definitely not firmly rooted in a known past any more. One might add that, precisely because it is now lived without a historical perspective, it lacks both a foundation and the possibility to criticize it.

Moreover, many people fear that mass communication, which slowly became more effective during the nineteenth century and whose message was usually directed at reinforcing consumer culture, as yet has contributed little of real significance to a solid foundation for the ideas and values which are called European. It is equally doubtful whether mass tourism, which replaced the more elitist 'cultural travel' and which has expanded so greatly since the second half of the twentieth century, has acquired a similar function.

Also, and notwithstanding the fact that in many European countries the same or comparable cultural institutions spread more or less the same ideas, indisputably many of the 'European values' have materialized in very different political-ideological systems. They were or are implemented in parliamentary-constitutional contexts and within these have become manifest as liberal, or social- or religious-democratic ideologies. However, they have often been interpreted from conservative-authoritarian perspectives as well which not infrequently resulted from either a social or a religious frame of mind, and in which the elimination of parliamentary-constitutional thought and action appeared and still appears to be a possibility or even a necessity. Moreover, the pretensions of this culture and its values at a unique humaneness have not prevented the horrors of war and the systematic oppression and even extermination of fellow human beings.

Therefore, we should pose the question whether the inhabitants of this Europe can rightfully maintain that the appellation 'European' designates more than a mere location within a region which, moreover, in the course of history has been diffuse and which certainly has not formed the culture of every 'European' in the same way and with the same depth while we might also ask whether, for many, it is not already long past?

Exploring these questions in this epilogue I am, after all, not offering a concluding analysis of the concept of Europe as an exercise in historical research. Nor do I propose to make any pronouncement on the direction that Europe should follow politically even though it is precisely on this point that the past has helped to shape the present. In the last instance, the importance of such an analysis can derive its meaning only from the function which people, Europeans, want to give to Europe, now, and in the future.

Against the background of these questions about the present and the times ahead it may be worth while to look more fundamentally at the content which people in the past wanted to attribute to 'Europe' because we, who use the name consciously or unconsciously with a certain intention, want to know what our 'being European' can and may mean. To ask what 'Europe' means is in essence asking about the moral-ethical load which every definition of a group identity necessarily carries. Indeed, 'European', used as an adjective, frequently seems to imply a criterion for quality. Therefore, the following nuancing of the complex reality of present-day 'Europe' seems apposite.

'Europe' is manifested outwardly as a relative unity. It partly legitimizes itself by pointing to certain economic and political choices and achievements that are said to imply moral choices as well. More importantly, it tries to defend certain values, the results of a rich cultural tradition. Yet one sees how between Europeans themselves, on every level of political or sociocultural organization, the description 'we' and 'the others' results in narrow-mindedness and restrictive behaviour. Frequently, even the freedom and, hence, the tolerance often given a central place in many definitions of 'the European tradition', are lacking, let alone that others are actually accepted.

For centuries, Europeans have been thinking in disconcertingly simple but nevertheless deeply felt insider–outsider oppositions that defined their world: the opposition of civilized vs. barbarian, Christian vs. heathen, believer vs. heretic, town vs. country, of 'high brow' vs. 'low brow' and, at a later period, of white vs. black; yet there were also the oppositions of north vs. south and west vs. east.[5] As to these latter two, easily the most visible oppositions, the influence of the Industrial and French Revolutions on the material and political-social conditions only strengthened this schematization. Since the early nineteenth century, north-west Europe has been inclined, more than ever before, to use the prosperity realized within its own region and the genesis of certain political institutions as absolute criteria to measure civilization and progress – as signs of a superior culture; moreover, these criteria have been applied both outside but equally within Europe. Over and above that, within Europe itself, too, the lack of understanding of other national or regional customs and traditions has led and still leads to attitudes towards others that sometimes are voiced only laughingly, but in times of opposition caused by scarcity or other restrictions, rather more fiercely and reprehensibly.

The question of European values, of freedom, tolerance and equal opportunity as living realities within a democratic system surfaced once again when, in the 1980s, a new phenomenon appeared – by many quickly and propagandistically referred to as a new 'enemy'. It was the phenomenon of the culture of the hundreds of thousands of migrant workers whom, since the 1960s, north-west Europe had brought in especially from southern Europe and from the countries along the north coast of Africa. It seems to me one may think of the phenomenon as a peculiarly poignant test for the strengths but also the validity of European values.

For many who live in Europe the two questions whether they feel European with the other inhabitants of this part of the world and which norms and values they share with each other seem less relevant than the need to be able to define themselves against others, the 'outside world': those who obviously have a different skin colour; those whose cultural expressions, especially in religion and in the various customs and norms resulting from it, diverge from or are precisely more pronounced than what most Europeans now consider 'normal'; those whose arrival can endanger European prosperity. One has to admit that the creation of such an opposition between 'us' and 'the others' stems from a need, felt world-wide, to ensure group safety, in which 'same' and 'different' serve as criteria on which distinction, self-assurance and power can be founded. Also, it seems clear that any system – the nation-state or Europe – can continue to provide cohesion only as long as it can remain true to its dream, and to the promises that dream holds, whether they be material or immaterial. This means that each and every system has its limits of capacity and that it cannot continue to expand uncontrollably unless, by some form of common consent, it alters its premises.

Certainly, the first 'wave' of 'immigrant' Europeans, often originating from the various and diverse cultures of the Mediterranean, has contributed to a very large extent to the unprecedented economic flowering which Europe has experienced in the 1960s and 1970s and which has made present-day society what it is. At the same time, it has resulted in a population of tens of millions of Islamic Europeans[6] – although it would be both dangerous and rather stupid to see or represent them as belonging to a 'monolithic' Islam, just as Christians themselves cannot so be represented. Knowing that these 'new' Europeans are often the second, third or even fourth generation to be born here, and yet casting doubt on their right to exist in Europe by drawing a dividing line between 'us' and 'them' is inhuman. Moreover, it also reflects a lack of insight into the very genesis of European culture itself, as the result of constantly recurring contacts with 'others' – often migrating into Europe from non-European regions.

Even if only as a result of the demographic factor, the cultures of these groups will increasingly play an active role not only in every 'national' culture which has received them, but just as much in 'European' culture. They are an undeniable factor in European society which will be changed by them as much as it will change them.

In Shakespeare's *Othello* (1611) the eponymous 'Moor' is the lead character. For Europe, the confrontation with the dark-skinned African, a believer in Islam, was one of the oldest historical confrontations with 'the other'. This tragic character, a Moorish admiral in Venetian service, was, one might say, Europe's first immigrant worker. Shakespeare sketched Othello 'objectively', that is to say, with his positive and negative sides, which are indicated as generally human. Moreover, Othello's opponent, the 'white' Iago, is the real scoundrel of the piece, as if the playwright wanted to indicate that stereotypes must be avoided. It has been suggested that, preferably, the 'Moor' be played by a white actor with a black mask, and Iago by a black actor with a white mask. Perhaps Europeans, of whatever background, should more frequently try such a form of 'role playing' in the drama of everyday life as well.

Shakespeare's plea for tolerance, however, seems to go still further. When Prospero in *The Tempest* eventually calls the 'wild' Indian Caliban his 'shadow', he recognizes the essential 'darkness' in himself, in every human being. Yet although tolerance can thus acquire a function as the self-criticism and, hence, the self-acceptance of any human amidst other humans, either permanent or not according to the extent to which a person enters into the confrontation with repeatedly new 'others', this certainly does not explicitly guarantee complete acceptance of the fundamentally different. Even if only in order to remain himself or itself, every human, every culture will consider certain behaviour or situations unacceptable as long as the confrontation has not led to gradual adaptation, change or inculturing. Tolerance without norms and values ends in arbitrariness and repression.

Whether the confrontation with 'the other' – the immigrant workers from the Mediterranean, the political exiles from Africa and Asia – will be a process of acculturation or of inculturation still cannot be ascertained. That Europe might perhaps return to its Mediterranean, partly Asian-African, origins is a fascinating thought. That the culture of any political unity in or of Europe during the third millennium of the 'Christian era' can be no longer specifically Christian seems to me indisputable.

Despite the nostalgia of many, Europe will be a world in which the church towers, the crosses and the ringing of bells will no longer almost instinctively evoke a multitude of emotions and images which, all-encompassingly, describe culture and solidarity. But among the group of Islamic Europeans, too, secularization will become stronger and the power of the mosques, the minarets and the muezzin to underline their group spirit will inevitably weaken as well. The same, perhaps, will happen to other religious cultures that have come to live in Europe. To provide these different cultural traditions which are now becoming the basis of Europe with a set of common values, with shared ideals, is one of Europe's greatest challenges.

The challenge is deepened because of another development. Since 1989, the communist regimes which have ruled the economy, politics and society of most states in central and eastern Europe for two or sometimes even three generations have collapsed, at least formally. The question whether these states and their inhabitants will take – or be given – the opportunity to adapt to the achievements of the western world cannot definitely be answered at present. Undeniably, the adaptation from an until recently totalitarian political and economic system to a situation in which a liberal- or social-democratic system and a free market economy count as the highest values will be extremely difficult.

The problem is all the more complex because it cannot be indicated clearly whether certain political or social choices also imply, either automatically or not, certain cultural manifestations. To ask but one question, is the consumer culture longed for by many in central and eastern Europe after decades of relative hardship necessarily paired with the western forms of democracy and secularization?

The process of adaptation certainly cannot be one-sided. For the present, western values seem to be triumphant everywhere and, therefore, dominant.

But whereas state-dominated socialism definitely does not seem to be a viable goal any more, we should not forget that one of its most important, underlying values, the wish to create a system of social justice, of human dignity, was created by Europe, and should be retained as a fundamental issue. Perhaps, it can be redefined as a capitalist society's form of radically reformist self-criticism – as it was, originally, in the nineteenth century. It is, one may argue, another of Europe's great challenges for the future.

The final question is, of course, which of its many ideals will prove strong enough to give Europe cohesion in the years to come. It is a question which historians may ask, but which they cannot 'scientifically' answer.

It is quite difficult to prove that man has an innate morality that keeps him from doing wrong, if only because the notions of right and wrong seem, at least partly, culturally conditioned. The quest for a 'global' ethics, a quest that many Europeans are now pursuing in order to find spiritual coordinates in a secularizing and increasingly global society, is real if obviously not yet successful.

Nevertheless, it seems obvious that people have moral instincts, at least those which serve to make them want to protect those they know and feel close to. In this sense, morality almost precedes social reality. It is imperative to preserve this morality as a weapon against the possible de-humanizing aspects of social structures with a high degree of organizational rationalism – the 'modernity' that now characterizes European society; in order to be able to do so, pluralism, with its political concomitant, democracy, seems the essential prerequisite. However, we cannot assume that everybody shares these views; as recent discussions between Europe and Asia show, Europe's certainty that the rights of the individual are of the first importance and that democracy is their best guarantee are off-set by Asian ideas about the primacy of the community's stability, to which the individual should be subordinate.

Nevertheless, to many Europeans, this notion of pluralism – both within the existing nation-states and, *a fortiori*, in the European Union – is the best cultural guarantee for a society that wants to foster ideals, and be fostered by it. It seems the best way to create a civilization in which culture keeps social structure in check. It helps to prevent society from being ruled by automatisms and one-issue movements. It checks the growth of authoritarian or even totalitarian attitudes and organizations. It forces people to take their own responsibility though, perhaps, at the danger of creating a situation in which no one person or group can claim the moral authority to provide the rules and regulations that help to give society the cohesion it needs.[7]

For the intellectual background of such ways of thinking one might refer to an analysis of present-day European culture as the one offered by the Jewish-Lithuanian-French philosopher Emanuel Levinas (1905–93), who survived the Nazi efforts to destroy the Jews. In growing opposition to the great German philosopher Martin Heidegger (1889–1976), whose *Sein und Zeit* (1927) had such enormous impact on European thinking between the two wars, Levinas held that 'to be' is not man's ultimate function, but 'being' is because it means living with the constant reminder of 'the other' and his needs. This does not lead to alienation, non-comprehension. On the contrary, it results in a basic form of humanism, an awareness of the other that generates an ethic with such basic moral precepts as 'thou shalt not kill' and 'thou shalt do unto others . . .'[8]

Indeed, there seems to be a consensus in Europe that looks at man in society under a threefold aspect: each man is unique, each person has to make his own choices for good and evil but, first and foremost, being human means taking responsibility for others, that means, protection of others to preserve the quality of society at large. Freedom, safety, prosperity for everybody seem the values European culture has come to cherish most; they transcend man's egocentric instinct for simple everyday survival. And yet, these values do not come natural: they have to be constantly reaffirmed within the context of the culture that holds them.

Confronting the uncertain future from the vantage point of the past, we should say that those Europeans who want the culture they have built and which they cherish to provide a continuing stimulus, in the context of myth and reality which 'Europe' now has become,[9] will have to evaluate constantly and critically the actual meaning of the great values and traditions which have been articulated and codified in the past – to be sure, by intellectuals to start with,[10] but from the late eighteenth century onwards by increasingly larger groups.

This participation is, of course, precisely the process which we should continue to foster. After all, intellectuals on their own will never make Europe into an experienced reality of the pretension that has grown in the past two-and-a-half thousand years,[11] or, as the Oxford professor of ancient history of Russian origin, Rostovtzeff, wrote: 'Our civilization will not survive unless it is a civilization not of one class, but of the masses.' Consciously or unconsciously revealing his own position as an intellectual, he added two questions:

> Is it possible for the lower classes to participate in a higher civilization without lowering its level and diluting its quality to the stage where it disappears? Is not every civilization doomed to disappear as soon as it filters through to the masses?[12]

Those phrases were written in 1926. They voice unpopular questions with uncomfortable presuppositions and political correctness seems to forbid their being openly uttered nowadays. However, silently they still play a role in every debate about culture, whether in the media or in politics or in academia. Undoubtedly, Europe's greatest challenge is to make certain that the values which it deems important are constantly reaffirmed and, indeed, practised by as large a part of its people as is possible. If Europe wants to preserve its cultural heritage, it requires, to paraphrase the German poet Novalis, ordinary people who share the same ideals; for, as he said, with a few words betraying his hopes and beliefs: 'Mit den Menschen ändert die Welt sich' ('the world changes as man changes').

Consequently, the most apposite answer to Rostovtzeff's implied question, 'What to do?', would be to pay as much attention as possible to sound education. For the transmission of any ideology, of moral values which can give a culture uniqueness and cohesion, remains the most important task of education, increasingly so since it is one of the few 'socializing institutions' still functioning within the traditional state for the whole of society. Yet this conclusion poses the question as to who introduces which values into that education? Within the indisputable globalization of culture, will there still be values which circumscribe some sort of national identity, as well as a European culture which is experienced as the logical sum of a number of such identities, through a complex of common roots?

At least, to create a climate for the continuing existence of these values, we should be concerned to raise historical awareness among as many Europeans as possible, realizing that there is an increasing danger that people will actually lose it; it has been argued that with the state and industry stressing the need for vocational or in-house training, and those who enter secondary and tertiary education increasingly involved in non-school activities, the lack of a common body of knowledge and values makes itself painfully felt.[13] Should this development be attributed to the fact that the knowledge of the cultures from which these values are supposed to stem is penetrating education to a lesser and lesser extent? Should it be blamed on the fact that such ideals, which were added to the 'canon of European values' especially in the economically dominant north-west of Europe after the Enlightenment and the French Revolution, for several decades were less than structurally guaranteed in Greece and Italy, the so-called cradles of civilization? Or should we raise an accusing finger at growing materialism, at a commercialization of life and culture which is all too easily explained by the influence of the United States?

If only to provide a critical perspective, education should certainly imply sound history education. For increased communication, especially as provided by the cinema and even more so by television and computerized information services has created a visual 'knowledge' of almost every aspect of the present as well as of the past that somehow can be shown. On the one hand this would seem to ensure the working of one of history's basic mechanisms, the increase of human interdependence, because people and the groups to which they belong, the social configurations, will have to continue to learn from each other; but precisely because of the deliberate irreality of much that is shown by the new media, the resulting encyclopedic memory runs the danger of being turned into an irreal, largely sentimental, less than human world as well. Indeed, it is futile to go on talking about the classical roots of European civilization and the way it has been intertwined in a process of creative tension with the Christian tradition if these and other aspects of European culture are not outlined, interpreted and, in their consequences for our own age, criticized both in teaching situations and, one has to add, in the modern mass media, which hold an enormous responsibility in this respect. Unless people know what their past is, they will not be able to make their choices on the basis of a sound perspective of tradition and renewal.

Therefore, history education in its broadest sense will have to give an adequate survey of the genesis of the economic, social and cultural structures which have developed in most (west) European countries in the course of past millennia; it will explain how and why fewer and fewer recognizable socio-cultural cores can be distinguished which, traditionally, have provided security: (extended) family, neighbourhood, religious community, and so on. It will ask whether, as some believe, life in the present lacks dimensions of identity; it will show that, perhaps, other forms are in the making.

Such education will emphasize the role of that traditional pillar of the European ideal, Christian religion and the Christian cultural tradition, showing that the Churches, both the united Roman Catholic Church as well as the Greek Orthodox and the many Reformed Churches, however controversial their policies, have for centuries been the bearers of culture, profoundly influencing Europe's norms and values – while, unbeknownst to many, Islamic civilization has been a force in European culture for centuries as well. It will analyse the process of disenchantment, in which formal belief in the supranatural power of the divine in the matters of this world has slowly declined, at least in most societies of western Europe. It will explain why, after the Second World War, in the west the Churches increasingly lost their authority to set strict norms for everyday behaviour while also, in a broader sense, losing their cultural authority. And it will sketch the genesis of other, more recent certainties, whether based on an intrinsic belief in the sciences or in forms of humanism and, sometimes, spirituality, that, while less institutionally powerful than the traditional Churches, yet seem to be emotionally satisfactory and, thus, culturally important to many.

It will analyse the growth of a more rationalist way of thinking and acting both in economic life and in the culture at large, and explain the accompanying ascendancy of the sciences; both processes have become evident since the sixteenth century and have increasingly dominated life in Europe since the eighteenth century. It will stress that these processes have created enormous prosperity and show how this situation has also led to all sorts of creative internationalization which now result in the 'globalization' not only of the economic but also of the cultural sphere. It will ask whether these developments threaten to accentuate and reinforce the declining belief in the value of group solidarity, traditions, culture and national identity or if, rather, cultural uniqueness and cohesion need no longer always be tied to a specific location: religion and science, music and film, for example, have transnational or even global dimensions easily accepted by many.

But precisely because the people born in the 1950s and 1960s will probably be the last 'Eurocentric generation',[14] the education of their children and grandchildren will have to show how, in the course of the past centuries, the appeal to the central values which had been, or were thought to have been articulated in the culture of classical Greece and Rome – freedom, individuality, creativity, democracy, in short pluralism – has been continuously adapted to suit changing needs. It will try to explain why this appeal yet had not sufficiently proven itself in the first half of the twentieth century. It also will show that, after the Second World War, it has regained its impact, even if reformulated.

Thus, exploring the past and, through it, the present, education will provide contemporary society with a basis; it is the best thing a society can do for itself. Assuming that one of history's purposes always will be to give guidance, to provide hope, it also has to be established that the validity of values does not result from historical example, only, but has to be proven from everyday practice. Therefore, I would venture to say that only by continuing to distinguish itself humanely, 'Europe' will continue to mean something. However, taking pride in one's cultural inheritance should not imply uncritically or unthinkingly imposing it on others. In the recent past, many of the values and other cultural forms that have originated in or been elaborated by 'Europe' have all too easily been termed 'universal'. We would do well to discard this much-discussed notion of universality as scholarly irrational and morally irrelevant. For indeed, the only test of any form of culture, of any set of values is whether or not it enhances the welfare of mankind. If Europe can convince the world that some of its more cherished traditions do have this function, its past will, indeed, contribute to a better future, both for Europe and for humankind.

Notes

Prologue

1. G. Erler, ed., *Johann Wolfgang Goethe, Werke, VIII, Faust*, Berlin 1984, Faust I, 77.
2. G. Colli, M. Montinari, eds, *Fr. Nietzsche: Kritische Gesamtausgabe der Werke*, III/2, Berlin 1973 [=Fr. Nietzsche, *Nachgelassene Schriften, 1870–1873: Ueber Wahrheit und Lüge im aussermoralischen Sinne I*], 378.
3. Some surveys: C. Curcio, Europa: *Storia d'un Idea* I–II, Florence 1958; J.-B. Duroselle, *L'Idée d'Europe dans l'histoire*, Paris 1965; H. Foerster, *Europa: Geschichte einer politischen Idee*, Munich 1967.
4. The dangers of such an approach are evident in the recent and surely ridiculous effort by H. Bloom, *The Western Canon*, New York 1994; of the twenty-six authors included, about three-quarters are Anglo-Saxon.
5. B. Geremek, *The Common Roots of Europe*, London 1996, gives an interesting, short survey of the genesis of the concept of Europe; he also argues that, at the end of the twentieth century, the notion of European civilization is felt rather more strongly in central than in western Europe. Ph. Longworth, *The Making of Eastern Europe*, London 1992, goes into the long history of the diverging paths of east and west. Ernest Gellner, *Conditions of Liberty*, London 1994, seems to view the ancient German lands as the frontier region between east and west.
6. See also P. Burke, 'Did Europe exist before 1700?', *History of European Ideas* 1 (1980), 21–9.
7. For example, A. Corbin, *Time, Desire and Horror*, Oxford 1995, viii–ix.
8. P. Burke, *Popular Culture in Early Modern Europe*, London 1978, 28; R. Chartier, *Cultural History: Between Practices and Representations*, Cambridge 1988, 30; B. Scribner, 'Is a history of popular culture possible?', *History of European Ideas* 10 (1989), 181–4.
9. Obviously, this is not to say that such theories cannot be fruitful. Yet I find, for example, G. Arrighi, *The Long Twentieth Century: Money, Power and the Origins of Our Times*, London 1994, not entirely convincing.

1 Before 'Europe': towards an agricultural and sedentary society

1. M.F. Ashley-Montagu, *Edward Tyson, 1650–1708, and the Rise of Human and Comparative Anatomy in England*, London 1943.
2. D.J. Boorstin, *The Discoverers*, II, New York 1991, 888–90.
3. For this and the following paragraphs: G. Bosinski, *Homo Sapiens*, Paris 1990; P. Mellar, C. Stringer, eds, *The Human Revolution*, Edinburgh 1989; R. Klein, *The Human Career*, Chicago 1989; C. Gamble, *The Paleolithic Settlement of Europe*, Cambridge 1986.

4. P. Mellar, *The Neanderthal Legacy: An Archaeological Perspective from Western Europe*, Princeton 1996. See also R. Foley, Humans before Humanity, London 1995.
5. See P. Bahn, J. Vertut, *Images of the Ice Age*, London 1988. The sexual interpretations of A. Leroi-Gourhan, *The Art of Prehistoric Man in Western Europe*, London 1968, are now being widely debated.
6. See the interpretations of J. Clottes, D. Lewis-Williams, *Les Chamans de la préhistoire: transe et magie dans les grottes ornées*, Paris 1996.
7. For a survey: Ph. Lieberman, *Uniquely Human: The Evolution of Speech, Thought and Selfless Behaviour*, Cambridge, Mass., 1991; J. Wind *et al.* eds, *Language Origin: A Multidisciplinary Approach*, Dordrecht 1992.
8. T.D. Price, A.B. Gebauer, eds, *Last Hunter, First Farmer*, Santa Fé 1995.
9. A valuable survey: A. Sherratt, *Economy and Society in Prehistoric Europe*, Edinburgh 1997.
10. D.R. Harris, ed., *Origins and Spread of Agriculture and Pastoralism in Eurasia*, London 1996.
11. See for a survey A.B. Knapp, *The History and Culture of Western Asia and Egypt*, Chicago 1988; M. Silver, *Economic Structures of the Ancient Near East*, London 1986.
12. An impressive, comparative and long-term study of this region is J. Krejci, *The Civilizations of Asia and the Middle East*, London 1990.
13. See M. Beard, J. North, eds, *Pagan Priests: Religion and Power in the Ancient World*, New York 1990.
14. B.J. Kemp, *Ancient Egypt: Anatomy of a Civilization*, London 1991; J.N. Postgate, *Early Mesopotamia: Society and Economy at the Dawn of History*, London 1992.
15. P. Mathiae, *Ebla: un impero ritrovato*, Milan 1977.
16. J. Chadwick, *The Mycenaean World*, Cambridge 1976.
17. J.P. Mallory, *In Search of the Indo-Europeans: Language, Archaeology and Myth*, London 1989. The Kurgan thesis has been most vociferously voiced by Maria Gimbutas, especially in the culmination of her life's work: *The Civilization of the Goddess: The World of Old Europe*, San Francisco 1991.
18. C. Renfrew, *Archaeology and Language: The Puzzle of Indo-European Origins*, London 1987.
19. N. Klengel, *Hammurapi von Babylon und seine Zeit*, Berlin 1977.
20. J.B. Pritchard, ed., Th.J. Meek, trans., *The Ancient Near East: An Anthology of Texts*, Princeton 1958, 138–67, *passim*.
21. N.J.G. Pounds, *An Historical Geography of Europe, 450 BC–AD 1330*, Cambridge 1973, 1–16.
22. See C. Bailey, ed., *Hunter-Gatherer Economy in Prehistory: A European Perspective*, Cambridge 1983.
23. J. Hoddes, *The Domestication of Europe*, London 1990.
24. See J. Bintloff, ed., *Europe's Social Evolution: Archaeological Perspectives*, Bradford 1984.
25. M. Gimbutas, *The Civilization of the Goddess: The World of Old Europe*, San Francisco 1991.
26. S. Piggott, *The Earliest Wheeled Transport, from the Atlantic Coast to the Caspian Sea*, London 1984.
27. E.M. Brumfiel, T.K. Earle, eds, *Specialisation, Exchange and Complex Societies*, Cambridge 1987.
28. See N.K. Sandars, *The Sea Peoples*, London 1978; A. Harding, *The Mycenaeans and Europe*, London 1984; J. Bouzek, *The Aegean, Anatolia and Europe: Cultural Interrelations in the Second Millennium BC*, Lund 1985.
29. See V.R.d'A. Desborough, *The Last Mycenaeans and their Successors*, Oxford 1964.
30. See P. Johnson, *Civilization of the Holy Land*, London 1979; J. Maier, *Geschichte des Judentums im Altertum*, Darmstadt 1989.
31. J.H. Hayes, J.M. Miller, eds, *Israelite and Judaean History*, London 1977.

32. S. Moscati, *The World of the Phoenicians*, London 1973.
33. O. Murray, *Early Greece*, London 1980; A. Snodgrass, *Archaic Greece: The Age of Experiment*, London 1980.
34. W. Burkert, *The Orientalizing Revolution: Near Eastern Influence in Greek Culture in the Early Archaic Age*, Cambridge 1992; orig. Munich 1984.
35. J. Bleicken, *Die Athenische Demokratie*, Paderborn 1986; C. Farrar, *The Origins of Democratic Thinking: The Invention of Politics in Classical Athens*, Cambridge 1988; J. Ober, *Mass and Elite in Democratic Athens*, Princeton 1989; D. Stockton, *The Classical Athenian Democracy*, Oxford 1990.
36. See the essay by Ch. Hedricks in R. Osborne, S. Hornblower, eds, *Ritual, Finance, Politics: Athenian Democratic Accounts Presented to D. Lewis*, Oxford 1993.
37. In a very interesting study, P. Vidal-Nacquet, *Politics Ancient and Modern*, London 1995, explores the ways in which widely diverse notions about Greek democracy have been formulated since the Renaissance, always to support contemporary ideas about politics.
38. From A. de Sélincourt, trans., *Herodotus, The Histories*, Harmondsworth 1972, III, 8–83, 238–40.
39. A fine survey: S. Blundell, *Women in Ancient Greece*, London 1995.
40. A.R. Hands, *Charities and Social Aid in Greece and Rome*, London 1968.
41. See A. Richlin, ed., *Pornography and Representation in Greece and Rome*, Oxford 1992.
42. W. Burkert, *Greek Religion*, Cambridge, Mass., 1985.
43. D. Cohen, *Law, Violence and Community in Classical Athens*, Cambridge 1995.
44. R. Buxton, *Imaginary Greece: The Contexts of Mythology*, Cambridge 1994.
45. Chr. Meier, *The Political Art of Greek Tragedy*, London 1993, focusing on Aeschylus, provides a very interesting discussion.
46. R. Meiggs, *The Athenian Empire*, Oxford 1972.
47. T.B.L. Webster, *Athenian Culture and Society*, London 1973.
48. J. Boardman, *The Greeks Overseas*, Harmondsworth 1973.
49. T. Champion, J.V. Megaw, eds, *Settlement and Society: Aspects of West European Prehistory in the First Millennium BC*, Leicester 1985.
50. B. Cunliffe, *The Celtic World*, London 1979.
51. N. Chadwick, *The Celts*, Harmondsworth 1984; N.N., *Au temps des Celtes, Ve–Ie siècle avant J-C*, Daoulas 1986.
52. J. Collis, *The European Iron Age*, London 1984.
53. See M.C. Fernandez Castro, *Iberia in Prehistory*, London 1995, which gives an excellent survey of the history of the peninsula in the first millennium BC.
54. J.-P. Mohen, A. Duval *et al.* eds, *Les Princes Celtes et la Méditerranée*, Paris 1988; B. Cunliffe, *Greeks, Romans and Barbarians: Spheres of Interaction*, London 1988.
55. A very readable survey: S. Moscati, ed., *I Celti: la prima Europa*, Venice 1991.
56. General surveys: W. Fritzemeyer, *Christenheit und Europa: zur Geschichte des europäischen Gemeinschaftsgefühls von Dante bis Leibniz*, Munich-Berlin 1931; P. Brezzi, *Realtà e mito dell'Europa dall'antichità ai giorni nostri*, Rome 1954.
57. The oldest known 'map of the world' shows the earth divided into two parts: *Lexicon der Alten Welt*, Zürich-Stuttgart, 1947.
58. De Sélincourt, *Herodotus*, IV, 37–45.
59. M. Führmann, *Europa: zur Geschichte einer kulturellen und politischen Idee*, Konstanz 1981, 7, n. 3.
60. F.M. Snowden, Jr, *Before Color Prejudice: The Ancient View of Blacks*, Cambridge, Mass., 1993.
61. J. Jüthner, *Hellenen und Barbaren*, Leipzig 1923; H. Diller, 'Die Hellenen-Barbaren Antithese im Zeitalter der Perserkriege', in *Grecs et Barbares: entretiens sur l'antiquité classique*, VIII, Geneva 1962, 37 sqq.
62. See D. Wood, *The Power of Maps*, London 1993.

63. P. Green, *Alexander to Actium: The Historical Evolution of the Hellenistic Age*, Berkeley 1990. The term 'Hellenism' was coined by the nineteenth-century German historian J.C. Droysen, in his famous study *Hellenismus*, 1836–43.
64. See also A. Bullock *et al.* eds, *Images and Ideologies: Self-definition in the Hellenistic World*, Berkeley 1995.
65. See R.S. Agarwal, *Trade Centres and Routes in Northern India (c. 322 BC – AD 500)*, Delhi 1982.
66. E.S. Gruen, *The Hellenistic World and the Coming of Rome* I–II, Berkeley 1984.

2 Rome and its empire: the effects and limits of cultural integration

1. E. MacNamara, *The Etruscans*, London 1990, but also, because of its use of recent archaeological material: G. Barker, Th. Rasmussen, *The Etruscans*, London 1996.
2. See, for example, J. Wernicke, *Die Kelten in Italien: Die Einwanderrungen und die frühen Handelsbeziehungen zu den Etruskern*, Stuttgart 1989.
3. R.M. Ogilvie, *Early Rome and the Etruscans*, Glasgow 1979.
4. See R.P. Saller, *Patriarchy, Property and Death in the Roman Family*, Cambridge 1994.
5. A. Alföldy, *Early Rome and the Latins*, Ann Arbor 1965; A. Keaveney, *Rome and the Unification of Italy*, London 1987.
6. J. Bleicken, *Die Verfassung der Römischen Republik*, Paderborn 1978; L.R. Taylor, *Roman Voting Assemblies*, Ann Arbor 1990.
7. J. Heurgon, *Rome et la Méditerrannée occidentale jusq'aux guerres puniques*, Paris 1969.
8. Z. Yavetz, *Slaves and Slavery in Ancient Rome*, Oxford 1988.
9. G. Rickman, *The Corn-Supply of Ancient Rome*, Oxford 1980.
10. P. Veyne, *Le Pain et le Cirque*, Paris 1976.
11. K. Christ, *Krise und Untergang der Römischen Republik*, Darmstadt 1979.
12. A.H.M. Jones, *Augustus*, London 1977.
13. See F. Millar, *The Roman Empire and its Neighbours*, London 1967.
14. H.H. Scullard, *Roman Britain: Outpost of the Empire*, London 1979.
15. A survey: J.F. Drinkwater, *Roman Gaul: The Three Provinces, 58 BC – AD 260*, London 1983, 35–53, 143–60.
16. For a survey: R.M. Cimino, ed., *Ancient Rome and India: Commercial and Cultural Contacts between the Roman World and India*, New Delhi 1994.
17. See, for example, M. Benabou, *La Résistance africaine à la romanisation*, Paris 1975.
18. R. Chevallier, *Les Voies romaines*, Paris 1972.
19. For the following: F. Millar, *The Emperor in the Roman World*, London 1977.
20. S.R.F. Price, *Rituals and Power: The Roman Imperial Cult in Asia Minor*, Cambridge 1984.
21. C.G. Starr, *The Roman Empire, 27 BC – AD 476: A Study in Survival*, Oxford 1982.
22. An up-to-date and interesting survey: J.S. Richardson, *The Romans in Spain*, London 1996.
23. F. de Zuleta, ed., *The Institutes of Gaius*, Oxford 1946, I, i–xi, xlviii–xlix.
24. N. Lewis, M. Reinhold, eds, *Roman Civilization: Selected Readings. II: The Empire*, New York 1990, 500–5, 509.
25. J.F. Gardner, *Women in Roman Law and Society*, London 1986. See for a nuanced view of patriarchical authority Saller, *Patriarchy*.
26. See Suetonius, in his section on Augustus of *De Vita Caesarum*, 89; P. Harvey, *The Oxford Companion to Classical Literature*, Oxford 1937, 451.
27. Horace, *Odes*, III, 6.
28. See F.M. Snowden, Jr, *Blacks in Antiquity: Ethiopians in the Greco-Roman Experience*, Cambridge, Mass., 1970.

29. S.F. Bonner, *Education in Ancient Rome*, London 1977; M. Beard *et al.* eds, *Literacy in the Roman World*, Ann Arbor 1991.

30. From J.A. Shelton, *As the Romans Do: A Sourcebook in Roman Social History*, New York 1988, 32–3, 106, 117.

31. J.P.V.D. Balsdon, *Romans and Aliens*, London 1980; B. Cunliffe, *Greeks, Romans and Barbarians: Spheres of Interaction*, London 1988.

32. This and the following quotations from B. Cunliffe, 'Iron Age societies in Western Europe and beyond, 800–140 BC', in B. Cunliffe, ed., *The Oxford Illustrated Prehistory of Europe*, Oxford 1994, 361, 362, 363.

33. B. Kruger, ed., *Die Germanen*, I–II, Berlin 1976, 1986; R. Christlein, *Die Alamannen*, Stuttgart 1978; P. Perrin, L.-C. Feffer, *Les Francs*, I–II, Paris 1987; W. Menguin, *Die Longobarden*, Stuttgart 1986.

34. A survey: M. Todd, *The Early Germans*, London 1992.

35. A discussion of the slow development of tribes into 'proto'-states: L. Hedeager, *Iron-Age Societies: From Tribe to State in Northern Europe, 500 BC to AD 700*, London 1992.

36. As examples: W.A. van Es, *Wijster: A Native Village beyond the Roman Frontier*, Groningen 1967; M. Stenberger, *Vallhagar*, Stockholm 1955.

37. N. Downs, ed., *Documents in Medieval History*, New York 1959, 9, 10.

38. A.A. Lund, *Zum Germanenbild der Römer: Eine Einführung in die antike Ethnographie*, Heidelberg 1990.

39. F. Dvornik, *The Slavs: Their Early History and Civilisation*, London 1956.

40. Ammianus Marcellinus, *History* (Loeb Classical Library), XXXI, ii.

41. Ammianus Marcellinus, *History* (Loeb Classical Library), XVI, iv.

3 An empire lost – an empire won? Christianity and the Roman Empire

1. M. Hengel, *Juden, Griechen und Barbaren: Aspekte des Judentums in vorchristlicher Zeit*, Stuttgart 1976.

2. M. Jack Suggs *et al.* eds, *The Oxford Study Bible*, New York 1992, 1271 sqq.

3. See E.P. Sanders, *The Historical Figure of Jesus*, New York 1993.

4. R.E. Brown, *The Birth of the Messiah*, London 1994.

5. R.M. Ogilvie, *The Romans and their Gods*, London 1979.

6. H.W. Obbink, *Cybele, Isis en Mithras*, Amsterdam 1965; M.J. Vermaseren, *Die orientalischen Religionen im Römerreich*, Leiden 1981.

7. For this and the following quotation: N. Lewis, M. Reinhold, eds, *Roman Civilization: Selected Readings. II: The Empire*, New York 1990, 542, 548–9.

8. R. MacMullen, *Christianizing the Roman Empire, AD 100–400*, New Haven 1984.

9. For a survey: W. den Boer, ed., *Romanitas et Christianitas*, Amsterdam 1973. Also R. Lane Fox, *Pagans and Christians in the Mediterranean World from the Second Century A.D. to the Conversion of Constantine*, Harmondsworth 1986.

10. See P. Brown, *The World of Late Antiquity*, London 1971, 53.

11. Lewis, Reinhold, *Roman Civilization*, 553–4.

12. B. Knopf, *Ausgewählte Märtyrerakten*, Tübingen 1929, third edition, no. 6.

13. Lewis, Reinhold, *Roman Civilization*, 556–7.

14. N. Downs, ed., *Basic Documents in Medieval History*, Princeton 1959, 17.

15. Cl. Pharr, trans., *The Theodosian Code*, Princeton 1952, XVI, x, 12.

16. Eusebius, *Historia ecclesiastica*, X, vii.

17. R. MacMullen, *Constantine*, London 1987.

18. See Lane Fox, *Pagans and Christians*, but also J. Blecken, *Constantin der Grosse und die Christen: Überlegungen zur konstantinischen Wende*, Munich 1992, 64 sqq.

19. See the analysis in E. Pagels, *The Gnostic Gospels*, London 1982.

20. R. Lim, *Public Disputation, Power and Social Order in Late Antiquity*, Berkeley 1996.
21. Pharr, *Theodosian Code*, XVI, i, 2.
22. Pharr, *Theodosian Code*, IX, xvi, 4.
23. Pharr, *Theodosian Code*, II, viii, 18.
24. Pharr, *Theodosian Code*, XVI, x, 12 and 19.
25. Pharr, *Theodosian Code*, XVI, v, 62.
26. See P. Heather, *Goths and Romans, 332–489*, Oxford 1994, who argues that the Goths entering the Empire were not yet a settled group.
27. P. Scardigli, *Lingua e Storia dei Goti*, Florence 1964 [translated as *Die Goten: Sprache und Kultur*, Munich 1973)].
28. Scardigli, *Lingua*, 95–132.
29. See E.A. Thompson, *Romans and Barbarians: The Decline of the western Empire*, Madison 1982.
30. See R. van Dam, *Leadership and Community in Late Antique Gaul*, Berkeley 1985, esp. 141–52.
31. J. Lindsay, *Byzantium into Europe: The Story of Byzantium as the First Europe (AD 326–1204)*, London 1952; J. Décarreaux, *Byzance ou l'autre Rome*, Paris 1982; M. Whittow, *The Making of Orthodox Byzantium, 600–1025*, London 1993.
32. J. Vogt, *Kulturwelt und Barbaren: zum Menschheitsbild der spätantiken Gesellschaft*, Wiesbaden 1976, 21. See also M. Pavan, *La politica gotica di Teodosio nella publicistica del suo tempo*, Rome 1964.
33. Vogt, *Kulturwelt*, 24.
34. Lewis, Reinhold, *Roman Civilization*, 627.
35. G. Cardona *et al.*, *Indo-European and the Indo-Europeans*, Philadelphia 1970; W.B. Lockwood, *A Panorama of Indo-European languages*, London 1972.
36. One among many vehement denials of any outside influence on India is P. Choudhury, *The Aryans: A Modern Myth*, New Delhi 1993.

4 Towards one religion for all

1. See J. Fischer, *Oriëns-Occidens-Europa: Begriff und Gedanke 'Europa' im späten Antike und im frühen Mittelalter*, Wiesbaden 1957.
2. G. Wijdeveld, trans., *Augustinus: De Stad van God*, Baarn-Amsterdam 1984, 760.
3. J.W. McCrindle, ed., *Cosmas: The Christian Topography*, London 1897.
4. See J.-G. Arentzen, *Imago Mundi Cartographica: Studien zur Bildlichkeit mittelaltlicher Welt- und Ökumenekarten unter besonderer Berücksichtigung des Zusammenhanges von Text und Bild*, Munich 1980, which, on plates 1 and 1a, has the Kosmas map.
5. R.L. Wilken, *The Christians as the Romans Saw Them*, New Haven 1982, 79 sqq.
6. Some testimonies in M. Führmann, *Europa: zur Geschichte einer kulturellen und politischen Idee*, Konstanz 1981, 23, n. 10.
7. See N. Cohn, *Noah's Flood: The Genesis Story in Western Thought*, Yale 1996.
8. The text is in Th. Mommsen, ed., *Monumenta Germaniae Historica: Auctores antiquissimi*, XIII, Berlin 1898, 149 sqq.
9. Some testimonies in Führmann, *Europa*, 23, n. 10.
10. J. Vogt, *Kulturwelt und Barbaren: zum Menschheitsbild der spätantiken*, Wiesbaden 1976, 39.
11. For the Merovingians see J. Wood, *The Merovingian Kingdoms, 450–751*, London 1993.
12. L. Duchesne, ed., *Liber pontificalis*, Paris 1886, 420.
13. B. Pullan, ed., *Sources for the History of Medieval Europe, from the Mid-eighth to the Mid-thirteenth Century*, Oxford 1966, 176–7.
14. P. de Letter, ed., *St. Prosper of Acquitaine, The Call of All Nations*, London 1950, 46.
15. See R. Fletcher, *The Conversion of Europe: From Paganism to Christianity*, AD 371–138, New York 1997.

16. P. Anderson, *Passages from Antiquity to Feudalism*, London 1974.

17. The text is in R. Rau, ed., *Briefe des Bonifatius: Willibalds Leben des Bonifatius*, Darmstadt 1968, 483, 30; 41–2; 493, 19–23.

18. J. Haldon, *The State and the Tributary Mode of Production*, London 1993, provides a stimulating reappraisal of developments in the west, compared with, especially, the Ottoman Empire.

19. See R. McKitterick, *The Frankish Kingdoms under the Carolingians, 751–987*, London 1983, but also the excellent survey by P. Riché, *Les Carolingiens: une famille qui fit l'Europe*, Paris 1983.

20. See R. Hodges, D. Whitehouse, *Muhammad, Charlemagne and the Origins of Europe: Archaeology and the Pirenne Thesis*, Ithaca 1983.

21. Bartholomew of Lucca, in the fourteenth century, quoted in J. van Laarhoven, *Europa in de Bijbel: kanttekeningen bij een middeleeuws concept*, Nijmegen 1991, 23.

22. J.W. Smit, 'Karel en zijn Kring', *Lampas* 18/2 (1985), 98–108.

23. See the discussion in *Nascità dell'Europa ed Europa Carolingia: un'equazione da verificare*, Spoleto 1981.

24. See a letter from Alkuin, A.D. 790, in E. Dümmler, ed., *Monumenta Germaniae Historica: Epistolae*, IV, Berlin 1895, 32.

25. W. Henze, ed., *Monumenta Germaniae Historica: Epistolae*, VII, Hanover 1928, 388, letter from Emperor Louis II to Emperor Basilius I.

26. Pullan, *Sources*, 27–8.

27. N. Downs, *Documents in Medieval History*, New York 1959, 33.

28. See B. Bischoff, *Manuscripts and Libraries in the Age of Charlemagne*, Cambridge 1994, 61.

29. See T. Stoianovich, ed., *Balkan Civilization: The First and Last Europe*, London 1992.

30. See R. Bartlett, *The Making of Europe: Conquest, Colonization and Cultural Change, 950–1350*, Princeton 1993.

31. A. Hofmeister, ed., *Ottonis Episcopi Frisingensis, Chronica*, V, prologue, in *Monumenta Germaniae Historica: Scriptores Rerum Germanicarum in usu Scholarum*, Hanover 1912, 227.

32. For the background the important synthesis by P. Riché, *Education et culture dans l'Occident barbare, VIe–VIIIe siècle*, Paris 1995.

33. For an example: V.I.J. Flint, *The Rise of Magic in Early Medieval Europe*, Oxford 1991.

34. J.C. Russell, *The Germanization of Early Medieval Christianity*, Oxford 1994.

35. See P. Biller, A. Hudson, eds, *Heresy and Literacy, 1000–1530*, Cambridge 1996; R. Copeland, ed., *Criticism and Dissent in the Middle Ages*, Cambridge 1996.

36. For a survey: C.H. Lawrence, *Medieval Monasticism: Forms of Religious Life in Western Europe in the Middle Ages*, London 1984. A useful reconsideration: L. Milis, *Angelic Monks and Earthly Men*, Woodbridge 1992.

37. For an example: N. Metzer, *Cultural Interplay in the Eighth Century: The Trier Gospels and the Making of a Scriptorium at Echternach*, Cambridge 1994.

38. See Bischoff, *Manuscripts*, 134 sqq. on the role of Benedictine monasteries.

39. See P. Dronke, *Intellectuals and Poets in Medieval Europe*, Rome 1992.

40. E.M. Wischermann, *Grundlagen einer Cluniacensische Bibliotheksgeschichte*, Munich 1988, 8 sqq.

41. P. Dronke, *Women Writers of the Middle Ages: A Critical Study of Texts from Perpetua (d. 203) to Marguerite Parete (d. 1310)*, Cambridge 1984.

42. See J.L. David, R.K. Ehrmann, eds, *The Letters of Hildegard of Bingen*, London 1994; J. Buehler, ed., trans., *Schriften der Heiligen Hildegard von Bingen*, Frankfurt 1980; P. Dronke, *Poetic Individuality in the Middle Ages*, Oxford 1970, 150–79.

43. For a later example: C.B. Bouchard, *Holy Entrepreneurs: Cistercians, Knights and Economic Change in Twelfth-century Burgundy*, Ithaca 1991.

5 Three worlds around the Inner Sea: western Christendom, eastern Christendom and Islam

1. I have borrowed the idea from G. Fowder, *Empire to Commonwealth: Consequences of Monotheism in Late Antiquity*, Princeton 1992.
2. For a survey: A. Hourani, *A History of the Arab Peoples*, Cambridge, Mass., 1991, and P. Crone, *Meccan Trade and the Rise of Islam*, London 1988, who argues that the trade routes, although profitable, were not a source of great riches and of a specific culture based upon it which would account for the genesis of Islam.
3. A. Özek, ed., *The Holy Qur'an with English Translation*, Istanbul 1992.
4. See H. Kennedy, *The Prophet and the Age of the Caliphates*, New York 1986.
5. For a survey: A. Dhanun Taha, *The Muslim Conquest and Settlement of North Africa and Spain*, London 1989.
6. See Ph.K. Hitti, *The Arabs: A Short History*, Chicago 1964, 120.
7. R. Morris, *Monks and Laymen in Byzantium, 843–1138*, Cambridge 1995.
8. D. Baker, ed., *Relations between East and West in the Middle Ages*, Edinburgh 1973.
9. R. Byron, D. Talbot Rice, *The Birth of Western Painting*, New York 1968; see also J. Beckwith, *Studies in Byzantine and Medieval Western Art*, London 1989.
10. D.J. Geanakoplos, *Interaction of the 'Sibling' Byzantine and Western Cultures in the Middle Ages and Italian Renaissance (330–1600)*, New Haven 1976, provides an extensive survey that yet shows the paucity of proof for really intense interaction.
11. A. Davids, ed., *The Empress Theophano: Byzantium and the west at the Turn of the First Millennium*, Cambridge 1996.
12. A. Papadakis, *The Christian East and the Rise of the Papacy*, Crestwood 1994.
13. For a survey: B. Gasparov, O. Raevsky-Hughes, eds, *Christianity and the eastern Slavs I: Slavic Culture in the Middle Ages*, Berkeley 1993; D. Obolensky, *Byzantium and the Slavs*, Crestwood 1994.
14. See R.P. Hughes, I. Piperno, eds, *Christianity and the eastern Slavs II: Russian Culture in Medieval Times*, Berkeley 1994.
15. For the background: W. Montgomery Watt, *Muslim–Christian Encounters: Perceptions and Misperceptions*, London 1992.
16. For a balanced survey: C. Cahen, *Orient et occident au temps des croisades*, Paris 1983.
17. H. Hagenmeyer, ed., *Fulcher von Chartres, Historia Hierosolymitana*, Heidelberg 1913, 130–8, *passim*.
18. N. Downs, ed., *Documents in Medieval History*, New York 1959, 75–6.
19. F. Gabrieli, trans., ed., *Arab Historians of the Crusades*, 1957; London 1964, 1984, 10–11, 79–80, 83–4, 82.
20. See S. Schein, *Fideles Crucis: The Papacy, the West and the Recovery of the Holy land, 1274–1314*, Oxford 1991; N. Hously, *The Later Crusades, 1274–1580: From Lyons to Alcazar*, Oxford 1992.
21. W. Stubbs, ed., *Willelmi Malmesburiensis, De Gestis Regum Anglorum*, London 1887, 394–8, *passim*.

6 One world, many traditions. Elite culture and popular cultures: cosmopolitan norms and regional variations

1. For the following: P. Anderson, *Passages from Antiquity to Feudalism*, London 1978; G. Duby, *The Early Growth of the European Economy: Warriors and Peasants from the Seventh to the Twelfth Century*, London 1978.
2. See H. Clarke, B. Ambrosiani, *Towns in the Viking Age*, London 1995.
3. B. Pullan, ed., *Sources for the History of Medieval Europe, from the Mid-eighth to the Mid-thirteenth Century*, Oxford 1966, 237–8.
4. 'Formulae Turonenses', edited by K. Zeumer, *Monumenta Germaniae historica: Formulae Merowingici et Karolingi Aevi*, Hanover 1886, 158.

5. L. Vanderkindere, *Ghislebert de Mons, Chronicon Hanoniense*, Brussels 1904, 13–14.
6. Vanderkindere, *Ghislebert*, 119–20.
7. See the 'iconoclastic' vision proposed by Susan Reynolds in her magnificent study: *Fiefs and Vassals: The Medieval Evidence Reinterpreted*, Oxford 1994.
8. J. Strayer, *On the Medieval Origins of the Modern State*, Princeton 1970.
9. J.A. Hall, *Powers and Liberties: The Causes and Consequences of the Rise of the West*, Oxford 1985, 125 sqq., is highly illuminating on this and related issues.
10. The case defended by J. Boswell, *Christianity, Social Tolerance and Homosexuality: Gay People in Western Europe from the Beginning of the Christian Era to the Fourteenth Century*, Chicago 1980, is definitely strong. It seems, however, that his argument for widespread acceptance of same-sex unions – in *A Marriage of Likeness: Same-sex Unions in Pre-modern Europe*, London 1995 – is less convincing.
11. J.B. Holloway *et al.* eds, *Equally in God's Image: Women in the Middle Ages*, New York 1990; M. Williams, A. Echols, eds, *Between Pit and Pedestal: Women in the Middle Ages*, Princeton 1993.
12. See R.I. Moore, *The Origins of European Dissent*, Oxford 1985, 58.
13. For an example, see A. Classen, ed., *Women as Protagonists and Poets in the German Middle Ages*, Göttingen 1991; H. Solterer, *The Master and Minerva: Disputing Women in French Medieval Culture*, Berkeley 1995.
14. For a survey of the many aspects of the cult of Mary through the ages: N. Perry, L. Echevarria, *Under the Heel of Mary*, London 1989.
15. M. Halissy, *Clean Maids, True Wives, Steadfast Widows: Chaucer's Women and Medieval Codes of Conduct*, Westport 1993.
16. Hall, *Powers*, 130–2.
17. For a survey: D. Sweeney, ed., *Agriculture in the Middle Ages: Technology, Practice and Representation*, Philadelphia 1996.
18. On indigenous developments in Europe: A. Pacey, *The Maze of Ingenuity: Ideas and Idealism in the Development of Technology*, Cambridge, Mass., 1976.
19. On the evolution of the water-mill since its early origins in the eastern parts of the Mediterranean: T.S. Reynolds, *Stronger than a Hundred Men*, Baltimore 1983.
20. J. Gimpel, *The Medieval Machine: The Industrial Revolution of the Middle Ages*, London 1977.
21. G. Duby, *The Early Growth of the European Economy*, Ithaca 1977.
22. A.Y. al-Hassan, D.R. Hill, *Islamic Technology: An Illustrated History*, Cambridge 1986.
23. For the following: J. Needham, *Science and Civilization in China*, 7, Cambridge 1986, *passim*.
24. A.P. Smyth, *King Alfred the Great*, Oxford 1995.
25. J. Krynen, *L'Empire du roi: idées et croyances politiques en France, XIIIe–XVe siècle*, Paris 1993.
26. Hall, *Powers*, 141 sqq.
27. For example, Krynen, *L'Empire*, for developments in France.
28. Ch. Tilly *et al.* eds, *Cities and the Rise of States in Europe, AD 1000 to 1800*, Oxford 1994, provides a sweeping interpretation. See also E. Pitz, *Europaeisches Staedtewesen und Buergertum: von der Spaetantike bis zum hohen Mittelalter*, Darmstadt 1991.
29. An interesting study is D. Harrison, *The Early State and the Towns: Forms of Integration in Lombard Italy, AD 568–774*, Lund 1993.
30. See the essays in R. Holt, ed., *Houses and Households in Towns, 1000–1600*, London 1998.
31. For a survey: D.C. North, *The Rise of the western World: A New Economic History*, Cambridge 1976.
32. Pullan, *Sources*, 265–6.

33. For the importance of the towns for the growth of the European concept of freedom, see R.W. Davies, ed., *The Origins of Modern Freedom in the west*, Stanford 1995.
34. Ph. Dollinger, *La Hanse*, Paris 1962.
35. R.S. Lopez, I.W. Raymond, eds, *Medieval Trade in the Mediterranean World*, New York 1955, 416–18, *passim*.
36. See Davies, *The Origin of Modern Freedom*, as well as G. Dilcher, ed., *Respublica: Burgerschaft in Stadt und Staat*, Berlin 1988.
37. W.-D. Heim, *Romanen und Germanen in Charlemagnes Reich: Untersuchung zur Benennung Romanischer und Germanischer Völker, Sprachen und Länder in Französischen Dichtungen des Mittelalters*, Munich 1984.
38. M.R. James, C.N.L. Brooke, R.A.B. Meyers, eds, *Walter Map De Nugis Curialium: Courtiers' Trifles*, Oxford 1983, 73, 173, 169, 183.
39. L. Wieland, ed., *Deutsche Chroniken. Monumenta Germaniae Historica: Scriptorum qui vernacula lingua usi sunt*, II, Hanover 1876; Zürich 1971, 115, 10; 116, 45; 133, 13–14; 139, 28–30; 150, 28–36.
40. See H.J. Graff, ed., *Literacy and Social Development in the West*, Cambridge 1982.
41. P. Strauch, ed., *Jansen Enikels Werke. Monumenta Germaniae Historica: Scriptorum qui vernacula lingua susi sunt* III, Hanover 1900. For the passages quoted in this chapter: 55, 2,847–53; 382, 20,021; 484–5, 24,837, 24,843; 498, 25,524 sqq.; 499, 25,576; 536, 27,393; 549, 27,661.
42. Strauch, *Jansen Enikel*, 535, 27,509–11; 535, 27,501–4; 536, 27,523–5.
43. His 'Noticia seculi' have been published by H. Grundmann, H. Heimpel, eds, *Monumenta Germaniae Historica: Staatsschriften des späten Mittelalters* I, 1, Stuttgart 1958; for this quote: 155–6.
44. See C. Beaune, *Naissance de la nation française*, Paris 1985, or its enlarged 2nd edition: *The Birth of an Ideology: Myths and Symbols of Nation in Late Medieval France*, Berkeley 1991.
45. F. Kempf, 'Das Problem der Christianitas im 12. und 13. Jahrhundert', *Historisches Jahrbuch* 79 (1960), 104 sqq.; P.E. Schramm, *Kaiser, Rom und Renovatio*, I, Darmstadt 1962, 3rd edition, 74 sqq.
46. R.F.M. Brouwer, trans., ed., *Dante Alighieri, De Monarchia en andere politieke teksten*, Baarn 1993, I, ch. 5; III, chs 13–15.
47. Ch.-V. Langlois, ed., *P. Dubois, De Recuperatione Terrae Sanctae*, Paris 1891, 1 sqq.
48. A. Gewirth, ed., trans., *Marsiglio of Padua: The Defender of Peace*, New York 1956.
49. See A. Erlande-Brandenburg, *The Cathedral: The Social and Architectural Dynamics of Construction*, Cambridge 1994.
50. L.J. Lekai, *The Cistercians: Ideals and Reality*, London 1977.
51. C. Stephen Jaeger, *The Origins of Courtliness: Civilizing Trends and the Formation of Courtly Ideals, 939–1310*, Philadelphia 1985.
52. A survey: A.S. Bernardi, S. Levin, eds, *The Classics in the Middle Ages*, Binghampton 1990.
53. An impressive case study: M.T. Clanchy, *From Memory to Written Record: England, 1066–1307*, Oxford 1992.
54. See I.D. Reynolds, N.G. Wilson, *Scribes and Scholars: A Guide to the Transmission of Greek and Latin Literature*, Oxford 1991.
55. For Notker Balbulus: G.H. Pertz, ed., *Monumenta Germaniae Historica: Scriptores*, II, Hanover 1829, 330; his *Gesta Karoli*, in R. Rau, ed., *Quellen zur Karolingischen Reichsgeschichte*, III, Darmstadt 1964, 344, 366; for Nithard: Rau, I, Darmstadt 1962, 386, 448.
56. For the background of the concepts 'little' and 'great' tradition: P. Burke, *Popular Culture in Europe*, London 1978, 28.
57. For a still masterful survey: M. Bloch, *La Société féodale*, Paris 1968; orig. 1939–40.
58. B. Reynolds, trans., *Dante Alighieri, la Vita Nuova*, Harmondsworth 1980, 97.

59. Good reading is provided by J. Sumption, *Pilgrimage: An Image of Medieval Religion*, London 1975; R. Stoppani, *Le grandi vie di pellegrinaggio del medioevo: le Strade per Roma*, Florence 1986.

60. A survey with many illustrations: N.N., *Santiago. Camino de Europa: Culto y Cultura en la Peregrinación a Compostela*, Santiago 1993.

61. D.G. Rossetti, trans., *The New Life by Dante Alighieri*, London 1904, sonnet 40.

62. N. Coghill, ed., trans., *Geoffrey Chaucer, The Canterbury Tales*, Harmondsworth 1960, 20–1.

63. A good survey of the many elements that made up the 'world of the knight' is R. Barber, *The Knight and Chivalry*, London 1996.

64. R. Lafont, *La Geste de Roland*, I–II, Paris 1991; W. van Emden, *La Chanson de Roland*, London 1995, gives the text of one of the many versions.

65. M.E. Lacarra, *El Poema de Mio Cid: realidad historica e ideologia*, Madrid 1980. The text has been translated by P. Such, J. Hodgkinson, *The Poem of my Cid*, Warminster 1987.

66. S. Reynolds, *Fiefs and Vassals: The Medieval Evidence Reinterpreted*, Oxford 1995.

67. G. Duby, *Les Trois ordres ou l'imaginaire du féodalisme*, Paris 1978.

68. Ch. Potoin, ed., *Oeuvres de Ghillebert de Lannoy, voyageur, diplomate et moraliste*, Leuven 1878.

69. See Th. Bender, ed., *The University and the City: From Medieval Origins to the Present*, New York 1988.

70. A survey that is also a plea for the notion that this specific culture dominated Europe till the end of the eighteenth century is R.W. Southern, *Scholastic Humanism and the Unification of Europe. I: Foundations*, London 1995.

71. Pullan, *Sources*, 104.

72. Migne, *Patrologia Latina*, 178, cols 1339–49.

73. G. Makdisi, *The Rise of Humanism in Classical Islam and the Christian West: With Special Reference to Scholasticism*, Edinburgh 1990.

74. A. Lewis, *The Islamic World and the West, AD 622–1492*, New York 1970.

75. B. Reilly, *The Contest of Christian and Muslim Spain, 1031–1157*, London 1992.

76. A synthesis: S.K. Jayyusi, ed., *The Legacy of Muslim Spain*, Leiden 1992.

77. Quoted in H.-J. Störig, *Geschiedenis van de Filosofie*, I, Utrecht 1972, 246–7.

78. N. Downs, ed., *Documents in Medieval History*, New York 1959, 134–5.

79. Pullan, *Sources*, 105–8.

80. For a history of the phenomenon of language as a constructor of identity: P. Burke, R. Porter, eds, *Language, Self and Society*, London 1991.

81. F.P. van Oostrom, *Het Woord van Eer: Literatuur aan het Hollandse hof omstreeks 1400*, Amsterdam 1987, 18–22.

82. S. Bertino, *Le Strade della Civiltà: I grandi itinerari della Storia di ieri e di oggi*, Milan 1984.

Interlude: The worlds of Europe, *c.*1400–1800

1. For a general survey of this 'world', which many would think of as the world of the Middle Ages see A. Gurevich, *Historical Anthropology of the Middle Ages*, Cambridge 1992. W. Rosener, *The Peasantry of Europe*, London 1994, provides a survey from the early Middle Ages to the present.

2. A. Cowan, *Urban Europe, 1500–1700*, London 1997, provides a very competent overview of life in Europe's cities.

3. B. Lepetit, J. Hoock, eds, *La Ville et l'innovation: relais et reseaux de diffusion en Europe, 14e–19e siècles*, Paris 1987.

4. See P. Hohenberg, *The Making of Urban Europe, 1000–1994*, Cambridge, Mass., 1995; G. Huppert, *After the Black Death: A Social History of Early Modern Europe*, Bloomington 1986, esp. ch. 1, 'The eternal village'.

5. The near all-importance of food has been sketched, albeit impressionistically, in two studies by P. Camporesi, *Bread of Dreams: Food and Fantasy in Early Modern Europe*, London 1989, and *The Magic Harvest: Food, Folklore and Society*, London 1993, as well as in his *The Land of Hunger*, London 1995.

6. W.H. McNeill, *Plagues and Peoples*, Oxford 1977.

7. Cf. R. Chartier, 'De praktijk van het geschreven woord', in Chartier, ed., *Geschiedenis van het Persoonlijk Leven 3: Van de Renaissance tot de Verlichting*, Amsterdam 1989, 95–139.

8. This, at least, is the outcome of the research by H. Roosenboom, *De Dorpsschool in de Meijerij van 's-Hertogenbosch van 1648 tot 1795*, Tilburg 1997.

9. See V. Fumagalli, *Landscapes of Fear: Perceptions of Nature and the City in the Middle Ages*, Cambridge 1993.

10. See P. Burke, 'The invention of leisure in Early Modern Europe', *Past and Present* 146 (1995), 136–50.

11. See C. Ginzburg, *The Cheese and the Worms: The Cosmos of a Sixteenth-century Miller*, London 1980, who deals with the methodological problems involved.

12. The best survey to date of this complex way of writing cultural history is P. Burke, *Popular Culture in Early Modern Europe*, London 1978.

13. For a survey of this field, on which opinions between scholars continue to clash: G. Duby, ed., *Amour et sexualité en Occident*, Paris 1991.

14. J. Delumeau, *Une histoire du paradis*, Paris, 1992.

15. G. Klaniczay, *The Uses of Supranatural Power: The Transformation of Popular Religion in Medieval and Early Modern Europe*, Cambridge 1990.

16. See the position taken in L. Milis, ed., *De heidense Middeleeuwen*, Brussels 1991.

17. A. Murray, *Reason and Society in the Middle Ages*, Oxford 1978, provides a fine introduction to the phenomenon of the mathematization of European culture. It does so rather more satisfactorily than A. Crosby, *The Measure of Reality: Quantification and Western Society, 1250–1600*, Cambridge 1996.

18. For a survey: M.L. Bush, ed., *Social Orders and Social Classes in Europe since 1500*, Harlow 1992.

19. For example, J. Kaplow, *The Names of Kings: The Parisian Labouring Poor in the Eighteenth Century*, New York 1972.

20. A survey of the attitudes involved: M. Sommerville, *Sex and Subjugation: Attitudes to Women in Early Modern Society*, London 1995.

21. N. Davis, ed., *Paston Letters and Papers of the Fifteenth Century*, I–II, Oxford 1971, 1976.

22. See N. Armstrong, L. Tennenhouse, eds, *The Ideology of Conduct*, New York 1987.

23. An interesting case: A. Pardailhé-Galabrun, *The Birth of Intimacy: Privacy and Domestic Life in Early Modern Paris*, London 1991.

24. The problem of childhood is one of the most discussed topics in recent cultural history. It seems that the original thesis about the 'invention' of childhood in the seventeenth century, voiced by Ph. Ariès, *L'Enfant et la vie familiale sous l'ancien régime*, Paris 1960, should definitely be revised; see e.g. S. Shahar, *Childhood in the Middle Ages*, London 1990; B.A. Hanawalt, *Growing Up in Medieval London: The Experience of Childhood in History*, New York 1993.

25. From the vast literature: S. Brauner, *Fearless Wives and Frightened Shrews: The Construction of the Witch in Early Modern Germany*, Amherst 1996, as well as R. Briggs, *Witches and Neighbours*, London 1997.

26. For a survey that compares the European experience to that of other cultures: A. Burgière *et al.* eds, *A History of the Family*, II, London 1996.

27. L. Bogaers, 'Geleund over de onderdeur: Doorkijkjes in het Utrechtse buurtleven van de vroege Middeleeuwen tot in de zeventiende eeuw', *Bijdragen en Mededelingen betreffende de Geschiedenis der Nederlanden* 112 (1997), 336–64.

28. Instances are given in P. Burke, *The Historical Anthropology of Early Modern Italy: Essays in Perception and Communication*, Cambridge 1987.

29. For example, E.M. Benabou, *La Prostitution et la police des moeurs au XVIIIe siècle*, Paris 1981.

30. Instances in M. Barberito, ed., *Giacinto Gigli, Diario di Roma, 1608–1670*, I–II, Rome 1994.

31. See R. van Dülmen, 'Das Schauspiel des Todes', in R. van Dülmen, N. Schindler, eds, *Volkskultur: zur Wiederentdeckung des vergessenen Alltags*, Frankfurt 1984, 203–45.

32. See A. Demandt, ed., *Mit Fremden leben: eine Kulturgeschichte von der Antike bis zur Gegenwart*, Munich 1995.

33. R.A. Houston, *Literacy in Early Modern Europe: Culture and Education, 1500–1800*, London 1988, 207.

34. See L. Trenard, 'L'enseignemant de la langue nationale', in D.N. Burke, ed., *The Making of Frenchmen: Current Directions in the History of Education in France, 1679–1979*, Waterloo 1980, 95–114; R.A. Houston, *Literacy in Early Modern Europe: Culture and Education, 1500–1800*, London 1988, 40 sqq.

35. E. Weber, *Peasants into Frenchmen*, London 1976.

36. P.J.A.N. Rietbergen, 'Beeld en zelfbeeld: "Nederlandse identiteit" in politieke structuur en politieke cultuur tijdens de Republiek', *Bijdragen en Mededelingen betreffende de Geschiedenis der Nederlanden* 107 (1992), 635–56.

7 A new society: Europe's changing views of man

1. See R. Jacoff, ed., *The Cambridge Companion to Dante*, Cambridge 1993.

2. A very perceptive study of the thinkers of the Renaissance is L.M. Baktin, *Gli Umanisti Italiani: Stile di Vita e di Pensiero*, Rome 1990. E. Garin, ed., *L'Uomo del Rinascimento*, Rome 1988, provides an attractive series of portraits of various Renaissance 'types'.

3. A masterly succinct survey is given by G. Nauert, *Humanism and the Culture of Renaissance Europe*, Cambridge 1995.

4. An exhaustive survey: A. Rabil, ed., *Renaissance Humanism: Foundations, Forms and Legacy*, I–III, Philadelphia 1988.

5. Piccolomini's treatise on Europe is in A.S. Piccolomini (Pius II), *Opera*, Basle 1551, 387 sqq.

6. W. Fritzemeyer, *Christenheit und Europa*, Munich-Berlin 1931, 18.

7. Fritzemeyer, *Christenheit*.

8. See Piccolomini's *Oratio de Constantinopolitana clade*, in his *Opera*, 682.

9. See Piccolomini's *Bulla de profectione in Turcos*, in his *Opera*, 923.

10. D.J. Geanakoplos, *Constantinople and the West*, Madison 1989; J.J. Yiannias, ed., *The Byzantine Tradition after the Fall of Constantinople*, London 1991; D.M. Nicol, *Byzantium and Venice: A Study in Diplomatic and Cultural Relations*, Cambridge 1992.

11. P.O. Kristeller, *Il pensiero filosofico di Marsilio Ficino*, Florence 1953; a German edition was published in 1972. Further: E. Garin, *La cultura filosofica del Rinascimento italiano*, Florence 1961; P.O. Kristeller, *Marsilio Ficino and his work after five hundred years*, Florence 1987.

12. R. Sabbadini, *Storia del Ciceronianismo*, Turin 1885, 82.

13. G. Christianson, Th. Izbicki, eds, *Nicholas of Cusa in Search of God and Wisdom*, London 1991.

14. A.G. Weiler, *Desiderius Erasmus: De spiritualiteit van een christen-humanist*, Nijmegen 1997, provides an up-to-date evaluation of Erasmus' spiritual significance. For a biography see L. Halkin, *Erasme parmi nous*, Paris 1987; trans. as *Erasmus: A Critical Biography*, Oxford 1993.

15. P.S. Allen, ed., *Opus Epistolarum Des: Erasmi Roterodami*, Oxford 1913, III, 587 sq., Erasmus to Cardinal Wolsey, 18 May 1519.
16. G.L. Hersey, *The Evolution of Allure: Sexual Selection from the Medici Venus to the Incredible Hulk*, Cambridge, Mass., 1996.
17. R.J. Clements, ed., *Michelangelo: A Self Portrait*, Englewood Cliffs, NJ, 1963, 37, 44.
18. G. Bull, ed., trans., *The Autobiography of Benvenuto Cellini*, Harmondsworth 1956, 15, 28, 29, 31, 37–8.
19. E. Garin, ed., *La Disputa delle Arti nel Quattrocento*, Florence 1947, 5–6.
20. The preceding is surveyed succinctly in G. Quazza, *La Decadenza Italiana nella Storia Europea*, Turin 1971.
21. P. Bange, ed., *De doorwerking van de Moderne Devotie*, Hilversum 1988; R.R. Post, *The Modern Devotion: Confrontation with Reformation and Humanism*, Leiden 1968.
22. M.M. Phillips, *Erasmus and the Northern Renaissance*, Woodbridge 1981.

8 A new society: Europe as a wider world

1. W.Ch. Jordan, *The Great Famine: Northern Europe in the Early Fourteenth Century*, Princeton 1996, is a good survey.
2. F. Chabod, 'L'Idea di Europa', *Rassegna d'Italia* II (1947), 7.
3. F.-M Arouet, Voltaire, *Le Siècle de Louis XIV*, Paris 1752.
4. E.J. Jones, *The European Miracle: Environment, Economies and Geopolitics in the History of Europe and Asia*, Cambridge 1987.
5. Francis Bacon, *Novum Organum*, London 1620 or later editions, aphorism 129.
6. M. Devèze, R. Marx, trans., eds, *Textes et documents d'histoire moderne*, Paris 1967, 77–8.
7. An excellent introduction is provided by L. Avrin, *Scribes, Script and Books: The Book Arts from Antiquity to the Renaissance*, Chicago 1991; a beautifully illustrated survey of all aspects of medieval manuscript production is J. Glenisson, ed., *Le Livre au moyen âge*, Paris 1988.
8. See P. Gumbert, *The Dutch and their Books in the Manuscript Age*, London 1989.
9. C. Bozzolo, E. Ornato, *Pour une histoire du livre manuscrit au moyen âge*, Paris 1983, especially part I: 'La production du livre manuscrit en France du Nord', 15–121.
10. H. Bresc, *Livre et société en Sicile (1299–1499)*, Palermo 1971, 187, table 2.
11. For the general background: Tsien Tsuen-Hsuin, *Paper and Printing*, Cambridge 1985 [= J. Needham, ed., *Science and Civilisation in China*, 1].
12. J. Moran, *Printing Presses: History and Development from the Fifteenth Century to Modern Times*, Berkeley 1973.
13. For the following: E.L. Eisenstein, *The Printing Press as an Agent of Change: Communication and Cultural Transformation in Early Modern Europe*, I–II, Cambridge 1979.
14. The problem of economic and technological stagnation in the east in general, and in the Chinese Empire in particular has been much discussed, lately, with very interesting but largely non-conclusive and always contradictory interpretations being brought forward by various authors. See M. Elvin, *The Pattern of the Chinese Past*, London 1973; C.A. Alvares, *Homo Faber: Technology and Culture in India, China and the West from 1500 to the Present Day*, The Hague 1980.
15. D.S. Landes, *Revolution in Time: Clocks and the Making of the Modern World*, Cambridge, Mass., 1983.
16. W. Schivelbusch, *The Railway Journey: The Industrialization of Space and Time*, New York 1986.
17. G.R. Elton, *Renaissance and Reformation, 1300–1648*, London 1963, 135–40.

18. The problematic nature of the term 'intellectual' as used in European cultural history is best illustrated by the following three studies, each a valuable contribution in its own right: J. le Goff, *Intellectuals in the Middle Ages*, Oxford 1993, originally Paris 1957; D. Masseau, *L'Invention de l'intellectuel dans l'Europe du XVIIIe siècle*, Paris 1994; C. Charle, *Naissance des intellectuels 1880–1900*, Paris 1990. I take an intellectual to be a person who, from a certain background of erudition or perhaps even specialized scholarship, participates in the wider debate regarding the functioning and direction of his culture and society.

19. See among others: E. Kaeber, *Die Idee des Europäischen Gleichgewichts in der publizistischen Literatur vom 16. bis zur Mitte des 18. Jahrhunderts*, Berlin 1907.

20. W. Schmale in his introduction to W. Schmale, N.L. Dodd, eds, *Revolution des Wissens? Europa und seine Schulen im Zeitalter der Aufklärung*, Bochum 1991.

21. R. O'Day, *Education and Society, 1500–1800: The Social Foundations of Education in Early Modern Britain*, London 1982, 13, 42.

22. D. Cressy, *Literacy and the Social Order: Reading and Writing in Tudor and Stuart England*, Cambridge 1980, 175–89.

23. F. Furet, J. Ozouf, *Lire et ecrire: l'alphabétisation des français de Calvin à Jules Ferry*, Paris 1977, 59–68.

24. K.P. Luria, *Territories of Grace: Cultural Change in the Seventeenth-Century Diocese of Grenoble*, Berkeley 1991.

25. J.M. Lloyd Thomas, ed., *The Autobiography of Richard Baxter*, London 1931, 3–4.

26. See R. Gawthrop, G. Strauss, 'Protestantism and literacy in early modern Germany', *Past and Present* 104 (1984), 31–55; G. Strauss, 'Lutheranism and literacy: a reassessment', in K. von Greyerz, ed., *Religion and Society in Early Modern Europe, 1500–1800*, London 1984, 109–23; R.A. Crofts, 'Printing, reform and the Catholic Reformation in Germany', *The Sixteenth Century Journal* 16 (1985), 369–81; R.B. Bottigheimer, 'Bible reading, "Bibles" and the Bible for children in early modern Germany', *Past and Present*, 139 (1993), 66–89.

27. For example, T. Watt, *Cheap Print and Popular Piety, 1550–1640*, Cambridge 1991.

28. See also P.E. Grendler, *Schooling in Renaissance Italy: Literacy and Learning, 1300–1600*, Baltimore 1989, 111 sqq.

29. H. Chisich, *The Limits of Reform in the Enlightenment: Attitudes toward the Education of the Lower Classes in Eighteenth-century France*, Princeton 1981.

30. This argument has been raised by A. Grafton, L. Jardine, *From Humanism to the Humanities: Education and the Liberal Arts in Fifteenth- and Sixteenth-Century Europe*, Cambridge, Mass., 1986, 17; see also G. Strauss, 'Liberal or illiberal arts?', *Journal of Social History* (1981), 361–7.

31. N. Kolowski, J.B. Lasek, eds, *Internationales Comenius-Kolloquium*, Bayreuth 1991; G. Michel, *Die Welt als Schule*, Hanover 1978.

32. R.A. Houston, *Literacy in Early Modern Euope: Culture and Education, 1500–1800*, London 1988, 83 sqq.

33. See, for example, R. Kagan, *Students and Society in Early Modern Spain*, London 1974; L. Brockliss, *French Higher Education in the Seventeenth and Eighteenth Centuries*, Oxford 1987.

34. See also: W. Frijhoff, 'Grandeur des nombres et misères des réalités: la courbe de Franz Eulenburg et le débat sur le nombre des intellectuels en Allemagne, 1576–1815', in D. Julia *et al.* eds, *Histoire sociale des populations étudiantes* I, Paris 1986, 23–64.

35. See also: H. Blumenberg, 'Der Prozess der theoretischen Neugierde', in his *Die Legitimität der Neuzeit*, Frankfurt 1966, 201–433.

36. N.G. Wilson, *From Byzantium to Italy: Greek Studies in the Italian Renaissance*, London 1992.

37. R. Myers, M. Harris, *Censorship and the Control of Printing in England and France, 1600–1910*, Winchester 1992.

38. A.R. Wentz, ed., *Luther's Works*, Philadelphia 1959, XXXVI, 66–7.
39. J.I. Packer, O.R. Johnston, trans., eds, *Martin Luther: On the Bondage of the Will*, London 1957, 80–1, 313–14.
40. For the following: M.U. Edwards, *Printing, Propaganda and Martin Luther*, Berkeley 1994.
41. R.W. Scribner, *For the Sake of Simple Folk: Popular Propaganda for the German Reformation*, Oxford 1994.
42. See T. Watt, *Cheap Print and Popular Piety, 1550–1640*, Cambridge 1991.
43. See for an illuminating example S. Anglo, ed., *Chivalry in the Renaissance*, Woodbridge 1990, 1–12, for Anglo's essay 'How to kill a man at your ease: fencing books and the duelling ethic'.
44. Especially by the great historian of the process, Norbert Elias, in his *The Civilizing Process. I: The History of Manners*, New York 1978.
45. E.C. Riley, *Don Quijote*, Winchester, Mass., 1986.
46. See A. Flores, M.J. Bernadete, *Cervantes across the Centuries*, New York 1947.
47. R. Palmer, *The Sound of History*, Oxford 1988, 1–29.
48. C. Kruyskamp, ed., *Mariken van Nieumeghen*, Antwerp 1982, vs. 227–30.
49. See L. Smith, *Reason's Disciples: Seventeenth-Century English Feminists*, Urbana 1982.
50. E.L. Eisenstein, 'Revolution and the printed word', in R. Porter, M. Teich, eds, *Revolution in History*, Cambridge 1986, 190–2.
51. On the problem of the frontiers of Europe: R. Bartlett, A. Mackay, eds, *Medieval Frontier Societies*, Oxford 1994.
52. See J.-Cl. Margolin, ed., *L'Humanisme portugais et l'Europe*, Paris 1984; M. Simoes, 'Camoes e a Identidade Nacional', *Peregrinaçao* 5 (1984), 3–8; J. Kaye, 'Islamic imperialism and the creation of some ideas of Europe', in F. Barker *et al.* eds, *Europe and its Others*, Colchester 1985, 59–71.
53. R. Beaton, *Folk Poetry of Modern Greece*, Cambridge 1980; R. Beaton, D. Ricks, eds, *'Digenes Akrites': New Approaches to Byzantine Heroic Poetry*, Aldershot 1995.
54. H.R. Cooper, *Judith*, Boulder 1991.
55. C. Barbolani, ed., *Juan de Valdes, Diálogo de la Lengua*, Madrid 1992, 132.

9 A new society: Europe and the wider world since the fifteenth century

1. I.M. Franck, D.M. Brownstone, *The Silk Road: A History*, New York 1986.
2. For a brilliant survey of this world: K.N. Chaudhuri, *Asia before Europe: The Economy and Civilization of the Indian Ocean from the Rise of Islam to 1750*, Cambridge 1990.
3. The most recent in a long line of authors who have doubted Polo's presence in China, F. Wood, *Did Marco Polo Go to China?*, London 1995, cannot really substantiate her claim.
4. J. Needham, *Clerks and Craftsmen in China and the West: Lectures and Addresses on the History of Science and Technology*, Cambridge 1970, 239 sqq.
5. N. Perrin, *Giving Up the Gun: Japan's Reversion to the Sword, 1543–1879*, Boston 1979.
6. C.G. Ekeborg, *Kort Berättelser om den chineska Landthusholdningen*, Stockholm 1757. A German translation followed in 1765; English and French ones in 1771.
7. A fundamental study is J.H. Elliott, *The Old World and the New, 1492–1650*, Cambridge 1992.
8. The most recent documentation can be found in *Amerika 1492–1992. Neue Welten, Neue Wirklichkeiten. Eine Dokumentation*, Berlin 1992, and *Amerika 1492–1992. Neue Welten, Neue Wirklichkeiten. Geschichte – Gegenwart – Perspektive*,

Berlin 1992. Besides these, H.J. König, *Die Entdeckung und Eroberung Amerikas*, Berlin 1992, is fascinating as well for the visual material of the time presented in it.

9. The already substantial amount of literature on the 'discoverer' greatly swelled in 1992. One of the useful titles is W.D. Phillips, C.R. Phillips, *The Worlds of Christopher Columbus*, Cambridge 1992.

10. W. Uitterhoeve, H. Werner, eds, *Christoffel Columbus: De Ontdekking van Amerika. Scheepsjournaal 1492–1493*, Nijmegen 1992, 48, 55, 65, 79, 80, 81, 84, 88, 114, etc., for mentions concerning Cipangu and Cathay.

11. Uitterhoeve, Werner, *Columbus*, e.g. 66, 71, 73, 78, 83 etc., on the beauty of the islands; 90, 100, on the beauty of language; 96, 97 on the absence of evil; 65, 97–8 on the natural belief in God; 93 on the absence of weapons and laws. For the quote: 116.

12. Quoted in D. Divine, *Ontdekkers van een Nieuwe Wereld*, Bussum 1973, 249.

13. Quoted in Divine, *Ontdekkers*, 245.

14. Quoted in Divine, *Ontdekkers*, 246.

15. For an overview of the influence of tobacco on different cultures of the world see J. Goodman, *Tobacco in History: The Cultures of Dependence*, London 1993.

16. R.N. Salaman, *The History and Social Influence of the Potato*, Cambridge 1949.

17. E. Forster and R. Forster, eds, *European Diet from Preindustrial to Modern Times*, New York 1975; R. Forster, O. Ranum, eds, *Food and Drink in History*, Baltimore 1979.

18. S.W. Mintz, *Sweetness and Power*, New York 1985.

19. A very informed case study: S. Gruzinski, *The Conquest of Mexico: The Incorporation of Indian Societies into the western World, sixteenth–eighteenth Centuries*, London 1993.

20. A. Crosby, Jr, *The Columbian Exchange: Biological and Cultural Consequences of 1492*, Westport 1972.

21. Crosby, *The Columbian Exchange*, 158–60.

22. For the following: H. Kellenbenz, ed., *Precious Metals in the Age of Expansion*, Stuttgart 1981; J.F. Richards, ed., *Precious Metals in the Later Medieval and Early Modern Worlds*, Durham 1983, especially 397–496.

23. H. Pohl, ed., *The European Discovery of the New World and its Economic Effects on Pre-Industrial Society, 1500–1800*, Stuttgart 1990.

24. See R. Pieper, *Die Preisrevolution in Spanien (1500–1640)*, Stuttgart 1985.

25. R. Ehrenberg, *Capital and Finance in the Age of the Renaissance: A Study of the Fuggers and their Connections*, New York 1963, 80.

26. H. Rowen, C.I. Ekberg, eds, *Early Modern Europe: A Book of Source Readings*, Ithaca 1973, 74–5.

27. Rowen, Ekberg, *Early Modern Europe*, 77.

28. On the problem: E. Zerubavel, *Terra Cognita: The Mental Discovery of America*, New Brunswick 1992.

29. See also J.B. Russel, *Inventing the Flat Earth: Columbus and Modern Historians*, New York 1910.

30. Two recent surveys: J. Brotton, *Trading Territories: Mapping the Early Modern World*, London 1997; J. Black, *Maps and Politics*, London 1997.

31. J. Fischer, F. von Wieser, eds, trans., *Martin Waldseemüller: Cosmographiae Introductio*, Ann Arbor 1966, 68–70.

32. See Bodin's *Methodus ad facilem historiarum cognitionem*, in P. Mesnard, ed., *Jean Bodin, Oeuvres Philosophiques*, Paris 1951, 223 sqq.

33. The following studies deal with this problem: S. Greenblatt, *Marvellous Possessions: The Wonders of the New World*, Oxford 1991; A. Grafton, A. Shelford, N. Siraisi, *New Worlds, Old Texts: The Power of Tradition and the Shock of Discovery*, Cambridge, Mass., 1992.

34. L.E. Huddleston, *Origins of the American Indians: European Concepts, 1492–1729*, Austin 1967.

35. K. Crossley-Holland, ed., *The Oxford Book of Travel Verse*, Oxford 1986, 364–5.
36. Crossley-Holland, *Travel Verse*, 365–6.
37. J.A. Levenson, ed., *Circa 1492: Art in the Age of Exploration*, Washington, DC, 1991.
38. Shakespeare, *The Tempest*, Act I, Scene II, 407–14.
39. Shakespeare, *The Tempest*, Act II, Scene II, 163–4, 166–8.
40. For the psychological background: O. Manoni, *Prospéro et Caliban: psychologie de la colonisation*, Paris 1984.
41. P.N. Carroll, *Puritanism and the Wilderness: The Intellectual Significance of the New England Frontier, 1629–1700*, New York 1969, 72, 112, 134.
42. R.H. Pearce, *Savagism and Civilization: A Study of the Indian and the American Mind*, Berkeley 1988, 23.
43. L.B. Wright, ed., *Robert Beverly: History of the Present State of Virginia*, Chapel Hill, NC, 1947, 235.
44. *Lawson's History of North Carolina*, Richmond 1937, 251–2.
45. A short but excellent survey of the process is U. Bitterli, *Cultures in Conflict: Encounters between European and Non-European Cultures, 1492–1800*, London 1993.
46. D. Heikamp, *Mexico and the Medici*, Florence 1972.
47. G.Th.M. Lemmens, 'Die Schenkung an Ludwig XIV. und die Auflösung der brasilianischen Sammlung des Johann Moritz 1652–1679', in G. de Werd, ed., *Soweit der Erdkreis reicht: Johann Moritz von Nassau-Siegen, 1604–1679*, Cleves 1979, 265–93.
48. P.J.A.N. Rietbergen, 'Zover de aarde rijkt. De werken van Johan Nieuhof (1618–1672) als illustratie van het probleem der cultuur- en mentaliteits geschiedenis tussen specialisatie en integratie', *De Zeventiende Eeuw* 2–1 (1986), 17–40.
49. J.-M. Apostolides, *Le Roi-machine: spectacle et politique au temps de Louis XIV*, Paris 1981.
50. Th. Hetzer, *Die Fresken Tiepolos in der Würzburger Residenz*, Frankfurt 1943; see also C. le Corbeiller, 'Miss America and her sisters: personifications of the four parts of the world', *The Metropolitan Museum of Art Bulletin*, April 1961.
51. *Federschmuck und Kaiserkrone: Das barocke Amerikabild in den Habsburgischen Ländern*, Schlosshof im Marchfeld 1992.
52. S. Münster, *Cosmographia Universalis*, Basle 1559, 40–1.
53. See also U. Nef, *Cultural Foundations of Industrial Civilization*, Cambridge 1958.
54. S. Purchas, *Hakluytus Posthumus or Purchas His Pilgrimes*, New York 1965 [originally *Works of the Hakluyt Society, Extra Series I*, London 1905], 248, 249, 250, 251.
55. Purchas, *Pilgrimes*, 251.
56. M. Eliav-Feldon, *Realistic Utopias: The Ideal Imaginary Societies of the Renaissance, 1516–1630*, Oxford 1982; J.C. Davis, *Utopia and the Ideal Society: A Study of English Utopian Writing, 1516–1700*, Cambridge 1981, 299.
57. Pearce, *Savagism*, 86.

10 A new society: migration, travel and the diffusion and integration of culture in Europe

1. Much has been written on the development of the travel story, which became a literary genre in the course of time, and on the use of such stories as historical sources. I mention only B.I. Krasnobaev *et al.* eds, *Reisen und Reisebeschreibungen im 18. und 19. Jahrhundert als Quellen der Kulturbeziehungsforschung*, Berlin 1980, and A. Maczak, H.J. Teuteberg, eds, *Reiseberichte als Quellen Europäischer Kulturgeschichte. Aufgaben und Möglichkeiten der historischen Reiseforschung*, Wolfenbüttel 1982.
2. D. Brewer, *Chaucer and his World*, London 1978.

3. A.W. Pollard *et al.* eds, *The Works of Geoffrey Chaucer*, London 1923, 1.
4. J. Brouwer, ed., *Spaansche reis- en krijgsjournalen uit de Gouden Eeuw*, Groningen 1932; Brouwer, *Kronieken van Spaansche soldaten uit het begin van de tachtigjarige oorlog*, Zutphen 1933.
5. J. van Bakel, P. Rolf, eds, *Vlaamse soldatenbrieven uit de Napoleontische tijd*, Bruges 1977.
6. For an impression, see A. Kopecny, *Fahrenden und Vagabunden: Ihre Geschichte, Ueberlebenskunste, Zeichen und Strassen*, Berlin 1980, and C. Kother, *Menschen auf der Strasse: Vagierende Unterschichten in Bayern, Franken und Schwaben in der zweiten Hälfte des 18. Jahrhunderts*, Göttingen 1983.
7. J. Edwards, *The Jews in Christian Europe, 1400–1700*, London 1988; J.I. Israel, *European Jewry in the Age of Mercantilism, 1550–1750*, Oxford 1985.
8. See M.A. Shulvass, *The Jews in the World of the Renaissance*, Leiden 1973; B.D. Cooperman, ed., *Jewish Thought in the Sixteenth Century*, Cambridge, Mass., 1983; D.B. Ruderman, *Jewish Thought and Scientific Discovery in Early Modern Europe*, New York 1995.
9. For an overview see M. Yardeni, *Le Refuge protestant*, Paris 1985, especially 129–54, 179 sqq. and 201 sqq.
10. For example S. Jersch-Wendel, *Juden und 'Franzosen' in der Wirtschaft des Raumes Berlin/Brandenburg zur Zeit des Merkantilismus*, Berlin 1978, especially 182 sqq.
11. P. Jeannin, 'Guides de voyage et manuels pour marchands', in J. Céard, J.-Cl. Margolin, eds, *Voyager à la Renaissance*, Paris 1987, 160.
12. See, for example, G. Miselli, *Il Burattino veridico . . . per chi viaggia*, Rome 1682.
13. V. von Klarwill, *Fugger-Zeitungen: Ungedruckte Briefe an das Haus Fugger aus die Jahre 1568–1605*, Vienna 1933.
14. K. Pisa, *Schopenhauer: Kronzeuge einer unheilen Welt*, Vienna 1977.
15. R.L. Latham, *The Illustrated Pepys*, London 1983, *passim*; in this splendidly illustrated work, in which Latham summarizes his monumental eleven-volume edition of the diary, there are many passages which illuminate this statement in more detail.
16. Julius Bellus, *Justinopolitani Hermes Politicus sive de Peregrinatoria Prudentia Libri tres*, Frankfurt 1608; S. Von Birker, *HochFürstlicher Brandenburgischer Ulysses*, Bayreuth 1669.
17. P.J.A.N. Rietbergen, 'Prince Eckembergh comes to dinner: food and political propaganda in the seventeenth century', *Petit Propos Culinaires: A Journal of Culinary History* VI (1983), 45–54. See also S. Bertelli *et al.* eds, *Rituale. Cerimoniale. Etichetta*, Milan 1985; M. Jeanneret, *A Feast of Words: Banquets and Table Talk in the Renaissance*, Oxford 1991 (originally Paris 1987).
18. See for the following paragraphs: N. Elias, *Die höfische Gesellschaft*, Darmstadt 1969; translated as *The Court Society*, Oxford 1983; R. von Krüdener, *Die Rolle des Hofes im Absolutismus*, Stuttgart 1973.
19. For a survey: G. Walton, *Louis XIV's Versailles*, Harmondsworth 1986.
20. See L. Norton, *Saint-Simon at Versailles*, Hamilton 1985.
21. See Ph. Beaussait, *Lully, ou le musicien du soleil*, Paris 1992.
22. An entertaining and informative study is B. Ketcham Wheaton, *Savouring the Past*, Baltimore 1983, esp. ch. 7 and following.
23. P.J.A.N. Rietbergen, 'Den Haag, 20 april 1660: de bruiloft van Susanna Huygens', *De Zeventiende Eeuw* III–2 (1987), 181–9.
24. E.B. Johnson, ed., *The Letters of the Right Honourable Lady Mary Wortley Montagu, 1709–1762*, London 1906, *passim*.
25. For example, H. Bots *et al.* eds, *Noordbrabantse Studenten, 1550–1750*, Tilburg 1979, *passim*.
26. J. Pesek, D. Sanan, 'Les étudiants de Bohême dans les universités et les académies d'Europe centrale et occidentale entre 1596 et 1620', in D. Julia *et al.* eds, *Histoire sociale des populations étudiantes*, I, Paris 1986, 89–112.

27. R.A. Houston, *Literacy in Early Modern Europe: Culture and Education, 1500–1800*, London 1988, 85.

28. W.Th.M. Frijhoff, *La Société neerlandaise et ses graduées, 1575–1814: une recherche sérielle sur le statut des intellectuels*, Amsterdam 1981, 83 sqq., 102, 106.

29. For example, J.G. Klinger, *Commentario de promotionibus studiosorum iuris ad iter iuridicum pertinentibus*, Leipzig 1744; Th. Bartholinus, *De peregrinatio medica*, Copenhagen 1674.

30. See H. Zimmer, *Die Dientzenhofer: Ein bayerisches Baumeistergeschlecht in der Zeit des Barock*, Munich 1976.

31. P.J.A.N. Rietbergen, 'Magnaten en Maecenassen in Zwedens *Stormakstid*: Magnus Gabriel de la Gardie (1622–1686) and Carl-Gustaf Wrangel (1613–1676)', *Artilleri* III–3 (1986), 67–80; IV–1 (1986), 35–50.

32. We are well informed about the experiences of all these sorts of trips by the travellers from at least one country, England, during the seventeenth century: J.W. Stoye, *English Travellers Abroad, 1604–1667: Their Influence in English Society and Politics*, London 1993; J. Lough, *France Observed in the Seventeenth Century by British Travellers*, Stocksfield 1984.

33. One example among many is P.J.A.N. Rietbergen, 'Papal policy and mediation at the Peace of Nijmegen', *Acta. International Congress of the Tercentenary of the Peace of Nijmegen, 1678–1978*, Amsterdam 1980, 29–96.

34. A. Frank-Van Westrienen, *De Groote Tour: Tekening van de educatiereis der Nederlanders in de 17e eeuw*, Amsterdam 1983; J. Black, *The British and the Grand Tour*, London 1985.

35. N.N., *Het Italië-gevoel: Nederlandse schrijvers over Italië*, Amsterdam 1989.

36. H. Harder, *Le Président de Brosses et le voyage en Italie au dix-huitième siècle*, Geneva 1981.

37. The expression is derived from a fascinating study by J. Pemble, *The Mediterranean Passion: Victorians and Edwardians in the South*, London 1988. He mainly describes the motives for and experiences of nineteenth-century English travellers, yet also exposes structures which already determined the southerly tendencies of northerners during the *ancien régime*.

38. As an example: G.J. Hoogerwerff, ed., *De twee reizen van Cosimo de' Medici, prins van Toscane, door de Nederlanden (1667–1669)*, Amsterdam 1919.

39. W. Bray, ed., *The Diary of John Evelyn*, I–II, London 1950, I, 101, 102, 107–8, 128, 136, 139, 140, 161–2.

40. An excellent survey: A. Maczak, *Travel in Early Modern Europe*, London 1995.

41. Such lists can be found in: *Carpentras, Bibliothèque Ingouimbertine*, Mss. 1821, folios 494, 496 and 497.

42. P. Charbon, *Au temps des malles-postes et des diligences: histoire des transports publics et de poste du XVIIe au XIXe siècle*, Strasbourg 1979.

43. L.E. Halkin, ed., *Desiderius Erasmus, Colloquia*, Louvain 1972, 333–8.

44. One such professional guide was the seventeenth-century Englishman Richard Lassels, who recorded his experiences: R. Lassels, *Description of Italy, With Instructions for Travellers*, London 1660.

45. Pitcher, *Bacon, Essays*, 113.

46. Pitcher, *Bacon, Essays*, 114.

47. Pitcher, *Bacon, Essays*, 113.

48. M. Rassem, J. Steigl, *Apodemiken: eine räsonnierte Bibliographie der reisetheoretische Literatur des 16., 17. und 18. Jahrhunderts*, Paderborn 1983.

49. J. Locke, *Some Thoughts Concerning Education*, London 1693, 189–201.

50. Carl von Linné, *Oratio, qua peregrinationum intra patriam asseritur necessitas*, Uppsala 1741.

51. P.J.A.N. Rietbergen, 'The Library of a Guelders country squire: Thomas Walraven van Arkel van Ammerzoden (1630–1684): a contribution to the history

of Dutch aristocratic culture in the seventeenth century', *LIAS* IX-2 (1983), 271–84.

52. See H. Peres, *L'Espagne vue par les voyageurs musulmans de 1610 à 1930*, Paris 1937.
53. W. Bray, ed., *The Diary of John Evelyn* I–II, London 1907; for this passage, see I, 118.

11 A new society: the 'Republic of Letters' as a virtual and virtuous world against a divided world

1. For a short introduction: F. Wacquet, H. Bots, *La République des Lettres*, s.l. 1997.
2. A.B. Grosart, ed., *The Complete Works in Verse and Prose of S. Daniel*, I, London 1885, 106.
3. Michel de Montaigne, *Essais*, Paris 1580.
4. Most of these plans were published and commented on in German translation by K. von Raumer, *Ewiger Friede: Friedensrufe und Friedenspläne seit der Renaissance*, Munich 1953.
5. Von Raumer, *Ewiger Friede*, 321.
6. Von Raumer, *Ewiger Friede*, 89 sqq.
7. See: G. Kanthak, *Der Akademiegedanke zwischen utopischem Entwurf und barocker Projektmacherei*, Berlin 1987, especially 64 sqq. An example is R. Hahn, *The Anatomy of a Scientific Institution: The Paris Academy of Sciences, 1666–1803*, Berkeley 1971.
8. O. Ranum, ed., *National Consciousness, History and Political Culture in Early Modern Europe*, Baltimore 1975, 54 sqq., 73 sqq.
9. Juan de Mariana, *Historia de Espana*, Book 26, ch. 1.
10. M. Warnke, *Hofkünstler: zur Vorgeschichte des modernen Künstlers*, Cologne 1985, 314.
11. M. Cherniavsky, 'Russia', in Ranum, *National Consciousness*, 118–43.
12. P.J.A.N. Rietbergen, 'Onderwijs en Wetenschap als instrumenten van cultuurpolitiek: Rusland in de tweede helft van de zeventiende en in de achttiende eeuw', *Ex Tempore* 11 (1992), 147–59.
13. See W.F. Reddaway, ed., *Documents of Catharina the Great*, Cambridge 1931, the *nakaz* of 1767, ch. 1, sec. 6.
14. See A. Dietz, *Zur Geschichte der Frankfurter Büchermesse, 1462–1792*, Frankfurt 1921.
15. See H. Kiesel, P. Münch, *Gesellschaft und Literatur im 18. Jahrhundert*, Munich 1977.
16. Pitcher, *Bacon, Essays*, 114.
17. See the map in R. Mandrou, *Des humanistes aux hommes de science*, Paris 1973.
18. M. Lowry, *The World of Aldus Manutius: Business and Scholarship in Renaissance Venice*, Oxford 1979.
19. For a case see H.-J. Martin, *Livre, pouvoirs et société à Paris au XVIIe siècle (1598–1701)*, I–II, Geneva 1969, 1064, 1073.
20. See C. Berkvens-Stevelinck *et al.* eds, *Le Magasin de l'Univers. The Dutch Republic as the Centre of the European Book Trade*, Leiden 1992.
21. G.C. Gibbs, 'The role of the Dutch Republic as the intellectual entrepot of Europe', *Bijdragen en Mededelingen betreffende de Geschiedenis der Nederlanden* 86 (1971), 323–49; Gibbs, 'Some intellectual and political influences of the Huguenot émigrés', *Bijdragen en Mededelingen betreffende de Geschiedenis der Nederlanden* 90 (1975), 255–87.
22. J. Marx, 'La Bibliothèque impartiale', in M. Couperus, ed., *L'Etude des periodiques anciens*, Paris 1972, 89–108.
23. See, too, for background information: E.L. Eisenstein, 'The cosmopolitan enlightenment', in her *Grub Street Abroad*, Oxford 1992, 101–30.

24. H.H.M. van Lieshout, *Van Boek tot Bibliotheek: de Wordinggeschiedenis van de 'Dictionnaire Historique et Critique' van Pierre Bayle (1689–1706)*, Grave 1992.
25. P.J.A.N. Rietbergen, 'Light from the North: Christian Constantijn Rumph, Gisbert Cuper and cultural relations between Sweden and the Dutch Republic during the last quarter of the seventeenth century', in J.A. van Koningsbrugge *et al.* eds, *The Netherlands and the Balticum, 1524–1814*, Nijmegen 1991, 315–42.
26. For the following, see P.J.A.N. Rietbergen, 'Witsen's world: Nicolaas Witsen (1642–1717) between the Dutch East India Company and the *Republic of Letters*', *Itinerario* IX–2 (1985), 121–34.
27. J. Bouchard, 'Les relations épistolaires de Nicolas Mavrocordatos avec Jean Le Clerc et William Wake', *O Eranistis* 1 (1974), 67–92; Bouchard, ed., *N. Mavrocordatos, les loisirs de philothée*, Athens 1989.
28. For the following, see P.J.A.N. Rietbergen, 'Dutch and Spanish "Enlightenments"? The case of Gerard Meerman (1722–1777) and Gregorio Mayans y Siscar (1691–1781)', in Rietbergen, ed., *Tussen Twee Culturen: Nederland en de Iberische wereld, 1500–1800*, Nijmegen 1988, 105–34.

12 A new society: from Humanism to the Enlightenment

1. See on this subject A. Grafton, *Defenders of the Text: The Traditions of Scholarship in an Age of Science, 1450–1800*, Cambridge, Mass., 1993.
2. A French translation was made in 1934 by A. Koyré, a German one in 1939 by Cl. Menzer.
3. M. Devèze, R. Marx, eds, *Textes et documents d'histoire moderne*, Paris 1967, 119–20.
4. On Galilei: P. Redondi, *Galilei eretico*, Turin 1983, which, although not accepted by all scholars in the field, is a stimulating study.
5. See Redondi, *Galilei*.
6. Cited from G. de Santillana, ed., *The Age of Adventure: The Renaissance Philosophers*, New York 1956, 159.
7. See Bax, ed., trans., *The Signature of All Things, with Other Writings by Jacob Boehme*, London 1926, 14, II, no. 8.
8. Bax, *Boehme*, 268.
9. Francis Bacon, *Novum Organum*, London 1620.
10. R. Descartes, *Discours sur la méthode*, Paris 1637.
11. C. Wilson, *The Invisible World*, Oxford 1995.
12. A good background study: M.F. Cohen, *The Scientific Revolution: A Historiograpical Enquiry*, Chicago 1995.
13. R.S. Westfall, *Never at Rest: A Biography of Isaac Newton*, London 1981.
14. I. Newton, Foreword to *Philosophiae naturalis principia mathematica*, London 1687.
15. A.J. Krailsheimer, trans., *Blaise Pascal, Pensées*, Baltimore 1966, 48, 95.
16. For a survey of developments in science: R. Olson, *Science Deified and Science Defied: The Historical Significance of Science in Western Culture. II: From the Early Modern Age Through the Early Romantic Era, ca. 1640 to ca. 1820*, Berkeley 1990.
17. A. Thomson, ed., *La Mettrie: Machine Man and Other Writings*, Cambridge 1996.
18. R.M. Adams, *Leibniz: Determinist, Theist, Idealist*, Oxford 1994.
19. For an introduction, see H.E. Allison, *Benedict de Spinoza*, London 1987.
20. J.H. Spalding, F. Bayley, eds, trans., *Heaven and its Wonders, and Hell: From Things Heard and Seen: by Emmanuel Swedenborg*, London 1920, nos 318, 328.
21. See: A. Schopenhauer, *Die Welt als Wille und Vorstellung*, I, 125 ff, and II, 366, in A. Hübscher, ed., *A. Schopenhauer, Sämtliche Werke* I–VII, Wiesbaden 1972.
22. For a survey: D. Goodman, *The Republic of Letters: A Cultural History of the French Enlightenment*, Ithaca 1994.
23. A very inspiring analysis is D. Roche, *La France des lumières*, Paris 1994.

24. H.C. Payne, *The Philosophes and the People*, New Haven 1976.
25. R. Porter, M. Teich, eds, *The Enlightenment in National Context*, Cambridge 1981.
26. For example, R.B. Sher, *Church and University in the Scottish Enlightenment: The Moderate Literati of Edinburgh*, Princeton 1985.
27. Th.J. Schlereth, *The Cosmopolitan Ideal in Enlightenment Thought*, Notre Dame 1977.
28. H. Vyverberg, *Human Nature, Cultural Diversity and the French Enlightenment*, New York 1987.
29. For a brief overview: Ph.N. Furbank, *The Encyclopédie*, Milton Keynes 1980; P. Swiggers, 'Pre-histoire et histoire de l'encyclopédie', *Revue Historique* 549 (1984), 83–93; J. Lough, *The Encylopédie*, London 1971, Geneva 1989.
30. U. im Hof, *Das gesellige Jahrhundert: Gesellschaft und Gesellschaften im Zeitalter der Aufklärung*, Munich 1982; R. von Dülmen, *The Society of the Enlightenment: The Rise of the Middle Class and Enlightenment Culture in Germany*, Cambridge 1992 (originally Frankfurt 1986).
31. O. Dann, ed., *Lesegesellschaften und bürgerliche Emanzipation: ein europäischer Vergleich*, Munich 1981.
32. See J. Bernal, *Black Athena: The Afroasiatic Roots of Classical Civilization*, London 1987.
33. F.M. Turner, 'Why the Greeks and not the Romans in Victorian Britain', in G.W. Clarke, ed., *Rediscovering Hellenism: The Hellenic Inheritance and the English Imagination*, Cambridge 1989, 61–81. For Germany, see B. Näf, *Von Perikles zu Hitler? Die athenische Demokratie und die deutsche Althistorie bis 1945*, Berne 1986.
34. See P. Kitromilides, *The Enlightenment as Social Criticism: Iosipos Moisiodax and Greek Culture in the Eighteenth Century*, Princeton 1992.
35. See D. Ringrose, *Spain, Europe and the 'Spanish Miracle', 1700–1900*, Cambridge 1996.
36. E. Sisman, ed., *Haydn and his World*, Princeton 1997.
37. A. Harrington, *Reenchanted Science: Holism in German Culture from Wilhelm II to Hitler*, Princeton 1996.
38. A. Faivre, *Mystiques, theosophes et illuminés au siècle des lumières*, Hildesheim 1976.

13 Europe's revolutions: freedom and consumption for all?

1. Quoted in G. Wurzbacher, R. Pflaum, *Das Dorf im Spannungsfelde industrieller Entwicklung*, Stuttgart 1961, 13.
2. F.A. Pottle, ed., *Boswell's London Journal, 1762–1763*, London 1982, 159.
3. See M.C. Moine, *Les Fêtes à la cour du Roi Soleil, 1665–1715*, Paris 1984.
4. A. Chéruel, ed., *Mémoires de Saint-Simon*, XII, Paris 1857, 461 sqq.
5. For a case study: J.H. Plumb *et al.* eds, *The Birth of Consumer Society: The Commercialization of Eighteenth-Century England*, Bloomington 1982.
6. See D. Roche, *The Culture of Clothing: Dress and Fashion in the Ancien Régime*, Cambridge 1995.
7. See F.B. Kaye, ed., *Bernard Mandeville: The Fable of the Bees*, Oxford 1924.
8. For a survey: B. Gottlieb, *The Family in the Western World from the Black Death to the Industrial Age*, Oxford 1987.
9. See B.W. Robinson, R.F. Hall, *The Aldrich Book of Catches*, London 1989, 79, no. 56.
10. A survey: H. Cunningham, *Children and Childhood in Western Society since 1500*, London 1995.
11. N. Elias, *The Civilizing Process. I: The History of Manners. II: State Formation and Civilization*, Oxford 1982.
12. See J. Barry, C. Brooks, eds, *The Middling Sort of People: Culture, Society and Politics in England, 1550–1800*, Basingstoke 1994, esp. 1–27; D. Blackbourn, R.J. Evans,

eds, *The German Bourgeoisie*, London 1991; P.M. Pilbeam, *The Middle Classes in Europe, 1789–1914: France, Germany, Italy and Russia*, Basingstoke 1990.

13. See D. Roche, *Les Republicains des lettres: gens de culture et lumières au XVIIIe siècle*, Paris 1988. An important case: C. Lougee, *Le Paradis des Femmes: Women, Salons and Social Stratification in Seventeenth-Century France*, Princeton 1976.

14. F. Chabod, 'L'Idea di Europa', *Rassegna d'Italia* II (1947), 3.

15. See H. Bots, ed., *Henri Basnage de Beauval en de histoire des ouvrages des savans, 1687–1709*, I–II, Amsterdam 1976.

16. P.J.A.N. Rietbergen, 'Pieter Rabus en de "Boekzaal van Europe", 1692–1702', in H. Bots, ed., *Pieter Rabus en de Boekzaal van Europe*, Amsterdam 1974, 1–102.

17. See on the moralizing nature of many weeklies: W. Martens, *Die Botschaft der Tugend*, Stuttgart 1968.

18. P.J. Buijnsters, 'Sociologie van de Spectator', *Spiegel der Letteren* 15/1 (1973), 1–17.

19. P. Clark, *Sociability and Urbanity: Clubs and Societies in the Eighteenth-Century City*, Leicester 1986.

20. M.C. Jacob, *Living the Enlightenment: Freemasonry and Politics in Eighteenth-Century Europe*, Oxford 1992.

21. R. Stadelman, *Preussens Könige in ihrer Tätigkeit für die Landeskultur. II: Friedrich der Grosse*, Leipzig 1882, 333.

22. G. Schmoller, ed., *Acta Borussica*, I/2, Berlin 1892, 8.

23. Stadelman, *Preussens Könige*, 287.

24. R. Chartier, *Les Origines culturelles de la revolution française*, Paris 1991.

25. Among the numerous introductions, for background information one might read Ph. Deane, *The First Industrial Revolution*, Cambridge 1979, and J. Goodman, K. Honeyman, *Gainful Pursuits: The Making of Industrial Europe, 1600–1914*, London 1988. An illuminating case study is D. Sabean, *Property, Production and Family in Neckarshausen, 1700–1870*, Cambridge 1990.

26. H. Ch. Mettin, ed., *Fürst Pückler reist nach England: aus den Briefen eines Verstorbenen*, Stuttgart 1958, 107 sqq.

27. For a non-English case study: R. Sandgruber, *Die Anfänge der Konsumgesellschaft*, Vienna 1982, which deals with Austria in the eighteenth and nineteenth centuries.

28. O. Wilde, *The Picture of Dorian Gray*, London 1891, chs 8 and 6.

29. A. Joubin, ed., *Eugène Delacroix, Journal. 1822–1863*, Paris 1981, 346–7.

30. See R. von Dülmen *et al.* eds, *Volkskultur: zur Wiederentdeckung des vergessenen Alltags, 16.–20. Jahrhundert*, Frankfurt 1984.

31. For a survey: R. Wendorff, *Zeit und Kultur: Geschichte des Zeitbewusstseins in Europa*, Opladen 1980.

32. K. Jantke, D. Hiler, eds, *Die Eigentumslosen*, Freiburg-Munich 1965, 178.

33. *Journal des Débats*, 18 April 1832.

34. See the fine study by J.M. Meriman, *The Margins of City Life: Explorations on the French Urban Frontier, 1815–1851*, New York 1991.

35. Quoted in P. McPhee, *A Social History of France, 1780–1880*, London 1993, 203.

14 Progress and its discontents: nationalism, economic growth and the question of cultural certainties

1. For a very perceptive study of similarities and continuities in this field, see R. Wuthenow, *Communities of Discourse: Ideology and Social Structure in the Reformation, the Enlightenment and European Socialism*, Cambridge, Mass., 1989.

2. A comparative survey of the sociopolitical consequences: G.A. Ritter, *Der Sozialstaat: Entstehung und Entwicklung im internationalen Vergleich*, Munich 1989; as well as S. Padgett, W.E. Patterson, *A History of Social Democracy in Europe*, London 1991.

3. Henri de Saint-Simon, *Le Système industriel*, Paris 1821, 19.
4. For further arguments: S. Woolf, *Napoleon's Integration of Europe*, London 1991.
5. B. Anderson, *Imagined Communities: Reflections on the Origin and Spread of Nationalism*, London 1983.
6. For a general survey: B. Tobia, *Una patria per gli Italiani: spazi, itinerari, monumenti nell'Italia unita (1870–1900)*, Rome 1991.
7. For the concept: P. Nora, ed., *Realms of Memory: Rethinking the French Past*, I, New York 1996.
8. See S. Collini, *Public Moralists: Political Thought and Intellectual Life in Britain, 1850–1930*, Oxford 1991.
9. For the background see P. Greenhalgh, *Ephemeral Vistas: The Expositions Universelles, Great Exhibitions and World Fairs, 1851–1939*, Manchester 1988.
10. P.E. Schramm, *Neun Generationen: Dreihundert Jahre deutscher 'Kulturgeschichte' im Lichte des Schicksals einer Hamburger Bürgerfamilie, 1648–1948*, Göttingen 1963, I, 295.
11. For example, D. Blackburn, R.J. Evans, eds, *The German Bourgeoisie: Essays on the Social History of the German Middle Class from the Late Eighteenth to the Early Twentieth Century*, London 1991; see also the essays in J. Kocka, A. Mitchell, eds, *Bourgeois Society in Nineteenth-Century Europe*, Oxford 1993 (originally Munich 1988). Pamela Pilbeam, in her wide-ranging *The Middle Classes in Europe, 1789–1914*, Basingstoke 1990, has raised the question of the continuity of the pre-revolutionary urban patriciate and the new industrial elite.
12. For example, E. Weber, *Peasants into Frenchmen*, London 1976.
13. See, too, H.J. Graff, *The Legacies of Literacy: Continuities and Contradictions in Western Culture and Society*, Bloomington 1987.
14. Kocka, Mitchell, *Bourgeois Society*, 430, table 16.3.
15. See S. Collini, *Matthew Arnold: A Critical Portrait*, Oxford 1994.
16. M. Arnold, *Popular Education and the State*, London 1861; Arnold, *Schools and Universities on the Continent*, London 1868.
17. J. Dover Wilson, ed., *M. Arnold, Culture and Anarchy*, Cambridge 1971, 129 sq.; M. Arnold, *Essays in Criticism* I, London 1865, 18.
18. G.W.E. Russell, ed., *M. Arnold, Letters* I, London 1895, 4.
19. *Culture and Anarchy*, 138.
20. *Culture and Anarchy*, 195.
21. Quoted by J. Dover Wilson in his introduction to *Culture and Anarchy*, XXXV.
22. P. Anderson, *The Printed Image and the Transformation of Popular Culture, 1790–1860*, Oxford 1994.
23. See O. Dann, ed., *Lesegesellschaften und bürgerliche Emanzipation: ein europäischer Vergleich*, Munich 1981, 22, 159 sqq.
24. See the details in F. Parent-Lardeur, *Lire à Paris au temps de Balzac: les cabinets de lecture à Paris, 1815–1830*, Paris 1981, 171, 172, 178.
25. G. Jäger, J. Schönert, eds, *Die Leihbibliothek als Institution des literarischen Lebens im 18. und 19. Jahrhundert. Organisation, Bestände, Publikum*, Hamburg 1980, 11 sqq.
26. Quoted in H. Nicolson, *Tennyson: Aspects of his Life, Character and Poetry*, London 1923, 1960, 235.
27. *La Regenta*, written by L. Alas (1852–1901), whose pen-name was Clarin, was translated in English in 1984.
28. See L. Sauer, 'Romantic automata', in: G. Hoffmeister, ed., *European Romanticism: Literary Cross-Currents, Modes and Models*, Detroit 1990, 287–306.
29. S. Butler, *Erewhon*, London (Everyman's Library) 1951, 144, 145, 147.
30. See M. Schneider, *Geschichte als Gestalt: Gustav Freytag's Roman 'Soll und Haben'*, Stuttgart 1980.
31. This is the drift of most of the essays in M.I. Finley, ed., *The Legacy of Greece: A New Appraisal*, Oxford 1981, and R. Jenkyns, ed., *The Legacy of Rome: A New*

Appraisal, Oxford 1992, even if the limitation of culture to art and literature in the latter volume is debatable.

32. See P.J.A.N. Rietbergen, 'Een Europeaan droomt: Novalis tussen Europa, Christendom en Wereld', in his *Dromen van Europa: een cultuurgeschiedenis*, Amersfoort 1993, 255–81.

33. From Alexander Dru, ed., *The Letters of Jakob Burckhardt*, London 1955, 97; 107–8, 145–8, 150–1, 219–20.

34. A. Corbin, *Time, Desire and Horror: Towards a History of the Senses*, Oxford 1995.

35. H. Kaeble, *Auf dem Weg zu einer europäischen Gesellschaft: eine Sozialgeschichte Westeuropas, 1880–1980*, Munich 1987.

36. See K. Tenfelde, ed., *Arbeiter und Arbeiterbewegung im Vergleich*, Munich 1986, which compares developments in Britain and Germany.

37. For the background: A. Corbin, *Le Territoire du vide*, Paris 1988; translated as *The Lure of the Sea: The Discovery of the Seaside in the Western World, 1750–1840*, Oxford 1994.

38. For the complexity of Europe's attitude towards nature: K. Thomas, *Man and the Natural World: Changing Attitudes in England, 1500–1800*, Harmondsworth 1982.

39. For a survey: A. Daumard, *Oisiveté et loisirs dans les sociétés occidentales au XIX siècle*, Amiens 1983.

40. See S. Easton *et al. Disorder and Discipline: Popular Culture from 1550 to the Present*, Aldershot 1988.

41. Quoted in J.M. Merriman, *The Margins of City Life: Explorations on the French Urban Frontier, 1815–1851*, New York 1991, 67.

42. An important introduction to the problems involved is W. Kaschuba, *Volkskultur zwischen feudaler und bürgerlicher Gesellschaft: zur Geschichte eines Begriffes und seinen gesellschaftlichen Wirklichkeit*, Frankfurt 1988, as well as Van Dülmen, Schindler, eds, *Volkskultur, passim.*

43. Quoted in G. Schönbrunn, ed., *Das bürgerliche Zeitalter*, 1815–1914, Munich 1980, 826.

44. See V. Lidtke, 'Recent literature on workers' culture in Germany and England', in Tenfelde, *Arbeiter und Arbeiterbewegung*, 337–62.

45. A good biography: M. Marnot, *Joseph Haydn: la mesure de son siècle*, Paris 1996.

46. See W. Weber, *The Rise of Musical Classics in Eighteenth-Century Orchestral Concerts: A Study in Canon, Ritual and Ideology*, London 1992; J.H. Johnson, *Listening in Paris: A Cultural History*, Berkeley 1995.

47. One of the best analyses of, especially, Schubert's solo songs still remains the one written by the singer who was probably their most convincing performer in the twentieth century: D. Fischer-Dieskau, *Auf den Spuren der Schubertlieder*, Munich 1976. A good biography: P. Guelke, *Franz Schubert und seine Zeit*, Laaber 1991.

48. See S. Finkelstein, *Composer and Nation: The Folk Heritage in Music*, New York 1960.

49. Quoted in P. McPhee, *A Social History of France, 1780–1880*, London 1993, 125.

50. See A. Briggs, *Victorian Things*, London 1988.

51. M. Miller, *The 'Bon Marché': Bourgeois Culture and the Department Store, 1869–1920*, Princeton 1981.

52. See G. Vickert, 'The theory of conspicuous consumption in the eighteenth century', in P. Hughes, D. Williams, eds, *The Varied Pattern: Studies in the eighteenth Century*, Toronto 1971, 253–67.

53. See the English translation: Jean-Jacques Rousseau, *The First and Second Discourses*, New York 1986, 4–5, 175, 180–1.

54. D. Hume, *Treatise on Human Nature*, Oxford 1978.

55. J.S. Mill, *Principles of Political Economy*, originally London 1848; Toronto 1965, 753–96.

15 Europe and the other worlds

1. For a survey, albeit a not always balanced one: A. Crosby, *Ecological Imperialism: The Biological Expansion of Europe, 900–1900*, Cambridge 1986.
2. G. Lantzeff, R. Pierce, *Eastward to Empire: Exploration and Conquest on the Russian Open Frontier to 1750*, Montreal 1973; M. Rywkin, *Russian Colonial Expansion to 1917*, London 1987; G. Diment, Y. Slezkine, eds, *Between Heaven and Hell: The Myth of Siberia in Russian Culture*, New York 1993.
3. D. Arnold, *Environment, Culture and European Expansion*, Oxford 1997.
4. See D. Gregory, *Brute New World: The Rediscovery of Latin America in the Early Nineteenth Century*, London 1992.
5. See P.J.A.N. Rietbergen, 'Aan de vooravond van "het Groote Missie-uur": een onderzoek naar de Nederlandse missiebeweging gedurende de eerste helft van de negentiende eeuw en de rol van "missietijdschriften" daarin', *Nederlands Archief voor Kerkgeschiedenis* 70 (1990), 75–108.
6. R.H. Pearce, *Savagism and Civilization: A Study of the Indian and the American Mind*, Berkeley 1988, 69.
7. J. Hector St John de Crevecoeur, *Letters from an American Farmer*, London 1782. Here quoted from the Everyman's Library, London, edition, 5.
8. The following quotations are from *Letters*, 11, 24–5, 13, 41, 41–2, 43–4.
9. W. Cather, *O Pioneers!*, New York 1913; Harmondsworth 1989, 301.
10. See W.C. Davis, *The American Frontier: Pioneers, Settlers and Cowboys, 1800–1890*, New York 1992; J.D. Unruh, *The Plains Across: Emigrants, Wagon Trains and the American West*, New York 1992; and the illustrative volume of eyewitness accounts in *Westward Expansion*, New York 1992.
11. For a general overview see D. Baines, *Emigration from Europe, 1815–1930*, London 1991.
12. The novels appeared between 1949 and 1959; G. Eidevall, *Vilhelm Mobergs emigrantepos: studien i verkets tillkomsthistoria, dokumentära bakgrund och konstnärliga gestaltning*, Stockholm 1974.
13. Upton Sinclair, *The Jungle*, New York 1965, 29.
14. The following quotations are from *The Jungle*, 32, 59, 64.
15. H. Croly, *The Promise of American Life*, New York 1909, 17–25, *passim*; 452.
16. W. Irving, *The Sketch Book*, London, 2.
17. P.E. Lovejoy, *Transformations in Slavery: A History of Slavery in Africa*, Cambridge 1983.
18. For a case study: H. Gruender, *Christliche Mission und deutscher Imperialismus*, Paderborn 1982.
19. For a survey of British attitudes: R. Robinson, J. Gallagher, *Africa and the Victorians: The Official Mind of Imperialism*, London 1981.
20. F.J. McLynn, *Hearts of Darkness*, London 1992; S. Lindquist, *Exterminate All the Brutes*, London 1997.
21. D. Massarela, *A World Elsewhere: European Encounters with Japan in the Sixteenth and Seventeenth Centuries*, New Haven 1990.
22. G.K. Goodman, *Japan: The Dutch Experience*, London 1986.
23. For a survey: N. Cameron, *Barbarians and Mandarins: Thirteen Centuries of Western Travellers in China*, Oxford 1989.
24. See D.E. Mungella, *Curious Land: Jesuit Accommodation and the Origins of Sinology*, Honolulu 1985.
25. See E. Evett, *The Critical Reception of Japanese Art in Late Nineteenth-Century Europe*, Ann Arbor 1982.
26. S. Wichmann, *Japonismus: Ostasien-Europa. Begegnungen in der Kunst des 19. und 20. Jahrhunderts*, Herrsching 1980.
27. See N.A. Silberman, *Digging for God and Country: Exploration, Archaeology and the Secret Struggle for the Holy Land, 1799–1917*, New York 1982.

28. S. Mills, *Discourses of Difference: An Analysis of Women's Travel Writing and Colonialism*, London 1991.

29. This, of course, has been the central, though debatable, argument of E. Said, *Orientalism*, London 1978, which he repeated in his *Culture and Imperialism*, London 1993.

30. A survey: M. Jacobs, *The Painted Voyage: Art, Travel and Exploration, 1564–1875*, London 1995. See also D. Mackay, *In the Wake of Cook: Exploration, Science and Empire, 1780–1801*, London 1985.

31. A. Olearius, *Neue Beschreibung der Moskovitischen und Persischen Reiche*, Leipzig 1656, 184.

32. See W. Leitsch, 'Westeuropäische Reiseberichte über den Moskauer Staat', in A. Maczak, H.J. Teuteberg, eds, *Reiseberichte als Quellen Europäischer Kulturgeschichte*, Wolfenbüttel 1988, 153–76.

33. Basic reading is the fine study by L. Wolf, *Inventing Eastern Europe*, Stanford 1994; for this: 7–8.

34. See D. Chirot, ed., *The Origins of Backwardness in Eastern Europe: Economics and Politics from the Middle Ages until the Early Twentieth Century*, Berkeley 1989.

35. D. Groh, *Rusland und das Selbstverständnis Europas*, Neuwied 1961, 65 sqq.

16 The 'Decline of the Occident' – the loss of a dream? From the nineteenth to the twentieth century

1. C. Harding, S. Popple, *In the Kingdom of Shadows: A Companion to Early Cinema*, London 1997.

2. W. Lautemann, M. Schlenke, gen. eds, *Geschichte in Quellen*, Munich 1980, 825.

3. A good introduction to the period is J. Barzun, *Darwin, Marx, Wagner: Critique of a Heritage*, New York 1958, esp. 38–55: 'The evolution of evolution'. See also R. Olson, *Evolution: The History of an Idea*, Berkeley 1989.

4. The study of Darwin has become a veritable industry. There is an avalanche of recent biographies. Instructive is L.S. Bergmann, 'Reshaping the roles of Man, God and Nature: Darwin's rhetoric in *On the Origin of Species*', in J.W. Lee, J. Yaross, eds, *Beyond the Two Cultures: Essays on Science, Technology and Literature*, Ames 1990. *Proteus: A Journal of Ideas* VI/2 (1989), is entirely devoted to the various aspects of Darwin's life and works.

5. See the very perceptive study by S.E. Hyman, *The Tangled Bank: Darwin, Marx, Frazer and Freud as Imaginative Writers*, New York 1962, which has not received the attention it deserves.

6. For example: G. Levine, *Darwin and the Novelists: Patterns of Science in Victorian Fiction*, London 1988.

7. Ch. Fox *et al.* eds, *Inventing Human Science*, Berkeley 1995.

8. D. Knight, *The Age of Science: The Scientific World View in the Nineteenth Century*, Oxford 1986, provides an excellent introduction.

9. P. Costello, *Jules Verne, Inventor of Science Fiction*, London 1978; G. Proteau, *Le Grand Roman de Jules Verne: sa vie*, Paris 1979.

10. B. Holm, *Selma Lagerlöfs litterära profil*, Stockholm 1986.

11. See Barzun, *Darwin*, passim.

12. E. Förster-Nietzsche, ed., *Nietzsche's Werke XVI*, Leipzig 1912, 402. It has to be said that a text titled *Der Wille zur Macht: Versuch einer Umwerthung aller Werthe*, as presented by Elisabeth Nietzsche as Nietzsche's chief work, does not exist. What exists is a collection of 'aphorisms', very difficult to interpret. See M. Montinari, 'Vorwort', in G. Colli, M. Montinari, eds, *Friedrich Nietzsche: Sämtliche Werke. Kritische Studienausgabe*, 14, Berlin 1980, 1–12.

13. See Colli, Montinari, eds, *Fr. Nietzsche: Kritische Gesamtausgabe der Werke*, VI/2, Berlin 1968) [= Fr. Nietzsche, *Also sprach Zarathustra: ein Buch für Alle und Keine*], 33, 8–1.

14. See B. Reardon, 'Ernest Renan and the religion of science', in D. Jasper, T. Wright, eds, *Critical Spirit and the Will to Believe*, New York 1989, 199–205.

15. For example, W. Loth, ed., *Deutscher Katholizismus im Umbruch zur Moderne*, Stuttgart 1991.

16. M. Artola, *Antiguo Régimen y revolucíon liberal*, Barcelona 1978; L.G. San Miguel, *De la Sociedad Aristocratica a la Sociedad Industrial en la España del Siglo XIX*, Madrid 1973.

17. See the texts in Foerster, *Die Idee*, as well as H. Wehberg, *Ideen und Projekte betreffende die Vereinigten Staaten von Europa in den letzten 100 Jahren*, Bremen 1984.

18. See G. Colli, M. Montinari, eds, *Fr. Nietzsche: Kritische Gesamtausgabe der Werke*, VI/2, Berlin 1968 [= Fr. Nietzsche, *Jenseits von Gut und Böse*], 209, no. 256.

19. See J.G.A. Pocock, *The Machiavellian Moment: Florentine Political Thought and the Atlantic Republican Tradition*, Princeton 1975.

20. See M. Elvin, *The Pattern of the Chinese Past*, London 1973.

21. A. Tennyson, 'Locksley Hall', in *Poetical Works of Alfred Lord Tennyson*, London 1917, 103.

22. For the case of Britain, which is the best researched: J.M. Mackenzie, ed., *Imperialism and Popular Culture*, Manchester 1896.

23. M. Lowsky, *Karl May*, Stuttgart 1987.

24. R.D. Gray, *Goethe the Alchemist*, Cambridge 1952.

25. A very readable biography has been written by P. Gay, *Freud: A Life for our Time*, New York 1988.

26. A balanced, up-to-date analysis is given by F. Forrester, *Dispatches from the Freud Wars*, Cambridge, Mass., 1997.

27. See L.B. Litvo, *Darwin's Influence on Freud*, New Haven 1991.

28. H.D. Cater, ed., *Henry Adams and his Friends: A Collection of Unpublished Letters*, New York 1970, 499–500.

29. H. Adams, *The Education of Henry Adams: An Autobiography*, Boston 1918, 379, 380, 381–2, 383.

30. See the study by H.A. Klomp, *De relativiteitstheorie in Nederland*, Groningen 1997.

31. See H. Hartmann, *Max Planck als Mensch und Denker*, Frankfurt 1953.

32. Chr. Butler, *Early Modernism: Literature, Music and Painting in Europe, 1900–1916*, Oxford 1994.

33. A. Stassinopoulos Huffington, *Picasso, Creator and Destroyer*, New York 1988, ch. 4.

34. See D. Roberts, *Benedetto Croce and the Uses of Historicity*, Berkeley 1987.

35. Quoted in R. Wohl, *The Generation of 1914*, London 1980, 240, n. 1.

36. H. Pirenne, *Mahomet et Charlemagne*, Paris 1937.

37. For example, P. Barker *et al.* eds, *After Einstein*, Memphis 1981; D.P. Ryan *et al.* eds, *Einstein and the Humanities*, Westport 1987.

38. G. Blasberg, *Krise und Utopie der Intellektuellen: kulturkritische Aspekte in Robert Musils Roman 'Der Man ohne Eigenschaften'*, Stuttgart 1984; G.M. Moore, *Proust and Musil: The Novel as Research Instrument*, New York 1985.

39. For the background: E. Timms, ed., *Unreal City: Urban Experience in Modern European Literature and Art*, New York 1985.

40. The very negative interpretation of Lang's film by Siegfried Kracauer in his *Von Caligari zu Hitler: eine psychologische Geschichte des deutschen Films*, Frankfurt 1979, originally 1949, seems unfounded, induced by Kracauer's wish to detect a growing glorification of totalitarianism in every movie made in these years. Rather, I think Lang's vision to be a generally pessimist one.

41. For the background *Revue du Dix-Neuvième Siècle* 13, 1983, and *Cahiers Victoriens et Edwardiens* 31, 1990. Also Th.P. Dunn *et al.* eds, *The Mechanical God: Machines in Science Fiction*, Westport 1982.

42. J.B. Kerman, ed., *Retrofitting Blade Runner*, Bowling Green 1991, especially in 110–23, as well as the illuminating analyses by J. Douchet, 'La Ville Tentaculaire', N.N. *Cités-Cinés*, La Villette 1987, 61–71; F. Chaslin, 'Dans les villes crépusculaires', ibid., 103–109. See also: Y. Biró, *Profane Mythology: The Savage Mind of the Cinema*, Bloomington 1982, 57–62.

43. M. Brod, ed., *Franz Kafka, Amerika*, Frankfurt 1953, 38.

44. For Huizinga's reactions: W.E. Krul, 'Moderne beschavingsgeschiedenis: Johan Huizinga over de Verenigde Staten', in K. van Berkel, ed., *Amerika in Europese ogen: Facetten van de Europese beeldvorming van het moderne Amerika*, 's-Gravenhage 1990, 86–108.

45. K. Harpprecht, *Thomas Mann: Eine Biographie*, Reinbek 1995.

46. See R. Wohl, *A Passion for Wings: Aviation and the western Imagination, 1908–1918*, New Haven 1995.

47. H.J. Fügen, *Max Weber*, Hamburg 1991; D. Käsler, *Max Weber: An Introduction to his Life and Work*, Munich 1988.

48. For the above, mostly B. Moore, *Social Origins of Dictatorship and Democracy: Lord and Peasant in the Making of the Modern World*, New York 1966.

49. For a survey of the historiography of this very complex problem see P. Lambert, *The Weimar Republic and the Rise of Hitler*, London 1997.

50. See R.I. Moore, *The Formation of a Persecuting Society*, Oxford 1987.

51. Z. Baumann, *Modernity and the Holocaust*, London 1989.

17 Towards a new Europe?

1. In Brecht's final version of 1930, the title was changed into *Das Badener Lehrstück vom Einverständnis*, which better indicated the central theme: man's basic need to accept death.

2. G. Alperovitz, *The Decision to Use the Atomic Bomb*, New York 1995.

3. See M.J. Nye, *From Chemical Philosophy to Theoretical Chemistry: Dynamics of Matter and Dynamics of Disciplines*, Berkeley 1993.

4. Watson himself wrote a highly readable first-hand account: J. Watson, *The Double Helix*, London 1968.

5. See C.P. Snow, *The Two Cultures: and A Second Look: An Expanded Version of The Two Cultures and the Scientific Revolution*, Cambridge 1964, as well as J.S. de la Mothe, *C.P. Snow and the Struggle for Modernity*, Austin 1992. Significantly, Snow's text was translated in German as: *Die Zwei Kulturen: literarische und naturwissenschaftliche Intelligenz*, Stuttgart 1967. Also F. Leavis, *Cultures: The Significance of C.P. Snow*, Cambridge 1964, as well as D. Thompson, ed., *The Leavises*, Cambridge 1984.

6. See *Unesco Statistical Yearbook, 1991*.

7. See A.P. French, P.J. Kennedy, eds, *Nils Bohr: A Centenary Volume*, Cambridge, Mass., 1985; G. Holton, *Thematic Origins of Scientific Thought*, Cambridge, Mass., 1988.

8. For a very lucid survey: S. Greenfield, *The Human Brain*, London 1997.

9. See A.H. Guth, *The Inflationary Universe*, London 1997.

10. A survey: D.W. Urwin, *The Community of Europe: A History of European Integration since 1945*, London 1995.

11. See the important, 'demythologizing' study by A.S. Milward (with G. Brenner, F. Romero), *The European Rescue of the Nation-State*, London 1993, as well as A.S. Milward, *The Reconstruction of Western Europe, 1945–1951*, London 1984.

12. See A. Milward, V. Sorensen, 'Interdependence or integration? A national choice', in A.S. Milward *et al*. eds, *The Frontier of National Sovereignty: History and Theory, 1945–1992*, London 1993, 1–32.

13. E.J. Hobsbawm, T. Ranger, eds, *The Invention of Tradition*, Cambridge 1983; E.J. Hobsbawm, *Nations and Nationalism since 1780: Programme, Myth, Reality*, Cambridge 1990.

14. This has already been argued by L. Kohr, *The Breakdown of Nations*, London 1957; more recently: Chr. Harvie, *The Rise of European Regionalism*, London 1993.

15. For the following see R. Kroes, *De Leegte van Amerika*, Amsterdam 1992.

16. For example, R.F. Kuisel, *Seducing the French: The Dilemma of Americanization*, New York 1993. For a parallel study: R. Willett, *The Americanization of Germany: Post-War Culture, 1945–1949*, London 1989.

17. P.M. Lutzeler, 'Bachman und Bernhard an Böhmens Strand: Schriftsteller und Europa oder die Entdeckung des Homo Europaeus Enzensbergensis', *Neue Rundschau* 102/1 (1991), 23–35.

18. S. Harding, D. Phillips, *Contrasting Values in Western Europe: Unity, Diversity and Change*, Basingstoke 1986; S. Ashford, N. Timms, *What Europe Thinks: A Study of Western European Values*, Aldershot 1992; and the reports of the European Values Studies Project, published in Tilburg, The Netherlands, from 1993 onwards.

19. For a survey: R. Williams, *Dream Worlds*, Berkeley 1982, 298–384, *passim*.

20. E. Durkheim, *Formes élémentaires de la vie réligieuse*, Paris 1912.

21. See M. Birman, *All that is Solid Melts into Air*, London 1982; A. Ross, *No Respect: Intellectuals and Popular Culture*, London 1989.

22. See M.A. Bienefeld, *Working Hours in British Industry: An Economic History*, London 1972.

23. J.M. Keynes, *Essays in the Art of Persuasion*, London 1931, 365 sqq.

24. For a general survey: R. Williams, *Culture and Society, 1780–1950*, London 1961.

25. G. Poujol, R. Labourie, *Les Cultures populaires*, Toulouse 1979.

26. W.W. Rostow, *The Stages of Economic Growth*, Cambridge 1961.

27. See P. Yonnet, *Modes et masses: la société française et le moderne, 1945–1985*, Paris 1985.

28. See P. Brantlinger, *Bread and Circuses: Theories of Mass Culture as Social Decay*, New York 1983.

29. J.K. Galbraith, *The Affluent Society*, New York 1958, 139 sqq.

30. See R. Butsch, ed., *For Time and Profit: The Transformation of Leisure into Consumption*, Philadelphia 1990.

31. From G. Cross, *Time and Money: The Making of a Consumer Culture*, London 1993, 193 sqq. This perceptive study has been of great value in the writing of this section.

32. V. Packard, *The Status Seekers*, New York 1959; W. Whyte, *The Organization Man*, New York 1956.

33. See R. Inglehart, *Cultural Shift*, Princeton 1990.

34. See P. Blyton, *Changes in Working Time: An International Review*, New York 1985.

35. W. Gossin, *Le Temps de la vie quotidienne*, Paris 1974.

36. A. Veal, *Sport and Recreation in England and Wales*, London 1979; J. Bishop, P. Higgett, eds, *Organizing around Enthusiasm: Mutual Aid in Leisure*, London 1986.

37. J. Dumazedien, *La Révolution culturelle du temps libre, 1968–1988*, Paris 1988.

38. Report of the Dutch Bureau for Social and Cultural Planning (The Hague), May 1995.

39. This is the argument persuasively sustained by Cross, *Time and Money*, *passim*.

40. For the background: L. Tilly, J.W. Scott, *Women, Work and Family*, London 1987.

41. U. Hannerz, *Cultural Complexity: Studies in the Social Organization of Meaning, States, Markets, Movements*, New York 1992.

42. A penetrating survey: H.J. Gans, *Popular Culture and High Culture: An Analysis and Evaluation of Taste*, New York 1974.
43. See *ILO Yearbook of Labour Statistics: Retrospective Edition on Population Censuses 1945–1989*, Geneva 1990.
44. E.J. Hobsbawm, *The Age of Empire, 1870–1914*, London 1987, esp. ch. 5.
45. P. Bairoch, *Two Major Shifts in Western European Labour Force: The Decline of the Manufacturing Industries and of the Working Class*, Geneva 1988.
46. See J. Rifkin, *The End of Work: The Decline of the Global Labor Force and the Dawn of the Post-market Era*, New York 1995.
47. F. Ewald, *L'Etat-providence*, Paris 1986.
48. A. Gray, J. McGuigan, eds, *Studying Culture: An Introductory Reader*, London 1993.
49. The point is much discussed; see, e.g., F. Zweig, *The Worker in an Affluent Society*, London 1961, as opposed to J. Goldthorpe *et al. The Affluent Worker in the Class Structure*, London 1971, although both rely heavily on the somewhat atypical case of Britain.
50. On Guardini: H. Kuhn, *R. Guardini, der Mensch und das Werk*, Darmstadt 1961. In 1962, Guardini was awarded the Erasmus Prize.
51. See Hannerz, *Cultural Complexity, passim.* The *Polity Reader in Cultural Theory*, Cambridge 1994, significantly starts with mass communication.
52. See P. Berger, 'Social sources of secularization', in J.C. Alexander, S. Seidman, eds, *Culture and Society: Contemporary Debates*, Cambridge 1992, 239–49.
53. R. Wilson, W. Dissanayake, eds, *Global/Local: Cultural Production and the Transnational Imaginary*, London 1996.
54. R. Shields, ed., *Cultures of Internet*, London 1996.
55. For a survey of various opinions: F. Webster, *Theories of the Information Society*, London 1996.
56. J. Ellis, *Visible Fictions: Cinema, Television, Video*, London 1992, esp. 109 sqq., 270 sqq.
57. Chr. Jenks, ed., *Visual Culture*, London 1995.
58. Ph. Drummond, R. Patterson, eds, *Television and its Audience: International Research Perspectives*, London 1988.
59. R.C. Allen, *Speaking of Soap Opera*, Chapel Hill, NC, 1985.
60. For a survey: M. Mitterauer, *Sozialgeschichte der Jugend*, Frankfurt 1986.
61. R. Floud *et al.*, *Height, Health and History*, Cambridge 1990.
62. From the *Financial Times*, 11 April 1991, quoted in Hobsbawm, *Age of Extremes*, 326.
63. E.J. Hobsbawm, *The Jazz Scene*, New York 1993.
64. Stravinsky, though presenting himself as a 'cosmopolitan', was far more influenced by Russia's musical past than he cared to admit: R. Taruskin, *Stravinsky and the Russian Tradition*, Oxford 1996.
65. For the role of television in the public domain: M. Price, *Television, the Public Sphere and National Identity*, Oxford 1996.
66. O. Marquard, 'Moratorium des Alltags: Eine Kleine Philosophie des Festes', in W. Haug, H. Warnung, eds, *Das Fest*, Munich 1989, 684–91.
67. See P. Manent, *An Intellectual History of Liberalism*, London 1994.

Epilogue: Europe – a present with a future

1. G. Erler, ed., *J.W. Goethe, Werke*, VIII, Berlin 1984, 77.
2. Quoted in W.C. Bark, *Origins of the Medieval World*, Stanford 1958, VII.
3. This vision was defended by A. Finkielkraut, *L'Humanité perdue*, Paris 1997.
4. F. Fernandez-Armesto, *Millennium*, London 1995.
5. An elegant though limited survey written by Josep Fontana, *Europa ante el espejo*,

Barcelona 1994, has been translated in several European languages; however, he omits the important north–south and east–west oppositions.

6. G. Nonneman *et al.* eds, *Muslim Communities in the New Europe*, Reading 1996.

7. Z. Bauman, *Modernity and Ambivalence*, London 1990.

8. E. Levinas, *Totalité et infini*, The Hague 1961.

9. P. Brezzi, *Realtà e mito nell'Europa dall' antichità ai giorni nostri*, Rome 1954, 22.

10. M. Beloff, *Europe and the Europeans: An International Discussion*, London 1957.

11. A. Lemaire, *Twijfel aan Europa: Zijn de intellectuelen de vijanden van de Europese cultuur?*, Baarn 1990. The contribution by C. Nooteboom, *De ontvoering van Europa*, Amsterdam 1993, as the reflection of someone who calls himself a 'European' traveller and thinker, is a disappointment.

12. M. Rostovtzeff, *The Social and Economic History of the Roman Empire*, Oxford 1926, 486–7.

13. R. Barnett *et al.* eds, *The End of Knowledge in Higher Education*, London 1997.

14. See C.W. Bynum, 'The last Eurocentric generation', *Perspectives* 34/2 (1996), 3 sqq.

Index

À la recherche du temps perdu, cycle of novels by Proust, 414

Abelard, Peter, monk and scholar, 152

Académie Française, 292

Accademia Platonica, at Florence, 181

Adam, the father of Man, 284

Adams, Henry, American intellectual and author, 411, 412

Adenauer, Konrad, German politician and statesman, 430

The Affluent Society, by Galbraith, 437

Aeneas, main character in the eponymous poem by Virgil, 51

Aeschylus, Greek playwright, 33

Akademie der Wissenschaften, or Prussian Academy of Sciences, 292, 296

'Akritic songs': Byzantine poetic genre, 225

al-Khwarizmi, Islamic mathematician, 106

al-Ma'mun, caliph, 106, 107

al-Rashid, caliph, 107

Alanus, descendant of Japhet, 88

Alaric, leader and king of the Goths, 75

Albeniz, Isaac, Spanish composer, 407

Alexander the Great, King of Macedonia, 34, 35, 43, 44, 59

Alfonso, the Learned, king of Castile, 153

Alfred, the Great, king of Wessex, 129, 137

Ali, Muhammad's son-in-law, 104

Alkuin, monk, one of Charlemagne's advisers, 93, 94

All my Loving, a song by Lennon and McCartney, 451

Alskog Tjangvide, with limestone tomb showing the Germanic cosmology, 82

Also sprach Zarathustra, by Nietzsche, 404

Altamira cave paintings, 5

Amerbach, Johann, publisher at Basle, 295

The American Village, poem by Freneau, 257

Amerika, Europa . . ., by Fröbel, 407

Amerika levend en denkend, or 'America living and thinking', by Huizinga, 417

Ammianus Marcellinus, Roman writer, 52, 55, 56, 57

Amphion Anglus, collection of songs by Blow, 293

Amsterdam Town Hall, 252

Andreae, Johann Valentin, German author, 257

Anti-Barbari, text by Erasmus, 183

Antiquités celtiques et antediluviennes, by Boucher, 4

Apologeticum, Tertullian's text in favour of the Christians, 66

L'Apprenti Sorcier, musical piece by Dukas, 427

Aquinas, Thomas, Christian theologian and philosopher, 110, 154, 155, 182, 303, 406

Arcadius, Roman emperor, 74

Arcana Coelestia, by Swedenborg, 312

Archimedes, Greek scientist, 35

Ardèche cave paintings, 5

Aristotle, Greek philosopher, 23, 34, 49, 83, 86, 106, 140, 181, 196, 214, 299, 309, 413

Arkwright, Richard, English factory owner and inventor, 340

Arminius, or Hermann, German war leader against the Romans, 54

Arne, Thomas, English composer, 316

Arnold, Matthew, English author, 356, 357, 438, 444

Aron, Raymond, French sociologist, 437

Asser, bishop of Winchester, biographer of Alfred the Great, 129

L'Astrée, novel by D'Urfée, 269

Atahualpa, last emperor of the Incas, 240

Atlas, the first part of Mercator's *Cosmographia*, 247

Au Bon Marché, one of the first, French, department stores, 363, 371

Au Bonheur des Dames, or *The Ladies' Paradise*, novel by Zola, 371, 372

Augustine, Christian saint and author, 81, 86, 87, 203, 303

Augustine, monk and Christian saint, buried in Canterbury cathedral, 90, 144

Augustus, Gaius Octavius, the first Roman emperor, 41, 42, 43, 44, 48

Averroës, or Ibn Rushd, Islamic scholar, 154, 303

Avicenna, or Ibn Sinna, Islamic scholar, 154

Bach, Johann Sebastian, German composer, 273

Bacon, Francis, English statesman and philosopher, 196, 200, 279, 280, 294, 299, 304, 306–7, 309

Bacon, Roger, English monk and scholar, 128

Baedeker, the first, German travel guide, 361

Barbaro, Daniele, Venetian scholar, 301

Barberini, Francesco, cardinal, 268

Barbie dolls, 434

Barlaeus, Caspar, Dutch writer, 252

Barnabas, writer of a very early 'Life of Jesus', 61

Basil I, Byzantine emperor, 94

Baugulf, abbot of Fulda, 95

Baxter, Richard, English theologian, 210

Bayle, Pierre, French publicist and philosopher, 286, 289, 297, 308

Bayreuth, shrine to Wagner and his music, 354

Beatles, English pop group, 450, 452

Beethoven, Ludwig van, German composer, 370

Behaim, Martin, German globe maker, 244, 245, 246

Benedict of Nursia, Christian saint, founder of the Benedictine Order, 99

Bering, Vitus, Danish-Russian explorer, 375

Berkeley, George, English philosopher, 312

Berkeley, George, English poet, 249

Berlin, song by Fischer Z, 452

Berlin, Symphonie der Grossstadt, film by Walter Ruttmann, 422

Bermuda, poem by Marvell, 248

Bernard, monk and Christian saint, founder of the Cistercian Order, 141

Bernini, Gianlorezno, Roman architect and sculptor, 252

Bessarion, Johannes, Byzantine scholar and book collector, 197, 214

Beverly, Robert, American poet, 250

Bezuchov, Pierre, character in Tolstoy's *War and Peace*, 353

Bibliothèque Impartiale, scholarly periodical, 296

Biedermann, German periodical, 332

Bird, Isabella, Scottish explorer, 395

Blade Runner, film, 417

Blow, John, English composer, 293

Boccaccio, Giovanni, Florentine writer, 150

Bodin, Jean, French political theorist, 243, 248

Boehme, Jakob, German philosopher, 304, 411

Boekzaal van Europe, Dutch learned periodical, 332

Bohr, Nils, Danish physicist, 414, 428

Boniface, Irish monk and saint, 91

A Booke called the Treasure of Travailers, by Bourne, 280

Borges, Jorge Luis, Argentinian writer, 377

Bosch, Hieronymus, Netherlandish painter, 193

Boswell, James, English diarist, 325

Boucher de Perthes, J., French scholar, 4

Bourbon, Henrietta Maria of, French princess, 266
Bourne, William, English author, 280
Brancion: fresco cycle at church of, 113
Brandenburg Concertos, by Bach, 272
Brasiliaensche Land-en Seereise, by Caspar Barlaeus, 252
Brecht, Bertolt, German playwright, 422, 423
British Museum, 254
Brown, Ford Maddox, English painter, 382
Bruni, Leonardo, Italian humanist writer, 190
Bruno, Giordano, Italian philosopher, 304, 411
Burckhardt, Jacob, Swiss historian, 363
Burke, Edmund, English political thinker, 331
Burlamacchi family, 266
Burnet, Gilbert, English theologian and historian, 297
Butler, Samuel, English novelist, 359

Caesar, Gaius Julius, Roman general and dictator, 8, 40, 41, 53
Caesar, Petrus, printer at Ghent, 203
Caliban, character in Shakespeare's *The Tempest*, 249, 250, 462
Calvin, John, Swiss Church reformer, 206
Camino de Santiago, pilgrims' road to Santiago de Compostela, 143, 445
Campanella, Tommaso, Italian freethinker and author, 257
Campra, André, French composer, 332
Canterbury Tales, a cycle of stories by Chaucer, 147, 148, 260
Casimir III, king of Poland, 184
Cather, Willa, American novelist, 379
Catherine, the Great, tsarina of Russia, 293, 380, 396
Cato, the Elder, Roman politician, 40
Cautio criminalis, a text on legal procedure in criminal affairs, 286
Cavallini, Pietro, Italian painter, 141
Cecilius Metellus, Roman politician, 49
Cellini, Benvenuto, Italian artist, 189, 272
Cervantes, de Saavedra, Miguel, Spanish author, 222
Chambers, E., English encyclopedist, 314
Chambers, Robert, Scottish scholar, 400

Chanson de Roland, epic tale, 148, 149, 225
Chansons de Geste, genre of epic tales, 149
Chaplin, Charles, American actor, 417
Chardin, J.-B., French painter, 330
Charlemagne, or Charles, the Great, king of the Franks, first Holy Roman Emperor, 92, 93, 94, 95, 96, 107, 111, 136, 208, 265, 284, 351
Charles I, king of England, 267
Charles III, king of Spain, 312
Charles IV, emperor, king of Bohemia, 184
Charles Martel, king of the Franks, 89, 111, 112
Charles V, emperor, king of Spain, 239, 242, 243, 246, 266
Chartres Cathedral, 141
Chaucer, Geoffrey, English civil servant and writer, 147, 148, 150, 170, 260
Chesterton, G.K., English author, 446
Chlodwig, leader and king of the Franks, 75, 89
Die Christenheit oder Europa, essay by Novalis, 362
Christina, queen of Sweden, 274
Chrysoleras, Manuel, Byzantine neo-platonist scholar, 181
Cicero, Roman orator and author, 51, 179
Citeaux, main monastery of the Cistercian Order, 141
Città del Sole, Campanella's major work, 7
Clarin, or L. Alas, Spanish novelist, 358
Cleisthenes, Greek politician, 23
La Clemenza di Tito, opera by Mozart, 272
clocks, 127
Clouet, François, French painter, 325
Cluny, main monastery of the Cistercian Order, 100
cocoa, 236
Codex, collection of imperial Roman decrees, 48
Codex Argenteus, manuscript copy of Wulfila's Bible in Gothic, 72
coffee, 236
Colbert, J., French statesman, 292
Collingwood, R., English historian, 457
Colloquia, text by Erasmus, 238, 279
Cólon, Hernan, son of Columbus, 234

Columbus, Christopher, Genovese mariner and explorer, 204, 232, 233, 234, 236, 237, 244, 245, 248, 374, 434

Comenius, or Komensky, Johann Amos, Czech scholar and author, 212

Confessiones, one of St. Augustine's main works, 86

Confucius, Chinese scholar and political theorist, 198, 390

Constantine, first Christian Roman emperor, 67, 68, 69, 71, 83, 87, 138, 192

Constantius Augustus, Roman emperor, 70

Contra Christianos, a work by Porphyry, 87

Cook, James, English explorer, 395

Cook, Thomas, 'first', English, travel agent, or tour operator, 437

Copernicus, or Kopernigk, Nicholas/Niklas, Polish scholar, 301, 302, 303, 309, 405, 423

Corneille, Pierre, French dramatist, 149, 332

Corpus Iuris Civilis, main Roman law code, 46

Cortés, Hernan, Spanish conquistador of Mexico, 234, 235

Cosmographia, Mercator's major collection of maps, 247

Cosmographia universalis, 248

Coster, Laurens Janszn, Dutch printer, 299

Council of Trent, 207

Cracow University, 184

The Creation, or *Die Schöpfung*, oratorio by Haydn, 318

Crick, F.H.C., English molecular biologist, 424

Croce, Benedetto, Italian philosopher, 415

Croly, Herbert, American journalist, 383

Cruise Missiles, song by Fischer Z, 452

Culture and Anarchy, by Arnold, 356

Cuper, Gisbert, Dutch politician and scholar, 297, 298

Curio, Johann, Hamburg publicist, 355

Cusanus, or Chrypffs, Nicholas, scholar and scientist, 182

Cyrillic writing, 109

Cyrillus, Greek Orthodox monk, and saint, 109

D'Urfé, Honoré, French author, 269

Da Gama, Vasco, Portuguese mariner and explorer, 204, 229, 232

Da Palestrina, Giovanni Pierluigi, Italian composer, 192

Da Sangallo, Aristotle, Italian artist, 187

Da Vinci, Leonardo, Italian scholar and artist, 272

Daguerre, L.J., French inventor, 398

Daimler, G., German technician, 398

Dali, Salvador, Spanish painter, 222, 407

Daniel, Samuel, English poet, 285

Dante Alighieri, Florentine poet, 139, 143, 144, 177

Darwin, Charles, English biologist, 386, 387, 402–5, 409, 411

Darwin, Erasmus, physician and poet, 400

Das Ende der Neuzeit, by Guardini, 444

Das Leben Jesu, by Strauss, 405

David, king of the Jews, 20

David-Neel, Alexandra, Danish-French explorer, 395

De Bello Gallico, Caesar's story of the war in Gaul, 53

De Buffon, G.L.E., French biologist, 400

De Camoes, Luis, Portuguese poet, 225

De Civitate Dei, one of St Augustine's major works, 86, 203

De Coelo et Inferno, by Swedenborg, 312–13

De Falla, Manuel, Spanish composer, 222

De Gasperi, Alcide, Italian statesman, 430

De Iure Belli ac Pacis, or 'On the Right of War and Peace', by Hugo Grotius, 204

De l'esprit des lois, by Montesquieu, 334

De la vicissitude . . . des choses de l'Univers, by Le Roy, 291

De la Fayette, Mme, French authoress, 270

De la Gardie, Magnus, Swedish statesman and patron of the arts, 274

De Lamarck, J.B., French biologist, 400

De la Mettrie, J.O., French scholar, 311, 428

De Lannoy, Guillebert, Burgundian nobleman and traveller, 150, 157

De las Casas, Bartolomé, Spanish monk, missionary and historian, 233, 234

De Mariana, Juan, Spanish historian, 292

De Monarchia, political treatise by Dante, 139

De Nugis Curialium, or 'On Courtiers' Trifles', by Walter Map, 136

De Peiresc, Nicholas Fabri, French scholar, 278, 294

De regimine iter agentium, by Grutarolus, 278

De Revolutione Orbium Coelestium, by Copernicus, 302

De servo Arbitrio, or 'On the bondage of the will', by Martin Luther, 218

De Valdes, Juan, Spanish historian, 225

Dead Sea Scrolls, 59

Decameron, collection of stories by Boccaccio, 150

Déclaration des Droits de l'Homme et du Citoyen, 336, 337, 338

Decree of Milan, 67

Defensor Pacis, political treatise by Marsiglio of Padua, 140

Le Défi americain, by Servan-Schreiber, 436-7

Defoe, Daniel, English author, 251

Delacroix, Eugène, French painter, 344, 345

Della Faille family, 266

Democritos, Greek philosopher, 85

Der Mann ohne Eigenschaften, novel cycle by Musil, 416

Der Untergang des Abendlandes, by Spengler, 415

Der Zauberberg, Thomas Mann's major novel, 418

Der Zauberlehrling, by Goethe, 427

Descartes, René, French mathematician and philosopher, 306, 307, 308, 309, 428

The Descent of Man, by Darwin, 402

Description of a Christian Republic, Andreae's major work, 257

Di Lasso, or De Lattre, Orlando/Roland, Netherlandish composer, 272

Diaghilev, S., Russian impressario, 409

Diaz de Vivar, Rodrigo, Spanish warrior, hero of the Poema de mio Cid, 149

Diaz del Castillo, Bernal, companion of Cortés, 234, 235

Dickens, Charles, English novelist, 348, 359

Dictionnaire, by Moreri, 296

Dictionnaire Historique et Critique, by Bayle, 296, 308

Didactica magna, Comenius' major work, 212

Dientzenhofer family of architects, 272

Dietrich, Marlene, German actress and singer, 422

Digests, collection of Roman private law texts, 48

Diocletian, Roman emperor, 62

Dionysios, Greek fertility god, 29

Dioscurides, Greek scientist, 106, 181, 301

Discours sur la Méthode, by Descartes, 308

A Discourse, by Lewkenor, 282

Divina Commedia, Dante's main work, 177

DNA, 424, 425

Doré, Gustave, French artist, 347, 348

Dormition of the Virgin, church of, at Moscow, 293

Drake, Francis, English buccaneer and naval commander, 240

Dreyer, Carl, Danish film maker, 419

Du Contrat Social, by Rousseau, 313–14

Dubois, Pierre, French political theorist, 139, 140, 407

Dukas, Paul, French composer, 427

Dürer, Albrecht, German painter, 188, 249, 272

Durkheim, Emile, French sociologist, 435

Eccles, John, English physicist, 428

Edict of Villiers-Cotterets, 215

Edict of Nantes, 289

Effi Briest, novel by Fontane, 358

Eggenbergh, Johann, prince of, Austrian diplomat, 268

Ehrenstrahl, D. Kl., Swedish painter, 274

Einhard, monk, Charlemagne's biographer, 93

Einstein, Albert, German physicist, 413, 414, 428

Elementai, Euclid's mathematical treatise, 35

El ingenioso hidalgo Don Quijote de la Mancha, by Cervantes, 222

Eliot, George, or Evans, Mary Ann, English novelist, 358

Elizabeth I, queen of England, 210, 354

English Men of Letters series, 353

Enikel, Jansen, Viennese chronicler, 138, 139

Die Entführung aus dem Serail, opera by Mozart, 288

Epistola de litteris colendis, Charlemagne's memorandum on learning, 95

Epistolarum . . . centurio prima, by Lipsius, 272

Erasmus, Desiderius, Dutch scholar, 183, 193, 218, 238, 279, 294

Eratosthenes, Greek scientist, 35

Erewhon, novel by Samuel Butler, 359

Escurial palace, 252

Essay concerning Human Understanding, by Locke, 308

Essay towards the . . . Peace of Europe, by Penn, 290

Eszterhazy family, of Hungarian magnates, patrons of Haydn, 369

Et Dukkelhjem, or The Doll's House, by Ibsen, 414

Etymologiae, encyclopedia written by Isidore of Seville, 73

Euclid, Greek mathematician, 35, 413

Euripides, Greek playwright, 27, 29

Europa, mythological Phoenician maiden, abducted by Zeus, 33

Europa und Amerika, by Von Schmidt-Phiseldek, 407

Die Europäische Bund, by Von Schmidt-Phiseldek, 407

Eusebius, biographer of the emperor Constantine, 69

Evelyn, John, English diarist, 275, 283

Ezekiel, Jewish prophet, 58

Fable of the Bees, by Mandeville, 327

Fairest isle, all isles excelling, air by Purcell, 293

Faraday, M., English chemist, 398

Fatima, Muhammad's daughter, 104

Faust, play by Goethe, xvii, 318, 408, 456, 457

Feíjoo, Benito, Spanish monk and author, 317

Ferdinand III, 'King of the Romans', 266

Ferdinand, king of Aragon, 153

Ficino, Marsilio, Floretine neo-platonist scholar, 181, 186

Finnegans Wake, novel by Joyce, 427

Fischer Z, German pop group, 452

Flaubert, Gustave, French novelist, 358

Fontainebleau palace, 273

Fontane, Theodore, German novelist, 358

Formey, Samuel, German Huguenot scholar, 296

Formulae of Tours, a set of models for legal practise, 121

Fountain of the Four Rivers, by Bernini, 252

François I, king of France, 215, 242, 273

Frankenstein, Mary Godwin Shelley's major novel, 359

Franklin, Benjamin, American politician and writer, 377

Frazer, James, English anthropologist, 404

Frederic I, emperor, 151

Frederick II, the Great, king of Prussia, 235, 334, 335

Freneau, Philip, American poet, 257

Fresnel, A.-J., French physicist, 398

Freud, Sigmund, Austrian psychologist, 411

Freytag, Gustav, German novelist, 360

Friedrich Wilhelm, king of Prussia, 351, 352

Fröbel, J., German author, 407

Frobenius, Johann, publisher at Basle, 295

Fugger, Jacob, of the German banking family, 242, 243, 264, 265, 266

Fulbert, bishop of Chartres, 120

Fulcher of Chartres, historian, 115

Fundgruben des Orients, scholarly periodical, 394

Gabriel, one of the archangels, 113

Gaius, Roman legal writer, 47

Galbraith, J.K., American economist, 437

Galen, Greek physician, 35, 106

Galilei, Galileo, Italian scientist, 301, 302, 303

Gallerie des Glaces, at Versailles, 268

Gance, Abel, French film maker, 419

Il Gattopardo, by Lampedusa, 451

Gauguin, Paul, French painter, 391

Genesis, the first book of the Old Testament of the Bible, 88

Gengangere, or Ghosts, play by Ibsen, 414

Gerusalemme Liberata, Tasso's major poem, 192

Gibbon, Edward, author of the Decline and Fall of the Roman Empire, 49

Gigli, Giacinto, Roman diarist, 170

Gilgamesh, Summerian epic, 22

Giner, Francisco, Spanish intellectual and educational reformer, 406

Giotto, di Bodone, Italian painter, 141, 177

Godwin Shelley, Mary, English feminist and novelist, 359
Goethe, J.W., German author and philosopher, xvii, 317, 318, 331, 353, 363, 411, 427, 457
The Golden Bough, by Frazer, 404
Gösta Berling's Saga, novel by Selma Lagerlöf, 403
Granados, Enrique, Spanish composer, 407
Graun, Karl-Heinrich, German composer, 253
Great Exhibition, at the Crystal Palace, London, 342
Gregorian chant, 108
Gregory I, the Great, pope, 90
Gregory III, pope, 89
Gregory IX, pope, 156
Grimm, Jacob and Wilhelm, German scholarly brothers, collectors of folk tales, 165
Grosses Vollständiges Universal-Lexicon, by Zedler, 314
Grutarolus, G., German author, 278
Guardini, Romano, German-Italian scholar, 444, 445
Guido of Arezzo, tenth-century musicologist, 408
Gundulic, Ivan, Serbic poet, 225
gunpowder, 128
Gutenberg Bible: the first printed book in the West, 199, 200
Gutenberg, Johann, German inventor, credited with the invention of printing, 199, 200

Hahn, Otto, German physicist, 424
Hall, John, English author, 281
Ham, or Cham, patriarch of the H/Chamites, or Africans, 88
Hammurápi, Babylonian king, 12, 13, 14
Handel, Georg Friedrich, German composer, 273
Hannibal, Carthaginian general, 40
Hausmann, Raoul, French artist, 425
Hawking, Stephen, English astronomer and physicist, 428
Haydn, Joseph, Austrian composer, 317–18, 369
Hedin, Sven, Swedish explorer, 395
Heidegger, Martin, German philosopher, 464
Heisenberg, Werner, German physicist, 414, 423

Hekataios of Miletos, Greek writer, 32
Helen, princess of Troy, character in the *Odyssey*, 22, 27
Henry IV, king of France, 289
Henry, the Navigator, prince of Portugal, 229
Henry V, play by Shakespeare, 238
Herder, J.G., German philosopher, 257, 397
Herodotus, Greek historian, 24, 30, 32
Hertz, H.R., German physicist, 398
Heyn, Piet, Dutch buccaneer and admiral, 240
Hildegard, abbess of Bingen, 100
Hindemith, Paul, German composer, 422
Hippocrates, Greek physician, 106
Historia Brittonum, a seventh-century Christian history, 88
Historiai, Herodotus' history of the Near East, 24
History of the Goths, by Isidore of Seville, 72
Historia Animalium, or the 'History of Animals', text by Aristotle, 49
History will teach us Nothing, song by Sting, 453
Hobbes, Thomas, English philosopher, 299, 310
Holbein, Hans, German painter, 325
Hollanda, Francesco de, Portuguese painter, 187
Hollywood movies, 434
Homer, Greek poet, 21, 30, 35, 51, 181
L'Homme machine, by La Mettrie, 311
Horace, Roman poet, 49, 51
House of Wisdom, academy of sciences at Baghdad, 106
Hroswitha, abbess of Gandersheim, 100
Hubble, Edwin, American astronomer, 414
Hugo, Victor, French author, 407
Huizinga, Johan, Dutch historian, 364, 417, 433
Hume, David, Scottish philosopher, 312, 373
Husayn ibn-Ishaq, Nestorian physician, 106
Hus, Jan, Czech Church reformer, 217
Husayn, Muhammad's grandson, leader of the Sh'ites, 104

Ibn Majid, African sailor and nautical scholar, 229

Ibsen, Henrik, Norwegian playwright, 414

Icarus, Greek mythological figure, 420, 456

Iconismus, a work by Kircher, 286

Iliad, 21, 27, 181

Imitatio Christi, Thomas à Kempis's major text, 193

Imperial Academy, at St Petersburg, 293

Institutio Oratoria, Quintilian's treatise on oratory, 50, 179

Institutiones, Gaius' main legal treatise, 46

Irving, Washington, American author, 384

Isabella, queen of Castile, 153

Isaiah, Jewish prophet, 58

Isidore, archbishop of Seville, Christian author, 72, 88

Isolde, Celtic legendary figure, 31

Ives, Samuel, English composer, 328

Izz ad-Din ibn al-Athir, Islamic historian, 116

James, Henry, American author, 385

James, William, American psychologist, 428

Japhet, patriarch of the Japhites, or Europeans, 88, 284

Jehol: Chinese imperial summer palace, 253

Jena University, 318

Jenseits von Gut und Bösen, by Nietzsche, 407

Jeremiah, Jewish prophet, 58

Jerome, Christian saint and author, 74, 75

Jerusalem, site of the Jewish temple, 20, 262

Jesus of Nazareth, 59 *passim*, John of the Cross, Christian saint and mystic, 446

John of Damascus, Christian scholar, 110

Jones, William, English Sanskrit scholar, 393

Journal Asiatique, scholarly periodical, 394

Journal of the Discovery of the Source of the Nile, by Speke, 386

Joyce, James, Irish writer, 427

Judita, epic by Marulic, 225

The Jungle, novel by Sinclair, 381

Justinian, Byzantine emperor, 45, 108

Juvenal, Roman poet, 49

Ka'ba, the House of Worship at Mecca, 103

Kafka, Franz, Czech writer, 416, 417, 431

Kant, Immanuel, German philosopher, 312–13

Karateyev, Platon, character in Tolstoy's *War and Peace*, 353

Karlstejn Castle, frescoes at, 184

Kepler, Johannes, German scholar, 303, 309

Keynes, John Maynard, English economist, 436

King Alfred, opera by Arne, 316–17

King Arthur, Celtic legendary figure, 31

King Arthur, opera by Purcell, 293

King James' Bible, 210

King's College Chapel, Cambridge: vaults and windows of, 141

Kingsley, Charles, English author, 403

Kircher, Athanasius, German Jesuit scholar, 305

Kitab al-Fawa'id, nautical treatise by Ibn Majid, 229

Koch, Robert, German bacteriologist, 398

Kölnische Zeitung, German newspaper, 342

Komensky, Johann Amos *see* Comenius

Kosmas, monk, first Christian cosmographer, 82, 83, 84, 244, 246

Kremlin palaces, Moscow, 293

Kristianikè Topographia, Kosmas' cosmological treatise, 83

Kritik der reinen Vernunft, by Kant, 312

Kritik der praktischen Vernunft, by Kant, 312

Krupp, German industrial family, 346, 347

Die Kultur der Renaissance in Italien, by Burckhardt, 363, 364

Lafargue, Paul, French sociologist, 435

Lagerlöf, Selma, Swedish author, 403

Lang, Fritz, German film maker, 73, 417, 419

Lâon Cathedral, 141

Lascaux cave paintings, 5

The Last of England, painting by Ford Maddox Brown, 382

The Laws of Imitation, by Tarde, 436

Le Clerc, Jean, Dutch Huguenot publisher and scholar, 298

Le Roy, Louis, French publicist, 291

Leavis, F.R., English author and literary critic, 426

Leeu, Gherard, Netherlandish printer, 234

Lehrstück, play by Brecht, 422, 423

Leibniz, G.W., German philosopher, 257, 293, 297-8, 312

Lemaitre, Georges, Belgian mathematician, 413

Lennon, John, English singer, 451

Leopold II, emperor, 273

Les Desillusions du progrès, treatise by Aron, 437

Les Loisirs de Philothé, novel by Mavrocordatos, 299

Lessing, G.E., German author, 312

Letters from an American Farmer, by St John, 378

Leviathan, socio-political treatise by Hobbes, 310

Levinas, Emanuel, Jewish-French-Lithuanian philosopher, 464

Lewkenor, Samuel, English author, 281

Liber Sancti Jacobi, manual for pilgrims to Santiago, 144

Lincoln, Benjamin, American general and writer, 377

Linnaeus, Carl, Swedish biologist, 281

Lipsius, Justus, Netherlandish humanist author, 272

Livingstone, D., Scottish missionary and explorer, 382

Locatelli, Domenico, Italian composer, 273

Locatelli, Giovanni, Italian composer, 273

Locke, John, English philosopher, 281, 286, 289-90, 298, 308

London, a Pilgrimage, picture book by Doré, 347

looms, 127

Louis II, emperor, 94

Louis XIII, king of France, 216

Louis XIV, king of France, 216, 253, 263, 268-9, 273, 284, 303, 326, 336

Louis XVI, king of France, 363

Luke, one of the disciples of Jesus, and writer of a gospel, 60, 61

Lully, Jean-Baptiste, French composer, 269

Luther, Martin, German monk and reformer, 206, 217-19, 303

Luzac, Elie, Dutch Huguenot publisher and publicist, 296

McCartney, Paul, English singer and composer, 451

Machiavelli, Niccolò, Italian political scientist, 190, 195

Macmillan, English publishing house, 353

Macpherson, James, English poet, 316

Madame Bovary, Flaubert's major novel, 358

Madonna, pop singer and actress, 453

Magellan, Ferdinand, Portuguese mariner and explorer, 245

Magliabecchi, Antonio, Florentine librarian and scholar, 297

Magna Carta, English constitutional document, 131

Mahomet et Charlemagne, by Pirenne, 416

Mandeville, Bernard, Dutch-English publicist, 327

Mani, Persian prophet, 62

Mann, Thomas, German novelist, 418

'Manual for Tailors', 220

Manutius, Aldus, Venetian scholar and publisher-printer, 214, 295

Map, Walter, English-Welsh civil servant and courtier, 136

Maria Theresa, empress, 318

Mariken van Nieumeghen, Dutch play, 62, 223

Mark, one of the disciples of Jesus, and writer of a gospel, 60, 61

Márquez, José Garcia, Columbian writer, 377

Marsiglio of Padua, Italian scholar, 140

Marulic, Marco, poet from Split, 225

Marvell, Andrew, English poet, 248

Marx, Karl, German philosopher and historian, 364, 402

Mary, mother of Jesus, cult of, 124

Massenet, Jules, French composer, 222

Master Eckhart, Christian mystic, 446

Matthew, one of the disciples of Jesus, and writer of a gospel, 59, 61, 87

Mavrocordatos, Nicholas, Greek ruler and scholar, 298

May, Karl, German author, 410

Mayans y Siscar, Gregorio, Spanish scholar, 299

Mazarin, Jules, Italian-French statesman and cardinal, 292

Mechanical Head, 'assemblage' by Hausmann, 425

Medea, play by Euripides, 27

Medinet Habu temple, 19

Medici, de' Cosimo, Florentine ruler and patron of the arts, 181

Medici de' family, Florentine bankers and dynasts, 252

Medici, de' Lorenzo, Florentine ruler and patron of the arts, 185

Medici, de' Maria, Florentine princess, 267

Meerman, Gerard, Dutch diplomat, bibliophile and scholar, 299

Melanchton, Philip, German theologian, 303

Mendel, Gr., Austrian monk and geneticist, 398

Mensch en menigte in Amerika, or 'Man and Mass in America', by Huizinga, 417

Mercator, Gerard, Dutch cartographer, 246, 247

Methodius, Greek Orthodox monk, and saint, 109

Metropolis, film by Lang, 417

Michelangelo Buonarotti, Italian artist, 185, 187, 189, 192, 252, 261

Middlemarch, George Eliot's major novel, 358

Mill, John Stuart, English economist, 373

Milton, John, English poet, 318

Minucius Felix, Roman author, 61, 64

Mithras, Persian god, 63

Moberg, Vilhelm, Swedish author, 380

Monnet, Jean, French statesman, 430, 458

Monostatos, character in Mozart's opera *The Magic Flute*, 288

Montaigne, de Michel, French philosopher, 286, 288–9

Monte Cassino, the first monastery of the Benedictine Order, 99

Montesquieu, de Charles, French political thinker, 196, 324

Monteverdi, Claudio, Italian composer, 192

Montezuma, last Aztec emperor, 235, 253

More, Thomas, English statesman and author, 257, 291

Moreri, Louis, French scholar, 297

Morton, W.T.G., American anaesthesiologist, 398

Moses, Jewish leader and law giver, 58

Moisiodax, Iosipos, Greek intellectual and author, 316

Mostaert, Jan, Dutch painter, 249

Mozart, Wolfgang Amadeus, Austrian composer, 273, 288, 370, 396

La Muette de Portici, opera by Aubert, 353

Muhammad, founder of Islam, 102–5, 111, 113, 137

Multinationals Bite, song by Fischer Z, 452

Münster, Sebastian, German cartographer, 248, 255

Museion, at Alexandria, 35

Musil, Robert, Austrian writer, 416

Mussolini, Benito, Italian dictator, 421

Mussorgsky, M., Russian composer, 409

Napoleon Bonaparte, French general, dictator and emperor, 315, 316, 351–3, 359

Napoleon, film by Gance, 419

Napoleonic Code, 351

Nassau, Maurice of, prince of Orange, Dutch statesman and military innovator, 202

The New Republic, American periodical, 383

Newton, Isaac, English mathematician, physicist and philosopher, 308–10, 312, 411, 413

Niaux cave paintings, 13,

Die Nibelungen, film by Lang, 419

Nibelungenlied, early German epic, 73

Nicot de Villemain, Jean, French diplomat, 235

Nièpce, J.-N., French chemist, 398

Nietzsche, Fr., German philosopher, xvii, 286, 404, 407

Nieuhof, Johan, traveller in the service of the Dutch East and West Indian Companies, 253

Nijinsky, Vaslav, Russian choreographer and dancer, 451

Nils Holgersons underbara resa, or 'Nils Holgerson's Strange Voyage', by Selma Lagerlöf, 403

Nithard, monk and historian, 142

Noah, biblical figure, 22, 88

Noris, Enrico, cardinal, 297

Notker Balbulus, monk and historian, 142

Novalis, or Von Hardenberg, Friedrich, German poet, 362, 407, 411, 431, 465

Novum organum, major work of Francis Bacon, 196

O Pioneers, Willa Cather's major novel, 379

Octavius, dialogue by Minucius Felix, 61

Odin, Germanic god, 82

Odyssey, 21, 27, 51, 181

Olearius, Abraham, German traveler, 396

On the Origin of Species, by Darwin, 402

On Travel, essay by Bacon, 279

Oppenheimer, J. Robert, American physicist, 424

Opticks, or 'Optica', one of Newton's major works, 305

Orang-Outang, sive Homo Sylvestris, by Tyson, 3

Organon, work by Aristotle, 196

Orpheus Britannicus, collection of songs, 293

Os Lusiadas, Portuguese epic by Camoes, 225

Osman, Serbic epic by Gundulic, 225

Osmin, a character in Mozart's *The Escape from the Seraglio*, 288

Othello, play by Shakespeare, 462

Otto I, emperor, 100, 123

Otto II, emperor, 109

Otto, N.A., German technician and inventor, 398

Pachomius, Christian saint, founder of the first monastery proper, 99

Packard, Vance, American sociologist, 437

Palladio, Andrea, Italian architect, 221

paper-making, 127

Paradise Lost, poem by Milton, 318

Pascal, Blaise, French philosopher, 310

La Passion de Jeanne d'Arc, film by Dreyer, 419

Paston, Margaret, English noblewoman and writer of letters, 168

Paul, apostle and Christian author, 64

Paul III, pope, 302

Penelope, Odysseus' wife, character in the *Odyssey*, 27

Penn, William, English statesman and religious leader, 290, 291, 407

Pensées, by Pascal, 310

Pentateuch, the first five books of the Old Testament of the Bible, 58

Pepys, Samuel, English diarist, 267, 369

Periplous, mariner's manual from Marseilles, 31

Perrault, Charles, French writer and collector of folk tales, 165

The Persians, play by Aeschylos, 33

Peter, the Great, tsar of Russia, 293

Petronius, Roman author, 179

Philip Augustus, king of France, 133

Philip II, king of Spain, 237, 239, 252, 272

Philip IV, king of France, 136

Philosophiae naturalis Principia mathematica, by Newton, 309

Picasso, Pablo, Spanish painter, 407, 414

The Picture of Dorian Grey, novel by Wilde, 343

Pieterpad, or St. Peter's Way, pilgrims' road to Rome, 143

Pincio Gardens, open-air gallery of national heroes in Rome, 353

Pirenne, Henri, Belgian historian, 416

Pius II, or Aeneas Sylvius Piccolomini, pope and humanist author, 180, 181

Pizarro, Francisco, Spanish conquistador of Peru, 240

Planck, Max, German physicist, 413, 414, 423

Plantijn, Christoffel, publisher at Antwerp, 295

Plato, Greek philosopher, 23, 27, 33, 83, 86, 106, 140, 181, 214

'Pleiades' series of French classics, 353

Pletho, Byzantine neo-platonist scholar, 181

Pliny, the Elder, Roman writer of a 'Natural History', 54

Pliny, the Younger, Roman author, 43

Plotinus, neo-platonist philosopher, 86, 87

Poema de mio Cid, Spanish epic tale, 149, 225

Politeia, Plato's treatise on politics, 23

Politika, Aristotle's treatise on politics, 23

Politische Geographie, by Ratzel, 389

Polo, Marco, Venetian traveller, 199, 227, 229, 233, 247, 295

Polyglot Bibles, 182

Porphyry, neo-platonist philosopher, 87

Portinari family, 265

Poseidonios, Greek writer 53

potato, 235, 242

Prince, pop singer, 453

La Princesse de Clèves, novel by Mme De la Fayette, 269

Il Principe, or 'The Prince', Machiavelli's major work, 190

Principles of Psychology, by James, 428

Prodigal Son, painting by Bosch, 193

Programma XLII de peregrinationis, by
Thomasius, 281
Prometheus, Greek mythological figure,
359, 456
Prosper of Aquitaine, Christian saint, 90
Prospero, character in Shakespeare's *The
Tempest*, 250, 462
Proust, Marcel, French author, 414
Prudentius, Christian scholar, 89
Ptolemy, Greek cosmographer, 35, 204,
244, 246
Punch, English satirical journal, 386
Purcell, Henry, English composer, 293
Purchas, Samuel, English collector of
travel tales, 255, 256
Pythia, Greek oracle at Delphi, 32

Quintilian, Roman paedagogue and
writer, 50, 51, 179
Quo Vadis? A Just Censure of Travels, by
Hall, 281

Racine, Jean, French playwright, 332
Raleigh, Walter, English buccaneer and
naval commander, 240
Rameau, J.-Ph., French composer, 332
Rameses II, Egyptian pharaoh, 19
Raphael(lo) Santi, Italian painter, 187,
292
Ratzel, Friedrich, German scholar, 389
La Reggenta, Clarin's major novel, 358
Renan, Ernest, French scholar, 405
Republic, one of Plato's texts, 106
Richelieu, J.-A. Duplessis, de French
statesman and cardinal, 292
Riddarhus at Stockholm, frescoes at, 274
Ring des Nibelungen, cycle of operas by
Wagner, 354
The Rising Glory of America, poem by
Freneau, 258
Robert, monk and chronicler, 115
Robinson Crusoe, novel by Defoe, 251
Robur the Conqueror, novel by Jules
Verne, 403
Romance of the Rose, tale of courtly love,
149, 177
Romanen om Utvandrarna, Moberg's epic
novel, 380
Rome, 260, 261
Röntgen, W.C., German chemist, 398
Rostovtzeff, M., English historian, 465,
466
Rostow, W.W., American economist,
436

Rousseau, Jean-Jacques, French
philosopher, 266, 286, 313–14, 372
Royal Society, 298
Rubens, P.P., Netherlandish painter, 274
Rublev, Andrej, Russian painter, 110
Rudolph II, emperor, 303
'Rule Britannia', song by Arne, 317
Rumph, Chr. C., Dutch envoy at
Stockholm, 297, 298
Rutherford, Ernest, English physicist,
423
Ruttmann, Walter, German film maker,
422

Le Sacré du Printemps, or The Rite of
Spring, by Stravinsky, 451
Said al-Andalusi, Islamic legal scholar,
153
St Petersburg, churches and palaces at,
273
St Basil's cathedral, at Moscow, 293
St James' shrine at Compostela, 144
St John, Hector, French-American
writer, 378, 380, 416
St Michael the Archangel, church of, at
Moscow, 293
St Peter's, the main church of Roman
Catholic Christianity, 88, 252, 261
St Simon, Duke of, diarist at Versailles,
269, 325, 326
Saint Simon, Henri, count of, French
social theorist, 349, 350
Salisbury Cathedral, 141
Samfundets Stotter, or The Pillars of
Society, play by Ibsen, 414
San Clemente, Rome: Mithraic frescoes,
63
San Vitale, Ravenna: Byzantine mosaics,
45, 177
Sarmiento, Martin, Spanish monk and
author, 317
Saturday Night Fever, film, 451
Savery, Roelant, Dutch painter, 149
Schelling, Fr.-W., German philosopher,
318
Scheherazade, one of the main characters
in the *Thousand and One Nights*, 106
Schiller, Friedrich, German author, 317
Schlegel, Friedrich, German linguist,
396
Schopenhauer, Arthur, German
philosopher, 266, 313, 393
Schopenhauer, H. Fl., German
merchant, 266

Schopenhauer, Johanna, née Trosiener, 266

Schubert, Franz, Austrian composer, 370

Schumann, Robert, French statesman, 430

Schuwalow-vase painter, 27

scriptoria, centres of manuscript book production, 198

Sein und Zeit, Heidegger's major work, 464

Semmelweis, I.P., Hungarian obstetrician, 398

Serlio, Sebastiano, Italian architect, 221

Servaas, or Gervase, bishop of Maastricht, saint, 144

Servan-Schreiber, J.-J., French politician, 436

Shakespeare, William, English playwright, xxv, 238, 249, 353, 462

Shamash, Summerian sun god, 12, 13

Shem, or Sem, patriarch of the Semites, or Asians, 88

Sic et Non, treatise by Abelard, 152

Sidgwick, Henry, English politician and intellectual, 357

Le Siècle de Louis XIV, by Voltaire, 195

Simon, also known as Petrus, the 'first of the apostles', the first pope, 87

Sinclair, Upton, American novelist, 381

Skokloster castle, 274

Sloane, Hans, German collector of books and curios, 254

Smith, Adam, English economic theorist, 196

Snow, C.P., English civil servant, scientist and author, 426

soap opera, 449

Society of Jesus, 220, 232

Socrates, Greek philosopher, 27, 28

Soll und Haben, novel by Freytag, 360

Solomon, king of the Jews, 20

Solon, Greek law-giver, 23

Sophocles, Greek playwright, 29

Sorbonne University at Paris, 146, 155

Soriano, Michele, Venetian diplomat, 243

Spaak, Paul-Henri, Belgian statesman, 430

Spanish peppers, 236

The Spectator, English periodical, 332

Speke, John, English explorer, 386

Spengler, O., German scholar, 416

Spinoza, Baruch de, Spanish-Jewish-Dutch philosopher, 312, 319

Stanley, H.M., Welsh journalist, 395

Statenvertaling, or Dutch State Authorized Bible, 210

The Status Seekers, by Packard, 437

Steen, Jan, Dutch painter, 330

Stephan, Heinrich, German postmaster-general, 399

Sting, English singer, 453

Stonehenge sanctuary/temple, 17

Stoss, Veit, Bohemian sculptor-painter, 141

Strabo, Greek geographer, 52, 204

Strangers and Brothers, cycle of novels by Snow, 426

Stratford-upon-Avon, Shakespeare's shrine, 353

Strauss, D. Fr., German theologian and scholar, 405

Strauss, Richard, Austrian composer, 222

Stravinsky, Igor, Russian composer, 451

Strettweg bronze chariot, 18

Sturm, Jacob, humanist scholar from Strasbourg, 213

Suasso family, 265

Summa Theologica, Aquinas' main work, 110

Sunna, the corpus of texts explaining Muhammad's teaching of Islam, 105

Susato, Tilman, Antwerp music publisher, 273

Svea, allegory of Sweden, 274

Swedenborg, Emmanuel, Swedish philosopher, 312–13

Symposium, one of Plato's main works, 86

Synesius, Roman orator, 74

syphilis, 237, 242

Tacitus, Roman historian, 49, 53, 54, 55, 155

Talbot, W.H.F., English physicist, 398

Tarde, Eugène, French sociologist, 436

Tasso, Torquato, Italian poet, 192

Tchaikovsky, P.I., Russian composer, 409

The Tempest, play by Shakespeare, xxv, 249, 462

Tennyson, Alfred, English poet, 357, 358, 409

Teresa of Avila, Christian saint and mystic, 446

Tertullian, Roman author, 66

The Times, English newspaper, 265

Themistius, Roman orator, 74

Theodora, Justinian's wife, empress of Byzantium, 45
Theodosius, Roman emperor, 69, 74
Theophano, Byzantine wife of emperor Otto II, 109
Thomas à Becket, English statesman, martyr and saint, 144, 147
Thomas à Kempis, or Thomas Haemerken, Netherlandish writer, 193
Thomasius, Johannes, German author, 281
Thomsen, Chr. J., Danish scholar, 3, 4
Thousand and One Nights, collection of (Arabic) tales, 106
Tiepolo, Giovanni Battista, Italian painter, 253, 273
Timaios, one of Plato's works, 86
Tinne, Alexandrine, Dutch explorer, 395
Tischbein, W., German painter, 363
Tizian, or Tiziano Vecelli, Italian painter, 325
tobacco, 235
Tokugawa family, rulers of Japan from the seventeenth to the nineteenth century, 390
Toledo School of Translators, Spanish academy, 154
Tolstoy, Leo, Russian writer, 353
Tomasi di Lampedusa, Giuseppe, Italian writer, 451
tomato, 236
Toscanelli, Paolo, Florentine geographer, 245
Le Tour du Monde, French periodical of travel stories, 361
Trajan, Roman emperor, 43
Die Traumdeutung, by Freud, 411
Tripitaka, the Buddhist canon, 198
Tristan, Celtic legendary figure, 31
Tristan und Isolde, opera by Wagner, 403
Turing, Alan, English mathematician, 424
Two Treatises of Civil Government, by Locke, 298
Tyson, E., English physician, 3

Ueber die Sprache . . . der Indier, by Schlegel, 396
Upanishads, ancient Indian texts, 391
Urban II, pope, 114, 117
Urban VIII, pope, 268, 303
Usama ibn Munqidh, Islamic nobleman and diarist, 116

Utopia, Thomas More's major work, 257, 290

Valhalla, the seat of the Germanic gods, 82
Van Arkel, Thomas Walraven, Dutch country squire, 282
Van Campen, Jacob, Dutch architect, 252
Van den Vondel, Joost, Dutch poet, 252
Van Gogh, Vincent, Dutch painter, 391
Van Scorel, Jan, Netherlandish painter, 272
Van Swieten, Gerard, Dutch-Austrian courtier and writer, 318
Vedas, ancient Indian texts, 76, 391, 446
Verdi, Giuseppe, Italian composer, 354
Verne, Jules, French author, 403
Versailles palace, 252, 268, 269, 317, 325, 326
Verses on the Prospect of Planting Arts, by Berkeley, 249
Vespucci, Amerigo, Florentine navigator, 245
Vestiges of the Natural History of Creation, by Chambers, 400
Victoria, queen of England, 357
La Vie de Jesus, by Renan, 405
Virey, J.J., French medical publicist, 371
Virgil, Roman poet, 51
Virtù, the creative potential of man, 178
Visconti, Luchino, Italian film maker, 451
Visegrád palace, 184
Vita Constantini, Eusebius' 'Life of Constantine', 69
Vita Karoli, Charlemagne's biography by Einhard, 96
Vita Nuova, cycle of sonnets by Dante, 143
Vitry, Jacques de, French clergyman, 155
Vitruvius Britannicus, English architectural treatise, 293
Vitruvius, Roman architect, 221, 293
Vivaldi, Antonio, Italian composer, 253
Vix-kratèr, Celtic bronze wine vessel from France, 31
Vladimir cathedral, 110
Voltaire, or François-Marie Arouet, French philosopher, 195, 266, 313, 335, 396
Von Behring, E.A., German pharmacologist, 398

Von Bismarck, Otto, chancellor of Germany, 399
Von Freising, Otto, German historian, 97
Von Gluck, Chr. W., German composer, 409
Von Hammer-Purgstall, Joseph, Austrian orientalist, 394
Von Hofmansthal, Hugo, Austrian author, 415
Von Humboldt, Wilhelm, German politician and intellectual, 356, 438, 444
Von Pückler-Muskau, Prince, German traveller and author, 341, 342
Von Roes, Alexander, German civil servant and writer, 139
Von Schmidt-Phiseldek, Fr., Danish politician and author, 407
Von Siemens, W., German industrialist and inventor, 398
Vossische Zeitung, Berlin newspaper, 368
Voyage to the Moon, novel by Jules Verne, 403

Wagner, Richard, German composer, 73, 354, 403, 404
Waldseemüller, Martin, German cartographer, 245, 246
Walter of Henley, author of a famous agricultural treatise, 126
War and Peace, epic novel by Tolstoy, 353
Wasa, Gustavus, king of Sweden and military innovator, 202
The Water Babies, novel by Kingsley, 403
watermills, 125
Watson, J.D., American biochemist, 424
Weber, Max, German intellectual and sociologist, 420
Weimar, Goethe's shrine, 353
Weissenstein palace near Pommersfelden, 253

Welser family, 266
Die Welt als Wille und Vorstellung, by Schopenhauer, 313
Wenceslas, king of Poland: Bible of, 148
Wilde, Oscar, English author, 343
William, duke of Aquitaine, 120
William III, prince of Orange, king of England, et cetera, 334
William of Malmesbury, monk and chronicler, 117, 118
William of Roebroeck, monk and missionary, 128
William, the Conqueror, duke of Normandy, king of England, 129
Willibald, monk, biographer of St Boniface, 91
Winchester Cathedral, 141
windmills, 125
Winnetou, the red Gentleman, character from novel by May, 410
Witsen, Nicholas, Dutch politician and scholar, 297–8
Wortley Montagu, Lady Mary, English noblewoman and writer of letters, 270
Wrangel, C.G., Swedish military leader and patron of the arts, 274
Wristcutter's Lullaby, song by Fischer Z, 452
Wulfila, or Ulfilas, bishop of the Goths, 72, 109
Würzburg episcopal palace, frescoes at, 253, 273
Wycliffe, John, English Church reformer, 217

Zagorsk monastery, frescoes at, 110
Die Zauberflöte, opera by Mozart, 288
Zedler, J.M., German author, 314
Zeus, Greek god, 32, 33
Zola, Emile, French novelist, 371, 372
Zoroastrianism, Persian cult, 35
Zur Kritik der politischen Oekonomie, by Marx, 402